KING

OF THE

CATS

BOOKS BY WIL HAYGOOD

Two on the River
(Photographs by Stan Grossfeld)

King of the Cats:
The Life and Times of
Adam Clayton Powell, Jr.

KING
OF THE
CATS

THE LIFE AND TIMES OF
ADAM CLAYTON POWELL, JR.

WIL HAYGOOD

A Peter Davison Book

HOUGHTON MIFFLIN COMPANY

Boston   New York

1993

For information about permission to reproduce selections
from this book, write to Permissions, Houghton Mifflin Company,
215 Park Avenue South, New York, New York 10003.

Library of Congress Cataloging-in-Publication Data

Haygood, Wil.
King of the cats : the life and times of Adam Clayton Powell, Jr.
/ Wil Haygood.
p.   cm.
"A Peter Davison book."
Includes bibliographical references and index.
ISBN 0-395-44094-7
1. Powell, Adam Clayton, 1908–1972.   2. Legislators — United
States — Biography.   3. United States. Congress. House — Biography.
4. Afro-Americans — Politics and government.   5. Afro-Americans — New
York (N.Y.) — Politics and government.   6. Harlem (New York, N.Y.) —
Politics and government.   7. New York (N.Y.) — Politics and
government — 1898–1951.   I. Title.
E748.P86H39   1993
973.92'092 — dc20
[B]   92-31771
CIP

Text design by Anne Chalmers

Printed in the United States of America

DOH 10 9 8 7 6 5 4 3 2 1

FOR
THOMAS F. MULVOY, JR. —
SUCH A FINE MAN

I gratefully acknowledge the generosity of the Alicia Patterson Foundation in providing a fellowship during the research and writing of this book.

— W. H.

ACKNOWLEDGMENTS

This biography was originally planned as a three-year project, but the spool of thread grew longer and longer. The Virginia countryside, where I located the still-standing slave cabin in which Adam Clayton Powell, Sr., was born, led to Harlem, which led to Berlin, which led to Washington, which led to Rome, which led to San Juan. Adam Clayton Powell, Jr., like many volatile political figures (Huey Long among them), left no personal papers behind. In the end it took six years, a journey of interviewing and combing through archives that took me across much of America and twice into Europe and the Caribbean. There were so many who helped along the way. My thanks, however, must begin with my employer, the *Boston Globe*. Jack Driscoll, the editor of the newspaper, granted me the necessary leaves of absence to complete this biography. There were times when I believed his passion for this project was equal to mine. At the *Globe* I also wish to personally thank Benjamin Taylor, executive vice president; Thomas F. Mulvoy, Jr., managing editor of news operations; and William O. Taylor — a grand publisher to work for. Together, their encouragement was constant, and offered at critical junctures.

Peter Davison, my editor at Houghton Mifflin, is a renowned poet, an accomplished editor, and a man of gifted sensibilities. I'm fortunate to have benefited from the entire sweep. He brought uncommon insight and faith to this biography, shepherding it through three drafts, making it better at each stage, never doubting. He has my deepest thanks and affection. Also at Houghton Mifflin I wish to thank Joe Kanon; John Sterling; Liz Duvall, whose keen reading of the manuscript made it better; and Erica Landry, Peter Davison's former assistant. Nan Talese, now a publisher at Doubleday, originally signed this project during her tenure at Houghton Mifflin. I am grateful for her confidence. Esther Newberg, my tireless agent, is a blessing. She has lavished time and attention on both book and author.

I found librarians and archivists indispensable, opening doors and offering suggestions along the way. I must thank the staffs of the following libraries for granting me courtesies: the Franklin D. Roosevelt Library, in Hyde Park, New York; the Harry S. Truman Library, in Independence, Missouri; the Dwight D. Eisenhower Library, in Abilene, Kansas; the John F. Kennedy Library, in Dorchester, Massachusetts; the Lyndon B. Johnson Library, in Austin, Texas; and the Gerald R. Ford Library, in Ann Arbor, Michigan. Also, for providing ample work space during my visits, I wish to thank the staffs of the New York City Municipal Archives; the Schomburg Center for Research in Black Culture, in New York City; the Library of Congress; the National Archives; the American Baptist Historical Society, in Rochester, New York; the Institute of Jazz Studies, in Newark, New Jersey; the Yale Divinity School, in New Haven, Connecticut; the A. Philip Randolph Institute, in New York City; the Ohio Historical Society, in Columbus, Ohio; and the West Virginia Department of Culture and History, in Charleston.

The library staffs of the *Washington Post,* the *New York Times,* the *Los Angeles Times,* the *Boston Globe,* the *Miami Herald, Le Monde,* and the *San Juan Star* were also accommodating during my visits, and they too have my gratitude. Rev. Calvin Butts of the Abyssinian Baptist Church allowed me access to the church's archives. During two visits to Colgate University, John Hubbard of the university's communications office was of immeasurable assistance.

I owe a large debt to the family members of Adam Clayton Powell, Jr., who welcomed me into their homes and gave so freely of their time in sharing memories. I thank Isabel Powell, Preston Powell, Adam Clayton Powell III, Adam Clayton Powell IV, Beryl Slocum Powell, and Yvette Powell. Hazel Scott's life has been sadly underdocumented and perhaps underappreciated. I've attempted in these pages to rectify the slight. Her musician friends were generous with their time, and I thank Bobby Short, Buck Clayton, Red Callender, Leonard Feather, and Wesley Carter.

Much of this book is based on interviews I myself conducted. Four individuals deserve special mention. In 1941 Maurice Rosenblatt became Adam Clayton Powell's first political campaign manager. It was Rosenblatt who fostered a relationship between Powell and the Manhattan Jewish organizations that aided his political rise. Rosenblatt was full of information, not only about Powell but about the times in which they both lived and dreamed. Marjorie Lawson, who rented Powell the upstairs of her Victorian home when he first arrived in Washington in 1945, offered numerous insights about Powell's early years in the nation's capital. I enjoyed our two meetings immensely. Before Powell's ultimate defeat in 1970, there was only one candidate who stood to alter his political career. In 1946 Grant Reynolds defeated Adam Clayton Powell in a New York City primary; Powell looked vulnerable. But in the end, and in one of the most treacherous moves engineered by a politician, Powell defeated Reynolds and drove him completely from the political arena. I finally located Grant Reynolds in Florida. He had never talked at length about that memorable campaign, and he has my gratitude for doing so. And for six years Lem Wells, a Harlem political insider, provided helpful information and answered every query without delay. He also helped open doors. I thank him for caring so deeply.

One of the genuine pleasures of working on this book has been meeting the acquaintances of Adam Clayton Powell, Jr. — fellow congressmen, White House officials, Baptist ministers, Harlem waitresses, railway station porters. Whether friend or foe, they were usually eager to talk, and never allowed their political stripe to dim their enthusiasm. "Too many people don't know about Adam Clayton Powell. By the way, whatever *happened* to him?" asked Tom Curtis, the former Missouri representative who helped spearhead Powell's ouster from Congress, when I called him. Then he invited me to his summer home in Michigan to talk.

In addition to the above-mentioned, the following people made themselves available for interviews, and I thank them all: Sherman Adams, Carl Albert, Clifford Alexander, Don Anderson, Jack Anderson, Howard Armstrong, William Ayers, Chester Bagley, Don Baker, Thomas Barr, Benton Becker, Howard Bell, Don Berens, Richard Bolling, Jimmy Booker, William Booth, St. Claire Bourne, Nigel Bowe, Ben Bradlee, David Brinkley, Peter Bromley, Neville Brown, Herbert Brownell, Herbert Bruce, William F. Buckley, Jr., Art Carter, Robert Carter, Robbie Clark, Marvel Cooke, James Corman, Daniel Crosby, Hycie Curtis, Lloyd Cutler, Maxine Dargans, Christine Davis, Russell Derrickson, Lloyd Dickens, Charles Diggs, Hattie Dodson, Richard Donohue, Strat Douthat, Carl Elliott, William Epps, Justin Feldman, Doris Gamser, William Geohegan, Ollie Harrington, Jim

Harrison, Wayne Hays, Grace Hewell, Herbert Hill, Bea Hines, Corrine Huff, John Hupper, Andrew Jacobs, Marian Javits, Thomas Johnson, J. Raymond Jones, Arthur Josephson, Eugene Keogh, Francis Keppel, Arthur Kinoy, Paul Klein, William Kunstler, Carl Lawrence, Acy Lennon, David Licorish, Harry Lipsig, Leonard Macaluso, Louis Martin, George McGovern, James Meredith, Gene Miller, E. Fred Morrow, Bob Moses, John Oakes, Lawrence O'Brien, Jim O'Hara, Jack Packard, Edward Peeks, Marilyn Perry, William Phillips, Stanley Pinder, Samuel Proctor, Roman Pucinski, Thomas Quinn, Maxwell Rabb, Charles Rangel, Dan Rappaport, Joseph Rauh, George Reedy, Herbert Reid, Grant Reynolds, Morton Robson, Creswell Romer, Franklin D. Roosevelt, Jr., James Roosevelt, Billy Rowe, Jawn Sandifer, Wesley Saunders, Arnold Sawislak, Michael Schwartz, Harry Sease, Robert Seavey, Olivia Stokes, Eddie Sylvester, Gardner Taylor, Frank Thompson, Jeanne Thomson, Viola Topson, Morris Udall, Jack Valenti, Lionel Van Deerlin, Gore Vidal, Jesse Walker, Mike Wallace, Fredi Washington, Robert Weaver, Aaron Wells, Basil Whitener, Doxey Wilkerson, Roger Wilkins, Edward Bennett Williams, Henry Williams, Howard Williams, Harris Wofford, Deborah Wolfe, Lester Wolff, and Louise Wright.

Additionally, I would like to thank the following friends and colleagues for their unstinting support over the years: Martin Berg, Ben Bradlee, Jr., Patti Doten, Mark Feeney, Ellen Goodman, Stan Grossfeld, Paul Hendrickson, Jonathan Kaufman, Ben Lay, Timothy Leland, Steve Le Vine, David Lieber, Mark Muro, Lincoln Millstein, Sean Mullin, Mark Muro, Martin Nolan, David Nyhan, Richard Rhodes, Andrew Sheehan, Matthew Storin (executive editor of the *Boston Globe* and among the first, during a previous tenure, to encourage me to come to the newspaper), Robert Taylor, David Warsh, Tom Winship, and Geoffrey Wolff.

CONTENTS

Acknowledgments · ix

List of Illustrations · xv

Prologue: THE YOUNG THINKERS · I

I COLGATE, 1926–1930 · 7

II YOUNG ADAM POWELL, 1930–1945 · 21
Interlude: Adam Clayton Powell, Sr. · 58
The Succession · 72

III THE RISE OF A PHOENIX, 1945–1952 · 107

IV SHIFTING GROUND, 1953–1957 · 177

V THE GLORY, 1957–1963 · 235

VI AND THE POWER, 1964–1966 · 297

VII THE FALL, 1967–1968 · 335

VIII REDEMPTION BY THE
CONSITITUTION, 1969–1972 · 379

Epilogue · 417

Notes · 423

Bibliography · 442

Index · 447

LIST OF ILLUSTRATIONS

following page 78:
1. Adam Clayton Powell, Sr.
   Mattie Powell
   The Powell clan in West Virginia, 1885
2. Little Lord Powell, age four
   Adam Clayton Powell, Jr., with his nanny, Josephine
3. Colgate yearbook photograph, 1930
   Preaching in 1941
4. Adam and Isabel Powell, newly married
   Adam in Oak Bluffs, ca. 1942
   Isabel Washington Powell, Oak Bluffs, 1935
5. Being sworn in to the New York City Council, 1942
   The would-be congressman and his lieutenants
6. Hazel Scott, 1939
   Hazel and Adam signing their marriage license, 1945
   Hazel with Count Basie, Teddy Wilson, Duke Ellington, and Mel
      Powell, 1948
   The Powell entourage en route to Haiti, ca. 1952
7. Hazel, Skipper, and Adam in Germany in the 1950s
   Father and son in New York, 1962
   Hazel Scott in Paris with friends, 1958
8. Grant Reynolds stumping Harlem, 1946
   Powell's campaign poster

following page 270
1. In the Abyssinian Baptist Church, 1960
2. Declaring for Eisenhower, 1956
   Talking to reporters

3. With J. Raymond Jones, Whitney Young, and Hulan Jack, 1967
   With Martin Luther King, Jr., 1965
4. With Congressman Jacob Javits, 1953
   Stumping for John F. Kennedy, 1960
5. With President Kennedy, 1962
   Chairman Powell and President Johnson, 1966
6. A committee hearing on 114th Street, 1965
   Powell's Washington staff in 1962
7. In Harlem, 1963
8. Yvette, Adamcito, and Adam Powell, San Juan, 1962
   Adamcito goes for his father's pipe at Villa Reposa, 1963

following page 366
1. Esther James at her New York libel trial, 1963
   Powell about to be sentenced for contempt of court, 1966
2. Democratic leaders, January 1967
   Powell's legal team
3. The Celler committee
4. On the way to preach, 1966
   On Bimini, reading the rules of the House aloud, 1967
   On the steps of the Capitol after being excluded from Congress, 1967
5. In Watts, January 1968
   On *The Dick Cavett Show*, 1969
   After reinstatement in the House, 1969
6. Reading the election returns, 1970
   Aboard *Adam's Fancy* in Bimini, 1971
   With Darlene Expose, Adam III, and Beryl, 1971
7. At the Long Island House of Detention, 1970
8. Hazel Scott, Adam III, and Rev. David Licorish after Powell's funeral
   Mourners

KING

OF THE

CATS

PROLOGUE:
THE YOUNG THINKERS

ഗ∿๛๏ He was raised by a shy and private mother, by middle-aged church ladies who mirrored his mother's image, by a dark-skinned nanny named Josephine, and by a stern father whose advancing age he would easily manipulate. Little Adam Clayton Powell, Jr., was first introduced to the ladies of the Abyssinian Baptist Church on West 40th Street when he arrived with his family from New Haven in 1908. Parishioners strained to see the baby beneath the blanket, paraded down the center aisle of the church. All agreed he was a lovely child to look at. Mattie Powell doted on her baby boy, singing him sweet lullabies, rocking him to sleep. Josephine dressed him beautifully, in silk stockings and knickers, tiny patent leather shoes, a Persian lamb coat to ward off winter winds.

Home, directly across from the church, was in a dangerous stretch of urban landscape featuring saloons, prostitutes, and ongoing criminal activity. Tammany Hall blessed the area, supplying it with crooked politicians and gullible police officers. Given a rueful name — the Tenderloin — the area was a hard place to raise children. The Powells had two, Blanche, their winsome and frail daughter, and little Adam, ten years younger. Adam's flowing blond locks gave him a decidedly feminine look, and his light complexion threw playmates off. Many wondered whether he was black, white, or Italian. In crowds he became what his friends wanted him to become, white in white crowds, black in black crowds.

Life at home was comfortable. Meals were lavish affairs, owing to his father's huge appetite: "codfish cakes made the preceding night and tossed up in the outside air to make them 'light,' baked beans cooked all night long on the back of the stove with plenty of black molasses on top and huge hunks of salt pork inside." Meal consumed, hands wiped on monogrammed napkins, Adam would dash off to play with friends.

His first school was P.S. 5, his first playground the church. The nooks and crannies of the Abyssinian Baptist Church provided a world unto themselves. Thomas Waller — girth later gave him the nickname "Fats," and raw talent his fame — was an especially endearing play-mate. The two would climb through the church window and sneak to the organ, where Waller would tap out tunes. During parades through Manhattan the boys made good use of the church rooftop, looking down on Tenderloin activities.

Adam's mother, Mattie, walked easily in the role of devoted min-ister's wife. Harry Sease, a long-time Abyssinian church member, recalled Sundays when she went into church, looked around — she seemed to know every parishioner by name — and became alarmed when she noticed that certain people were absent. Nudging Sease, she would demand that he drive her to their homes following the service. More often than not, said Sease, her instincts proved correct: illness had laid these parishioners low. Mattie Powell would walk into the kitchen of a sick parishioner and begin cooking; she would find brush and bucket and hand them over to Sease, instructing him to begin cleaning. Abyssinians looked after Abyssinians.

When Adam Clayton Powell, Jr., turned twelve, his father was al-ready fifty-five, nearly old enough to be his grandfather. Father and son did not play games together; the elder Powell was a severe man, save for a love of fishing and the water, which he passed along to his son with paternal devotion. The young Powell entertained himself, but mostly out of his father's reach. He became an avid reader, in-cluding racy sex magazines among his literary tastes; he smoked hand-rolled cigarettes in private; he roamed around Coney Island in the company of his eccentric sister. Some Sundays he skipped the first session of church (there were always two) to go boating in Central Park, always allowing himself, according to church member Hattie Dodson, enough time "to rush back to church" for the day's final session.

When his family moved from midtown Manhattan to the emerging black Harlem as a new Abyssinian church was being built on 138th Street, Adam had to adapt to new surroundings. An engaging youth, he did so quickly. He formed a group within the new church, and gave it a name: the Young Thinkers. On Sunday afternoons he led the group into the church basement, where they pulled out chairs in the recreation room and began talking. There never was any doubt that Adam was the leader, recalled Chester Bagley, a group member. Discussions varied: local issues one week, national the next, then international; Bagley remembered lively discourse about the future of Russia. "It made you think," he said of the talks. Adam delighted in staging impromptu debates with other youth clubs in Harlem, in particular the renowned Beaux Arts Club, which drew members from the finest families of Harlem. The arts were a popular subject; Adam seemed fascinated by the theatrical crowd. Race, however, was rarely a dominating issue. "At that time we weren't having racial problems," explained Bagley. "Blacks hadn't begun to kick their heels up."

There was one subject that Adam discussed frequently, so frequently it made other members of the Young Thinkers blush, and that subject was sex. "Sex was always a big topic," said Bagley. "Adam had no trouble talking about sex, quite openly, even in those days." Bagley wondered how he had come to know so much about sex, and Adam confided in him that his father had taken him away one weekend and told him all there was to know about the subject. From that point on, Adam imagined himself a connoisseur of women. He rarely dated church girls — the fruit was too close to the tree. Distanced from his father's eye, he smoked a pipe, became a ladies' man, pointed out to Bagley the beautiful girls he aimed to woo.

In 1922, as befit the son of a prominent New York minister, Adam began high school studies at the prestigious Townsend Harris Hall. The school was located in the Washington Heights section of Manhattan, on the City College campus; the buildings stretched from 138th to 140th Street, circling St. Nicholas and Amsterdam avenues. Townsend Harris Hall, so proud of its rigorous academic reputation that it refused to call itself Townsend Harris High School, served as a laboratory for the brightest young minds in Manhattan. Its graduates were guaranteed admission to City College without having to take that college's stiff entrance examination. Townsend students completed their high school education in three years, the supposition being that they were very serious, and that serious young men were in a hurry. The school had a reputation for ruthlessly dropping students with failing grades. Those who flunked a course had to take it over. Electives were limited to languages — French, Latin, and Spanish; an appreciation of the arts was encouraged. Suit and tie were required dress. Once admitted, a student became known as a Harrisite.

As a Harrisite, young Powell seemed to enjoy himself. Academically and athletically, he excelled. He became a member of the Spanish Club. His height made him valuable to the basketball team; in springtime he ran track. His lack of weight kept him from varsity football, but pride forced him onto the class football squad. Classmates remembered a poised young man, bright and quick, not yet a leader but hardly a follower — an approachable loner.

Under their yearbook photographs, the graduating seniors in Powell's year shared their choice of college, which reflected the range available to bright young men: the Naval Academy, Harvard, Columbia, and City College, Powell's school of choice. A little ditty, an ode to be remembered by, also appeared beneath each classmate's photograph. "After Adam came Eve, and she's after him yet" appeared beneath Powell's portrait.

His first semester at City College was disastrous. "Gals" were to blame, recalled Chester Bagley. Family tragedy undercut his attempt to rally in his second semester. On March 26, 1926, Blanche Powell died.

A stenographer, Blanche had breezed between Wall Street and her New York neighborhoods — first the West Forties; then, when the family moved uptown, black Harlem — with an ease that belied ongoing racial frictions. Caught between white Manhattan and black Harlem, she rid herself of a preoccupation with race by simply ignoring it. Bohemian, waiflike, and very pale, she reduced race to a game, to mere ruse. Racial realities demanded that she, like her father, think on her feet. The moments when father and daughter passed themselves off as white took place around strangers, men and women with whom they had no link. Having crossed over, they knew they could always cross back again, realizing that true safety was the dividing line between white and black Manhattan: Harlem, their cocoon. In Harlem, acquaintances dared not question their racial pride: the Powells were well known, not only conservative but prosperous, beyond reproach.

When Blanche fell ill, she was taken first to a hospital, then to a sanatorium when her condition was recognized as grave. Her death was laid to peritonitis, a lethal ailment in those pre-penicillin days. Those who knew her were forced to confess that they had never truly known her. She was "a bit strange and mysterious even to her closest friends," her eulogist said, in words touched by understatement. Thousands attended the funeral. Huge bouquets of flowers — orchids, roses — overwhelmed the Abyssinian altar. From the balcony, the white-robed choir sang hymns during the service; many couldn't take their eyes off the pearl-white casket.

The Powells were now beset by crisis. Their daughter was dead; their son was dismissed from City College at the end of his second semester. Adam Senior spent time on the road, lecturing, assuaging his own grief. His wife, always private, uttered barely a word about her pain. Adam Senior and Mattie Powell knew they had to balance sympathy for their son with reality. Young Adam could not be left to roam the streets of Manhattan. The family huddled. It was decided to send him away to school. He needed discipline. Discipline, coupled with an education in the countryside, seemed the perfect tonic. Relying on the help of a friend from his days as a minister in New Haven, Adam Senior arranged for his son to enter Colgate University, in Hamilton, New York.

Not surprisingly, when Adam Clayton Powell, Jr., went away to college, he had yet to decide what his own miscegenation meant — whether it would define his life or not; whether it was a curse or a blessing.

I

COLGATE

1926–1930

C OME EVENING, long shadows fell across the shoulders of the young men strolling on the Colgate University campus, still a lush green as the school year began in 1926. Set in the Chenango hills of upstate New York, it was an all-male school with an all-male faculty, sober scholars drumming moral and religious maturity into their charges. Pines and firs and cedars — "everlasting trees which hide the morning" went a renowned Colgate verse — stretched along the campus pathways. The young man taking long strides across the campus alone — alone now because he courted anonymity, although years later acquaintances recalled a figure seemingly always alone — was Adam Clayton Powell, Jr., miles from his home in Harlem. Sent here by a concerned father following two disastrous semesters at the City College of New York, he had been lectured to reform. Family name and future were both at stake.

It was not Yale or Harvard, schools that Colgate men mockingly referred to as "Eli Yale" and "fair old Harvard"; it was Colgate, and it clung tightly to its own mystique. Colgate men survived fierce winters and the remoteness of their campus. They climbed steep hills to reach classrooms and sat daily on benches in chapel to give prayer. Sport was encouraged, and they played in hale and hearty fashion. A year before young Powell's arrival, the football team, often playing against larger schools with larger players, went undefeated, and Powell was interested in joining George Hauser's gridiron team. To be a Colgate man was to endure; Colgate was not an institution for the effete.

Four other blacks, athletes all, arrived on campus along with Powell. He knew none of them. Merton Anderson, the lone senior among the group, was eager to play mentor. For several years Anderson, who came from a small Pennsylvania town, had been the only black at Colgate, but this year was different. There was a sophomore transfer student, Ray Vaughan, and the athletic department had brought two additional blacks to the campus, John Enoch and Daniel Crosby. Their presence seemed to reflect more a desire to win at sport than outright progressivism by the administration, but Anderson was nevertheless anxious to tell the newcomers about Colgate, the traditions and the academic rigors, especially the isolation and the brutal winters that lay ahead. After classes one evening Enoch, Crosby, and Vaughan walked over to Anderson's dormitory room. When they arrived, Anderson greeted them with interesting news. He had been tipped off that there was another black on campus. The unknown student, he had also learned, was not an athlete. He was exasperated. "I can't find him," he said to the others. Anderson suspected that whoever the missing student was, he was passing himself off as white. At Colgate blacks roomed with other blacks or alone.

Adam Clayton Powell had quietly settled into Anderson Hall, where his roommate, Howard Patterson, from Brooklyn, assumed that he was white. Powell was finding the Colgate environment vastly different from that of City College. City College was near his old high school, near friends and girls, and so near his home that he had lost his ability to concentrate. Here there was peace — woods to walk in and hills to climb. Traipsing into town, he quickly found the corner store popular with all Colgate students, and he hoarded tobacco and bought any of the dozen New York newspapers that kept the young men of Colgate abreast of world news. Hamilton was only a small village that abutted the campus and existed for the life that Colgate students gave to it. Young Powell wasted little time in wooing his first date, the daughter of a local white Baptist minister.

On weekends during the early part of the year, before the crunch of examinations, Colgate students often boarded the train in nearby Utica for New York City. There were Broadway shows to see, flappers to admire. Powell had told campus acquaintances that his father was a minister in New York, so one weekend a group of students who were in town looked up the address of the church. To their amazement, it was in Harlem — in the black section of Harlem. Back on campus and giddy with the news, the students set about spreading the word: the minister's son at Colgate was black, not white.

"We had no idea," recalled Howard Patterson, Powell's roommate.

Patterson was not predisposed to liberal experiments and demanded an immediate removal from the room. He was relieved when it was all "handled down at the admissions office."

Many on campus did not know what to make of the scandal. Whites were more bemused than anything else, as Powell had committed no crime. His fellow blacks, however, saw it differently. Merton Anderson's worst suspicions, of an anonymous student trying to pass himself off as white, had proven true. He felt that such an act was unforgivable, and for the remainder of his college career he avoided Powell. Anderson was as light-skinned as Powell, and while the act was surely not a crime, to him, prideful of his heritage, it meant one thing and one thing only: an attempt to hide one's background, in essence one's self.

Alone in his dormitory room, engulfed by the embarrassment and guilt most poseurs must confront when discovered, Powell had time to ponder the consequences of his actions. He could not have expected to pass as white much longer without being caught. It had been a mere game, albeit a dangerous one. For decades light-skinned blacks had posed as white when benefits could be gained, when the practicality of such a deception made sense. Thus, traveling in the South, Adam Powell Senior had often passed himself off as white at opportune moments — when nearing a lynching party, for instance. His stories of lynchings were rooted in reality: he had seen such horrors with his own eyes. In 1924 he had traveled through Germany, becoming fascinated with the country, its history and landscape, but he had been careful to travel "incognito" there, too. Hadn't Adam's sister, Blanche, passed herself off as white before her death?

As a little boy, Adam Powell Junior had climbed to the rooftop of the Abyssinian Baptist Church and looked down on parades led by the enigmatic Marcus Garvey, proponent of racial pride and black activism. Seated in the pulpit next to his father, he had been raised on sermons and deeds of racial progress. Now his very being had come to this — the shame and anger on Merton Anderson's face. The episode was a galvanizing moment in his life. On the Colgate campus, fall gave way to winter. For weeks, eighteen-year-old Adam Clayton Powell, Jr., walked the campus alone. Somehow he would have to redeem himself, to take back lost pride.

He wasted little time. He slipped a note beneath the door of Daniel Crosby's room, "apologizing and asking for friendship," recalled Crosby. Hearing of Ray Vaughan's difficulty with his German classes, he slipped a note beneath Vaughan's door, too: Powell picked up foreign languages quickly and was doing extremely well in German; he was available to tutor.

Vaughan and Crosby were football players. Young Powell went out for the team, as a split end. Though tall, he lacked brawn, for which he paid dearly. Practice mates pummeled his lithe body. As spontaneously as he had appeared on the practice field, he vanished from it. Football "just wasn't for Adam," explained Leonard Macaluso, a freshman football player who went on to break various Colgate rushing records. Still, "he was always hanging around the football field." (Amazingly, in the years to come, profiles of Powell would allude to his athletic prowess at Colgate, mentioning not only football but track. *Time* magazine would refer to him as a javelin thrower. He did little to change the inaccuracy of the reports. There is no record that he played in a football game or threw the javelin during his Colgate years. "Some of the boys used the term *played* rather loosely," recalled one of his classmates. "If they went out for the team, they said they were on it. They really weren't." Powell did maintain a lifelong fascination with football, though, speeding to games at Yale to watch the Eli and to Shea Stadium to watch the New York Jets.)

Powell also got himself initiated into Alpha Phi Alpha, the renowned fraternity for young black men. There was no Alpha Phi Alpha chapter at Colgate, which never had enough black students to organize one. Walking by Powell's room, Vaughan, Enoch, and Crosby noticed the Alpha insignia, which he had conspicuously affixed to his door at eye level. The three were perplexed, and also quite impressed. "How he became an Alpha I'll never know," said Crosby.

Soon talk of Powell among these three blacks, who shared a suite of rooms, turned from disdain to admiration. The freshman from Harlem was energetic, personable. "Let's let him room with us," Crosby said to his roommates. (Anderson, the senior, lived alone.) When they relented, Powell eagerly moved in. Now he was no longer alone on campus. He regaled his roommates with stories of Harlem and New York City, encouraged them to call him "Ad," shared his vast record collection. Coon Saunders and Paul Whiteman melodies — they were among his favorites — blared from his Victrola. He mesmerized them with stories of the white girl he had been dating in Hamilton. (Powell asked a white classmate, Howard Armstrong, to inform the girl that he would no longer be dating her.) "Adam,"

Crosby said, "you are something else." During the next four years Crosby would come to realize the profundity of his comment.

ᑕᗰᗆ

Fathers sent their sons to Colgate to learn of hard work and discipline, virtues that were personified by George Cutten, the university president. Cutten was something of an ascetic; among his publications was one that bore the title "The Threat of Leisure." Religion was an integral part of campus life; if one wished, one could major in biblical literature. During the 1920s chapel remained a uniform part of Colgate life, and although students were no longer required to troop into chapel at 5 A.M., as they had been years earlier, daily worship remained compulsory. The Colgate-Rochester Seminary was nearby, and they were encouraged to take classes there. (Some students mockingly referred to the seminary as "the angel factory.") Sport shaped character, and nothing provoked campus solidarity as much as the Colgate football team, the Big Red. At football games President Cutten braved autumn winds on the sidelines without coat and hat. The habit was quickly picked up by the young men of Colgate, and soon it became a test of character: to love Colgate was to arrive at football games in bone-chilling weather minus overcoat and hat. The decade was wicked, the young appeared spoiled; the young men of Colgate, however, would not be allowed to be so affected.

Powell braved wintry Saturday outings without coat and hat to cheer on the Big Red. He cracked the books on dark evenings. After selecting his major — biblical literature — he unveiled his streak of independence. Just as he had rebelled against his father's Calvinist leanings, so must he rebel against Colgate. The opportunity arose during planning for the school's annual winter carnival.

The carnival, held in February, was a rite, one of the more festive seasonal events on campus. Every year fraternity houses constructed huge ice replicas on their lawns, trying to outdo the previous year's efforts. Colgate men invited their girlfriends to campus. Guests arrived from Saratoga and Poughkeepsie by way of the Ontario and Western Railroad. There were toboggan races, ice-skating across Taylor Lake, outdoor hockey, skiing; the woods were covered in snow.

The festive event of 1927 brought gloom to the five black men of Colgate, who wondered where they would find dates. Powell knew. He set out on a romantic recruiting mission, which landed him back in Harlem. When he returned he had girls with him, Harlem girls. The sudden appearance of so many black girls on campus caused a stir. "Kids were sitting in windows looking at these colored girls," recalled Crosby, whose date, compliments of young Powell, was Mildred Handy, from a well-known Harlem family with a musical tradition. Powell's date was Isabel Washington, a New York City actress. The young couples enjoyed themselves in their suite and on campus. In private they toasted life, drinking alcohol that Powell had smuggled onto the campus. Over the years, Crosby said, Powell brought an abundance of liquor to Colgate, not to drink himself but to sell to classmates. It was, after all, Prohibition. There was money to be made.

There were other ways in which young Powell made Colgate life more enjoyable for his roommates. He watched professors and told his classmates which ones he thought were racist. Many professors thought he was white; they could hardly tell otherwise. He was poised, always well dressed. But his Harlem friends were not forgotten. Al Campbell, on the lam from the police, found refuge in his dormitory room, and Powell confided to Crosby and others that he believed his father had sent spies to determine whether Isabel Washington was hiding out there, too. (If so, she was never caught.) Powell was also rarely short of spending money. Ray Vaughan, Johnny Enoch, and Daniel Crosby worked at college, Vaughan as an assistant in the gym, Enoch as a short-order cook in Hamilton, Crosby as a bartender at a fraternity house. Adam Powell played poker. "He'd be back and forth to the white kids' rooms," said Crosby. "They'd be playing poker. We were too poor to play poker." Powell had advantages.

A year before Powell's arrival at Colgate, Scribner's published F. Scott Fitzgerald's *The Great Gatsby,* in which the narrator recalls advice given him by his father: "Whenever you feel like criticizing anyone, just remember that all the people in this world haven't had the advantages that you've had." Classmates remembered years later how generous Powell was with his advantages. He invited Crosby and others to Harlem, to stay at the Abyssinian church, and treated them to dinners and took them on dates. "We would get to Harlem," recalled Crosby. "It was fascinating to us. I was from this jerk town, Hartford." He noted, however, one strange thing about their invitations: they often arrived only to find that Powell was not there, he was either down in Greenwich Village or out on Cape Cod. "He never bothered with us much," explained Crosby, "but he always said that when we visited, we had to stay at the church."

In choosing biblical literature as his major, Powell was influenced by his father. He performed well academically his first year at Colgate. There were two A's and four B's, the lone C coming in rhetoric. Then, in his second year, signs of the old Adam resurfaced; he spent his weekends in New York, and there were four C's and a D. Summers he worked, redcapping at Grand Central Station or toting bags at the exclusive Equinox Hotel in Vermont, where he also had time for leisure pursuits — "chasing the Vermont girls" as he himself recalled years later.

There remained two years for young Powell to make his mark at Colgate, to prove worthy of the faith his father had placed in him or to fail.

ᕝᗯᕐ

Howard Armstrong arrived at Colgate the same year as Powell. From Yorkville, New York, he was the son of a teacher, grandson of a farmer. He became Powell's best white friend on campus. Pursued by white girls who did not know of his racial background, Powell would urge Armstrong to rescue him: "Will you tell her I'm black, so she'll back off?" Visiting Powell's room, Armstrong would see him with his roommates and get the strangest feeling: "My impression was Adam didn't have much to do with them." Armstrong often found Powell hunched over his desk, either reading mail or composing letters. He immediately thought of Powell as a politician-in-training. "I would go in there and he would show me his correspondence files," explained Armstrong. "He would take delight in showing me letters — two stacks, one had been answered, one had not been answered. He had correspondence coming in and going out all the time. These were from any number of people he knew." They talked politics and the future. They went on weekend jaunts, to either Utica or Syracuse, riding through the lovely upstate countryside in Armstrong's Dodge, which he had purchased for fifty dollars, money he had earned by working for a town haberdasher.

Syracuse had both the Loew's State Theater and Loew's Bigtime Vaudeville. The two young men also liked the big-band music the Syracuse hotels were noted for. "Once we dipped into a bar in Utica," recalled Armstrong. "Remember, this was during Prohibition. The bartender decided Adam wasn't white. I was ready to give him an argument. Adam said, 'Well, no, let's not start any trouble.' " Even more, Armstrong enjoyed his trips with Powell into black Harlem. "We went to a dance one night, a big room; he knew them all. He was in his environment, I'd say." One evening they strolled down to the East River to see a girlfriend of Powell's off to Europe. Armstrong remembered a particularly enjoyable evening at the Powells' home, with Adam Senior engaging the young Colgate student in discourse. "You know we blacks are not jealous of you whites," he began. "In some respects we feel superior." Armstrong barely moved as the elder Powell went into a conversation about black women, dark-skinned women and light-skinned women, and the joy of having women of various hues to choose from. Later that day Adam Junior treated him to an evening at the whites-only Cotton Club. Armstrong concluded that the Powells' wasn't a house of traditional Baptist ministers.

Academically, Powell rallied during his junior and senior years at Colgate. His course work was dominated by A's and B's. No longer hindered by mathematics and sciences — course work that demanded a methodical mind — he could unleash his freewheeling intellect to its full advantage. "American Diplomacy," "The History of England and the British Commonwealth," "The Recent Novel," "The Modern World," "Old Testament Times," "International Law," and "Social Diagnosis" were the kinds of courses he devoured and mastered. They stretched a mind, forced it to search for options, to acknowledge that history was in perpetual motion. In his biblical literature classes, professors found him so adept that they asked him to address his fellow students as a lecturer. Powell spoke some Spanish, but German became his foreign language of choice. (Far back in his mother's ancestry lay a German heritage, and in years to come he took vacations in the German countryside.) He also received a little celebrity during visits from his father, who was invited to the campus by President Cutten. Following the crash of 1929, Powell Senior addressed the faculty and students of Colgate, trying to ease their worries. "You've got to have faith in God to pull you through," he told them.

Perhaps as a buffer against the woes that awaited the Class of 1930, the Colgate administration planned grand celebrations for their commencement. Four days of festivities, billed as the grandest ever planned, highlighted the school's tribute to its senior class. There were dances and social teas, promenades in the sunshine, the arrival of alumni. Seniors exchanged photographs and home addresses among themselves. "Now listen here guy," Powell wrote on his photograph to Howard Armstrong — "the perfect Colgate man," according to Powell — "if I'm ever trying to prepare a sermon in afterlife, and you bust in on me, for cripe's sake, give a guy a break . . . When I'm old and gray — optimistic, what? — and my thoughts revert to Andrews Hall — 1st floor, I can't help from being rejuvenated. I'll think of Howie . . ." There was indeed an address on the back: 132 West 138th Street, home of the Abyssinian Baptist Church — "your future hotel," he advised Armstrong.

Powell's senior picture shows him in a three-piece pin-striped suit, silk tie, collar closed by a stickpin. His hair is swept cleanly back, although on the right side a tuft is out of place, giving his countenance a slight raffishness. The ears are large but the facial features soft and handsome. His eyebrows curve upward, away from dark eyes. It is a photograph of both comfort and mystery. For all the world to see, he looked like many handsome white Colgate graduates in the Class of 1930, which, of course, he both was and wasn't. Beneath the yearbook photographs of the other blacks were listed their athletic involvements — baseball, football, basketball. There was nothing beneath Powell's picture but the Alpha Phi Alpha insignia, a distinction none of his classmates enjoyed. This achievement failed, however, to tell the true story. He had left a permanent impression on his classmates, black and white, but especially black. He had brought culture into their lives, entertained them, taken them to Harlem, won them over as friends.

He had also matured. A month earlier he had given his first sermon in the Abyssinian pulpit, before the usual congregation of about four thousand people. He had been "ordained without any divinity training," a visitor wrote of that Sunday sermon, "but he can handle the people." The company of his contemporaries did not intrigue him as much as the company of older men and women. His self-confidence was strong, leaving those in his wake believing that he felt supreme, that "there never was a height higher than he was," as a church acquaintance put it. He told Daniel Crosby that if he did become a minister, he would not be like his father; he would preach economic and racial justice.

The new graduates knew little, with the exception of what they read in the newspapers, about the crash on Wall Street, soon to engulf America. The Colgate administration had offered financial aid to seniors whose parents were suddenly strapped for cash. To survive

Colgate was to be helped by Colgate. Beyond the confines of the university, however, lay the real world. James Colgate, the family heir, addressed the senior class at commencement. He found no reason to mince words. "Do not fool yourselves," he warned them. "Life has stricter rules, harsher judgments, and more cruel limitations than any of you have known in your college life. It is a hard game, and its rules are inexorable."

Powell had overcome his first crisis in life, the brief notoriety he had received in his attempt to pass as white. ("Never let that happen again," his father had warned him.) He would not be the tragic mulatto, seesawing between racial identities. He would instead accept being black and give it a wonderful spin, demanding to be accepted in both worlds, black and white, while arriving at the door of each with rebellion in his eyes. Scandal had yielded shame during his first months on campus, but it had also shown the way toward triumph. Never again would the Merton Andersons of the world question his racial identity. Now he knew who he was. The attributes he would need — cunning, wit, arrogance, and intelligence — to take on labor and church leaders, senators and representatives, ambassadors, and even American presidents, were now in evidence.

Colgate had provided his last chance, and he had endured. The trees were green again, the valley as lush as always in early summer. There would, however, be no looking back on Colgate for Powell; he would attend no rah-rah reunions. Although he continued to invite classmates to Harlem, only one friend would last. That was Daniel Crosby, who had first encouraged his fellow blacks to allow Powell to room with them; Crosby, the darkest-skinned black on campus, the football player who had had to stay behind when the team went south to play Vanderbilt.

Powell's senior year had been so accomplished that he was excused from taking final examinations, the reward for outstanding academic achievement. On those classmates who had doubted him, he now had the last laugh. At commencement, John Hoben delivered the class poem. Each senior had been given a small maroon leather booklet with the senior program printed inside. For the first time ever, the Colgate seniors held torches — yet to be lit — as they circled Taylor Lake. Alumni began singing the alma mater; townsfolk had gathered on the hillsides. The class president began walking around the lake, lighting each torch with his own until all were aflame. Dusk turned to darkness. Reflections of flames bouncing across the lake made it look like there was fire beneath the surface. The scene was majestic, and the problems of a depressed nation seemed far, far away. Along with the other seniors, young Adam Clayton Powell, Jr., knelt and dipped his torch in the water. With the flame doused, he walked out into the world.

II

YOUNG
ADAM POWELL
1930–1945

FOLLOWING HIS GRADUATION from Colgate University, Adam Clayton Powell, Jr., sailed for Asia and northern Africa, the trip a gift from father to only son. Traveling east, he did not stop until he reached Damascus. His sense of style carried well. He walked across the ruins in a white jacket and two-toned bucks. "Just a snap of me taken by an Arab — I didn't know it. This is from my furthest point beyond in Syria," he wrote to Isabel Washington, his Harlem sweetheart. "Coming home!" Before coming home — the journey lasted three months — he pocketed bottles of fragrant oils to give to her.

His immediate career path, mapped out by a wise and aging father, was hardly unusual for the twenty-two-year-old son of a prominent Baptist minister. There would be graduate studies at nearby Union Theological Seminary, supplemented by an understudy's role at his father's church. Powell Senior had a father's patience, but there was much for the younger Powell to prove to the deacons. They had known a boy who had shown up for church with liquor on his breath (he kept a supply of breath mints handy to cover the smell), a boy who frequented nightclubs and talked energetically of women and sex. Union Theological Seminary, then, would shape the mind; understudying at the church would shape the character. But the Harlem that he had left in 1926 was very changed when he returned from abroad in the fall of 1930.

The Depression had wreaked havoc on human lives. Factories across America were either closing or had closed. Families were scavenging in big and small towns alike. The previous March, thousands of unemployed people had staged a protest in New York City's Union Square, only to be violently dispersed by policemen with blackjacks.

Harlem, its economic strength never secure, had become crippled overnight. Nowhere was the plight of its people more profound than beneath the Third Avenue railroad tracks on the edge of the South Bronx. There the women of Harlem gathered nearly every morning in hopes of being picked to do "day work." They were met by housewives from the Bronx and Manhattan, who walked beneath the thundering tracks to look for their maids for the day. Sometimes a housewife would walk up to a woman, look her over, and pass her by, continuing through the open area where other women stood waiting to be selected. When one was chosen, she would follow the housewife home and clean her house, and clean it very well, in hopes of being selected again the next day or the next week; she would scrub and scrub, and when she left later in the day, she was fortunate to have money in her hands. The going rate ranged from one to four dollars.

The women of Harlem waited under the tracks in the mornings because their husbands or fathers had been put out of work. Somehow money had to be raised. Rent had to be paid and food placed on the table. In Harlem, one of the more dreaded noises was the balled fist of the real estate agent knocking on the door. Every week men and women heard the echo of that fist, because in Harlem rents were demanded on a weekly basis, and those who could not meet the payments had to leave. There was much more than misery beneath the railroad tracks, however. There was fear, none more palpable than the fear caused by rumors that another boatload of refugees had just docked in Hoboken and that the newcomers were heading for Harlem, looking for jobs that were not there, hiking the competition for what meager employment there was to a fierce level.

Within months of the crash there were breadlines in Harlem, lines that would last for years. Tired figures stood in long lines, watched by the police officials who dispensed meal vouchers. Tensions ran so high that fights broke out. Imaginative out-of-work cooks sold meals from storefronts for as little as fifteen cents; civic officials pleaded with churches to feed the hungry; schoolteachers were asked to treat children with a little more understanding. Illness became prevalent, and the sick were sent to Harlem Hospital, an institution that lacked the community's trust and respect. As fall turned to winter and the breadlines lengthened, there were blank stares on the faces of the hungry children. Figures huddled in alleyways, and people warmed their hands over the haze of bonfires up and down Harlem's streets.

The elder Powell knew he had to act. Riding along the streets in his Packard, with his son conspicuously and often by his side, he grimaced with pain. The wrenching poverty reminded him of how he had lived as a boy in West Virginia. When desperate appeals were made to private citizens and charitable organizations, money came in from the Rockefeller philanthropies, and men like Seward Prosser, the influential banker, and Adam Clayton Powell, Sr., the Abyssinian stalwart, stepped forth. In New York City, charitable donations provided for the creation of an Emergency Work Bureau, which Prosser headed. Workers were to be paid fifteen dollars a week for an assortment of menial jobs. "No man can be moral in Harlem on fifteen dollars a week," Powell feared. But there was opportunity in the Emergency Work Bureau, and he realized it. It was an opportunity for his son.

Young Powell, already named business manager of the church, was appointed to administer the work relief bureau for Harlem, operating out of the basement of the church. Setting up a staff in the basement, he worked with the kind of energy the times demanded. He sent young men, his aides (some of them were older than he was), out to buy discounted food, and when they returned hours later, their arms loaded with sacks of food, they would hand the food over to the church ladies. The ladies would then scurry to empty the contents into big iron pots, and the hungry would be fed; and Mattie Powell would stand there, proud of her son. Every evening, as dark spread over Harlem, the needy would be summoned to the church to eat and to get shoes and clothing, and the young minister would shake hands and pat backs and get to know the men and women who had been raised in his father's church. Word quickly spread about him. "Have you heard about Adam, up in Harlem, feeding the hungry?" a Colgate classmate asked Daniel Crosby. In a few short months, young Powell and his staff had provided 28,500 free meals and given away an estimated 17,000 pieces of clothing and 2,000 pairs of shoes.

The work was like having a government job, but it was more than that, because it did what government was supposed to do and sometimes could not. Powell was just too busy to attend classes at Union Theological Seminary, so he sent church secretaries over to take his class notes. When seminary officials complained about the practice, he quit the seminary in a huff. Directing a staff, feeding the hungry, and appealing to the congregation for collections were so much more vital than sitting at a desk.

Adam Clayton Powell, Sr., was a Republican. A Republican president had freed his mother from slavery. Party loyalty, and his standing in the New York community, had inspired a correspondence with President Hoover. The letters were insignificant — praise from a Harlem minister — but Powell's devotion to the Republican ticket encouraged New York Republicans to name him a presidential elector at the 1932 party convention. The news was given wide play in the Harlem newspapers. Accepting the honor, the elder Powell, with his son at his side (tall and thin and not yet wearing a mustache, young Powell looked hopelessly collegiate), vowed to use "all the God-given energy of my hands, head, and heart" to help Hoover's re-election campaign. As a Republican he refused to hold Hoover responsible for the Depression, instead blaming Harlem's woes on unchecked vice, which had been allowed to flourish by the Democratic administration of Governor Franklin D. Roosevelt and the shifty men who ran Tammany Hall, he claimed. But he was careful not to offend New York City officeholders. He waged his battles on terrain he could navigate, which meant the church and the pulpit. A huge congregation listened as he read his written sermon "A Hungry God," a flinty appeal to his fellow Harlem clergymen, whom he criticized for their lavish ways and their lack of attention to the needy.

Proud, educated at Yale, where he had adopted a Yankee's stolid vision, Powell Senior could no longer remain silent about the evangelists on the streets of Harlem. His fellow ministers were charlatans offering "hypocritical prayers." "The preachers, churches, and lodges that remain indifferent this winter to our sorely depressed people will soon be gone and forgotten forever." Sacrifices must be made, and they would begin in the Abyssinian pulpit. Powell announced that he would forgo a pay raise, a new car; he would give over a portion of his salary to charity. He demanded no less from other ministers. But the ministers not only refused to follow his advice and warnings, they turned their tongues against him, fiercely attacking his penchant for European vacations and his comfortable living style: "In his magnificently furnished dining room alone is a five-thousand-dollar suite of carved furniture . . ." The din rose. "Let not your ambition for a cheap notoriety spoil your real work," said another critic.

It became painfully clear that the elder Powell no longer held emotional sway over Harlem. His son, forced to watch the angry challenges, neither forgot nor repeated Powell's battles with the Harlem clergy. In due time he found his own enemies: politicians and city administrators, the men who ran Tammany Hall, officials of the NAACP. He dismissed clergymen in the hunt for bigger targets. For now, he remained busy, working feverishly to prove to his father that he could take on added responsibility.

He also had something else to prove to his father: his independence. In the midst of the social turmoil sweeping Harlem, he challenged his father over the woman he wished to marry.

⚭

Born in Savannah, Isabel Washington had been sent north to a convent in Pennsylvania as a young girl. Her sister, Fredi, joined her there later. Isabel rebelled against the school's discipline; she particularly did not like having her mail censored. Upon graduation, she visited an aunt in Washington; Savannah was not big enough for her or her dreams. Stepping off the train in an elegant dress and a Panama hat, she had barely a dollar to her name. Fortified by her relatives, she continued north, to New York City, and even further north, to Harlem, where a grandmother lived in a walkup on 135th Street.

Harlem was noisy, crowded, and active. Isabel liked it right away. For blacks, there was no other place like it. She would become a showgirl, then a star. Isabel Washington did not lack confidence. "I had a very beautiful voice," she stated proudly. Her confidence paid off in trouper's luck. Hanging around the stage door of *Running Wild*, a theatrical presentation, she ingratiated herself to cast, crew, and management. When a singer fell ill, she was given her chance. From there, other opportunities followed. She danced in the chorus at Connie's Inn and at the famed Cotton Club, joining other young women who had an intriguing trait in common: light skin color, an attribute that increased their chances of gaining employment in New York entertainment circles. On Broadway she appeared in *Bamboola, Singing the Blues,* and a show aptly titled *Harlem.* She also made true on her promise to have her little sister, Fredi, follow her to Harlem. Not only was Fredi more talented than Isabel, she was more aggressive, more attractive — and her skin was even lighter. Fredi Washington became a legitimate dramatic star. In 1933 she appeared on Broadway with Paul Robeson in *The Emperor Jones,* and a year later she was lauded for her performance in the Hollywood film *Imitation of Life,* in which she played the daughter of a woman who passes as white.

Isabel Washington pushed on. Her first marriage, to the photographer Preston Webster, ended in divorce but produced a son, also named Preston. A short while after her divorce, a dancer friend asked Isabel if she knew Adam Clayton Powell. She confessed that she had heard of him, but they had never been introduced. On one of his weekend forays into Harlem from the Colgate campus, young Powell sat in the audience of *Harlem*. He rushed a fan's note to Isabel, calling her a "fabulous" actress. Sensing mutual attraction, Isabel's friend arranged a brunch at her apartment. When the doorbell rang, in walked young Powell — "this long, skinny guy," Isabel recalled. After the meal, there was more chatter, then the long skinny guy hailed a taxi; Isabel and her friend had a Broadway show to do.

Powell began rushing home from Colgate "practically every weekend," as Isabel remembered. He introduced her to his friends and to the Abyssinian congregation. His trip abroad after college graduation was arranged by the elder Powell as much to encourage him to forget about Isabel as to allow him to see the world. Instead, the romance flourished. Isabel was a divorcée with a son, but she was more than that. She worked in nightclubs; photographs of her in Harlem newspapers were alluring and suggestive, with a bare shoulder turned directly to the camera's eye. Although producers had approached her about appearing in a road version of *Showboat*, she lacked serious dramatic credentials and the respectability that came with such training. Powell Senior could not bring himself to understand his son's wishes; there were good young women in the pews of the Abyssinian Baptist Church, quiet women from quiet homes, and his son had forsaken them because of his infatuation with a showgirl.

But the young couple were intent on marrying. They considered the consequences of a life without the Abyssinian Baptist Church and devised a plan for financial salvation. They would take to the road together, gently barnstorming. Adam would give sermons and lectures, and following his appearance onstage, Isabel would emerge from behind the curtains to sing recitals. They were young and attractive; they would not starve. They were confident of their ingenious plans. "Take your money," Powell snapped to his father outside church one day, when the two were standing shoulder to shoulder, Isabel nearby, taking a kind of gleeful pride in the dramatics. Isabel saw their predicament in terms of royalty, believing that Powell would have to abdicate his throne for her. Isabel had an active imagination.

Powell Senior, now sixty-eight years old, could not take much more of the battle. He acceded to his son's wishes. Acquaintances of the younger Powell were impressed. "I called it his first triumph," explained St. Claire Bourne, a Harlem resident during the turmoil. "He got the congregation to accept Isabel and his marriage."

Everyone was quick to agree that Isabel would have to be baptized. In the eyes of church members, she was not yet the equal of their minister's son. As she stood at the edge of the baptismal pool, Isabel could not help feeling that the elder Powell still did not sanction this marriage. She knew it better when he dunked her head in the water, his hand to the back of her head. The air drained from her lungs, and she was unable to breathe with the tall old man's strength at the back of her neck. Her imagination went into high gear. She felt that he was trying to drown her. She could see nothing, and she felt her muscles tighten. Suddenly her head was yanked from the water and she gasped for breath, water splashing and the congregation sighing. Born again as an Abyssinian churchwoman, she was deemed fit to marry an Abyssinian man, Adam Junior.

The groom was kept busy. Friends threw him not one but four stag parties, although those making arrangements for the wedding were careful to prepare a modest celebration, less they be accused of over-indulgence in times of despair. Still, the occasion was marked by joy. In a community where there had long been a certain amount of currency attached to dash and drama, the wedding of a glamorous young couple was a cause for celebration. Invitations to the wedding, on March 8, 1933, were considered prizes. Crowds braved a pelting rain to begin lining up outside the church in early morning, though the ceremony was not scheduled to begin until noon. Detectives were quietly placed in the church, because the bride had been threatened for taking one of Harlem's most eligible bachelors, and with the newspapers still peppered with stories of the kidnap and murder of the Lindbergh baby, Isabel Washington was not taking any chances. She worried incessantly about possible harm to her little son, Preston.

When the bride entered the church, she looked up at the balcony, and there, leaning over and shrieking her name, were many of her showgirl friends, envious but wishing her well. Isabel had come a long way from Savannah, and like her, they knew it. The reception was a quiet affair, with slices of cake and drinks. Then Adam whisked his wife away to a farm in the Virginia countryside. Isabel enjoyed her rustic honeymoon, with the exception of the repeated requests that she milk a cow. Farm life and the countryside held no appeal for her; that was one of the reasons she had left Savannah. As for the groom, he had an engaging ability to ingratiate himself in almost any surrounding. On a farm Adam became a farmer, doing farm chores and asking intelligent questions. His wife thought the talent unique. Rising in early morning, she was apt to find her husband bent beneath a cow, drawing milk.

❧

The radicalism that shaped the political consciousness of Adam Clayton Powell, Jr., in the early 1930s had its beginnings in national campaigns waged by both Republicans and Democrats in earlier years. Disaffected members of both parties formed the Progressive Party in 1912 to bolster the fortunes of their presidential nominee, Theodore Roosevelt, no longer a politician in retirement but one hungry for battle. Roosevelt's Progressives were an eclectic mix of easterners and midwesterners, sprinkled with small numbers of women and southerners. They included American Labor Party members, Socialists, and Republicans — not mere Republicans, but, as befit the game hunter in their standard-bearer, Bull Moose Republicans. Their enemies were big business, greed, and public corruption.

Blacks, however, continued to give their support to the Republican Party of Lincoln. Roosevelt had proved too unpredictable. He had drawn praise from blacks for inviting Booker T. Washington to the White House for dinner in 1901, then scorn for dismissing the renowned Twenty-fifth Regiment after a clash with civilians in Brownsville, Texas, in 1906. Angered at their treatment, members of the unit marched through town with weapons drawn; a white civilian was killed and two were wounded. The dispute made national headlines, evoking heated debate, and pity, on both sides of the divide. To blacks, there was no better unit than the Twenty-fifth; its members had distinguished themselves gallantly in the Spanish-American War, and some were middle-aged soldiers with more than two decades' worth of service. To southerners, the episode was a manifestation of armed blacks running amok, something they were not about to tolerate. By inviting Washington to the White House, Roosevelt had already piqued southerners' feelings. He could ill afford more political damage below the Mason-Dixon line. Shrewdly waiting until after the elections, he dismissed the entire regiment (the actual deed was done by his secretary of war, William Howard Taft). Black pride was severely wounded. Once as "enshrined in our hearts as Moses," as Powell Senior said, Roosevelt was afterward considered a Judas.

Blacks were hardly the only flaw in the Progressives' plan of attack against the major parties. A lack of organization haunted them; they saved their best for their 1912 convention, allowing fistfights and chaos to reign. Save for small factions, the party lay dormant until 1924, when once again it was called to action. Liberals found themselves angered by the Democrats. Bitter debate marred the Democratic convention, where southerners, with their Ku Klux Klan followers, gained power over the party. The Republicans held a fairly smooth convention in Ohio — too smooth for the Wisconsin senator Robert La Follette and his followers. La Follette came in second to Calvin Coolidge at the convention, and he was just angry enough to ride the tide of the Progressive Party as its new standard-bearer. His Progressive credentials were impeccable: he had championed child labor laws and challenged the railroad magnates. The New York congressman Fiorello La Guardia thought La Follette's message was so attractive that he abandoned the Republicans that year to campaign for the Progressive ticket.

Progressives meant to reform politics, to fight for better labor laws, better control over the political nominating process, and more rights for minorities and women. Their dreamy idealism, however, was one thing; their lack of experience in running national political campaigns another. As in 1912, they went down to defeat. But it was undeniable that they had unleashed a movement, a passion to challenge municipal government.

Few municipalities felt their passion as did New York City beginning in the late 1920s. New York exhibited the constant clash of good government and bad government, idealists and the entrenched. In 1929 La Guardia took on Mayor Jimmy Walker in a campaign that became a gutsy attack against Tammany Hall and corrupt government. La Guardia was trounced; nevertheless, the political winds were shifting, and in New York City, the men gaining influence now were men like Samuel Seabury, the patrician judge appointed by Governor Roosevelt to investigate Tammany Hall corruption; and Albert Bard, a Harvard graduate obsessed with the idea of good government, which he found embodied in the movement for proportional representation, about which he was trying to educate the voters and the ultimate aim of which was to rid New York of its board of aldermen in favor of a more democratic city council; and La Guardia, beaten in his last run for Congress and beaten as a mayoral candidate but still full of energy; and tall, lean, smiling Stanley Isaacs, the Bull Moose Republican; and Robert Moses, the parks commissioner, savvy and un-smiling; and young Adam Clayton Powell, Jr., up in Harlem but on his way downtown where the other reformers were.

In 1930 New York City was ripe for progressive men on the march. The mayor gave them their first local challenge: Tammany Hall. In the good days, the days before the Depression, Mayor Walker had been tolerable, Broadway shtick and all. Giving up a career as a songwriter (one of his more creative titles was "There's Music in the Rustle of a Skirt"), Walker, like his father, became a Tammany man, first going to the state assembly in Albany, then winning election as mayor in 1925. Jimmy Walker was a man easy to like. He dressed beautifully and had a wicked gleam in his eyes. In reality he was a cold-blooded politician, a Tammany creature who ran City Hall like a fiefdom, with cold-blooded emissaries beneath him shaking down the city. When the citizenry looked to Walker and his City Hall to ease the pain of the Depression, to give them food and clothing, not entertainment, they saw an administration unraveling because of charges of municipal payoffs and corruption, corruption that ate at the moral fiber of government itself.

Governor Roosevelt had to do something; the volume of the com-plaints grew and grew. In 1930 he appointed Judge Seabury to in-vestigate, and Seabury, a long-time warrior in the good-government battles of New York City, relished the task. He hired young attorneys, who went at their assignment relentlessly. Young lawyers burst into his office offering to work for him, wanting to have a hand in bringing down the Walker administration; many were so eager that they worked without pay. Seabury's two-year investigation uncovered a stunning array of corrupt practices. Building permits were issued il-legally; no-show jobs seemed a permanent fixture of the administra-tion; judges were on the take; Tammany minions were such adept shakedown artists that not even prostitutes escaped their grip. There were safe deposit boxes stuffed with thousands, and Seabury's probe turned toward income tax records, fatal to Walker and his adminis-tration. Before the end came, however, Walker was summoned to appear before Seabury's investigating committee. "Drive carefully, we don't want to get a ticket," the witty mayor said to his chauffeur on the morning he headed to his testimony.

Seabury suggested to Roosevelt, already a presidential nominee — and a nominee who had been gruffly treated at the 1932 convention by the Walker-led Tammany forces — that he remove Walker from office. Long an anti-Tammany figure, Roosevelt was nervous. Tammany corruption had been exposed before, and Tammany was still around, and its presence would still be felt on election day. Walker, however, saved Roosevelt from the dilemma by resigning from office and sailing for Europe with Betty Compton, his mistress, on his arm. Joseph McKee, president of the board of aldermen and the man who would ignite Adam Clayton Powell, Jr.'s political ambitions, took over as acting mayor until a special election could be held.

The 1932 elections did little to abate Tammany Hall's suffering. Roosevelt resoundingly defeated Herbert Hoover. Herbert Lehman, lieutenant governor of New York and himself a reformer, was elected governor, and he would be the first governor (Roosevelt included) to pay genuine attention to the black community of Harlem. In New York City, then, the reformers had beaten back Tammany Hall. Although John O'Brien, a Tammany Democrat, won the special election for mayor, the reformers did not plan on letting up. Their army of bold and energetic men was about to advance on the city. Leaders would be sought out and reputations made.

◦◦◦

Conrad Vincent had been one of five black doctors hired at Harlem Hospital in 1925, a move blessed by Tammany Hall, its eye always keenly on future elections. Harlem Hospital was the only hospital in New York City that catered to the medical needs of blacks; the other hospitals were segregated. But as the years passed, Vincent, enthusiastic at the breakthrough in 1925, turned angry. The black doctors were not given challenging assignments. As for the black nurses, they were segregated within the confines of the hospital. Vincent, speaking on behalf of the black staff and thereby taking the most risk, also complained that the care of black patients at Harlem Hospital was abysmal. Having allowed vice to flourish in Harlem, from prostitution to bootlegging to numbers racketeering, New York officials could hardly have been surprised at the crimes that resulted. Murders, robberies, and crimes of passion were all played out in high, if sad, spirits in the Harlem newspapers. Crime and poverty deepened the community's health crisis. Syphilis rates in Harlem were nine times higher than in white Manhattan; the pneumonia and tuberculosis statistics were as alarming. Black babies had half the chance of surviving of white babies.

Harlem Hospital, on the corner of 136th Street and Lenox Avenue, frightened many in the community. "The butcher shop," they sometimes called it; at other times, simply "the morgue." In the hospital during the Depression years, one saw patients sleeping in hallways, their groans eerily echoing down the corridors. For 200,000 Harlemites, there were 250 beds. "When I take my life in my hands I want peace, quiet, and harmony," one resident said. "I don't want to be around the strife and turmoil of Harlem Hospital."

When an NAACP-appointed committee was formed to investigate Vincent's allegations, Adam Powell Senior and Heywood Broun, the crusading *New York World-Telegram* columnist, refused to serve, believing that the committee's work would be compromised with Louis Wright, the director of the Department of Surgery at the hospital, as one of its members. Such was the reach of Tammany Hall that it held enormous sway over the activities of Harlem Hospital. Wright's position had been endorsed by Frederick Morton, Tammany Hall's black leader in Harlem. Morton ruled with an iron fist; his club, the United Democratic Club, was known reverently as "Morton's White House." Wright's position as a board member of the NAACP gave him credentials as a civil rights advocate, and since he had not made any complaints about conditions at the hospital, it followed logically that Vincent was merely an emotional man, ungrateful for an opportunity.

Squeezed between the NAACP and Tammany Hall, Vincent needed an outsider, someone with a progressive mind, someone who could rally the community, and above all, someone willing to go downtown and fight; in heart and mind, Conrad Vincent needed a progressive, someone willing to challenge the parameters of limited liberalism so appreciated by the men sitting behind the desks over at the NAACP offices. In young Adam Clayton Powell, Jr., Vincent found his ally — an uptown reformer, in fact a progressive, willing to march downtown and take on the opposition. Not only had Powell drawn attention for his relief efforts in Harlem, he had protested the case of the Scottsboro boys, nine Alabama youths falsely accused and sentenced to death for the rape of two white women. One of the more interesting twists in the case involved Ruby Bates, one of the victims, who recanted her story and became an accuser of the entire Alabama justice system. Pained by a guilt-ridden conscience, Bates had come to Harlem, and from Harlem traveled the East Coast making appeals on behalf of the accused, with Powell at her side.

Desperate for a replacement for Walker, Tammany Hall had turned to surrogate court justice John O'Brien. Although O'Brien had won the special election, he still faced a battle in the regular 1933 municipal elections. A Tammany man first and a justice second, he was Tammany's kind of mayor. He was also uncreative and reviled by the reformers in New York City. But he prepared energetically for his fall campaign.

One day the doors to his office swung open and in walked young Adam Clayton Powell, come to complain about conditions at Harlem Hospital. Ordinarily complaints from a Harlem minister — any Harlem minister — might not have rated high on the mayor's list of priorities, but this was an election year: Harlemites voted. O'Brien's tone toward Powell, however, was condescending. He treated the minister as a neophyte, as someone else who had come to extract promises from the Tammany table, and sent him on his way empty-handed. "Go on back to Harlem, boy, and don't fan the flames," he told him. It was all that Powell needed.

Back in Harlem, he swung the doors of his father's church wide open and waved in thousands of protesters, emotional protesters: the men and women who had been treated, who had relatives who had been treated, at Harlem Hospital; the men and women who had long criticized the service by the staff; the men and women who had long walked the corridors searching for a black nurse, a black doctor, and had been unable to find one; the men and women whose children had been born at the hospital. It was the only hospital there was. No matter what its administrators said, these people believed Conrad Vincent. They came to the Abyssinian church for a meeting — it was more protest than meeting — and they settled in the pews, and they listened to the young minister who had gone downtown to get answers and instead of getting answers had been treated condescendingly.

"If nothing is wrong in Harlem Hospital, then why is O'Brien nervous?" Powell asked them. He had a way of making them feel that he was angrier than they were. "If nothing is wrong," he bellowed, looking out over the gathering, "then why are you assembled here tonight?" He knew as well as they knew: something was wrong. And they were looking to the young Abyssinian minister to lead them. This was not moral preaching against a distant enemy, against the forces in Washington or the Deep South officeholders. It was preaching against the enemies who were nearer, who were right downtown, a bus ride away. It was preaching against the men who ran municipal government and Tammany Hall, the men in suits whom Harlemites saw only on election eve; against Frederick Morton, the black Tammany official, sure in arrogance and aloof in manner. Young Adam Powell no longer looked like a callow collegian. A mustache now added a look of maturity. The body was bulkier, the strides more purposeful. The minister's son was coming of age.

When Powell returned to City Hall the following month, he was not alone. There were fifteen hundred protesters with him, enough to cause alarm among New York police. Mounted patrols were called out to surround the protesters, who raised their placards high, their little children clutching at them amid the confusion and the snorting of the horses. It was exactly the kind of scene O'Brien could ill afford. Hospital officials had warned him against meeting with Powell again, but he could not have an army of protesters at City Hall while refusing to meet with their leader.

It was not the litany of demands made by Powell — more black doctors, an end to the segregation of black nurses in the hospital — that was surprising to the administration. It was his sheer bravado, his arrogance when he turned to Hospitals Commissioner J. G. William Greeff and demanded that he resign, citing "incompetency, inefficiency, and prejudice." For Tammany Hall the scene was nearly incomprehensible. A relatively unknown Harlem minister, at least unknown by downtown standards, was holding court in City Hall, making demands; and outside the windows there were vocal protesters, the young minister's supporters, who refused to go away. The men and women of municipal government could not take their eyes off Powell, who stared them directly in the eye. Then he strolled out, their gaze trailing him.

On the steps of City Hall, Powell posed with the doctors. It was a group pose, but it was also something else: Powell, coat draped over one arm, fedora in hand, had stepped just a step, but a powerful step, in front of the rest. He was their leader. They were older than he was, and they were doctors, the cream of the community, and he was their leader. There was a look of consternation on his face.

In June, his threats to Tammany Hall grew louder. With an eye on the upcoming mayoral election, he vowed to register ten thousand voters — "members of my church" — to fight the Democratic Party if changes were not made at Harlem Hospital. Tammany Hall did what Tammany Hall rarely had to do: it capitulated. In August, Commissioner Greeff, the man ultimately responsible for the direction of the hospital, resigned, only four months after Powell had turned on him at City Hall, demanding his ouster. Powell now joined the ranks of the men who had taken on Tammany Hall and extracted a victory. The moment was significant in his political career.

By going downtown and facing the enemy, he had shown that he was eager to lead, and he had shown that there were many in Harlem who were willing to follow him. He had gazed out over the congregation of his father's church and seen not merely people eager to pray on Sunday mornings but people eager to protest. Week by week, there were those in the congregation who looked around and noticed visitors in the pews, and the visitors, Catholics and Episcopalians, were from other Harlem churches, coming to hear the young Powell. A woman named Gwen Bourne sat there one Sunday, listening to him as he summoned would-be converts, and she could not hold herself back. She rose, and just as she began to walk toward the pulpit, Powell's voice pulling her, her husband caught her, and Gwen Bourne thought to herself, "I'm a Catholic!" and knew she couldn't proceed.

And there were those who noticed something altogether different about Powell now. He had begun using his body. He walked to be seen, eagerly stepping to the forefront of crowds. Once in a room, he could almost be felt. From the pews in church people could certainly see it. When he walked down the aisle of the church, his robe billowed; one church member once said that he must have a small fan beneath his robe because it billowed so much. He had the kind of presence that was drawing the attention of politicians in New York City in 1933.

⟨⟨⟩⟩

Edward Flynn, the cool, studied, suave Bronx Democratic boss, who had managed to remain untouched by the Tammany Hall scandals, had plenty of reasons to be concerned about the 1933 New York mayoral race. Flynn was a Roosevelt confidant. Tammany Democrats were not Roosevelt Democrats, and Roosevelt would not soon forget their efforts to sabotage his nomination at the party's 1932 convention, where he had been forced to a fourth ballot. Though Mayor O'Brien was a poor campaigner, he could not be dismissed, for his victory would continue Tammany's hold on City Hall. Such a result might prove dangerous for Governor Lehman and embarrassing for Roosevelt. Flynn needed a reform Democrat to take on the Tammany candidate. He approached Joseph McKee, the former board of aldermen president, who also hailed from the Bronx. But despite a show of support from Democratic reformers, who had given him 250,000 votes in the special election campaign even though he had not been an official candidate, McKee was not interested in the race. He retreated to his banking business.

The Republicans were also in a quandary. Their only hope, and they knew it, was to coalesce with the Roosevelt Democrats, to fuse the two parties together in an effort to slay the Tammany tiger. The men who had helped bring down Jimmy Walker, men like Moses and Seabury, were desperate. They believed fusion could work; they only needed a candidate.

He was short and thick-chested, and he walked like a man ready to swing his fists. He was a Republican, but a Republican who had bedeviled his party by swinging to the Progressives in the 1924 national elections. A son of immigrants, he had studied law, then been elected to Congress, where he championed labor laws and forged a national reputation. In 1928, he tried unsuccessfully to upend the Tammany reign of Jimmy Walker, then returned to Congress. In 1932, when his career looked so bright, Fiorello La Guardia was defeated. His constituents felt he had become too aloof and in his place elected another Italian, conspicuously short like La Guardia. He lived in East Harlem, Italian Harlem, which was never to be confused with central Harlem, black Harlem. Fiorello La Guardia, who loved New York City and hated Tammany Hall, became the candidate of the Fusion Party.

But Flynn, and thus Roosevelt, had genuine reason to worry about La Guardia. Fearless and emotional, he was a gutsy campaigner who connected with voters. It took him little time to prove his mettle. His speeches were passionate appeals to the city's electorate against Tammany Hall. His goal was nothing less than changing the New York political landscape. It could not have given Boss Flynn (who would not back O'Brien and was still desperately hunting for a candidate) comfort that of the announced candidates, O'Brien and La Guardia, it was La Guardia who had the greater emotional attachment to black Harlem. As a congressman, he had taken on southern Democrats, challenging them on the floor of the House, and forged alliances with labor leaders, both moves that endeared him to blacks. Leaders in black Harlem, eager for any kind of help on a national level, were quick to give support to their allies in Washington or elsewhere in New York.

Black Harlem itself had no clout, not downtown and certainly not in Washington. Harlem had been sliced up into portions that represented principally two ethnic groups, Jews and Italians. The Jewish and Italian districts cut across, up, and around black Harlem in an ingenious pattern that denied black residents any voting strength. Black Harlem thus remained a political stepchild, forced to take whatever congressional help it could get from La Guardia, Joseph Gavagan, and Vito Marcantonio, all of whose districts included it. Tammany Democrats proved their disdain for black Harlem by repeatedly refusing to support a black congressional candidate. In 1928 Hubert Delaney, a black New York City lawyer, ran for Congress against Tammany's candidate, Joseph Gavagan, with Republican backing. La Guardia marched into black Harlem pleading for help for Delaney. "Don't vote for me if you can't vote for Delaney," he bravely, but dangerously, told his followers. They followed his advice: both candidates lost.

When black Harlem looked at the mayoral election of 1933, Tammany was anathema, and La Guardia seemed to be a man who could be trusted. By early fall, the Fusion candidate, appearing at rally after rally, brusquely bursting forth, assailing Tammany graft and corruption, accompanied by Samuel Seabury himself, looked like the man to beat. But Flynn was not willing to concede so easily. The only hope was to play fusion with the Fusion backers of La Guardia — to go out and find a candidate who would fall in between Tammany and Fusion, a Democrat but a reform Democrat, someone who could reclaim the liberal votes that looked to be sliding toward the La Guardia camp.

Ed Flynn's best hope rested with Joseph McKee, his Bronx ally who had turned him down. Now, with Flynn promising White House support, McKee had a change of mind and entered the race. However, there was one problem. He could not run as an organization Democrat, because Democrats already had their man in O'Brien. His strategy would have to mirror La Guardia's strategy; party ideology would have to be widened and distant forces be summoned together. McKee's supporters formed their own party, the Recovery Party, and collected an impressive roster of businessmen and Rooseveltian figures, people who thought La Guardia not only crude but intemperate. Drawn to McKee's maverick candidacy, these men and women were not deterred by its notoriously late unveiling in September; the lateness seemed only to inspire them more. Samuel Leibowitz, stalwart defender of the Scottsboro boys, came aboard. Averell Harriman, the young railroad baron, appreciated the challenge. And Adam Clayton Powell, Jr., was asked to join the campaign. McKee, wisely making an appeal for the black vote, had not forgotten Powell's presence as he took on Mayor O'Brien at City Hall. For Powell the opportunity was welcome. He could show the big boys downtown, whose world seemed a world away from central Harlem, that he meant to play seriously.

Powell was named McKee's Harlem chairman. Immediately he saw the move as condescending: the black minister was to play chaperon and usher other blacks into the fold. So he rewrote his title to "chairman and director of the McKee Recovery Party campaign." Starting late and desperate for harmony, McKee seemed not to mind this grandstand play. For Powell, it was merely the beginning.

It was McKee's campaign, but there were times when Powell all but dwarfed him. Powell added a huge supporting contingent to his staff — women's groups, personal aides, and, of course, a publicity team. Then he traveled, from uptown to downtown and back again, giving speeches. Like McKee, he was always quick to identify himself not as a Tammany Democrat but as a Roosevelt Democrat. With aides swinging doors wide open for him, Powell strode from meeting room to meeting room, and soon it became clear that he was leading the charge not for McKee's campaign but for some unannounced campaign of his own. Powell Senior liked it all, the way his son was taking the lead. Still a Republican, he was not deterred from throwing a luncheon for McKee. For a while the McKee-Powell forces surged ahead in a few polls. It was clear that the campaign had been energized. Then, with a swiftness that was mortal, the McKee camp was delivered a blow from which it could not recover: a charge of anti-Semitism.

As a high school teacher, McKee had penned an article noting the exploding numbers of Jewish students in New York City high schools, as opposed to the numbers of Catholic students who were quitting to work. His dark implication was that Jews would someday take over New York. When the La Guardia camp brought forth the article again (actually, it had been exposed in an earlier campaign), McKee was ruined. Jewish allies came to his defense, but to no avail; he could not distance himself from the charge of anti-Semitism. The Roosevelt White House steered clear of the fray. La Guardia went on the attack relentlessly, lauding Jews and Judaism and defending New York's Jewish governor, Herbert Lehman. "Are you trying to draw a red herring across the cowardly, contemptible, and unjust attack that you have made and published against a great race so gloriously represented by our Governor?" La Guardia demanded to know. The more McKee, a deeply devout Catholic, tried to explain, the more he sounded guilty. In the days leading up to the election, La Guardia's troops gained daunting momentum. It was just not the newspaper endorsements or the huge rally at Madison Square Garden staged by the Fusion forces, it was the candidate himself, a man ready to crush all who stood in his way, especially Tammany and all that Tammany meant. On election eve, La Guardia was tough, carousing on New York's streets and calling Tammany men "punks" and "thugs" to their faces and demanding that they get out of his way. He had his redemption, defeating McKee with 868,522 votes to McKee's 609,053 votes; O'Brien trailed, with 586,672 votes. The "little flower" swept Harlem as well.

For New York, the events were dramatic. Not in sixteen years had the city been run by anyone save Tammany Democrats. And even though the victory was a defeat for the young Powell's candidate, it was not a defeat for Powell himself. Politics had energized him, had summoned the best of his talents. He had surged so far ahead of the McKee campaign that at times he himself looked like the candidate. It was not just the elation at having been named to an important post in a citywide campaign that thrilled him, according to David Licorish, an assistant minister at Abyssinian; it was the sheer joy that he seemed to get from campaigning, from working the streets, from addressing the voters. While he had lost, he really had not lost, recalled Licorish, because he had tasted "the sweet fruit" of political battle.

For Adam Clayton Powell, Jr., the election campaign had been a victory indeed. By distancing himself from his father's Republican politics, he claimed his own political ground. He took the mantle of a Democrat, but of an opposition Democrat. He had done what no Harlem minister had done before: entered the tricky world of New York City politics. The move from pulpit to political arena did not go unnoticed. "He is young and he is a minister," one Harlem publication noted derisively. "Youth has practically no record in Harlem politics." The sharpest salvo — and one with merit — accused him of turning the McKee movement into a "Powell movement."

The campaign that exposed Tammany weakness must be remembered for more than boosting the career of Fiorello La Guardia. It was also a campaign where names surfaced, names that in the coming years would mean much in New York politics, and beyond. Newbold Morris and Stanley Isaacs would be heard from, and Averell Harriman and Robert Moses. Because Powell was not looking for a mentor —

instead he was looking to lead — he did not seek to forge an immediate relationship with Ed Flynn. But Flynn had watched him, had appreciated his alliance with McKee, and had liked what he saw. And Ed Flynn, Roosevelt's emissary, did not forget the Harlem minister.

ᑲᐧᐤᑥ

The political activism that enabled the Fusionists to win City Hall did not extend into black Harlem. Having never received much from a New York City mayor, black Harlem, which threw its votes wistfully to La Guardia in the 1933 election, did not know what to expect from the new mayor and his administration. In turn, La Guardia did not quite know what to give it. The mayor gained a small measure of capital with blacks by appointing Hubert Delaney, the Republican attorney, as tax commissioner, but the community's woes were not high on his list of priorities. During the early months of his administration, La Guardia was forced to spend a great deal of time traveling back and forth between New York and Washington, cashing in chips with former congressional colleagues and forging a working relationship with the Roosevelt administration in order to get money. Tammany Hall had left New York City in a financial quagmire. Estimates of the city's debt to banks ranged from $30 to $60 million. Before he could save Harlem, La Guardia had to save New York City.

But black Harlem was impatient, and its impatience coincided with the arrival of a bevy of young thinkers and activists, their minds clicking. Benjamin Davis arrived from Georgia, Roy Wilkins from Missouri, and Herbert Bruce from the Caribbean. (Paul Robeson was on the international stage — he had played Othello in London — and did not yet include himself as an important influence in the emerging political thought of Harlem.) Pulled by the reputation of stalwarts such as W. E. B. Du Bois and A. Philip Randolph, already distinguished figures, the youngsters came to Harlem and found fertile ground for their own imaginations.

Du Bois, both enigmatic and angry, edited *The Crisis,* the NAACP magazine, mixing protest with literary flair. With a Harvard doctorate to his name (he was the first black to claim such an achievement), Du Bois found his job opportunities limited in white America, despite a reputation that had been cemented by his publication, in 1903, of *The Souls of Black Folk,* a book of trenchant essays that marked him as a genuine thinker and an opponent of Booker T. Washington's theory of accommodation. Having been the leader of the Niagara

Movement, Du Bois wished only to continue his protest from behind a desk after his arrival in Harlem. Born in Massachusetts, he had a Yankee's pride and disposition. He was aloof and wished to be left alone.

A. Philip Randolph had been delivering speeches around America a decade before the Depression hit, advocating socialism and frightening as many blacks as he inspired. Florida-born and with an Edwardian manner, he had ardently backed Eugene V. Debs's 1920 presidential campaign and was currently engaged in a bitter battle with the railroads to form a black porters' union. Relentless and steady in his determination and selfless to a fault, Randolph inspired an ally to remark in later years that he "stands four-square to all the winds." Although twenty-one years younger than Du Bois, Randolph had obtained such a reputation that he too was already considered a part of the old guard in the Harlem of the mid-1930s.

In Kansas City young Roy Wilkins had worked quietly in boycotts, pressing local grocers to hire black clerks. Evenings, he lectured before various church groups about race relations. Days, he wrote for a local newspaper, torn between a reporter's objectivity and the discrimination he saw in the community. Tall and thin, with a warm smile, he did not come to Harlem to be a newspaperman; instead, the work of NAACP activism was about to claim his soul. "My newspapering days were over; a new way of life lay just up the tracks," he wrote in his memoirs about the journey to Harlem.

Educated at Morehouse, Amherst (where he played football), and Harvard Law School, Ben Davis had returned to his native Georgia to defend Angelo Herndon, who was accused of distributing Communist leaflets in Atlanta. Even though Davis demanded that blacks be placed on the jury, a Georgia court sentenced Herndon to eighteen years on a chain gang. Davis appealed to the U.S. Supreme Court, where he won, gaining instant fame. His father, Benjamin Davis, Sr., was a Republican national committeeman, comfortable in the belief that the cold eye cast by Republicans on matters of race was less cold than that of southern Democrats. There also was something of the Deep South in the elder Davis, a love of both land and tortured history: he named his son Benjamin Jefferson Davis. When the son arrived in Harlem in 1933 and took an apartment on 126th Street, he arrived as an acknowledged Communist. His visions of the South were more suspicious than his father's.

And there was Herbert Bruce, a small man with mellifluous diction, who in time would be given the moniker (as a sign of both derision and respect) "the mighty midget." Bruce had actually arrived in Harlem at the age of thirteen aboard a ship from Barbados. But now, having worked to forge a link between black Tammany boss Fred Morton and the Harlem reformers, he too was ready to make his mark. After allowing the elder Powell to use his restaurant to host the luncheon for mayoral candidate Joseph McKee, Bruce realized that the time had come to assert his own political ideas.

In the mix of old and new faces now in Harlem, a fierce competitiveness to get one's ideas across emerged. The competition had an Olympian intensity to it. Minds raced against one another; invitations were sent out for dinners and soirées. In collective brainpower the group of uptown blacks conceded little to the young lions downtown — Newbold Morris and Stanley Isaacs, Averell Harriman and Fiorello La Guardia. The uptown Harvard degrees were as well earned as those downtown, the uptown ambitions as genuine. The young men met for food and drink at Bruce's Monterrey Club, noted for its Parisian ambience. They also met at the Abyssinian Baptist Church. Young Adam Powell would forge his reputation in the heat of the thinkers gathered in Harlem, then surge ahead of the group; admiring the talents of the newcomers, he adopted some of their traits, only to hone those traits for himself.

As a community in desperate straits, Harlem was susceptible to radical movements. Having been energized by the Bolshevik Revolution and pained by the ongoing disorganization within the ranks of the Progressives, the Communists seized on Harlem in the early 1930s with the zeal of an invading army. Labor officials, writers, streetcorner speakers, they aimed to upset the political order. Their presence became intoxicating. The quickest way for a white Communist to demonstrate his commitment was to show up at one of the weekend retreats in upstate New York with a black recruit, and the quickest way for a black Communist to show his savvy was to show up at a retreat with a white recruit. Powell was intrigued by the Communists, not only by their thinking but by their unabashed radicalism and ability to summon crowds at a moment's notice. He welcomed them into his father's church. The older deacons, apt to be Republicans and quiet Tammany Democrats, complained bitterly to the elder Powell, who, having seen his son's independence during his courtship, did not wish to engage in more father-son battles and did nothing. Young

Powell was intent on standing his ground, and did, telling the Communists that he would leave the church, would "walk out with you," if they were denied admittance. In person, he was careful and shrewd, supporting them without joining their ranks.

Now in Harlem there were bright young political thinkers and there were Communists. There were also street-corner evangelists, and among those who garnered the most attention were two who lived under aliases. First was Father Divine. Alternately giving his real name as Frederick Edwards and George Baker, he had come to Harlem and gained a reputation as a savior among the poor and homeless; intellectuals considered him a charlatan. Claiming to be "the only living God," Father Divine fed the hungry and established retreats on Long Island. Often backed by a gospel choir in public appearances, he seemed an effete caricature of Marcus Garvey. Hounded by police, he would ride out the decade with his reputation tarnished by arrests.

Second was Sufi Hamid, whose real name eluded everyone. Hamid arrived in Harlem from Chicago at the dawn of the Depression. At times he masqueraded as a linguist, until he emerged as a full-time evangelist. He meant to shock and did. Dressed in Nazi riding boots and a green turban always accentuated with silk accessories, Hamid wailed from Harlem corners, deriding the lack of blacks working in Harlem stores. Forcing a limited number of merchants to hire blacks, he gloated in his success. But the stand-off pitted Jewish store owners against the anti-Semitic Hamid, who was called "Black Hitler" by his critics. Arrested for inciting a riot, he lost his opportunity to boycott when Judge Samuel I. Rosenman issued a court order prohibiting boycotts. Watched closely by the FBI, Hamid left Harlem in the 1940s; it was later reported, to the FBI's relief, that he had vanished in an airplane accident.

Powell scorned both Hamid and Divine; followers of the latter he characterized in Steinian language as being "truly a lost generation." But conditions were bad in Harlem, and people needed hope. Survival involved crowding into tenements, families and extended families doubling and tripling up because of the constant influx of people. Young men would ask directions to the Harlem YMCA, and when they found no vacancies, they would take to the streets, their belongings rolled up under their arms or stuffed into old wicker suitcases. In winter the cold tore through the unheated tenements, and in summertime the furnace-hot dwellings challenged tempers. And every week came the knock, the rapping on the door from the landlord or an employee the landlord sent to collect rents, and yet another family was forced to move on.

New arrivals kept coming into Harlem because there was hope there. "In Harlem you might have to sit in the balcony, but at least you could get into the theater, whereas in the South you couldn't even get into the theater," recalled Howard Bell, who moved to Harlem in the 1930s to pursue a legal career and immediately went to the Abyssinian Baptist Church in search of comfort. As a graduate of Virginia Union University, Bell had heard much of Powell Senior (a strong financial supporter of the school) and Powell Junior. "The year before I arrived at Virginia Union," he remembered, "young Adam gave a speech that I heard was something else."

While Ben Davis ran — and lost — a succession of Communist-backed campaigns, Roy Wilkins settled less controversially into NAACP work and Herbert Bruce played host at his restaurant, plotting his own political moves, torn between Tammany clout and his streak of independence. Du Bois, the intellectual eminence, brooded, earning money as a writer and speaker. Young Powell flirted with the Communists, challenged the NAACP from the pulpit — he deemed the organization, of which his father was a vice president, too conservative — and invited the young thinkers of Harlem to his apartment and church.

He also demanded more action from the La Guardia administration. As the season of the activist dawned in Harlem, Powell turned up everywhere. Toward the end of 1934 a local newspaper ran a contest to determine Harlem's most popular figure. During the first two weeks of the polling, the leader was not Davis or Wilkins; nor was it Bruce or Du Bois; it was twenty-six-year-old Adam Clayton Powell, Jr.. And while he did not win the contest (it was won by a black realtor), there were few who could deny that he was surely on the rise.

Meanwhile, down in Washington the bright young planners of the New Deal were working feverishly. Their magic had not yet reached black Harlem, but that did not keep blacks from pinning their hopes on FDR. There was a new cast of characters in Congress following the 1934 elections. Democrats had increased their numbers in the House to 318 members; now there were fewer than a hundred Republicans. In Chicago, Oscar DePriest, the black Republican congressman, was soundly defeated by black Democrat Arthur Mitchell.

Mitchell's campaign speeches rode the fervor of the New Deal, suddenly fashioning DePriest, with his pro-Hoover sentiments, into a relic. As the first black Democratic congressman from the North, Mitchell was a bellwether: blacks increasingly shifted their aspirations to the Democratic Party.

Closer to home, in New York City, La Guardia remained busy with administrative tasks, probing into municipal minutiae, browbeating aides, worrying secretaries, and threatening cabinet secretaries. He seemed oblivious to the plight of black Harlem. No one there extracted demands from the fiery mayor; indeed, no headlines anywhere in America spoke of racial rioting during the first half of the 1930s. But on March 19, 1935, it happened, and it happened in the center of black Harlem. A Puerto Rican teenager stole a knife from the Kress department store on 125th Street and was arrested by the police. Onlookers gathered. They were soon joined by Communists, who passed out leaflets decrying the police and intimating that the boy had been brutally beaten, which he had not. Bricks began crashing through windows: the jobless wanted jobs. The police began making arrests; afternoon light turned to darkness; sirens continued to wail. Three lay dead in the Harlem night. More than 125 were arrested. La Guardia, as he was wont to do in times of crisis, bounded to the spot. He looked perplexed and hurt as he stepped over and around the debris, trailed by aides. Though the damage was confined to central Harlem — black Harlem — it reflected on La Guardia's administration, his priorities.

Black Harlem confused Fiorello La Guardia. In 1928 it had backed Jimmy Walker, the Tammany Democrat, instead of La Guardia, the Progressive. Even in 1932, when residents went Democratic for Roosevelt nationally and voted for the Fusion ticket locally, he was unsure of the depth of their loyalty. Not long after he assumed office, he received a letter from a black Harlem attorney named Francis Rivers, who warned him of the emerging gulf between his platitudes and his aloof administration. Rivers suggested an immediate meeting to discuss the situation, but he found it harder than he had imagined to crack the wall around La Guardia; mayoral aides turned a deaf ear to his plea.

In Congress, La Guardia had looked and sounded strong in battling racism and taking on the monopolies. But as mayor he had yet to make his presence felt in black Harlem. He had not walked into the stores, owned by Italian and Jewish merchants, to demand fair treatment of blacks in hiring. He had unleashed tirades against Tammany Hall corruption but not against discrimination in Harlem, a community that could not be soothed by long-ago speeches, a community that became the test of his progressivism. "This very conventional family man," explained a La Guardia biographer, "did not know what to make of the open prostitution, broken families, and social problems rampant in this black mecca. He was sure that it had something to do with poverty and limited opportunities enforced by the environment, but he was unsure how much of it had to do with a culture that he had no basis for understanding."

Over the next few months La Guardia appointed commissions to study the woes of Harlem, and when the results pained him — the commissions found a wide array of problems, from poor schools to inadequate medical care to a lack of jobs — he read the reports and did not quite believe in the misery and indignation of the residents. Fusion had not found its way into the crowded tenements stretched along 125th Street. Fusion had not yet improved health care in Harlem. "Fusion has done little, if anything, to improve conditions in Harlem, notably in its hospitals," cried the *New York Post*.

"What is worse, these hovels have no heat, only coal grates. When the coal book from the Home Relief Bureau expires, the dwellers comb the neighborhood for fuel. Janitors in the surrounding district have to stand guard over coal deliveries until they are moved in. During December I saw five tons of coal that had been deposited in front of Lenox Avenue and 113th Street vanish in boxes, pails, paper bags, quicker than you could say Fiorello La Guardia — that is, if you weren't too weak or too starved." This was the voice not of an upset Harlem relief worker but of Adam Clayton Powell, Jr., railing from the pages of the *Evening Post*. Members of the community streamed into his church office, complaining, sobbing; he feared more rioting. "A great majority of these are men and women who have worked and held decent jobs in the past, but who have no reason or self-discipline when their bellies are rubbing their backbones."

What Powell saw in the mind and actions of Fiorello La Guardia following the Harlem riot was inaction and indecisiveness, that point where a liberal is satisfied with some gain as opposed to no gain. La Guardia was a man of the people. He lived in East Harlem. He could not help seeing the pain on the faces. Reformers were in the midst of his administration. And yet, among his reformist allies were some who liked reform but only to a limit, those like Robert Moses, the parks commissioner, who sided with the reformers but whose ideas of reform stopped just short of 110th Street. Moses-the-reformer did not wish for proportional representation, the one reform that might bring voting strength to black Harlem. Moses-the-reformer did not rush to build parks in black Harlem.

It was that moment of weakness in liberals that excited the young Adam Clayton Powell. He saw tottering and falseness, and he saw the opportunity to strike; and over the years he struck in a cold-blooded fashion and often without warning, forcing liberals either to come over to his camp, his ideology, or suddenly to suffer from having the degree of their commitment brought under sharp suspicion. Powell attacked a long list of liberals — Thomas Dewey and Harry Truman, Adlai Stevenson and Richard Bolling and Jack Kennedy — and forced them onto his playing field, squeezing, and sabotaging, and holding hostage their liberal consciences, and returning them only when he had extracted political favors, only when he had stopped the tottering.

Now Fiorello La Guardia was tottering. Now the emotional mayor was growing angry at having his commitment questioned. Young Powell had him right where he wanted him. Across Harlem there were community meetings; men and women slid into the Abyssinian pews, anger feeding anger. At one meeting Powell turned to a friend, the businessman Lloyd Dickens, and said he wished he had a knife, because if he did he would slash his skin and let all the white blood in his body drain out. Dickens, an Oklahoman by birth and an immigrant to Harlem for opportunity, was as light-skinned as Powell. He thought the comment overly emotional, but he liked hearing it. Dickens was about to embark on a prosperous real estate practice in Harlem. There would come a time when the opportunity would arise for him to put his money behind certain political candidates. Like Ed Flynn, he would not forget Adam Clayton Powell, Jr.

⸙

Isabel Powell became active in Abyssinian church activities. Along with her husband, she hosted civic events. Friends were enamored of them and taken with their collective grace. "It was like a movie, a dream. You couldn't believe there was such a beautiful couple on earth," recalled a friend. Isabel, already madly in love with her husband before their marriage, found herself falling even more in love with him. Every morning, dressed in a bathrobe, his pipe already lit (she tried to curb his pipe smoking but could not), he brought her coffee in bed. She saw for the first time the effect he had on others. When he began wearing white linen suits to church ("He wore tweeds beautifully" as well, she confessed), Isabel noticed that Sunday after Sunday, more and more other young men of the Abyssinian Baptist Church, especially the ushers, began to wear white linen suits, too. And she also noticed how the women looked at her husband as he left the church to stroll through the streets of Harlem. "I thought the women were going to *die*," she explained.

More than anything, Isabel was grateful at how quickly her husband had taken to her son, Preston, whom he adopted. Adam Powell taught the boy what a son needs to know. He taught little Preston Powell about the importance of money, of earning and then saving it. He gave him chores, among the most delightful of which was running a projector from the back of the church, the lens aimed at Minister Powell catwalking back and forth in the pulpit. It made Preston feel like a movie director. He was just as delighted on those mornings when the church was so crowded that he was given the responsibility of stringing wire and hooking up loudspeakers so Powell's voice would be carried outside the church, to those unable to get a seat inside. And after the sermon began, little Preston often went outside to make sure that the voice was coming through loud and clear, and he would look up and down the streets and notice windows being pulled up and men and women leaning out, listening to the voice of his new father. It gave him such a thrill to know he had a part in this voice booming up and down the sidewalks of Harlem.

There were Sundays, too, when Powell would impulsively leave the pulpit and stride straight out the door of the church, robe still on, billowing in the open air now, and head up Seventh Avenue, Preston scooting along to keep up. They would go in and out of buildings, Powell stopping on stoops, tapping friends on the shoulder, turning them around, saying, "Missed you in church today, brother." There were days when Powell would don his robe and take off for the bars, the Red Rooster and Small's Paradise, not to drink but to admonish those who had recently missed church. Then he would move on, across the street, through the doors of another establishment, dark and full of music and men and women sitting on barstools, and suddenly the barstools would turn around in the dim light and Powell would stride along, smiling, tapping people on the shoulder. And Preston took in the darkness and the mysterious mood of the makeshift bars, the way his new father seemed to know everyone, how they all rushed up to him to talk and to shake his outstretched hand. And there were nights when Preston was awakened by his father's voice in his bedroom, because Powell wanted the little boy to meet yet another friend — never just any friend, but an important friend. On one occasion Preston was introduced to Joe Louis; on another, to Louis Armstrong; on still another, to Matt Henson, the Arctic explorer.

Adam and Isabel Powell liked to travel. They went horseback riding (he rode well, she remembered) in the Connecticut countryside, taking advantage of the hospitality provided by friends of his father's, old men and women who had known Powell Senior from his days at Immanuel Baptist Church in New Haven. Summers they traveled to Martha's Vineyard, beginning their journeys at the Hudson River pier, rolling the Pierce-Arrow onto the ferry. Once on Martha's Vineyard, they drove to the village of Oak Bluffs, where they owned a ginger-bread cottage that was painted green, tucked off the main road, and offered a simple view of trees and ocean beyond. Adam hung his fishing equipment inside, on a wall. When he made a catch worth showing off, he would hold the fish shoulder high and parade around, pipe clenched in his grinning mouth. In summer he grew a raffish beard, something he could not do while in the pulpit. Evenings were given to dinner engagements, and he dressed brightly, in yellow suits and matching yellow socks and shoes. Isabel was partial to lightweight print dresses and snappy hats. Nights in Oak Bluffs were silent, save for crickets and the rush of the ocean; but sometimes there would be the high-pitched voices of theatrical friends. "They had bourbon parties," a church member said of the times in Oak Bluffs. "You never saw such royal entertaining as up there."

Just as his father had taught him, Powell taught Preston how to sail, how to tack and jibe, how to anticipate the rise of the wind once on the water, how to leave and approach a mooring. He taught him how to clam, how to crab, and how to fish. Sometimes, sailing near Oak Bluffs, they were accompanied by Isabel's friend from her Cotton Club days, Hycie Curtis. Curtis was very thin, had long legs, smoked cigarettes, and loved the way the theater had penetrated her life, giving it ballast and intrigue. Powell would look at his wife and Hycie and demand that they go up to the front of the boat and strike their best feminine poses. "He wanted us to go through that bay just like those rich white girls," recalled Curtis, "hair blowing in the wind."

Their world of travel extended, however, far beyond the boundaries of Martha's Vineyard. With Wingee, Powell's one-armed chauffeur, behind the wheel, they traveled south, through Maryland to Georgia, Alabama, and Mississippi, looking for opportunities for Powell to give lectures in small churches and meeting halls and to extend his line of contacts. Often Powell would have Wingee pull over to the side of the road so he could commence giving history lessons to young Preston. Wading out into a cotton field, he would lecture the boy about cotton, what the crop had meant to blacks. He showed Preston cotton fields in Alabama and turpentine camps in Georgia where farmers blown out of work by the Depression eked out a meager living. "Adam had a lot of friends along the way, and we'd stop," explained Preston. Entering Florida, where blacks thought the Powells were white and looked at them in amazement, Powell became excited about big-game fishing.

When Adam and Isabel Powell traveled alone, they went by train. Still, Isabel was amazed at how many of the porters knew her husband. They both delighted in engaging in little dramas along the way. Seated in the white section of the dining car, they would listen to the other diners talk disparagingly of blacks: "Nigger this and nigger that," recalled Isabel. Meal finished, Powell would rise, look around the dining car — porters in clear view — raise his voice, and comment to the whites with whom he had just sat and dined, "Well, it was nice talking to you, but you happen to have been talking to Nee-groes." The black porters, their backs stiffening, would want to applaud but would realize the prudence of not doing so, and their hands remained still. Powell would stride off jauntily, passing white diners and hearing the echo of clanging silverware in their nervous hands, with his wife, the actress, striding at his heels. Powell also traveled alone, as his father had done years earlier — and still was doing, but more infrequently — to give speeches at the small black colleges that dotted the American South. One day he arrived on the campus of Virginia Union University in Richmond, his father's alma mater and a school that always heartily welcomed both men. (Powell Senior was a loyal financial benefactor.) A student by the name of Samuel Proctor had been sent to escort him. "I had read a lot about him," said Proctor. In his address to the students, Powell spoke about "brotherhood and justice and the fallacies of white supremacy," according to Proctor. "This was before we won any civil rights victories. As college students, we were impressed. In the South we didn't hear many speeches like that."

If Powell caused the pride of the students to swell, he also caused their suspicions to arise. "He looked so different from black people," explained Proctor. "They lived in small towns. They might have been intimidated by his rhetoric. They could not conceive of a black man who spoke so boldly." There was something else that Proctor noticed, and that was that Powell seemed, when away from groups of students and faculty, strangely aloof. Proctor found the young minister reticent about opening up on a personal, more intimate basis. On the morning he went to Powell's room to escort him to the train station for his departure — perhaps this would be the time to ask personal questions about the church, about Harlem, about other parts of the South — he found the room empty. Powell had already gone. (Many years later, when he succeeded Powell in the Abyssinian pulpit, Proctor was forced to remind himself that his assessment decades earlier had had merit: he had never been invited into Powell's home, and never even knew where that home was.)

Adam Clayton Powell, Jr., charmed his wife's friends, and it made her realize even more why she adored him so. Her friends liked his unpredictability. Before his marriage in 1933, he would bound into Hycie Curtis's apartment, look around, and ask for the gin. He'd grab the jug, raise it over his shoulder, and down hearty swigs. This would make Curtis nervous, because Prohibition was in effect, and yet it also delighted her — the gin on his lips, the huge hand gripping the jug, the way he would smile, gulping like someone gulping life itself. "Adam," she would demand, "pull the shades before somebody sees you!"

On soft Manhattan nights Adam and Isabel could be seen strolling on the Hudson River pier, taking two tickets from the outstretched hand of Joe Ford and then embarking on a boat ride. An extremely dark-skinned man who had arrived in Harlem following a bout with Texas law enforcement figures, Ford hustled jobs in and around Harlem; some nights he sold tickets on the pier. He was canny enough to ingratiate himself to Tammany Hall, and to men like Clarence Neal, who oversaw the nominating process for Tammany Hall. As an errand runner, as a man with a checkered past, as the kind of man who seemed to know no bounds when thinking creatively, Joe Ford was welcomed by Tammany Hall as a conduit to the Harlem community. Neal did not like Herbert Bruce, the "mighty midget," whom he thought to be too arrogant. When Neal began talking to Ford about rising young men in Harlem, he mentioned Powell, whom he characterized as an intellectual. Then Ford ingratiated himself with Powell, who in time gave the Tammany gofer a job inside the church. This move would prove to be a mixed blessing.

It took steady vigor in 1930s Harlem to gain and maintain a reputation as a rising young man. Herbert Bruce began his own political club, recruiting allies; he was seen at Yankee baseball games, a season ticket stuffed in his wallet. Roy Wilkins got to know the writers and artists of Harlem, forging a friendship with George Schuyler, the *Pittsburgh Courier* columnist who had been a protégé of H. L. Mencken's. Ben Davis ran for, and lost, most political offices that came his way, managing to maintain a deep appeal among Communists because they believed that his time would come. But no matter how frenzied one's activity, something else mattered in Harlem, and that was one's own newspaper by-line. The most desirable location was the pages of the *Amsterdam News*. The *News* was owned by C. B. Powell (no relation to the Abyssinian Powells), and it covered politics energetically, although its reputation suffered from its brazen rush to print crime-of-passion stories. There was also the *Age,* owned and operated by Frederick Moore. Its politics were conservative, and Moore's politics were no secret — he had performed public relations duties on behalf of the Republican National Committee. The liberal and radical newcomers avoided the *Age* and found space in the *Amsterdam News*. Soon Harlem readers were being treated to the musings of both Wilkins and Ben Davis.

But they did not enjoy the kind of reverence from the *Amsterdam News* that Powell did. In 1936 employees of the newspaper, complaining of low wages and protesting the owners' attempt to stop them from joining Heywood Broun's newspaper guild, went on strike, parading in front of the building. Marvel Cooke, one of the striking journalists, looked up one day on the picket line and noticed Powell walking with them. He had such a "great stride," recalled Cooke. But police sirens seemed to make him jittery. He would disappear; there would be no jail for him. When the strike was settled, the owners hired one of their more vociferous critics, and they wasted little time in trumpeting his arrival: "Adam Clayton Powell, Jr., militant young minister, pastor of Abyssinian Baptist Church, and graduate of Colgate University, will join the editorial staff as columnist, delving into social and economic problems." The February 8, 1936, advertisement went on to describe Powell as the "liberal champion of the lowly and oppressed."

There were those in the community, particularly journalists who took themselves with utter seriousness, who never could respect Powell as a journalist. They had been writing for years, had paid dues, had written columns without pay or happily accepted the ten or fifteen dollars they sometimes received for their work. Powell wasted no time in showing readers how incessantly his mind ticked over. He wrote on a wide variety of subjects. There were columns about politics (he considered himself a Jeffersonian Democrat; he read Jefferson's version of the Bible). There were columns about southern lynchings ("The Florida pines stretched high, the mottled blue shone through, the July sun was hot, the brown earth rich with green, but the tree from which he hangs is dead"). There were sprightly columns about his sunny travels. There was, as well, a breathless quality to his writing — here was a man always on the move, dictating his columns into a dictaphone, then turning the dictaphone over to his secretary, Hattie Dodson, because there was so much to do, so many places to be. "Negroes," he wrote in his column on April 11, 1936, "we are at a crossroads. Left or right. Freedom or oppression. Quo Vadis?"

At the expense of more serious journalists, Powell had fun with his column-writing. Steadily the din of critical voices rose, none louder than that of George Schuyler. In 1933 Roy Wilkins devised a scheme to go undercover to investigate reports that black field workers were being paid a paltry ten cents an hour by the Army Corps of Engineers to build bridges in the South. Wilkins recruited Schuyler, whom he thought "mordant" but obviously resourceful, to accompany him. When they got back to Harlem, Wilkins and Schuyler were summoned by Powell Senior to speak at the Abyssinian Baptist Church about their findings. Powell Senior, of course, was an NAACP official. But Wilkins was made to feel nervous at the church. His address was rudely interrupted by "provocateurs," as he recalled — men and women he knew to be Communists, men and women whom the young Powell, also in attendance, had seemed to befriend. These people called Wilkins and Schuyler frauds, and Powell Junior did not rise to their defense. He had, of course, seen the same South Wilkins and Schuyler had seen, but he had seen it while being driven by a chauffeur, while dressed comfortably, while in little danger.

Little wonder, then, that Schuyler resented Powell. A year after his appearance in the church, when he wrote a column about young men on the rise in Harlem, he dismissed Powell as being merely hungry for "publicity and power." Over the years, Schuyler's disdain for the minister only increased. "I wonder what that yellow nigger is up to now," he would ask fellow journalists.

༺❀༻

In the winter of 1936 New Yorkers went in a direction that startled Democratic officials, by voting overwhelmingly — 923,186 to 555,217 — for proportional representation, the device to guarantee representation at City Hall for those minorities who had been kept out of the political process over the years. The vote was seen as a rebuke to Tammany Hall, and had as its inspiration the 1926 voter revolt in Cincinnati. In their bold move, New Yorkers replaced the old board of aldermen with a city council. The municipal possibilities were now untold. The reformers had undeniably gained ground, and Stanley Isaacs, Newbold Morris, Samuel Seabury, and Albert Bard had won a victory. Others, like Robert Moses, who had spoken gallantly of reform but now waffled, believed that proportional representation would usher radicals and Communists into the Democratic Party, causing endless compromises. And there was young Adam Powell, who knew, better than most, that proportional representation would provide an opportunity in black Harlem, a gate for a leader to go through. It was time to begin assembling a machine. Powell named Joe Ford "church counselor," a vague title no one took seriously; Ford was to help him forge an alliance with Tammany Hall.

There was one more thing. The seventy-two-year-old Adam Clayton Powell, Sr., was about to turn the Abyssinian Baptist Church over to his son. With the maturing of the young Harlem activists and the arrival of the proportional representation movement, the timing could not have been better. The church had the biggest Protestant congregation in America: its membership rolls had swelled to upwards of fifteen thousand people. It had emerged as a powerful voice. Its minister, whose history was rooted in a Virginia slave shack, had earned respect over the years, had shaped its image; it would be left to his successor to shape the destiny of the Abyssinian Baptist Church.

Powell Senior announced his plans to resign in 1937. The announcement differed from his resignation bluffs of previous years, which had been made to extract favorable votes from the congregation and board of deacons. Now, with political winds sweeping Harlem and more and more young people joining the church and demanding a voice, the time had come to step aside. Ministers come and go, the well-read Powell Senior told the congregation — he was fond of poetry and literature and in later years cultivated a literary friendship with the Anglo-Irish writer George Bernard Shaw — but the church, "like Tennyson's brook, must go on forever, without let or hindrance." Now, with the end of his reign near, he was comfortable in playing down his contributions. His descent from the Abyssinian pulpit was considered the end of an epoch.

To amuse themselves, the Harlem newspapers printed stories about behind-the-scenes intrigue at the church in naming a successor. They overplayed comments from old board members. In reality, few members of the church hungered at the prospect of looking into the pulpit and seeing someone new. Powell Senior had been in control since 1908; he had physically moved the church, browbeating when he had to, caressing at other times. But eager reporters raced against one another for scoops, their active imaginations telling them that a battle must be looming between Powell Senior, the aging, conservative deacons, who did not favor young Powell, and the more progressive deacons and younger church members, who did back Powell. Their scenario, however, suffered for lack of accuracy.

For years the elder Powell had been quietly training his son to be his successor. He took him to meet influential politicians, to chat with the men downtown whom he had dealt with during his early years in Harlem. He took him on the road, introducing him to the men and women he respected, quiet men and women with resolve, women like Nannie Burroughs and Mary McLeod Bethune, who were making their own reputations as civil rights advocates. This was hardly the time for the deacons to assume a radical posture; as Abyssinian deacon Harry Sease explained, the elder Powell had long given his board members gifts, had long been accustomed to sending them on enjoyable out-of-town trips when he felt a problem brewing, when he felt a need to soothe egos. Now he wished to give his son a church, a congregation.

Abyssinian was a church primed for its successor, and there was genuinely little mystery as to who the successor would be. Abyssinian was, after all, a Powell church. It operated on decisions made by Powell men. One needed only to see the elder Powell climbing into the pulpit, or leafing through an old Bible, his hands as large as the Bible itself, or, just as impressively, turning the corner on 138th Street with head held high and chest out, to know that it was better for him to go out while the image still carried weight and significance. "I acquiesce in your stepping down," a friend told him, "only because you have shown Junior so well how to step up."

Powell Senior's legacy was a quiet one, and one without scandal. He had not become as well known as his fellow Virginian, Booker T. Washington, and over the years, even in Harlem, there had been other ministers — notably Reverdy C. Ransom — who enjoyed a more riveting celebrity. But he was known among the American church community as a man of resolute sensibilities. He wrote for Christian journals, added his name to civil rights causes, addressed audiences coast to coast, and exhibited flashes of philanthropy. He had an ability to change with the times. A lifelong Republican, he told a *New York Times* reporter in 1936 that he backed Roosevelt, that he wanted the president to be given another four years so he might carry out his "high ideals."

More than three thousand people crowded the church on the night of Adam Clayton Powell, Sr.'s retirement. Accompanied by his wife, Mattie, the strapping minister processed down the central aisle. The congregation rose and eyes welled. "It was an exciting evening," recalled Olivia Stokes, a member of the congregation who delivered words of praise that night. Community leaders, along with church officials, dueled with one another in extolling the minister, each salute more profuse than the previous one. The aging minister had come a long way from roaming through the woods in the aftermath of the Civil War.

⟋⟍ INTERLUDE ⟋⟍

Adam Clayton Powell, Sr.

THE LAND IN and around Franklin County, Virginia, set deeply in the Tidewater region, where the soil is rich and jet black, rolls gently south toward the North Carolina border, east toward the ocean. The Blue Ridge Mountains rise in the distance like bare knuckles. For generations the region's soil has been perfect for tobacco, and farmers have reaped rewards from the crop. In the years leading up to the Civil War it was not unusual for a farmer to find that as little as five acres could yield more than three thousand pounds of tobacco.

Throughout the 1850s Llewellyn Powell had been one of the more successful farmers in the county, tobacco being the primary crop of his 236-acre farm.

Born in 1811 of German descent and married in Franklin County at the age of twenty-nine to Elizabeth Sample, Llewellyn Powell, along with several other farmers in the region, was considered part of the local aristocracy; his very name connoted power and authority. Powell did not work his farm alone. He owned twenty-one slaves. His slave quarters, just yards behind his plantation house, which sat on a rising hill, consisted of two shacks, a chimney separating one from the other. One of his slaves was Sally Dunning, eighteen years old at the outbreak of war. Her mother, Millie Dunning, was also a slave. Their lives were about to change dramatically.

Because the Civil War threatened their way of life — an agrarian economy fueled by slave labor — true Virginians, the landed gentry of Jefferson's beloved countryside, wasted little time in deciding their course of action shortly after the war's outbreak. On April 17, 1861, they seceded from the Union. In Franklin County, Llewellyn Powell and other farmers began nightly patrols on horseback to guard against Union invasion.

In 1864, Sally Dunning became pregnant by her owner. Whether her baby would be born in freedom or slavery depended on the battles taking place across the South and in the Virginia countryside. But after several seasons of war, it had become apparent that southern might was being defeated. Southerners did not lack for vivid fantasies, however, and some put forth the proposition that blacks join with the Confederacy and fight for the continuation of their own enslavement. In spite of this dubious proposal, on April 9, 1865, Robert E. Lee and Ulysses S. Grant signed the necessary documents to bring peace to the land for the first time in four years, ensuring that Sally Dunning's baby would be born free.

On May 5, 1865, Sally Dunning, in no shape to travel from the plantation, gave birth to a boy. Doubtless the other former slaves present tried to provide as much comfort as possible for her and her newborn. The first name given the baby, Adam, was from the Bible; his last name, Powell, came from his mother's former owner. His middle name, Clayton, was a mystery.

Like his mother, little Adam Clayton Powell was a mulatto, extremely light-skinned because of miscegenation. The boy grew up not knowing who his real father was, and his mother apparently chose to forget. When he asked about his mother's father, Charles Powell, he was told that the man was German and "handsome and brilliant." (As he grew into middle age, Adam Clayton Powell developed a fascination with things German, traveling to Germany and passing the lore of the land on to his children. His son studied the language in college and also traveled to Germany for vacations. But as the tyranny of Hitler's evil spread during World War II, the Powells ceased to mention this fascination.)

On November 2, 1867, Sally Dunning married Anthony Powell, a short, dark-skinned man with proud eyes, himself a former Franklin County slave. Both bride and groom were listed on their marriage license as illegitimate. They eked out a meager living in Virginia as sharecroppers. Reconstruction had made the region both lawless and unpredictable. In 1875 the family moved to West Virginia — the journey took two days by train — to work a farm near Colesburg. They had children of their own, some of whom left the region, others of whom chose to stay. Sally Powell stayed. She died seventeen years after their arrival in West Virginia — not yet fifty, but a free woman. The son she gave birth to in the afterglow of slavery was living in Ohio on the day of her burial, a Sunday in July, and was unable to attend the funeral.

Because of the brief notoriety her son achieved before he left West Virginia, Sally Powell might have been genuinely surprised at what Adam had become. Guarding a farmer's land, young Adam Clayton Powell had shot at intruders, hitting one with buckshot in a most unwelcome posterior area. Afterward, many wondered what was worse for Powell, his aim or the fact that the intruder was white. Fearing that he would be "lynched or murdered," he fled the area. "The Earlies [a neighboring family] spirited him out of here," explained Edward Morris, Powell's nephew. By the time of his mother's death, Powell had become a busy minister in a little sin-haunted Ohio town. On the Sunday of his mother's funeral he preached not one sermon but three.

When Adam Clayton Powell left West Virginia in 1884, he surfaced a few miles over the state line, in Rendville, Ohio, a coal mining town. Young Powell arrived there seeking peace of mind — and employment. He found one but not the other. The town was unsettled by labor strife; white miners were striking over wages. The coal company quickly began hiring blacks, young Powell among them, to work the mines. Angry whites threatened retribution. The situation grew tense enough for the Ohio governor to call out troops, who spent several days and nights in the area, "bayonets gleaming in the moonlight," until they were confident enough to retreat.

The anger never lifted from Rendville, and turned the small town, which had merely a boarding house, a hotel, a post office, a few saloons, and a dry goods store, into a coarse and untrustworthy place. Adam Clayton Powell sensed something "lawless and ungodly" about it. Its vices appealed to him at first, and he joined the action. As a gambler, however, he fed the stereotype of the hick from West Virginia, lost among quicker and savvier minds. His wages were a hundred dollars a month — more money than he had ever made in his life — and gambling debts ate them away. The morning after an especially ruinous Saturday, with his wages gone, young Powell was walking the town's main street and taking stock of his life when he passed a church. The noise drew him inside. He knew little of church life. A hell-raising minister was shouting from the pulpit, urging the sinners of Rendville to repent, to quit drinking, quit gambling. In midsermon the minister went silent, then collapsed. The unsophisticated among the crowd considered the event mystical, and a chill swept over them. Powell later confessed that the stunt had pierced his own "wicked heart."

Within days a revival-like fervor overcame the mining town. Liquor was emptied from barrels; there were day-long prayer vigils; mines were shut down. In time Rev. D. B. Houston, the minister who had collapsed in such a theatrical fashion, recovered enough to invite five men of Rendville to join the ministry, convincing them that their presence at church on the morning of his collapse made their indoctrination inevitable. Adam Clayton Powell had little to lose. Young and impressionable, he was prepared to accept a religious movement. On the eve of his twentieth birthday, he joined the ministry. Born again, and realizing that he was in dire need of education, he enrolled in the Rendville Academy. Then, after three years of study, he announced himself ready to leave — to "hoist sails and try another ocean." Howard University was an esteemed black college in the nation's capital. A degree from that institution could add a different kind of gait to a young man's stride.

❧

Ambition aside, it took money to enroll at Howard, and Adam Clayton Powell had none when he reached Washington, D.C. Instead of hunching over a desk at Howard University, he found himself working at Howard House, a restaurant and hotel, corner of Pennsylvania Avenue and Sixth Street. But the white owner of Howard House sensed his eagerness to learn and encouraged him by suggesting books to read. Powell read the plays of Shakespeare, the psalms in the Bible; he was careful to save his earnings. By 1888 he had earned enough to begin school — not at Howard, however, but at Wayland Theological Seminary, also in Washington (and later part of Virginia Union University). For the next four years he studied diligently, pausing only briefly for summer vacations and the consummation of a romance. He had met Mattie Fletcher Schaefer during his West Virginia youth; smitten, he never forgot the girl. Also extremely light-skinned, she was blessed with high cheekbones and flowing black hair. The young couple were married in July 1889, a year after Powell's seminary study had begun.

Classmates became quite impressed with Powell during his years at Wayland, so impressed that in 1892 they chose him as commencement speaker. An imposing figure at well over six feet, he delivered his address in a cutaway coat. There was little time for celebration. Adam Clayton Powell had a wife to support and needed a job.

It was the custom (and has remained so through modern times) for young Baptist preachers in search of a church to have their name put on the grapevine. A Wayland Seminary graduate, especially one who had given the commencement address to his class, was sure of garnering attention. It did not take long for Powell to attract job offers. Once sent for by a church, a minister had to prove himself: community leaders had to be impressed; the congregation had to be won over. Summoned to St. Paul, Minnesota, he arrived with high hopes, but they were quickly dashed as he encountered a controversy between the resident minister and the congregation. The congregation felt the minister had overstayed his welcome; the minister felt otherwise, and dared them to evict him from his pulpit. Not wanting to begin his career in such rancorous surroundings, Powell simply left.

By the end of the year, Ebenezer Baptist Church in Philadelphia had invited him to appear in its pulpit. Ebenezer's financial lot would have worried an experienced minister, let alone a newcomer. The young minister was offered a salary of thirty-two dollars a month and told that unless the church's financial fortunes improved, it would be placed on the auction block. Powell quickly proved his mettle as a fund raiser, raising enough money to keep the church from being sold. Over the next year, however, Ebenezer's problems did not subside, and Powell found his complaints about his paltry salary straining relations with his congregation. After a little more than a year's service, he had accumulated four weeks' worth of paid vacation. Ebenezer granted him the time but, citing hard times, balked at vacation pay. Powell saw this as an indignity and abruptly resigned.

A train took him and his wife as far as Atlantic City. They needed work, and almost any kind of work would do. Mattie Powell took a job as a seamstress, and the Reverend Adam Powell became a waiter, striding among tourists at the ageless Windsor Hotel. There was at least one consolation: Adam Clayton Powell had grown fond of the water, and the Atlantic stretched as far as the eye could see. For recreation, he fished. The dream of having a good healthy church of his own remained alive.

It was considered a rite of passage at the turn of the century for American ministers to engage in missionary work. Such work brought distinction to their pulpits and communities; they were travelers, they had ventured out into the world to help others. In 1893 Rev. George Jackson, esteemed pastor of the Immanuel Baptist Church in New Haven, Connecticut, accepted a job as a missionary to Africa — "Away to the station, with our guns and dogs," he announced upon departure. His decision left the Immanuel pulpit open. Adam Clayton Powell dropped his waiter's outfit and traveled to New Haven in hopes of convincing the congregation that he was the man to replace Jackson. The congregation was so impressed with him — and with his steady wife, Mattie — that they offered him a starting salary of sixty-five dollars a month, double his Philadelphia salary.

New Haven was a tough manufacturing town that had prospered from immigrant labor. It was also the home of Yale University. Blacks lived in a degree of comfort regarding race relations — "a freer air," as one account described their lot. They found work in factories, hotels, and at Yale, where they worked as porters and maids, dusting rooms and waiting on students. Yale jobs gave New Haven blacks pride. Adam Clayton Powell planned to build his personal ministry in life by challenging the congregation he preached to. The Immanuel congregation, under the impression that they were well heeled because of their proximity to Yale, had become slowed in their vigor. Complacency had set in; the new minister proclaimed the congregation "spiritually dead."

Powell made the hour of Sunday church services earlier. He recruited new members. A local bank was inspired by his leadership and donated money for building improvements. He invited curious Yale students to the church; evenings, he and Mattie took them into their home for discourse and food.

Finding no history of Immanuel, Powell wrote one himself — "A Souvenir of the Immanuel Baptist Church, Its Pastors and Members" — then scurried to sell copies of the book to meet the payments on the money he had borrowed to print it. In 1895 he made one of the more fortuitous moves in his career: he enrolled in the Yale Divinity School. His study lasted just one year, but in that time he was able to study great philosophers and theologians, to make new acquaintances, to affix the name Yale to his *vita*. Not many black ministers could boast of study at Yale. Powell used the education for all it was worth, writing about it, purposefully dropping it into conversation; at the end of his year of study, he was (stretching the term a bit) a Yale man.

He began to lecture, traveling throughout America, spreading his name and the gospel. The words in his lectures (with titles such as "The Stumbling Blocks of the Race," "Broken, but Not Off," and "My Black Cats") were more cautious than radical, imploring blacks to strive for independence, to lift themselves up. He became a thinker like Booker T. Washington, the founder of Tuskegee Institute, who had struck vibrant chords as the first conservative black intellectual in America, especially after President Theodore Roosevelt invited him to the White House. Over the years, however, many blacks, led by W. E. B. Du Bois, distanced themselves from Washington's pronouncements, believing them too weak and compromising. Powell, however, remained a devoted ally. Curiously enough, in his spare time he studied the lives of three men whose politics differed greatly from Washington's: John Brown, William Lloyd Garrison, and Frederick Douglass. Now and then he even lectured on this triumvirate.

The New Haven years saw Powell gain a measure of financial security. He bought a house in town. He voted Republican but refused to have anything to do with New Haven political candidates and officeholders. In 1898 Mattie Powell gave birth to the couple's first child, a daughter, whom they named Blanche. In 1900 Powell, as a result of his growing prestige, found himself in London, sent to join an international church convention. While abroad he visited Paris for the first time; upon returning, he readied a lecture called "Twelve Days in Balmy France." In 1904 Virginia Union University conferred a doctor of divinity degree on him. Immanuel continued to grow with Dr. Powell in its pulpit. In May 1908 Adam Clayton Powell celebrated his forty-third birthday, and his wife was pregnant with their second child. Powell had now been in New Haven fifteen years; he felt restless and "too full of energy." It was time to set new goals. He had clearly outgrown Immanuel.

Powell received a visitor from New York City, Rev. C. S. Morris, the pastor of the Abyssinian Baptist Church. The church had a long and troubled history. Morris himself was living proof. For months he had tried to convince the congregation to move the church to a new locale. They balked, challenging him until he suffered a nervous breakdown, which was covered excitedly by the New York press. Morris convinced himself, upon recovery, that his grip on the congregation had slipped beyond repair. Adam Clayton Powell's reputation had spread, so that Morris came to New Haven in November 1908 on a recruiting mission. He offered his most gallant pitch, telling Powell that he was "the only man" in America who could save the church. The two ministers talked long into the evening. Powell finally accepted.

The news was heartbreaking for the Immanuel congregation, which held three farewell events for Powell. The minister was showered with gifts, among them a gold chronometer. He was lauded by the New Haven press. Admirers offered a great deal of praise, one claiming that Powell's success lay in the fact that he preached "real sermons" and had "life and fire."

Weeks after her husband had accepted the offer in New York City, Mattie Powell gave birth in New Haven, on November 29, to her second and last child. It was a boy. Reflecting the mixture of blood in his parents — more white than black — the baby had brown eyes but blond hair, Caucasian rather than Negroid features.

In December, the Powells — Adam Senior, Mattie, Blanche, and the new baby, Adam Clayton Powell, Jr. — left New Haven for the short trip to New York. They arrived at the height of the holiday season, just weeks after Abyssinian had celebrated its hundredth anniversary.

გ~⁊

In 1807, sixteen members of the Gold Street Baptist Church in New York City, tired of being forced to sit in segregated pews, complained to the church hierarchy. Not the least of their problems was that their view of the minister was blocked, owing to their forced seating arrangement. They simply wished for an unencumbered view. Gold Street leaders saw no need to accommodate them. Rebuffed, the members, who were of Ethiopian heritage, their lineage stretching back to the land of Abyssinia, decided to build their own church. Promises of financial assistance were made by Ethiopian merchants in New York. The move by the sixteen members was unique, inasmuch as it was the first of several moves that forged a working alliance between slave-descended blacks and Ethiopians. The Gold Street revolters' plan was quickly recognized as desperate, and word of their plight spread. It hardly helped their cause that they were without a leader, a unifying voice. But when news of their ordeal reached Boston, home of Abolitionist fervor, help was quickly sent.

Rev. Thomas Paul's reputation, and pedigree, among Boston Baptists was unassailable. He had been born a free black in Exeter, New Hampshire; his father was a Revolutionary War veteran. In 1805, when a group of blacks rebelled against sitting in a segregated pew in a Boston church, they appealed to Paul. He raised money from white businessmen, hired blacks to build a church on Beacon Hill, and saw the construction of the African Meeting House on Charles Street in 1806. It was from inside that church, for decades and decades into the future, that some of the most passionate pleas for black freedom and rights would flow. Paul became a troubleshooter for black congregations up and down the East Coast. The African Meeting House dispatched him to New York City to mediate the Gold Street crisis.

Paul's touch was deft. He arrived in New York more as a conciliator than as a rebel-rouser and helped the small congregation raise money throughout the summer. Then he departed to resume his church duties and Abolitionist work. The sixteen New Yorkers moved into a church on Anthony Street in lower Manhattan; little more than a wooden shack, it was not expected to be a permanent home, but it was a roof under which they could worship. In honor of their Ethiopian heritage, they called their new home the Abyssinian Baptist Church.

Their woes mounted quickly. For years they were unable to raise enough money to purchase a permanent home, and they were forced to move about Manhattan, from dwelling to dwelling. In 1835 they admitted, in candor, that "a cloud has, for some time past, been hanging over our temporal affairs"; but they remained resolute. In 1848 they renewed their fund-raising efforts with enthusiasm. Before the goal was met, however, panic struck the congregation. In 1851 several members, former slaves, bolted from the group in fear of bounty hunters acting under the Fugitive Slave Act. Those who stayed remained hearty, yet realistic. By 1854 the shrunken congregation, without a pastor, found themselves worshipping on Broadway. Periods of financial hope reappeared; a new minister took the pulpit. But the stability did not last long. On July 13, 1863, horror struck. Irish longshoremen out on strike, with the fear of being drafted to fight for blacks humming in their ears, turned their rage on black strikebreakers. In a bizarre orgy of violence, they looted, burned, and attacked newspaper offices. Their murderous spree saw 105 blacks killed, six of them by rope. It took federal troops sent from Gettysburg to return a degree of calm to New York City. The riots caused Abyssinian worshippers to endure "a year of great anguish."

William Spellman remained in the Abyssinian pulpit until 1885, nearly a thirty-year reign. His leaving was contentious. His style was considered autocratic; at times worshippers were forced to pay to sit in the best pews, an extreme form of charity giving. Spellman did not go quietly: he stole church books and documents, then boldly started a church in Brooklyn, taking as many Abyssinians with him as he could. Ministers came and went until 1902, when the church recruited the popular Charles Morris, who had made his reputation in Norfolk, Virginia, by closing down several drinking establishments. Morris's tenure began comfortably enough. He managed to move the congregation into relatively secure quarters on 40th Street. But then he saw what others in Manhattan were seeing — that real estate in Harlem was becoming available to blacks. Huge churches could be built in Harlem for far less than downtown. But the congregation, weary of moving so often over the years and forced once again to make sacrifices, balked. The more they balked, the more Morris fought. Gossip ran through the pews. In the emotional world of Baptist power politics, gossip fanned by the right bellows can have woeful results for any minister. Driven to nervous breakdown, Morris traveled to New Haven to convince Adam Clayton Powell to take over a proud — and stubborn — congregation.

❧

Turn-of-the-century New York City had changed from a visionary place to what the novelist Henry James called "a terrible town." For all its grandeur and commerce, the city found itself reduced to battle between immigrant and new arrival, Irish and Jew, Italian and black, all fiercely battling to claim a part of the turf. Many suffered from the freedom that, as James put it, merely granted them the right to "grow up to be blighted." Reports of overcrowding did nothing to deter migration. Caught between the gamble of remaining in the South and migrating to the unknown northern city, blacks chose the unknown. Between 1900 and 1920 more than 200,000 blacks left the South, some by railroad, some even by foot. In New York City, blight was nowhere more commonplace than in the West Forties, that district referred to as the Tenderloin, and as the black Tenderloin when blacks began to populate it. Tammany politicians cast a cold eye on reform in the crime-ridden Tenderloin. Many of the police were crooked; graft was rampant. It was an area full of flophouses, prostitutes, saloons, and wandering children. To eat, many children turned to scavenging and pickpocketing. Vagrants outmuscled hoodlums and grifters — "ravening wolves," a minister called them — for living space.

Abyssinian Baptist Church, located on West 40th between Seventh and Eighth avenues, in the red-light district, gave its members a bird's-eye view of the wicked activity. It was this New York City — "a valley of Bacca," as one resident termed it — that Rev. Adam Clayton Powell found when he took over the Abyssinian pulpit in 1908. It did not take him long to realize the unpleasantness of his surroundings. His response came quickly, just after the beginning of the new year, when he launched a "gospel bombardment" from the pulpit, attacking pimps, prostitutes, gamblers, all those engaged in criminal mischief. He appeared energized by his bombardment, even welcoming Reverdy C. Ransom to join him in his crusade. The energetic and sharp-tongued Ransom came with delight to the task. The two ministers minced few words, and their sermons often turned to tirades. At times Powell became so worked up, jerking his arms in expression, that his cufflinks flew off his sleeves; members of the congregation would lunge at them "like a football."

The bombardment attracted the interest of the media, and soon both Powell and Ransom were being trailed by reporters. Surreptitiously given the names of members of his congregation who were operating houses of ill repute, Powell would stare at them hard from the pulpit, letting them know what he knew, until they left. Walking along a street one day with little Adam, he nearly stepped into a sack of excrement thrown at him from an apartment building. The minister figured he was making progress.

A few years later, it became apparent to Powell that many of the characters he had identified earlier were still on the streets, still doing business. His gospel bombardment was simply no match for Tammany's lack of interest in curbing vice. In 1913 church officials suggested that he take a vacation, fearing that his exhaustion would result in a nervous breakdown. When he returned from his respite, he concluded that there was only one thing left to do, and that was to move Abyssinian out of the red-light district. As whites began to flee Harlem with the lowering of real estate prices during World War I, blacks moved in. Poets, writers, and artists arrived, and the migration developed the feel of a renaissance. In time, churches relocated to Harlem. Powell could envision Abyssinian's future. It lay uptown.

Old habits are not easily broken, however. In the Abyssinian history lay the ruination of many ministers whose objectives had clashed with those of their congregation. To succeed, Powell had to outwit his parishioners. He knew the more numbers he had on his side, the more favorably church members would view his policies. In 1915 he launched a series of citywide revival meetings; membership at Abyssinian rose by four hundred. But in time the astute congregation caught on to Powell's long-term goals. At a 1916 business meeting he was accused of making a behind-the-scenes effort to sell the church and the valuable property it sat on — "trying to kill the goose which lay us a golden egg," as a member put it. By 1919 he was predicting that fifteen churches would be built in black Harlem within the next five years. Doubters were forced to watch as he purchased a home uptown with a limestone front, the interior trimmed in mahogany.

Part of Powell's prediction of an economic explosion in Harlem was based on a curious phenomenon: the gadding about of Marcus Garvey. Garvey, a Jamaican, first showed up in Harlem in 1916. His plans were grand, his confidence dazzling. Elaborately costumed and proclaiming himself a messiah, he launched a crusade in an effort to inspire blacks to return to Africa. Boats were constructed, nurses hired, maps unfolded. Himself dark-skinned, Garvey attracted dark-skinned blacks. Racial pride coursed through his pronouncements. His followers multiplied, and his emotional grip held sway in the emerging black Harlem, a locale that Powell saw as "the symbol of liberty." As Jews and Italians fled central Harlem, blacks carved their own niche. The streets above 125th, sweeping north all the way to 145th, began turning black. As Adam Clayton Powell, Sr., roamed Harlem, preaching trial sermons, he became ever more assured of success in building a church for the Abyssinian congregation, a permanent home, an edifice of power and architectural signficance.

The minister's enthusiasm was infectious. In the spring of 1920 Powell spied six vacant lots at the corner of West 138th Street and

Seventh Avenue. A cabaret had previously claimed part of the spot. He imagined his church rising on the vacant land. All he needed was money. That summer he launched a series of tent meetings on the site, raising money for the church. Loyal Abyssinians participated, ignoring the stifling heat. Soon they raised enough money to make a $15,000 down payment, with $5,000 going to Charles Bolton, the architect, who happened to be black. Powell added seven hundred more members to the church's rolls during the tent meetings. The fund-raising effort went on for two straight years. Powell set a frenetic pace, and his demands were intense. He asked the congregation to donate 10 percent of their earnings to the church's construction. The more they gave, it seemed, the more they were asked to give. The emerging black neighborhood had seen money-hungry evangelists come and go and heard idealistic cries from street corners. Abyssinians had every right to wonder what deep hole their hard-earned dollars might drop into, but Powell dismissed their fears and increased his pleas.

When Bolton presented his final plans at a cost of $300,000, not the $200,000 Powell and the congregation had imagined, it was all the critics within the congregation needed to justify their anger. Many felt they were being misled. Gossip suggested financial mismanagement. Finally, building was delayed. In a bulletin issued in May 1921, the church blamed the delay on high labor costs and "extortionate charges of money lenders" and predicted groundbreaking the following September. Members had raised $2,500 during the previous year for church construction, a figure far below their goal. "This amount would have been doubled had all the members followed the Lord's plan for giving," the bulletin ruefully announced.

Powell saw the lack of financial contributions as a direct attack on his leadership. Undeterred, he devised a plan to raise the money himself: he took to the road, swinging south, in and out of small towns, preaching in churches, then standing by as collection plates were passed for money to construct his church up in Harlem. The travel undoubtedly was grueling for the fifty-six-year-old minister, but he kept going. Yet when he returned to Harlem, a malaise had set in among the congregation. They were tired of fund raising, tired of spending nights beneath tents, tired of the flow of businessmen back and forth to the church, tired of reaching deep into their pockets. So much money had already been given, and there was not one brick in place.

The big city wore Powell down. There was only one thing left to do — resign, which he did, surprising the congregation with an announcement from the pulpit. He would travel America as an evangelist, selling Bibles and sermons, preaching to the masses. They laughed, until they realized he was serious. Then he demanded a voice vote, at which time the congregation, back to the wall and suddenly made nervous by Powell's threats, rose in unison to support him. His shrewd gamble paid off.

The following days and weeks were dramatic. Church officials got together and finally completed a deal to sell their 40th Street property. Financial contributions escalated. As Powell later recalled, "The pastor and the trustees pushed buttons and the money flowed." Bolton's architectural plans were at last finalized. And on April 9, 1922, the day of groundbreaking, thousands could be seen walking toward the corner of 138th Street and Seventh Avenue: men dressed in top hats, their hands covered with white gloves; women in their finest, bonnets on their heads to shield them from the sun's glare; children in lace and knickers; the Powells, father, mother, Blanche, and fourteen-year-old Adam Junior, with band music ringing in everyone's ears.

Thirteen months later, preceded by a parade led by Sunday School children, Abyssinians walked into a huge Tudor and Gothic structure of blue stone, the interior walls made up of Italian marble, with a pearly white baptismal pool, pews downstairs, and, in the upstairs balcony, room enough to seat several thousand on the grainy, shining brown wood. There was a basement and an activity room, a picture of Jesus high above the pulpit. It was the kind of structure — so huge and imposing, so special — they knew they would never leave; they would never have to pack up and move again; they were home. That very month Powell celebrated his fifty-eighth birthday. Dedication ceremonies lasted from May 20 to June 17.

With his church built, Adam Clayton Powell, Sr., had cemented his reputation. Religious journals asked him to pen articles; invitations to speak came his way. Tired, he left America to vacation in Germany; Berlin and Munich were among his favorite cities. He sailed the Rhine, trekked through the Black Forest, engaged in intellectual discourse ("You could find more culture among the servants in a Berlin hotel than you could find on a college campus in America"), and sat inside huge cathedrals.

In time, his pulpit became an admired place to appear and speak. Judge Robert Wagner, Harlem congressman Joseph Gavagan, author

Mary McLeod Bethune, and others came and spoke of politics and goals not yet realized. Outwardly, Powell appeared apolitical, but the men and women he invited to his pulpit were hardly apolitical; while they ran the political spectrum, Democrat and Republican, their underlying trait was that they were progressives.

In church circles throughout America, Powell became a model, a symbol of fortitude and perseverance. And still the minister was not finished. During the next several years he continued to badger his congregation gently for money, week after week, month after month, until the entire $300,000 mortgage was paid. Many black churches in America had been paid for by white philanthropy; the Abyssinians who sat in the pews of the new church on 138th Street were especially proud that they had paid for their church with their own money. In January 1928 the mortgage was finally paid in full, according to Hattie Dodson, whose family moved from West 40th to 138th Street with the church and whose own life became intertwined with that of the Abyssinian Baptist Church. Dodson, along with the rest of the congregation, watched as Powell held the mortgage document aloft in his hand during a service, ensuring that not only those at ground level but those in the balcony of the church could see, and struck a match. He too watched as it burned before their very eyes, turning to ashes. The congregation owed no one.

Now Abyssinians were free.

༺✳༻ The Succession ༺✳༻

IT WAS NOT ENOUGH to give one simple Sunday to the installment of Adam Clayton Powell, Jr., in the winter of 1937. There would be pageantry and pomp. Among the elder Powell's last acts in the Abyssinian pulpit was overseeing his son's ascension. As was expected, the salutes during the four-week event took on a new direction. Now praise was heaped on the younger Powell. On the evening of his installation, the old deacons, aging men who still found him too liberal for their tastes, could do little save tap their shoes and nod at the momentous occasion taking place. "Majestic Sweetness Sits Enthroned" was the selection of the Abyssinian choir. The elder Powell's advice to his son was simple: "Preach with all the power of your soul, body, and mind the old-time simple Gospel, because it is a fountain for the unclean, food for the hungry, drink for the thirsty, clothing for the naked, strength for the weak, a solace for the sorrowing, medicine for the sick, and eternal life for the dying." He encouraged his son to preach such words until his tongue was "paralyzed in death."

The congregation had had glimpses of the young Powell on the stump. They had seen his energy. But they did not know what a politically minded minister, full of pride, full of arrogance, in fact full of himself, taking hold of a congregation of ten thousand souls and taking hold of it in the wake of proportional representation, could do. Adam Clayton Powell, Jr., was now twenty-nine years old. A massive church had been given to him. There was little doubt among the congregation, old and young, critic and admirer, about how he saw the Abyssinian pulpit. "He saw it as an opportunity," explained Olivia Stokes, who was both encouraged and made nervous by Powell's ascension. She knew he would be an active force in the church, but she also saw potential for calamity: "His father called him to preach — not the Lord."

From this moment on, life at Abyssinian would never be the same. Those rooted deeply in the disciplines of the church could see it clearly; those less rooted, those more willing to gamble with their minister, those less tied to secular constraints, would witness a change at Abyssinian. Political activity would become embedded in the church's grain; the sway of the conservative deacons would become less and less meaningful, until it all but disappeared. Young Powell gloried in the challenge. "Once Adam made up his mind, you couldn't change it," recalled Harry Sease, who trained under Powell Senior and became a deacon during Powell Junior's tenure. More important, however, Powell would use the Abyssinian stage as a bully pulpit against Tammany Hall, against those who would deny black Harlem its rights, against merchants in the community. In the pantheon of Abyssinian ministers, young Powell had now taken his place.

His immediate agenda was to break the stranglehold of nonblack employment in the stores that lined 125th Street.

⟶✦⟵

Before the 1920s central Harlem had been mostly a Jewish enclave, home to immigrants who had reached America's shores and turned their fortunes around by learning a trade, then perfecting it. Jews had acquired businesses along 125th Street. Blumstein's department store was one of the more popular; Hygrade's was more typical of an everyday business operation. But with the influx of blacks in the 1920s, Jews began their exodus into the Bronx and out to Long Island. Their businesses remained behind, tied to dreams, and because they were tied to dreams, their owners hired family members and acquaintances of trusted family members, the idea being to stretch the dream from generation to generation. Now and then the Jewish hold on Harlem businesses was challenged by a Joe Louis or an A'Leia Walker (the cosmetics empress), prominent blacks who were inspired to invest in the neighborhood. But mostly the businesses were owned and operated by Jewish merchants.

Blacks lived above the stores, next to the stores, and around the corner from the stores. They shopped in the stores — Woolworth's was a favorite, with its weekly bargains — sometimes becoming well enough known as shoppers to open lines of credit. Blumstein's advertised handsomely in the Harlem press, with pictures of tall white models in dresses and hats and shoes. Blacks were quite welcome; their money was as good as anyone else's. On Sundays, 125th Street resembled a bazaar. It was so crowded because everyone appeared to be out shopping, though with money scarce, quite a bit of window shopping was going on as well. But when these same people asked about possible employment, the mood changed. Hale and hearty store owners turned cold. There were no jobs, they said, simply no jobs. That applied not only to the department stores but to many of the restaurants as well. In Harlem in 1937 you could walk into Frank's Steakhouse (it was widely believed that Frank served the best steaks in Harlem), sit anywhere you wished, and order a nice juicy slab of beef. But when you looked up to order your nice juicy slab of beef, you would be looking into the face of a white waiter or waitress, because Frank did not hire blacks. Frank, who came from Greece, hired other Greeks.

Jewish store owners in Harlem hired their own — other Jews — and not blacks. And blacks, who paid their electric and gas bills to Con Edison and the other big monopolies, could not get jobs at the utility companies, because the utility companies did not hire blacks either. Buses cruising through central Harlem, picking up black passengers, were driven by white Irishmen (to get a job driving a bus, you benefited from having a letter from your local parish priest).

In the aftermath of the 1935 Harlem riots, Jewish store owners were hit with a $147,000 bill for broken glass. And they could not quite understand the anger. Hadn't Jews given to the United Negro College Fund? Hadn't Jews been instrumental in founding the National Urban League and in supporting the NAACP? Hadn't Samuel Leibowitz, a Jewish lawyer, braved southern bigotry to defend the Scottsboro boys? But the gulf between charity and the dignity of a job was vast and spoke volumes about cultural differences. And when Judge Samuel Rosenman enjoined Harlemites from picketing because he feared rioting, he all but derailed on-site picketing of the Harlem stores. Young Powell had to find a way to fight the law, to bring the law over to the side of the picketers.

In 1933, with his Howard University law degree, young Belford Lawson set up his shingle in the nation's capital. He was blessed with a wonderful speaking voice, a mellifluous voice with traces of his Roanoke, Virginia, birthplace in it. He was also quite serious, neither drinking nor smoking. "He was a very disciplined person," said his wife, Marjorie. In time he achieved a reputation as a dependable attorney who knew the best legal minds over at the Howard University Law School.

When a group of Washington blacks calling themselves the New Negro Alliance began picketing a local grocery store ("Do Your Part! Buy Where You Can Work! No Negroes Employed Here!" said their placards), they caused a ruckus. The store owners went to court and the picketers were slapped with an injunction. They went to see Belford Lawson. Agreeing to take the case, Lawson planned to fight it as a labor rights issue, and he planned to take it to the Supreme Court. He felt he was on to something. Adam Clayton Powell, Jr., also felt he was on to something. If Lawson could win, then picketers would have the force of law behind them.

Lawson began traveling to New York and appearing in the Abyssinian pulpit, explaining the case he was fighting down in Washington, pointing out how it had much in common with the plight of Harlemites who wanted to picket the stores on 125th Street, how the picketers in Washington were just like them, common people who simply wanted an opportunity to work in the stores where they shopped. Tall and well built — he had been the first black to crack the varsity football team at the University of Michigan, where he received his undergraduate degree in 1924 — Lawson, like Powell, cut an imposing figure in the Abyssinian pulpit.

"The case was of great interest," Marjorie Lawson, also an attorney, explained, "because it was a new way of thinking." It reached the Supreme Court docket in the fall of 1937, as *New Negro Alliance* v. *Grocery Co.* The decision, reached in October, was profound. It held that citizens living in a particular community could boycott a store or business if they felt they were being denied equal opportunities, and that while picketing, they were protected by the Norris–La Guardia labor act.

By bringing Lawson into the Abyssinian pulpit, Powell showed that he did not plan to think, and operate, like an ordinary minister. Marjorie Lawson couldn't help but to notice the difference in the two men, how Lawson eschewed the limelight for the courtroom and how Powell rushed toward the limelight. "Adam saw politics as a way to power," she said. "Belford saw politics as a way to deal with injustice." Belford Lawson basked quietly in his victory. Young Powell made noise with it.

La Guardia's Manhattan was a segregated city, and the segregation was nowhere more starkly displayed than in the job market. Powell could persuade all the disparate groups — the Communists, those who belonged to the NAACP, the still emotional Garveyites, the plain curious, and of course the jobless — to join his enterprise, because now, thanks to Lawson, he had the law on his side. He formed a group that called itself the People's Committee; Abyssinian Baptist Church became its headquarters. The members' orders were to march. "We walked down Lenox Avenue," recalled Olivia Stokes. "The employment campaign was really a stirring thing. It was the kind of thing that was very significant. It stirred up Harlem." The marchers, the discipline of the marchers, "excited and elated" Powell, she added.

On any given day in Harlem, Powell could rally forces to picket a dozen stores. "You were aroused by all the picketing," said Stokes. Blacks about to cross a picket line to go into a store were shamed with catcalls. Others also led the picketing of the late 1930s — there was Rev. William Lloyd Imes, studied and disciplined, and Arnold Johnson, a Cuban described as a "suave, handsome young radical" — but Powell walked the picket lines in a white suit, stirring the crowds, taunting those who dared to break the line and cross over to shop at Blumstein's or order a steak at Frank's Steakhouse. His admirers grew. "I didn't fall in love with him," said Edith Sease, one of the picketers. "I fell in love with his picketing and demonstrations." The People's Committee covered Harlem "from river to river," according to Harry

Sease, looking for pawnshops, grocery stores, any business that was practicing discrimination. "They went floor to floor, checking to see whether there was a Negro," he said. "Made pawnshops hire Negroes."

Some businesses relented and hired blacks, but light-skinned blacks only. Adam Powell wanted dark-skinned blacks, blacks whom the public could clearly see were black. "When Blumstein's first hired Negroes," recalled Sease, "Powell told them, 'When I come in here from the front door, I want to see colored girls, and I want to see colored girls sitting at the lunch counters.' " The employment victories started to come. Metropolitan Life Insurance, which had two insurance policies, one for whites and one for blacks, would not hire blacks. Powell dispatched Joe Ford, now on the Abyssinian payroll, to buy a policy. Policy in hand, Ford threatened that other blacks who held policies would drop them if the company did not hire blacks. Metropolitan Life relented.

The picketing campaign went on for months and months, with stout-footed men and women picketing six days a week, taking Sundays off for church, joined during the marches by girls from the entertainment business, then by the minister himself, Powell, in a double-breasted suit. He met with merchants and attempted to negotiate. Sometimes the merchants mentioned money, asking how much Powell would take simply to go away. "But Adam couldn't be bought off," Roy Wilkins said later.

When the Powell-led forces picketed Con Edison, Harlemites darkened their homes on certain nights and opted for candles. The young minister suggested that people pay their bills in pennies, to disrupt business. In April 1938, Con Ed surrendered and announced that it was hiring four blacks to work.

The buoyancy of the movement energized Powell and his followers. "Everyone was crazy about him," recalled Lloyd Dickens, one of many who followed Powell's movements closely and plotted his entry into New York politics. It was more than Powell's timing, how he could show up on a picket line, then vanish, how he joked with the showgirls when he was there. When he showed up, the picketers wanted to stay a while longer; crowds gathered to watch him. Herbert Bruce, the fiery young politician whose animus toward Tammany Hall never abated, knew Powell's strength and came grudgingly to admire it: "He looked like a movie actor."

In those delirious months of the boycotts, young Powell carved a name and a reputation for himself. He was shrewd enough to have the law on his side. Herbert Bruce was not the only one who was amazed; so were officials of the NAACP, who had thought Powell undisciplined. But they heard the stories of how merchants had tried to buy him off, offering cash money, and how he had refused them, time and time again. Few in Harlem knew how to take advantage of victory as well as Powell. When the first buses with black drivers began rolling through Harlem, he gathered a crowd; as the buses passed, with black hands on the steering wheels, he knelt and kissed the ground — being careful not to dirty his suit.

In the spring of 1938, delivering a commencement address to graduates of Shaw University, in Raleigh, North Carolina, which conferred on him an honorary doctorate of divinity, its highest honor, Powell talked about his economic philosophy as well as his disdain for other black leaders. "The hour for Negroes to move ahead has long since struck," he told the graduates. "We've got too many Uncle Toms among our leaders. We've got to streamline our race and come to realize that mass action is the most powerful force on earth." Nothing gave him as much delight as tossing barbs at light-skinned blacks like himself. "Prejudices within our own race are doing us more harm than many outside discriminations," he said. "These prejudices are built upon the idea that we should set up a class system based on wealth and family background. Because of the differences in the color of our skins and because a few of us can trace our ancestry back a few generations, we refuse to follow and all want to be leaders. In most cases, if we move our family tree six inches, we find ourselves either in a cotton patch or among mangrove trees. What we need is a closely knit, militant race with a new leadership."

In Powell's voice could be heard the old cry of the Progressives, his appeal for economic parity echoing their appeal. Months before delivering this address he had returned to his alma mater, Colgate, for the first time. "The time has come for the Negro to close ranks," he urged from the Hamilton campus. His wife, Isabel, accompanied him, and they made good their early threat of how they would make their living: after Powell's address, Isabel sang spirituals from the choir of the Colgate chapel.

⌒❦⌒

There was something else in black Harlem that bore watching, that, with Hitler's rise, posed dangers on America's shores as well as in

Adam Clayton Powell, Sr., New Haven minister, 1908

Mattie Powell, New Haven, 1908

The Powell clan in Pratt, West Virginia, 1885. Grandpa Anthony Powell is on the left; Dee Powell, brother of Adam Clayton Powell, Sr., is at right.

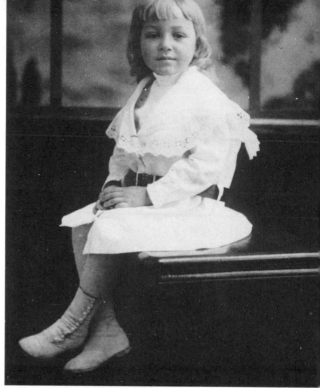

Little Lord Powell, age four, 1912

Adam Clayton Powell, Jr., with his nanny, Josephine

Colgate University yearbook photograph, 1930

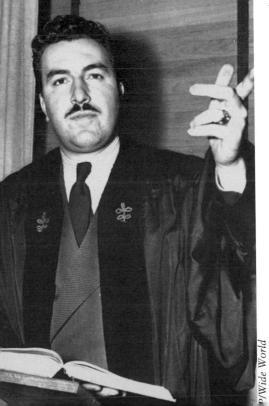

Preaching in 1941

Adam and Isabel Powell,
newly married, 1934

Below left: Adam and friend in Oak Bluffs, Martha's Vineyard, ca. 1942
Below right: Isabel Washington Powell, Oak Bluffs, 1935

Above: Being sworn in to the New York City Council, 1942. *From left to right:* Joe Ford, Mattie Powell, Adam and Isabel Powell, Adam Clayton Powell, Sr., and Mayor Fiorello La Guardia

Below: The would-be congressman and his lieutenants, marching on the U.S. Capitol, 1942

Top left: Hazel Scott, 1939
Top right: Hazel and Adam signing their marriage license, Stamford, Connecticut, 1945

Hazel Scott with (*left to right*) Count Basie, Teddy Wilson, Duke Ellington, and Mel Powell, ca. 1948

The Powell entourage en route to Haiti, ca. 1952

Hazel, Skipper, and Adam in Germany in the late 1950s

Father and son in New York, ca. 1962

Hazel Scott in Paris with her second husband, Ezio Bedin (*left*), and Dizzy Gillespie, 1958

Grant Reynolds stumping
Harlem, 1946

Powell's campaign poster

Europe — anti-Semitism. The fear left behind by Sufi Hamid and his followers remained palpable. If blacks and Jews were to coexist in Harlem, with one group trying to manage businesses, the other trying to extract employment from those businesses, there would have to be conciliation.

On the University of Wisconsin campus, in the middle 1930s, a young man named Maurice Rosenblatt had majored in political economics. To major in political economics on the Madison campus was oftentimes to hear, and catch, the fever of the New Deal. Many of the instructors had been Progressives, followers of La Follette and his huge dream; some had even gone off to Washington to work for Roosevelt. When Rosenblatt walked off the campus in 1936, he walked off a Progressive, a La Follette man.

For a couple of years he did odd jobs, such as serving as promotions man for the Wisconsin State Fair. In 1938 he put his savings in a shoebox and took off for New York City, where his sister, Bernice Evans, was working in Harlem relief agencies. She had been repelled by the sight of black women being eyeballed from head to toe in their attempt to get day work. Maurice Rosenblatt discovered that jobs were hard to come by, but eventually he found work as a researcher with the Amalgamated Labor Union magazine. He became fascinated by the Jewish-black relationships in Harlem — and by the spread of anti-Semitism. "My sister Bernice said there was somebody putting poison in the melting pot," he later explained. Rosenblatt suspected that German agents, trying to gain sympathy for Hitler, were spreading rumors among blacks that Jews were destroying Harlem. In Harlem, Jews were characteristically department store managers and owners or rental agents. Inasmuch as eviction notices were a common occurrence, and inasmuch as blacks had not broken the stranglehold on employment, Rosenblatt quickly concluded that there was a reason the more radical speakers were espousing anti-Semitism: Jews had a significant role in the economic plight of black Harlem. He proposed a community plan, whereby Jewish merchants would meet with black leaders to begin an open dialogue. Then he would take his next step: jobs for blacks.

But when Rosenblatt presented his plan to the Anti-Defamation League, he was met with derision. "They said it's ridiculous for the Negro not to love us," he recalled, adding that he heard the familiar names Rosenwald and Guggenheim, the names behind the charitable organizations that aided blacks. Because he was Jewish, Rosenblatt thought his reasoning would carry weight. It did not. "One thing the Jews never understood in New York is that when people stand in breadlines, they generally want to kill the baker." Jewish leaders dismissed him. "They thought I was naive to fight anti-Semitism." He thought their own methods strange: "They'd hire impoverished ministers to go out and say Jews are nice people."

Friends described Maurice Rosenblatt, five-foot-eight and quietly intense, as "brilliant." There was something of the bulldog in him, the La Follette passion and spirit. The more his sister told him about Harlem's inequities and the further Hitler's army advanced, the harder Rosenblatt worked to achieve his goal. He began visiting rabbis and black clergymen in Harlem, telling each group that they could work with the other group. In early 1941 he unveiled his committee, the New York City Coordinating Committee for Democratic Action. Its purposes were to alert people to the German menace and to bring about fair play for Harlem's dispossessed. Among its members were Herbert Agar, Rev. William Lloyd Imes, A. Philip Randolph, Rabbi Jerome Rosenbloom, Rabbi David De Sola Pool, Frederic R. Stettenheim, and Adam Clayton Powell, Jr. The more Rosenblatt spoke with the older residents of Harlem, the more often he heard them mention young Powell, and he quickly sensed that they had faith, they expected great things from him. "They considered him their fair-haired boy," he said.

Meanwhile, America was in no mood to take a risk with a newcomer in the presidential sweepstakes, but in 1940 the Republicans offered a newcomer anyway. Wendell Willkie was no politician — an Indianian, he was the president of a utility corporation — but he surged ahead at the Republican convention, defeating Thomas Dewey's forces, who had steamrolled through the primaries only to be whiplashed by their own hubris at the Philadelphia convention. But Willkie proved to be a poor campaigner on the stump, losing his voice on the trail, and Roosevelt, who had sought to reassure America that it would not enter the war, swept to victory.

As the months passed and war became imminent, blacks were forced to decide between patriotism and expressing their continued anger by refusing to fight. Oddly enough, war offered them one new opportunity: employment. Still, blacks looking to the federal government for sustenance found little. Despite valiant efforts by New York senator Robert Wagner, there was still no law prohibiting lynching. Antilynching bills invariably made it out of the House, only to be stymied in the Senate by powerful southerners. Fearing a southern backlash, Roosevelt did not put the weight of his office behind the legislation. The president also disappointed many by refusing to sign legislation creating the Fair Employment Practices Commission (FEPC).

A. Philip Randolph devised a plan to focus Washington's attention on the plight of American blacks. Billed as the Negro-March-on-Washington, it showed the union leader at his greatest. Randolph and others, including Powell, imagined that the march would finally prove to Washington that while the black vote might be in contention, black dignity and pride were not: blacks would fight, but first they would demand equality when seeking employment. There were those who thought the Negro-March-on-Washington was ill-timed and dangerous; while Randolph took his cue from support he received around the country, from crowds that greeted him from Georgia to Michigan, Washington insiders were aghast at the idea. Mayor La Guardia, dispatched by the administration to plead with Randolph, warned that blacks would be killed marching through the capital. Both Roosevelt and La Guardia were pushed into positions contradicting their liberal beliefs. Randolph persisted in his resoluteness, and in the end Roosevelt gave in, creating the FEPC and enabling Randolph to cancel the planned march.

Back in New York, Maurice Rosenblatt needed someone to help him raise money for the overseas war effort, particularly for Zionist causes. Two underground groups in Palestine, Stern and Irgun, were the beneficiaries of his efforts. Rosenblatt needed someone who could rivet a crowd, someone who had earned respect in the Harlem community, someone who saw the Zionist cause as inextricably linked to the black cause in the fight for freedom. He turned to the fair-haired boy of the Harlem elders, Adam Clayton Powell. Powell began to join him at rallies in and around New York City, and his name became linked to Zionism.

As the months passed, the tremors of war became more violent, especially after Hitler's invasion of Russia on July 22, 1941. At a Madison Square Garden rally that went on and on, Powell hopped up from his seat, pulled a hundred-dollar bill from his pocket, and bellowed, "If a black man will give a hundred dollars for freedom, what will you Jews do?" He stood there with the bill in his hand, and Rosenblatt saw hands dipping into pockets, the crowd reaching for money. He then realized that Powell had the ability to galvanize. They raised more than $100,000 that night.

In and around Harlem, throughout New York City, Powell could no longer ignore invitations to enter the elective political arena. There were risks, of course. His entry into McKee's 1933 campaign had drawn scorn from the Harlem media. There was much sentiment in favor of Randolph, glowing from his FEPC victory. But the more the young Powell became known and respected, uptown as well as downtown, the more impossible it became to ignore him. "He became involved whether he wanted to or not," according to Herbert Bruce. So the mystery turned on which office he would seek. He could run for state assembly and go to Albany. Albany, however, seemed beneath his prowess and imagination, and rural New York, with its memories of Colgate, held no appeal for him. That left Congress. But barring unusual circumstances, one needed the support of Tammany Hall to win a congressional seat, and Tammany showed no enthusiasm for supporting black candidates from Harlem. It would be another thing if a district were carved in black Harlem, but this was yet to be.

Powell could look around and see that for all its complexities and anguish, proportional representation had indeed changed the face of New York City Hall. The city council was far more diverse than the one-party aldermen rule had been; it comprised various factions, including Stanley Isaacs as the Jewish Bull Moose Republican, Newbold Morris as president and patrician Republican, and representatives of the American Labor, Democratic, and Republican parties. But for all its novelty and reformist posturing, it remained a council without a black face on it. No one knew how long the experiment of proportional representation would last. Just as it had been put on the ballot, it could be taken off the ballot. And Powell was not unknown to council members; he knew Isaacs, who lived on the border of Harlem. Morris kept a list of up-and-coming New Yorkers, men and women he might be able to support if they sought city council seats; Powell's name was on the list, where he was again described as "brilliant." So Powell's goal became the city council.

Among Powell's political strengths was his unpredictability. On a summer Sunday morning, he stood square to his flock and announced his intention to enter the hurly-burly world of New York politics as a candidate. From pew to pew the noise spread: the whispers, then the amens; the amens, then the shouts. And it went on and on, because this is what the people had wanted, and needed, to hear. They had walked the streets until they were tired. They had listened to the voices in this pulpit for decades, men and women talking of FEPC legislation and antilynching bills. They needed to know that the gates could be flung open. They lived in a world clamped within six square miles — black Harlem — and they needed bigger boundaries, wider boundaries. So they raised their voices while seated in their pews, their backs alternately touching and moving away from the fine grain as their emotions spiraled. And when the volume became deafening the young minister knew he had told them the right thing. Suddenly they looked less like a flock than like the beginnings of a political machine. According to one account, the shouting went on for twenty minutes.

News of Powell's announcement spread quickly. He had not consulted with elders, with Harlem district leaders — they were Tammany men whom he disdained. But Randolph and Wilkins and the NAACP had not had any advance warning of his candidacy either. Herbert Bruce was disheartened by his move: "Although we didn't get along, I realized he would have been a powerful force for us because of his ability as a rabble-rouser." Maurice Rosenblatt felt he owed Powell favors for his help in fund raising; furthermore, this was just the kind of campaign — against the odds, maverick — that moved Rosenblatt. It had the sure spirit of progressivism. He joined Powell's campaign as its primary fund raiser.

Rosenblatt took advantage of the contacts he had made when he formed the New York Coordinating Committee for Democratic Action and returned to members of that group. With war at America's back, he knew just how to play his hand. He would start off talking to potential donors about how he needed money for the war, to defeat Hitler, but then, depending how much he had ingratiated himself, he would switch the emphasis on where the money might end up and mention Powell's campaign, and explain how Powell had spoken energetically on behalf of Jewish causes and how his campaign could use a little money as well.

Rosenblatt had a low voice, soft and raspy, with a midwestern twang; he was well read; he seemed to know everyone in New York City. He went to Fred Stettenheim, Walter Lippmann's cousin, and left with a small contribution for Powell. He went to the representatives who worked with Sidney Hillman, the labor organizer. He went to anyone he figured would be willing to give money. If they were willing to give to the war effort, he figured, he could talk them into giving to the Powell effort. "I'm talking fifty bucks," he recalled about how much he averaged. And as the days and weeks passed, Rosenblatt became more and more energized. "A black had never been elected to city council!" He knew how strange it sounded to some of those he sought funds from, and yet he sensed exhilaration in others. Sometimes he conducted his fund-raising trips alone; at other times Powell came along. To see them together, Powell and Rosenblatt, riding around in taxicabs, going from donor to donor, was to see two hungry young men, taxi door slamming and Rosenblatt paying the fare, the two climbing steps, walking down hallways, pulling up chairs, and making their plea for a little contribution.

When the campaign began to roll through Harlem, it was unlike anything the community had seen before. Campaigning as a foe of Nazism, as an all-out patriot, Powell began rallying his congregation from the street corner during the week, from the pulpit on Sundays. "We started going up and down the street with a bandwagon," said Acy Lennon, one of Powell's aides. "We took the city by storm." Powell was running not as a machine man but as an independent. The move was shrewd and reminiscent of La Guardia's stormy mayoral campaign in 1933. Backed by his People's Committee, Powell's campaign looked like both a candidacy and a movement. When his organization mailed out 200,000 sample ballots to voters, it was careful to explain the intricacies of proportional representation — and how to mark the complex ballots. Church members canvassed; doctors and nurses canvassed.

The downtown newspapers did not know what to make of Powell's candidacy and for the most part chose to ignore it. Then the news began to flash, late on the eve of voting. "Powell Leads City," said the *New York World-Telegram*. The *Herald Tribune* called his accumulation of votes "extraordinary" and "amazing." In the end he did not lead, but he had amassed enough votes — 63,736, for third place — to become the first black to win a seat on the New York City Council. It was a stunning surprise. Powell had proven he could cross racial lines. Admitting its misreading of his candidacy, the *New York Times* concluded that there had been "two surprises" in the elections, that of Peter Caccione, the Brooklyn Communist, and Powell. His council victory caught the attention of the national media, and *Time* magazine said that his juggernaut had "amazed Manhattan politicians." To Maurice Rosenblatt, the victory realized La Follette's dream: hard-driving progressives could upend the political order.

There were many victory soirées for Powell. One, populated by labor leaders who had helped in the campaign, was held at a fashionable Manhattan brownstone. Rosenblatt arrived with Helen Simpson, grande dame, progressive Republican, and wife of the New York GOP leader Kenneth Simpson. After dinner, Rosenblatt said, everyone crowded around Powell, touching him, asking questions — "it was the laying on of hands on Adam." Powell took over, quickly answering all questions, being witty, towering over most of the men, catching the eye of the women. Standing next to Rosenblatt, her eyes glued to Powell, Helen Simpson leaned over and whispered, "He's wicked, isn't he?" And Rosenblatt noticed the way she said it — how it sounded, more than anything, like a compliment. "She didn't say it in any kind of a vengeful way, you see. But she just knew he was naughty."

As a council member, Powell anticipated a lot of work; he also intended to be heard. He dashed off a letter to Stanley Isaacs, his fellow councilman: "It may seem presumptuous on my part, as the youngest and one of the newest members of the Council, to offer any suggestion, and yet on the other hand because of those facts, I may be in a better position to do so." He went on to suggest an immediate meeting of the council, recommending that the council consider dropping "party designations" to show unity in the face of the pending war. There was also a warning. While Powell was admittedly "a registered Democrat, a Negro, and a Protestant," he said the only distinction anyone on the council should take seriously was that of "independent."

He was sworn in to the New York City Council on January 1, 1942, by Mayor La Guardia. America had been at war less than a month. His mother and father stood at his side, along with his wife, Isabel, wearing something silky and furry draped over her arms, and Joe Ford, the Tammany emissary with the shady reputation.

As councilman, Powell formed an alliance with Isaacs, and together they offered liberal housing legislation. But one of the more peculiar effects of proportional representation was that it pitted liberal against liberal, not liberal against conservative. Consensus was rarely to be found as members from the Bronx and Manhattan found themselves fighting members from Brooklyn and Queens. When they tired of fighting each other, they turned their anger on La Guardia, criticizing him for being out of town so much, and began organizing council committees to investigate his administration. Isaacs and Powell both seesawed back and forth between outright criticism and support of La Guardia. At one time the borough president of Manhattan and loyal to La Guardia, Isaacs now believed the mayor to be a man who "varies in loyalty to himself and the things he used to stand for." Powell harangued La Guardia about the city's refusal to build decent housing for the poor. It was not that New York City did not build housing; Robert Moses' reputation as a builder was deserved. It was that the housing plan for the poor was inferior and even indecent. As a Moses biographer later put it, the builder was busy "dividing up the city by color and income." The housing bills that Powell and Isaacs offered went down to defeat time and time again. But Powell did not intend to be deterred by the late council sessions, which often turned tempestuous.

There was, in fact, little about the business of sewage problems and streetlights that interested him. He turned his attention more toward his People's Committee and the war effort. And he was quick to use his position as councilman to promote his national image. Speaking before an integrated church group in Boston, he gave a rousing address about America's war effort and black personnel. "You cannot isolate the Negro in this war! You must make America safe for democracy before you go out to make the world safe for it." He described how blacks were made nervous by the conflict — "the Negro people are not sold on this war" — because of the brutalities that had greeted them when they returned home from World War I. "We measure democracy this morning with the yardstick of the Negro, and there is no group in America more loyal. This is an hour in which to go forward in the battle for democracy, this is a time to sound the alert and never to sound the all-clear until we have attained liberty and justice."

Powell had to make a quick decision as to whether to go the way of Paul Robeson and Du Bois, who were advising blacks to stay out of the military, or strike the pose of patriot. He adopted a devilish compromise, choosing the cry of the patriot mingled with the voice of protest. At the Mecca Temple in Manhattan in 1942, he appeared with Eleanor Roosevelt, who was presiding over war rallies coast to coast. Maurice Rosenblatt was there, and when Powell spoke, Rosenblatt understood his strategy. "Everybody was giving these routine speeches. Adam throws in this sour note — 'The Negro people are not sold on this war!' Sure, he supported the war, but he was cutting out his own message too," Rosenblatt said. When he turned to look at Eleanor Roosevelt, she was looking at Powell. "I could see Mrs. Roosevelt was absolutely awed by this man. She was just awed. Everybody was."

For Powell, it was wonderful to be a New York politician involved in the war effort; it was exhilarating to appear beneath the unfurled banners in light-colored suits, suits that on anyone else might have looked theatrical but on him looked just right, to appear on stages throughout the city, sometimes accompanied by a beaming Adam Powell Senior. There were radio appearances with Tommy Dorsey and Ingrid Bergman, efforts to sell war bonds. War had its romantic side, too. In New York it provided an opportunity for beautiful black actresses to become involved in the fight for freedom, by displaying their sex appeal. In Hollywood, Lena Horne had baffled studio executives, forcing them to acknowledge her miscegenation: she was extremely light-skinned, and her roles were inferior to her talent. But she played the war heroine gamely, attending rallies and urging on the troops, and her photograph was treasured by black soldiers abroad. Fighting by her side in New York City was Hazel Scott, an ingenue and a renowned pianist who gave tirelessly of her time to the war effort. They all — Duke Ellington, Lena Horne, Hazel Scott, and New York City's lone black councilman — merged their voices, Powell racing from radio spot to stage to radio spot by evening's end. Black troops went off eagerly to war; "Hitler, count your men!" became one of their more notable battle cries from the foxholes. But the black conscripts had to suffer the brutal rules of segregation, and the first-term councilman would not let New York forget that. Appearing at a Salute to Negro Troops rally, Powell shouted that blacks must be "taken out of the glory holes of battleships and put on the deck and into the pilot seat of planes."

Adam Clayton Powell also delighted in pricking New York's high society. At a Waldorf-Astoria function he sat on the dais with Governor Lehman and other Democratic officials. When he was introduced as "one of the most outstanding citizens of this state, member of city council, head of the largest church in the city of New York, the Reverend Adam Clayton Powell," Herbert Bruce couldn't help but notice the hushing of voices and the craning of necks, because from the audience Powell looked like a white man. "People started moving chairs to see him," Bruce explained. When he rose, eyes trailed him. Such moments came easily to Adam Powell. "I'm here tonight," he began, "not as a member of the city council, not as a minister of a church, but I come here tonight as a Negro!" Now they knew: he *was* Powell, and he *was* black. "That shook everybody up, all the white folks," said Bruce. And as Herbert Bruce sat there, watching

Powell like everyone else, he realized, why he couldn't hate him, even as a political enemy: because Powell threw himself to the winds, because Powell made him feel proud. "He's the kind of guy you can't dislike," Bruce remarked years after that affair. "If he rang that doorbell now — he's dead and gone now — before he got to that chair, he'd hug me. Even if I had just finished calling him a yellow son of a bitch. That was Adam Clayton Powell."

༚ཀྵ༚

Charlie Buchanan, who operated the Savoy Ballroom, one of the classier dance haunts in Harlem, was a Powell ally and eager to promote him. They decided that Powell needed better media coverage; in fact, they decided that he needed a newspaper all his own. The paper would have two purposes. One would be to blunt the criticism Powell received from the conventional Harlem papers; the other, to drum his political ideas and aspirations into the electorate. They raised money from Mo Gail, the Jewish entrepreneur who actually owned the Savoy Ballroom. The paper would be called *The People's Voice.* Office space was found above Woolworth's, at 210 West 125th Street. The Apollo Theatre sat across the street. Powell had no difficulty recruiting a staff. There were plenty of writers and artists in Harlem. Once he had picketed the *Amsterdam News,* later he had written for it; but now he raided it, hiring away both Marvel Cooke and St. Claire Bourne, two of the paper's most respected staffers. Others came to the church for interviews and were hired on the spot. There were rumors that Eleanor Roosevelt herself might contribute an occasional column. The rumors heightened interest in the newspaper, and proved to be just that — rumors — although Powell was not above asking the first lady for a financial contribution. Ferdinand Smith joined the staff as a columnist from the labor movement; Benjamin Davis represented the radical fringe; Fredi Washington wrote about the arts. Washington couldn't write a lick, but that didn't matter. She had contacts off Broadway and on, and was one of the rare New York critics who had actually acted on stage and in film. Furthermore, she was Powell's sister-in-law. Ollie Harrington, a Yale man and a gifted artist, became the paper's cartoonist.

Powell dived into the venture with abandon. To write, to be a writer, to own a newspaper and be a publisher — there were endless possibilities. Few on the staff, however, failed to recognize the real purpose of the venture. "I think that Powell saw it as a political asset more than anything else," recalled Harrington. "It was quite obvious he was using the paper for his own purposes, but nobody minded it. That's what the paper was for." Harrington quickly noticed Powell's attributes. "He was very perceptive," he said. "He understood people quickly, then sized them up, then proceeded to overwhelm them." Like others, Harrington soon came under the spell. He found himself cavorting through Harlem with Powell, spending weekends at Oak Bluffs, fishing and boating. "Powell was a very charismatic person. A fantastic ego person," explained Harrington. "He considered himself about the best person in the world, and people accepted that. He was always utterly in command. Many considered him a con man, but a superior con man." And "I never saw Adam Powell sad in all the time I knew him. He was always flamboyantly happy."

Marvel Cooke, who had tired of the lurid headlines in the *Amsterdam News,* was perhaps the most talented writer on the staff. She was amazed at Powell, how he had suddenly fashioned himself into a publisher, how he would walk and talk like a publisher. "He came in with such nerve," she said. "We wanted to be different, striking in as many ways as we could," recalled St. Claire Bourne, who was hired after an interview at the church. One of the more gifted writers to arrive at the newspaper was a young woman from Connecticut, Ann Petry. New to Harlem, she found the community both impressive and riveting. To see children walking the streets with keys tied to strings around their necks — a common sight in Harlem, where the young hung around waiting for parents, or parent, to get off work — was a shock to Petry, who had grown up in a middle-class environment. Her mind took in too much for mere journalism, and she began work on a novel.

News of the maverick paper raced quickly among black newspaper owners. They did not like it — without having seen it — believing that its claim to independence was deceitful. "Oppose New N.Y. Tabloid Backed by White Group," said the *Chicago Defender.* "New York Proposes a White Newspaper with a Colored Front," said the *Baltimore Afro-American.* When the first issue hit the stands, after a prepublication bash in the lobby of the Golden Gate Ballroom, the staff was thrilled; it "looked beautiful to us," remembered Bourne. Powell's tabloid was more *PM* than *Front Page; PM's* publisher, Marshall Field, a liberal philanthropist, allowed Powell to use his printing press. There was an undeniable spirit — and, with Powell as publisher, egotism — behind the venture. Perusing the newspaper on any given

Wednesday (it debuted in February 1942), one might find an article written by Paul Robeson or a Langston Hughes poem, an excerpt from Richard Wright's novel-in-progress or a photograph of the lovely Hazel Scott. Powell's reporters wrote energetically of blacks at war, of poverty in New York City, of the lack of housing coming from the La Guardia administration. In Powell's weekly column, "Soapbox," dictated while he was being driven through Manhattan by his chauffeur, he hammered away at injustice far and wide. Blacks whom he considered Uncle Toms became weekly targets of ridicule.

Although other black publishers derided him as a would-be William Randolph Hearst, Powell ran a tight newspaper. "Everybody was overworked" explained Doxey Wilkerson, one of the many radicals who worked for Powell. Wilkerson, who had been recruited from Howard University, had worked with Gunnar Myrdal in his pioneering study of race relations in 1939–1940. He remembered Powell striding into the office, always seeming in a rush, pushing an assortment of documents onto his desk. "When Powell called me and said he was coming in," said Wilkerson, "I knew he had a story about himself. Of course we fully cooperated." At its peak, it was not unusual for *The People's Voice* to sell 40,000 to 50,000 copies a week. Staff loyalty was intense; "it was a crusade for them," according to Wilkerson. Once when their offices burned in a fire of suspicious origin, the staff produced the paper without missing a deadline.

The tall and extremely dark-skinned man seen hanging around *The People's Voice* was Solomon Harper — "a little weird," recalled Ollie Harrington, "but the sweetest guy." In truth Harper's life had been tragic. One of twelve children born into a sharecropper family in Mississippi, little Solomon was awakened one night and forced to watch through a window with his brothers and sisters while a mob lynched his father. Considered precocious and a mathematical whiz, he escaped the South and took a degree from Syracuse University. In time he became an inventor, creating gadgets used by railways and aerial devices. In 1915 he was cited by the NAACP for an award; great things were predicted for him. But Harper found the routes to patents tricky and never received his just financial rewards. The more he tried, through court procedures, the more of a maze he seemed to run into, and the more he lost his grip on reality. Harper became a lost soul, turned to communism, rummaged for a living. When he showed up at *The People's Voice,* hardly equipped to do anything, Powell refused to ask him to leave. "He didn't have a job there, but

Adam Powell let him hang around," explained Harrington. "I'm sure he gave him a little spending money." Anyone passing through the newsroom of *The People's Voice,* then, passed by Solomon Harper, and few knew of the brilliance he had exhibited and the tragedy of his fall. Governor Lehman tried to get him financial assistance, as did Eleanor Roosevelt. But nothing ever came of the efforts. At *The People's Voice,* Solomon Harper, the dark-skinned Mississippian, seemed to represent all that could go wrong with a human life.

༄

For years there had been talk — and hope — of redrawing one of the congressional districts in Harlem to allow for a seat that would primarily serve its black population. In the late 1920s blacks had attempted to run for Congress from the twenty-first district, where the majority of blacks were concentrated, only to realize how strong white voting strength remained. In order for a black to be successful, the district lines would have to be redrawn. Curiously, the Justice Department of the Roosevelt administration kept a huge dossier on potential black political districts across America. In an effort to determine a district's degree of patriotism (or lack of patriotism), agents gathered evidence of rallies and riots and information on leading figures in particular communities. In Harlem, Powell was identified as someone to watch closely.

Herbert Bruce was among many who had pressured Governor Lehman and the legislature to create a congressional district for black Harlem. "I made a couple of trips to Albany," explained Bruce. "I don't think he wanted to do it. But I think he realized it was going to happen anyway." Editorials appeared in *The People's Voice* calling for reapportionment; otherwise, Powell was relatively low-key. He was still settling into his role as city councilman. But he was low-key for a reason. Behind the scenes he had his man, Joe Ford, negotiating with Clarence Neal of Tammany Hall. Bruce, as a Harlem political leader, expected to be wooed to run for the seat, but his relations with the Tammany machine were strained. Tammany thought that Bruce, who had formed his own political club, was uncontrollable, and there were many who thought the "mighty midget" suffered from a Napoleon complex. Neal found him arrogant. When Bruce realized that Powell and Ford were aligning themselves with Neal, he became livid.

Finally, late in 1941, Governor Lehman forced a recalcitrant state legislature to enact legislation creating a new district, the twenty-second, which would provide a black congressman by tightening the boundaries around central Harlem's black enclave. The seat, however, would not be filled until the 1944 elections. Although blacks in Harlem had waited a long time for the possibility of political inclusion, it was within their grasp.

⟨❧⟩

The massive freedom rally planned for Madison Square Garden on the evening of June, 16, 1942, was designed to serve a variety of purposes. There were to be heightened appeals for equality, and as well, the event would provide an opportunity to salute A. Philip Randolph for his tireless efforts on behalf of FEPC legislation. The New York press made nearly daily mention of the rally; artists and writers and actors and representatives of every political persuasion (including an infiltration of FBI informants) would be in attendance. Powell offered to attend and bring the disparate groups together. He imagined himself as the minister-councilman soothing the masses. Randolph's lieutenants were wary of him, often wondering whose interests he was more devoted to, his own or the masses'. It was at such events, wide open and with thousands watching, that he was at his most dangerous and unpredictable. But to ignore his offer would have seemed petty; after all, he was the only black in New York City with a voice downtown, in City Hall. Powell was added to the roster.

For Randolph, the moment was heady. Four months earlier he had received the prestigious Spingarn Medal from the NAACP on behalf of his civil rights work. There were few who cared about civil rights who denied that Randolph deserved such a night — although of course it wasn't really his night at all, because Randolph himself worked tirelessly to make sure it wasn't, to make sure that various groups were represented and had a chance to speak. But it became his night nonetheless. More than 20,000 people were on hand, "all but one end of the very top packed solid with Negroes," as a participant later noted. As Randolph entered, surrounded by his Pullman porters, whoops echoed high into the air; a band struck up "Hold the Fort, for We Are Coming"; banners billowed; old men stood straight. The Pullman porters were Randolph's men, his army. They were proud men, men who worked and lived on tips, men who sent their children to black southern colleges, men who rode trains cross-country, attending to white passengers and displaying fine manners —

because the finer their manners, the quicker their "Yes, sir," their "No, sir," their "Why of course, ma'am," oftentimes, the better the tip. They were men who dressed up when they had to, and on this night they were dressed; men who folded their money around money clips; men who left Harlem and other cities at all hours of the day, to catch the next train, their clothes in the bag swinging from their arm. They were Randolph's men, and they were proud to see him walk into Madison Square Garden that night.

Randolph, ever the gracious host, took a seat on the podium, insisting that others speak first. He watched and listened to speaker after speaker. Young Powell rose to thunderous applause. Acy Lennon, his aide and driver, stood at the back of the Garden and strained to spot Powell's face on the stage; through the crowd, he saw "this bright yellow face" up there, beaming.

Powell's speech was an ode to protest — and to himself. He talked of the strikes and pickets that had gained New York blacks jobs they had never held before. "It was because we protested," he reminded the gathering, "that Negro people in New York have a councilman in City Hall." There was an undeniable feeling that the speech was leading somewhere. The Baptist preacher in Powell knew how to begin a story from the outer edge, then zero in and end in dramatic fashion. ". . . And it is because of the new Negro that I must, regardless of time and energy or previous commitments, run for the Congress of the United States, so that we may have a national voice speaking from the national capital. . . . It doesn't matter what ticket or what party — my people demand a forthright, militant, anti–Uncle Tom congressman!"

Madison Square Garden erupted in pandemonium. Randolph's troops were outraged. Now, for the very first time, Governor Lehman's reapportionment law had changed reality; now the twenty-second New York congressional district was more than a piece of legislation; now it began to take a shape, a form, and a tone. If there had been an incumbent congressman, Powell's announcement, so early, would have seemed ridiculous. But there was no incumbent. The seat was without a history, and by striking first, Powell had given it a history, a defining moment, a beginning. "My cry today and until I die," he went on, "is let my people go — now!" The pandemonium would not calm, and time ran out on Randolph, the man of the hour, who never had the opportunity to speak.

Young Powell had picked up enemies, but he had also rocketed himself, through his shrewd and cunning move, into the front-runner position for the seat. He had turned the Randolph salute into a Powell sendoff. The waving banners, the Pullman porters, the artistic community, the filled auditorium of Madison Square Garden — Madison Square Garden, which had played host to presidential nominating conventions — had become Powell's on this night. The crowd spilled out onto the streets of Manhattan, which, because of the many black faces milling about, "looked like Harlem" to Langston Hughes (who assumed the task of writing Powell's campaign song, "Let My People Go — Now!"). Hughes dashed off a note to a friend, telling of the rally, concluding that Powell "had run off with the honors." If there were those who had been surprised by Powell's announcement, Herbert Bruce did not count himself among them. "You could never figure out what Adam was going to do."

Although Randolph had not given any indication that he would run for the congressional seat, some of his supporters felt that he had been stung, that any hopes he might have entertained were now dimmed. A colleague warned him not to be despondent, telling him that the campaign for the twenty-second congressional seat would be the "dirtiest, muck-racking campaign" in the whole country.

Now, only six months after joining the council, Powell was less a city councilman than a congressional candidate. His headquarters — the Abyssinian Baptist Church — was open every day of the week. His maverick campaign employed a wide array of individuals. Few were more important than Joe Ford, Odell Clark, and Benjamin Davis, three dark-skinned men. Clark worked with the unions, Ford handled the overall campaign, and Davis, in addition to recruiting radical leftists, managed legal matters. Billboards were posted around black Harlem, but were often quickly ripped down and kept as souvenirs. The NAACP kept its distance from the campaign — a strange posture, since the association's vice president was Adam Powell Senior. Young Powell told Roy Wilkins that he was "much concerned" that Wilkins did not attend the People's Committee meetings.

Powell's campaigning style was full-throttle, and because he had announced so early, he had to create his own opposition. That opposition consisted of Hitler, the foes of democracy, southern Democrats, and Uncle Tom blacks. And now *The People's Voice* became what many had always thought it was born to become, a cold partisan sheet backing Powell's political aims. On the issue after his announcement, stretched at the very top of the newspaper — above the fold, above the five-column photograph of troops marching through America, above the two words "Attention: Axis!" — was the bold headline ADAM POWELL TO RUN FOR CONGRESS. Powell did not confine his campaigning to Harlem. He went to Washington in November, leading a group of men (including the young photographer Gordon Parks, who was working for the Farm Services Administration, trailing them to capture the moment) into the chambers of the House and Senate to push for an antilynching bill. Capitol guards stopped the group and turned it around. Back in the Abyssinian pulpit, Powell told the story, getting all of it right, the drama and emotion, with the exception of whom the Capitol Hill police had pulled a gun on. It had not been Powell, as he told the congregation. A police officer had looked at Benjamin Richardson, one of Powell's aides, and because Richardson would not back away, had pulled his gun. Since Richardson was on the Abyssinian payroll, he thought better of challenging Powell's version.

Months after his announcement, Powell was running in New York by crisscrossing America. For grand effect he gave his tour a title, "The Conflicting Forces of the New Negro and Southernism." He went from Hollywood (where he conferred with Orson Welles, himself a political activist; perhaps it is merely coincidental that Hazel Scott was also in that city, for movie and nightclub work) to Detroit, then to Indianapolis. In midwestern cities he spoke of union rallies and the need for black and white workers to forge alliances. He told a group in Philadelphia that they must canvass and picket, so that when blacks returned from the war they would "return to a Democracy which they will enjoy." But it was surely in New York City that Powell was at his most riveting. In New York the ballroom doors were swinging open for the huge patriotic rallies — there were big bands, kisses being blown to sailing-away soldiers, war bonds being waved in the air; there were speakers: Paul Robeson, Vito Marcantonio, Eleanor Roosevelt, and Powell. "Adam used to walk into these places — it was almost like the president," recalled Howard Bell, one of Powell's parishioners. "When he walked into the ballroom, people were turning, looking, clapping." The war rallies convinced Powell of untold possibilities; "The new Negro," he felt, "is getting stronger." At every stop and from every podium, he piggybacked on the name of Franklin D. Roosevelt, although the administration had yet to acknowledge his campaign.

Powell could now call upon certain individuals in Washington for favors. One was Frank Horne of the Federal Public Housing Authority. "Is there any way for me to have furnished weekly the names of all Senators and Congressmen of areas where Negroes vote and just how they have voted in subcommittees and in the general body?" he asked Horne. "Then we can really start putting our finger on them." Groups in Washington wanted to meet him, and the radical Republican senator from North Dakota, William Langer (they called him Wild Bill), asked for a meeting to talk about "mutual" ideas.

While Powell was in midstride, a wave of antiwar riots broke out across America, first in Detroit, then in Texas, then the so-called zootsuit riots in Los Angeles. In Detroit, twenty-one people died. "The question that now concerns us is not will we win the peace, but will we win the war, and if so, which one — abroad or at home?" asked Powell. In early July 1943, he issued a warning to the New York City Council. "If a riot breaks out in New York, the blood of innocent people, white and Negro, will rest upon the hands of Mayor Fiorello La Guardia and Police Commissioner Lewis Valentine." New York City that summer was jittery, and the anger above 125th Street, caused by the lack of jobs and by the tales of returning soldiers of segregation and unfair treatment in the military, was genuine. "These are dark days for the common man," said Harlem's congressional candidate. Four weeks later, his prophetic statement came true.

Most riots took just one spark, and this one began in the lobby of Harlem's Braddock Hotel. A woman refused to pay her hotel bill, citing bad service. Police were summoned. Robert Brandy, a soldier home from battle, stepped in. Voices were raised between the woman and a police officer; Brandy sought to intervene, and found himself engaged in fisticuffs with the officer. Breaking loose and bolting, he was felled by a bullet from the officer's gun. The bullet struck only his arm, and he survived, but Brandy was arrested along with the woman. In Harlem, on an August night in 1943, the episode was enough to fan flames. Word raced along the streets that a black soldier had been shot by a white police officer, and it raced into the ears of the unemployed, the idle, and the hungry. Crowds gathered quickly. They picked up stones and rocks and bricks and sent them crashing through store windows. A contingent of police officers was summoned.

A young actor not long in Harlem came up out of the subway system, and when Sidney Poitier looked around 125th Street, he saw looting and fire, looters fleeing from the zing of bullets. Behind the wheel of one of the cars navigating the streets during the riot was James Baldwin, on his way to a graveyard to bury his father. The broken glass, the fleeing black bodies, the screaming voices, the insistent wailing, were all taken in. "It seemed to me that God himself had devised, to mark my father's end, the most sustained and brutally dissonant of codas," he wrote. Roy Wilkins was on a city bus, and was forced to duck as a brick came flying through the window. The city mobilized six thousand uniformed police officers, and the new governor, Thomas E. Dewey, put the National Guard on alert. All along 125th Street stores were attacked, food looted; women foraged for goods, some standing resolute as officers jumped from the back of police wagons with pistols drawn.

The riot pained La Guardia. He feared that children would go hungry if the stores were not restocked immediately, but his critics told him that children were already going hungry. For La Guardia it meant that once again, a significant portion of his metropolis was in pain, prone to riot, and vengeful. He pointed to his record, to his attention to social services, to deeds done in Congress. "It is harder to look up from records and look at facts," said a *PM* editorial, "and the facts are that all our schools and playgrounds and housing and speeches have not been enough." The dead were all black, and the riot pained Harlem more than it did La Guardia. Inasmuch as the soldier who had been shot, sparking the riot, was black, raw nerves of patriotism and equal rights were touched. "Had it been a Negro civilian, however prominent, who was shot, there would have been no riot," the NAACP's Walter White believed. City Councilman Adam Clayton Powell, Jr., knew the reasons for the riot, which he refused to characterize as a race riot, calling it instead an economic riot, the direct result of "blind smoldering resentment against Jim Crow of Negro men and women in the Armed Forces . . . the increasing rents and failure of the OPA [Office of Price Administration] to establish rent control . . . the wide flourishing of the black market in Harlem." Powell and his ally, Stanley Isaacs, blamed a lack of housing and recreational facilities in Harlem, charges that hit directly at Robert Moses. Moses reacted swiftly to the criticism, hinting that Powell and Isaacs represented the "lunatic fringe" on the council. Pressure extracted an apology, but few were unaware of Moses' sentiments toward Harlem.

Once again Powell flung the doors of his church open for community meetings, and once again he surged to the forefront of the elected officials lamenting Harlem's woes. Again Harlem seemed unsure of its future, seemed a place so separate from Manhattan, so misunderstood, as to be a mystifying world of its own. However, if one was waging a campaign in Harlem, there was plenty to wail against and many among the angry ready to be led. Powell stayed on the stump. "I helped you with your strikes when many other leaders scurried like rats during the Depression," he reminded one group. He masterfully dispatched his aides throughout the community to take advantage of their individual strengths. He sent his wife (it was politics, and sacrifices had to be made) into the entertainment community to rally the actors and entertainers. David Licorish, his West Indian assistant at the church, was told to focus on the West Indian community. Benjamin Davis, whom Powell was now backing for his own city council seat, thus ensuring Communist support for himself, worked on the Communist party. Ferdinand Smith, the labor columnist for *The People's Voice,* shored up labor support. And there were the ladies of the Abyssinian Baptist Church — "some of the most combative women in Harlem," according to Ollie Harrington — who worked tirelessly for Powell, handing out literature, registering voters, holding teas in their apartments.

Amid all of this, the war rallies continued, huge affairs that often turned exuberant and sweaty. On any given night there might be music from Duke Ellington and Mary Lou Williams and Coleman Hawkins. Hazel Scott was seen more and more frequently; she was described at one such affair as "looking like Hollywood, wearing a full-length mink cape," and playing the piano so well that she "wrecked the house." The rallies now were not just for Powell but for Marcantonio's re-election campaign, Davis's city council effort, and Roosevelt's run for the presidency. But Powell dominated them, merging patriotic fervor with progressive ideas.

Hazel Scott began taking more than a casual interest in Powell, trailing him in her limousine after the rallies, too shy to get out of the car and say anything, just watching him, because what could she say to a married man? But they invariably found time to say plenty to each other during the halcyon months of Powell's first congressional campaign, and in time it became apparent, to friends of both Scott and Powell, that the interest between them concerned more than Powell's political future. To relax, Powell often took Isabel down to Greenwich Village to hear music; Isabel later expressed shock that her husband had dared to take her to hear none other than Hazel Scott.

Powell's campaign continued to crest. The presidential election year was advantageous for the candidate. With no real opponent yet — Powell had brazenly entered all three party primaries — he took off after Governor Dewey, the GOP presidential candidate. Dewey was a New York Republican — that is to say, he had liberal notions and had been among the first governors to endorse the FEPC — but he was upstate New York, not the big cities and certainly not New York City. Moreover, when it came to the national campaign, Dewey abandoned much of his liberalism and waded into the land of indecision, struggling to win the right-wing votes of his party — and wading deeper into that area where Powell struck quickest. Powell dismissed him in a battering array of speeches, and he dismissed Dewey's small cadre of black appointees, calling them "men on horseback," without direction.

Finally Powell communicated with the Roosevelt administration. The White House sought advice from the Bronx Democratic boss, Ed Flynn, backer of the 1933 McKee mayoral campaign, who was well versed in New York City politics. He knew Powell and described him to the administration as worthy of support — "a very decent fellow." From this point on, the White House kept an eye on Powell's campaign.

It took months before the Abyssinian Baptist Church (doubtless under the influence of the more conservative members) broke with tradition and entered Powell's campaign wholeheartedly. When it did, eight months before the primaries, it did so with force. The church not only pledged $10,000 to the campaign, it formed a nonpartisan committee to work around the clock for Powell, granting him carte blanche to marshal forces inside the church. He picked up endorsements — for example, the Negro Labor Victory Committee, which claimed to represent 300,000 workers, pledged $15,000 — and each endorsement gained him strength.

Oscar DePriest, the old, gray-haired, defeated black Chicago congressman, came to Harlem to campaign for Powell. When a draft-Randolph committee came into action, Randolph killed it, refusing to make "compromises" he thought beneath him in the political arena. In February, Powell hit the road again, the FBI noting his movements at every stop. The hinterlands intrigued him. He told a Youngstown, Ohio, crowd that there was no peace for blacks across America, that there was just a war "for the four freedoms, and we shall demand ours after the peace or the black, brown, and yellow races will start

World War No. 3." But the hinterlands never intrigued him for long stretches of time, because there was nothing to match the thrill of coming back into Manhattan, rushing through the crowds at Penn Station, conferring with church officials or the actors and artists backing his campaign, picking up the newspapers — the *Times* and the *Herald Tribune*, the *World-Telegram* and the *Sun*, the *Post* and the *Journal-American* — and seeing what they were writing about the campaign, then picking up his own newspaper and reading the favorable coverage of his march toward Congress.

When Tammany Hall's Edward Loughlin, operating on orders from Clarence Neal, threw his backing to Powell, it was out of desperation Tammany had never supported a black candidate for office, but with Powell's momentum, it became a wise choice. The Tammany endorsement infuriated Herbert Bruce. He told the *New York Times* he could not endorse Powell because he feared that Powell, once in Washington would bring about "bloodshed" between the races.

Three opposition Democratic candidates finally emerged: William T. Andrews, Eardlee John, and George Harris. None had Powell's name recognition in Harlem. And none was invited to Washington that March, as was Powell, to address an audience at the National Press Club and to lunch with Vice President Henry Wallace ("I had lunch with Henry Agard Wallace" the other day, announced Harlem's beloved name-dropper). Powell became shameless in the art of self-promotion. An unsigned article appeared in the May 27, 1944, *People's Voice*, mentioning a strike that he had helped negotiate: "The resettlement was on the basis of several proposals made by the brilliant editor and public servant."

The Republican Party finally found its candidate. She was the Harlem attorney Sara Pelham Speaks, who boasted a fine community reputation, having graduated from the University of Michigan and New York University Law School. Many raised an eyebrow at the mention of Sara Speaks. Respected as she may have been, she had no political experience. The move looked extremely naive on the part of the Republicans — or else they were using Speaks as a sacrificial lamb. Her political strategy against Powell was low-key, in a community not given to the low-key in any endeavor. "You get nowhere by rabble-rousing," she believed. Powell's campaign manager, Joe Ford, promised that "we'll give her a good fight if she wants it." Speaks managed to pick up the quick endorsement of the Republican *Herald Tribune*, which did not see much to gain in Powell going to Washington and sitting as a Democrat in a House controlled by race-baiting southern Democrats. But the newspaper warned Speaks that going against the "political machine backing" of Powell would be anything but easy. Now that Powell had a GOP opponent, the national media once again took an interest in him; they were lavish with praise, referring to him as a "spellbinder." And in Harlem Powell hardly let up, plagiarizing Tom Paine: "This is a year when we must cut off fair-weather friends, sunshine patriots, and summer soldiers within our ranks." At times it seemed that groups were vying with one another to endorse Powell. In early May, the Independent Non-Partisan People's Committee threw its support behind him, dropping $1,000 into his campaign kitty and hearing him proclaim "an unceasing war against all individuals or groups who through mudslinging and lies try to oppose this People's Movement." Powell waged his campaign in the streets of New York and the boot camps of southern military bases, traveling back and forth between the two, making every effort to be in the Abyssinian pulpit on Sundays, because the pulpit provided such a wonderful campaign forum, and on Sunday mornings there was no better, more exciting place in Harlem. To Powell, the twenty-second district race was not merely for a Harlem seat; it was a national campaign. "During those days," recalled Howard Bell, "every Sunday you had no seats. People were standing around the walls. Each service was packed." And as you were leaving church during the campaign, you would be met at the door by an usher dressed in starched whites, and the usher would press a little card in your hand, and as you stepped from the door into sunshine you could read the card: "Let's go friend. Make Adam Clayton Powell the first Negro Congressman in the United States from the East."

The fires that fell across Powell's path were quickly put out. Herbert Bruce accused him of courting the Communist vote. Powell publicly disavowed Communist links, yet actively backed Ben Davis for his council seat. Even the Communists understood survival. Ministers who attacked him were rebuked: "The cloistered hall of religion today needs the fresh air of militancy." In June 1944 the first polls were released. Of the Democrats, 92 percent supported Powell; 74 percent of Republicans supported him, and 83 percent of the American Labor Party. Powell's three Democratic opponents withdrew from the race, leaving only Speaks between him and victory. He looked unstoppable.

In June both national parties held their conventions in Chicago. (The last time presidential conventions had been held in time of war was in 1864, during the Civil War.) Dewey became the GOP standard-bearer, and after noisy infighting, Roosevelt, whose health was a worry, decided to accept the nomination of the Democrats for the fourth time. There was, however, drama among the Democrats. Vice President Wallace was pushed aside for the Missouri senator Harry S. Truman. Few knew Truman. Among blacks, the very fact he was a southern Democrat was cause to worry. Powell dismissed the Republicans' convention and the "love song [they] crooned" to blacks, believing their platform to be no more open than in years before. He enthusiastically attacked Dewey, referring to him as the "pal of the poll-tax, anti-Roosevelt southern Democrats, as the thief of the soldier vote, and as the darling of the Big Business advocates of back-to-Hooverism and mass unemployment."

Following the conventions, it could hardly have pleased the Speaks camp that a Republicans for Powell Committee was formed. Among its organizers was the estimable J. Finley Wilson, exalted ruler of an estimated two million Elks nationwide. Wilson's endorsement was a clear coup, especially since Wilson was a well-known Republican. He hadn't voted for a Democrat since Al Smith, but he began urging Harlemites to do as he was now willing to do — to vote Democratic, to vote for Powell and place "principles, issues, and men above party."

The last stretch of Adam Clayton Powell, Jr.'s first campaign for Congress was a thing of grit and beauty. On July 10 a bandwagon began rolling along Harlem streets, and over the next several days Powell made speeches when it stopped at corners. By the end of the street-corner caravan, he had put in seventy-five speeches. Ralph Cooper, an impresario who made his reputation by introducing acts at the Apollo Theatre, would work the crowds into a frenzy before introducing Powell. "I just introduced a sort of theatrical note to the entire presentation," said Cooper. "I was the equivalent of the warm-up. Lot of laughs. When we got them into the proper frame of mind, we would introduce Adam." And from corner to corner they went, microphones on top of the wagon, Cooper beautifully dressed, Powell beautifully dressed, Powell's photographs everywhere. They rolled up and down Seventh Avenue, trailed by crowds. It was the kind of campaigning that Speaks considered beneath herself, preferring teas and quiet conferences among her advisers and backers. But Powell enjoyed it. He enjoyed the give-and-take, the bantering, his tall body emerging from car and rising atop car hood, atop ladder, his hand reaching out to the Harlem voter, his body leaning down to hear a whisper — he enjoyed it all. Especially the entertainers, because they enjoyed him; he had backed them and helped form the Negro Actors' Guild. So wide was Powell's reach in the Harlem community, so huge his number of volunteers, that on primary night he emerged as the victor not only in Democratic columns but in the Republican and American Labor parties as well. Now no one stood in his path; the November elections would be a mere formality. The dream had come alive. Black Harlem would have its congressman.

There was little need to campaign for himself after the primary, so Powell campaigned instead for Roosevelt, for the national ticket. In Chicago, appearing before a group of J. Finley Wilson's allies, repaying a campaign debt, he vowed that the day of the "so-called Big Negroes and Big Shots" was coming to an end. He addressed a group of independent voters in Boston who had heard Congresswoman Clare Boothe Luce's stump speech for Dewey and her attacks on Roosevelt the night before. Denigrating that "Luce talk," Powell urged a vote for Roosevelt. He finished out the weeks before the November election by working himself to exhaustion, attacking Dewey, traveling, sending broadsides out over the airwaves: "The people have purged this community of carpetbaggers, compromisers, and Uncle Toms." He prided himself in bringing together disparate groups in the Harlem community, particularly the "emancipated" Republicans. Unsigned poems came across the candidate's desk:

> When Powell goes to Congress
> We'll have a voice at last!
> Not timid or irrelevant,
> Like voices in the past,
> But one clear and outspoken
> And not afraid to speak,
> A champion of all people,
> Defender of the weak.

☙

Tired by the primary victory, Powell, on doctor's orders, sought rest. Along with his wife, he went to Oak Bluffs, to the summer home, the small oasis where they had spent so many summers. Adam Clayton Powell, however, had taken his wife to Oak Bluffs to tell her that he was ending their marriage; he was having an affair (though he did not tell her of it yet) with Hazel Scott. Walking from the ocean's edge to the porch, from the porch into the house, he stopped and told his wife that she would not be going to Washington with him. Isabel gasped for air. Married for eleven years, by her own admission spoiled ("I didn't even know how to make out a check"), she recoiled, stunned to silence. When she found her voice, it rambled; she asked him in a frightened tone what she should do, what should she do about love and sex? Coldly, he suggested celibacy. She simply exploded.

Back in Harlem, news of the split was swift. Powell dispatched his lawyer, Harrison Jackson, to work out a settlement. The old deacons did not know what to make of the news, but Powell was giddy with happiness. "Adam had the idea that if he had a problem," said Herbert Bruce, "everyone was to go along with him." Isabel was sure she would find comfort and sympathy among the Abyssinian congregation. She was wrong. There were those who felt that Isabel had aligned herself too closely with the light-skinned clique in the church, which Powell showed no favoritism toward. The congregation quickly rallied around their minister — their minister who was on his way to Washington. To dim any criticism, they vowed to put both money and backbone into his reputation.

Running into both Powell men at the church one day, Isabel could not hide her disgust. She called Powell Senior Satan, his son, her soon to be ex-husband, Satan Junior, then stalked off. The scandal meant little to Powell. "I thought you were a man of the cloth," someone asked. "I am," Powell said. "Silk."

Appearing back in his pulpit after his summer vacation, Powell saw the church packed, the rafters full; his church was busy. There were war conferences and community gatherings. In Harlem, there was still picketing activity. The war bond rallies were still taking place. To Powell there was no place like Harlem in the autumn of 1944. "During the past six years we have come out of the valley and we have come out together," he cried.

In an October 10 radio address, Powell unleashed an attack on Dewey that was scathing; he had turned himself into a full-time Roosevelt backer. He assailed Dewey as the "Albany Flash" and said that his international thought went no further than a Times Square shuttle train. "His claim to experience as a commander-in-chief is based upon fighting gangs in New York City."

A week before the election, Powell and Henry Wallace walked the streets of New York City, "cheered by crowds along the way," reported the *Times*. At the last minute, the Roosevelt forces had hired Louis

Martin, an energetic young Democrat from Michigan, to work with black voters. When Martin arrived in Harlem to help with Powell's campaign, Powell assured him that he needed no help at all. And of course Powell *didn't* need any help; both he and Roosevelt were victorious. His two-and-a-half-year campaign had come to an end. His strike-first posture had proven wise. In the winter of 1944 the mood of Harlem shifted from woe to hopefulness. The congressman-elect would soon be leaving for Washington. Adam Clayton Powell had emerged ahead of the other Harlem figures — the ones with law degrees, the ones with political reputations, the ones who considered him too radical. He had the grand prize. "He used to make the statement that he was better than his critics because he *chose* to be black," Martin recalled.

Harlem, so celebrated for its cultural renaissance, was now on the cusp of a political renaissance. In gaining his historic victory (and few could deny that the victory had been earned), Powell had broken through the doors of Tammany Hall. He had out-Tammanied the political club made infamous by Boss Tweed. Little did Tammany know — and certainly not Clarence Neal, who had become fond of Powell — that this was the man who would bring it to its knees, who would one day usher in the beginning of the end of Tammany's powerful reign.

Powell had rallied the masses of Harlem, the light- and the dark-skinned, but especially the dark. This was the beginning; this was triumph. Telegrams congratulating him poured in. There were rallies, huge sendoff affairs; at one he showed up in an evening suit and took his place on the dais with Mary McLeod Bethune.

The congressman-elect picked two secretaries for his staff: one, Hattie Dodson, light-skinned; the other, Maxine Dargans, dark-skinned. Now separated from his wife, he departed for Washington after the holidays — alone.

III

THE RISE
OF A PHOENIX
1945–1952

R ECONSTRUCTION WAS MORE than a gritty dream for blacks. For them it meant that the Fifteenth Amendment — the right to vote — had come to life. They would utilize that precious right for all it was worth. Old men and women, shoeless and penniless, whose ancestors had spent decades on plantations in bondage, could walk to meetinghouses and county offices in southern towns and vote. It was the one act that immediately set them on level ground with their former plantation owners; each of their votes carried as much weight as each of their former owners' votes. Those who could neither read nor write (and many couldn't) marked X; a vote was a vote, and much blood had been spilled to earn it.

During the years of Reconstruction, from 1865 to 1877, the risky Republican-backed Fifteenth Amendment, loathed by Democrats, did exactly what Democrats feared: it changed the political landscape of the American South. Soon enough, in state legislatures all across the region, there appeared black elected officials. Mississippi and Alabama, Georgia and South Carolina, North Carolina and Louisiana, once powerful slave-holding states, were now forced to endure social change. In 1870, Joseph H. Rainey of South Carolina arrived in Washington as the first black ever elected to the House of Representatives. Fifteen other blacks followed him into Congress during Reconstruction. They were an eclectic bunch — former tailors, businessmen, and merchants, their numbers evenly divided between freeman and former slave. Congressman Robert Smalls of South Carolina had emerged from the Civil War with a hero's medal, won for piloting a ship in battle. All sat, not unexpectedly, as Republicans, their debt to the party of Lincoln. They pleaded for civil rights legislation, and warned of Reconstruction backlash in the backwoods of their home counties. Their pleas fell upon deaf ears, and their bills rarely made it to the floor.

Black Alabama Congressman Benjamin Turner introduced a novel idea, the creation of a national land commission to ensure that former slaves would receive land and would be able to hold on to it when they received it. The bill never came to a vote. The manic wind that blew the black congressmen into Washington was not destined to last. Southern lawmakers redrew districts; literacy and poll taxes were devised; Grant's government sat idly by as waves of violence swept the South. An especially murderous rampage in Clinton, Mississippi, in 1875, where dozens of unarmed blacks were murdered by whites, served as harbinger of things to come. (Mississippi had sent Hiram Revels and John Lynch, both black, to the Senate and the House.) Blacks pleaded with Washington to send troops to protect their right to vote. Grant's government lay mired in scandal; brave whites saw their appeals to help blacks ignored. Both Charles Sumner and Thaddeus Stevens, the great voices of democracy who had designed and fostered Reconstruction, died unable to keep it from being sabotaged. One by one the black elected officials in Washington were sent home, losing elections at an alarming rate.

In time the South reverted to what it had long been — a land dominated by white officeholders. Out of office, the former black congressmen found their opportunities limited. Many refused to return home, choosing to teach and lecture in the North, where their former-congressman status imbued them with honor. Alonzo Ransier, a black South Carolina congressman, returned to Charleston after his stint and took a variety of odd jobs to survive, the last as a street sweeper. He died in 1882, broke.

George White, a North Carolina congressman, arrived in Washington in 1897, well after Reconstruction. He was elected because of a peculiar set of circumstances: an independent, he crossed party lines and drew votes from both Democrats and Republicans. The game could not last, and he surely knew it. Still, he held on to his seat until the century had turned. In 1901 White stood before his fellow congressmen to deliver his parting words (rarely did a black congressman leave Congress without a denunciation), which were tinged with sadness and bracketed by a vow. "Phoenix-like," he promised, speaking of the black man in Congress, "he will rise up some day and come again." For decades the white congressmen of the South thwarted this ɔrediction, allowing a feudal system that denied blacks the right to ⱴote to flourish.

Nearly three decades later, with the great black migration from ﾐouth to North in full swing, Oscar DePriest was elected on the Republican ticket in Chicago. Born in Alabama, DePriest moved to Kansas with his family before swinging north to settle in Chicago. First he went into real estate, then into ward politics, where his job was to deliver black votes to the white political machine. He succeeded in fine fashion, and in 1928 his reward was election to Congress. He arrived trailed by scandal, his name having been stretched across Chicago newspapers because of vice and gambling charges. (Few in Chicago paid any attention.) Once in Washington, DePriest, who wore a large bone-white Stetson, quickly sought to diffuse expectations. "I have no race consciousness of the kind that is consumed in the vain notions of social equality," he awkwardly said. He worried less about national black aspirations than he did about his own survival. He wished to integrate the House cafeteria, then argued with black students at Howard University who saw his means of doing so as too genteel. They picketed, which made DePriest nervous and drew him to attack their methods. He found the New Deal too radical and opposed it, even as gaunt Chicagoans scavenged the stockyards of his district for food.

After three terms, blacks voted DePriest out, choosing Arthur Mitchell, an FDR Democrat, to replace him. A guileless politician, Mitchell floundered for four terms in Washington and is remembered merely as the first black Democrat. In 1942, he was defeated by William Dawson, who came of voting age a Republican but strategically switched to being a Democrat after FDR fever had heated black aspirations. Dawson convinced himself that he could be most effective (his goals were never clearly stipulated) by being silent in Washington. He was so nervous that he didn't socialize, he abhorred publicity, and he warned the press that his comments, which were few and far between, were off the record. His long-time secretary, Christine Davis, remembered him, not surprisingly, as "a retiring man." Dawson had no intention of shouldering the burden of black ambitions. The black congressmen of Chicago arrived in Washington with parochial debts to ward politicians back home, and they steered clear of the national limelight.

It was not until 1945 that the first northern black congressman to appeal to both parties, like George White, arrived in Washington. He

arrived free of political debts and free to roam the corridors of power
And his arrival in Washington gave hope to blacks east to west, north
to south, who were praying in that cold January of 1945 that he was
as one publication put it, "the Negro chosen by some destiny" to lead
the march toward equality from the halls of Congress. Adam Clayton
Powell, Jr., went to Congress as a ghost of Reconstruction, his mind
on the unfinished work of America.

◦◦◦

Hattie Dodson was a slender woman, fastidious in her habits, ele
gantly mannered, and raised in the Abyssinian Baptist Church. Her
voice was soft, her features more plain than beautiful, but the com
bination of her talents and her utter devotion made her admirable
among Abyssinians; it made them think of her as a beautiful young
lady.

Hattie Dodson's love for Adam Clayton Powell, Sr., was platonic
the love of a religious young girl awed by the elderly minister in the
pulpit, the minister whom her mother served diligently as a church
organizer. Her family had been among the thousands who had wor
shipped at the church when it was on West 40th Street (she was the
last to be baptized there), and she had proudly taken part in the
building festivities of the church on 138th Street, standing with her
family and thousands of others in the open sun. She had considered
it an honor to serve as one of the minister's secretaries while still in
her teens, helping to lighten the load of Dorothy Brooks, his persona
secretary. In huge Baptist organizations, secretaries took on huge re
sponsibilities, from acting as gatekeeper to handling business affairs
Adam Senior expected two things from his secretaries: propriety and
discretion. Scandal was to be avoided at all costs, and gossip kept to
a minimum; church business was the church's business, not the pub
lic's. Brooks's skills became Hattie Dodson's skills.

But Hattie's devotion to Adam Junior was more than platonic
Members could see it; "Hattie loved him," recalled church member
Olivia Stokes. Hattie withstood his marriage to Isabel with grace, and
their 1944 breakup with still more grace. In moving to Washington
and leaving behind the Harlem she loved and her mother and father
she was forced to endure the rebirth of rumors that her emotiona
attachment to him had not abated. Over the years she even withstood
occasional cruel needling from Powell himself — "the virgin Hattie,"
he would sometimes say when introducing her.

Eager to set up Powell's congressional office, Hattie arrived in war-ime Washington and quickly felt the city's tenseness. Armed men ;uarded government buildings; sirens sometimes blared. Washington was a starkly segregated city, and she soon realized how many rules ind limitations affected her. There were stores she could not go into. 'I wasn't used to it," she explained.

Meanwhile, Belford Lawson, the attorney who had won the landnark job discrimination suit in Washington that had inspired the Harlem boycotters, and his wife, Marjorie, offered to host a party or Powell. "What we had in mind was for the community to meet nim," recalled Marjorie. "And we wanted him to have a middle-class, upper-class introduction." Even before his arrival, as Lawson remembered, her friends were excited about Powell. "They were curious. He was this new black congressman. Here was somebody from New York, :he eastern seaboard."

When Powell arrived in Washington, Hattie Dodson had already organized his office. In the House office building, the two stepped into an elevator. There were two white men inside. The door closed. 'We're just waiting for that nigger to come down here from New York," one man said to the other. Hattie turned to Powell. "His face :urned red; mine turned red," she recalled. "He didn't say a word."

On January 3, 1945, at noon, Adam Clayton Powell was escorted :hrough the House chambers by William Dawson of Chicago and sworn in as a member of the 79th Congress, the first congressman to represent the newly established twenty-second district of New York. Old deacons from the Abyssinian Baptist Church leaned down from the gallery. Hazel Scott, wonderfully attired and coiffed, looked on. There sat Adam Clayton Powell, Sr., although Mattie Powell was ailing and unable to attend. Still, it must have been a proud moment for the elder Powell, who had once worked in Washington as a menial laborer. An old man nearing his eightieth birthday, he had believed, when others didn't, in the talents of his unpredictable son. "Just wait and give him more time. Let him develop," he had told Franklin Delano Roosevelt, Jr., who had spoken at the Abyssinian church.

President Roosevelt, looking wan, was inaugurated for his fourth term. After attending the inauguration, the new congressman from Harlem attended his first White House luncheon, with Hazel Scott at his side. (The invitation had been addressed to Mr. and Mrs. Adam Clayton Powell; Hazel replaced Isabel, who never forgave either of them for denying her the opportunity to grace the White House.)

From the White House — no one dared to ask about "Mrs. Powell" — Congressman Powell and Hazel Scott went to a soirée in his honor at the Mayflower Hotel, thrown by Robert Hannegan, Democratic national chairman.

Marjorie and Belford Lawson lived well, in a fifteen-room Victorian mansion overlooking Washington's Logan Park. Living in Washington since the late 1930s and involved in civil rights causes, they had been sorely disappointed that none of the black Chicago congressmen had appealed to their sense of mission. They had high hopes for the thirty six-year-old Powell. More than a hundred guests, black and white, reflecting the Lawsons' wide circle of friends, arrived at their home to welcome Powell. The whiff of scandal that trailed him to the nation's capital did nothing to dim his luster, and Marjorie Lawson knew why: "He was so handsome and charming." Confident, never demure, and keen at reading the faces of strangers, for she had been playing to crowds since childhood and was fond of the grand entrance, Hazel Scott arrived at the party in full stride. Her white dress was fitted ("tight," allowed Lawson), and her hair was wrapped in a white turban held in place with a diamond stickpin. Such a light color against her brown skin made for a striking contrast. Powell held his own at the affair, but the attention shifted to Hazel, who had a dazzling smile. "She had every man in the room hanging on to her every word," recalled Lawson. Normally Hazel would have been annoyed at being asked to play the piano on a social occasion — it made her feel cheap, as if she had to sing for her supper — but there was a beautiful baby grand in the Lawsons' living room, and she ambled over and took a seat, taking a crowd with her. Playing on this occasion would be different. Instead of playing to the gathering, she was playing to the man she had fallen in love with. "She was a sensation," said Lawson. "People were titillated."

As for Powell, he merely enjoyed himself. (He never, during his stay in Washington, made a habit of socializing with high society, which was populated by light-skinned blacks, blacks like himself. He knew their secret, and his habit was to mock and scorn it. "His mind was all concentrated on poverty and race," explained Lawson.) He and Hazel left the party as they had come, confident and in good spirits. It delighted them to leave the partygoers stunned in their wake. Marjorie Lawson was perplexed. "It was a bad introduction to Washington society," she thought. "It didn't accomplish what we wanted."

Adam Clayton Powell's first residence in Washington was the top floor of the Lawsons' huge home. On the weekends that he didn't return to New York, Hazel came down from New York in her chauffeured limousine, accompanied by servants, whose running in and out upset Lawson. For a while she tolerated the noise that surrounded a traveling musical celebrity — the servants, the ringing telephone — but then she tired of it and asked Powell to tell Scott.

Like most other freshman congressmen, Powell was expected to sit and learn, and sit and learn quietly. The House was an intricate place, a place where anonymity might well swallow a congressman up, but it also gave the opportunity to form the behind-the-scenes friendships and alliances that often served to boost his career in later years. Since little was expected of them, freshman congressmen often gave little, and rarely became known outside their home districts. (Emmanuel Celler, a Brooklyn Democrat elected in 1924, pitied the freshman congressmen and called them "lost souls.") An exception was J. William Fulbright, a liberal Arkansan who arrived in Congress in 1943 and proceeded to introduce the resolution that engineered America's participation in the United Nations.

Powell paid the obligatory visit to Sam Rayburn, who placed him on the Indian Affairs and Labor committees. Elected to the House from Texas in 1913, Rayburn had risen through the complex system of House politics, the protégé of powerful men like Joe Cannon and John Nance Garner, all the way to the Speaker's high-backed chair. The younger congressmen found it wise to listen to him. The congressman from Harlem was different. Adam Clayton Powell had no predecessor. He was hand-picked by no one. He arrived in Washington with independence. Rayburn realized as much. "Don't try to go too fast" was Rayburn's standard advice to newcomers, but he expanded on it for Powell: "Adam, everybody thinks you're coming down here with a bomb in each hand. Maybe you are. But you don't throw them. Feel your way around. You have a great future."

So for the first month Powell was quiet, much to the chagrin of reporters. "They convinced me that my maiden speech in the House should be constructive," he told one reporter, "and on as high a plane as possible." He kept himself busy learning the rules of the House. Vito Marcantonio, his fellow Harlem congressman, an expert on them, offered advice and encouragement. Marjorie Lawson rarely saw Powell; he would arrive home late. The door would swing open, and there he would be. Often he dashed right upstairs, his long legs covering the steps in double time. Other times he sat with her and talked.

She was raising a little baby, and her husband was often on the road. Powell talked about everything, she recalled — his plans and ideas for Congress, what he could do, and the interesting people he was meeting, not so much in Congress but in and around Washington. Often on weekends he rode the train to New York City; Saturdays were for Hazel, Sundays for the church.

But there were weekends when he remained in Washington, Scott was on the road, and Belford Lawson was away tending to legal business. On such weekends Powell would grab Marjorie and tell her she was going out for the evening, and she would be surprised to find herself in a roomful of artists, liberals, writers, men and women interested in talking about race and politics in a relaxed manner. And Marjorie Lawson, who had thought she would introduce Powell to Washington society, began to notice how the party, host and all, gravitated toward him, got close to his conversations. She grew fond of the outings, of Powell's driving fast through the Washington streets and introducing her to yet more "rich white liberals," who were fascinated by his arrival in Washington and by what he might do. "Those were elegant parties," she recalled. "They were people interested in liberal causes. And they were interested in seeing this interesting man."

Powell had a small Washington staff: Hattie Dodson was secretary, and Waldo Parrish took dictation, trailing Powell with a dictaphone in his hand. Congressmen often ran their offices with merely an aide or two to answer constituent mail. But in addition to his Washington staff, Powell kept aides on his congressional payroll at his Harlem office: the Abyssinian Baptist Church. Dodson adapted to Washington as best she could. Christine Davis, William Dawson's secretary, befriended her, and some evenings she and Powell would go for long walks (Washington winters being so much more tolerable than New York winters) and gaze at the magnificent buildings. Sometimes they found themselves down on the Potomac, at water's edge. Powell liked the water. Circling back, still on foot, they passed restaurants, and Adam Clayton Powell would turn to Hattie Dodson, point to the restaurants, and say, "You know, I can't go in there." She knew all too well what he meant. He went in anyway. He challenged waitresses and waiters, walking up on them with his imposing body, knowing he confused them with his light skin, primed for argument, then stalking to his seat, his boldness serving to dim curiosity about his racial background. Dodson knew the look of waiters who recognized what that background was. When black waiters who were too afraid to serve blacks gave Powell an especially discerning look, she knew they realized he was black. His assault on public restaurants gave him perfect grist for Sunday morning sermons. He told his congregation that he went in those places, right through the front door — not for himself, he wasn't eating for himself, but for them and their children and their grandchildren, for Georgia's blacks and Mississippi's blacks and Alabama's blacks, for blacks everywhere.

One day Hattie Dodson walked down to the House cafeteria. She was refused service. Shocked, she fled. Powell urged her back to the cafeteria, to stand in line until she was served. He was prepared to make a scene. Finally the supervisor came out. "Go on and serve her," he said. Claiming victory, Powell spread the word that the House cafeteria had been desegregated. "He knows that's not true," said Christine Davis. When someone jerked a tray out of her hands, she told Dawson, who quietly took the matter up with Sam Rayburn. Arrangements were made for Davis to be served too, but nobody announced any desegregation policy in the House cafeteria. Dawson and his staff grew angry at Powell. Dawson brooded in silence. He did not talk to the press. Congressman Powell did.

The Congress of 1945 was a Congress that had long been muscled by President Roosevelt. It was full of Republicans who believed that if not for the weakness of Herbert Hoover, this patrician former governor from Hyde Park, New York, might never have made it into the White House. He had humiliated them by driving a wedge between their patriotism and his legislation. His policies had ensured that the black trek across the road from Republican to Democrat had begun, that fewer and fewer blacks would be susceptible to pleas for faithfulness to the party of Lincoln.

The Democratic congressmen were mostly southern men, grandsons of Civil War veterans, come to Washington to continue an intellectual war against the North. Growing up, they had heard stories of the Civil War, the war that had sent their grandfathers to early graves and widowed their grandmothers, and of the havoc Reconstruction had wreaked on their beloved South. Many came from rural districts in the low country, and many still employed blacks as field workers and maids. They were men in bow ties and suspenders, men in straw hats, men who had come as far north as they cared to come, because this town, Washington — "the most southern city north of Richmond," it was called — had such a southern feel to it. Many preferred not to live in the District, with its overwhelming black population which spread from Anacostia across the entire city. They purchased homes in Virginia and Maryland; in good weather they reclined on wicker chairs in the open air, sucking in the fresh air coming through the trees in the distance, while black maids and butlers took empty glasses and disappeared into their kitchens.

With no chance of attaining the presidency, southern politicians put their talents into maintaining control of Congress. It was not ironic at all to southern congressmen that John Rankin, a segrega-tionist from Mississippi, controlled the financial fortunes of the over-whelmingly black population of the District of Columbia. From county steps in Mississippi, Rankin had long excoriated blacks; he had also done it from the floor of the House. This is what the con-gressman from Harlem faced. Unlike William Dawson, Powell could not stand idly by in the face of insult. There was simply too much to do for him to sit and learn. He had known cautious men, men who had jeered at him, who had confused his pace, his activities, with what they perceived to be hunger for notoriety. Results — jobs for blacks in the stores of Harlem; black drivers on the previously all-white Harlem buses — were the only thing he truly understood. He had no respect for men who went slowly. It was inevitable that Adam Clayton Powell would do battle with this Congress.

The Mississippi congressman was proud of his nickname, Lightnin' Rankin. He was an avowed anti-Semite, once having risen on the floor of the House to attack the columnist Walter Winchell by calling him "a little kike." In early 1945, a week after Rankin had launched yet another bizarre assault on Jews, the congressman from Harlem stood to offer his maiden speech. "Last week democracy was shamed by the uncalled for and unfounded condemnation of one of America's great minorities," Powell said. "I am not a member of that great minority, but I will always oppose anyone who tries to besmirch any group because of race, creed, or color. Let us give leadership to this nation in terms of racial and religious tolerance and stop petty bick-ering in this body."

Days later Rankin accused Frank Hook, a Michigan congressman, of consorting with Communists. Hook called Rankin a "dirty liar." Rankin rose from his seat and marched toward Hook, a former coal miner, which was an unwise move. Hook met him with blows; the two had to be separated. Powell stood again. "The time has arrived to impeach Rankin, or at least expel him from the Democratic Party."

They were bold words, especially for a representative who had been in Congress less than eight weeks. What amazed Marjorie Lawson about Powell was his attitude toward other congressmen. "He acted as if he were their superior. I think he overwhelmed them."

In the early months he voted for an antilynching amendment, an extension of rights for District of Columbia residents, naturalization for Native Americans — votes that were crushed by the alliance of conservative Republicans and southern Democrats. He voted to oppose funding for the Rankin and Dies committees, which had been set up to hunt for subversives. He spoke out against discrimination against black nurses. He used newfound contacts to keep his adopted son, Preston, now in the navy, far from battle; the boy spent the last year of the war on a naval base in Virginia.

In New York City, Powell addressed a rally by supporting Henry Wallace for secretary of commerce, a nomination fiercely opposed by conservatives. Powell saw the battle as all-important; he was already on the Wallace-for-President bandwagon for 1948. "Those opposed to Wallace say he is a dreamer," Powell told the gathering. "We need a dreamer." Pragmatically, he kept attention on his Harlem constituency, sending the obligatory press releases, traveling back and forth weekly to the Abyssinian pulpit. His newspaper, *The People's Voice*, ran laudatory (though not lavish) stories about his congressional work. One issue in early 1945 carried an advertisement for a contest. Those who clipped ten coupons from the newspaper — the catch being, of course, that you had to purchase ten successive issues — and forwarded them to the congressman's office would receive a photograph of the congressman, "suitable for framing."

Three months after Adam Clayton Powell's congressional career began, tragedy struck his family. Mattie Powell died, following a long illness on April 22. She was eulogized in Harlem as a caring woman, a woman who had given much to the Abyssinian Baptist Church — as much, in her own way, as her husband and son. "An ideal preacher's wife," began one eulogy, "a safe and wise counselor, a veritable Gibraltar of strength in her husband's life . . ." Many had Mattie Powell stories. She was a kind lady who sent blankets and other items back to relatives in West Virginia every Christmas, who always encouraged the bright young men of Harlem to respect black women. She had carried the mantle of first lady of the Abyssinian church with high purpose. She was a "regal" woman, said long-time church member Olivia Stokes, yet approachable.

There were those in the congregation who imagined that the death would be enough of a shock to drive Powell back into the arms of his wife; he and Isabel were still legally married. Those people had only to walk into the funeral and look at the beautiful flowers the congressman had placed on his mother's casket to know that it was not to be: the flowers were from Adam Powell and Hazel Scott, who arrived at the funeral hand in hand. "I thought that was the height of immorality," said Stokes.

Ten days before Mattie Powell's death, gloom had swept America, and particularly black America, at the news of Franklin Roosevelt's death. "Born of landed gentry," one Harlem editorial remarked, "he became, for this generation, the symbol of the rights of all citizens." As FDR's body rolled north on a train from Warm Springs, Georgia, whites and blacks hunched along the land sliced by the tracks — blacks who had rarely voted and blacks who couldn't vote — all touched by the hugeness of the man and frightened of the unknown, which was already spreading. Powell wasted little time in contacting the new president. He promised Truman the same support he had given Roosevelt, then requested a conference "soon as possible" to talk about "the entire program of the Negro people." At the bottom of the telegram a presidential aide wrote, "This is the colored congressman." In Harlem, Powell led memorial services in honor of Roosevelt and grieved with his congregation.

In June he divorced his wife. In the settlement, Isabel received the cottage at Oak Bluffs, where they had spent summers, and cash, the amount undisclosed. She had not come to the agreement easily; hopelessly believing in a chance at reconciliation, she had sequestered herself in the Abyssinian-owned apartment she had shared with her husband, daring anyone to put the pastor's wife "out on the street." But in the end, accompanied by her sister and dressed stylishly, she rode a train to Reno, Nevada, and obtained a divorce. Ever the trouper, she entertained USO troops while in Nevada. "I was like a bird thrown from a nest," she remembered of her painful divorce. She returned from Reno, however, with her confidence intact. "I never felt better in my life," she announced, "but I feel so sorry for Adam."

⟨∾⟩

The marriage of Hazel Scott and Adam Clayton Powell, Jr., was announced for August 1. Barney Josephson, the jazz impresario who was to host the reception, sent beautifully etched invitations out to more than a thousand people. The announcement hit the wire services, and the news spread from coast to coast. Even in a nation still at war, celebrity marriages spread their balm. In black America, the wedding of Adam Clayton Powell and Hazel Scott was something more — the stuff of grand romance and intrigue.

Born in Port of Spain, Trinidad, on June 11, 1920, Hazel Dorothy Scott had arrived with her parents, Alma and R. Thomas Scott, in the United States in 1924; she had celebrated her fourth birthday aboard ship. The Trinidadian family brought a strong racial pride with them. But R. Thomas Scott, trained as a scholar in England, found that his academic prowess was not appreciated in America. Reduced to odd jobs, he fell into deep depression. Alma Scott, a musician, supplemented the family income by playing with various bands and by giving music lessons in their Bronx home. Upon her husband's death, when Hazel was fifteen, she became the family's sole support. Forced to survive independently, to care for both her daughter and her mother, Alma adopted a fierce work ethic, which she passed on to Hazel. First she joined Lil Armstrong's all-female band. Then she formed a band of her own, the American Creolians.

While her parents worked, Hazel passed the time with her grand-mother and learned to speak fluent Yiddish from Jewish playmates. One day when she was four years old, she climbed onto the piano stand and began picking out a tune. From another room, her grand-mother called out, wondering who was playing the instrument. Be-wildered, she rose to find little Hazel playing away, a tune called "Little Jesus." The child had near-perfect pitch. She was pronounced a genius, first by family, making the utterance suspect, then by Juilliard professors, giving it legitimacy. Hazel's natural gifts encouraged Alma to add her to the band she was then playing with; the girl was all of five years old. Alma never taught her daughter how to cook, because she feared what stovetop burns might do to Hazel's hands.

Mother worked daughter hard; Hazel Scott spent her childhood in the adult world of music, playing for pay. Alma wished to make sure that she would always be able to take care of herself financially. When Harlem was struggling through the Depression in 1933, thirteen-year-old Hazel was being introduced at her first Manhattan recital. Three years later she was confidently hosting her own radio show. Broadway beckoned, and she made her debut at eighteen in *Sing Out the News,* stunning the audience with her version of "Franklin D. Roosevelt Jones." In 1939 she was featured at the New York World's Fair. That same year she formed her own all-female band (it was short-lived) and even found time to do some arranging for Coleman Hawkins's band. At nineteen she was mature beyond her years. Men adored her company, and found her salty language, picked up in nightspots, to be titillating. They mistook her sensuality for promiscuity. "Everyone wants to sleep with you," she once confided. "If you don't, you've got problems. When you brush off the bosses and geniuses in the front office, you automatically become a lesbian. If you do go along with these idiots, you're a bum. Name it and take your choice." She made other women jealous, and didn't mind. It was not that she was going places; at nineteen, Hazel Scott had already been there. She needed to take her career to its next level, to become a crossover star, a success among whites as well as blacks. Barney Josephson helped make it happen.

Born in Trenton in 1902 into a family that put stock in liberal and often radical values (one brother became a noted labor lawyer, defending indigent clients, often without compensation; the family shared pictures of lynchings with their children, to teach them of the horrors), Barney Josephson grew up picketing in front of theaters that barred blacks. The experience drew him into Harlem, that teeming black mecca, where he caught Duke Ellington on the stage of the Cotton Club. His conscience kept him from completely appreciating the experience, however, because he noticed that blacks were allowed onstage, to perform, but not in the audience.

A brother helped him realize a dream: an integrated nightclub, called Café Society, in Greenwich Village. It opened in December 1938. "The club was small, a cellar club," explained Arthur Josephson, Barney's nephew. "It had murals on the walls painted by leading illustrators of the day. Had a little short bar. Then there were tables in the middle of the floor, along a wall. And there was an intermission pianist at all times." The debut singer was Billie Holiday. She sang "Strange Fruit" there; the song was about blacks hanging from trees in the South — strange fruit — and her rendition was hailed as haunting and unforgettable.

Holiday's presence and the club's integrated policy put Café Society on the map. "You'd get these rednecks," remembered Arthur Josephson, who frequented the club often in its early years, despite the fact that he was under age. "I remember one in particular, big blond naval officer, came in, sat down, he had all that gold shit over him. He looked around, said something to the waiter. Waiters all were instructed to say, 'That's the policy of the club. You wish to complain, you speak to the owner.' Barney would say, 'That's the way it is and you can leave.' Barney would pick up the tab, and if they got salty, they were told they would be removed." The doorman's name was Harry. He was huge, a Sephardic Jew. Everyone called him Harry the Turk. He handled customers like the blond naval officer. "You would go," recalled Josephson. "It would be like someone locking your arm in a vise."

The club mixed jazz with comedy. Both Zero Mostel and Imogene Coca became popular. There were three shows nightly, the first at nine, the second at midnight, and the finale at 2 A.M. Police officers walking the beat often stuck their heads in to partake of the music. But Josephson appeared partial to piano players. Art Tatum and Earl Hines and Joe Turner and Teddy Wilson all tickled the ivories at Café Society. None of their engagements became as popular as that of Hazel Scott, who followed Billie Holiday as a featured attraction. Scott rarely sang — her voice was low and sweet, but she had trouble in the high register — but everyone came to hear her play piano. Bare-shouldered, with a lone lamplight on her, and, because she had been influenced by Holiday, a gardenia often in her hair, she played a version of piano that was considered novel. The feat demanded rare versatility. First the pianist had to become expert at playing the classics — Bach, Beethoven, Chopin, Rachmaninoff — and then at playing jazz. In the jazz realm, Scott had been influenced by Hines and Tatum. During performances she would "swing" the classics, stopping in the middle of a Chopin riff and trilling the keys with some Tatum-inspired takes. It was an astounding feat. Purists of either discipline, classical or jazz, might have felt that their music was being compromised, but those who had only a fair knowledge of music were impressed, and praise flowed.

The college kids from Princeton came up to see Scott play; Eleanor Roosevelt, hardly a socialite, showed up with her son, Franklin Junior. Scott was shrewd enough to realize the oddity of it all — a black woman being appreciated more for playing wicked versions of the classics than for playing the classics themselves. "My stuff is hybrid," she once sought to explain. "I'm not grim enough for the classics."

There were apartments upstairs from Café Society, and the critic Leonard Feather occupied one of them. He would take the elevator downstairs, stroll into the club, take a seat, and listen to Hazel Scott, who dazzled him. "Café Society was her breakthrough," he recalled.

"She had an exuberant personality." The public began talking not of Billie Holiday's stint at the club but of Hazel Scott's. Liking his friendship, Scott began picking up Feather some evenings in her limousine, and together they would hit the New York nightspots. "She was very vivacious, interested in that whole music world," said Feather. "Almost like a fan." He began doing public relations work for her, hustling all over the city to get her on the cover of music magazines. Despite her popularity, she still had to hew to society's racial realities, and Feather considered it a coup when he could get her on a magazine's cover.

Lloyd's of London insured her hands. She was fond of carrying a single red rose wherever she went. Harry Winston, the famous New York jeweler, made her jewelry; she liked diamonds, and anything of art deco design.

In 1940 Barney Josephson opened another club, on 58th Street. Café Society Uptown was larger than its downtown counterpart, and the club's ambience was lusher. Admirers of Hazel Scott dreamily convinced themselves that Josephson had built the club solely for Scott. Its clientele was also noticeably more glamorous. It was at Café Society Uptown that Arthur Josephson first saw Adam Clayton Powell, who strolled in one evening. "I remember him at the bar, chatting with Paul Robeson. Oh God, was he suave. He was always dressed just this side of flashy."

Hazel Scott began to tour in the early 1940s. Following a performance in Chicago, a critic wrote in the *Daily News* that Scott "knows and can play the classics, as she demonstrated yesterday at the outset of her program, but she knows, too, how to swing them into the comprehension of boogie-woogie fans without doing violence to the soul substance of her composers." She further surprised audiences when she sang in a variety of languages: Yiddish, French, then Italian. At the piano she looked sultry (she kept a handkerchief nearby to dab at any beads of sweat). Charlie Parker recorded his version of Gershwin's "Embraceable You" to her piano playing. Soon she became an outright star. She purchased a home in Mount Vernon, away from the noisy city. There she lived with her mother and grandmother, three prideful West Indian women who went about their daily life in quiet splendor, driven to and from errands in a limousine. When Hollywood called, Scott went west. Pride prohibited her from playing maids, as Billie Holiday had been forced to do. She was mentioned for the role of the pianist in a picture called *Casablanca* — Humphrey

Bogart was one of her biggest fans — but by the time casting had been completed, the pianist's gender had been changed, and Dooley Wilson was given the part.

The movies she appeared in were forgettable; she had bit parts alongside Mae West and Red Skelton — a mere ornament, the anonymous lady on piano: Hazel Scott. In 1943 she appeared in *The Heat's On*, starring Mae West, a Vincente Minnelli movie called *I Dood It*, and another movie called *Something to Shout About*. Unhappy with movies, she managed to pick up additional spending change while out in Hollywood; $1,500 a week they paid her for playing at the Mocambo Saloon.

Scott was an ardent Roosevelt supporter, and her appearances at political rallies in New York City drew notice in the press. She went from Roosevelt rallies to rallies for Adam Clayton Powell. The two began dining out; "21" and the Stork Club were favorites. Hounded by the press as "the other woman" in Powell's marriage, Scott coolly played coy until the divorce was announced. On July 24, a week before their own wedding, she and Powell showed up together in Stamford, Connecticut, at the local courthouse, where they obtained a marriage license. Scott could no longer hide her infatuation. Smiling (the press had obviously been tipped off), she put both hands around Powell's wrist as he signed the document, a boutonnière resting in the lapel of his suit coat.

They were married at the Bethel AME Church in Stamford. The groom dispatched his chauffeur to pick up the Scotts. He and his father, racing to the affair in another car, suffered a blowout in Greenwich, but an understanding tollbooth attendant drove them the remaining miles. Bride and groom were elegant, the groom in morning attire, as was his father, the bride in a white Chantilly lace dress with diamond clips at the shoulder. She held gardenias and white orchids in her hand.

After the ceremony, it was off to Manhattan, to Josephson's Café Society, for the reception. Twenty-five New York police officers were on hand to hold back the growing crowd outside the club who wanted to get a peek at the couple. "Park Avenue's women of means with their pugnosed puppies" were seen outside. While the Gene Fields Trio played and a *Life* photographer snapped pictures, guests mingled, among them Langston Hughes, Carl Van Vechten, Bill "Bojangles" Robinson, Vito Marcantonio, and New York City mayoral candidate William O'Dwyer. The arrival of the wedding cake, which took several men to unload from the back of a truck, caused a minor sensation. Shaped like a miniature White House, it stood more than two feet high. Inside the cake, noticeable only to those who bent to peek, was a lone figure standing at the door of the White House, dressed in a minister's robe. Normally resilient in bright lights and noise, Hazel Scott found herself weakening on her wedding day, and she became dizzy and eventually fainted. *Life,* calling Powell a "political curiosity indigenous to the city," gave the marriage a two-page spread in its August 13, 1945, edition, the cover of which showed a wartime jet flying through the sky. The next day, August 14, Truman signed the documents that ended the war in the Pacific.

The Powells honeymooned (following a night at the Waldorf) on Long Island, in Quogue, where they found privacy in a white cottage set in a rustic area. Hazel playfully called Adam "Daddy." They walked the beach — blue skies, endless ocean — hand in hand. They made plans for their future. She had her music, he had his politics, and now they had each other.

Hazel Scott and Isabel Powell could not have been more different. There would be no dunking of Hazel Scott's head in the Abyssinian pool. She would go to church, but only when she felt like it. She would not sacrifice her career. She would not be deterred by the congregation's moodiness. They would have to accept her as she was: twenty-four years old, semiwealthy, and strong-willed. With Isabel out of the picture and Mattie Powell dead, the Abyssinians needed a first lady. Long independent, Scott lacked the temperament for such a role. She was the minister's wife, but she never needed the congregation's support to boost her ego; nor did they ever give it. Raised a Catholic, she refused to give herself wholly to the Protestant faith. In the church her critics became legion. They abhorred her language, which was sometimes brutal. "Hazel was pretty," admitted a church member, "but nasty." She was also, the same person added, "sexy and loud."

But there was no denying that together, Adam Clayton Powell and Hazel Scott were a Gershwin couple set down in postwar America, vowing, by example, to raise the race. They became a celebration unto each other. Whenever she was slighted on the road because of the color of her skin, she immediately reported to her husband, in Congress, who would either pick up the phone or threaten to expose discrimination against his wife on the floor of the House. She tried to teach him how to play piano; he was too impatient. "If you walked into the Stork Club," recalled Franklin D. Roosevelt, Jr., "you'd see them sitting in a corner. I'd gravitate to their table. Hazel would brighten up, start talking about some subject that interested me. They knew how to live it up. They were a marvelous couple. She was young and pretty. Adam was the Greek god." Whenever Roosevelt was around Powell, he found himself noticing things that made him admire the Harlem congressman even more: how in restaurants he seemed to know every waiter by name, as he knew photographers'; his manners, which Roosevelt thought exquisite; his neckties, "tasteful but colorful"; how Powell had adapted so well to the jazz world. (Jazz musicians spoke admiringly of Powell's jazz knowledge; he was one of the few politicians, they said, who knew exactly which instruments a wide variety of musicians played.) And Powell made Roosevelt feel good by talking about his father and his uncle, Teddy, in a warm way.

Theirs, however, was much a nighttime friendship. "I had to worry if I got too close to Adam," explained Roosevelt. "People would say 'Adam is using Mr. Roosevelt,' or 'Mr. Roosevelt is using Adam.' I'd say to Adam that that's the wrong way for our relationship to evolve, and Adam would say, 'Franklin, I couldn't agree more.'" Once Hazel Scott told young Roosevelt that she could get him a screen test for the movies; he was too shy, and held the offer as a compliment.

When Scott showed up at Broadway openings in fur, her admirers were unaware that she had come out with two furs, unable to make up her mind which one to wear. She and Powell traveled with a maid and a cook, and they were as romantic as the sepia-toned couples in the all-black movies being shown in the segregated movie houses across America. Their marriage, as Powell described their early years together, consisted of "warm, golden brown hotcakes on a winter morning; lazy summer afternoons on our Long Island beach; beer and crackers and cheese on our terrace, relaxing evenings at the neighborhood movie house and in the living room before the fire with Rachmaninoff's Second Piano Concerto coming out of the phonograph."

⟨⟩

Following the congressional recess and his honeymoon, Powell returned to Washington, a week late. He did not stay long. His bride had a concert engagement in Philadelphia. They checked into the Ritz-Carlton. Later that evening, when Scott went onstage to give her performance, Powell took a box seat, which enabled him to look down on the stage and acknowledge well-wishers who waved up to him. Scott's virtuosity enthralled the audience. She performed Bach and Scarlatti and Chopin. Her fingers "flew like birds over the most difficult passages," noted a critic.

Back in Washington, the couple, at Powell's instigation, launched an ingenious plan, one with dynamic political overtones. For the Washington debut of Hazel Scott, who had already graced the stage of Carnegie Hall in New York City, something grand was needed. Constitution Hall, with its wide, U-shaped theater, with its rich history as an homage to the Revolutionary War era (pictures of Jefferson and Washington hung from the ivory walls), with its magnificent facade of Alabama limestone, fit the bill perfectly. An agent for Scott booked the hall through the organization that controlled its bookings, the Daughters of the American Revolution. Founded in 1890, the DAR was committed to historical preservation and, naturally, genealogical research. Admirers of art, its members put a premium on culture. Distinguished women joined its ranks. In 1945 Congresswoman Clare Boothe Luce was a member, but its most renowned member that year was surely First Lady Bess Truman.

The Daughters of the American Revolution drew the line with the issue of race; they did not allow blacks to perform on the stage of Constitution Hall. They were swift in their refusal to allow Scott to perform. They were not unfamiliar with such requests; in 1939 they had denied permission to Marian Anderson. First Lady Eleanor Roosevelt had protested by quitting the organization, but the ladies of the DAR were not swayed by her protest and remained resolute in their decision. Anderson, however, had another important ally in the White House: Harold Ickes, FDR's interior secretary. Ickes, a former NAACP official in Chicago and a man who had long-time credentials in the Progressive Party, arranged for Anderson to perform at the Washington Mall, with the Lincoln Memorial as backdrop, on Easter Sunday 1939. Thousands attended. In addition to other songs, Anderson sang "God Bless America."

Adam Clayton Powell had yet to meet President Truman. He introduced himself by way of telegram: "Request immediate action on your part in the situation of my wife Hazel Scott concert pianist being barred from Constitution Hall because she is a Negro." Truman wired back five paragraphs, the essence of which was that he could do nothing, that this was the business of the DAR and the DAR was a private organization. Matters hardly ended there. Powell hoped at least that Bess Truman, taking a cue from Eleanor Roosevelt, would announce her resignation from the DAR to protest its discrimination. But Bess Truman liked the little DAR affairs, evocative of life in Missouri and her southern upbringing. She announced that she was appalled by discrimination, then walked proudly into the Sulgrave Club on October 12 for a DAR tea party. It was hardly just another tea. "Tea for Fifty Ladies," *Newsweek* quipped, sarcasm spilling through the article.

In New York City, rushing down the street with aides during yet another rally, Powell was informed of this development. He dashed into a phone booth and telephoned reporters, giving them his comment before they asked. Mrs. Truman was no longer first lady, he said; she was now "the last lady of the land." The remark was more than a little explosive; Adam Clayton Powell was assailing the wife of the American president. First his comment hopped onto the news wires; then the White House switchboard lit up. Harry Truman wrote letters to his wife almost daily when she was in Missouri. Harry Truman was greatly devoted to his wife and his daughter, Margaret. Hard-driving Harry Truman was the last man to sit by while his family was being criticized. "That damn nigger preacher," he snapped to aides, in private, the next day.

Bags of mail taking positions on the issue arrived at the White House. One person wrote to Mrs. Truman of the blacks who had died in the war: "In light of their sacrifice it is a shocking fact to realize that you refused yesterday to give up a cup of tea and a box of cookies to support the thesis for which they died." The issue wound up on the front pages of the nation's newspapers, on radio broadcasts. Powell refused to let it die. American soldiers, black soldiers, were returning from war, and this was what they were made to realize in the nation's capital: a black pianist who had performed to raise war bonds was not being allowed to perform on the stage of Constitution Hall. But Powell played it as an irony, and wrapped President Truman up in the emotional bonds of race.

A New Jersey chapter of the DAR adopted a resolution condemning the Washington chapter for its "perpetuation of racial prejudices." Clare Boothe Luce, who knew both Powell and Scott, tried to intervene. She stopped short of resigning from the DAR, but she did inform the organization that she would switch her membership to another chapter if the discriminatory policy was not rescinded. Her threat carried no weight with the ladies. "Mrs. Luce's Action Fails to Sway

DAR," said the *New York Times* headline. It was not only in Washington that the news story was major. Now it was humming across America. "Minnesotans Criticize DAR for Refusing Hall to Pianist," said a story in a Minnesota newspaper. "A Problem Haunts DAR and the GOP Out In Iowa," read a *Chicago Sun-Times* headline. A *New York Times* editorial writer wrote with passion criticizing the DAR: "It can't stand for the American patriotic tradition and close its doors to the descendants of Crispus Attucks, the first American to fall in the Boston Massacre."

As for Scott, she went on tour, leaving the Washington spotlight to Powell alone. He was in no hurry to relinquish it. Colleagues warned him that the fallout could be dangerous, and Herbert Bruce paid a visit to try to convince him to ease up on the Trumans — but "Powell was not interested in bringing about a truce of any kind," Bruce recalled. In Harlem the congressman donned his minister's robe, climbed into his pulpit, spread his arms, looked from pew to ceiling, from ceiling to pew, and told his congregation that he had been warned that he was risking his political future, that it all had gone too far and gotten out of hand. President Truman was angry.

But Powell really could not help himself; his fight wasn't one of protocol, it was a "fight for justice," as he explained to his flock. He received nothing but support from them. In Harlem, cultural pursuits were a prized activity. Mothers sent their children to study music with teachers who had come of age during the Harlem Renaissance, teachers who were happy to pass on what they knew, so that the children might someday pass it on themselves. The DAR had not only affronted Hazel Scott, it had affronted all the little black girls and boys, all the black women and men across America, who played the piano with passion and grace.

The two influential New York senators, Robert Wagner and James Mead, were also drawn into the debate, and supported Powell and Scott. "The attempt to extend race prejudice into the field of art and music is to my mind the most striking demonstration of the utter unworthiness of race prejudice in any form," Wagner told Powell.

The imbroglio was not lost on the members of the House of Representatives, of course. Mississippi's John Rankin, hearty defender of the DAR, clashed with John Coffee, a Democrat from Washington, while spectators looked on from the galleries. Rankin knew who the DAR critics were: they were Communists. Howls came from the gallery. Sam Rayburn urged quiet. Coffee said he strongly opposed "the drawing of the color line" at Constitution Hall — a hall, he pointed out, that benefited from government tax breaks. Powell announced the formation of an activist group that would lobby against the DAR's practices. He had President Truman on "the political ropes," a Washington minister confided. "On the other hand," said a newspaper in Missouri (Truman's back yard), "Powell has certainly seized a dramatic way to strike at prejudice, and like Cato (who had warned of the cracking of the Roman empire) is serving the nation by calling attention to danger."

Ten months after his arrival in Washington, Adam Clayton Powell had rocked the city and the White House. He had made southerners his mortal enemies. The White House now knew him. The old black men and women who cleaned Constitution Hall, wiping the stage their people were not allowed to perform on, knew him. The black women who scrubbed to send their children to piano lessons knew him. The ladies of the DAR certainly knew him. All America knew him.

The phoenix had risen.

Too few Democrats, and no southern Democrats, came to his aid in the Constitution Hall debate, so Powell went after his fellow party members, saving his Republican blast for later. There was still no antilynching law, he told a six-thousand-strong rally at the Golden Gate Ballroom. Though the FEPC existed, it was still without teeth. The poll tax was still alive. In the House, he claimed, Rankin had usurped the authority of Majority Leader John McCormack. He predicted that the Democrats would take a beating in the 1946 elections, that Dewey would win the New York governorship again, that a Republican might well slip into the White House in 1948. He intimated that he had heard rumors about southern Democrats going into New York with offers of money for someone to run against him, and he warned Democrats, especially black Democrats, that "no hand-picked Negro" in New York City could sway the black vote. He said he had, in fact, been undecided about running for re-election — that is, until now, until this very moment. "I have a happy home life, and my work here consumes a great part of my time, but I am going to run again just for the evilness of it." He would not worry about money. There were labor groups who would help. There was his wife's income. There was his own income. There were the hands along the pews, from the front pew all the way to the back pew, from side to side and balcony to balcony — the hands of the men and women and children, too, of the Abyssinian Baptist Church, who reached into purses and wallets and laid money in the church plate. He would not worry about money. "And I'll match dollar for dollar every one they put up, whether it be $25,000 or $50,000."

Using his newfound notoriety, Powell traveled to Detroit to campaign for mayoral and city council candidates. Rumors that he would bolt the Democratic Party trailed him. They were untrue, Powell said; he preferred to fight "from within" the party.

The year drew to a close, and the Powells were keeping quiet about some good news. Hazel was pregnant. Ed Sullivan, the entertainment columnist, broke the story, and then there was hardly anyone who didn't know. Hazel gushed about it all, her pregnancy and her marriage to "this good man," as she described her husband. The Abyssinian congregation was excited. "About June there will be another big noise here beside me," the minister announced.

Those in Adam Clayton Powell's district could only marvel at their congressman's first year in Congress. He had established an independent voice. He had taken on Democrats from states where the poll tax was still in existence, where blacks had to pay for the right to vote. His staff — Odell Clark, Acy Lennon, Maxine Dargans, Joe Ford, all employed in either church or congressional office, all from the Deep South — was proud of him. "How they can make the headlines. We love 'em," swooned a Harlem columnist about Powell and Hazel Scott. Earl Brown, a Harlem political commentator who was a lifelong critic of Powell, could not contain his effusiveness about the congressman's "enigmatic, unpredictable" first term. Powell's voting record had been the kind of progressive record the *New Republic* magazine could not ignore, and it named him to its 1945 honor roll.

In early 1946 Dial Press published Powell's first book, *Marching Blacks,* an all-out attack on the South that urged southern blacks to leave the region and go north. It did not receive recognition for its prose, nor did the author expect any. As a writer, Powell had a charming lack of hubris ("I never posed as a writer, like some other people"). The book had a breathless tone that read as though it had been spoken into a dictaphone — which it had been. Taken as a treatise, however, it could not be ignored. "The South evidently does not want blacks, even though it needs them, or it would not treat them so cruelly," wrote Powell. "Some blacks in the South are happy with their lot as slaves. Let them remain. There are others who, though blacks, have reaped great profits from the misery of their fellow blacks. Let them stay and starve. But to the vast millions who have been suckled with the milk of freedom from the depths of black bosoms — let them leave!"

The *New York Times* reviewer was caught off-guard by Powell's bold premise and gave the book a chilly reception. "Many good causes have had intemperate advocates," the reviewer wrote. "Whether such intemperance in the long run advances or retards the cause in which it is exerted is not susceptible to precise determination." The last thirty words of the review are notable for their forced tragicomic tone: "Dr. Powell, like William Lloyd Garrison and John Brown, would brook no compromise. It is greatly to be hoped that his intransigence will have a happier outcome than did theirs."

Culling his reviews, Powell decided that the most stinging criticisms came not from whites but, surprisingly, from blacks, who chided him for his logic, or lack thereof. Ben Richardson, an assistant minister at Abyssinian and a ghostwriter for Powell's speeches, did not ghostwrite *Marching Blacks,* but he did review it for *The People's Voice.* Inasmuch as his editor there was Powell, he admittedly had a risky assignment. It was also the kind of thing that made for good publicity. Richardson held little back. He thought the book "dated" and argued that Powell's idea would lead to mayhem. "However, and I say this in great kindness," he wrote, "the suggestion that Negroes in the South come North in these days of crisis, ill housing, unemployment, labor-capital struggle, and racial tensions, is an invitation to catastrophe for millions of the oppressed." Richardson's review forced Powell to conclude that "white liberals are way ahead of so-called Negro liberals."

In the end, of course, Powell's thesis proved quite inviting; blacks marched. Beginning in the 1940s, more than five million blacks left towns like Selma, Alabama, and Atlanta, Georgia, Hattiesburg, Mississippi, and Raleigh, North Carolina, to go north to places like Cleveland and Chicago and Detroit and Harlem. In Harlem they might be lucky enough to get a job driving a bus, or work in one of the recently desegregated department stores on 125th Street. "Walk out," Powell had urged southern blacks. "Leave your doors and windows, if you have any, wide open."

Inasmuch as he had no pretensions about literary endeavors, Powell did not waste much time with book promotion. There was too much work to do on Capitol Hill. One of the more exciting pieces of legislation he drew up during his first years in Washington was an amendment — suitable for attachment to all sorts of bills — that would stop federal funds from going to states that discriminated against blacks. It was a classic maverick's amendment, similar to one that had first been offered in 1819 by another New York congressman, James Tallmadge, in his attempts to halt the spread of slavery. The practice of offering such an amendment on the floor of Congress had been out of fashion for so long that Powell's legislation instantly took on a life of its own. It affected both southerner and northerner, both liberal and conservative — the entire Congress. It became known as "the Powell amendment." Liberals alternately decried and applauded it. They were angered when forced to vote Powell's conscience, and their own, by supporting it, because they knew that ultimately it would be crushed by the conservative alliance of Republicans and southern Democrats, yet they had no way around it. If they voted against it, they would land themselves in the same camp as segregationists. "He made you feel guilty if you didn't vote for it," recalled Joseph Rauh, who went to Washington years before Powell as an ardent New Dealer.

In each session, whether he gained one convert or two, Powell held fast to the bill's purpose: to stop discrimination with government dollars. In February he attached the amendment to the federal school lunch program. Southerners cried out against it, and so did liberals, for they feared the amendment would kill the entire $100 million program. They pressured Powell to withdraw it. Powell knew better. Parents of white children voted, and if the lunch program was killed, they would know who to blame: their Alabama or Georgia or Mississippi or Texas congressman, not Adam Clayton Powell. The amendment passed, 258 to 109. The congressman from Harlem had his first national legislative victory. He was inspired.

Shortly after the novelist Richard Wright was denied service in a Washington restaurant (he had arrived in the nation's capital with Orson Welles to watch a musical based on his novel *Native Son*), Powell took to the floor of the House to offer a bill outlawing segregation in the District of Columbia, reminding his colleagues that he could not get admitted to theaters that were playing his wife's movies. The bill failed. (America lost the gifted Wright to Paris, where he lived until his death.) It was doomed to failure. An angry Powell predicted "a lot of changes in this body before the next Congress rolls around."

There were House members from the South who indeed wanted a change in the next Congress: they wanted to be rid of the representative from Harlem. A group of southern Democrats made a pilgrimage to New York for a private chat with Herbert Bruce, the black Tammany official. As a congressional candidate, Bruce would benefit generously from the Tammany machine. He was offered $35,000 to run against Powell. "They wanted to get rid of him," Bruce explained. A vocal critic during Powell's 1944 congressional campaign and a temperamental man, he desperately wanted to see Powell beaten. But he also wanted to maintain his Harlem organization, and a candidacy might dilute his strength. He declined the offer.

One of the best-known Republicans in America also had it in for Powell. New York's governor, Thomas Dewey, realized that Republicans could not wait until the campaign was well under way, as they had in 1944, to oppose Powell. This time they would organize the opposition early. And Dewey found just the right man to take on Powell. He was bright, quick, riveting on a stage, a war veteran, and, as the women quickly noticed, handsome. He was also a minister. Grant Reynolds, in fact, had many of the same qualities that had propelled the career of Adam Clayton Powell.

⟨✦⟩

Reynolds's father was an alcoholic, his mother a hard-working woman who kept the family together with a keen business sense. During the Spanish-American War she took her family to Key West and opened up a boarding house. She knew there would be customers, and there were. But when her marriage began to suffer, she sent Grant, born in Florida in 1908, to Detroit to live with relatives and continue his schooling. A bright youth, he gained admission to New York University. While in New York he worked in a variety of jobs to finance his education — waiter, taxi driver, salesman. Then, a semester short of graduation, he decided he wanted to study theology. Eden Seminary, in Webster Groves, Missouri, offered a scholarship. (While at seminary, Reynolds, who was the only black in his class, was once thrown off an all-white streetcar.) After graduation he ministered to a church in Cleveland before moving on in 1940 to New York City, where he worked as a social worker. He joined the army just before the bombing at Pearl Harbor. War changed his life.

With his education, he was able to enlist as a commissioned officer. He was assigned to Camp Lee in Virginia, where he complained about segregated quarters. Black commissioned officers had only so much clout in the segregated army. Tiring of Reynolds's complaints, the post commander summoned him, pointed toward an expanse of dirt, and told him that if he wanted integrated quarters, he should build himself a barracks on the open expanse of land, with his own hands. After standing silently for a moment, unable to determine whether the commander was serious or cruelly joking, Reynolds retreated to the black barracks. Shocked by the illiteracy of some of the black soldiers, he recruited teachers from nearby towns to tutor them. Reynolds became a base hero. "The boys loved me," he said. The post commander did not, and soon thereafter transferred Reynolds to Fort Devens in Massachusetts.

The army then sent Reynolds to Harvard University, where it was conducting a chaplains' school. Harvard campus or not, army personnel had to abide by guidelines; black and white chaplains slept in segregated quarters. "I told the guys we ought to protest this," he said. When he circulated a petition, Reynolds found that not one black other than himself would sign it. Uncle Sam could be unforgiving.

Grant Reynolds's next transfer was to Fort Wachuka, an army outpost in the Arizona desert. He hoped to start anew. As chaplain to black soldiers, he was given an office in a segregated black wing of the hospital. Walking outside one day, he noticed something startling: electrified barbed wire ringed the dormitory area where white nurses lived. There was no such wire around the black nurses' units. Reynolds figured the wire was a warning to black soldiers. He demanded an explanation. His commanding officer thought his questioning odd, but saw an opportunity, and told Reynolds to lecture the black soldiers about venereal disease.

When a small band of black soldiers was returned to the Arizona base after having gone AWOL, they were placed under arrest in an open area that was enclosed by wire. The days were hot; on cold nights friends tossed blankets to them. As chaplain, Reynolds imagined himself to be the ombudsman for black soldiers. One day he began snapping pictures of the stockaded soldiers, clicking away with a handheld camera. Summoned to the post commander's office and asked for the film, he lied and told the commander that he had already shipped it to a newspaper friend in Chicago. (Actually there had been no film in the camera.) This time Captain Grant Reynolds was disbatched to Camp San Luis Obispo, in California. He looked forward to leaving Arizona; the desert had brought on sinus problems, and he also found himself suffering migraine headaches.

Walking into an auditorium on the California base where Bob Hope was to give one of his shows, Reynolds looked at, then walked right by, the segregated seating section and took a place with white officers. Later, while in the base hospital having his sinuses checked in the hope of finding the cause of his migraines, he found himself being questioned by an army psychiatrist. Diagnosed as paranoid, he was quickly shipped to another hospital, in Santa Barbara. Sitting across from another psychiatrist, Reynolds was drilled about his attitudes toward race and discrimination. When the psychiatrist turned away from him to answer a telephone call, he leaned over far enough to notice that the thick file on the psychiatrist's desk had his name on it. The psychiatrist admitted that the army had an extensive file on Reynolds but told him not to worry. "You won't be railroaded here, chaplain," he said. Reynolds was told he would be treated as an outpatient; he was free to come and go, as long as he signed in every two days, and in time he would receive more definite orders.

He found the outpatient game strange but played it. With time on his hands, he enjoyed the California weather; he even found time to golf. He received invitations to social gatherings, where he met academic types, who were amazed at his army experiences. Soon he found himself on area campuses, talking about blacks and wartime, talks that invariably turned to his own woes.

When Grant Reynolds received a notice to appear before the medical discharge board, he allowed his paranoia to become full-blown: he believed the army was trying to force him out. The board told him that his migraines were causing him to become delusional. For his own good, they said, he was being given a medical discharge. However, officials in Washington refused the discharge, requesting an in-depth analysis of Reynolds's diagnosis. He was told to report to a neurosurgeon, who told him that he would have to undergo tests in which air would be forced from his spinal column up to his brain. The process sounded frightening. Reynolds balked, did some soul searching, and realized that if he did not go through with the procedure, he would probably be discharged dishonorably. For ten days following surgery he lay in the hospital. He had lost coordination and control over bowel movements; footsteps a hallway away banged in his eardrums. After his gradual recovery, his discharge was reviewed again. This time the army sent Grant Reynolds home, granting him a medical discharge.

By the time he arrived back in New York City in early 1944, he was something of a hero. Word had spread of his travails — of both his painful medical odyssey and his stance against segregation. In New York he was befriended by Thurgood Marshall, the NAACP lawyer; Hubert Delaney, a Dewey confidant; and Walter White, the NAACP director. All predicted a bright future for Reynolds. He was dispatched to Chicago, where he addressed a wartime NAACP conference. White was struck by his oratory and hired him as a lobbyist to work in Washington.

Reynolds replaced Leslie Perry, whose wife was suspected by NAACP officials of being a Communist; in times of war, suspicion was enough. In Washington, Reynolds found himself playing gofer to White. He felt underutilized. However, he was happy to find time — and encouragement — to write for *The Crisis,* the NAACP paper. His articles were trenchant pieces about segregation in the army, and they tore at a budding friendship between Roy Wilkins and Reynolds, because Wilkins, as *Crisis* editor, was careful not to attack the government during the war.

Writing made Reynolds restless. He wanted to do more: "I didn't have passion for anonymity." He thought the national campaign being waged between Dewey and Roosevelt was intoxicating. It was in Roosevelt's army that he had been abused, and now he found FDR saying nothing about military segregation. Dewey, a scrapper who appeared to be in perpetual motion, was saying plenty. He supported the FEPC, his minority hiring record in New York was considered progressive, and Reynolds liked what he heard. He began campaigning for Dewey, taking to the stump all over New York City, becoming widely known and heard in Harlem, where residents called him "Captain Reynolds." A. Philip Randolph contacted him and suggested that he form an organization to expose segregation in the military, which became the Committee Against Jim Crow in Military Service and Training.

Dewey's strategists liked Reynolds. He had a military record (Dewey did not), and he was willing to assail both military and New Deal policies. Reporters dubbed him "Pretty Boy"; he didn't like the moniker, but women did. In 1944, to add even more luster to his background, he entered Columbia Law School. After he moved into a dormitory on campus, he was able to renew acquaintances with people he had known in his youth. Everywhere on the campus there was talk of politics. Grant Reynolds, home from the war and angry about his military experiences, was soon in the thick of it.

∽∾∾

Dewey kept busy addressing audiences across America in his 1944 presidential campaign, attacking Roosevelt and his New Deal policies, blaming the latter for a bloated government and for the number of American troops committed overseas. He also attacked the administration's links with Tammany Hall and union bosses across America. For a liberal New York governor, Tom Dewey was capable of sounding shrill and appearing Machiavellian. He hinted at Communist sympathizers in the government and questioned Roosevelt's love of country. Grant Reynolds followed his lead, telling audiences that the New Deal was more promise than delivery, that blacks had been short-changed, that the true beneficiaries of the New Deal were the fossilized southern congressmen who had become powerful chairmen. All blacks gained from the president's policies, he said, was an introduction to the welfare rolls.

When Dewey wound up his 1944 campaign with a rally at Madison Square Garden, Reynolds was seated on the platform next to Gloria Swanson, the actress. He gave a rousing speech — so rousing that he received a standing ovation. Dewey couldn't take his eyes off Reynolds; he was stunned, and the crowd was standing and clapping and smiling. "What are you trying to do, steal the show?" he asked. Then Dewey looked at Reynolds and said, "I want to see you later."

Dewey lost the 1944 election, but his forces immediately started preparing for the contest in 1948. They realized that the governor's New York strength was always upstate; he was not a downstate, big-city man like FDR. If Dewey could make inroads into Harlem next time, it would be a notable achievement; such inroads would have to include an attempt to dilute Powell's voting strength. Over the next several months Dewey emissaries met with Reynolds to discuss challenging Adam Clayton Powell in the 1946 election. When Reynolds mentioned his financial responsibilities, he began receiving funds from Republican sources. "Dewey made it possible for me to get some spending change to take care of rent," he recalled. Actually, Dewey did considerably more. He enabled Grant Reynolds to acquire a coveted liquor license — "worth twenty thousand dollars" at the time, by Reynolds's own estimate — and Reynolds promptly opened a liquor store at the corner of 158th Street and St. Nicholas Avenue.

There can be little doubt that Dewey saw something of himself in young Grant Reynolds. Like Dewey, Reynolds attended Columbia Law School, and like Dewey, he took on Democratic forces while forging his own alliance of progressives. In 1946 Dewey was between presidential campaigns; he had time to keep an eye on downstate congressional elections. He appointed Reynolds to a job as corrections commissioner, giving him additional visibility in Harlem and the prestige of a gubernatorial appointment. (Although it was a nonpaying position, the Dewey camp made sure Reynolds was compensated. "Every month I got a little money from the party," he explained.)

Incumbency in Congress was no guarantee of election; La Guardia's ouster from Congress was a painful reminder. A tall, handsome minister and military veteran with NAACP and Dewey contacts and a growing list of Harlem supporters could be dangerous to a first-term congressman. Grant Reynolds was electrifying Harlem, and Adam Clayton Powell realized as much. He told Edward Dudley, a New York Democratic Party official, to arrange a meeting. Powell suggested evening cocktails at Café Society; Reynolds agreed. He was kept waiting. He boiled. Finally he looked toward the door, and in strolled Powell. Reynolds recalled years later how beautifully dressed the congressman was, and that his car sat outside, double-parked.

Good at cutting to the quick and hardly interested in small talk with a man on the march in his back yard, Powell told Reynolds that he had no future in the Republican Party, then suggested that his only hope at survival was to join the Democratic Party: there well might be a job on Powell's staff. Reynolds was taken aback. "I told him I couldn't do that. I told him I'd make my own future." Powell bade a curt farewell, then stalked out the door, leaving Reynolds with the tab: "I go there at his invitation and I pick up the tab!" Double-stepping, Reynolds followed Powell onto the street and asked for a lift to Harlem. Just before they entered Central Park, Powell gunned the engine and roared off by the side of another vehicle in a madcap race. Grant Reynolds concluded that Adam Clayton Powell was a strange man.

Reynolds announced his candidacy in early March, and quickly received the GOP endorsement. What he did not have was residence in Harlem. The problem was quickly solved when Fannie Robinson, estranged from her husband, Bojangles Robinson, offered Reynolds the use of her apartment in the handsome Dunbar Apartments. (Fannie took up with another lover, in New Jersey, for the time being.) In the beginning Reynolds remained in law school, attending classes by day and giving campaign speeches at night. A local reporter mused that his challenge might provide Powell with his "first real test" as a politician. Reynolds took to the stump with enthusiasm. He launched his first salvo on a radio program, not at Powell the politician but at Powell the author, attacking *Marching Blacks* as little more than a "deplorable conglomeration of deliberate distortions." He attended teas and socials. He appeared before church groups and expounded on his views of Harlem's future. There was too much self-criticism in Harlem, he allowed, too much of an "antagonistic attitude" toward life, especially among youngsters. He made allusions to what he perceived as Powell's weaknesses: the psychic wound within the church caused by Powell's divorce and quick marriage to Hazel Scott; Powell's party being the party of the southern Democrats, the very Democrats who opposed integration and kept the poll tax alive; Powell's attacks on Harry and Bess Truman. Day by day and week by week, from late spring into summer, Grant Reynolds saw his campaign camp swell. Army buddies walked through the doors of his headquarters; the Harlem author Zora Neale Hurston licked envelopes; A. Philip Randolph's wife helped out. In the evenings some of his fellow law students showed up to work. Joe Louis, the boxer, threw his support to Reynolds, saying, "Keep punching and we'll win in November."

Yet for all of Harlem to see, it appeared that Reynolds was campaigning against a phantom. Congressman Powell had yet to acknowledge his opponent publicly. Begging for an opportunity to debate Powell, Reynolds was greeted with silence. Finally, in a move of desperation, he offered a thousand-dollar bond guaranteeing his own appearance at such a debate. More silence from the Powell camp. Reynolds kept his pace up, campaigning up and down Harlem's streets, shaking hands and becoming familiar.

Campaigning was not on Adam Powell's mind; he was more worried about his wife's pregnancy and the arrival of his first child. On July 17 Hazel Scott gave birth to a son at Sydenham Hospital. The cesarean birth was hard for her, but afterward Powell stood outside in the sunshine, passing out cigars, waving to onlookers, and praising his newborn son, who had been given his name: Adam Clayton Powell III.

As expected, Powell received the Tammany endorsement. Vito Marcantonio saw to it that he also received the American Labor Party endorsement. As he had done in 1944, Powell entered the GOP primary, looking for a victory that would effectively knock Reynolds from the race and deliver a painful blow to Dewey. But when Harlemites emerged from the polls, they had given Grant Reynolds five hundred votes more than they had given Powell. "Powell Setback Called Sign of Shift by Negroes," claimed the *New York Herald Tribune*. Reynolds called the victory an "awakening." Of course, the real election was months away, in the November cold, but now, in the Harlem heat, the Republicans looked strong and Powell looked weakened. Flushed with victory, Reynolds (who scored a record coup by garnering the backing of the Liberal Party as well) announced that he would take a vacation. "I'm already resting," Powell snapped. He took the defeat with equanimity, saying that he would retreat to his new home in the Westchester hills, because his wife and son needed him, and "forget politics until September fifteenth." True to his word, he remained in White Plains, greeted daily by summer breezes and the cries of a baby. He did not worry about politics.

Reynolds, however, now had the kick he needed. The pace of events picked up, and he was forced to drop out of law school. Working out of the Lafayette Theater, which had been closed but was opened for him by an owner with Republican sentiments, he saw interest in his campaign heighten. Summoned by Clare Boothe Luce, he was given names of potential financial contributors. (Reynolds was vain enough to believe that Luce's interest in his campaign reflected her romantic interest in him, and wise enough to keep the belief to himself.) She sent him to John Hay Whitney, who lived off family investments, raced horses at Hialeah in winter, and gave handsomely to Republican causes, and to Walter Hoving, the president of Tiffany's. Both men gave "handsome contributions" to his campaign, recalled Reynolds, who added, "Nobody in Harlem gave me a dime."

The challenger continued to request a debate. Powell finally sent Vito Marcantonio to debate Reynolds, and the evening of charge and countercharge was quickly forgotten. Powell did not, however, ignore the insurgent campaign of the Workers' Party candidate, Ernest McKinney, who might siphon votes and strengthen Reynolds. Powell's lawyer was able to get McKinney removed from the ballot on a technicality.

As the weeks passed, such was the fever of Reynolds's campaign

hat it drew national figures into Harlem on his behalf. Clare Boothe
_uce came and told a church audience that the Democrats, the party
of conservative southerners, were guilty of "betrayal" in their treatment of blacks, and she scorned Powell for belonging to such a party.
The actress Fannie Brice gave to Reynolds's campaign. Reynolds
poarded a rented bus in the evenings to travel the streets, and his
army cohorts, in fedoras, stood guard because of the many threats of
physical harm. Night after night Reynolds barnstormed up and down
the streets of Harlem. "It was exciting," he remembered. "We'd put
signs up, go from street to street. Every night we were out on the
streets, because that's when people were available. I'd never get home
until one or two o'clock in the morning. I was so exhausted when
I'd get home that a hot bath would send me to bed. Nothing for me
to do except get my vocal cords together and get ready for the next
night's crusade."

Friends had told him the campaign would get vicious, but with
Powell for the most part absent from Harlem, Reynolds did not believe
it. And when Isabel Powell approached him, offering to share check
receipts that would surely have a harmful effect on Powell's candidacy
(Powell had put her on his payroll, but she did no work), Reynolds
refused, choosing to stay on high ground.

Marjorie Lawson, Powell's friend from Washington, was now in
New York City, like Reynolds attending Columbia Law School. She
watched the campaign fever spread to the Columbia campus and
watched as it entranced Harlemites. She knew why Reynolds had
claimed such a following. "They were very much alike," she said of
Powell and Reynolds. In Harlem, the gamblers were handicapping the
race two to one in favor of Reynolds.

Adam Clayton Powell chose to come into Harlem just days before
the election, and he came to ruin Grant Reynolds. "Adam came out
on the street like a wild man," recalled Reynolds. It was not, however,
on the streets that Powell delivered the blow that would assure the
collapse of Reynolds's candidacy; it was at a Golden Gate Ballroom
rally attended by Eleanor Roosevelt and Tammany officials, the kind
of huge pre-election rally sure to warrant wide press coverage. On
the Tuesday night preceding the election, Powell arrived at the Golden
Gate along with other dignitaries. Before his arrival he had secured
a copy of Reynolds's army medical record from a War Department
source. The record, full of Kafkaesque accusation and innuendo, was
all that he needed. On the podium he launched into a long tirade

about Reynolds's medical history, intimating that Reynolds was mentally deranged and delusional. The revelations sent a buzz through the crowd.

His salvo delivered, Powell vanished once again to White Plains. Reynolds's former employers at the NAACP were appalled by Powell's action, but the NAACP remained aloof from political campaigns. Reynolds characterized the move as a "dirty, unspeakable trick," but his backers knew he was finished before the next morning's newspapers hit the streets. "There wasn't anything I could do but call him a scoundrel," he explained. "I denounced him for using his influence to get my files. It destroyed me."

Marjorie Lawson was shocked. "Ruthless" is how she later characterized Powell's tactic: "It was mean." "Bitter" was the New York Times's assessment of the campaign. The bitterness edged right up to election night eve. Rumor swept Harlem that election day would be marred by intimidation and the stuffing of ballot boxes. Lewis Valentine, the former police commissioner whom Powell had battled as a city councilman, now in charge of election security for the twenty-second district, promised to "move in on terrorists the moment they are spotted."

On the day New Yorkers went to the polls, newsmen were looking for Powell. He did not show in the morning, when he might have been expected to greet voters on their way to the polls, nor did he show in the afternoon, when he might have greeted voters returning home from work. When he finally showed up it was early evening and he strolled into town with all the nonchalance of a fighter going to do a necessary bit of business. "I've been in bed all day," he said, ambling from car to voting booth, cameras clicking. "My doctors say it's fever." This did not resemble a worried politician.

As evening deepened, it became obvious that the darkness would yield no happiness for Grant Reynolds. Powell defeated him by more than thirteen thousand votes, a two-to-one margin. This was why the gait had been easy, the confidence overbearing. Grant Reynolds never ran for political office again. Powell regarded him as an enemy forever; he belittled him at every opportunity in the years to come. Asked at one rally whatever became of Reynolds, Powell looked out over the gathering and said, "He's somewhere trying to pass his bar exam." In fact, the Republicans took care of Reynolds. He became general counsel to the chairman of the Republican National Committee and stayed in the post until 1964, when the GOP championed Goldwater, whom Reynolds could not support. The results of Powell's election aside, Republicans scored coup after coup in 1946. They picked up fifty-four House seats and added twelve senators, among them the New Yorker Jacob Javits, soon to become one of Powell's allies. Marcantonio won, but barely; his denouement was not far off. Dewey was sent back to Albany, despite a strange occurrence: protesters had stormed the state capitol during his campaign, demanding better jobs and housing. Dewey had met with them briefly, extolled the virtues of his liberalism, and, in so many words, told them that if they thought New York government was insensitive, then they might look to the South for proof that New York was ahead of other states in terms of progressivism. Dewey's victory was big, especially in the rural regions. It did not take much contemplation by political commentators to realize that the governor in Albany had once again become the Republicans' leading candidate for the upcoming presidential election.

Now, having dodged the bullets that sent fifty-four of his fellow Democratic congressmen down to defeat, Adam Clayton Powell walked tall through Harlem. He had spent hardly a cent on the campaign. He had entered the contest late, and with unabashed arrogance. "The thousands of dollars poured into Harlem could not buy the Negro vote," he said after his victory. "We have served notice on cheap politicians to stay out of Harlem." All he wanted to do now, he confessed, was return to Congress and fight for the "rights of the common man."

Not many in New York City realized how much Hazel Scott had contributed to his success. As a native West Indian, she drew West Indian votes into his camp. "You had a bloc of West Indian voters in Harlem who had a better turnout record than American blacks, 75 percent against 50 percent," recalled Louis Martin, the Democratic Party operative.

In time, the critics would come to realize that only Adam Clayton Powell could defeat Adam Clayton Powell, and now, in 1946, walking through Harlem with his hair swept back, skin smooth, mustache thin, body tall and erect, well-wishers reaching for him, reaching to touch him, he looked good. He was thirty-eight years old, and smart enough never to mention his handsomeness. By seeming unaware of it, he made it that much more lethal. He posed for photographs with a movie star's gift for the best angle, a movie star's awareness of the camera. He had given himself an aura, a kind of political magic. "Send Him Back!" had been his simple campaign slogan. He had reduced politics not to campaigning, not to billboards, but to destiny. He painted his enemies not as Harlem clubhouse politicians but as entrenched southern Democrats and conservative Republicans in Washington who controlled legislation, who would not free his bills, who would not free the liberals in Congress, who would not free his constituents — his people.

He announced that he was going back to Washington, that he was disturbed by segregation at New York's Sing Sing prison, that he would offer a bill to halt it, that Grant Reynolds, who had been doing prison consultancy work on behalf of the state, should heartily support such a move "or resign." It would be more than a decade before Adam Clayton Powell, Jr., suffered another serious challenge to his Harlem domination.

⟜✺⟝

Among the new House members in the 80th Congress were two future presidents, Richard Nixon, elected in California in a bitter fight against Jerry Voorhis, a liberal Democrat; and John F. Kennedy of Massachusetts, a World War II hero. Both freshman congressmen joined Powell on the Labor Committee. As was customary, President Truman threw a party for new members of Congress. Every member received an invitation except Adam Clayton Powell. Truman never forgot Powell's attack on his wife, and as long as he remained president he prevented Powell from entering the White House. There were, as well, no White House patronage favors for the Harlem congressman. Hazel Scott and Adam Powell did not suffer from the slight; they made the rounds of the embassy parties. They were seen quite frequently at the Cuban embassy, where the music was Afro-Cuban, a fusion of bebop and Latin rhythms that was becoming the rage along the New York–Havana axis.

In the winter of 1947 Republicans exulted. The liberal coalitions of radicals, laborites, and Communists were fraying at the edges and were about to be placed under fierce attack. The House was no longer Democratic; it was Republican. Truman and his aides could count, and they knew problems awaited them. Some could not imagine the scope. With the dawn of the cold war, the House Un-American Activities Committee was about to go into high gear. "I believe we all must agree," Nixon told his colleagues, "that now is the time for action as well as words." John Rankin saw the HUAC as nothing less than "the grand jury of America."

For years Adam Clayton Powell had dodged the Communist label. "I make no brief for communism," he stated in the House. "It has plenty who can and do speak for it. I am not a Communist and I am not in favor of communism. However, I must defend the right of any individual to maintain whatever particular view he holds until such a view is declared illegal by an act of Congress." Then, in typical Powellian fashion, he challenged his colleagues. "Those of you who are so afraid of Red scares should have the guts to make communism illegal. Until then it is legal."

Those who wanted to pin the Communist label on Powell needed only to look to New York for ammunition. In *The People's Voice,* Communist sympathies ran strong. Both Marvel Cooke and Doxey Wilkerson were open sympathizers, as was Max Yergan, a writer who had recently returned from South Africa, where he had worked on behalf of the YMCA and undergone a radical political transformation. With the war over and the unveiling of the Smith Act, a federal law allowing the imprisonment of those believed to be plotting to overthrow the government, this was dangerous. In Powell's absence, Wilkerson assumed a lot of responsibility for day-to-day operation of the newspaper. Proud and stubborn, he swung the paper's tone even more leftward, giving plenty of space to the views and ambitions of city councilman Benjamin Davis. Davis's columns openly advocated Communist positions, and he used *The People's Voice* as Powell had used it, to further his own ambitions.

But Powell had always been a progressive, cold-bloodedly using Communists to rally support, and Davis's antics made him nervous. His allies warned him that ongoing connection with the newspaper would be ruinous. Under pressure, Yergan resigned, and, amazingly, adopted a rightward stance with the same zeal with which he had previously adopted a leftward stance. Powell fired Wilkerson. "It was purely political," recalled Wilkerson, who wasted little time in attacking Powell and the newspaper in columns for the *Daily Worker,* accusing *The People's Voice* of giving in to redbaiting and Truman's policies. Marvel Cooke left as well, fully convinced that the government had planted a spy in the newsroom. She was quickly followed by Fredi Washington, Powell's sister-in-law, whose employment had been uneasy ever since Powell had left Isabel. The promising young

Ann Petry also departed. She had won a Houghton Mifflin literary fellowship. Her novel *The Street,* a grim, eloquent retelling of Harlem desperation, brought her sudden fame when it was published in 1946. Skittish about that fame, however, she soon left Harlem, retreating to the quiet surroundings of her hometown, Old Saybrook, Connecticut. Bitterness among the staff members grew. St. Claire Bourne left for home one day with plans to return to the newsroom, then was notified by courier that he was fired. Internecine squabbling about whose politics to support — Communists', Democrats', Socialists', Adam Clayton Powell's — brought forth fissures that could never heal. In 1947 Powell had no further use for the newspaper and relinquished his interest; a year later it filed for bankruptcy.

Meanwhile, Powell's antilynching bill and other pieces of legislation were going nowhere. Much seemed lost. Congressmen who condemned the abuse of citizens' rights in the hunt for Communists themselves became suspect. Vito Marcantonio, a thinnish man with an Italian accent, did not care about the criticism. Many of his colleagues had already labeled him a Communist. He was a lawyer who knew the law, and House rules, extremely well. In the renowned "Hollywood Ten" case, in which ten screenwriters were issued contempt citations for refusing to testify to the HUAC, he warned his colleagues that they were ignoring the law. "The issue is the Constitution, and the Constitution protects all, including Communists," he said. "When you attempt to circumvent that proposition, you are subverting the very democracy you say you want to defend."

⟨✦⟩

Hazel Scott never took to Washington (save in cherry blossom season), and Powell rushed back to White Plains as frequently as possible. During the May recess he was back in New York City, attending to church business and spending time with his wife and son. He affected an aristocratic mien, sitting around his home in the evenings with an ascot covering his neck, a pipe in hand. His wife would play the piano, a photograph of the congressman atop her Steinway. "If you must know," she told a *New York Post* feature writer in 1947, "my marriage is the utopian platter of the century." She had begun playing professionally again, and was booked for an engagement at the Roxy Theater. On the evening of her performance, she and Powell climbed into the car and rolled toward Manhattan. En route Powell suffered chest pains, which turned out to be caused by a heart attack — "severe and sudden," his doctors later reported. Scott remained calm as her husband was rushed to the hospital.

Powell requested and received an indefinite leave from Congress. Scott packed her ailing husband and her son, and together the family was driven by their chauffeur to their Long Island summer home, so that Scott could nurse her husband in the cool serenity of open land and sea. For several months the restless Adam Clayton Powell was forced to rest. Scott, wanting no talk of church or politics to worry her husband, prohibited visitors. The recuperating congressman relaxed under the summer sun, watched his little boy crawl across the grass, listened to the sounds of nature. Now and then his father would call from New York, passing on the rumors sweeping Harlem: that Powell might resign, that the heart attack had been worse than reported; that a dozen morticians in Harlem were offering to bury the congressman free (at that rumor, Powell laughed). By summer's end his strength had returned, but not quite enough for the battles of New York and Washington. Hollywood was different. That was his wife's world, a world where he could sit back and watch. After a trip to the West Coast, he returned to New York, in time to attend the hundred-and-thirty-ninth anniversary of the Abyssinian Baptist Church. Dressed in formal attire, posing for photographers and chatting with friends, Powell looked well.

Later, in a replay of the kinds of activities he had engaged in during the Depression, he walked into the church's nearby recreational area, looked around, and envisioned a store that would sell fruits and vegetables at lower rates than Harlemites were forced to pay at the neighborhood stores. This is what people liked about their minister-congressman: how he could imagine on the spot, how he could flail his arms and tell his aides to bring tables and chairs, to buy loads of fruit and vegetables, to create a food store right before their eyes. By the end of the first day all the items in the makeshift store had been sold. The *New York Times* found the idea intriguing enough to send a reporter out. "The best price seemed to have been on lemons, which went rapidly at about half of the current market price," the *Times* reporter wrote about the first day of activity. "Condensed milk was sold for about four cents under current retail prices. The price on sweet potatoes was reported at less than that displayed outside the church on a huckster's wagon."

In January 1948 Powell announced that he was "back in shape and ready to fight on all fronts." He made plans to reassemble his picketers "to get jobs in all companies" that were doing business in Harlem. Hounded for answers as to whom he would support in the upcoming presidential election, he said he would "follow his conscience," all the while letting it be known that he was interested in the breakaway candidacy of Henry Wallace, the one-time Roosevelt cabinet member who had felt so betrayed by Roosevelt holdovers that he abruptly resigned from the Truman administration. Few knew much about Dwight Eisenhower's party affiliation — courted by both parties, he was playing coy — but Powell, using more hope than hard evidence, referred to him as "a progressive" and intimated that the Columbia University president was the kind of Republican he could be convinced to support. Democratic officials had begun warning Democratic congressmen with noticeable Labor Party support that they would be jeopardizing their political futures if they supported candidacies such as Wallace's, and Truman was besieged with woes; various southerners had taken to the floor of the House and Senate to ask him not to run for re-election. When Truman submitted a civil rights program on February 2 ("my civil rights program," Powell called it; he indeed did have the only anti–Jim Crow bill sitting — lamely — before Congress), he quickly realized the fragility of his southern support.

In March an interdenominational group of ministers honored Powell for his "pioneer work" in the New York City Council and Congress. Addressing the group, he said that he saw a dangerous world, one where there were still battles to be fought, where ministers everywhere were too silent. "Hold to your Scripture and preach on Sunday," he advised them, "but on Monday, speak to the people." Politically, he said, he had no quarrel with New York Republicans — Governor Dewey's civil rights record was admirable — but he would do battle with the GOP everywhere else. Emmanuel Celler, the Brooklyn congressman who shared the dais, praised Powell for "striking out against the bigots in Congress" and told the audience that those in Harlem who were unwilling to fight to keep Powell in Congress were crazy.

By summer's end, Americans would be faced with more choices in a presidential election than they had experienced in a while. In Harlem the sentiments seemed to run clear. Harlemites did not mind Dewey in Albany, but they displayed no eagerness to send him on to Washington. Wallace had magnetism, but his campaign was risky. It had black leaders, with the exception of Powell, in an uproar. Men like Walter White, of the NAACP, feared that Wallace's candidacy would take away votes from Truman, enabling Republicans to capture the White House.

For its sheer bravado, there was nothing quite like Wallace's candidacy. Wallace and his running mate, the Idaho senator Glen Taylor, known mostly as a former cowboy musical celebrity, set out across America in the summer of 1948 on a campaign swing, the whispers that Communists were within their ranks growing louder the farther south they traveled. They floated along on principle and determination, chased and cursed by southern men, women, and children who thought they were little more than a band of Communists in political heat. In Birmingham, Taylor walked through a COLORED ONLY doorway to protest segregation. He was promptly arrested. Refusing to eat in segregated diners, the two men and their traveling party stayed in black-owned hotels. (Emerging in the morning, they were followed by hustling photographers in saddle shoes, neckties flying over their shoulders.) Wallace referred to his new Progressive Party as an army, and he walked straight ahead as if following a beam of misdirected light. Two newspapers endorsed him, the *York* (Pennsylvania) *Gazette* and the *Daily Worker,* the Communist newspaper.

Outraged by Truman and his ideas for the Democratic Party, a group of southern Democrats formed the States' Rights Party and held a convention in Birmingham, where they nominated Strom Thurmond, the governor of South Carolina, as their presidential candidate. Their strategy was to create an electoral stalemate and throw the entire election into the House of Representatives, but their day-long convention was considered bizarre enough to keep many powerful southern Democrats, fearful of House retribution, from attending.

Both major party conventions were held in Philadelphia. The Republicans descended on that city in late June. Governor Dewey went in as the front-runner and departed with the nomination, with Governor Earl Warren of California as his vice presidential nominee. The Democrats arrived the following month, the ghost of Roosevelt hovering on their consciences. Many did not trust Harry Truman, wondering whether he was up to a bitter campaign. But cold reality forced them to turn to him. Truman accepted his party's nomination, and in his surprising acceptance speech many heard the old rallying cry of New Deal fervor.

Meanwhile, in New York City, Adam Clayton Powell kept his political thoughts to himself until June. Following his Easter sermon he officiated at the marriage of Maria Ellington to a most eligible bachelor, the crooner-pianist Nat King Cole; afterward everyone dashed to the Waldorf for the reception.

Weeks later Powell walked into Small's Paradise, a kitschy little bar that sat within shouting distance of the Abyssinian church, and, surrounded by well-wishers and good drink, announced that indeed he would run for Congress again. He was snubbed at a New York rally for Truman. The Wallace candidacy, with its bold plank calling for across-the-board civil rights enforcement, subsidized housing for the poor, and universal voting rights, appealed to his idealism, but following the snub, an aide warned that the congressman just might "knock the whole town out by declaring for Dewey." Powell was more pragmatic than his critics thought, however, and his ability to read the political winds was unique. (The Wallace platform, which Vito Marcantonio had endorsed heartily — in a move that would soon haunt him — also called for nationalization of banks and railroads, an end to military training, and an accommodation with communism.)

Appearing at an East Side rally on October 25, Powell stung the Wallace forces, who had hoped for his support, by telling the crowd that he was "from top to bottom" committed to backing the Democratic ticket. (Again he had made Democrats nervous by waiting until the last moment — three days, in fact, before Harry Truman, needing every vote he could get, rolled through Harlem in the first-ever campaign swing by a president into the black mecca.) "Get mad and stay mad with men like Tom Dewey," Powell said. He reminded his listeners of the celebrated case on Long Island involving the Ferguson brothers, two black youths home from the military who had been shot dead by a police officer who accused them of resisting arrest and disorderly conduct. The officer said he shot in self-defense, fearing that one youth was reaching for a gun. A gun was never found, and the officer was never indicted. Governor Dewey, despite appeals, refused to reopen the case. "His hands still drip with the blood of the Ferguson brothers, and the voters of this community will remember that next Tuesday!" Powell shouted. He thumped for a sixty-five-dollar-a-week minimum wage for the heads of Harlem households, urging "black and white, Jew, Gentile, and Catholic to fight and fight until these wage gains have been made."

Adam Clayton Powell made one speech during the congressional campaign in which he blithely predicted he would beat the GOP nominee, Harold Burton, a former plumber, by a three-to-one margin.

Burton and Powell were more friends than enemies, and were often seen together in nightclubs along 125th Street. Powell "is not in the good graces of Tammany Hall," Burton told Harlemites, unaware that he was merely reminding them of Powell's streak of independence. On election day Powell smiled and waved at well-wishers while entering the voting booth. It was hard to miss his wife, Hazel, a fur draped over her shoulders.

Powell's prediction of a three-to-one victory over Burton was a bit low. He defeated his opponent 63,062 votes to 13,995 — better than four to one.

Genuine drama was played out in the presidential campaign. Truman, who knew flinty politics from his Missouri days, took to the stump by train across America, wearing spiffy double-breasted suits, a bit of handkerchief showing from the breast pocket, and attacking Republicans with both fists. Dewey's own fists were balled, but he was advised not to punch. Truman couldn't stop punching. Never mind the polls, which continued to show him trailing. He went from city to city, seeking to rebuild the old New Deal coalition. In Harlem and other urban centers, he was applauded by blacks, who were grateful for his civil rights pronouncements. The *Chicago Tribune,* both Republican and reactionary, rushed a headline ("Dewey Defeats Truman") into print and legend — and paid dearly. Truman crushed Dewey, despite the States' Righters and the Progressives, and Democrats took control of the House again, gaining seventy-five seats, which gave them 263 seats to the Republicans' 171. They also rode back into power in the Senate, picking up nine seats, for a total of fifty-four to forty-two. New Democratic voices would soon be heard from, among them those of Senator Hubert H. Humphrey, the cherub-faced former mayor of Minneapolis; Lyndon Johnson, who had moved from the House to the Senate in a controversial election victory in Texas; and Adlai Stevenson, the governor in Illinois, who was soon regarded, on the national scene, as a rather attractive mystic.

New Yorkers had appreciated Thomas Dewey more than the nation at large had. In New York, he could exhibit true passion; on the national stage, it eluded him. On the national stage, he looked something of a small-time technocrat, moving too slowly, burdened by the weight of the truly conservative wing of the Republican Party, which was dominated by men like Ohio's Robert Taft. But Dewey had brought no small achievement to New York government — integrity and compassion — and he had goaded Republicans nationally to search their minds for the same. "It's been grand fun, boys and girls," he announced on leaving his election night hotel suite, with the bitter defeat of two presidential elections to haunt him. The language appeared to reduce everything to a mere collegiate squabble. New York's governor hurt, and he feigned joy: "I've enjoyed it immensely."

It had in fact been a grueling campaign. Everyone seemed to need a vacation. Truman found his in Key West. Dewey took his family to Arizona. The Powells sought refuge in the Bahamas.

᙭᙭᙭

Harry S. Truman's inauguration made history, for it was an integrated affair where blacks and whites mingled. Coarse segregation still reigned in the nation's capital, but the inauguration provided a delicate touch that gave hope to huge ambitions. The New Deal coalition looked to Truman for leadership on issues that still moved them — civil rights, housing, medical care. There was hope that the Fair Employment Practices Commission might someday soon have more than mere investigative powers. Democrats had numbers on their side in both House and Senate. But Truman was still blocked by the resolve of southern Democratic committee chairmen to prevent progressive legislation — in particular, any legislation involving civil rights.

House Labor Committee Chairman John Lesinski, of Michigan, a hard-nosed man as passionate as Truman, had the task of trying to orchestrate passage of the bill to strengthen the FEPC. Adam Clayton Powell threatened to attach his amendment again — he risked minimal damage, inasmuch as he was already excommunicated from the White House — if the bill appeared near passage in a weak form. Lesinski was open to suggestions. Powell had one: blackmail. If Lesinski named him to chair the FEPC subcommittee, Powell would not introduce his amendment. The tough Labor chairman had no choice. "First Negro to Preside at Drafting of Civil Rights Legislation in Congress," the *New York Herald Tribune* headline read.

Among those across America who were proud of Powell's ascension, the NAACP could not be counted. For years the civil rights organization had pressured politicians to support the FEPC. Now they found it in the hands of Powell. They still held a grudge over what he had done to Grant Reynolds in the 1946 election. The organization's leaders did not trust Powell, and yet they wanted in on any FEPC action. They dispatched Paul Klein, a young New Yorker with a passion for civil rights, to Washington, and gave him two instructions: he was to do everything he could to help the FEPC obtain real powers, and he was to have nothing to do — socially, at least — with Adam Clayton Powell. Klein realized, in fact, that he was being sent to Washington at least in part to spy on Powell. "They gave me a job I thought was impossible," he remembered.

A short man with intense eyes, Klein was a Cornell graduate whose social commitment had been honed while he was working for Senator Robert Wagner. Now he was working for the National Council for a Permanent FEPC, a clearinghouse for all groups interested in the FEPC. The NAACP was naturally among its primary backers. So nervous was the NAACP about Powell that Klein was instructed to avoid all job overtures. The NAACP did not wish to have someone working on its behalf listed on Powell's payroll.

When Klein told Powell that he had been sent by A. Philip Randolph ("a grand old man," Powell said), it was all the congressman needed to know. Powell told Maxine Dargans, his secretary, to take instructions from Klein. Klein was given an office within Powell's suite so that he could round up witnesses to appear before the FEPC subcommittee. He grew in admiration for Powell, but he quickly realized that the congressman had no interest in "the nuts and bolts" of legislation.

Powell relished the subcommittee chairmanship. In a move he thought strategic, he placed Richard Nixon ("young, pink-faced, fluid, and fluent" was his description years later) on the subcommittee. "He did that on purpose," Klein explained. "He felt he could swing Nixon around." Powell then called forth a wide array of witnesses. Throughout Washington he drummed up support for the FEPC. An auditorium at the Labor Department was made available to FEPC supporters, and Powell showed up for a rally, accompanied by Klein. When Powell's turn to speak came, he rose and his voice rose with him. "He made this rip-roaring speech," Klein said. "The theme was 'The people want this!' and 'The people deserve this!'" As Klein sat there, he saw the emotions swell in the crowd until it became feverish: "I felt he was going to walk right out of there and walk over to the White House with the people."

The FEPC testimony was passionate, but so was the opposition. The FEPC was "unconstitutional, unenforceable, and unwise," said an Alabama lawmaker. The bill to give it permanent, meaningful powers was communistic, cried a Florida lawmaker; it was a Truman bill, snapped Powell in reply. Chairman Lesinski was forced to bypass the subcommittees whose goal it was to do the administration's work on the House floor. Speaker Sam Rayburn undercut him by forcing him to present FEPC testimony to the southern-dominated House Rules Committee, where the bill would certainly die. Lesinski also felt he was being undercut by Graham Barden, a segregationist member of the Labor Committee, who thought the FEPC opened the door for federal intervention in private business and offered to bar private schools from receiving any public assistance. Archbishop Francis Spellman entered the fracas, charging Barden with being both "anti-Catholic" and "anti-Negro" — a surprisingly blunt critique from the conservative Spellman.

Congress not only refused to increase the FEPC's powers in the 1949 session; it did not loosen the grip of segregation on the nation's capital, either. In dire warnings to both Dixiecrats (the conservative southerners) and northern liberals, Powell suggested that there would be reprisals. "Let me speak to you frankly as a Negro," he said in the well of the House, "and let me tell you great northern liberals that regardless of what Uncle Tom Negroes may inform you, the Negro people would rather continue living in the slums fighting for their God-given civil rights than to have public housing and be Jim Crowed, segregated, and discriminated against." There was sarcasm in his words, and the "great northern liberals" could surely feel it. He held up a bill — attached to it was the Powell amendment — that, if passed, would desegregate Washington's public facilities. "Here is our first test," he began, and he went on: "Here now is the opportunity before the eyes of our nation to stand up and be counted, to let America know whether we campaigned on the basis of hypocrisy or on the basis of sincerity and honesty."

He had forevermore drawn a line in the sand between himself and his fellow liberals. Both Dixiecrat and liberal would constantly be reminded of where he stood. He stood on immovable ground, where the quest for equality would not be shifted. He stood where Smalls and Ransier and the other black Reconstruction congressmen had once stood. He stood to be recognized, but his bill to desegregate public facilities went down to defeat.

The first few months of Truman's second term were painful. Domestic legislation lay dormant. And soon Truman would be engulfed by a crisis of frightening proportions: the scare, fanned by the public and politicians alike, that Communists had infiltrated the government. Richard Nixon was about to make his national reputation by exposing a State Department employee named Alger Hiss. Accusations would

:ouch politicians, teachers, actors, and nightclub singers. As well, Truman was about to be surprised by war.

ᏺᐤᏺ

During his summer recesses, Adam Clayton Powell traveled the world, a habit he began after college graduation. His travel, which became more frequent as his wife's career entered full swing and Congress tightened its already tight lock on liberal legislation, later gave rise to accusations of chronic absenteeism. Harlem understood its congressman and his appreciation for cultured climes, but few others understood his peripatetic habits. He undertook his trips at times on behalf of committee work, and at other times for the sheer pursuit of pleasure. Powell would not take a back seat to liberal, Dixiecrat, or hedonist.

It was the age of the magnificent ocean liner, with huge ships docked at the pier along the Hudson River, beautifully dressed New Yorkers disappearing belowdecks and steaming away. Powell loved the water, and took easily to the Old World charm of ocean liners. In the summer of 1949 he and Hazel Scott traveled to Panama. She had concerts to give; he would address groups of the Panamanian government. In foreign ports they docked with the flair of traveling royalty, a handsome couple taking time to pose for photographers, little Skipper (as Adam III was called) and the nanny in tow.

After docking in Panama, Powell held court at the Tivoli Hotel, where he protested the ill treatment of Panamanian workers and inquired if those who had toiled in building the Panama Canal were receiving adequate retirement benefits. Some of the workers' voices rose in anger, and he vowed to take their complaints before the U.S. Congress. For several days the couple visited nightclubs, entertained and were entertained, and obligingly signed autographs. Powell wooed the Panamanian National Assembly. "First, I have fallen completely in love with your country, and this is the sentiment of my wife and our son," he began his address to the assembly. "On the night before our boat docked, as my little boy was going to bed, I was telling him to say his prayers so that he would go to heaven. He said, 'No, I do not want to go to heaven. I want to go to Panama.' "

Powell wasted little time in getting around to the subject of American politics. "We are living today in one world, and whether we be Jew or Gentile, Protestant or Catholic, black or white, Americans or Panamanians, we are all equals in today's society. Unfortunately, there are some people of my nation who are ignorant. They think that they are better than anyone else. I wish to assure you that those people do not represent the majority thinking of the American public."

A U.S. government official was impressed with the Powells' visit. "There can be no question . . . that Powell's evident interest in Panama, his personal charm, his adroit use of flattery, and his showmanship made a favorable impression not only on political leaders but on the Panamanian public in general," he cabled back to Washington. "In this connection due emphasis should also be placed upon the immense success of Miss Scott's concerts and to the considerable and uniformly favorable newspaper publicity accorded to both of the Powells."

But travel had its painful moments. Less than a year later, when traveling through Canada, Hazel Scott was forced off a train because of her skin color. An angered Powell fired off a letter to Edward Miller, assistant secretary of state. "I know this is not in your province," he began his missive, going on to assail the Canadian responsible for his wife's removal. "If this happens again, I intend to air it with a full speech on the floor before the House."

Adam Clayton Powell had a habit of returning to Harlem after trips abroad. Walking the streets after a quick drink in one of the bars, he would spot a milk crate, place it on the corner, jump on it, and thunder forth — part travelogue and part sermon, but mostly a renewed call to action, his fist pumping the air. And word would spread that he was back in Harlem, down on the corner, and people would come out of the restaurants and bars, down the steps of their apartments, to hear his voice. They would leave playground benches and the nearby newsstands, crossing streets and slowing traffic, until hundreds were gathered around him, and his three-hundred-pound bodyguard, Acy Lennon, would watch nervously as they kept coming to see and hear their congressman. Often Powell would get so worked up, especially in summertime, that he would yank off his suit jacket, then his tie. Harlem remained his community, yet Adam Clayton Powell no longer lived in Harlem. He maintained an apartment on St. Nicholas Avenue as a voting residence, but his New York home was in White Plains. His congressional office was the Abyssinian Baptist Church itself; "no appointment necessary" proclaimed the congressional stationery.

Harlem had become increasingly crime-ridden, from numbers rackets protected by the police, to the burgeoning petty crimes that commanded ample space in the community's newspapers, to the murderous crimes of passion that seemed to thrill readers. Some of it was born of deprivation, some of it committed by go-for-broke criminals. Every five years or so, America was forced to yank its attention to Harlem in the aftermath of yet another riot. It would not be one of Adam Powell's legacies that he changed the face of Harlem. He could bring in money with federally funded programs; supporters got patronage jobs; schools were funded. But even at the peak of his powers, still years in the future, Harlem remained defiantly impoverished, a legacy of dashed dreams. His contributions were more national than parochial.

Powell understood all too well the broken glass on Harlem streets, and he knew how it had fallen there. But he refused to live among the broken glass even while in New York. Harlemites believed he still adored their community, and loved to see him on a street corner, wailing; to see him emerging from a bar and crossing a street and hugging a constituent; to see him in the Abyssinian pulpit, then to look up to the balcony and see all the visitors — it was easy to understand why they believed he continued to love Harlem. He could still enjoy the clubs, the Red Rooster and Small's Paradise, the Apollo, the tantalizing mix of ethnicity. But Harlem was such a small and confining community. A figure of elegance could hardly halt its deterioration, and that pained him. He grew fonder of downtown clubs, particularly "21," the Stork Club, and Barney Josephson's Café Society.

Seated at a table at the Stork Club one night (the waiters could be so unobtrusive they seemed to glide), Powell and Scott were joined by Franklin D. Roosevelt, Jr. Of all the Roosevelt children, he looked most like his father, with the huge body and huge head, the dark eyes; unlike his father, he suffered a reputation as a cad but didn't mind. The night was getting on, and the lure of Harlem pulled — not for Powell, but for Franklin Junior. "Adam, how about showing us Harlem?" he asked. "I'd love to take you up there," Powell responded, but he warned: "Remember, it's not like it used to be." Roosevelt detected traces of sadness in Powell's voice. Dreamy Harlem was long gone.

Two years earlier, addressing a group of insurance officials whose aim it was to do business in Harlem, Powell had said, "I welcome you to Harlem as one who loves Harlem, not for its slums, not for its crimes, not for its injustices, not for its ghetto and its unfair treatment of the Negro, but for what Harlem symbolizes. Negroes north and south, east and west, Negroes from the Caribbean and Africa, have come here and established a degree of unity that cannot be approximated in any other city in the United States of America." Harlem had given him a state of mind and a balled fist. And in his travels, he told the world of Harlem, his Harlem, and how it had fed America with culture, how it had sent him to Congress.

He returned on Sundays to Harlem, to his church, and those in the pews never complained about his absences. They knew he was in Washington, or somewhere on the globe. Denied so much for so long, they were black America: field hands come north, waitresses, cooks, bus drivers, day laborers, Pullman porters, railroad men. They could feel themselves in the halls of Congress alongside him, could feel themselves crossing the Atlantic on choppy waters; and they continued to give their breathless "Amen" to him and his well-being. Some Sundays, particularly when Powell was in yet another firestorm, Adam Powell Senior, now affectionately referred to as "the old man," would appear, to show confidence in his son. There in the Abyssinian pulpit the Powells would stand side by side, two men in flowing robes, regal men with the common touch, in a church that was once only a tent. At such a sight the congregation brightened, and Harlem seemed its own special world.

❧

Before his election Truman could not have imagined his woes toward the end of 1949 and into 1950. Alger Hiss was convicted of espionage charges, giving rise to speculation that the government was rife with Communists and Communist sympathizers. Richard Nixon seized the country's mood. Hiss, he allowed, was merely "a small part of the shocking story of Communist espionage" in America. A besieged Truman still imagined that an FEPC bill had a chance of passage in early 1950. Led by Adam Clayton Powell, Democrats once again took the bill to the floor of the House for a much-anticipated showdown in February. Powell urged Congress "to give dignity" to itself by keeping the measure alive, but again it was defeated by the combination of southern Democrats and conservative Republicans. Powell told a commencement audience in Ohio in June that Congress had done nothing less than sell "the Negro down the river again."

That same month the United States was dragooned into war against North Korea, which had struck South Korea "like a cobra," as General MacArthur put it. The pictures on the front pages of newspapers of helmeted soldiers charging up hills reflected a mean and distant skirmish which made blacks painfully aware that wartime accommodations remained segregated, even if the military did not. Paul Robeson again urged blacks to avoid going to war. "I have said it before and say it again," he told a Madison Square Garden gathering, "that the place for the Negro people to fight for their freedom is here at home." Adam Powell, who could swing from radical to patriot in the same breath, took issue with Robeson. "In the hour of crisis, we will be loyal to our nation," he said, "reserving the right, however, to criticize constructively as we did in World War I and World War II."

While war raged, Truman was trying to deal with the threat of communism in his own government. The McCarran Act, prohibiting travel by Americans who were thought to be subversive and passed over Truman's veto, was a direct result of Capitol Hill furor. Robeson's passport was taken away; Du Bois, aging and battered yet still full of pride, was arrested for passing around peace petitions; J. Edgar Hoover's FBI men infiltrated campuses, looking for subversives. Richard Nixon rose in the eyes of Republicans and, for much of America, began to emerge as a hero, the brave young congressman ferreting Communists out of the government. In New York, Benjamin Davis, the Communist-backed city councilman, was defeated at the polls in 1949 by Earl Brown, a political columnist who had the backing of Republican, Democratic, and Liberal sources. Davis's defeat energized the coalition forces and put Representative Vito Marcantonio, who had long benefited from Communist support, on notice.

As for Powell, he worried little about his brief associations with Communist sympathizers. He dared anyone to accuse him of following the Communist line. When they did, he eagerly talked of civil liberties and civil rights with a fearlessness known to few other politicians. Behind his bravado lay a streak of pragmatism. During the Korean conflict he assured House colleagues that he would put the Powell amendment on hold. American Labor Party officials wished to back him in the 1950 elections; Powell refused their support, abiding by a Tammany edict that Democrats distance themselves from the Communist-backed party. Powell planned to survive the Red scare and Tammany's resurgence, so he adopted, conveniently, the role of "good Democrat." Immediately, his onetime protégé Benjamin Davis became one of his critics, attacking him in the Harlem press. Thus Powell escaped the taint of having followed the Communist line.

His wife wasn't so fortunate. Scott's name appeared on a list of Communist sympathizers linked to the entertainment industry and to Barney Josephson. Police and fire officials began appearing more frequently at Josephson's clubs; the staff felt harassed. Men in suits who did not seem to be enjoying themselves were conspicuous; the FBI was quite aware that the only truly integrated nightclub in Manhattan might attract Communist Party followers. Adam Clayton Powell struck a Sir Galahad pose in relation to his wife; anticipating that she would be summoned before the House Un-American Activities Committee, he encouraged her to volunteer to testify. The move was risky but shrewd.

Sitting across from her inquisitors in a closed room on Capitol Hill, Hazel Scott asked if she could make an opening statement. Congressman John Wood, a Democrat by way of Georgia, agreed, but only because "you are the wife of one of our colleagues." Scott's testimony was direct and even brave. In a strong and unyielding tone, she told committee members that they might very well have important work to do, but she wondered whether they had not become victims of "headline-seeking superpatriots." Several pages of testimony later, she summed up her appearance, ending on a note that had the finality of a piano composition that had begun smoothly only to come to an end with the echo of keys that had been struck with determined passion:

> Now that you gentlemen have heard me so patiently, may I end with one request — and that is that your committee protect those Americans who have honestly, wholesomely, and unselfishly tried to perfect this country and make the guarantees in our Constitution live. The actors, musicians, artists, composers, and all of the men and women of the arts are eager and anxious to help, to serve. Our country needs us more today than ever before. We should not be written off by the vicious slanders of little and petty men. We are one of your most effective and irreplaceable instruments in the grim struggle ahead. We will be much more useful to America if we do not enter this battle covered with the mud of slander and the filth of scandal.

Hazel Scott drew praise for her testimony. In the months and years afterward, however, her concert bookings in the United States showed a marked decrease.

∽✴∾

America in 1950 was engulfed by hysteria, fragile race relations, and the looming House and Senate elections. Congressmen who had not expressed extraordinary vigilance against communism would be held accountable. Liberal politicians were looking over their shoulders. In California, Representative Nixon was contesting Helen Gahagan Douglas in a Senate race that quickly took on a cruel edge, with Nixon accusing Douglas of Communist sympathies. Douglas drew support from the liberal Hollywood crowd and others who appreciated her brave protection of individual liberties. Nixon's camp was made up of rock-solid conservatives and was buoyed by the swelling belief that his involvement in the case of Alger Hiss could only benefit his future. Like Powell, Douglas had been a freshman in the 79th Congress, and like Powell's, her voting record had been consistently liberal. She voted with her conscience, and the price was dear. Indeed, the price of being a shameless liberal was costly in the 1950 elections not only in the valleys of southern California but in the streets of Italian Harlem.

A tough young reformer by the name of Carmine DeSapio had been elected to Tammany Hall from Greenwich Village. Among his first duties was purging those who had not been loyal to Tammany. Vito Marcantonio, who had single-handedly held together the leftist coalitions in New York City, had been an ardent supporter of Henry Wallace. Tammany, having been battered throughout the Roosevelt years, would no longer tolerate such insurrection, and withdrew its support of Marcantonio, throwing it to James Donovan, a slight bespectacled man familiar on the local political scene.

Marcantonio fought back. Taking to the streets on top of a sound-truck, bullhorn in hand, he noticed that the crowds had dwindled. He had served in Congress eight terms, forming an alliance of Jews, blacks, Italians, and Puerto Ricans and fighting for his constituents, who lived in the filthy Harlem tenements, worked dangerous jobs down on the docks, and often, because of the capricious economic winds, found themselves out of work. Marcantonio had been La Guardia's protégé and believed what La Guardia believed: that the little man must be helped. Many felt that his passion exceeded La

Guardia's. A short man in a snap-brim hat and three-piece suit, he led marches up the steps of the capitol in Albany, with foot-stompers and rent strikers trailing behind. His had been a passionate voice in favor of FEPC legislation and fair housing. He had been one of the earliest mentors of Adam Clayton Powell and grew to admire his fellow New York congressman (although he once confided to the Senate aide George Reedy that he thought it strange how, when Powell entered a room full of blacks, he would always scan the room, walk over to the darkest-skinned person there, and throw his arms around that individual). Marcantonio's law training had taught him to be vigilant about civil liberties, and time and time again he had taken to the House floor in defense of those accused of communism.

James Donovan defeated Vito Marcantonio by thirteen thousand votes. The concession speech was less sad than it might have been, given the outcome, and even had a certain ardor: "I want to thank you all for putting up a grand fight. We will have to learn the technique of a gang-up. I am not worried. You are not worried. Go home tonight with the full realization that the ultimate victory belongs to us." Marcantonio spent the rest of his life defending pacifists, such as W. E. B. Du Bois, and radicals, never caring much about money and rarely taking a fee. He was found dead of a heart attack on a New York City street in 1954, the year in which the Supreme Court ruled segregation in schools illegal, confirming an argument he had long made.

Rumor invaded Harlem that the NAACP's Walter White might run against Powell in the 1950 election. White had just married a white woman, and there were those who wondered how that might affect the race. White didn't run, but Governor Dewey found his man in Elmer Carter, a Harvard graduate and an employee of the State Committee Against Discrimination. Carter considered himself a coalition candidate, the representative of both the Republicans and the Liberals. Powell considered him "a dupe of political manipulators." Addressing a Harlem rally on behalf of Carter, Dewey used words to strike fear and summon visions of Dixiecrats: "We have launched the banner to cure the evils the Democrats left in this state and let me tell you that if you don't elect Republicans this year, the Democrats will come back and put you back where you were before." Marcantonio's fate did not haunt Adam Clayton Powell. He made but one campaign speech, then unleashed his church workers and the remnants of his People's Committee to trounce Carter, 35,028 votes to 14,819.

Nixon defeated Douglas in California, in a campaign whose treachery lived for many years as lore. Not many grieved for either Douglas or Marcantonio that year. Marcantonio's defeat by the Tammany machine was less a coup than a political threat made good. Carmine DeSapio had gone into politics with a shady past, having kept company with gamblers and racketeers, and with a fierce admiration from Italians, whom he had led in a challenge to the Irish hierarchy of Tammany Hall. After growing up in Greenwich Village and earning a college education, DeSapio went from running errands for Tammany Hall to being backed by Clarence Neal and Ed Flynn. An eye ailment caused him to wear dark glasses, which gave him a sinister demeanor, but oddly, he was considered both respectable and ruthless. Victory in the ethnic rivalry had given his name and career a legitimate boost. Hungry for respect, he now walked as a reformer, vowing to rid Tammany of its corruption. Marcantonio was his first major victim.

Having pushed into Italian Harlem with good results, DeSapio began looking toward black Harlem, which bewildered him, and the machine of Adam Clayton Powell. If he could gain control of black Harlem, it would signal another step in his efforts to restore a degree of Tammany control over New York Democrats. Tammany had become a pariah in the national party, which was under the influence of southern Democrats, whose last friend in Tammany Hall had been Jimmy Walker. Herbert Lehman, now a senator, was not a Tammany man; La Guardia, who had died in 1947, after surrendering the mayoralty in 1945, had despised Tammany; Franklin D. Roosevelt, Jr., had gone to Congress in 1949 by defeating a Tammany-backed candidate. Tammany was desperate to reassert control over New York City and even to take back the governor's seat. DeSapio, then, glanced at Harlem from behind his dark glasses and plotted his move. The machinery of Adam Clayton Powell, "the good Democrat," would have to be brought under control.

◦✦◦

Truman's administration, gripped by scandal, could not rid itself of malaise. Various figures, including Senator J. William Fulbright, had been put in charge of conducting investigations on Capitol Hill. The administration found itself in disarray, hounded by charges of communism from the outside, battered by corruption from within. Truman's popularity dipped to 23 percent. Republicans sensed fissures in the Democratic Party. Another presidential election year was looming. Where was Adam Clayton Powell? Atop a mountain.

He had been in Europe, traveling; Hazel Scott spent much of 1951 performing abroad, and her husband went along as her business manager. Two months turned to three, which turned to five. Capping his visit in the fifth month, Powell, his son in tow, paid a visit to an army camp of Druze rebels in Lebanon, where he met "ancient warriors face to face." He climbed a mountain; posed with rebels, their rifles in the air, bandannas tied around their heads; and marveled at the sights all around. Looking north, the congressman could see the mountains of Syria "and the valley of Armageddon." To the south he could see where "the Mediterranean washed the ruins of an old fort of the Crusaders." He and his son shared delicacies, "the ceremonial bitter coffee of friendship, the sweet thick Turkish coffee, exotic foods, ate bread two feet around and only a quarter of an inch thick, sucked tangerines from Joppa, enjoyed black olives from Galilee and almonds smuggled in from Transjordan to be dipped in hot melted sugar."

Off the mountain, he prepared to return to the United States. He boarded the *Queen Mary* along with other passengers, and while crossing the Atlantic, slowed by "stormy seas," he wired his political informants on the mainland. Upon his arrival he would have announcements to make about presidential politics.

He returned to a country skittish about the future, to charges and countercharges made by a deposed general (MacArthur), and to major parties in high gear for the 1952 primary season. In his first public appearance, Powell said that everyone he had met while abroad, from Copenhagen to Jerusalem, had convinced him that America would be judged by how well it treated its minorities. "Negroes must fight to save America," he said. In Manhattan he attended an affair for the Negro Actors' Guild, a group he had long been associated with, a group that had been instrumental in both his city council and his congressional campaigns. He announced that he would lead a boycott of TV and radio sponsors who were not giving adequate work to black performers: "We will list the names of the products advertised and charge these concerns with denying Negro entertainers their moral right to work regularly. I will have hundreds of thousands of reprints made, and using my congressional privileges we together will mail them all over the United States to leaders and individuals, urging an immediate boycott." If the campaign didn't bring companies to their knees, he proposed a resurgence of picketing: "It was through mass picketing under my leadership that we broke down stores, bus companies, and public utilities, so that today Negroes are employed everywhere in New York City."

In March Powell's activities consisted of the usual elegant party and a thumping political announcement. He appeared at the United Nations Ball. When the National Council of Churches refused to attack segregation, he announced from the Abyssinian pulpit that his church would secede from the organization. The ministers of the council, Powell said, "have again crucified Jesus on the cross of bigotry, and modern-day Judases have sold him for thirty pieces of white supremacy silver."

In that same month Democratic House members were greeted with news that both stunned and relieved them. Harry Truman told a Jefferson-Jackson Day dinner audience that he would not run for re-election. Many took the news as a surprise; others saw it as inevitable. Truman's presidency had been battered, slowed, and nearly taken hostage by the Red hunters, and by southern Democrats whom he had angered by taking liberal civil rights positions. Harry Truman, the one-time haberdasher, simply wanted to go home. While the Republicans were moving closer and closer to Eisenhower (who had finally let it be known that he was a Republican), Truman liked Governor Adlai Stevenson, of Illinois, and could also support his former commerce secretary, Averell Harriman.

On June 16, Powell was honored by the Carver Democratic Club in New York. Throughout his political career, he appeared at club after club in Harlem, depending on the moment and the benefits to be gained, all the while refusing to become a permanent member of any of them. He realized that there was no political club more loyal to his goals than the Abyssinian Baptist Church, through which he could pit clubhouse politicians against one another. In return for the Carver Democratic Club honor, Adam Clayton Powell promised nothing save his attendance on the night of his award presentation. "We are going to Chicago to build a platform every bit as strong as Truman built," he told the dinner guests. "We can win this election, but not if we play in the same league of compromise which the Republicans have already monopolized."

The candidates were declared. On the Republican side, there were the conservative Robert Taft, of Ohio; the liberal Harold Stassen, of Minnesota; and, being wooed, General Dwight D. Eisenhower. Taft, an inflexible member of the old guard, frightened many. Some wondered whether the ardor of his father, the former president, had not caused him to reach beyond his natural gifts — not an uncommon malady. No one questioned Harold Stassen's ambition, but whether he could round up the horses was another matter. Eisenhower's popularity intrigued Republican leaders, and could not be dismissed.

With Truman clear of the fray, the Democrats had to look for new blood. Harriman had obvious appeal: he had foreign experience, was well trained in domestic officeholding, was a Wall Street scion, had a family name. But as Truman himself wondered, "Can we elect a Wall Street banker and railroad tycoon president of the United States?" A family fortune was hardly the least of Averell Harriman's attributes. He was blessed with blinding confidence. "I am the Democrat to beat," he believed, and launched a favorite-son candidacy. His political past included no election to political office since college — Yale's Skull and Bones Society.

At the top of Harriman's campaign staff could be found two New Yorkers: Franklin D. Roosevelt, Jr., as chairman, and Adam Clayton Powell, Jr., as vice chairman. Harriman's candidacy allowed New York Democrats, saddled with a reputation of infighting, to rally around a cause. The candidate struck out across America, traveling through points west in a swank railway car, giving genuine evidence along the way of the odds he faced. His patrician air was palpable. Aloof by nature, Averell Harriman found it nearly impossible to ingratiate himself with crowds.

Estes Kefauver had emerged from the Washington corruption hearings as something of a hero and a sure-fire presidential aspirant. But his Tennessee regionalism posed an obvious problem for voters in the North and Northeast. Adlai Stevenson — who did not hunger after the nomination, a factor that, oddly enough, gave him some appeal — emerged quickly on the presidential scene, but too quickly for anyone to know the range of his popularity.

On May 1, at the Biltmore Hotel in New York City, the New York Democratic Committee met to select their delegates-at-large for the Chicago convention. There were familiar names on the final list: James Mead, a former senator; Mayor Vincent Impelliteri; Senator Lehman. There was one unfamiliar name, that of Adam Clayton Powell, who thus became the first black delegate-at-large sent from New York to a major party convention. The selection confirmed his growing power.

The next day the New York delegation boarded a fifteen-car train for the journey to Chicago, Powell dressed in a beautiful light-colored suit, silhouetted against the evening's darkness, his aides rushing to talk over last-minute matters with him. The Harlem congressman had promised devotion to his candidate, Harriman, but not to the party line. Powell's warning was clear. If "a Republican type of civil rights platform" was passed by the Democrats, he said, he would not be bound by it. Such a plank, he said, would force him to change course and campaign merely for state and local offices. Other Democrats ignored the threat.

The Republicans arrived in Chicago for their convention first, and they arrived eager and hungry; gone were the sentimental moods of the past. Dewey and MacArthur drew attention, as did Stassen, but they faded soon enough. Eschewing sentiment in favor of cold reality, Senator Everett Dirksen said, "Re-examine your hearts before you take this action" to those willing to rise up on behalf of Dewey. "We followed you before, and you took us down the path to defeat." Taft, mature enough to know that nothing was guaranteed in politics, nevertheless believed he saw a gentleman's agreement being forged on his behalf. Reaching for the nomination, he saw it taken by men and women marching across the convention floor for Eisenhower. Eisenhower sealed the top half of the GOP ticket; the vice presidential nod was given to Senator Richard Nixon. Few could deny the potency of such a combination. Eisenhower represented military might and expertise for the conduct of the Korean War; Nixon was the man who sent Alger Hiss to prison. The Republicans left Chicago feeling heady.

The Democrats arrived nervously. Their convention would last six days and on the first day the lack of unity was obvious. Their memories darkened by the Dixiecrat revolt, Democrats were genuinely unsure of their nominee. The liberal faction was appalled by the weak civil rights plank. Adam Clayton Powell felt confident that he could exert influence. He overestimated his powers, but before the convention's end he found a way to compensate.

It was William Dawson, not Adam Powell, who got attention as the black congressman at the convention. A quiet man who was not above working with Dixiecrats, he had made few enemies in Congress. Dawson had a friend in Harry Truman, and in Chicago, among his ward leaders, among the South Side blacks, he was at home, and he was proud to be home. The Democrats were not about to lose the opportunity to display Dawson, a black face in a city with a huge black voting population. Roaming the convention floor with an ease all but absent from his congressional duties in Washington, Dawson made speeches, was invited to back-room committee meetings, and dwarfed Powell, who quietly fumed. Behind the scenes, senators Lehman and Humphrey had both, along with Powell, fought for a stronger civil rights plank. Dawson found no problem with the original plank, which had been weakened at the behest of southern Democrats.

Adlai Stevenson came over from Springfield to welcome the conventioneers and to torture them with his proclaimed lack of interest in the nomination, but if he came to the nomination kicking, he also came with honed oratorical skills. He spoke of "the stark reality of responsibility in an hour of history haunted with those gaunt, grim specters of strife, dissension, and materialism at home, and ruthless, inscrutable, and hostile power abroad." He warned that "sacrifice, patience, understanding, and implacable purpose may be our lot for years to come." Truth, the need to tell the truth, seared his conscience. "Better we lose the election than mislead the people," he said, "and better we lose the election than misgovern the people." The words were beautiful, the tone mystifying.

After giving his acceptance speech, Stevenson made a calculated move. In a city full of blacks fresh from southern states, in a city where the Harlem congressman, Adam Clayton Powell, was already on edge, he selected the Alabama senator John Sparkman as his vice presidential nominee. Sparkman summoned forth visions of southern injustice: black necks snapped beneath tree limbs, the Scottsboro boys. Powell struck, and quickly. With a wave, a turn of his shoulders, he led a group of black delegates and bolted from the convention, causing pandemonium in the entire gathering. He saw Sparkman's nomination as one of "the great tragedies of our times," and felt that Sparkman, along with the weak civil rights platform, would be impossible to sell in the North — "sheer death," as he put it. "They can cram a candidate down our throats, but they cannot make us vote for him."

Uttering demeaning remarks about Dawson, Powell vowed to campaign for only state and local Democratic candidates, and he predicted that Eisenhower had victory "on ice." His anger shocked the reserved Dawson, who explained, "I am not a publicity seeker." Roosevelt Junior, who had come to the convention to push Harriman but was willing to settle with Stevenson, was alarmed at Powell's actions; "That was the time Adam and I fell apart," he recalled. New York reporters covering the convention chased after Powell for quotes; he promised more once he had returned to Harlem. His critics emerged en masse. A labor official dismissed him as "confused in his thinking and leadership."

Never again would Adam Clayton Powell attend a presidential convention where his own powers were not respected and his own role clearly defined. His dire warnings had fallen on deaf ears en route to Chicago. Having fought against southern Democrats ever since his arrival in Washington, he found it hard to be asked to campaign for one.

Many imagined that his Chicago performance had been ruinous. They failed to understand Powell. It was nothing less than victorious. In Chicago, Adam Clayton Powell was not playing to the Democratic Party delegates; instead, he was playing to the men who worked in the stockyards, the women who cleaned the hotels where the conventioneers stayed, the teachers in the segregated school systems, and the parishioners of the Olivet Baptist Church, the largest black congregation in America next to his own. And he was playing to the poor people in the shantylike tenements along Federal Street, and to the middle-class black homeowners along South Park Boulevard, and to the factory workers in nearby Gary, Indiana, and to the critics of William Dawson. When he left Chicago, his critics knew how sharp his sword could be; his admirers saw how quickly it could be drawn. Having been upstaged by Dawson and misled about the civil rights plank, he had seen no alternative but to steal the convention spotlight by making his exit, leaving fellow Democrats, a national audience, and William Dawson aghast.

As a politician, Powell was fond of metaphor, and talented enough to use it better than most. Back in New York, he wrote Democratic officials that the platform offered blacks a house with only a floor to walk across, when they were in desperate need of "walls and ceiling." He didn't like the Republican platform, either, but being a Democrat, he wanted to like the Democratic platform better. He did not. Both parties had sold blacks "down the river," he said. He alone waded toward the river's edge, to stop the tide he saw. His campaign was against his own party. He would pin powerful politicians, draw their consciences out into the open. Rallies and speeches were his weapons. "Mr. Civil Rights" is how he was introduced at one New York rally. "We will, of course, go to the polls this fall in larger numbers than ever before," he promised. "But we will vote only for our county, city, and state candidates, unless between now and November we can get firm assurances from Governor Stevenson and Senator Sparkman that they will campaign on a more forthright civil rights program than the ambiguous one adopted in the party platform." In Powell's eyes there were worse southerners than John Sparkman; he saw Spark man as a tool of the Democratic Party and pitied him. "Sparkman o Alabama has been a slave of the South. I think it's time that we Harlem Negroes set him free." Friends had told him to be cautious, and he in turn told the crowds that caution had never benefited his politica career and that they should abandon the Stevenson-Sparkman ticket If not, Powell predicted that the only tune crooned on election nigh would be "Stars Fell on Alabama." Carmine DeSapio, hungry fo unity, was reduced to silence. "If this is Armageddon," said Powell "let it be Armageddon."

The Stevenson camp, operating their national campaign out o Springfield, Illinois, heard Powell's noise, and it stung, speech afte speech, rally after rally. The candidates could ill afford for such pro nouncements to continue through the late summer. Making an east ward swing, Stevenson wisely sought out Powell in mid-August. I was the phone call Powell had been waiting for. Having been avoidec in Chicago, he could now publicly affirm his power: a presidentia candidate was coming to him and asking for help.

Powell and Stevenson met in New York City, at the Biltmore, on August 29. Powell made demands, and Stevenson, with little choice, accepted them. If elected, he vowed to eradicate segregation in Washington, D.C., and to wage an intense battle against segregation and for civil rights nationwide. To undo the damage already done, to campaign for the ticket, Powell demanded campaign expenses and money to pay a staff. Once Stevenson had agreed to that detail, he was able to leave New York with the support of America's most visible black politician. "We are 100 percent in back of him," Powell said.

Harlem Republicans scurried again to find an opponent willing to face Powell in the November elections. The congressman's showing in Chicago, and Stevenson's capitulation, had given him daunting strength. Lest DeSapio risk fraying what unity there was among his supporters, Tammany backed Powell's re-election.

Before Powell began spending time on his own campaign, he dashed to London with Hazel Scott. Both were becoming Europhiles. From London, where there were engagements and sightseeing, he phoned the States to schedule a press conference for his arrival, at which time he would launch his re-election campaign. On the day of his expected return, reporters and Democratic pols and well-wishers showed. Powell didn't: still at sea. In early October he surfaced in Harlem to announce that he was running "on an unbroken record of twenty-two years of fighting for civil rights."

Richard Baltimore, a New York attorney, had been chosen as the Republican nominee. Powell longed for battle, but he thought Baltimore was a weak candidate; "There are too many good Republicans in Harlem who have worked with people and have done much in securing better housing and civil rights," he pointed out. That said, he turned his attention quickly to the national campaign, appearing up and down the East Coast before crowds whose enthusiasm for Sparkman was noticeably lacking. Governor Dewey even called Sparkman "the white supremacy candidate."

In need of an emotional boost, the Stevenson campaign arrived in Adam Clayton Powell's Harlem in late October. The crowds on rooftop and balcony, in windowsill and doorway, were electric; Truman had had such a greeting, warm and noisy and wide-eyed. Walking alongside Powell, Stevenson could hardly navigate the crush of people. The two politicians strolled down 125th Street, the rise of voices everywhere. They stopped at the Hotel Theresa, which had played host to Eisenhower weeks earlier. Eisenhower had held a breakfast in Harlem, and in introducing Stevenson, Powell said that Eisenhower had tried to buy off Harlem by treating voters to free coffee and doughnuts. Ike was not to be trusted, he went on, claiming that he was "double-dealing, double-crossing, and double-talking." He did not spare Nixon either. Referring to the senator as a "Nixiecrat," he said he knew Nixon's record better than any other Democratic politician did because he had worked with Nixon in 1948 on his FEPC subcommittee. Seeing Nixon up close, he had not been pleased. "For weeks we held hearings, and I must report to you tonight that Nixon is a died-in-the-wool, unalterable Nixiecrat of the worst type." "Stevenson Wildly Cheered in Harlem," said the *New York Times* headline.

A day later a massive rally was staged on Stevenson's behalf at Madison Square Garden. By four o'clock the Garden had filled up; Stevenson was not expected until nine. It was David Dubinsky's International Ladies' Garment Workers Union — laborites. They did not particularly care for Powell — he pushed them too hard on the race issue, and they resented it — but he was scheduled to address the gathering. He was, after all, the Manhattan congressman who had hosted Stevenson the night before.

Powell and Paul Klein, who occasionally assisted Powell with his speeches, had spent days on his remarks; then, just before Powell entered the Garden, he tossed the speech away. "He walked out there," recalled Klein, "in this noisy place, and people quieted down. And he said, 'Last night, Adlai Stevenson came to Harlem in front of the Hotel Theresa and we had a rally for him. And the people from Harlem sent me down here to tell you we're gonna roll up a bigger plurality than we ever did for Franklin D. Roosevelt!'" The crowd roared; men tossed hats. Powell scanned the Garden: a hostile crowd had become his crowd. "There was an animal magnetism involved," Klein said. "The whole place went crazy. It took them ten minutes to calm the place down."

But Stevenson was stung by the *Times*'s endorsement of Eisenhower. A feeling began to emerge across America that Stevenson lacked foreign policy experience. American troops were still trudging across the hillsides of Korea, and Eisenhower promised a Detroit audience that if elected, he would visit Korea. The vow struck a nerve: General Eisenhower, Ike, back on the battlefield. It didn't exactly ring of derring-do; his bravery was unquestioned. It rang of timely statecraft.

Nixon, however, brought the Republican campaign to a dangerous crawl when it was revealed that he had been the beneficiary of a secret campaign fund. Eisenhower thought of dumping his running mate. Then Nixon went on national television and explained how he was a simple man, how in fact his finances were meager, how his family had been frugal, how they had cared for a dog named Checkers, a humble little gift. It wasn't a beautiful speech, but it was deft, and it played enormously well to a riveted television audience. Nixon, having toyed with GOP fortunes and the severe men who ran that party, was forgiven.

The beautiful-speech maker of the 1952 presidential campaign was Adlai Stevenson. In his oratory, Stevenson was a man of near poetic sensibilities. The nation had heard as much at the Chicago convention: "Here, my friends, on the prairies of Illinois and of the Middle West, we can see a long way in all directions. . . . Here there are no barriers . . . to ideas and aspirations. We want none; we want no shackles on the mind or the spirit, no rigid patterns of thought, and no iron conformity. We want only the faith and the conviction that triumph in free and fair contest." On the wild prairies of a campaign, however, Stevenson could not summon the horses to take him across. Sparkman proved to be a heavier burden than the Democrats had imagined —

captive of the South, as Powell had put it. A nation engaged in foreign conflict and worried about the Communist threat did not go to bed on election eve thinking Democratic.

On election night, Adam Clayton Powell and Hazel Scott attended a People for Powell party in New York, then went to the Waldorf to be with other Stevenson supporters. "From the beginning I have been certain my husband would win," Hazel told the press, "and hopeful for Mr. Stevenson." Adlai Stevenson lost by six million votes. He took the defeat with equanimity, but it was a powerful blow for the Democrats, who also lost control of the House and were one senator shy of a Senate majority. Now Roosevelt's ghost would be pushed aside. Blacks simply had not been able to rally around Stevenson and Sparkman. Powell, however, crushed Richard Baltimore, receiving 71,512 votes to his opponent's 15,832.

༒

Adam and Hazel made the rounds of election night parties accompanied by Adam Powell Senior and his new wife, Inez. Following the death of his first wife, the elder Powell had grown lonely. Many had seen it, watching the aging minister playing chess with youngsters on the stoop of the Abyssinian church, appearing more eager for companionship than the children. When he married Inez Means in Los Angeles in 1946, rumors that she was white swept Harlem and entered the gossip columns ("80-Year-Old Dad of Congressman Has Blond Bride"). Adam Junior joked that his father had been jealous — of Hazel. Was Inez Powell white? From her photographs, it is hard to judge otherwise. She had blond hair and light skin; in a room with white women she would have been indistinguishable. The elder Powell, still a giant on Harlem's streets, hushed the gossip simply by saying that it was not true, that there was a sufficient amount of black blood in his new wife for her to be black; enough was enough. The matter was dropped.

Seven months after the election, on June 12, 1953, Adam Clayton Powell, Sr., died, at eighty-eight. He had spent the last years of his life, more often than not, away from the busy streets of Harlem. There were trips south, to warmer climes; Inez came from South Carolina. His pursuits were leisurely: reading and writing, corresponding with old allies. A fervent believer in education, he donated money to philanthropic causes. He fished until the end, his driver taking him out to Sheepshead Bay, where he would crawl into a little boat and cast line and sinker, the wind blowing through his flowing white hair. The obituaries were effusive, and spoke of a man of quite humble beginnings who had grown and matured to shape modern Harlem and build one of the largest congregations in all of America. The son of a slave, he had educated himself, put a son through college, and witnessed the son's entry into the United States Congress. He was buried in Queens, in a plot beside his first wife, Mattie, and his daughter, Blanche. (The remaining place in the plot had been purchased for Adam Junior.)

In a way, of course, the death freed Adam Clayton Powell, who became the sole surviving member of his immediate family. "I think he was scared to death of his father," said Marjorie Lawson. "He admired him, but he was like an adolescent breaking away." Photographs lined the walls of Powell's office, but the only photograph he kept near, atop his desk, was a family portrait that showed his mother and father, his sister Blanche, and himself as an infant on his mother's lap.

IV

SHIFTING GROUND

1953–1957

L ITTLE FRIGHTENED Harlemites as much as the throng of police officers that descended upon them during times of crisis — hundreds of officers climbing from the back of police trucks, wielding billy clubs and marching into crowds with arms raised; officers galloping down 125th Street, horses wheeling and maneuvering to catch looters; officers running, circling picketers and rent strikers; officers smashing down doors in search of numbers runners and racketeers. To the average New York police officer, young, male, Irish, often with a military background, whose uncle, father, or grandfather might well have preceded him onto the force through a Tammany appointment, black Harlem was another world. It was a land of mystery, of anonymous black faces, cars speeding and horns blaring, lurid headlines in the weekly newspapers; it was a place (Hell's Kitchen was another) that the old officers reminisced about, telling tales of gangster lore. Owney Madden and Dutch Schultz were big names associated with Harlem violence in the 1930s; then there were the Harlem riots of 1919, 1935, and of course 1943. For decades officers who had disappointed the top brass were not fired but sent to duty in black Harlem.

The undercurrent of organized crime that stained Harlem could hardly have flourished without official collusion. Over the years various mayors — William Gaynor, and especially La Guardia — tried to rein in the police force and cure it of criminal collusion, but the department was too huge and impenetrable. It resisted all calls to set up a civilian board, and kept enough support in Tammany Hall to prevent such requests from becoming reality. While the majority of the police force was considered dutiful and honest, it took only a few to spread the disease of corruption; low wages were a formidable inducement to accept bribes, and one crooked cop in each station house was enough to keep the department mired in allegation and suspicion. The NYPD was a force unto itself.

In early 1953, two black men were arrested and subsequently handcuffed and beaten at the West 54th Street station house in Manhattan. The beatings roused Powell, providing him with his most potent opportunity to assail the department. He spent the early part of the year dashing back and forth between New York and Washington (he boasted to friends that he could make the trip in three hours' time, instead of the railroad's four, in his Jaguar sedan) to lodge an array of complaints against the police, including brutality, corruption, and payoffs. Because the beatings had occurred in Jacob Javits's congressional district, Javits joined Powell's attacks, giving them the clout of bipartisan attention. Brutality was not the least of the charges; the most explosive was Powell's accusation that the department had struck a deal with the FBI to refrain from investigating such reports. Moving fast, Powell took his attack to the floor of the House. The department just as quickly issued denials. Powell called for the firing of police commissioner George P. Monaghan; his fellow New York congressman Isidore Dollinger seconded his demand. That two blacks had been attacked by police officers was hardly enough to warrant congressional attention; that Powell had unearthed an agreement between the NYPD and the FBI indeed was. By focusing on the agreement, he could, of course, bring attention to the charges of brutality.

Powell and Javits pressured Kenneth Keating, a New York Republican, to convene a House subcommittee hearing to air the charges. As the hearings got under way, Keating grilled Monaghan, asking if such an agreement had been struck. When Monaghan told Keating he had "no recollection" of it, the congressman snapped, "Is that as strong as you can put it?"

"Yes," the commissioner answered. Then he turned his big body to Adam Clayton Powell in the hearing room, wagged a finger, and dramatically blurted his reaction to the allegation: "That was a lie, Clayton, and you know it."

Monaghan was not fired, and the hearings reached no conclusive outcome; the code of silence within the police department was all but unbreakable. Powell's allegations were not without foundation, but the proof, and the full-scale investigation that would root out the proof, lay nearly two decades in the future.

Among the trips that Powell took in the spring of 1953 was a jaunt to West Point. The academy was, after all, in his home state. He had heard reports that there was segregation at the academy, that a black military unit had been assigned to act as waiters in dining halls and dishwashers in kitchens. He descended upon the school for a "review," as he called it. And indeed, some of those scrubbing the barracks, those in the kitchen, were black soldiers relegated to such jobs. "Negroes do not want to fight communism with a frying pan," the New York congressman said of conditions at President Eisenhower's alma mater.

ᏸᎳᏯ

As Powell began his fourth term in Congress, much of America had long since adjudged him an aberration, a noisy black in the corridors of power, a figure whose career would surely be cut short in due time — if not by party defeat, then surely by scandal. Few realized, and fewer appreciated, his resilience.

Adam Clayton Powell planned to make his special mark in the House of Representatives. It was the one place where he was free of his father's grandest accomplishment, the Abyssinian Baptist Church. The younger Powell had given much to the church, but there were those (and they would be around for years to come) who, when mentioning it, were quick to refer to "old man Powell," because he was the organizer of the modern-day Abyssinian church. "He built a spiritual church the likes of which we haven't seen since," one member said years later. In Congress, Adam Clayton Powell, Jr., could amass his own legacy. There was no other place where America's disparities were on such raw display, almost daily, and no other place where those disparities were played out in motions that could go from gentlemanliness to fevered hatred in the time it took to return from afternoon recess to the House chamber. Always a wonderful thinker on his feet, Powell found the environment heady. He had long since fathomed why Congress both pained and challenged him. It was a place of timid souls, men bound by class, region, and party, men who walked in Rayburn's shadow, men who positioned themselves for committee assignments, men who were quiet, so quiet that they eventually disappeared into anonymity. Not all, of course, were quiet. There were men like Jacob Javits, Kenneth Keating, Emmanuel Celler, William Langer, and Vito Marcantonio, and women like Helen Gahagan Douglas; but the latter two were now gone. Only a few understood Powell and recognized his vision. Ever since he had entered the House, he had appeared to the majority of representatives as exotic, untamed, and dangerous — as exotic as he had been to his fellow students at Colgate, as untamed as he had been to members of the New York City Council, as dangerous as he had been to some members of his father's church.

Some Democrats — progressive Democrats — were dismayed at the prospect of Eisenhower's moving into the White House. Deep in his soul, Adam Clayton Powell, who was elected as a Democrat and who voted with the progressive Democrats, still considered himself an independent, not of party but of mind. In his political background lay a coalition of disparate parties: socialist, Communist, American Labor, Republican, and Democratic. The Republicans who had begun taking over the nation's capital did not frighten him. While he could not reconcile himself to the rigidity of the national Republican Party, he owed part of his own political rise to the New York Republican Party, the party of Bull Moose republicanism, liberal Republicans, Republicans like Theodore Roosevelt, Fiorello La Guardia, Stanley Isaacs, even Tom Dewey, all independent thinkers. Never allowed access to Harry Truman's White House, Powell determined not to suffer a similar fate with the Eisenhower White House. Viewed by many Republicans as a threatening and indecent figure, he had only one recourse now: to appeal to the decency in the Eisenhower administration and draw it, and the Eisenhower people, out into the open.

The Republican men and women invading Washington in January 1953 had every right to be dizzy with excitement. It was their first inauguration since 1929, since Hoover. The inaugural festivities were grand affairs, the men in Homburgs, the women in mink. Eisenhower took the oath of office with his hand laid on the Bible he had read while he was a West Point cadet.

The new president unabashedly filled his cabinet and administration with well-to-do businessmen; better them than "New Deal lawyers," Eisenhower concluded. One of the more interesting personnel dramas involved E. Frederick Morrow. Morrow, born in New Jersey and educated at Bowdoin College in Maine, came from a long line of Republicans. He considered GOP party loyalty nothing less than an act of bravery for a black man. "It was like having a horrible disease, to be a Republican," he recalled. When the Eisenhower campaign caught on, he left his job at CBS, where he worked with Edward R. Murrow, and joined the effort. As a professional black committed to the cause, he stood out. The harder he worked, the more nervous Republicans became: somehow he would have to be rewarded with a job. He was promised a job in the White House. A black had never been appointed to a White House executive position. After the election, Morrow's phone stopped ringing; he was reduced to badgering the president's office about his promised job. Others phoned on his behalf. Finally the White House relented, and Morrow was named an assistant to Eisenhower. He quickly warned administration sources that he wanted nothing to do with civil rights, having convinced himself that doing so would open him up to charges of being treated as a token — which, of course, was exactly how he had been treated.

Adam Clayton Powell knew the people who made up the Eisenhower administration; he knew their types. Their thoughts and opinions on the great moral question of the day, race, would have to be bent. New methods would have to be devised to bring them onto his ground. Morrow might have been Powell's conduit, but Morrow was caught in his own dilemma: the more he was perceived to be a *black man,* the less whole he felt. So he went about his daily White House routine with a casualness that belied reality, playing golf on Virginia courses in the afternoon sun, shying from discussions of civil rights at work. Powell understood his dilemma but held little pity. He would toy with Morrow — the light-skinned Powell serving as example of black pride to the dark-skinned Morrow.

Herbert Brownell and Maxwell Rabb also joined the administration in high-level positions. Powell knew both, Brownell from New York political circles and Rabb from Capitol Hill. "I was always impressed," Rabb said of Powell, whom he found a "very charismatic figure; he had a very winning way." Rabb had been an able assistant to Senator Henry Cabot Lodge, recently defeated by John Kennedy, and was now secretary to the cabinet. Brownell, whom Eisenhower named attorney general, had been Dewey's long-time political lead man in New York City and was now the lone cabinet member who found the discussion of social issues invigorating. He also imagined himself the only member of the cabinet ever to have visited the Abyssinian Baptist Church.

Oveta Culp Hobby, the sole woman in the cabinet, had been drawn to Eisenhower's attention because of her military background; during World War II she had served as head of the Women's Army Corps. As a Texas Democrat, she sympathized with the Dixiecrats. (William Hobby, her husband, was a significant financial contributor to southern Democrats, especially Lyndon Johnson.) Eisenhower named Hobby to head the Federal Security Administration, but within months she became the secretary of the new Department of Health, Education, and Welfare.

America's knowledge of its new president had been gleaned mostly through his wartime adventures. Inasmuch as he emerged a hero, and America victorious, knowledge of his personal convictions and beliefs was scant. He had been born in Texas, raised in Kansas, attended West Point, and spent a career in a segregated army. In World War II he approved using blacks in various military roles (following years of bitter complaint), and he had been labeled by many blacks — in a gesture that turned out to be painfully premature — a progressive. After the war he had served with some discomfort as president of Columbia University. In the postwar years, with military veterans utilizing the GI Bill, a university could benefit from a president who knew the Pentagon and had military contacts.

In reality the new president was a cautious man whose speeches lacked both sweep and romance. Truman had lacked poetry but not experience. He often told aides of horrific Ku Klux Klan activities he had seen while growing up in Missouri. His creation of the Civil Rights Commission was considered a bold step for a Democratic president dependent on southern Democrats. Roosevelt and Truman had both given assistants the specific job of keeping track of minority matters. Eisenhower had no such assistant. In the early months of his administration other matters were fraying his nerves: communism and the Soviet threat. Running headstrong in Congress was Wisconsin's senator Joseph McCarthy, already dramatically assailing the State Department for being rife with Communist sympathizers. Eisenhower was shy about taking on McCarthy. Such caution had its perils.

Eisenhower's attention was quickly snapped elsewhere, into the machinations of his own military and the continued segregation on military bases. Black veterans who had been wounded in Korea were mending in segregated veterans' hospitals, where they were treated like second-class citizens; black children on military bases were being obliged to attend segregated schools. In the first months of the Eisenhower administration a small cadre of blacks — a lobbyist, a traveling pianist, and Adam Clayton Powell — conspired to bring the issue to the president's desk.

The pianist, of course, was Hazel Scott, who covered the United States from back road to big city, playing piano but becoming her husband's alter ego as well. In February she found herself in Tennessee, performing two engagements for veterans, one in Murfreesboro, the other in Nashville. She traveled in high style — she knew no other way — but her conscience remained close to the ground. For Scott the engagements were goodwill work without performance fees, a little Ellington and a little Bach for maimed soldiers, the least she could do. Conditions in the Tennessee veterans' hospitals shocked her. Soldiers were segregated by race, not only in the wards but in her audiences as well. She could hardly keep quiet. Her only recourse was her husband. When the information reached Powell, he wired the White House. "How can we expect to defeat communism when Negroes who have been wounded and lost parts of their bodies in fighting Communists in Korea are brought to segregated hospitals in America?" he wanted to know, especially since Eisenhower had vowed to end segregation on military bases and in hospitals. The Harlem congressman demanded an investigation.

The White House instructed J. T. Boone, the chief medical director of the Veterans Administration, to deal with Powell. Boone's response was littered with fear, trepidation, and conceit. He told Powell that the veterans' hospitals were in fact drawing up plans to desegregate, but that black patients themselves were to blame for slow implementation, because they had become accustomed to segregation. He also feared that there would be riots if word leaked throughout the Tennessee communities that ailing black veterans were sleeping and eating with ailing white veterans. Boone confidently informed Powell that patients undergoing shock treatment were allowed to recover in integrated environments.

In March, Powell appeared before a House committee, castigating the government for spending vast amounts of money to support segregated school systems on military bases. Black servicemen, he said, had sent complaints to his office, telling of having to send their children off-base to segregated schools. He cited a variety of military posts, among them Fort Sam Houston and Fort Bliss, in Texas (the home state of Speaker Sam Rayburn and cabinet member Oveta Culp Hobby); Fort Sill, in Oklahoma; and Fort Belvoir, in Virginia. The complaints, Powell said, had come to him from transplanted military families, families from Pennsylvania and Minnesota and New York, families accustomed to integration. "They are serving their country in the Armed Services, and, as a penalty for such service, they are forced to send their children, who have never previously been exposed to segregation, to schools for colored in the communities surrounding the posts."

Clarence Mitchell, an NAACP lobbyist who was alone among the NAACP hierarchy in trusting Powell (although at times nervously), had a habit of slipping Powell information gleaned from NAACP field offices. Mitchell was given further proof of segregation on military bases. He encouraged one of his favorite reporters, Alice Dunnigan, of the Associated Negro Press, to question Eisenhower about this at press conferences. The energetic Dunnigan all but badgered the taciturn Eisenhower, who said that he could not see how federal funds could be used to promote segregation on military bases, "legally, or logically, or morally." Powell's strategy had worked. Eisenhower instructed his staff to begin the unfinished work of desegregating U.S. military bases.

It was hardly a revolution, but on various military bases soldiers armed with screwdrivers began removing WHITE ONLY signs. Lest anyone cause a commotion, the task was performed at night, and those who inquired were told that the signs were being taken down to be washed. The issue remained touchy for Eisenhower, as his biographers have noted, and he felt no urge to interfere with southern sentiments on public integration. Military bases were another matter. He could simply order it done with a stroke of the pen. And in reality the risks were minimal. More often than not, military bases were far removed from the public eye, in remote areas surrounded by rural stretches of land. At West Point, the secluded academy behind Bear Mountain and above the Hudson River, the all-black waiters-and-dishwashers detachment was disbanded.

In April 1953, in an obvious nod to southerners, Eisenhower named Oveta Hobby to her cabinet position. Among the massive goals of the newly created Department of Health, Education, and Welfare was the continuing, and total, desegregation of military bases. Hobby found it more than a little difficult to confront her fellow Texans on this issue. A born southerner and a long-time critic of the New Deal who saw integration as a dangerous social experiment, she adopted a laissez-faire attitude toward the assignment and busied herself with other matters. Word of her lackluster performance spread quickly along the NAACP grapevine, and Clarence Mitchell informed Powell. The Harlem congressman had to plot a careful strategy. He would have to go after Hobby and hope that his criticism of her would blemish the president's image.

Adam Clayton Powell had been a newspaperman. He knew what an afternoon deadline in Washington meant, knew how White House staff members reached eagerly for the afternoon papers, scanning the headlines, then national news, then foreign news. If a story was unfavorable toward the White House, it meant that the president's aides might have an uneasy night, especially if the story cut deep, if the headline wouldn't go away. The White House received his telegram on June 4, 1953, in the early afternoon, just when the *Washington Evening Star* arrived at the White House. The *Star* generously, and favorably, covered Powell's Washington exploits, and he had given it a scoop: the entire contents of his telegram. It printed a page-one story, above the fold; the headline, "Hobby Note Flouts Segregation Order, Powell Charges," would not go away. The administration's honeymoon was over.

Powell managed little restraint. White House staff members were sabotaging integration; appointees were ignoring Eisenhower; the president was losing his grip; time was running out. "The hour has arrived for you to decisively assert your integrity," he told the president. "You cannot continue to stand between two opposite moral poles." He described Hobby's insubordination. "This detracts from the dignity, integrity, and power of your office," Powell said, the moral tone rising higher and higher. "I have faith in you as a man of good insight, decent instincts, and a strong moral character. I beg of you to assert these noble qualities. The free world is looking to you as its last hope. Strong leadership is imperative now; tomorrow may be too late." Eisenhower might well have winced at the last line: "For fear that this might not reach you, may I have the courtesy of a personal reply?"

Anger swelled at every level of the White House when the telegram was read. Maxwell Rabb was stunned. "Things appeared to be going along very well," he recalled. "It was the first big crisis." The administration felt ambushed. "I had never seen such consternation in the Eisenhower ranks," added Rabb. "They were utterly unprepared for this." Why hadn't Powell gone through normal channels, the military-trained Eisenhower wanted to know.

The president instructed Sherman Adams, his top assistant, to do something. Adams, a blunt-spoken operative who had learned his politics in New Hampshire, planned to defuse the situation quickly, but first he made some preliminary phone calls to military bases. He grew perplexed when he found that Powell's charges had merit. Adams didn't know Powell, but he concluded that a congressman who would have such an explosive telegram delivered to the White House, and have it given wide coverage in the newspapers, was not to be taken lightly. He wrote letters to Powell, tore them up, then rewrote them. Adams was reluctant to admit insubordination on Hobby's part. Instead of contacting Powell, he turned to Rabb, who rushed to Powell's office for a face-to-face chat, not even bothering to phone ahead.

Squeezing a moral issue, bringing it out into the open, partaking in the debate and the sparring, watching the telegrams fly, watching the newspapers seize the moment, knowing the issue would reverberate up to Harlem and beyond, is what Adam Clayton Powell liked best — knowing the phones would start ringing in his office, as his constituents called to tell him how proud they were and to encourage him to keep it up. Rabb was a blur to Maxine Dargans, Powell's secretary, as he waltzed right by her and into Powell's office, where Powell sat smiling. "Max, I've been expecting to see you," he said.

Rabb had, in fact, come to strike a bargain. He told Powell that this administration would be different, that it would not be an administration of platitudes. No promises would be made to blacks, then broken. He mentioned the FEPC and Roosevelt's inability to give it meaningful powers, and said that Eisenhower would do things differently, "without the idea of publicity." The deal he presented was intriguing. Rabb offered Powell an opportunity to become an ally in the Eisenhower administration's battle against segregation. He would have to work behind the scenes, Rabb said, for obvious reasons, but an open line of communication would be available. Rabb asked Powell to travel to both domestic and foreign military bases on behalf of the administration, and to report directly back to the White House. He only demanded assurances that Powell would refrain from criticizing the administration in print. Powell liked the bargain, and agreed. For the first time since going to Washington, he was about to have access to the White House — a Republican White House.

Eisenhower sent a telegram in response to Powell's, in which he vowed he would not take "a single step backward" from the distance he had come in the field of civil rights (it wasn't far). "There must be no second-class citizens in this country," he said. Then the missive took on ominous tones, tones of indecision. Eisenhower believed that 'the spirit of these objectives" would not be achieved by him alone; he did not have the mandate to reach any further than the rule of law. He imagined that victories would come "one by one."

In communicating with Powell, the Eisenhower administration publicly, if nervously, displayed its respect for the Harlem Democrat. Powell lifted Eisenhower's telegram beyond its measured tone, imbuing it with literary touches and sweeping historical connections, calling it "a Magna Carta for minorities and a second Emancipation Proclamation." The press picked up the claim, no doubt wondering if Ike's simply worded telegram was the same one Powell was referring to. A "Magna Carta for minorities" might have been something released with fanfare, a "second Emancipation Proclamation" with more than that. Instead, this was a telegram released by a single congressman on a hot June day on Capitol Hill. The nation was living in "troubled hours," Powell told Eisenhower, and he assured him that the "senior Congressman of all parties from Manhattan," the "first Negro Congressman to be elected in modern times from the Eastern Seaboard," would engage with enthusiasm in the goal of equal rights. He warned as well that he would be on constant lookout for saboteurs inside the White House.

Powell had struck a nerve, throwing the new administration off-balance. But he had also provided it with an emotional sendoff into uncharted territory, that of desegregation. Eisenhower had no one else to turn to in the matter of black affairs and desegregation, and his quick overture had appealed to Powell's independent streak. "He was an enigma at that time," recalled Sherman Adams, who considered himself a "country boy," forced to think fast to keep up with Powell. Over time, Adams and other members of the Eisenhower administration found themselves admiring the Harlem congressman, if secretly. "I guess you could say we leaned on Powell quite a lot," he added. "Powell, at those early stages, was a political asset, and we treated him as such." When Powell strolled into Adams's office and sat down and began talking, Adams found himself becoming more and more entranced. Powell "was an intensely interesting experience — an expert at political chicanery, and not in a bad sense," he said.

Charles Thomas, an undersecretary of the navy, was dispatched to review the military bases that Powell had pointed out were still segregated. His first stop was in Norfolk, Virginia, where, months after Eisenhower's initial order, he found drinking fountains, cafeterias, and bathrooms still segregated and COLORED signs still posted. Following orders, Thomas had the base desegregated. But he knew other bases might not be as easy, and he told Eisenhower that many areas in the South would require caution. At Norfolk he told soldiers he was there because of Adam Clayton Powell. Everyone, he later reported, either "knew or knew of Mr. Powell." He believed that Powell meant nothing but trouble, that the Harlem congressman was someone who "could not be trusted."

Slowly segregation fell away on the navy bases. As soon as Rabb got word that the signs had been removed from another base, he reported to Powell: Norfolk and Galveston, San Diego and Charleston. "The first weekend we went to work," he said, "we did all the water fountains. Over the weekend the signs were quietly removed."

Eisenhower held no vision of integration beyond the borders of military bases, and no intention of forcing federal law to ease the plight of blacks. There would be no effort at new FEPC legislation. A sip of water on an integrated military base hardly ensured a sip of water in segregated Birmingham, Alabama; Fayetteville, Arkansas; or McComb, Mississippi. Eisenhower expected southern communities to resolve the problems of segregation on their own. But the hour was approaching when he would no longer be able to avoid challenging segregation beneath ringing school bells.

Powell had begun praising Eisenhower in his speeches and sermons to groups as he traveled around the country. In an October sermon before his own congregation, he brushed aside criticisms directed toward the president, telling his flock that he could "bear witness" that progress had been made in the months since Eisenhower had taken office; when the president had given his word to Adam Clayton Powell, he had kept it. The number of black Republicans in Harlem may have been steadily dwindling, but there were still those among the Abyssinian congregation who remembered when the word *Republican* had been uttered with warmth; they could remember which party Adam Powell Senior had supported. Powell told his flock that he was indeed a Democrat, but that, more important, he had been born with a label — just like them — that transcended political identification and in troubled times enabled him to vacillate: by birth and breeding, he was "an American."

Clippings about Powell's appearances began coming across Rabb's desk. Having taken deep cuts in the ranks of black voters since Roosevelt's day, Republicans did not plan to allow Powell's newfound religion to go unnoticed. Smooth and decisive, Rabb acted quickly. "You might be interested in seeing how a difficult Democrat, who originally blasted the Eisenhower administration, has reacted to a little friendly treatment," he told Leonard Hall of the Republican National Committee.

Powell's pronouncements worked beautifully with the White House. "I rather enjoyed working with Powell," recalled Sherman Adams. "You'd sit with him and you'd think he was a sage of wisdom about the race problem. He was about the smoothest guy I ever saw. He was a magnificent diplomat. I always felt he had an intuition about how to act."

Having forged a relationship with Adams and Rabb, Powell went after Morrow, the lone black on the White House staff, who continued to remain aloof from civil rights matters. Powell called Adams one day and told him he was going to have a gathering in Harlem the following Saturday and there would be some things on the agenda the administration might be interested in. He wanted Adams to send someone. Adams instructed Morrow to go.

After flying to Manhattan, Morrow took a taxi to Harlem, to Frank's Place, a popular restaurant and Powell hangout. "Adam met me at the door, a martini in his hand," recalled Morrow. The presidential aide looked around and saw no one else; he was puzzled. "I knew they'd send you," Powell said. The comment was cutting; Morrow thought Powell was making fun of his status in the administration. Swirling his drink, Powell turned and called out to other ministers and assistants, who were hidden behind partitions. Then, looking back and forth between them and Morrow, he said that he might well be a Democrat but he had the Republicans down in Washington eating out of his hand; they were so afraid of him that they'd send one of their own when he demanded it. Morrow was livid, and wanted to turn and leave, but Powell turned on the charm. He slapped Morrow on the back, offered a drink, a seat. It was Saturday in Harlem — black America's soul, Adam Powell's Harlem — and he told E. Frederick Morrow to relax.

⟋⟍⟋⟍

Adam Clayton Powell was paying scant attention to the Committee on Education and Labor. The 1950 elections had catapulted Graham Barden, from the low country of North Carolina, into the chairman's seat. With Barden's ascension, Powell's fortunes took a nosedive.

Powell, the quixotic northern liberal, was given little to do by Barden, the quintessential Dixiecrat.

Barden was born in rural North Carolina in 1896 into a family of cotton farmers. Following college, where he used his bulk to good advantage as a tackle on the football team, he took a law degree at the University of North Carolina. Before entering politics, he became a schoolteacher and a successful football coach. His career as a state representative lasted just three terms. His congressional constituency comprised farmers and timber men and fishermen, women who cooked on iron stoves, poor and near-poor southerners distrustful of a government that had once sent marauding soldiers galloping through their pine woods. The counties in and around New Bern, where Barden lived, were unlike the areas around Raleigh and Charlotte, which had come to know moderation on the racial front. In Washington, Barden turned against the liberal experiments of Roosevelt's New Deal, endearing himself to the voters in his district.

Graham Barden rarely held committee hearings. When he did, he railed against big government, social programs, and federal intervention in schools. The Education and Labor Committee took on a volatile nature. "It was so controversial — strong pros and cons on every issue that came up," recalled William Ayers, a Republican committee member from Ohio. Carl Elliott, a Democrat from Alabama, also a member of the committee, knew the Barden philosophy well. "Barden didn't have much ambition," he said. "He regarded it as his duty to hold down all the changes that would shake up things in the South in the slightest."

Chairmen were powerful men with unchecked powers, the men who actually ran Congress and controlled the flow of legislation; they were called barons for a reason. Barden, "a rough, tough son of a bitch," in Elliott's terms, had the ability to stifle legislation. "The committee of little education and no labor," liberals called his committee. "The Barden committee stopped every liberal-to-moderate idea any president ever had," explained Richard Bolling, who in 1950 was beginning to form a coalition that would soon challenge Barden: Americans for Democratic Action. Barden's constituents feared federal education bills, said Bolling. "They were honestly afraid of school bills. They thought the federal government was going to take over their children." Bolling began holding meetings of moderate southerners and liberal Democrats, to devise a scheme to take on Barden and, in reality, to realign Congress itself. According to Frank Thompson, a Democrat from New Jersey, "Barden envisioned himself as Horatius at the bridge. He was going to stop any labor legislation, any school legislation, and by God, he was going to stop any civil rights legislation."

Adam Clayton Powell represented everything Graham Barden was against. The relationship between the two men was reduced to pro forma letters and played out as a painful minuet, with Powell telling Barden he would be going away on yet another mission, Barden pleasantly and quickly offering letters of introduction. Barden treated Powell "more or less with contempt," recalled Carl Elliott. Powell "knew how to get money and get it quietly" from Barden, claimed Russell Derrickson, a member of Barden's administrative staff. "He got in a lot of travel time on the committee." Northern Democratic congressmen stood nervously by as Powell, caught between his Dixiecrat chairman and the Eisenhower camp, gravitated toward the latter.

Powell continued to travel around America. In February 1954 he told more than two thousand people at a union rally in Chicago that Eisenhower had a wonderful civil rights record, that he had done more to restore the Negro "to the status of first-class citizenship" than anyone since Lincoln. The energetic Rabb came up with a plan to exploit the situation. He convinced Stanley High, a personal friend and a senior editor of *Reader's Digest,* to approach Powell about writing an article on Eisenhower and blacks. The journalist in Powell could hardly resist.

Back on September 8, 1953, Chief Justice Frederick Vinson had died of a heart attack in his Washington apartment. Vinson had been unable to unify the Supreme Court on the issue of race. (Justice Felix Frankfurter had been one of his harshest critics. "This is the first indication I have ever had that there is a God," Frankfurter coldly told a clerk upon news of Vinson's death.) Attorney General Brownell began championing Earl Warren, the popular governor of California and Thomas Dewey's running mate in 1948, as Vinson's replacement. Warren's sense of *noblesse oblige* during the backbiting 1952 GOP campaign had appealed to Eisenhower, and Brownell's recommendation carried considerable weight; Eisenhower named Warren, who belonged to the moderate wing of the Republican Party, to succeed Vinson. Among the more significant cases facing Warren was a school desegregation case that had been filed in Topeka, Kansas, eighty-nine miles from Abilene, Eisenhower's birthplace.

On May 17, 1954, the Warren Court issued its landmark *Brown*

v. *Board of Education* decision, striking down segregation in schools. "In these days, it is doubtful that any child may reasonably be expected to succeed in life if he is denied the opportunity of an education," Chief Justice Warren wrote. "Such an opportunity, where the state has undertaken to provide it, is a right which must be made available to all on equal terms." Few fathomed right away the ramifications of so sweeping a decision. The Harlem community saw no reason to celebrate, but its congressman understood the depth of the change. The decision was nothing less than "democracy's shining hour," he wrote for *Reader's Digest,* and "communism's worst defeat."

After reading the typescript of Powell's article, Stanley High, who was enthusiastic about it, had a few small queries. He looked in vain for Powell. The congressman was traveling through Europe and Africa on a one-man congressional investigation of military bases, with bouts of leisure as shock absorbers. He would usually arrive at a base unannounced, but his little son noticed how quickly word would spread, how the soldiers, especially the New York boys, would rush to see him, and how pretty soon he would be at a table, playing cards and joking. But that was not all. Often he would summon his wife, and Hazel Scott would arrive with a few musicians she had managed to pick up in Paris, and there would be a little jam session for the troops. Powell liked the muddy bases, the bonhomie of the young soldiers. "That was not living in the lap of luxury," recalled Adam Powell III. Powell always sent messages back to the White House after his investigations. "There is no place in Orléans, on the base or in the city, where an enlisted man can take his date or dependent to dance," he wrote from France. Blacks could not get waited on in bars in the town of Chaumont, and were forbidden even to enter some of the small English towns.

An exasperated High finally had a correspondent reach Powell in Europe, and the article was readied for publication. High mailed advance copies to the black press. "The President and the Negro: A New Era!" was published in the October 1954 edition of *Reader's Digest.* "As a Democrat," Powell wrote, "I nevertheless believe that Dwight Eisenhower is proving to be the President of all the people and that, not Negroes only, but all the people will be better and America stronger because of it." Rather conveniently, he remained abroad. Democrats were engaged in the heat of their congressional campaigns; mere weeks from election day, they were treated to a pro-

Eisenhower article in a widely circulated magazine by a member of their own party.

Eventually Powell made his way back to the United States. Though he himself was up for re-election, there was a congressional campaign in Detroit he was more interested in. Charles Diggs, a black state senator, had abandoned that job to run for Congress against George O'Brien, the incumbent and a fellow Democrat. O'Brien had the support of the Irish Democratic machine; Diggs, that of the black churches, for his father was a successful mortician. Diggs scored a surprising victory in the primary, beating O'Brien three to one, which left only a weak GOP opponent in his path. When Powell appeared at the Ebenezer Baptist Church in Detroit, he screamed from the pulpit, "Elect Charlie Diggs! Detroit needs him! Michigan needs him! The world needs him!" A crescendo built. "The crowd was going crazy," recalled Diggs, who won the election and joined Powell in Congress.

Powell skipped his own campaign, making only one cameo appearance in Harlem on his own behalf, even though his opponent had a lot to say, most of it about Powell's ethics.

Being a man in a hurry, Harlem's congressman drove roadsters. His Jaguar and Nash Healey were low to the road and took corners effortlessly. The Jaguar was a soft-top, the Nash Healey an even more beautiful machine. The Nash Healey, however, had been acquired in a questionable way. David Kent was a New York builder who in 1952 began building low-cost rental apartments in Queens. Powell became interested because the building contract stipulated that the complex would be integrated from the beginning. So intrigued was Powell that he began talking about the rental units from his Abyssinian pulpit, and he appointed two church aides, Acy Lennon and William Hampton, to set up offices in the basement as rental agents for Kent. Tooling out to the Queens site in the Jaguar one day, Powell, while chatting with Kent, noticed a Nash Healey. He would like one, he told Kent, but he couldn't afford it. Kent offered a $3,000 loan. Powell purchased his Nash Healey. Two years later, in 1954, the Federal Housing Administration, finding out that Powell had paid back less than 10 percent of the loan over the period, launched an investigation. Did Powell exercise any undue influence on the FHA to help Kent secure his building loans? The FHA planned to find out.

Harold Burton, Powell's GOP opponent, thus had his campaign

ammunition: Powell's links to David Kent. During the hearings, Powell swung the probe away from possible undue influence and turned it into a public outcry against the lack of affordable integrated housing in New York. The charges, he said, were nothing more than a "Republican-sponsored drive to destroy what little nonsegregation has been started" in the New York housing market. Instead of explaining his remarkably low loan repayments, he lectured his inquisitors to spend more time investigating Jim Crowism in that market. In its final report, the FHA reported no undue influence on Powell's part. Powell breezed to re-election victory against Burton.

The news in New York State was Averell Harriman, who was elected governor to succeed Thomas Dewey, albeit by a less than reassuring eleven thousand votes. Harriman was an unlikely choice to become New York's governor. Lacking the warmth and common touch that had personified his predecessors, he shook hands with the downstate devil — Tammany Hall — to win the close election. Harriman, who had seen his first presidential campaign fizzle before his eyes, had high ambitions. Albany would be the base from which he would launch another presidential run; Carmine DeSapio vowed Tammany's kinetic support.

⌘

While he had been in Washington, Adam Clayton Powell had turned an increasing amount of power in his church over to Joe Ford, his campaign aide and link to Tammany Hall. Ford had no family or spiritual link to the church, but no one questioned his ascendancy in the church hierarchy. The church, after all, served as Powell's district headquarters. Abyssinians chose to ignore the lurid stories in the Harlem press about Ford's adulteries and the alimony suits of his former wives. They were mindful that to question Ford was to question Powell, who demanded loyalty from church members. To quiet even the hint of criticism, Powell "stacked his deacon board full of flunkies," as Olivia Stokes recalled, adding that Powell also charmed by giving gifts: "By his gift giving, he eased his irritants."

Ford did not lack ideas, however, to appeal to the Abyssinian congregation. A self-trained accountant, he operated an income tax agency, with Powell's blessing, in the basement of the church. Somehow, in their little apartments, Harlemites found that money evaporated quickly. They pulled huge pots down in the evenings to cook ham hocks and collard greens — an Old South diet, a cheap diet — and yet food was still expensive; that is why their minister had gone into the recreation hall and opened a food store. They parceled money and saved when possible, but it was so hard to save. Powell Senior had given the church a tradition of doing things to ease the congregation's plight, by establishing a community center, a nursing home. Powell Junior could not resist trying to extend the tradition. So Joe Ford, in tandem with Acy Lennon, Powell's bodyguard (whom Ford had trained, quickly and inefficiently, as a tax preparer), went down into the Abyssinian basement to set up a tax service. Abyssinians facing the IRS deadline took their forms in the yellow envelopes, walked down 137th Street, turned into the church, went down to the basement, and had their taxes prepared — at a discount. They appreciated any help they could get. And they came face to face with Joe Ford and Acy Lennon and Hattie Dodson, Powell's faithful secretary, who also became a part of the service.

The signatures of the tax preparers and the novelty of the enterprise quickly drew the attention of the federal government and the hard gaze of IRS auditors. Powell Senior had known that many a church had fallen because of financial irregularities, and had been scrupulous in the church's financial endeavors and careful to surround himself with men of unquestioned integrity. Powell Junior lacked such a gift, blindly allowing his aides to earn extra income against the backdrop of the Abyssinian family. Acy Lennon's mind was not quick enough to decipher piles of beguiling numbers. Hattie Dodson confused her service to Powell with admiration and unrequited love. Joe Ford aspired to too many enterprises to be an expert at any one; as a tax preparer, he sorely overestimated his talents. The mix was fatal. When the government uncovered proof of tax evasion in 1954, Dodson, Ford, Lennon, and William Hampton, a church aide, were summoned before a New York grand jury.

Dodson's and Lennon's testimony did not help them. In May 1956 Hattie Dodson was convicted of nine counts, including tax evasion, claiming false dependents, and receiving illegal funds. A month later she was sent to prison for seven months. In October 1956 Lennon was also sent to the federal penitentiary, to serve a one-year sentence. In a bold move to silence the inevitable speculation of racial persecution, the government had Samuel Pierce, one of the few black federal attorneys, announce the indictments. The government called the Abyssinian tax service nothing more than "an intricate tax scheme." The scandal sent a collective sigh along the streets of Harlem, in and out of the competing churches that kept an eye on one another.

Before Hattie Dodson was convicted, Abyssinians found themselves bracing for her courtroom appearance, for she was much loved. On the stand, Dodson, unaware that she was but a small figure, that the government was after larger prey, steeled herself. She had become involved in a scheme involving misleading tax forms. Somehow on her tax form she had listed several dependents; she had no children. There was pain in her personal life. Her marriage to Howard Dodson, blessed by Adam Powell, was one of convenience. Howard Dodson, the Abyssinian choir director, was a kind man, but he was a homosexual, a fact that perplexed many in the church. He too was named as a conspirator in the tax fraud. On the witness stand Hattie Dodson fought the charges feebly. Few understood the move, or her motives, if in fact she had done what she was convicted of. She lived simply; she was a woman of modest means and never appeared eager for material gains. Many believed that she had been duped into the scheme by Ford. One thing was for sure: on the witness stand, Hattie Dodson was in pain for her church. Abyssinian was everything to her. She hated the questions from the government lawyers, endless questions, and she hated the innuendo about Powell. What she knew of the scheme — the cold facts — she kept to herself and took to her grave. Hugged by parishioners, she departed from New York City one evening for the women's federal penitentiary in Alderson, West Virginia, to begin serving her sentence. One of Hattie Dodson's bravest acts was taking the blame for her husband; all charges against Howard Dodson were eventually dropped. Some parishioners felt that Powell had betrayed Hattie Dodson, and thus the church itself. "We thought it was terrible," recalled Olivia Stokes. "She was left high and dry."

The older deacons, the deacons whose loyalty was more to Powell Senior than to Powell Junior, had always feared this moment: that calamity would land right in the lap of the Abyssinian pulpit; that Powell Junior lacked discipline; that there was a price to be paid for allowing political operatives into the sanctuary of the church. They had warned the elder Powell, as gently as possible, that his son's lack of discipline could lead to woe, could exact a price. Now that day was upon them. Powell Senior had been dead for little more than a year, and three church members had been sent to prison.

Acy Lennon quickly lost weight in prison. A simple man whom

Powell treated at times with condescension and at other times sympathetically, he could barely read and write. He did not hear from Powell while in jail; Hazel Scott sent sweets. When he was released, a political ally of Powell's offered free suits, which Lennon accepted because all of his own clothing was too big.

After seven months, with time off for good behavior, Hattie Dodson was released from federal prison. "She came back to the church as if nothing had happened," Olivia Stokes explained.

As for Joe Ford, the architect of the tax service, he never served a day in prison. The government struck an interesting deal with the savvy Ford.

∽ₐₓ∾

John Foster Dulles had a penchant for railing against what he called "Godless communism." Eisenhower's secretary of state, having once had Alger Hiss in his employ, reeked of nervousness on the issue. "There are no Communists in the Republican Party," he heartily proclaimed at the 1952 GOP convention. During the Indochina crisis in 1954, Dulles advocated intervention. He blamed Truman and a Democratic Congress for China's "fall to communism"; American prestige had been damaged, and the hawkish Dulles vowed it would not happen again. But he had a hard time rallying allies. In the end, Eisenhower himself, ever mindful that he had been elected as a peacetime leader in a country still wounded by the Korean conflict, refused to send troops.

But American might — and arrogance — worried President Sukarno of Indonesia, who thought that the nations of people of color were being overlooked in international development and that the United States was among the culprits. In Third World nations, one thing about America was paramount: it had had the will to drop the atomic bomb. In 1954 Sukarno began mapping plans for a conference of Asian and African leaders, in an attempt to form an alliance. Beneath the prospect of a meeting, however, lay something more: the hope that pro-West countries might debate Communist-aligned countries in an open arena. China was invited, but so too were England and the United States; the anti-West leaders of Burma, India, and North Vietnam were sent invitations, and so were the pro-West forces of Pakistan, the Philippines, Lebanon, Ethiopia, and a host of sub-Saharan countries that were worried not only about colonialism but about nuclear warheads being tested in their deserts. The conference was announced for April 15, 1955, to be held in the West Java city of Bandung, a remote mountain resort.

Dulles, buried deep in cold war paranoia, thought the idea of meeting with Communist-dominated countries and leaders absurd, and went so far as to advise Eisenhower against even acknowledging the invitation. Ike followed his advice. Dulles busied Nelson Rockefeller, then a White House aide, in writing background papers supporting the administration's decision to avoid the Bandung conference. The United States thus had no official representation at the first Third World conference ever.

Adam Clayton Powell considered himself the spiritual equal of the emerging black African leaders who would be at Bandung. As a young man fresh out of college, he had journeyed to Asia and Africa. He could not miss the historic meeting. He appealed to Dulles, reminding him, "I'm known throughout Africa." Dulles refused to budge. "Dulles was very jealous of his prerogatives, and he didn't want any congressman interfering," recalled Herbert Brownell. Powell found no supporters among his fellow congressmen, many of whom held opinions similar to those of Missouri congressman Thomas Curtis, who felt that Powell would simply use the conference to launch attacks against his own country. Max Rabb was Powell's last hope. Rabb tried, but quickly found that he held little sway against the machinery of Dulles's State Department. "Ike doesn't want me to go," Powell said to his wife and son at dinner one night.

Powell still had contacts in the black press, so he proposed to a handful of black publishers that they provide him with press credentials in return for firsthand dispatches. Black publishers were known for their parsimoniousness. Although they were interested in the conference, the cost of sending a reporter around the globe played with their blood pressure levels; but here was Powell, willing to pay his own way. They could hardly refuse. With his press credentials guaranteed, Powell wangled an invitation from the Indonesian government and took off for the airport on April 8 as a foreign correspondent and de facto representative of the absentee U.S. government. Dulles was not amused. As Powell readied to board his airplane, a man walked up to him, handed him a camera, and asked if he would mind taking pictures of the Chinese as a little favor to the government. Powell took the camera and bade farewell to his family and to the CIA operative who had handed him the camera.

The conference held particular resonance for American blacks, who were eager for respect on the international stage, even if it had to come vicariously, through the efforts of black African nations. American newspapers sent their top correspondents. Homer Bigart covered the event for the *New York Herald Tribune,* Carl Rowan for the *Minneapolis Tribune,* Robert Alden for the *New York Times.* Richard Wright, the American novelist and expatriate, left the Left Bank of Paris to attend.

Powell first surfaced on the tarmac in Manila, a shoulder bag flung over his shoulder, a press card dangling from his neck. Former senator Homer Ferguson, now the U.S. ambassador to the Philippines, met him and invited him to stay at his residence for the night, then was forced to tell Powell he could do nothing further for him — on orders from the government. The next morning Powell left Manila on an Indonesian jet. Among his fellow passengers was General Carlos Romulo, heading the Philippine delegation. At Jakarta, thousands jammed the airport to see the arriving dignitaries. Music blared and children hustled for autographs. When Powell finally arrived in Bandung, on April 15, he found that the host government had made available a spacious apartment; on Third World soil, he was accommodated as a dignitary, not a mere journalist.

A dazzling array of leaders gathered at Bandung: Chou En-lai, of Communist China; Abdel Nasser, of Egypt; Jawaharlal Nehru, the Indian prime minister; Sukarno; and twenty-five other delegations. (The U.S.S.R.'s leaders were moodily absent. They sent regrets, a telegram lauding the gathering, and a team of *Pravda* reporters.) Of the world's 2.5 billion people, 1.4 billion were represented.

And there was Powell, of the United States, representing nobody.

The delegates, up close with one another for the first time, appeared surprised to learn that the others were human instead of caricatures. Many expected Chou En-lai, as the representative of the rigid Chinese leadership, to prove explosive; at Bandung he spoke reasonably, and while he did not concur on some of the issues, such as human rights, he appeared eager to reach points of unanimity. Sukarno worked diligently to produce harmony, and in the end, those who attended adopted several principles of agreement, including adoption of the UN charter that sought to control atomic weaponry and a continuing denunciation of colonialism.

If the conference had ended there, the Communist countries might well have considered it a success. But it did not. *Pravda* reporters hunted for Powell. They were eager to hear his comments, and they

wanted to know in particular about American racism. The congressman turned preacher. Telling the gathering that he was but "two
generations removed from slavery" yet had risen into the halls of
Congress, Powell pointed with pride to American gains in the field
of race relations. He talked about how blacks were receiving better
jobs in the South, and he urged other nations to look to the American
example for working out racial problems. He pointed to the recent
Supreme Court decision, *Brown* v. *Board of Education.* The *Pravda*
reporters, having anticipated an all-out critique of the United States,
lost interest. Other journalists gathered close. Homer Bigart sensed
that the mood of the conference was changing: "Before Powell had
finished, I noticed the TASS man closing his notebook and putting
his pen away. Such a disappointment for him."

Soon, an event halfway around the world, in a tiny Indonesian
resort that many Americans had never heard of before, was appearing
on the front pages of American newspapers. Powell created a sensation. He had taken the stage to wave the flag and had become, wrote
Alden in the *Times,* a "vigorous" spokesman for America. "It is
perfectly obvious," a *Herald Tribune* editorial said while the conference was still under way, "that things have not gone at Bandung
the way the Chinese protagonist, Premier Chou En-lai, anticipated.
Rep. Adam Clayton Powell, as an American observer, set the tone
for much of the proceedings with his dramatic defense of the way the
United States has faced up to the racial problem." A *New York Daily
Mirror* editorial was just as effusive: "In our opinion, Rep. Powell's
unofficial trip will pay off in a great deal of official and unofficial
good will for our country, and its ideals." It ended with an "Attaboy,
Adam!"

Before returning home, Powell issued a shot at Dulles, claiming that
unless the American government paid attention to Third World countries, "an anti-white" movement might be spawned in retaliation
against a "narrow-minded and unskilled foreign policy."

When Powell landed in New York, he was greeted by his wife and
son. "How's it playing here?" he quickly asked. "It's been on the
front pages every day," Hazel replied. Then the TV cameras began
closing in. Later that night, at home, little Skipper didn't want to go
to bed; he wanted to see if his father would be on the news. "Can't
stay up late," his father often told him. "You'll get bags under your
eyes like Duke Ellington." But this time he relented. "Good evening,
ladies and gentlemen," John McCafferty began his nightly report on

Channel 4. "What kind of a day has it been? It's been a day when Adam Clayton Powell returned from Indonesia." "Wow, that's you!" Skipper said, turning to his father.

Long eager to play on the international stage, Adam Clayton Powell had now hoisted himself onto it. Conservatives who had ridiculed him for his "radicalism" now had to contend with his all-out Americanism. "One of the really astonishing stories in Washington is that of the Negro congressman, Adam Clayton Powell," wrote Ralph McGill, the *Atlanta Constitution* columnist and editor, who went on to criticize Dulles's State Department: "Why they didn't want him to go and why we did not send greetings is a troublesome mystery." C. L. Sulzberger, writing in the *New York Times* about the government's apprehension in dealing with Communist countries, said that it might do well to listen more closely to Powell, "who appears to have fought some successful battles for the United States in Bandung."

The raves spilled over onto the floor of the House. Ray Madden, an Indiana Democrat, praised Powell for turning the Bandung conference into the "first worldwide moral defeat for Communist aggression." Congressman Gerald Ford, who hosted a talk show beamed back to his Michigan constituents, invited Powell to discuss Bandung on his show. The *New Republic* said that Powell "did more than anyone else" at Bandung, while "representing more than half the world's population, to persuade delegates of America's decency in racial relations." The liberal weekly did not lose sight of closer terrain, noting that Powell must "sit in the rear of buses if he travels in the South, can't stay at certain hotels, or eat in many restaurants."

Some in the black press were bewildered. The *Pittsburgh Courier* was careful in its praise, claiming that Powell had "showered American racial policies with saccharine praise," which had indeed impressed southern congressmen but puzzled some blacks. Yet the *Courier* admitted that it was not immune to being mesmerized by the Harlem congressman, even if the compliment was backhanded: "Whatever the reason, we are glad to see this new Congressman Powell in the role of defender of God's country."

In mid-May Eisenhower finally met with Powell to discuss the conference. The New York Democrat was full of advice. He told Eisenhower he should meet as soon as possible with the heads of state of Far Eastern nations, a move he thought would help "annihilate the propaganda drive of Red China." He told the president that embassy personnel abroad were nervous because of McCarthyism, which had been sweeping America. He appealed for the appointment of blacks to ambassadorial positions: "One dark face serving the U.S. over there would do much more good than millions of U.S. aid." There was an additional matter. Powell warned Eisenhower that his fellow Democrats — especially Herbert Zelenko, a liberal congressman from New York, and other liberals — were about to attempt to exploit the issue of segregation across the country.

On the streets of Harlem now, Powell's smile was wide, his suit brightly colored. He was preaching about Bandung, and the crowd swelled, kept swelling, and there, in back of the street-corner crowd (she tried to get close but couldn't) stood Isabel, the first wife. Her eyes kept glancing around; she knew the voice; she stood on tippytoes like almost everyone else that afternoon. She had been walking home and had noticed the crowd, the slowing of cars; in the distance she had seen the bright suit. They hadn't seen each other in a long time. She got closer — not as close as she wanted to, but close enough so that for a quick moment their eyes caught. She looked directly into his; she felt that he saw her, his head swiveled in her direction. Yes, she was sure, was positive, she told herself as she walked on home, he must have seen her, he had looked in her direction and smiled. Who else would he have looked at like that? With such intensity? It was just a moment, but she was sure it was their moment. Isabel Powell, ten years after the breakup of her marriage to Adam Clayton Powell, was still refusing to remarry, still carrying a torch for her ex-husband. That summery night in Harlem she walked home feeling light on her feet.

☙❧

Powell wasted little time in exploiting his heightened popularity. He journeyed south. In 1955 interesting events were unfolding in Alabama. Baptist ministers in Montgomery, led by the young Martin Luther King, Jr., were plotting protest movements. Educated in Boston, King advocated Gandhi's philosophy of nonviolence, and he was a riveting presence. (Powell had turned to his wife one evening and asked, "Who is this little nigger Martin Luther King, Jr.?") The strategists had devised a plan to break the discriminatory Montgomery bus company economically by having blacks walk to work.

Powell perplexed southern black ministers, who had become political leaders in their communities. He thought these ministers had fallen under the wing of white philanthropy, and that the civil rights hierarchy, with the exception of Clarence Mitchell, was too slow and plodding. The real battles lay in Washington.

Powell avoided the huge Baptist gatherings that made ministers familiar with one another. Once he made a huge auditorium full of ministers and their guests wait for his appearance. He was such a huge draw, handsome and fond of electrifying entrances; they waited and waited, heads swiveling back and forth to the doorway. "The place was jam-packed," recalled Gardner Taylor, one of the ministers. Time passed, and still no Powell. Taylor took a phone call. It was from Powell, who said that he would not be able to make it. The next day Taylor received another phone call from Powell, who wanted to know how big the crowd had been.

Baptist ministers were vividly aware that Powell had no direct link to civil rights organizations. He traveled with no entourage and employed no brain trust. He was a quintessential loner in thought and action, and a nakedly political animal, motivated by the pain and despair of the downtrodden. Often he wondered to friends just how much black blood coursed through his own body. Bounding among three worlds — dark-skinned black, light-skinned black, and white — he smiled at slights from all three.

He encouraged the Montgomery organizers to proceed with their planned bus strike, and described the similar strike that he had led a decade before in Harlem. He told them of the maids who had stopped riding the buses into Manhattan, how the boycott had finally worked. Bayard Rustin, a King aide listening to the speech, found it compelling. Still, one speech from a northern congressman was hardly enough to launch a crusade in a small Alabama town.

Among southerners, Alabama politicians stood out from their political neighbors in Georgia, Mississippi, and Louisiana. They were hardly go-for-broke liberals like the politicians from the border state of Missouri. But Alabama's congressional delegation was noted for its moderation on the issue of race. Carl Elliott, who represented Jasper, Alabama, was passionate about education; he delivered books to rural Alabama communities. Lister Hill, in the Senate, often voted with the liberals — except on matters of race. And James Folsom, the governor when Powell arrived in 1955, was a populist who spoke eloquently of the plight of blacks in his state: "Negroes constitute 35 percent of our population in Alabama. Are they getting 35 percent of the fair share of living? Are they getting adequate medical care to rid themselves of hookworm, rickets, and social diseases?"

Both Powell and Folsom had been cut from populist cloth; both men cared about education, blacks, and the poor. Powell spoke to the Alabama Education Association, the black teachers' organization, of the state's political hope, citing men such as Folsom, whom he called "a big, open-hearted fella." Folsom invited Powell to the governor's mansion, and sent his chauffeur to pick him up. Folsom was planning to run for Democratic national committeeman, an honorary post; perhaps Powell could offer insight. The meeting went well, the two politicians talking of current events in relative solitude; the press was unaware of the spontaneously called meeting.

Before leaving the state, Powell ran into a reporter who, wanting information about Powell's address to King's organizers, asked him how his visit went. Careful not to leak King's strategy, Powell simply said that his visit had gone fine. "I was out at Jim Folsom's," he added. "We had a few drinks." The comment sent the reporter rushing back to his newspaper, and news of the event raced around the state. Suddenly Folsom and Powell were being discussed in feverish tones. Their meeting loosed raging stereotypes about both men. As well as being an open supporter of the Montgomery boycotters, Powell represented everything that many white Alabamans loathed. He was from New York — worse, from Harlem — and women, white and black, looked at him approvingly. Similarly, "Kissin' Jim" Folsom had had many publicized affairs with younger women. There was a fine line in Alabama between tolerance and rage, and even Carl Elliott, the moderate congressman, said that the meeting "was unbelievable to me."

Folsom endured the firestorm, but he never quite understood how such a simple meeting had become such a powerful footnote in the state's political history. In 1958 he ran for the Senate. He lost, and he lost every other campaign he waged over the next fourteen years.

Months after Powell left Montgomery, the black citizens still had not launched their bus boycott. On December 1, Rosa Parks, a tailor's aide, boarded a city bus. When two whites got on, the driver turned to Parks and asked her to give up her seat. She refused. Her arrest launched the year-long boycott. Abyssinians sent money to help the boycotters. The movement served to catapult young Martin Luther King into the national limelight, and hastened his arrival in Adam Clayton Powell's Washington.

America remained at peace during Eisenhower's first term, but his military planners believed that by the year 1960 a military reserve unit of 2.9 million men and women would be needed. Powell could not envision a future of segregated military units, and threatened to dust off the Powell amendment. Eisenhower needed southern votes, not an antisegregation amendment, to get the reserve bill passed; 'This is no place to attach social, political, or any other kind of legislation," he said. But Powell persisted and gathered enough votes to stall the bill. "Bias Issue Blocks Reserve Program," said the *New York Times* headline. Desperate, the administration sent Vice President Nixon into Harlem to rally support. The move was nervy. Nixon's itinerary included a tour through Harlem and a dinner at which Powell was scheduled to give the opening prayer.

Julius Adams, an *Amsterdam News* reporter and a strong Dewey backer, led Nixon through Harlem. Nixon said he hoped that racial advances could be made by "persuasion rather than compulsion," a reference to the actions of Powell and his allies. Nixon, who had struck up a genial acquaintance with Martin Luther King, Jr., thought the administration's civil rights goals were gaining ground because of "a statesmanlike and temperate attitude" on the part of black leaders. Powell skipped the dinner. A telegram was sent. "Best wishes to everyone," it said, "including Vice President Nixon."

Debate about Eisenhower's military bill continued. Senator Leverett Saltonstall, the Massachusetts Republican who was his party's ranking Armed Services Committee member, was pushed to the edge in trying to explain his support for both integration and a bill that would add to the number of segregated military units. "No one believes more strongly or has worked harder than I in behalf of equal rights for every American," he told a college class in Vermont. "But I believe even more strongly that our national security is paramount to any and all other considerations." Powell enjoyed this double-talk, but his critics pointed out that his amendment might gain a victory in the House, only to lose in the Senate. He replied that as he was a representative, he would worry about the House and the House only. He told the *Washington Post* that Eisenhower was being tricked by anti–civil rights forces, and that his good deeds were in jeopardy of "being lost."

On July 3, as the House members gathered to vote on the military reserve bill, including Powell's amendment, the air, one observer noted, was charged "with the echo of the Powell challenge." These were the moments that drove Clarence Mitchell, the NAACP lobbyist into Powell's camp. When he heard Adam Clayton Powell striding down the corridors of the Capitol, heard the click of his heels, saw the large silhouette in the distance, he felt better, felt that a bill favorable to the cause of equal rights might now have a chance, and if not a chance, at least it would be talked about, aloud, on the House floor. Powell wanted to know, from both John McCormack, the Democrat, and Joseph Martin, the Republican, both leaders of the House, both Massachusetts men, how they could "walk by the monument to Crispus Attucks in Boston" and oppose his antidiscrimination amendment without shame.

Social conscience once more gave way to parochial consideration in Washington, and Powell's amendment went down to defeat. Carl Vinson, born in Georgia eighteen years after the end of the Civil War, hammered the bill through the House. "Even if unintentionally," wrote a citizen to the New York Times, Powell had performed "a genuine service by forcing the nation to stand and take thought in a matter which does reach close to all issues of individual liberty and civil rights in a democratic society." On July 14 the Senate passed the bill, eighty to one, the dissenting vote cast by North Dakota's William L. Langer. One consolation for Powell was that the reserve bill would not force reservists of integrated units to be transferred to segregated units.

Powell then turned to the administration's school construction plan. The shortage of school buildings across America had prompted Eisenhower to announce an ambitious building program. Southerners had no intention of backing the program, since the schools would have to be integrated because federal dollars were involved. As well, the Brown desegregation decision hovered over the future of all schools. HEW secretary Oveta Hobby showed up at House Education and Labor Committee hearings with a thick set of notebooks and proceeded to reel off statistics about classroom shortages. When Powell wondered aloud how the administration could build schools without an antisegregation amendment and Chairman Barden gruffly counseled him against urging "social reforms," the battle was as good as launched. Powell laid down his amendment in committee, holding the classroom bill hostage.

The West Virginia congressman Cleveland Bailey's passion for schools burned deep. Children in the hollows of his mountainous district had to crowd into dilapidated and ill-equipped schools. Forced to choose between the Powell amendment and new, but segregated, schools, Bailey, a lifelong liberal, chose the latter. "Bailey was getting older, and wanted the honor of advancement any way he could," explained Carl Elliott. At a committee debate Bailey accused Powell of trying to wreck the schools bill. "Liar," Powell called out. Sixty-nine-year-old Cleve Bailey lifted himself from his chair and charged at Powell. Powell, at least forty pounds heavier than the rail-thin Bailey, had no reason to fear him, but Bailey let loose with an uppercut, catching Powell off guard and sending him sprawling against some chairs. Several congressmen quickly rose and separated the two. They agreed that the incident would go no further, but secrets were hard to keep on Capitol Hill. Newspaper reporters got wind of the scuffle and sought Bailey out. On the House steps, the West Virginian posed like a prizefighter, with a fist balled and an arm cocked.

Debate about the school construction bill lingered for months, emotions rising throughout the summer and even into the winter. The bill's fate hung in the balance until 1956, an election year, when the issue was placed at the top of Eisenhower's domestic agenda.

Eisenhower's popularity showed no indication of waning in 1955, but he was not invulnerable to criticism. In August the Gallup Poll reported strong feelings that the president "encourages segregation." Max Rabb thought the charge ludicrous, but figured the administration had no one to blame but itself. "We have been more than tender in soft-pedaling our accomplishments," he told Sherman Adams. "Perhaps it is time to give some serious thought to this whole problem."

Once again the Powells spent the summer abroad. Skipper Powell came to recall those trips fondly — sailing across the ocean, his father getting special permission from the captain to take his son belowdecks, where Skipper stared at the machinery with wide eyes as the liner hummed across the sea; and the evenings aboard ship, where lavish black-tie dinners were accompanied by candlelight and music. The Salzburg festival in Austria was a regular treat, with the classical music of Powell's favorite German composers, such as Mozart, floating across the green parks. Wading out into knee-deep water, his father's flask filled with whiskey, Adam Powell taught his son how to read a trout stream.

While the Powells were abroad, a brutal murder took place in the American South. Emmett Till, a fourteen-year-old from Chicago, was visiting relatives in Money, Mississippi. On a dare he walked into a store, stared at a white woman, and said, "Bye, baby" as she left; some accounts allege that he whistled at her. Whatever the exact slant of his communication, the boy did not realize the gravity of it. He soon vanished, and his body was found in a river. He had been shot through the right temple, the bullet exiting from the back of his head. The murder shocked many across America; Till's mother insisted that her son's casket be open at the funeral, so the world could see. Two white suspects were acquitted in a kangaroo court by an all-white jury. "The verdict has been one of the most tremendous victories propaganda-wise for international communism," Powell said when he returned, stepping off the ocean liner *United States* with a trench-coat over his arm, his wife and son at his side. "I consider the only thing to do now is for the Department of Justice to exhaust every angle of investigation and that an emergency session of Congress be convened to enact a federal antilynching bill." Congress called no emergency session. Attorney General Brownell wanted to intervene but in the end saw no recourse through the federal court system.

Again the administration pressed its school construction bill. Joseph Martin, the House Republican leader, swung over to the Powell forces, citing the Supreme Court decision on desegregation. "I don't think you can do otherwise," he said. The columnist Walter Lippmann became incensed: "Mr. Powell is a Democrat and Mr. Martin is a Republican. They would do well not to play politics with the public schools." But the Harlem congressman was backing his fellow liberals against a wall. Arizona's Morris Udall felt the pressure and suggested a bill that would provide more money to schools that promised to make a conscientious effort to abide by the desegregation decision. Udall had waded out into that murky area of indecision that Powell abhorred, and Powell refused to take up the suggestion. Meeting in Atlantic City in February 1956, the National Education Association voted unanimously to refute the Powell amendment. Tempers continued to flare. Eisenhower finally conceded that the law of the land included the *Brown* decision, and concluded that "a vote against Powell would seem to be a vote against the Constitution." But the admission did not alter the president's stance. He wanted schools more than integration.

Powell went after southerners, vowing to attach his amendment to legislation geared to fix the prices of staples such as sugar and corn — "the lifeline of southern farmers," as he put it. He told southerners that he had taken an oath upon coming to Congress, and that he could not vote to give money to law-breaking communities that would not abide by the Supreme Court decree. "The reason he could get his amendment adopted in the House," recalled Carl Elliott, "is that so many people were afraid of Powell. See, these old southerners coming from the plantation families down here, well, they knew all the tricks. Powell didn't pay much attention to them. He was a showman. When he got his twenty or thirty minutes, the House got quiet. And he'd make the finest speech you ever heard for his side, and he'd catch that train back to New York."

When Senator John Bricker of Ohio threw his support behind a Senate amendment that resembled Powell's, liberals knew it was a devilish prank. Bricker opposed all forms of civil rights; by backing the amendment, he was in effect helping to discourage the bill's passage. Having conservatives such as Bricker suddenly in Powell's camp pained liberals. "Here is Powell with this right-wing son of a bitch," said Joseph Rauh, a lawyer for the Leadership Conference on Civil Rights. "You could support the Powell amendment only on moral grounds, not on practical grounds." And therein lay the rub for Rauh and others. "Nevertheless, on balance, I thought you had to be for the Powell amendment."

The NAACP, suspicious of jumping aboard any bandwagon guided by Powell, could not resist joining the fray in support of the amendment. The organization took out a full-page advertisement lauding it and assailing southern legislators. "It is this tight clique of legislators from eight states, not the Powell amendment group, which holds a gun at the head of the school aid bill," the advertisement said. "It is this minority which demands that it be given its candy, in the form of outlawed segregation, else the children of the forty law-abiding states shall not have their meat and vegetables in the form of badly-needed classrooms."

Southern and northern sentiments clashed fiercely in the final debate on the bill. The administration lost, but its loss was Powell's victory. No schools that extended segregation would be built with federal funds.

One thing was for sure. The Powell amendment had become such a powerful weapon that it had entered the national lexicon. Trucks would not roll to build segregated schools backed by federal monies, nor would shovels be swung. The Harlem congressman had become the amendment, and if his legislative device was not quite as powerful as a presidential veto, it was contentious enough to begin to shape the upcoming presidential election.

Meanwhile, in Montgomery the boycotters persisted. Many were being jailed. Among clergymen, Martin Luther King was the most prominent. The sight of ministers and women being herded into jail was disturbing to much of the national television audience. Powell scored the arrests as "a victory" for communism "behind the dark curtain" of Montgomery. "The arrest of my fellow clergymen," he told the White House, "is a new low in American barbarism." The administration steered clear of the Montgomery impasse, but Sherman Adams and Fred Morrow were worried. Morrow warned that Powell — a formidable "opportunist," as he put it — would reap benefits from the crisis if someone within the administration did not intervene. He urged Eisenhower to send him south as an intermediary. But Eisenhower was nervous about offending southern politicians. Morrow's plea was ignored.

Powell demanded that the White House convene a conference on the situation in Montgomery. If it did not, he said, the president would lay himself open to questions about his health (Eisenhower had earlier suffered a mild heart attack); there would be many, Powell implied, who would wonder, and be forced to conclude that the president might not be "physically fit" to run the government for another four years. Appearing on the Howard University campus, Powell told students that Eisenhower was dodging the issue in Montgomery and was guilty of "passing the buck," that he was "trying to wash his hands like Pilate of the blood of innocent men and women in the Southland."

Powell called for a National Observance Day of prayer on March 28 to bring attention to the Montgomery crisis. "We'll decide whether the Negro is ready for a spiritual movement, and if so, who would be able to lead it," he said. Randolph, Wilkins, and King — especially young King — all heard Powell's echo. Powell issued ominous warnings that he might form a third party. With that in mind, he informed his congregation that the situation in Montgomery was so bad that he might have to resign from the pulpit to devote his entire energies to desegregation work. Such announcements sent shivers through the Abyssinian congregation. It would not be the last time Powell threatened to resign; such pronouncements seemed to thrill him, and he would sit back and watch the congregation plead with him to stay.

It was with a degree of fanfare that a massive civil rights rally was staged at Madison Square Garden on May 24, 1956. Eleanor Roosevelt, A. Philip Randolph, Roy Wilkins, Adam Clayton Powell: the familiar gang of four knew the hall well, had participated in many rallies under its old roof. This rally, however, had a southern dimension. Among those prominently featured were Autherine Lucy, the first black to attend (under armed guard) the University of Alabama; Gus Courts, who had attempted to vote in Mississippi and had been shot for doing so; and Martin Luther King, Jr., fresh from the boycott. One of the more curious participants was the screen actress Tallulah Bankhead, of the Alabama Bankheads. Her father, William, had been a congressman; her uncle, John, a U.S. senator. Tallulah turned her back on Alabama, hitching herself to liberal causes and excoriating her native state in her husky voice. "Bigoted, stupid people" across the South, she told the gathering, were impeding democracy's march. The NAACP's Roy Wilkins issued a warning to the presidential contenders that they would be watched and judged as to their performance on civil rights during the campaign.

In the midst of the rally, Randolph grew nervous; Powell had yet to arrive. Many in the audience had come to hear him. Randolph sent Bayard Rustin, who found out that Powell was across the street, waiting in a hotel to make his entrance. Rustin nervously told Randolph, who realized there was nothing to do except wait and hope.

While yet another speaker, Ann Hedgeman, was at the lectern, the Garden lights clicked off. Slight tremors, a nervousness, ran through the crowd. All of a sudden a spotlight came on and zoomed to the back of the Garden, to land on a tall figure standing alone: Adam Clayton Powell. The Garden erupted; his Abyssinians erupted. And he stood there, still; then he began walking, cutting a swath right down the middle of the Garden, the spotlight trailing every step of the way. Chants exploded: "We want Adam," "We want Adam." Adam Clayton Powell, in the flesh, wanted King and Rustin and the others to remember: his New York City; his Garden.

There were sixteen thousand people gathered to hear him speak. He played the partisan crowd for all it was worth. Ike, he charged, was being double-crossed by his own staff; the administration was using every force "North and South, Republican and Democrat, to hold back democracy, to nullify the Supreme Court decision, to interpose Jim Crow between the people and equality." He went on and on, the adrenaline flowing hard and quick, until Randolph, now permanently wary of Powell on a stage, warned Rustin to get a message to Powell that he was running late. Rustin scribbled a note and walked to the lectern and laid it down for Powell to read: "Dear Adam, Mr. Randolph wants you to know two things: 1) We must be out of here by 10:30, and 2) Mrs. Roosevelt has yet to speak."

Minutes later, Powell picked the note up and read it. Then he heaved his chest out a little more, and the Harlem congressman said, "I have a note here handed me by Bayard Rustin, anyone know who he is? And he says we have to be out of here by ten-thirty. Has this Bayard Rustin never heard about freedom? The only reason we would have to leave here is because we would have to pay more money to stay. Everybody in here who is in favor of paying for our freedom raise your hands." Hands, thousands and thousands of hands, went up. "You must pay for freedom," he continued. "And if we want to stay here until noon tomorrow we will stay, and we will speak to this nation, and we will let them know that we will pay for our freedom. But Mr. Randolph, you need not worry, Abyssinian Baptist Church will pick up the check!" And he walked off, and Autherine Lucy and Martin Luther King would not forget Adam Clayton Powell when they returned south.

Randolph was stuck with the bill for the extra hours, which came to $6,000.

⁂

There was just a little mystery about the shape of the GOP presidential ticket. Eisenhower's mild heart attack had fueled rumors about his health and his commitment to a second campaign. But he recovered well and the ticket was set, with Nixon again as his running mate.

Adlai Stevenson and Estes Kefauver had traveled across the cold landscape of New Hampshire, Minnesota, and on into Iowa, scratching their way through the presidential primaries as the Democratic front-runners. Powell forced himself into the presidential debate. Stevenson and Kefauver were being hounded by questions about the Powell amendment. The amendment, and thus Powell, rattled through the campaign like an old saber.

On the presidential stump Stevenson was quoting Toynbee and, paradoxically, avoiding the issue of race, in contrast to Kefauver, who issued a plea for a sweeping federal plan that would combat mob action and ensure equal rights for all Americans. Kefauver saw no way that President Eisenhower could avoid enforcing the Constitution. Stevenson did not believe that the government should intervene in southern communities for the sake of integration. He proclaimed an "allergy to hollow promises" and claimed that too many politicians believed that "promises pay, that they are indispensable to victory, and that keeping them is far less important than making them." Asked in a meeting with a group of blacks whether he would support using federal troops to back integration efforts, Stevenson said absolutely not: "That is exactly what brought on the Civil War. It can't be done by troops or bayonets. We must proceed gradually, not upsetting habits or traditions that are older than the Republic."

That Stevenson uttered such a comment was not surprising; it had the tone of a slightly interested academic conversing on someone's verandah. That he uttered it before a group of blacks, offering honesty in lieu of passion, proved a fatal flaw in his approach to politics. He himself soon sensed his inability to connect with the liberal Democrats: "Evidently what they want to hear about is civil rights, minorities, Israel, and little else, and certainly no vague futures." Time and time again Stevenson said that he was not in favor of the Powell amendment. "I ask this question of Mr. Stevenson and his crowd," Powell said. "How can new Jim Crow schools, built in states that are defying the Supreme Court, help even gradualism?"

Stevenson twisted in the wind, Kefauver picked up steam, and Harriman staked ground as the most unyieldingly liberal candidate, though it kept moving beneath him. In Minnesota Kefauver defeated Stevenson and gained momentum, but he suffered a crucial setback when Stevenson took California and became the man to beat. Kefauver and Harriman both showed up at the Democratic convention needing huge favors and luck.

Meanwhile, Powell kept up his attacks on Eisenhower. Speaking on a radio program from Washington, he charged the president with being surrounded by "a palace guard" who were attempting to return to the "good old days of segregation." He said that administration advances in the District of Columbia and in the Veterans Administration were being threatened because segregation was returning to the military. Powell alternated his criticisms — one week for the Democrats, the next week for the Republicans — taunting both parties. Southern Republicans had hastily signed the Southern Manifesto, a bipartisan statement of dissent from the Supreme Court's desegregation ruling and Eisenhower's tabled civil rights bill. Three southern Democrats, however, refused to sign: Lyndon Johnson, of Texas, and Estes Kefauver and Albert Gore, both of Tennessee. (It was Gore who had accused the Eisenhower administration of not governing but "gazing into the fairways of indifference," a mocking reference to the golfing habits of many in the administration.)

Powell continued to baffle the administration. "We are going to shame the wrong elements of the white South so that they are going to get down on their knees and cry out, 'Oh, God, what must I do to be saved?' " he declared from a Manhattan pulpit. "Eisenhower thought Powell was hurting his own cause," recalled Herbert Brownell, who added that Eisenhower couldn't help but give Powell credit for "dramatizing it." "I guess Powell thought dramatization was more important than anything else," Brownell speculated. "He was an independent thinker."

In New York, Carmine DeSapio, who would be able to claim that he was a national power broker if he could shoehorn Averell Harriman into the White House, had grown weary of Powell and his primary-season attacks on Democratic candidates. Powell had pushed Stevenson to the wall on the segregation issue, and had all but ignored Harriman. It was not what Carmine DeSapio of Tammany Hall envisioned as loyalty. New York Democrats did not name Adam Clayton Powell a delegate to the 1956 Democratic convention, to be held in Chicago.

Powell ignored the August convention, leaving the Democrats to wrestle with their consciences. He summered, again, in Europe. It wasn't all play. He had become particularly worried about the increasing frequency with which black soldiers were charged with raping white women in European cities. In Germany he attended a rape trial, of seven black soldiers accused of raping a white girl, to show moral support, but it helped little; the soldiers received forty-year sentences.

The Democrats arrived in Chicago ready for a bruising battle among themselves. It was a convention that pitted liberal against liberal, with factions jockeying for position. No one wanted a replay of the 1948 and 1952 displays of disunity. With that in mind, the delegates adopted a new policy whereby Democratic National Committee members who did not support the ticket, or who planned to bolt, would be removed. Machine men like DeSapio rallied behind the plan.

Stevenson, victorious in the primaries, arrived in Chicago as the front-runner, but his remarks about the Powell amendment had raised questions, especially among unwavering liberals, who looked at him and saw brittleness and uncertainty. Truman questioned Stevenson's understanding of foreign policy and came to the convention as a

Harriman backer, as did Eleanor Roosevelt. But Stevenson won the nomination. Liberals felt slighted on the issue of civil rights and forced to accept a platform they thought weak. "Stevenson's position was very moderate on civil rights," recalled Joseph Rauh, who attended the convention. "I can see where Adam would have had a fit. Stevenson beat us down on civil rights." Stevenson could not decide on a running mate, and in a dramatic flourish opened the convention up to elect the vice presidential candidate. Kefauver and Massachusetts senator John Kennedy battled for the nomination. When Kennedy pulled into the lead, Albert Gore threw his delegates to Kefauver, igniting his run and putting him into the lead to stay.

Arriving back in New York City, Powell expressed a "wide-open" outlook on the November elections. He demanded meetings with Stevenson and Eisenhower. Merely the overture to the GOP candidate should have alarmed Democrats, but it didn't. Many began to wonder if Powell would dare to support a Republican ticket. *Newsweek* saw folly in such a move. "As a Democrat," the magazine wrote, "the veteran Negro congressman enjoys seniority which he'd have to give up if he left the party." Stevenson was chilly to the idea of meeting with Powell, then froze completely and refused.

At certain moments in the campaign Stevenson caught fire, but the moments were too few. He could not connect with the voters; he looked perplexed shaking hands. By trying to intellectualize the debate about the racial gap in American life, he seemed to trivialize it. Big-city machine bosses, dependent on black voter turnout, issued warnings that his attacks on the Powell amendment would backfire. But Stevenson did not believe it. Many now saw Powell, who had accused Eisenhower of being caught between two moral poles, in a similar position. If he supported Stevenson, he would be capitulating to the whims of the national Democrats and the threats of DeSapio and other Democrats in Manhattan. To support Eisenhower would be political suicide. But Adam Clayton Powell could not support Adlai Stevenson, for Stevenson sat in that gray area made comfortable by men with timid souls. A man who believed that defeat for the right reasons was better than victory for the wrong reasons was not a man to draw support from Adam Clayton Powell. Stevenson represented everything that Powell despised in a politician: the compromise, the lack of ruthlessness, the feigned liberalism. It was America, not the Harlem congressman, that was caught between two moral poles. Powell knew who Stevenson's secret critics were: big-city bosses who questioned Stevenson's commitment to and understanding of machine politics, and the true liberals, who were amazed at Stevenson's overtures to the South. They comprised the very three groups — big-city bosses, liberals, and southerners — who suffered from Powell's attacks. Backed into a corner, Powell, without consulting anyone, quickly made a decision. He had always been more of an independent than a party follower. A meeting with his old friend Max Rabb was arranged.

Rabb sat stunned, listening to Powell. Powell wanted to come out and support Eisenhower. "Are you sure?" Rabb kept asking. He also asked Powell if he was aware of the consequences. Sometimes, Powell told Rabb, "you've got to transcend the party." Rabb immediately saw wondrous possibilities. He could barely contain himself. He quickly set up a White House meeting between Powell and Eisenhower.

The two met on October 11 for thirty-five minutes. Warned in advance, reporters and photographers crowded the White House press room. Emerging from the meeting in a double-breasted suit and knit tie, cadging a cigarette from press secretary James Hagerty, Powell faced the reporters and cameras and jauntily announced his decision. He was now ready to lead a movement of "disillusioned liberal Democrats" away from Stevenson and into the Eisenhower camp.

At times Powell looked not at the reporters but at their notepads, as if he were guiding their pens and pencils across the page. They wrote furiously, then scurried to make their deadlines; the news was riveting. Many imagined that a back-room deal had been made. With the exception of Eisenhower's promise to fund — handsomely — Powell's campaign travels, because the Harlem congressman liked to travel first-class, there was no deal. On the surface, the move indeed looked dangerous for Powell, but in actuality the risks were minimal. The national Democratic Party was guided by his natural enemies. He did not fear retribution in opposing them.

Other considerations were surely anticipated by Powell. Eisenhower's popularity remained high, and America was at peace. Stevenson faced an uphill battle, and the odds were long. Many black Baptist ministers, especially in the South, were leaning toward Eisenhower and Nixon. Their positions would soften his stance. King, for instance, though silent, was leaning toward the Republican ticket.

The one Tammany trait that Powell held dear was money. For endorsements and speaking engagements he demanded money up front, and it would be no different when Republican officials mapped out his "Democrats for Eisenhower" campaign. In fact, because they were Republicans, he would rub them a little harder. They would bring the money to him, and he would tell them to bring cold cash. There were three places in Harlem where Adam Clayton Powell liked to have his money delivered, either under the guise of church business or amid the chatter of evening cocktails: his office at the Abyssinian Baptist Church, the Hotel Theresa, and a little corner booth he favored at Small's Paradise. An Eisenhower emissary delivered Powell's money to him at the bar of Small's Paradise, in a brown bag. Powell sat with Jimmy Booker, a Harlem newspaperman who dabbled in public relations work. The amount was only a portion of the $50,000 budget; the administration wanted to make sure Powell kept his commitment. (Powell being Powell, estimates of the total figure escalated, as if to validate chicanery. Fred Morrow later spread rumors that it was $100,000.)

Adam Clayton Powell could rally blacks better than any other politician in America. His itinerary included St. Louis, Baltimore, Detroit, Chicago, Cleveland, Los Angeles, and San Francisco, and he vowed he would swing votes. It was a challenging and emotional campaign. There were rumblings along the trail that Democratic officials were threatening reprisals against him in the next Congress — "if he is elected," as Emmanuel Celler angrily put it. Powell told a Cleveland audience that if he was punished in any way, it would prove that Democrats had truly "thrown away" the black vote. At a rally in Newark he vowed to keep campaigning for Eisenhower and against Stevenson, "even if it means the end of my political career." In some cities people were simply happy to see and touch him. Adoring fans crowded around him; local ministers came out to have their photographs taken alongside him; civic organizations hustled to present him with awards. Powell told a crowd of ten thousand people in Gary, Indiana, that Eisenhower's contributions in the field of civil rights had been greater than any other president's. Detroit's blacks, intensely Democratic — they had been instrumental in electing the much-admired Democratic governor, G. Mennen "Soapy" Williams — were curious about Powell's switch. "My quarrel is not with northern Democrats," he had to explain. "My quarrel is with the Dixiecrats." Powell's clout still had a profound impact on Detroit. The labor leader Walter Reuther agreed with Stevenson about not backing the Powell amendment — that is, until Detroit labor leaders, representing thousands of black voters, forced him to change his stance.

Powell was greeted by defiant picketers in Los Angeles. Police protection was heavy, and his speech was delayed for two hours. He knew better than to attack the entire Democratic Party, the Roosevelt and Truman loyalists, so he aimed his ire, again, at southern Democrats. "Anyone [like Stevenson] who is endorsed on the one hand by Eleanor Roosevelt and on the other hand by Eastland of Mississippi," he boomed, "has to be either a hypocrite, a liar, a double-talker, or a double-dealer."

Brownell and Rabb, the two members of the Eisenhower administration he knew best, came to realize just why they admired Powell so: he took such gambles, gambles that he made look like sheer gallantry, and he seemed to enjoy life as much as they sometimes enjoyed politics. Brownell had once been in Germany, at Berchtesgaden, Hitler's hideaway, and Powell was the "first person I walked into when we were sightseeing." Sherman Adams had been in Germany in 1955, near the Austrian border, in an occupied area. "One of the amenities I was given," he explained, "was the right to catch some fish. I went out to this pond. I was casting. I looked up above this dam, and who do you suppose was sitting there? Powell. He had a bottle." Adams thought Powell was something of a playboy, but also more — a cunning political operative. In Washington, in the evenings, Rabb liked watching Powell descend the Capitol steps — "he had this camel's hair coat" — because the Harlem congressman looked so alone and yet of the world at the same time. "He was feared," said Rabb. "He was a power. You knew he was there." Brownell, too, appreciated Powell's sense of independence. "He fought just as hard against Democratic leadership as Republican leadership," Brownell said. "You couldn't control Adam Clayton Powell."

Rabb and Brownell knew the more European Powell — the whiter Powell. Fred Morrow knew the Harlem Powell, the dangerous opportunist, the black Powell. Where others were charmed by Powell, Morrow kept his doubts, and his distance.

Powell had thrown the Harlem political scene into disarray. New York City officials began threatening him, and he threatened back, telling them that he liked Jacob Javits and was considering throwing his support to the GOP Senate candidate. Javits was a liberal Republican, and certainly not a timid man — Powell's kind of politician. DeSapio was furious. Powell was now predicting a 30 percent swing in the black vote from Democrat to Republican.

Toward the campaign's end, Powell landed in the haven of his own pulpit, where he needed to offer no explanation or apology. "In 1956 no one can afford to be a slave to anything — neither physical colonialism nor a mindset," he said. "Anyone who doesn't have an open mind is a slave." In and around Harlem cards were being passed out: "The Party of Eastland is the Party of Nullification, Vote Republican."

Blacks in record numbers voted for the Republican ticket in 1956, sending Eisenhower to a resounding victory. Nationwide, the president won by more than 10 million votes. More blacks voted the Republican ticket than at any time in the previous twenty-five years; the tallies made Powell seem prescient. Stevenson, in fact, never seemed to recover from his squabbling with the energetic Harry Truman, who had gone on the attack, assailing his credentials, both domestic and foreign. Democrats feared that the shift might imply a trend or, worse, might be permanent. Powell easily won re-election, much to DeSapio's dismay. And Jacob Javits was elected to the Senate.

⚬⚭⚬

Marian Anderson, beautiful and serene, sang at Eisenhower's inaugural festivities. Basil Whitener, a North Carolina congressman, took a southern friend along. When a gentleman raised Anderson's hand to his lips and kissed it, Whitener's friend said, "Well, look at that. You don't see that kind of thing back home, a white man kissing a colored woman." Whitener turned to his friend and said, "That's no white man. That's Adam Clayton Powell."

After the election, Democratic Party officials wasted no time in disciplining Powell. Two of his patronage employees were fired from jobs on Capitol Hill. "Let's put it this way," Congressman Harry Sheppard said. "The Patronage Committee is charged with taking care of Democrats. Period." The move irritated black America, especially since the House leadership had been loath to discipline the Dixiecrats in 1948. Fearful that Powell might lose his seniority, black ministers convened a conference in Philadelphia to show support. Roy Wilkins cautioned Speaker Rayburn that the party would be hurt if it punished Powell and if people believed that he was being punished because of his insistence on civil rights legislation rather than for backing the GOP ticket. Wilkins told the gruff Rayburn that the price for Powell's punishment would be heavy at future polls.

Attacks on Powell caused black Americans to ponder their own vulnerability. Debate among the civil rights hierarchy led to only one conclusion: leaders who were not in total agreement with Powell, such as Wilkins, had to come to his aid; there was little choice. Powell watched gleefully as they rallied, and offered them nothing in return for their support. "The isolated move against Powell will strengthen the national suspicion that the Southern Democrats have moved into full command of their party on Capitol Hill," the *New York Post* said in an editorial. "It will intensify Negro disenchantment with the Democratic Party." Then the paper laid a hand-wringing question on the lap of House liberals: "Will liberal Democrats accept this formula without protest? Is the Democratic Party really bent on total self-destruction?"

Powell's allies in the trenches would not forget the risks he had taken in the presidential election year. He had pinned Eisenhower, the war hero, to the wall over the issue of decent schools for black children. Then he had forced liberals to the limit. Then he had gone beyond the limit by supporting Eisenhower and striking a match to the conscience of every liberal in Washington.

～※～

At year's end, when the Powells returned from their winter vacation — in the Virgin Islands, that year — they were met with some unfortunate news. The government had announced plans to indict them on a litany of tax evasion charges. Those who imagined that Powell had backed Eisenhower to avoid the pending indictment were quickly proven wrong. The indictment was really the work of Roy Cohn and T. Coleman Andrews. Cohn had been Senator Joseph McCarthy's lawyer and had left Washington after the infamous Army-McCarthy hearings with his reputation tarnished, though it was fervently polished in right-wing and conservative circles. T. Coleman Andrews was the IRS commissioner, and had also been the States' Rights Party presidential candidate in the 1956 elections. A Virginian, Andrews owed his appointment as commissioner to the powerful Virginia senator — and segregationist — Harry Byrd. Cohn had urged Andrews to keep looking into the Powells' tax affairs; he was sure there was something there.

Herbert Brownell had his doubts about Andrews: "He was really an extremist." Before the indictment, Andrews asked Brownell to review the case. "When I looked into it," he recalled, "I didn't think there was anything to it." Brownell had been uncomfortable about the earlier tax trial against the Abyssinian church, and thought that Hattie Dodson's prison sentence was unjust. But he was loath to raise his voice. He was trying to get a civil rights bill passed; there was no room to antagonize yet another southerner, T. Coleman Andrews. Furthermore, he knew that he would not stay around for the completion of Eisenhower's second term. He was planning to return to his law practice. When conservative columnists in New York City (William F. Buckley, Jr., and George Sokolsky) drummed up the issue of Powell's possible indictment, before it had been handed down, the Justice Department found itself squeezed. "I did feel we had to bring it to trial, to dispose of the charge that we were protecting Powell," Brownell explained. "I felt the case was so small that it would appear to the black community that we were persecuting Powell."

Blacks reacted with strange silence to Powell's indictment. Perhaps it was because tax indictments of highly successful blacks had a kind of inevitability that lessened the sting; Jack Johnson, Bojangles Robinson, Joe Louis, all had problems with the Internal Revenue Service. Even Martin Luther King was incurring difficulties with his state income taxes. Powell was no different; now it was time for him to take his medicine. Resigned blacks realized that they could do little except wish him well and pray that he hired talented attorneys. Immediately claiming innocence, Powell accepted the indictment so calmly that it was the posture either of a man convinced of his innocence or of a man blindly fearless of the clout of the United States government.

The 85th Congress began its caucus meetings on January 2. Tension focused on two representatives: John Bell Williams, a Mississippi Democrat who had refused to support Stevenson and thrown his support to the Dixiecrat candidacy of T. Coleman Andrews, and Adam Clayton Powell. The debate grew bitter, and for Rayburn, it was dangerous. If he were to discipline Powell and not Williams, he would leave himself open to obvious charges. Black ministers once again rallied on Powell's behalf, arranging a meeting with Rayburn, where they warned of dire consequences if Powell was punished. There would be no purges, Rayburn announced, quieting worry in the black community.

There was a new member of the Education and Labor Committee, George McGovern, of South Dakota. Gaining an additional member gave liberals on the committee — particularly Powell (although he was wary of upsetting the seniority system), Lee Metcalf, Frank Thompson, and Carl Elliott — an opportunity to demand that Barden form subcommittees to do research for education legislation. Barden hated subcommittees and never allowed them to be formed, but now, sensing growing antagonism to his leadership, he created five. As the most senior member on the committee next to Barden, Powell was expected to chair one of the subcommittees. Little did he know that Barden and the others had struck a deal: no subcommittee would be given to Powell, because members were afraid he would add the Powell amendment to legislation.

However, discussions were going on behind Barden's back to undercut his powers as committee chairman. "I couldn't go along with them on that," recalled Carl Elliott, who was eventually given the subcommittee due to Powell. "I had faith in the seniority system." The liberals were paying Powell back for forcing their hand. Powell was angry, but committee members did not try to console him. He turned to the Eisenhower administration for help, but it told him there was nothing it could do.

Powell's infighting with the committee was interrupted in early 1957 by his interest in foreign affairs. He wanted to go to Ghana to partake in that nation's independence celebrations. The ceremony carried spiritual significance for American blacks, who imagined that their destiny was attached to Africa's, Africa's freedom was an echo of their own. The administration owed Powell favors; he thought it time to collect. He was in no mood for another Bandung-like episode. Martin Luther King, Jr., who had developed a cordial relationship with Vice President Nixon, had already made plans to attend the celebrations, and Powell, the northern minister, was not about to be upstaged by King, the southern minister.

The White House came up with several ideas for Powell, the most unusual of which had him traveling as an aide to Nixon. Sam Rayburn squashed that idea. Max Rabb, who felt that the administration owed Powell, grew worried. He confided to Sherman Adams that "anyone who goes to bat for us in the future will know that he will be heavily penalized and that we will not be able to help him." Conscious of sentiments in the black community, the administration knew it had to acknowledge at least one of the three black congressmen in office, even though all three were Democrats. William Dawson steered clear of explicitly black affairs and Rayburn opposed Powell, so the administration turned to Charles Diggs, the Detroit congressman. Fred Morrow went as Nixon's personal aide. The American delegation, headed by Nixon, departed on February 28.

At an outdoor cocktail party in Accra, Fred Morrow looked up and was astonished to see a figure in a white dinner jacket, drink in hand, walking toward him. It was Adam Clayton Powell. "He was prancing around, meeting everyone," Morrow remembered. A chat with Mrs. Nixon; small talk with A. Philip Randolph and Lester Granger, of the National Urban League, and of course King; drink being switched from one hand to the other, the huge hand extended — Powell greeted everyone in sight. He had come to Ghana on his own, and drew attention everywhere he went. At another outdoor affair, he was dressed in a white linen suit and an ascot.

At the independence ceremony, Powell stood in downtown Accra with Congressman Diggs and watched the British flag being lowered and the Ghanaian flag raised, the green and black colors of Africa going up, he and Diggs with "tears streaming down our faces," as Diggs recalled. Adam Clayton Powell had long spoken of African nations and their links to American aspirations. What he had witnessed at Bandung was flourishing before his eyes here in Africa: Third World independence. It all sharply contrasted with events taking place back in the American South: a wave of bombings, attacks on synagogues and churches, the arrest and jailing of ministers and children.

〜✺〜

In 1957 the White House was besieged with appeals to do something about increasing southern violence. Eisenhower pointed to his pending civil rights bill — a bill that many liberals had already attacked as too weak. Eleanor Roosevelt, who used her newspaper column, "My Day," to espouse liberal causes, assailed Eisenhower — and Adam Clayton Powell. Her passions never wavered from those of the proven liberals in the Democratic Party, and she could not fathom the political eccentricities of Powell, who she believed was playing a "dangerous game" by making promises to blacks on behalf of the Eisenhower administration. "Rep. Powell would do a more effective job if he would get behind some of the other people who propose amendments that have a chance of passing," she wrote.

Back on American soil, Powell appealed to Eisenhower to make a speech condemning the violence: "Not behind the iron curtain, but within the United States, men of God are being arrested, houses of worship are being bombed, and American citizens are continually meeting with physical violence." Powell reminded Sherman Adams that he had gone out on a limb for the administration and now was subject to "bitter criticism" in his district, "among Negroes," and, of all people, by Eleanor Roosevelt.

Greeted with White House silence, Powell saw no recourse but to go south himself, into the quagmire. Addressing a group of ministers (some of whom had recently been arrested) at an April rally in Atlanta, he predicted that equality for blacks — "this day of destiny" — would occur between 1963 and 1965. On that claim he proved prescient; not so when he told the audience that the domination of Congress by Republicans and Dixiecrats was ending. He scorned southern white political leaders for their program of gradualism. "Go slow" was merely a code, he said, for "stop, stand still, do nothing."

The triumvirate of King, Wilkins, and Randolph had tried not to deal with a creature so nakedly political as Adam Clayton Powell. Straining to see the minister in him, they too often saw only the wicked politician. But now the three needed Powell, who was alone among powerful blacks in having access to the White House. They were threatening another march on Washington and wanted Powell to get them in to see Eisenhower. They invited him to attend a planning meeting on April 5.

In the White House, Max Rabb was nervous about a march, so he asked Powell to let him know what happened at the meeting. He then told Sherman Adams why the meeting was making him so nervous: "We are getting too firm a hold on the friendship of Negroes to risk the damaging effects of a spectacular effort designed to criticize the President." Sitting in on the meeting with a dual purpose — to participate, and to observe and report back to Rabb — Powell lobbied against a march and recommended instead a day of observance in honor of the *Brown* v. *Board of Education* anniversary. His position was backed by Clarence Mitchell of the NAACP, and it struck a chord. Rabb enthusiastically reported to Adams that Powell had changed the "entire character" of the meeting. The march was now a prayer pilgrimage. Of course, the White House still was not free of worry. "There is always the possibility that a prayer pilgrimage cannot be kept under control," Rabb told Adams.

Because the administration had allowed Powell through its doors, it had to suffer his criticisms. During an Easter sermon before his congregation, Powell said that it was "inexcusable" that Eisenhower hadn't spoken out about violence against blacks in the South, and that "we need leaders who will not excuse themselves from acting on inconsistencies in our society." The iron curtain was one thing, he said, but "let us look behind our own curtain."

Beneath the granite shadow of the Lincoln Memorial, the prayer pilgrimage took place on May 17. A crowd of between twenty-five and thirty thousand people gathered — southern and northern, black and white, young and old. Newsmen with cameras crowded the podium during each speaker's appearance. King spoke. Randolph spoke. Gospel hymns filled the air. Those who didn't trust the cagey Powell, among them now as both spy and legend, could not deny his sheer power. In a gray double-breasted suit (King wore his minister's robes), hair blowing in the wind, an American flag just behind his right shoulder, his face and mouth contorting, he preached and thundered, crying, "We are sick and tired of the two-party hypocrisy!" He called for boycotts and sit-ins, sweeping his logic up in international relevance: "Asia and Africa will never trust America, because they know we're ruled by a hypocritical bipartisan Jim Crow policy." Again he spoke of forming a third party. This was not his affair; he had come simply to prove his mettle against the array of southern preachers. So now he thundered with a passion drawn from both anger and distance. He was a political animal, trusting no one save himself; Harlem had taught him always to be on guard.

It should have cut deep, but didn't, when Fred Morrow issued ominous warnings to the White House about inaction on the civil rights front. Morrow told Adams that "the rank and file of Negroes" felt the administration had "deserted" them and warned of widespread unrest. He suggested that Eisenhower meet with "two or three outstanding Negro leaders" immediately.

As for Powell, he kept up his busy schedule. One Friday he arrived in New York City and proceeded to do the following: give a speech at a dinner affair, sit for a television interview, confer with his church trustees, deliver a sermon before a prayer group, and lay a crown on a beauty queen's head. Overworked, he fell ill in the pulpit and was rushed to the hospital, leaving parishioners frightened that he had had another heart attack, which he hadn't. Dr. Aaron Wells, Powell's physician, blamed his exhaustion on stress. The doctor suggested rest. Powell took his advice and departed for Europe.

After nearly two years of debate, Eisenhower's civil rights bill was positioned for a vote during Powell's absence. A. Philip Randolph urged an outright veto. The baseball legend Jackie Robinson, a Republican, held a similar view. "We disagree that half a loaf [is] better than none. Have waited this long for bill with meaning — can wait a little longer," he told the White House. "I am for the whole loaf," said an NAACP board director. The bill practically flew through the House, with fingerprints of Dixiecrats all over it. Senator Lyndon Johnson, now the majority leader, led the bill's passage through the Senate, arm-twisting and cajoling his fellow senators. But Eisenhower lost a crucial voting rights amendment to the Dixiecrats, and blacks were forced to settle for half a loaf. Following the vote, Fred Morrow could sense the anger. Blacks were being forced to accept a bill that gave only "lip service to democratic ideals," he told his superiors. Blacks did not know whether to cry or to celebrate, and for the most part kept a studied silence.

Floating home aboard a steamer, Powell felt vindication and a need to celebrate. This was the reward for supporting Ike in 1956. "After eighty years of political slavery, this is the second emancipation," he proclaimed. He lauded King's planned voter registration drive: "I will assist him by sending in expert political workers to aid in this effort. I personally will come South anywhere and at any time as needed, as I did to spark the Montgomery bus boycott." In anticipation of his arrival stateside, Powell gave politicians of all stripes fair warning: "Negroes must not ally themselves with or think in terms of either party, but should concentrate on the issues and the position of the candidates in relationship to these." And he warned that it was time for "big-city northern Democrats to do some painful soul-searching."

Before Powell stepped off his ocean liner, school bells across America had already begun to ring for fall classes in 1957, and the ineffectiveness of Eisenhower's civil rights bill was quickly realized. In Little Rock, Arkansas, nine black students tried unsuccessfully to integrate Central High School. Orval Faubus, the Arkansas governor, who was running for a third term, opposed integration. The White House warned Faubus that he was disobeying the law of the land. Faubus listened, then called out the National Guard to ring the school building. The White House applied pressure. Scenes of the school-children, with their study materials in their hands, being forbidden to enter the school — being stopped, in fact, by armed guards — engrossed the nation.

Powell picked up news of the event while at sea. Upon debarking, he demanded a meeting with Eisenhower to discuss the situation. "I have just returned from Europe, where American prestige is at its lowest ebb," he said. The president, vacationing in Newport, agreed to see him but set no date.

The emotions building across the United States forced Eisenhower to send troops, no-nonsense paratroopers from Kentucky's Fort Campbell, to protect the children in Little Rock as they went to school. Angry crowds taunted the soldiers, who were armed with rifles and bayonets. They butted heads; the children walked a cruel gauntlet. Senator Richard Russell assailed Eisenhower for sending in the troops. "I must say that I completely fail to comprehend your comparison of our troops to Hitler's storm troopers," Eisenhower told Russell, explaining that "in one case military power was used to further the ambitions and purposes of a ruthless dictator; in the other, to preserve the institutions of free government."

Many waited for news of Powell's meeting with Eisenhower, now designed to include other civil rights leaders as well. A month passed and the meeting still had not taken place. "This is giving aid and comfort to the enemies of democracy," Powell impatiently said to the White House. Unbeknown to him, Roy Wilkins had urged against holding the meeting in the aftermath of the Little Rock crisis. Wilkins feared Powell's political agenda; so did the White House. The meeting was delayed.

⟨∾∾⟩

Skipper Powell had an appreciation of his parents' prowess in public life, yet no matter how busy they were, they doted on him when they were around. "The amazing thing was that every Saturday they would be back at home," he recalled. On Saturday mornings father and son would rise early and wax the Jaguar (if mother had had a concert the night before, she would sleep late, with father and son's blessings). Afternoons, there would be games of touch football on the lawn, Hazel tossing the ball as well, "much to my mother's agent's horror." Then there would be a trip to the Parkway Theater; "They would sit right through those kiddie shows, Abbott and Costello." Evenings, they would end up at Sardi's. Nights, after dinner, back home, father and son would descend into the basement to polish their shoes for the next morning's church service. "I remember his study always smelled of pipe tobacco," Adam III said. "He had twenty, thirty pipes." Books lined the walls of Powell's study; there were several pairs of eyeglasses lying around. He rarely wore them in public — too vain. A huge globe dominated the room. Often father would point out to son the countries he was about to visit. And often, early on Sunday morning, around 4 A.M., Skipper would hear noise in his father's study. It was his father, working on his sermon.

But there was another side to Rev. Adam Clayton Powell, one that his family never saw and that he exercised on weekends when his family duties were not pressing. In the 1950s he began slipping into Greenwich Village on weekends to attend "beard" parties, Manhattan affairs where discretion was all, where men and women were matched up beneath chandeliered light. There would be chatter, then dinner, then privacy for the matched couples. The intrigue was the mystery: you never knew who your mate was married to, and if by chance you did, you were not supposed to mention it; in essence, you pretended you wore a beard.

Powell was sexually voracious. The women he was seen with — black one weekend, white the next — had little in common, except they were always gorgeous. "He was a man of great appetites," remembered Doris Gamser, a witness. She recalled how overwhelmed dinner-party guests would be when there was a knock on the door, and the door was opened, and in strolled Powell, who immediately began looking around the room for his prey. "He was overwhelming because he had such presence," she explained. "He was marvelous. He was quite a figure of a man. There was a mystery to him. There was an alertness, a penetrating gaze."

Doris Gamser was the young and attractive wife of Howard Gamser, a Greenwich Village labor lawyer who later went to Washington to work for Powell. She had never seen anyone quite like the congressman. When she went down to Washington, still very much a southern city in the 1950s, starkly different from New York (and especially from bohemian Greenwich Village), she would see the old southern congressmen in their suits and suspenders and straw hats, and she would see Powell, in his bright suits, and she would think to herself that his suits were as dramatic as the southern congressmen's suits, if not more so. "It was almost as if he took on the southern plantation gentlemen," she said. "It was dramatic." The "beard" parties were perfect for a married man such as Powell, who treasured his privacy. "Those of us who loved him respected that privacy," Gamser explained.

In the 1950s Mike Wallace had a hot New York City television show called *Nightbeat,* on which he interviewed Manhattan celebrities. Sometimes he kept company with those celebrities, among them

Adam Clayton Powell and Hazel Scott. "They were stars, not only in the black world but the white world," he said. "That was extraordinary." But Wallace saw what others saw: Powell roaming the Manhattan nights, sometimes alone, sometimes with a woman who was not Hazel. "I think just about every woman, black or white, was game for Adam," he pointed out, adding, "First of all, he was smart. And attractive, suave, daring, and gallant with women. His color really was golden. There was a kind of golden hue to it."

Paul Klein, who had been sent to Washington to work on the FEPC in 1949, had been told to avoid socializing with Powell, but he found himself pulled into Powell's web and became his Man Friday. On weekends the two would zip up to Manhattan (Klein, like Powell, owned a Nash Healey) and slide in and out of the swank supper clubs and nightspots. One of their favorite haunts was Sardi's. "He liked the show crowd," recalled Klein, whose parents owned an extravagant Central Park West apartment, where the likes of Langston Hughes and the singer Josh White were often seen. From Sardi's, Klein and Powell would be off to "21" or the Stork Club or Toots Shor's. Through Hazel, Powell had become a jazz aficionado. One of the more peculiar Adam Powell habits that Klein witnessed was his trait of hearing a good joke at one place — say, the Stork Club — then arriving at another club — "21" — and retelling it in an original fashion, as if the punchline had actually happened to him.

Klein found the whole scene a kaleidoscope of flings, Powell not so much wooing women — "all shades of black, white, an occasional Oriental" — as being wooed by them. One night in Chicago, after he and Powell entered a nightclub and took seats, the waiter came to tell Powell that a lady in the corner wanted to send him a drink over. "He had this exciting presence," explained Klein. In time Klein began to worry about the women, the conquests, and gave Powell's nightlife a Freudian spin, wondering if Powell's huge sexual appetite for women shielded a latent homosexuality. But surrounded by so many beautiful women on so many beautiful, jazzy nights, Klein dismissed his pop-psychology analysis as airily as he had come up with it. He only needed to stay close to Powell; he sometimes bedded the women in whom the congressman showed no interest. "I have to admit it didn't do too much for my ego," said Klein.

Rumors floated back to Hazel Scott. Some nights she would be playing piano in Manhattan and hear that Powell was in town, without her knowledge. After the show, recalled Wesley Carter, one of her friends, she would grab her fur, fling it across her arm, and leave in a fury. At other times she had only to pick up the daily newspapers and look at the gossip columns, which linked her husband with yet another woman. "He always told her the gossip columnists were out to get him," recalled Klein. But the infidelities hurt Scott. A discreet woman, she had married an indiscreet man. To sit in a pew in the Abyssinian Baptist Church Sunday after Sunday was to risk seeing one woman after another who had been personally invited to hear her husband preach, so Hazel's appearances in church began to taper off. Friends sensed marital discord. There were fewer and fewer soirées on the Powells' Westchester lawn.

The 1950s were not particularly kind to Hazel Scott. Work began to dry up, doubtless because of her testimony to the HUAC regarding her associates in radical musical circles. She remained a popular party guest, however. During a party on Long Island, where guests had scattered through the manse, she ended up with other guests in a bedroom where conversation was still going on. Her dress was cut out in the back. While she was standing, a woman who had been sprawled on the bed got up on her knees and began licking her back. "Honey," Scott said, "if you're doing that for yourself, fine; if it's for me, a little lower and faster, please."

Constantly challenged by the weight of race, she began to wish for simple freedom. She sued a Spokane diner that refused to serve her, and won a token judgment; the victory was in the judgment itself, not the monetary award. She began to close her shows with "Freedom Suite," an ode to human and civil rights that she had written herself. And once Hazel Scott walked into a Greenwich Village nightspot not to perform, just for a drink. Oddly enough, her escort on that occasion was Paul Klein, who knew her husband's secrets. They had drinks. When Klein reached for the bill, she glanced at it and became enraged. Klein could not figure out who or what she was angry about, the bartender or the huge bill, but he knew she thought the bartender was either trying to clip her or send a message that he didn't like to serve a white man and a black woman together. Scott called the bartender over, raised what remained of her last drink to his eye level, and poured the drink onto the bar. "You tell the owner that Hazel Scott pisses in his mother's milk." Then she stalked out.

Scott was, however, one of the first blacks to get work in Las Vegas, along with Sammy Davis, Jr., and Nat King Cole. She took her pride to the desert. A gangster — at the time she didn't know he was a gangster — once spotted her in a Las Vegas lounge, relaxing. "Get out of here," the gangster said. Scott wouldn't budge. "What are you going to do, kill me?" she replied. "What's so fucking great about living?" Bugsy Siegel left the proud woman alone.

When her marriage deteriorated beyond repair early in 1957, Hazel Scott moved to Paris, taking her son with her. She rented an apartment at 80, rue de Miromesnil, and became an expatriate. The Parisians adored her; she became a popular attraction at the world-famous Blue Note. Her French — a touchy issue with Parisians — was nearly flawless. American musicians liked to stop by her apartment and enjoy her soul food (ham hocks and collard greens, never easy to get in Paris) and flavorful West Indian dishes. "Everybody got a kick out of going to her place for dinner," recalled the trumpeter Buck Clayton. Sometimes the musicians talked about their favorite songs; "My Heart Belongs to Daddy" was one of Scott's favorites. "It was a song about a young girl," said Clayton, "who wouldn't do anything wrong with her man, who was older than she was."

Raised among artists, Hazel Scott treated creative people with deference. Cast members from the Comédie-Française stopped by; African students became friends, and many were invited to her home. Skipper Powell, now nearly as tall as his father, came home from his Paris school to find strangers in the apartment: James Baldwin, Artie Shaw, Max Roach, Buck Clayton, Dizzy Gillespie (Hazel loved to scoop up his beret and wear it around the apartment), Mary Lou Williams — his mother's friends, who became his friends. Scott appeared in French films, played the huge resort hotels, was escorted along the Champs-Elysées by handsome young Frenchmen. She did not miss America. Marian Javits, Jacob Javits's wife, had always thought that Scott was temperamental and angry, but then she ran into her in Paris. "In Paris she was happy," Javits remembered. "The chip wasn't there."

Scott's music changed noticeably. It became more serene. There was less of lending a boogie-woogie tilt to the classics; that had all been for curious white patrons who wanted something freakish. A mellowness came over her music. Her album *Hazel Scott — Relaxed Piano Moods,* which featured Charlie Mingus on bass and Max Roach on drums, was quiet, particularly "Peace of Mind" and Gershwin's "A Foggy Day in London Town."

Movies continued to interest her — the pay was good — and while she was in Paris she had a chance to play opposite Sidney Poitier, Paul

Newman, and Joanne Woodward in *Paris Blues*. It was about two jazz musicians — artists — struggling with everyday life and romance. As Poitier's love interest, Scott would play straight drama. She welcomed such a stretch, but the role eventually went to Diahann Carroll, a more experienced film actress. Hollywood had typecast Scott and she knew it: "Once you've played the priest, you can never play the gangster."

At times European reporters hounded Scott and asked about Powell, citing the latest report about him and another woman. She usually resorted to a stock answer, pointing out that since Powell was not homosexual, it was to be expected that he would chase after women. She was adept at the cutting comment; it masked hurt. She pleaded with the press to leave her alone. It was obvious that the marriage of Hazel Scott and Adam Clayton Powell, a marriage that had been so strong that at times it had seemed to represent nothing less than democracy itself, was over, and divorce was inevitable. Friends of both later swore they had seen it coming, blaming it all on the clash of two titanic personalities and virtually dismissing Powell's infidelities, which tore at the couple's bond.

V

THE GLORY

1957–1963

ADAM CLAYTON POWELL drove home to his fellow Education and Labor Committee members the point that America's educational needs remained unmet, that unequal education was bad for the entire country, by pointing to the cosmos. Immediately after the Russians launched Sputnik in October 1957, hysteria swept the United States. Many concluded that if the Russians could invade space, their technology must be superior to America's; their children must be smarter, their schools better. Politicians could ill tolerate the perceived gap. Senator Stuart Symington wanted to convene a special session of Congress to discuss the *beep beep beep* from space. The administration wasn't convinced that it had to worry about Sputnik; Sherman Adams believed that the event was little more than the Russians "playing basketball in outer space." Senator William Fulbright, however, thought the administration's inaction "disturbingly small-minded."

Adam Clayton Powell flew to Michigan to address a mass rally. Louis Martin, his old friend, picked him up at the Detroit airport. "The church was packed," recalled Martin. "People were hanging from the rafters." It fell to Harlem's congressman to elucidate Sputnik for the common people, for those whose children were attending segregated schools, for those at this rally in this Detroit church. In the pulpit, looking out at the masses in the balcony, in the recesses of the church, Powell announced that he indeed knew what the *beep beep beep* that was coming from the sky was. "All of America is trying to decipher the meaning of that noise," he told them. "I'm the only American that knows! That *beep beep beep* means that the walls of segregation are starting to come down! Jim Crow has got to go!" His spreading, thundering voice raised them to their feet, pew by pew, balcony to balcony. He had done what Louis Martin and Detroit congressman Charles Diggs, also in attendance, knew he could do: couple space technology with the plight of black Americans.

Powell shook hands, then reminded Martin that he had to go, couldn't linger; always in a rush. "All the ladies were excited when he showed up — ladies of both colors," Martin remembered. Later, in the car, speeding to the airport with Martin behind the wheel and the cold October wind whipping, Powell pulled a bottle out. Martin looked once, then, trying to keep his eyes on the road, again. It was a half-bottle of Scotch. The speech had gone so well, the crowd had been so huge, that Powell insisted that Martin share a nip with him. Martin couldn't resist the Harlem congressman: "He was a crazy guy."

Graham Barden, the incumbent Education and Labor chairman, was unmoved by Sputnik. He considered it beneath American dignity to attempt to duplicate a Russian feat. But Barden could not ignore the excitement of certain committee members. When Carl Elliott heard of Sputnik, he was traveling, trying to drum up support for education legislation; the news sent him rushing back to Washington. Led by Elliott, the committee pushed through the National Defense Education Act. "We had slipped the key in the lock," he recalled. The act enabled the government to provide loans to those who wanted to go to college. The idea was indeed novel, and the act the first of its kind. It did not, however, address the issue of education and race. The availability of government money did not ensure that a black student could gain admission to southern universities. Powell took little comfort in Elliott's inspired legislation, and vowed to meet up with the southerners on the issue another day.

With a midterm election looming, Powell decided to inch his way back into the Democratic fold. Herbert Brownell had left Eisenhower's administration at the beginning of his second term, and no one else in the White House espoused civil rights as vigilantly as he had. Powell had lost a favored ally. It was not a question of whether the Democrats would accept him; few Democrats in the country could expose the administration's weaknesses in such a scintillating fashion as he could. The administration he had once lifted up, he would now go about tearing down.

He began by predicting "another Little Rock" if more amendments were not added to the civil rights bill. That January Martin Luther King had confided to him that Nixon had promised King, while in

Ghana, to convene a meeting of government officials to attack discrimination in federal programs. "Seven months have gone by since that conference, and the government contract compliance committee has not even crossed the Potomac," Powell told the administration. He painted a bleak picture of the Russian advance in technology and the dispirited civil rights environment, and he warned that "time is not on our side."

At a February 6 press club meeting in Washington, Powell said that the administration needed to be pressured because of its "broken promises." There were not enough liberals in either party, he lamented, to forge the kind of consensus needed on civil rights. The only route now was to create a "holy alliance" of liberals from both parties. Powell had gone the remaining distance in severing his ties with Eisenhower. The split was inevitable.

Powell's shift pained the president. "Here's a man that's got everything," Eisenhower told Fred Morrow. "He's handsome, he's brilliant. But goddammit, he's tricky."

⟨◦⟩

Meanwhile, Governor Averell Harriman was sitting in Albany plotting moves for the presidential campaign of 1960, confidently looking past the 1958 gubernatorial race. From Albany one could understandably dream of Washington, as FDR had done. For Harriman, age was advancing, and if he was to cap his golden résumé, there was only one job that remained in America: the presidency. Of course, a Democratic victory would need a strong showing in the Northeast. In looking ahead, Harriman was nervous, and with reason. He had won his first governor's race by a scant eleven thousand votes. He had allies, among them Herbert Lehman and Eleanor Roosevelt. But Roosevelt was torn between the reform and the regular Democrats — emotional about the former, realistic about the latter. Powell's allegiance was to neither group. Roosevelt told Carmine DeSapio to do something about Powell, to get him in line with Tammany's ambitions.

In Washington, the old guard was now laughing at Tammany Hall. Tammany had lost much of its power; it was no longer comparable to the huge political machine in Chicago. DeSapio planned to change all that, but first he had to get rid of Powell. "DeSapio decided Adam had been a congressman too long," explained Robert Seavey, a clubhouse lawyer at the time.

When the rumors of a Tammany challenge began circulating, Powell made his way to Harlem. "I dare them," he said of the plot, prancing before his congregation. "If they buck me for re-election, then there will not be a Democratic governor in Albany next year." The possibility of a knockdown intramural fight in his own district, pitting him against Tammany Hall in a race where the winner would be declared solely by the voters, greatly excited him. It had been years — years! — since he had engaged in a hard-fought campaign. In some years he ignored campaigning completely; in others he campaigned merely to raise money — for himself. "When those old ladies press those dollar bills into Adam's hand, they're not giving that money to the NAACP — they're giving it to Adam" is how an NAACP staffer put it.

In order to stop DeSapio, who would have to rally the black district leaders in Harlem, Powell had to split the black forces, turning voters against the district leaders before the district leaders could turn the voters against him. DeSapio didn't realize how difficult the latter would be. Powell would not only pit black against black, black against white, Harlem against Tammany Hall, Republican against Democrat, but he would pit the Abyssinian Baptist Church against everyone who listened to Tammany Hall. Powell's game plan involved confusion, but beautiful confusion.

His first order of business was to evaluate the GOP candidates challenging Harriman in the governor's race. Oddly, Harriman considered his gubernatorial re-election a minor challenge; but Powell knew better. Jacob Javits, who had supported Powell in his clashes with the New York City Police Department, was Powell's friend as well as a candidate; Nelson A. Rockefeller represented a more realistic candidacy, and he was dangerous to Harriman. He had name recognition and he had money. He was a Republican, but his bent lay in the liberal direction. Like Harriman, Rockefeller had presidential ambitions. If Rockefeller made it to Albany, Averell Harriman was finished.

Adam Clayton Powell warned Harriman and the Tammany forces that they could lose at least twenty thousand gubernatorial votes by challenging him. A Republican challenge from Rockefeller, he predicted, would be nothing less than "the beginning of the end" of the Democratic Party in Harlem. Rockefeller or Javits might well win New York State with or without Harlem.

DeSapio was livid over Powell's intrusion in state politics. In mid-May he summoned his district leaders to determine Powell's fate. The click of heels of powerful men echoed down the hallways at Tammany headquarters at 331 Madison Avenue. Carmine DeSapio knew well what he wanted. To defeat Powell was to control Harlem; his reach would go deep into the Harlem tenements. It was little more than a ceremonial meeting; DeSapio had already made up his mind. "De-Sapio called us all in there," said Lloyd Dickens, one of the leaders, "and sat there and said they had to get someone else to run. Funny thing, they hadn't even selected anyone. They were just against Adam." DeSapio went around the table, asking for each one's position. "Put Adam out," came a voice; then another voice, "Put Adam out"; then another voice, the same litany. Then DeSapio came to Lloyd Dickens. Dickens, of course, went back with Adam Clayton Powell, to the days when Powell first began his climb. "I'm for Adam," he said. The others turned away from him. The vote was eleven to one.

Tammany had its enemy; now it needed a challenger. Thurgood Marshall, the NAACP lawyer, turned them down; he and Powell, he said, were fighting "for the same thing." City councilman Earl Brown was approached, as were state senator James Watson and Bessie Buchanan, a former Cotton Club dancer turned assemblywoman. All said no. FDR Jr. was considered — his last name carried cachet in Harlem — but the appeals made to him were weak. Mayor Robert Wagner remained clear of the fray. Elijah Crump, leader of the twelfth district, had the stamina to take to the stump and expressed interest. Powell recalled Crump to a group of Harlemites: "When Crump first came to Harlem, he didn't have any shoes on his feet and he didn't have any teeth in his mouth. Well, I gave him money to buy shoes and I gave him money to buy teeth for his mouth. Now look at him. Now he's trying to kick me in the ass and bite me in the back." Crump never recovered from Powell's devastating wit.

Tammany suddenly looked like a toothless tiger. Hulan Jack, the Manhattan borough president — it was largely a ceremonial position, although he received notice as the first black in America to gain such a position — was mentioned. Jack had risen through patronage, along with several other West Indians in Harlem. A Tammany man through and through, he was a lackluster campaigner. He began thinking twice about the idea. "If Jack refuses this challenge," Powell said, "whoever runs is simply running as Jack's stooge candidate."

Black district leaders looked to J. Raymond Jones, who had arrived in Harlem as a little boy, a stowaway aboard ship from a Caribbean island. Unable to gain admission to Tammany's Irish-dominated clubs in the 1920s, he had begun working uptown, in Harlem, in black political clubs. Jones, a beefy man, was rarely without his cigar. He was kind to underlings, dropping bits of wisdom, and canny enough to be given the name "the Fox." He was out of the Tammany spotlight now, working a patronage job for a judge downtown. Sometimes bored in the judge's chambers, he would stroll up to the roof, where he tended a little garden. Powell, as usual, was quicker than Tammany. He enlisted Jones as his own campaign manager. Jones was eager to cut his links (for the time being) to Tammany Hall. "If you know politics, you have no friends or enemies," he once said.

Powell began denigrating the black leadership in Harlem, telling one newcomer that it was "at the lowest ebb" he had seen in years. The congressman talked of forming a new alliance, of liberals and young ministers, to take on Tammany, to rid Harlem of its second-class citizenship. Campaigning against an unnamed opponent, he sought out the Puerto Ricans (his Spanish was rudimentary), and he sought out the West Indians (they remembered his West Indian wife, Hazel Scott), and he sought out the radical Republicans, and he went after the businessmen. He told them all about their stake in the American dream, explaining that he was down in Washington doing the tough work, taking on the Dixiecrats, and in order to continue that battle he had to do business with Tammany Hall. He formed a bipartisan Greater New York Leadership Council of businessmen — Tammany businessmen. It was Powell, he reminded them, who worked in Washington — not Carmine DeSapio.

On May 8, however, the anti-Powell forces received an emotional boost. The government finally handed down its tax indictment, on three counts, against Adam Clayton Powell. Dunbar S. McLaurin, one of Powell's allies, felt that the indictment was an attempt to attack "independent Negro leadership." Powell said little in response to it and merely looked about for an attorney.

On the Sunday after he was indicted, Powell was scheduled to preach two sermons at his church. It was Mother's Day. He did not show up. Overflow crowds poured into the church, trailed by reporters. "Let the poor man alone; go home now," a stylishly dressed woman urged a group of reporters. From church to church across the New York region, from Staten Island to Brooklyn, Mount Vernon to Harlem, sermons were preached that Sunday in support of Powell. The Abyssinian congregation issued a spirited statement: "We call on

he religious community to stand with us and to offer constant prayers
o Almighty God that his enemies may be confounded so that he can
:ontinue to fight wherever God gives him an opportunity for the rights
)f common men."

The assistant minister, David Licorish, delivered the Mother's Day
;ermons at Powell's church. Licorish, who was strongly devoted to
Powell, was not a man given to eloquence, and sometimes the words
flew from his mouth too fast for the congregation to comprehend
:hem. But when his minister was in trouble, he did not lack his own
fire. "As we near the promised land, evil forces are organized against
our leadership," he told the crowd. "But there is a restlessness in
Harlem."

Powell launched his campaign against Tammany Hall not from his
church and not from a Harlem street corner but from the federal
courthouse, where he had gone to plead not guilty to the tax charges.
Dressed in a long black-buttoned trenchcoat caught at the neck, and
flanked by two attorneys, Harrison Jackson and Edward Bennett Williams, he was trailed up the steps by nameless men in hats, adoring
fans, and clicking cameras. He brought power and danger with him.
He vowed to take on DeSapio for trying to purge him, vowed to unite
blacks and Puerto Ricans in their political ambitions, and picked up
$275 in campaign contributions. "God bless you," someone scrawled
on one of the contributions. "We will dump Tammany," he declared
before taking off.

Powell now began reminding voters that he was not just any congressman; seniority was on his side. He had spent thirteen years in
Congress; real power was within his grasp.

On May 17 the NAACP held a rally to commemorate the fourth
anniversary of the *Brown* v. *Board of Education* decision. Harlem
leaders were expected, but Powell had warned Jack and DeSapio to
stay off the streets. "We won't do what the Communists did to Vice
President and Mrs. Nixon in South America," he said. (Nixon had
just returned from South America, where he had been pelted by mobs.)
Hulan Jack could ill afford to duck Powell's challenge, but when he
showed up on the podium, he was booed, booed as he had never been
booed in Harlem, and he was visibly shaken. The cacophony of hisses
and boos grew louder. Suddenly Powell appeared on the scene, hustling
up onstage. His arrival looked timed, but it was wonderful. He raised
his arm for quiet, and Jack sat down, and Powell took the lectern. He
assailed "black leaders" (Jack could not have been comfortable), lit

into Nixon and Eisenhower, and said DeSapio was trying to turn Harlem into Mississippi. To Adam Powell this was no commemoration event; it was pure politics. He had Jack where he couldn't run, where he looked like so many other politicians — tottering in the wind. Powell kept talking from the podium, assailing Tammany, indirectly belittling Hulan Jack. The NAACP was livid; Powell had sabotaged their event.

DeSapio and his lieutenants must have been upset by the results of an informal *New York Post* poll on the upcoming election, which showed continuing widespread support for Powell. "I don't know if he did wrong or not," commented one New Yorker about Powell's tax indictment, "but I know he did all right for us Negroes. I'm going all down the line for him." Still, the *Post* feared that a political battle was about to engulf Harlem. "Nothing could be deadlier to the cause of civil rights than fratricidal war in Harlem," it said.

Governor Harriman was becoming nervous at Tammany Hall's inability to find an opponent for Powell. Possible candidates were summoned to his home and wooed, unsuccessfully. Tammany finally found its man in May: Earl Brown, the city councilman who had earlier turned down the invitation. Now squeezed by Tammany, Brown had no choice. He had followed Benjamin Davis, who had followed Adam Powell, onto the New York City Council. As a councilman he had distinguished himself by drafting (along with Stanley Isaacs) a landmark antidiscrimination housing bill for New York. Brown fancied himself a writer, and his work was published in Harlem periodicals as well as *Life*; his articles appeared in the latter infrequently enough to arouse suspicion that he was a mere token.

Earl Brown? Powell laughed coldly. "Lookdown Brown," he dubbed his opponent, giving him an embarrassing nickname, as he was apt to do to adversaries: Lookdown Brown, as in looking down at voters, looking down at white people, looking down at challenges.

Tammany dug in hard, but not as hard as Powell, who busied himself raising the clash to titanic proportions. It was more than a battle between two congressional candidates; it was a battle for political independence, to show America that Harlem was not boss-dominated as the South Side of Chicago was boss-dominated. "Negroes would reflect a dangerous yellow streak of cowardice were they to turn their backs on Powell in this crisis": the words came from A. Philip Randolph, generally a stoic man, not given to emotion. Randolph, of course, had his own motives. For years he had been locked out of

power politics in Washington, unable to get kind ears and good legislation for his Pullman porters, for any blacks. And now Powell stood
high on the seniority list in the Education and Labor Committee.

Abandoned as the official Democratic nominee, Powell made overtures to the Republican Party. Thomas Curran, the GOP boss, quickly
let it be known that he ran Republicans only. Curran was being challenged on other fronts. Young liberal Republicans led by John Lindsay
were challenging his candidates in the silk-stocking district. He had
enough problems. So Powell went to Harold Burton. Burton had run
against Powell twice, first in 1948 and again in 1954, but they laughed
together, drank in the Red Rooster together. They were friends. Burton's offices lay in the shadow of the Abyssinian church. "We must
act for the good of the people and select a candidate who is willing to take a forthright stand on civil rights," Burton said, throwing his support to Powell. Coming from a Republican district leader,
Burton's endorsement carried psychological weight. Powell took it
in stride, thanking the GOP for having "stood up like men and not
mice."

DeSapio failed to realize the precarious position he put the Harlem
district leaders in by asking them to abandon Powell. To them, whether
Democrat or Republican, Powell represented not only power but independence, something rare in the days before his ascendancy. "It is
a high price the Harlem Republican leaders are willing to pay to get
their party label on a House member," said the *New York Times* on
its editorial page. A month later, in a letter to the editor, a New York
resident predicted that Harlem voters would stay with Powell because
he had led so many protests and pickets throughout New York City;
they would stay with him not only in this election but "to the very
end."

It was June when Powell opened his campaign headquarters at the
Hotel Theresa, amid the clinking of glasses. The candidate was feeling
near-holy. "Love those who curse you," he said from his pulpit. Not
long after Randolph threw his support to Powell, Martin Luther King,
Jr., gave his. King said that Powell was being "assailed with desperate
weapons of political destruction" because of his independence and
"militant singleness of purpose." (Three months later, King went to
Harlem. He was stabbed in a store while autographing copies of a
book. The wound was perilously close to his heart, but he recovered
quickly. The stabbing did little to assuage southern feelings about
mercurial Harlem.)

Next the labor unions rallied behind Powell: the Brotherhood of Sleeping Car Porters; the Drug Store Clerks and Pharmacists Union (the pharmacists still remembered the days when, even with their pharmacy degrees, they could not get jobs in Harlem drugstores — until the picketing); the Bartenders Union; the Amalgamated Meatcutters — the laborers who stood to gain from having Adam Clayton Powell on the Education and Labor Committee in Congress. These were his people, butchers and bartenders and porters. Powell was rousing the masses, traveling from stoop to stoop, striding beneath the famed marquees along 125th Street, leaning for the outstretched hands. "Rabble-Rouser of the North," *Newsweek* called him in reaction to his relentless campaigning.

In June the Eisenhower administration finally met with the civil rights leaders in Washington. Wilkins, King, Granger, and Randolph were there. Powell, who had originally suggested the meeting, was absent, uninvited. The civil rights leaders, hardly on solid ground with the administration, had seen no need to fight for Powell's presence, especially after he had taken over the Harlem rally. Little, however, was achieved at the meeting. In a photograph that was taken, the smile on everyone's face masked doubt and frustration, doubtless the result of duplicity, including the administration's stalling on holding the meeting in the first place. Something was lacking in the photograph. It was edge and danger. It was Adam Powell. After the meeting, the civil rights leaders returned to their offices and the South. The Eisenhower administration returned to its cocoon.

Powell was busy, taking Manhattan.

༺∾࿇∾༻

J. Raymond Jones was under no illusion about his political capabilities and how much boost they could give Powell. Jones was already sixty years old. He would not be going to Washington. He was not, however, above consideration for a patronage job. Adam Powell could do something for him; he could get him a job in New York City, something a little better-paying than secretary to a judge downtown. Powell could, if Jones chose to run for a political office in New York, throw his weight behind him. As Powell's campaign manager, Jones put his skills in high gear, organizing volunteers and sending them into the tenements on recruiting missions. As the weeks passed, however, his celebrated billing became less and less a factor, not because of Jones's lack of commitment but because of Powell himself. Powell was unable to take orders from others; he was his own best strategist, his own best campaigner, his own politician. There was little for Jones to do except flank the candidate. It was Powell's campaign, and he treated it as opera, raising his voice on this street corner, lowering it in that pulpit, wearing a white suit one day, yellow the next, cream-colored the day after that — all fine Austrian-made suits.

With the primary looming, the *New York Post* gave space to both Powell and Brown, and both penned articles about their positions, which ran side by side. "The Battle of Harlem," the *Post* labeled the series. Brown staked out a defensive position. He wrote that Powell had been abandoned by the Democratic Party, that he refused to cooperate on civil rights legislation in Washington, that he spent too much time abroad, and that Brown himself was not an Uncle Tom, as Powell had called him.

Powell looked into the past. "Harlem in the thirties was an American tragedy, something we all like to forget," he wrote. "Destitute, gaunt women roamed the streets, searching garbage cans for food to feed the crying, hungry children. Angry men, unemployed, hungry and without hope, gathered on street corners. Violence, sickness, and frustration simmered and boiled, waiting only for someone to lift the lid to explode it into all of New York. My early career was dedicated to attacking the root of these troubles, the job discrimination against the black man. It wasn't an easy fight. It wasn't a one-man job. And it isn't over." The Harlem congressman intimated that only by looking back could he look forward: "I did what I did to help my people." He praised Brown — "rising quietly in the New York City Council and being for the Negroes and the Jews and against McCarthy" — but quickly concluded that that "differs greatly from rising in a hostile Congress and debating Carl Vinson of Georgia on segregation."

Powell kept walking, until he had covered nearly every block of pavement in Harlem, with Jones at his side. Boldly, he staged a rally in front of the Hotel Theresa, site of his headquarters and, ticklishly, of Earl Brown's as well. More than two thousand people gathered, among them labor leaders and musicians. Powell had a new Tammany plot for Harlemites: Tammany would be sending "hoodlums" into Harlem to disrupt the election, he said, men with rings on their fingers who would tear up the ballot sheets inside the booths. "If officials do not stop this influx of hired hoodlums, black and white," he told the crowd, standing before them in shirt sleeves in the August heat, "I hereby announce publicly that I will not be responsible in any way for what happens on primary day in this community." A. Philip Randolph said a few words. Dizzy Gillespie wailed on his trumpet.

In the end it did not matter about the tax indictment. And it did not matter that Powell was without Tammany support and Democratic Party dollars. It did not matter that Hattie Dodson and others had been sent to prison. Harriman, up in Albany with statewide influence, did not matter. In the summer of 1958 a strong surge of anti-Tammany sentiments swept New York City, from Harlem to Park Avenue, and it had undeniably been led by Adam Clayton Powell. Powell crushed Brown, 14,837 votes to 4,935. The blow to Tammany was devastating. DeSapio would never recover.

The political makeup of Harlem would also never be the same again. J. Raymond Jones was energized by the victories, which had exposed Tammany's weakness. Long generous with political advice, he began peering deeper into Harlem. He saw young men with potential: Percy Sutton, Herman Badillo, and young Charles Rangel, recently back from the Korean War. They could be trained. Powell had always seen young men as ruthless plotters, and had avoided clubhouses because they trained such young men. But J. Raymond Jones, the Fox, was once again in pursuit of Harlem's political future. When Powell returned to Washington, Jones began summoning the young men to his side.

Harriman, of course, had been given the Democratic nod for governor, and Nelson Rockefeller had won the GOP nomination. Rockefeller was hungry, and his quest posed significant problems for Harriman. Powell wasted little time in basking in the glow of his victory but demanded Tammany purges and dodged questions about whom he would support for governor. The *New York Post* quickly concluded that with his resounding victory he had the capability to "influence events on a national scale."

Powell had given Harlem hard-won respect. He now demanded it from Albany, and Albany heard him coming. As the *New York Times* put it, "In a close gubernatorial race Mr. Powell's support could be decisive and might materially affect Mr. Harriman's chances for a Presidential nomination in 1960."

In approaching Powell, the Harriman camp had reason to be jittery. Powell bargained, but hard. Demands were made. He wanted more jobs for blacks in the state government. DeSapio and Harriman were both on the Democratic National Committee; Powell insisted that they guard his seniority on Capitol Hill against Dixiecrat challenges.

And there was one more demand: Powell, who had missed the 1956 national convention, wished to be included in the 1960 Democratic convention in a meaningful manner. Harriman's supporters accepted the demands. Only then did Powell inform them that he would meet with Rockefeller anyway, as a matter of courtesy.

Powell dallied with the GOP — briefly — and they regretted it. He accused them of trying to buy him off. "I will name the names and dates when they sent people to me," he threatened, and the GOP kept silent.

Rockefeller was crisscrossing New York State with zeal and energy, in stark contrast to the sixty-seven-year-old Harriman. There was something almost intoxicating about Rockefeller. "Rocky," as he was sometimes called, traveled the state in a car, rolling in and out of the upstate hamlets, barnstorming, reaching over picket fences to take hands, sloshing across fields coated with manure. He stormed into cities, getting close to blacks and Puerto Ricans. Powell had told blacks about Rockefeller's money and how much of it had been made, was still being made, in the South African gold mines, "where slave labor is used at twenty-five cents a day." But blacks in New York State, and Harlem, knew something else: that Rockefeller money had been used in philanthropic causes; it was money that had worked against poverty. And they knew that Rockefeller had Jackie Robinson in his camp, and Robinson was a beloved figure. Campaigning in Spanish Harlem, Rockefeller spoke fluent Spanish. So rich, he knew he would have to come down to the people, and he did, with such vigor that it seemed to release something in him. He wanted to win.

Whereas you couldn't see Rockefeller's richness, Harriman's wealth lay visibly like a shawl around his shoulders. The same Harriman whose quick mind had tangled with Stalin and Churchill and MacArthur, who had established himself gallantly on the world stage, was awkward in the rough world of New York politics. His friends, who came from backgrounds similar to his, wondered why he had gotten down in the grubby world of clubhouse politics. "Averell's a Democrat and a fool," his friend Robert Lovett once remarked.

Vice President Nixon stumped America heartily that fall for Republicans, and was joined late in the campaign by Eisenhower himself. The Republicans had their problems, not the least of which was the scandal over Sherman Adams's acceptance of a vicuña coat from a businessman. They received a jolt on election night. As the numbers came in, so did the misery: the Democrats had taken a total of forty-eight House seats from them, and had taken twelve seats in the Senate as well. John Kennedy swept to a Senate seat by the largest margin ever in Massachusetts. Twenty-one governorships were at stake, and the Democrats made off with thirteen of them. But not the governorship in Albany: Rockefeller defeated Harriman by nearly half a million votes. It was such an enormous victory that Rockefeller automatically became a White House contender.

Adam Powell picked up four of five Tammany districts in Harlem, an acknowledged sweep. The Democratic losses in New York State, however, he blamed on "chaos at the top of the ticket." Nationally, the news was good. Liberals were on their way to Washington, young congressmen with vigor: John Brademas, of Indiana, and Robert Giamo, of Connecticut; Roman Pucinski, of Chicago, and James O'Hara, of Detroit. And no sooner did some of them arrive in Washington than they asked to be put on the Education and Labor Committee, because they had come from big cities, and their constituents cared about schools and wanted better wages. Sam Rayburn listened closely to the Young Turks.

⟨≈⟩

As winter turned to spring and spring to summer, Democrats began to choose a presidential candidate. Three U.S. senators — John Kennedy, of Massachusetts; Lyndon Johnson, of Texas; and Stuart Symington, of Missouri — were being prominently mentioned. Of the three, Powell liked Kennedy least, and in the summer of 1959 began blasting him in the press, urging blacks to ignore him because he had been a favorite of the Dixiecrats, particularly Alabama's John Patterson. What Powell saw in Kennedy was indecisiveness, as he had seen in Stevenson. In Symington he saw an unyielding liberal. But in Johnson he saw ruthlessness. There were such similarities between Texas and New York politics: a lack of gentility, the ability to strike first and fast when doing so. Johnson had rushed to the fore to support the 1957 civil rights bill. By doing so he had taken on, even threatened, his fellow southern Democrats. "The Negro, other minorities, and right-thinking whites" should not support Kennedy under any circumstances, Powell felt.

That winter Powell's work was interrupted by surgery at Bethesda Naval Hospital, where a tumor was removed from his chest. Addressing his congregation on the eve of the thirtieth anniversary of his being named to the ministry, Powell could not ignore the possibility of divine intervention. He asked the choir to sing "Ain't Got Time to Die." The tumor was benign.

He journeyed to San Juan to recover in the sun. As a member of the Interior and Insular Affairs Committee, he had been there before, to conduct hearings. Inasmuch as a growing percentage of his constituency was Puerto Rican, the Puerto Rican government tried hard to impress him. When the Harlem congressman returned, it sent a car for him, assigned him a military aide. And he was asked if he felt up to going on a date, because the government could take care of that as well.

Someone from Governor Luis Muñoz Marín's office called Yvette Flores, who came from a politically connected island family; she was single, and she was attractive. "I didn't want to go," she recalled, but the governor persisted, and who could turn down a persistent governor? She huffed, then told herself, "I'll do it for my country." The congressman from New York came and picked her up in his chauffeur-driven car. He had flowers, and she remembered that he clicked his heels — "very European" — when she opened the door. Dinner was nice, then he took her dancing, even though he didn't dance. She said she would sign a contract to teach him how to dance, laughing about it because she felt that he already moved like a dancer. He talked of jazz, and jazz clubs, and his trips around the world. She was young. His Spanish was hardly fluent, but she didn't mind, because he told her, assured her, that he was an admirer of Spanish culture, and pointed to his congressional district and the growing numbers of Puerto Ricans he represented with pride. Then he vanished, and she didn't hear from him for two months. She thought often of him, and yet there was nothing for two months. Then a postcard: "Missing you," it said. And nothing more. Then, a short while later, another postcard: "Still missing you." He began to phone late at night, and she would jump from bed and run across the room to grab the receiver.

In a few months Powell returned to the island again, on unofficial business — to see Yvette. They went swimming. Hoisting a huge fishing rod, he waded knee-deep into the ocean, with shorts on, and threw a line across the water. They went to parties and went to hear jazz, and some nights they took a boat across the sea to Havana, to chat awhile with Fidel and smoke his cigars and drink his wine. (Powell took Cuban cigars back to Washington, placed the box on his desk, and offered them to fellow congressmen, telling them that the cigars were freshly rolled, from Batista's Havana, which Castro would soon overtake.)

Powell had the ability to make Yvette feel like the only woman on earth. She liked the way he could stroll into a club and not dance, into a casino and not gamble. To her, this was control of oneself. She asked him what race he was, and he saw it coming: skin color. Puerto Ricans had a caste system based on its color line; lighter-skinned Puerto Ricans, those with Yvette's complexion, ruled the government. There were parallels to American blacks' own divisiveness on the issue. The way she asked made him nervous. In other situations he would have proudly said he was black, but now he didn't. He told her that he was a mixture of races — white, Indian, and black.

There was talk by the water of a life together, a home by the surf's edge, something built from the ground up. He began pointing out parcels of land, imagining architectural drawings. She did not know what to believe, whether the New York congressman was amusing himself (because after all, he was still legally married) or was serious. Yvette Flores knew of her own romantic feelings. She was hopelessly in love. Again he vanished, but not before saying he would come back for her. She did not quite interpret that as a marriage proposal. She did, however, rebuff other suitors.

⟨⟩

There was a tiny thrill of danger in playing the numbers in Harlem, and the risk contended with the monotony of a nine-to-five job. Many of those who had jobs — store clerks, waitresses, beauticians, shoe-shine men, bakers, laundry workers, janitors, the church-going citizenry — played the numbers. The practice had become so ingrained in the community that it was joked about. At times the Abyssinian minister would mention a psalm, then joke that the particular verse of Scripture — 3:18, for instance — might be the lucky numbers the next day.

The process was simple. A numbers runner would visit you during the day, at your job. If you were a barber, you would motion the runner to the back, select your three numbers, watch as he or she wrote them down, hand over a small amount of money, two or three dollars, then hope. You could bet as much as you wished, the average amount was one to three dollars. By early evening the runner would return to his or her bookie establishment, and you would simply wait for word; then the winning three-digit number would race along the streets like wildfire.

You rarely won at playing the numbers. And the more money you bet, the more elusive winning appeared. The odds were estimated at six hundred to one. If you lived in Harlem, you did not find those odds daunting. Estimates of how much money numbers running took out of Harlem varied wildly, from $50 million to $100 million a year.

How could such an extensive underground network of illegal gambling thrive in Harlem, thrive anywhere? First, it was a mob-controlled operation. The police department tolerated numbers running, which had been brought into Harlem in the early 1930s by Dutch Schultz, the gangster. Second, corrupt policemen on the mob payroll served as lookouts and informed the bookies when a bust was being planned. Now and then arrests were made and a net was dropped, but the arrests were few and the net thin.

Black criminals had a hand in running Harlem numbers, in jobs given to them by mobsters. But in the late 1950s the mob's kindness took a sharp turn, and blacks found themselves being elbowed out of the numbers racket on their own turf. One numbers runner told Powell that blacks in his position were being run out of Harlem, and that the police department had full knowledge. By the time Powell left the bar where he got this information, he had made up his mind. He would go after not only the mobsters but the police department, with which he had been warring for years. He left with the names of the few Harlemites who were still running numbers for the mob — in effect, of people who were working for the Italians as bagmen and bagwomen, who were putting other blacks in Harlem out of business.

Powell began dropping names to the New York media. Then he demanded that the police department pick up the alleged criminals. The police officials were not amused. Flagrant charges that there was corruption within their ranks had been leveled by a high-ranking congressman. They quickly launched raids on Harlem bookie joints, sweeping through back rooms, which they found, curiously, with little effort. Their action was little more than "a phony roundup" Powell charged. Sermonizing from his pulpit, he repeated the charges, then ordered refreshments for the police officers in attendance. "I am against numbers in any form," he roared. "But until the day when numbers are wiped out in Harlem — I hate to say this from the pulpit — I am going to fight for the Negro having the same chance as an Italian."

The phone at the Abyssinian Baptist Church began ringing — anonymous callers, threatening death. Powell was urged to get a bodyguard. He had one, three-hundred-pound Acy Lennon, who had a pistol holstered on his belt. The police suggested one of their own. "I don't need anyone dressed in blue," Powell snapped, "as long as I have God at my side." He alternately told his flock to kick the habit of running numbers and promised them that if numbers must be run in Harlem, then black lawbreakers should have equal rights with Italian lawbreakers.

Powell demanded probes, wiring Mayor Wagner, then Governor Rockefeller. What was needed, he said, was a commission, a huge commission with broad powers, to investigate crime in Harlem and the New York City Police Department. He had just the person to head such a commission: Adam Clayton Powell. He said it was important, because numbers running was "pauperizing" his district. Rockefeller and Wagner ignored his request.

Powell then took his demands to the floor of Congress. Aware that he would receive immunity there, he began reeling off the names of numbers runners in Harlem, names that had been dropped anonymously into his church mailbox, addressed to him. Few were better at performances on the floor of the House than the Harlem congressman; turning his head, turning his shoulders, playing to the galleries, waving his hand, stretching his long arms. There was a "continued and shocking disregard of law and order in my city and in my district in particular," he told his colleagues. He called for the badge of New York police commissioner Stephen Kennedy, and demanded to know why there were no black deputy police commissioners on the force and no black supervisors in Harlem. Strangely, Powell drew support from none other than Mississippi Democrat John Bell Williams, a segregationist. Williams too believed that New York police were "protecting white gamblers while not protecting Negro gamblers."

The debate festered without letup. Powell was invited to appear on Lester Wolff's New York television show, *Between the Lines,* broadcast over the DuMont network. The show was live, without rehearsal, and Wolff and his producers grew understandably worried when Powell missed his arrival time. Finally there he was, at the door. "He came in five minutes before the show," recalled Wolff, who thought Powell looked tired and harried. Wolff wanted to talk about one thing — Powell's debate with the New York Police Department and numbers running. Always a heady challenge for television interviewers, Powell gave Wolff everything he had hoped for. He named names, among them Esther James, just as he had done on the floor of the House; he vowed to keep pressure on the police department; he vowed to keep the issue in the news. Wolff thought the show went well; Powell rushed away afterward.

A short while later Lester Wolff received a telephone call. "You're a nice man," the woman on the other end said, before identifying herself as Esther James and going on to say that she was preparing to sue both Powell and Wolff — Powell for the charge that she was a bagwoman for the mob, and Wolff because Powell had made the charge on his show. Wolff received many such calls. In a way, it was the nature of the business. His show was insured by Lloyd's of London. But he did try to reach Powell to inform him of the threat. Powell's office brushed him off, telling him that Powell was too busy to pay attention to such threats.

Esther James, a Harlem grandmother with a criminal background, hired Raymond Rubin as her lawyer. Rubin was not a distinguished lawyer, but he would prove to be tenacious. And Raymond Rubin had been waiting for a case like this all his life. He was rebuffed by Powell's office. At his own office, which he shared with two other attorneys, he began to focus solely on James's libel suit, day in and day out, looking up precedents, cutting out clippings, and scattering them around his desk, then beneath the glass top that covered his desk. He took no money from James, assuring her that the case was winnable, that she could pay him when they won. Lloyd's of London settled with Wolff for $1,700. Rubin was sure he could get far more from Powell.

For Adam Clayton Powell, it was the beginning of a long nightmare.

It took Congressman James O'Hara, one of the Young Turks sent to Washington in 1958, little time to feel the Powell presence. "You could always tell when Adam was around," he said. "He had this Nash Healy. When I came to Congress, his office was in the Cannon building. He always used to double-park the damn car."

O'Hara and his fellow newcomers hadn't come to Washington to play games, and they hadn't come to sit around and wait for old congressmen to retire. They had come with progressive minds, and they wanted to put their progressive minds to work immediately. Graham Barden had been given the bad news early in 1959 that many of the new members of his committee were liberals. Joseph Loftus, a *New York Times* reporter, had slipped the new committee assignments to Barden, and he informed Barden of something else: that John Brademas, a Rhodes Scholar from Indianapolis, was not only liberal but a member of the NAACP. Barden realized that Rayburn had done this to him, had stacked his committee with northerners and liberals. And he didn't like it.

There was soon evidence that the new Democrats planned to challenge Barden's powers. When Barden passed over Powell for a subcommittee chairmanship, Roman Pucinski, of Illinois, stood up in conference and demanded to know why. Barden, taken aback at such a raw challenge to his power by a neophyte congressman, demanded that Pucinski sit down. "Mr. Chairman, I got here the same way you did, except that a lot more people voted for me than voted for you," Pucinski said. Then, staring even harder at Barden, he said, "I won't be treated like a sharecropper." The comment stung Barden.

The seniority system of Congress, which had protected the rise of Graham Barden, smacked of feudalism to these new congressmen. They vowed to do something about it, and joined with Wayne Phillips, a young liberal activist, to form the Democratic Study Group, whose purpose was to work on liberal legislation and at the same time to loosen the grip of chairmen — the barons of Congress. Powell did not join the little group. He joined ad hoc groups only when he saw direct gains for himself.

To peer into the House of Representatives at the beginning of 1960 was to see twenty-one committees, of which fifteen were headed by southerners. Of the sixteen committees in the Senate, ten were ruled by southerners. Politics looked to be a southern man's occupation and life. But the old southern congressmen could hear the chords of discontent all around, for now, week in and week out, civil rights and education and labor issues dominated the news. Graham Barden began talking to aides of retirement, and they thought such talk scandalous, because right behind Barden in seniority on the Education and Labor Committee stood Adam Clayton Powell. Barden saw behind Powell, to the young liberals. Furthermore, Powell was under indictment for tax evasion. Barden had a wide-lawned home in New Bern, North Carolina, which overlooked the Trench River. He had invested in the North Carolina timber industry. A pension would be forthcoming from Congress.

In January 1960 Graham Barden announced his retirement from

he House of Representatives. He hadn't even warned Sam Rayburn. "It was the best-kept secret in Washington," recalled James Harrison, a committee staff member. The committee members got together, wondering what to do for their retiring chairman. Some wanted to do nothing, because he had treated them with condescension; others thought a dinner would be appropriate. The vote was for a dinner, but Barden told them not to bother, and there was no dinner. One of Barden's last acts before he left Congress was to help defeat a minimum wage bill. The *Raleigh News and Observer* lamented that he had stayed "true to form to the very last."

The Education and Labor chairmanship was now within Powell's grasp. With it he could have a profound effect on American legislation; he could shape it, pass it, and unleash it. Carl Elliott had told him to respect the seniority system, and he had not joined the Young Turks in their efforts to curtail it. Seniority could work beautifully for him, if Rayburn and others would protect his ascension.

Old Powell allies, who had believed that Barden would never leave Congress, were now enthusiastic. "This opens up all kinds of promising opportunities," Chester Bowles, the former Connecticut governor and congressman and a long-time civil rights ally, told Powell. Bowles thought the committee would go from being a "burial ground for progressive views" to one creating liberal legislation.

The expected change at the top of the Education and Labor Committee could not have been more striking. A northerner was about to replace a southerner; a black was about to replace a white; a liberal was about to replace a conservative. William Dawson had been the first black to be named chairman of a standing committee, but his Committee on Government Operations did not initiate legislation; the appointment had in reality been a gift from southerners for Dawson's acquiescence. Education and Labor carried power. It could mandate what happened in schools and on jobs, the lifeline of a nation. Although Powell was the Dixiecrats' "Public Enemy No. 1," according to the *New York Times*, Rayburn and Lyndon Johnson, the majority leader, vowed to help make sure that Powell was given the chairmanship, because he had the seniority. Rayburn wanted Johnson pushed as a presidential candidate. Among southern blacks he would need help, which Powell could give. Rayburn and Johnson could not afford to abandon him now.

The labor leader George Meany was appalled at Powell's possible rise to the chairmanship. Powell had long tussled with labor unions

over segregation within their ranks. Attending a Florida conference
Meany told delegates that he felt Powell would be a "terrible" choice
to succeed Barden, and proceeded to turn the meeting into a refer
endum on Powell. A. Philip Randolph, in attendance, took issue with
him and spoke up enthusiastically for Powell's elevation. (Randolph
did not allow the issue to rest there. A short while later he formed
the Negro Labor Council to bring together black trade unionists in
a concerted effort to put pressure on segregated labor unions across
the country.) James Hoffa, the Teamsters president, threw his support
to Powell, and so did John L. Lewis, the president of the United Mine
Workers, who called it "sheer stupidity" for Meany to oppose Powell

The Democrats would have to win the White House in order for
Powell's grip on the chairmanship to be secure. Moreover, the Harlem
congressman would have to avoid being sent to prison.

⟨⟨⟨⟩⟩⟩

The following cast of characters gathered inside — and outside — the
Foley Square courthouse in lower Manhattan for Adam Clayton Powell's federal tax trial in March 1960.

Judge Frederick vanPelt Bryan looked as if he had been sent from
Central Casting: he was an aging man with unruly white hair and a
handlebar mustache, an Old World judge now at the dawn of a new
decade.

Edward Bennett Williams, Powell's attorney, was a staunch civil
libertarian, the past defender of blacklisted Hollywood writers, of
Frank Costello, the gangster, and of Senator Joseph McCarthy. He
was a lawyer who moved best among those thought to be doomed.
Tall like his client, he had wit, was a known raconteur, and accepted
the spotlight as a necessary part of his business. While attending Holy
Cross, he had become a champion debater. Courtrooms put Williams
at ease. "I had to try the case in front of a white judge, white jury,"
he remembered years later. "In those days juries consisted of white
people from the East Side of Manhattan."

Morton Robson was lead attorney for the government. After graduating from St. John's Law School, he had trained under the Manhattan district attorney Frank Hogan, becoming one of Hogan's most
valued recruits. For Robson the stakes were huge; the Justice Department down in Washington would be watching.

There was Murray Kempton, of the *New York Post*, newspaperman
and urban poet, torn between admiration of and disgust with the

defendant who came through the courthouse doors every morning smiling. There was Benjamin Davis, heaving his huge, battered body into the galleries with a pen in hand, catching quotes for the *Daily Worker*. Davis was still Harlem's angry apostle, a trained lawyer, wondering now, perhaps, what route his career might have taken if not for Harlem and the rush of politics in the 1930s, which had captured him as it had caught Powell. In 1949 Davis had been convicted of Communist activities, but three years in a Georgia prison had done little to dim his spirit.

And there was young William F. Buckley, Jr., the cool, self-assured patrician, who had founded the *National Review* in 1955 — in it he voiced weekly appeals to run the Eisenhower crowd out of Washington — and who had emerged from the haze of McCarthyism, with its ruined lives and maimed reputations, with his own reputation on the rise. The indictment itself was a victory for Buckley. In 1956, when the government was wavering about the case, Buckley had befriended Thomas Boland, a government lawyer who kept him abreast of grand jury movements. When both Boland and Buckley believed the grand jury was leaning against returning an indictment, Buckley printed a series of articles in the *National Review* attacking the administration for not bringing a case. Herbert Brownell believed that it was just such pressure that eventually led to the indictment. Many believed that Buckley had unduly influenced the original jury by sending copies of the articles to its members. "If he'd done it during the trial," Williams said, "he'd have gone to jail. Buckley was convinced there had been some fix." ("I believe we're all here because of penis envy," the acerbic Murray Kempton whispered to Buckley one morning as the trial was about to begin.)

And there was Powell, arriving in court with his arm draped around Williams's shoulder, a Homburg in the other hand. Old Harlem men, some ministers, others laborers, were there every morning awaiting him, having taken the A train and climbed the Foley Square steps into the neoclassical courthouse because they felt the threat to one of their own. "They were all men of old-fashioned dignity," Kempton wrote. "Since the trial has begun, most of the time there have been no seats for them and they stand outside, which is unfortunate for them but a general blessing of innocence and brotherhood in a corridor sadly in need of both."

The government's case was simple: it had to prove that Powell had deducted expenses on his 1951 and 1952 income tax returns for items that had been paid for by government funds given to him when traveling abroad on congressional business. In his opening remarks Robson predicted a case of "far greater magnitude" than the public imagined. Then, over the next weeks, he called forth an array of witnesses, led by the IRS agents and embassy officials who had come into contact with Powell and Hazel Scott during their travels. (The government did not pursue a case against Scott.) Scott's European theatrical agents told of parties that the couple had thrown from Paris to Monte Carlo, then in Rome; of money being spent, then more money being wired abroad to replace the spent money — money that Robson said Powell deducted from his taxes. Robson called Hattie Dodson to the stand. Before the trial he had paid her a visit in her Harlem apartment. "She was helpful when I first spoke to her," he recalled. On the stand, Dodson, once again asked to implicate her church — her minister — froze. "I can't remember," she began answering, over and over. "Incredible," Robson later said, laying the blame on Powell. "Powell was a strong influence on people — smart, very smart."

The prosecutor was not deterred. He brought forth a huge chalkboard and began charting numbers, adding and subtracting, writing figures up, down, and across the board, placing it in plain view of the jurors. Pointing to the figures, he cited inconsistencies in Powell's tax forms. Williams, however, noticed the looks on the faces of the jurors. They looked confused; they were not accountants. He began walking over to the chalkboard, feigning confusion, utter confusion; raising an eyebrow, peering closer — mocking. Then Williams produced his own numbers, and when he finished he came to different conclusions from Robson. His figures showed that Powell was still *owed* money by the government.

Williams called James Johnson to the stand. Johnson had formerly worked for the IRS and had filed Powell's taxes for one of the years in question. Williams went over the tax form with him and got Johnson to admit that he had made a mistake by taxing Powell on his $2,500 congressional expense allotment. And then Williams began wondering how much the government had spent to fly its witnesses to New York from Europe, whether they were staying in expensive hotels, how long they would be in the city. Edward Bennett Williams painted a picture of a zealous government spending a huge amount of the taxpayers' money to send Adam Clayton Powell to prison.

Turning the tables on the government, he made Powell look like a victim.

The strategy was working beautifully, and Robson sensed it. He sensed it from the actions of Judge Bryan. "He was pretty impressed with Powell," Robson explained. "He did something I had never seen before or since. He turned over the grand jury transcript to Williams. You are only entitled, as defense lawyer, to testimony of witnesses on the witness stand. We had quite a battle." And Robson sensed how much Powell was enjoying it. "At one point he winked at me. To him it was a bit of a game." At one point Robson produced a tax receipt from Cherio's, a restaurant, and there was confusion about where it was. "You know Cherio's," explained Powell. "That's where the theatrical crowd goes on Sunday nights, when Sardi's is closed."

Robson could not help but notice the women at the trial. There seemed to be so many — "good-looking, black and white," he recalled years later. One woman in particular, a striking black six-footer, caught his attention. Her name was Audrey Smaltz; she was a fashion model. When Robson found out that she knew one of the alternate jurors — and Powell — he suspected mischief. Smaltz was summoned to his office and grilled about jury tampering. She vehemently denied the accusation, left Robson's office, and shared the meeting with the press. The story made Robson appear desperate.

At night, Williams and Powell holed up in a New York apartment. They worked around the clock, breaking only for meals — more often than not, a burger and a beer at P. J. Clarke's. It was at the apartment that Williams collapsed one night from fatigue. He was amazed at Powell's stamina. "I never saw him nervous, about anything," recalled Williams. "He was a cool cat."

When Williams finished explaining the numbers, it was indeed the government that owed Powell money. Williams did not mention race; he went after incompetence. It was Powell who slyly interjected the issue of race. Williams asked Powell if he had tried in the past to straighten out the perceived tax woes with T. Coleman Andrews, the IRS commissioner. Powell said yes; Williams asked when. "It must have been before the middle of 1956," Powell answered, "for Andrews resigned his post to run for president on a segregationist ticket."

Williams transformed his case into one of governmental intimidation, and cited tax mistakes that had been made not by Powell but by the government. "These mistakes were made by seven experts from the Internal Revenue Service and five separate lawyers from the Justice Department," he told the jury in an impassioned summary.

Judge Bryan dismissed two of the charges, then sent the jury to determine its verdict on the remaining charges. After some time the jurors admitted they were deadlocked. To Powell and Williams, a mistrial was victory enough. Waving, Powell, who had turned the curious trial into a rather joyful interlude from other business, left the courtroom, trailed by the old ministers who had followed him there and watched by the beautiful women. He disappeared in a station wagon with THE ABYSSINIAN BAPTIST CHURCH stenciled on the side.

The congressman sent a telegram to his son in London, who later remembered hearing the light crinkly noise of paper being shoved beneath a door. "The people won. Dad." It said nothing else.

◈

Powell's legal victory served to energize his plans for the upcoming presidential campaign. The primaries were already under way; there was catching up to do. At an outdoor rally on 125th Street, ostensibly to fête Edward Bennett Williams (fifteen thousand people showed up), Powell could not stop himself from addressing presidential issues. He imagined that Nixon would head the GOP ticket but believed that Rockefeller would make the better candidate. He liked Rockefeller, a candidate who was "boss-free" and had "hard-hitting, partisan-free views." The wind was nippy, but his voice was strong. On the Democratic side he liked Stuart Symington and Lyndon Johnson, and thought that Eugene McCarthy, of Minnesota — "brilliant, militant" — was prime vice presidential material. He berated Senator Kennedy for his "softness on McCarthyism." He attacked, but did not name, "well-known Negro leaders" in America, calling them captives of old ideas and old strategies. Then he turned to the students who were boycotting in the American South: "I shall work, fight, picket, and boycott with them 100 percent." He was happy to be free. "Abraham Lincoln freed the slaves," he bellowed at the massive gathering. "Edward Bennett Williams freed Adam Clayton Powell!"

Williams was named Harlem's Man of the Year. Powell handed him a huge trophy — "like the Statue of Liberty," Williams said — and then everyone went to Sugar Ray Robinson's bar for drinks. One of Powell's aides took Williams's trophy, telling him that he was taking it to put a personal inscription on it and Williams would receive it again soon. Weeks, then months, passed. Williams did not receive it. He phoned Powell. "Where's my trophy?" he asked. Finally it arrived, but it wasn't the huge statue he had been given at the rally. It was smaller — much, much smaller, the size of two hands put together. Williams chuckled: this was the price of dealing with the congressman from Harlem. The inscription nevertheless made him proud. "Harlem's Man of the Year," it said. He was the first white man to be so honored. Williams placed the trophy in a very visible place in his Washington law office, so visitors would not miss it.

Two weeks after his trial, Adam Clayton Powell traveled to Princeton, New Jersey, to deliver a speech before the American Cliosophic Society, a prestigious debating organization. His one-sided debate touched on a variety of issues — the 1950s, liberals, blacks, and presidential politics. He chided Americans for "wallowing in the morass of mediocrity of the fifties." He promised that the new decade, "the challenging sixties," would contain surprises. He lamented that Jacob Javits, the New York senator, and Abraham Ribicoff, the governor of Connecticut, were not being legitimately considered as vice presidential candidates, which he attributed to anti-Semitism. Lyndon Johnson he thought to be "the most able man in the United States" but snared politically by regionalism. Northern liberals were scorned for "paternalism," the NAACP for relying always on legal methods. The Harlem congressman envisioned a new order, and saw growing maturity on the part of civil rights protesters: "It takes maturity to have your churches bombed, your children beaten, your houses burned, your people lynched, in the South by the mob and in the North by savoir-faire, and not to strike back but rather to stand together and thrust more relentlessly and thereby continue to score significant victories." The theme of maturity struck Powell as resonant. "A voter in my district who defied the mandates of the political boss and thereby didn't even let the Tammany Hall candidate get scarcely five thousand votes in a congressional election is mature," he said. He warned against the "tyrants of mediocrity" who were "leading this nation backward." Sarcastically citing a number of books that reflected the recent decade — *The Hidden Persuaders, The Status Seekers, The Lonely Crowd,* and *The Organization Man* — Powell reminded the bookish Princeton crowd to be wary of a little ditty: "Come weal, come woe, my status is quo."

The Democratic presidential primary contenders had waged a feisty battle during the early part of the year. Through the snows of New England and the rains of a midwestern spring, they were bracing themselves to face the heat of the Los Angeles convention. Senator Kennedy came out of the gate quickly, rolling up delegate votes. He had charm and style, a pedigree, but what was then considered a taboo religion when making a run for the White House: Catholicism. Hubert Humphrey could not be ignored. He was a go-for-broke liberal, the former mayor of Minneapolis, continuing the line of thinking that had been held by such fellow midwesterners as La Follette and Eugene Debs. Lyndon Johnson was a dark horse, but he was powerful, savvy, and shrewd, and he wanted the nomination badly. Blacks reeled at the thought of a southerner in the White House and did not give him much credit for helping pass the 1957 Civil Rights Act, because they believed the act was ineffective. Adlai Stevenson still had supporters, and they were still dreamy. Stuart Symington, the Missouri senator, had a streak of independence: he had left Truman's cabinet in a huff with Defense Secretary James Forrestal, and he had told Senator McCarthy, at the height of the McCarthy-Army hearings, to see a shrink. As a Missouri entrepreneur, he had hired blacks in appreciable numbers. Powell had made a stirring speech in the middle of Harlem on Symington's behalf, but Symington fever wasn't spreading across the country, because Symington, a sophisticated gambler, wasn't campaigning. He chose to skip the primaries, hoping to rally forces in Los Angeles.

As for John Kennedy, the same Senator Kennedy who refused to vote to censure McCarthy, Powell found him lacking in moral courage and denigrated him for accepting the support of the segregationist Alabama governor, John Patterson. "For a man from Massachusetts," Powell said, alluding to the Abolitionist tradition, Kennedy had an abysmal record on civil rights. That summer, Powell began making phone calls, urging black delegates around the country not to support Kennedy.

The Democratic Party this year, unlike in 1956, had to deal with Adam Clayton Powell. His victory against the Tammany machine had been decisive. If Democrats wanted to reclaim the White House, they needed every vote they could get. At one time thought to be politically dead, the Harlem congressman had resurrected himself; he was alive, vibrant, and threatening, marching once again against the status quo.

Adam Powell loved the parties in Los Angeles that summer, loved strolling down hotel hallways, immaculately dressed, then cutting a figure in a doorway, lines of smoke rising from the thin cigarillo in the huge hand. Whispers both greeted him and trailed him: the color of his skin wasn't black and it wasn't white. His skin color, of course, was somewhere in between, throwing those in his path momentarily off-balance, enabling him to rebalance them with both smile and greeting. Although the Harlem renaissance had ended thirty years before, he remained full of its dash and charm, which he had taken to Washington, to wherever he went, now to Los Angeles. "Peccadilloes, my boy, peccadilloes," he told the author Gore Vidal, who had heard rumors of his having once tried to pass as white.

Hollywood gravitated toward the convention. Frank Sinatra was there, so were Janet Leigh and Peter Lawford and Sammy Davis, Jr. Vidal was contemplating a run for political office in New York State and was hoarding advice. Carmine DeSapio was counting delegates, although at one relaxed party he was spotted chatting amiably with the novelist Christopher Isherwood. Norman Mailer needed no introductions. Powell showed up at one party, a beautifully cut white suit jacket on his back, and chatted with Gina Lollobrigida, the Italian actress, in a corner.

Southern blacks had arrived early, with plans to picket the Los Angeles Convention Center. The possibility worried congressional Democrats. They had been fired up by the 1958 elections. Momentum was on their side. They did not need confrontation at the convention. Powell, momentarily switching roles, to congressman from activist, had tried to halt the threatened picketing. Before going to California, he had contacted Bayard Rustin, Martin Luther King's aide, and told him that if King did not call off the plan, he would announce to the world that Rustin was sexually involved with King. The charge was patently untrue, but Rustin, a homosexual, grew nervous. King, however, held steady, and vowed that the picketing would go on as planned, which it did. The southern blacks, long wary of Powell, now had good reason to distrust him. To them, he could be as dangerous as a Dixiecrat.

Nonetheless, at an NAACP rally attended by 250 black delegates, the southerners saw how much they needed Adam Clayton Powell, how he could not be ignored. Sitting on the podium, Powell was the congressman on the cusp of real power. Beginning his address, his voice alternately rising and lowering in his best Harlem cadence, he talked about democracy, about the need to retake the White House, about the need for a "revolution of passive, massive resistance," his arms flying, the clock ticking, the delegates saluting, wiping their brows, praising him; King, Wilkins, Randolph yelling — this was Powell, the Powell they knew and had heard of and feared and mistrusted but whom they respected. "Powell had the crowd in a frenzy," recalled Eddie Sylvester, a delegate who was working on behalf of Kennedy.

Powell returned to his seat next to Frank Reeves, a Washington attorney who was one of his supporters, and Reeves, watching the applause spreading, leaned over and said to Powell that he couldn't do that again, raise the crowd up out of its chairs like that. "You watch," Powell replied. He stood, walked to the podium, and began talking again, picking up the old points, the fire spreading; and first Reeves, then Sylvester, became amazed as the delegates rose again. They could not stop shouting. Eleanor Roosevelt did not quite know what to think of Powell's address, which she described later as one of those "let's burn the place down" speeches.

Congressman James O'Hara, a Kennedy man, arrived at the convention early. One evening, before the convention had fully cranked up, he heard that Powell was to deliver a speech in a black church. Having never seen Powell preach, he grabbed a friend and made his way to the church. "There were very few white people there," he remembered. "I went out of curiosity. I sat in the back. I saw an Adam Powell I had never seen before. Here was Adam Powell speaking of the injustices in America, of a brighter tomorrow. I'm telling you, he was inspiring. The crowd was enraptured. He was just magnificent. Everyone in that hall was just going wild. And Adam knew it, and you could see him gaining strength on the podium. That was what kept him going. He was great."

Stevenson arrived, surrounded by the warm and uneven air of nostalgia. The tall Eleanor Roosevelt hovered near his side, and the speech introducing him to the convention, made by the young Minnesota senator Eugene McCarthy ("Do not leave this prophet without honor in his own party . . ."), had the sweet ring of populism and poetry. A rallying cry swept the convention center, summoning Stevenson from his suite. He appeared, quoted a poem by Robert Frost ("The woods are lovely, dark and deep"), then vanished, once again leaving

hose moved by him wondering whether he was more interested in
erse than in vote. The rallying cry was not enough, and Stevenson's
ollowers were forced to look at a mirror cracking before their very
yes.

Stuart Symington arrived in Los Angeles hoping for a deadlocked
onvention, took a hotel suite, and waited as history's clock began
o tick, hoping he would not have to dirty his hands. Eighty-six
lelegates gave him their votes. It was not enough, and Symington
:ame in third in the delegate count.

Lyndon Johnson had his allies, but also his detractors, who saw
wild odds against getting a Texas senator into the White House. But
ohnson, unlike Symington, didn't mind getting his hands dirty. He
·idiculed Kennedy's record in the Senate, and he talked disparag-
ngly about the Kennedy pedigree and the Kennedy money. "More
>rofile than courage" went the barb. He begged Rayburn for help,
ınd he loosed his Texan spirit on the convention — long arms, big
·oice, huge stride. And he still could muster only 409 delegate
·otes. Half of one of those votes came from Harlem's Ray Jones;
?owell, in an independent, and symbolic, gesture, cast his half-vote
·or Symington.

Kennedy had come to the nomination as the front-runner, having
nade himself known in small towns and big cities and primary elec-
:ions across America. He had worked long and hard, and had masked
ın undistinguished senatorial record with sheer confidence. The television cameras treated him kindly. He had avoided blacks during the
>rimaries, which is why blacks found him anathema; moreover, he
1ad cast his vote against a voting rights bill and was considered weak
>n labor issues.

There was much bitterness among the New York delegation, which
1ad gone to Los Angeles 114 votes strong. Stevenson was their sen-
:imental choice, and they could live with Symington. But the pendulum was swinging toward Kennedy. He was not one of them, not
>ne of their kind. Scanning his congressional record, they saw no
ındependence of mind, no fire in his conscience. And some of them
:ould not trust a man who had cavorted so brazenly with southerners.
The New York delegates had come from Manhattan and the Bronx,
from Queens and Brooklyn; they were long-time battlers on behalf
of immigrant dreams and liberal legislation, and they now faced a
man whose commitment they could not sense or measure. Among

them were middle-aged and aging heroes: the eighty-two-year-old
Herbert Lehman, one of the last great liberal governors of New York
the governor who had signed legislation creating Harlem's black dis
trict; Eleanor Roosevelt, keeper of the liberal flame; New York Cit
mayor Robert Wagner, Jr., son of the great New York senator an
proponent of laws against lynching, Robert Wagner; Emmanue
Celler, of Brooklyn — "Manny" to everyone in the delegation — who
had spent his early years in Congress fighting the forces of Calvi
Coolidge, his later years working for the judiciary and immigration
Charles Buckley, the Bronx boss and a Kennedy ally; DeSapio, in hi
dark glasses. There was Averell Harriman, the worldly Harriman, a
beautiful instrument on the grand stage, Europe, but not the smal
stage, Albany. In Los Angeles, between the two stages, he stood ful
of pride, full of possibility, serene in the knowledge that a victoriou
Kennedy camp would surely seek his services. And there, in a sof
suit, tall, erect, dangerous, his eyes always moving, watching and being
watched, his body moving like an ocelot, as Congressman Frank
Thompson liked to call him, was Adam Clayton Powell, six feet, four
inches tall, weighing more than two hundred pounds, prepared to
heal, or inflict, wounds.

When Kennedy won the nomination — on the first ballot, nearly
doubling Johnson's vote count, 806 to 409 — blacks shook their
heads violently, No, no, almost in unison, stirring the convention
awake. The Kennedy camp, with its Harvard minds hard at work, its
lawyers churning out position papers, was stumped. Now the Kennedy
juggernaut looked unsteady; Powell moved about threateningly.

Behind the scenes, Kennedy offered the vice presidential nomination
to Symington, which appeased the true liberal wing of the Democratic
Party, the wing that questioned Kennedy's heart. But then he snatched
it back, cornered by conservative southern senators, who warned him
that he would lose the race if he lost the South, which would certainly
happen without Johnson on the ticket. Putting Johnson on the ticket
was a genuine gamble, and many black delegates could hardly believe
it. But Powell, whose career was a trail of gambles, was delighted.
(Symington, wooed, then spurned, left the convention as he had come,
an elegant figure of not-quite-finished promise — the aging gentleman, his hands still clean.)

Kennedy delivered his acceptance speech at the Los Angeles coli-
seum. He was introduced by Adlai Stevenson, who could play, when
the battle was no longer ringing in his ears, the wonderful romantic

visionary, claiming that Kennedy was the man to solve the woes "of our troubled, trembling world." Kennedy talked of a new frontier, of assaults on poverty and ignorance, of tackling the "uncharted areas of science and space." He said that the United States was at "a turning point in history." He alternately looked at ease and, jabbing the air with his forefinger, defiant. He talked of human emotion and the concept of sharing. His address was brief, and not quite Stevensonian. But it was obvious he was geared for battle and ready to meet the Republicans head-on.

Powell committed himself to no one, once again offering up the distinct possibility of open confrontation. The Harlem congressman left Los Angeles angry, and national Democrats could not afford to allow Adam Clayton Powell's anger to brew. Kennedy would need the black vote, and blacks across America listened to Powell. But Powell was wise enough to know that Kennedy would have to come to him. The senator would have to find a way to diminish the issue of Catholicism, among blacks as well as whites. "Somehow," recalled Eddie Sylvester, "blacks were concerned that the Vatican would be involved with running the government." The black ministers who had attended the convention were not politicians. They listened and they prayed, deftly keeping their feet out of the roiling political waters. Powell's stock as a potential healer rose quickly. He emerged from Los Angeles as both congressman and Baptist minister. He knew well the currents of politics, and he knew his Bible. He needed only to retreat to Harlem and wait.

The Republicans convened in Chicago after the Democratic convention. There was less suspense over the ticket. Vice President Nixon chose Henry Cabot Lodge, the former United Nations ambassador, as his running mate; Lodge was somewhat of a surprise, since Kennedy had walloped him for the Senate in 1952. Both Goldwater and Nelson Rockefeller had been favorably mentioned, but both declined. Lodge's record on civil rights was liberal; party regulars grumbled that it might be too liberal. Among old-line blacks, there was little reason to worry about Nixon and Lodge. It was a ticket they could trust. It was the other fellow from Massachusetts whom they worried about. And shortly into the campaign, when the clergyman Norman Vincent Peale, a Nixon supporter, mentioned Kennedy's Catholicism, it became obvious that the Republicans planned to exploit the issue.

Back in New York City, lounging in a chair at Sardi's, Rev. Adam Clayton Powell said he sensed a "smoldering resentment" toward Kennedy among blacks. He also said that if the election were held during the summer, Kennedy could not take the state of New York. Such a pronouncement must have sent shudders through the Kennedy camp, which did not waste much time in contacting Powell. Sargent Shriver and Harris Wofford, working for Kennedy, wired Powell, making their plea. "We need your thrust," they concluded, getting a kick, given Powell's sexual reputation, out of the word *thrust*. "We all enjoyed the punch line, because it had a double meaning," recalled Wofford.

Kennedy's brain trust sent Louis Martin, Powell's friend from his first congressional campaign. As was often the case when an emissary was being sent to meet with him, Powell was waiting — with his own plan. After spending weeks painting the gloomiest of pictures for Kennedy, he told Martin that he might tour America, not only as congressman but as minister, climbing pulpits in urban America and assailing the fear of Catholicism. Martin listened with rapt attention. "Powell was important because the Kennedys had no strong ties with blacks in America," he explained, and he wasted no time in accepting Powell's support. "It was an important endorsement."

But it would take money. Adam Clayton Powell would not be shortchanged when it came to money. He wanted to travel like the most comfortable politician. He was edgy about slights. (Eisenhower's people had sent him across the country, then refused to pay until his badgering forced them to cough up.) Robert Kennedy disapproved of Powell's demands, but, reminded by others in his brother's entourage of how important it was to have a religious spokesman on their side, he relented. "Adam demanded to be paid exclusively from the pot of money we had at the speakers' bureau," said Sylvester. Since he had a bad back, he wanted hotel rooms — suites — with a bed board beneath the mattress. And he demanded a limousine at his disposal when he arrived in each city. "Bobby wanted you to do everything for free," recalled Marjorie Lawson, one of the first blacks on the Kennedy bandwagon.

So Powell became Kennedy's urban affairs consultant — not "black affairs consultant," because that would have been too condescending — receiving several thousand dollars per speech. Before he embarked on his nationwide tour, he honed his plan of attack close to

Declaring for Eisenhower,
1956

Overleaf: In the Abyssinian
Baptist Church, Harlem,
1960

Talking to reporters

With (*left to right*) J. Raymond Jones, Whitney Young, and Hulan Jack, 1967

Below: Two ministers' sons: Adam Clayton Powell, Jr., and Martin Luther King, Jr., 1965

With Congressman
Jacob Javits, 1953

Stumping for John F.
Kennedy in October
1960. *From left to right:*
W. Averell Harriman,
staff members, Eleanor
Roosevelt, Powell,
Kennedy, and Herbert
Lehman.

Above: President Kennedy handing Powell his pen after signing the Minimum Wage Act of 1962

Below: Chairman Powell and President Johnson, July 21, 1966

A committee hearing on 114th Street in 1965. *From left to right on the platform:* staff member Chuck Stone, Rep. James Roosevelt (behind flag), Chairman Powell, Rep. Ogden Reid, Rep. John Dent, Rep. Augustus Hawkins

Below: Powell's Washington staff in 1962. Corrine Huff is fourth from the left; Maxine Dargans is third from the right.

Facing page: The congressman in Harlem, 1963

AP/Wide

Above: Yvette, Adamcito, and Adam Powell, San Juan, 1962
Below: Adamcito going for his father's pipe at Villa Reposa, 1963

home, in New York City. So infrequently was Adam Powell seen away from his pulpit in ministerial garb that the effect could be dramatic. Years before, people had seen him striding from his pulpit, the black robe flowing, its lettering in scarlet, its white collar starched and circling his neck — striding down the street to Harlem Hospital to align himself with union workers, his flock trailing and the TV cameras whirring. Now here he stood in Central Park, attending a Kennedy rally in full ministerial garb, allowing as to how he was "shocked and amazed" at the "un-Christlike, ungodly, and un-American" attacks on Kennedy's religion. He said that such attacks could come only from Republicans or southerners — "bigots in the pulpit" — who refused to admit blacks to their churches. If the Republicans wanted to talk of religion, of church and state, Adam Clayton Powell would allow them that, but he would not miss the opportunity to talk about racism.

By September Powell was feeling sure that blacks, nationwide, would back the Kennedy ticket. "The persecuted cannot join in a persecution," he declared. His national campaign was launched on October 9 in Pittsburgh, where he vowed that he would sacrifice campaigning for his own seat to throw his full energies into Kennedy's effort. He traveled coast to coast, from Pittsburgh to Detroit, from Chicago to Cleveland, from Cleveland to Los Angeles. He met with ministers, then their congregations; then, in the evenings, in the cities, he attended huge Kennedy rallies. "I didn't know of any black American who could walk into a room and turn on the lights like Adam," said Louis Martin. "Big smile on his face, hearty welcome — elegant." There was the rush of a campaign, the flight from city to city, the waiting limousine, the big rally, the limousine speeding him back out to the airport. Brazenly, he stung Republicans in an all-out attack on Nixon. It had been revealed that Nixon had once sold a property with the stipulation in the deed that it could not be sold to a black or Jewish buyer. Powell traveled with a blown-up copy of the deed, a six-foot replica, and at opportune times before crowds he would prop the deed up. "He did that with gusto," recalled Wofford. Nervous about Powell ("You weren't sure what he would do next"), Wofford and other members of Kennedy's inner circle more often than not simply watched as Powell galloped along. "When he was on your side," Wofford added, "it was fun to be with him."

When Powell felt himself needing an infusion of funds — discretionary money — he phoned Martin and put the squeeze on him. It was subtle blackmail. "Adam had to have a lot of confidential help," said Martin. "I remember once giving him five thousand dollars. It was one Saturday; he was in the gymnasium of the House of Representatives. I gave it to him inside a book. We always took the position that when we gave Adam money, we were paying for the speeches."

Kennedy's supporters began traveling more and more into black areas, sending in advance teams. It was obvious that Kennedy had begun to connect with black voters. In the cities they saw Powell and then Kennedy, or Kennedy and then Powell, two handsome men with sharpened swords twirling against the Republicans.

As for Nixon and Lodge, they too were rolling across America, Nixon's cold war passions bracketed by Lodge's liberalism. There was still fear among conservative Republicans that Lodge was too liberal, that he was one of those Massachusetts Republicans, more Democrat than Republican. It was in Adam Powell's Harlem that Lodge met his Waterloo; staring into the faces of Harlem's men and women, sensing their dashed dreams and anguished hopes, he was moved, so moved that he announced that Nixon would break precedent by naming a black to the cabinet. Southerners were aghast, none more so than Nixon loyalists. The Kennedy camp had made no prediction on cabinet makeup. Nixon's people stiffened at Lodge's indiscretion. The utterance proved disastrous.

In October, Senator Kennedy had his destined date with Harlem. The event, a two-day National Conference on Constitutional Freedom, was considered something of a gamble by some of Kennedy's supporters. It was capped by an outdoor rally held in front of the Hotel Theresa. The grand ladies of Harlem came out in full force, with furs draped around their shoulders — distinguished women in hats and gloves, a few of them on the dais, flanking Eleanor Roosevelt. The former first lady still walked tall among Harlemites, still drew whispers, still was touched reverently. Men and women and children looked on from balconies, which had been decorated with red, white, and blue crepe paper. The area around 125th Street and Seventh Avenue was cordoned off. The air was crisp and clear. On the dais Powell, dressed in a three-button roll suit, stood next to Kennedy, who stood next to Herbert Lehman. Powell held his speech, bound between soft covers, in his hand. He talked of Kennedy, his friend Jack Kennedy, who had served in Congress with him, and he attacked the Republicans.

Kennedy talked of the sweep of history, which he could see from Harlem on that October day, with thousands of intent gazes upon him. He talked of foreign lands, where the names of American heroes, names like Franklin Roosevelt and Thomas Jefferson, were still revered. "They don't quote any American statesman today," he said. He talked of Africa and of Africans (and here the Harlemites could identify), who were so enamored of American democracy that they named their children after American heroes, after Washington and Jefferson. "There may be a couple called Adam Powell," he said, and when Powell leaned over and said, "Careful, Jack," there it was, the exchange of grins, the playful innuendo of sexual escapade. Laughter spread, and suddenly the citizens of Harlem could see how and why they could vote for this Kennedy, because he had some of the wit and polish of their own Adam Powell; they were seeing it up close, that there was some Powell in Kennedy, some wickedness, a reality of sex as romp and adventure, and this they liked. Louis Martin, who had attended many of Kennedy's rallies before blacks, thought that none had been better than the Harlem rally.

Toward the campaign's end, a ministers' convention was held in Los Angeles. In the audience were old Baptist ministers with "Nixon Now" buttons on. Powell went to change their minds. But just before his address, Ray Jones, who was beginning to form political ties with Bobby Kennedy, took a phone call. The news was good. Martin Luther King had been released from a jail in Georgia. The Kennedys had applied pressure — not Nixon, not Lodge, not the Eisenhower Justice Department, but the Kennedys. Ray Jones pulled Powell to the side and told him, and then, before he could tell Powell how to release the information to the ministers, he saw Powell, Rev. Adam Clayton Powell, of Harlem's Abyssinian Baptist Church, striding away toward the podium. Before him sat a sea of faces, men of the cloth, the "Nixon Now" buttons on their lapels staring him in the face. "Gentlemen, I bring you tidings of great joy," he began. "I have just talked to Robert Kennedy and he informed me that King is *free*. I tried to arrange for him to talk to you by telephone. I am sorry we were unable to arrange it." Jones was appalled, yet this was Powell at his most characteristic, creating pandemonium. The old ministers let out shouts of joy, and they clapped, and Powell grinned, and the ministers began moving in their seats, their voices cascading and merging, their faces looking up at the podium, at one of their own, a fellow man of the cloth. And Powell stood there before them, knowing fully that he received additional praise simply for delivering the news.

Powell made his way back east, winding up his cross-country tour in Jersey City. He said he was now convinced that Kennedy could win, and boldly predicted a two-to-one margin of victory.

⟨∽∾⟩

The election returns were both slow and dramatic, and the contest turned into an old-fashioned cliffhanger. Kennedy's victory margin was a mere 118,574 votes, with some elaborate arithmetic in Illinois. But it was victory nevertheless, and the door was about to open on what Powell had told the Princeton audience would be "the challenging sixties." Already the northern Democratic congressmen were preparing, pulling out the bills they had been working on, drumming up more ideas. Legislation that had died in the hands of Dixiecrats would be born again. There would be a new chairman of the Education and Labor Committee. The New Frontier was about to begin.

"We stand today upon the threshold of an unparalleled opportunity, for black and white, Jew and Gentile, Protestant and Catholic, northerner and southerner, to walk together across new frontiers into a great era of brotherhood," Powell told his congregation on the Sunday of election week. Now he would return to Washington, not just as a congressman but as the chairman of a major committee. Education was everything to blacks; labor, which meant jobs, second only to education.

It had been a long time coming, but now the tilt was in Adam Clayton Powell's favor. There would be money, a staff (for so long he had operated largely without a staff), the president's ear, unrivaled power. On November 30, Powell stood before the cameras outside the president-elect's Georgetown home, having emerged from a meeting where the two had discussed upcoming legislation, because there was so much to be done in the areas of education and labor. Powell carried briefing papers in the crook of his arm and had a look of earnest seriousness on his face.

Already he had begun issuing orders, gathering those members of Congress he would depend on. Oregon representative Edith Green was to get position papers ready on juvenile delinquency. Carl Elliott, the big, soulful Alabaman, was to study the educational systems of America and Russia and devise ways to close the gap, if there was a gap. The years were catching up with Cleveland Bailey, the passionate

West Virginian who had once charged Powell in a committee meeting. Powell put no reins on Bailey; he could study any facet of American education he wished. Congressman James Roosevelt, of California, was to study scholarship programs; Frank Thompson, the arts; and Herbert Zelenko, discrimination in unions — in George Meany's unions.

In late January, those who feared and admired Adam Clayton Powell — members of the Kennedy administration, union leaders, local politicians, church officials — met in New York City to give him a testimonial sendoff to Congress and his new duties. The event took place in the ballroom of the Hotel Commodore; A. Philip Randolph was master of ceremonies. President Kennedy had sent not one but two cabinet members: Abraham Ribicoff, secretary of health, education, and welfare, and Arthur Goldberg, secretary of labor. Eleven congressmen came, all members of the Education and Labor Committee. The Abyssinian church deacons showed in force. Eleanor Roosevelt had been invited to give the opening remarks, but she declined, sending a warm message. Powell had invited the FBI director, J. Edgar Hoover. This had to be nothing less than a tease. Hoover declined so quickly that Powell tauntingly sent another invitation, asking him if he was absolutely sure that he did not want to participate. (He was.) Angier Biddle Duke, Kennedy's chief of protocol, served as chairman of the event, and it was a glittering affair, with Sammy Davis, Jr., entertaining — slapping backs, moving about in his will-o'-the-wisp body, apparently having recovered from the slight he received from the Kennedy camp when they told him not to bring Mai Britt, his white wife, to the inauguration. One hundred and fifty labor officials were in attendance. The two cabinet members read a message from the president (laudatory, benevolent), then praised Powell's congressional record and expressed the administration's delight in having him as chairman of Education and Labor.

"There's a saying up in Harlem," Powell said to those gathered. " 'When we get our Negro up, all hell breaks loose.' " And as he looked out over them, friend and foe alike, he saw the past and the future, and it was the future he was concerned about. He vowed an investigation of the National Labor Relations Board. He vowed to look into scholarship programs. He derided "cheap imports" that struck at the American work force. "I come with a record in the field of labor that is one of the best of many men in Congress, and yet I come with my hands free, because labor has not been the force that has made me what I am today — the force has been the people," he claimed. He wanted young blacks to be given opportunity through apprenticeship programs, to be given a fair chance to carry the heavy tools of the union members.

This was the kind of talk that had long frightened George Meany, nowhere in attendance on this night. And this was the kind of talk, when reported in the next day's newspapers, that would delight Harlemites, that would give them hope, that encouraged them to keep faith in Powell, that kept them voting for him, election after election. The outside world could not understand. They washed dishes, and they worked for $1.10 an hour. They rode the subways into lower Manhattan, where they could not afford the rents, and scrubbed floors. They worked in grocery stores. They prayed for life's little essentials, and for miracles. Some — too many — were without jobs. For a long time, as their congressman reminded those gathered inside the Hotel Commodore, their "Negro" had been up. And when they were greeted by their congressman, saw him pass their way, saw him raise his arms, felt his hand upon their foreheads, they knew that the weather might not always be cold, that indeed there was a God.

⟨⟩

Among Adam Clayton Powell's first acts upon taking over as chairman of the Education and Labor Committee was to send a bouquet of flowers to Graham Barden, now retired to North Carolina. His staff thought the move classy. Then Powell had the office spiffed up. There were new drapes and new carpeting — all blue, like the sea. Fresh flowers were ordered; he insisted that there always be fresh flowers at staff meetings. (He had asked Rayburn for larger quarters and received them. "I worked like a dog in this campaign, as you probably have heard or will hear, but it was worth every bit of it," he told Rayburn. The implication was that the Democrats now *owed* Adam Powell.) When he called his first committee meeting, some staff members ambled in late. He pounded down a gavel. This was a new chairman, a new era. There would be no lateness. And when that meeting had ended, he hammered the gavel down again. Summoned with the noise of the gavel, they were dispatched with it. "He did all these things early on to let them know he was chairman," recalled a committee aide, Louise Wright.

For eight years there had been hardly any research in the arena of social legislation. Unbeknown to Powell, rebel Democrats had been meeting in Washington during Barden's last two years, devising plans for research. Promoting his own agenda, Powell dismissed their reports and ordered new ones, more sophisticated ones; he hired more staff. He wanted research on juvenile delinquency, hunger, education; they were the woes of not only Harlem but all of America. Adrian Field, an assistant to the committee, remembered "this very progressive, activist chairman taking over a moribund committee. He was one of the quickest-learning people I'd ever seen. He had eyes all over his head."

"He galloped," said Donald Berens, another aide. Sometimes Powell would disappear to the gym for a massage, and the phone would ring in Berens's office, and he would pick it up, and it would be the new chairman, summoning him to deliver yet another piece of correspondence to the White House right away. Sometimes Berens would accompany Powell, and they would hustle over to the White House and slip in a side door to avoid the press. (Once Berens was to meet the chairman at the Longworth building. Berens went to college in the evenings; his days were long, and he sometimes slept late. There he was, running down the hallway toward Powell, out of breath because he was late, when Powell raised his arm, slowly and steadily, and told him to stop running, never to run, to relax. He worked for the chairman and should not worry that the chairman was keeping people waiting; they must simply wait for the chairman.)

Washington had been a cold place for black intellectuals. They had never felt welcome on Capitol Hill. Now things would be different. Powell was deluged with applications from both white and black people, but never before had so many well-trained blacks been so hopeful about working in Congress. This was an education president; this chairman would have to move bills, and he needed good minds to help him do that.

Powell hired a huge staff. Experts went to testify before Powell's committee, and some of those experts were from the historic black colleges, the colleges that had provided both Powell and his father with lecture circuit money. Deborah Wolfe, a black educator with a doctorate, came aboard; she had graduated from Tuskegee Institute. "The place is crawling with Ph.D.'s," Powell quickly bragged. It wasn't really, but no one could deny that there were Ph.D.'s around. Wolfe would roam the halls of Congress, grabbing representatives who were leery of the work that was going on in Chairman Powell's office, leery of these education bills, and pull them in and have them try out this gadget, read that document. She wanted to show them that education was not scary, that the federal government did not intend to knock down school buildings, just to upgrade the schools, to get better education into the schools, and — here was the catch — to integrate those schools. "Deborah, don't you miss teaching?" her friends would ask. And Deborah Wolfe, spunky, unable to let up, unable to slow down, would say, "But I'm teaching Congress!"

"Powell had these eager beavers on the committee who wanted to change the world," recalled Jim O'Hara. "He pushed them. He said, 'Look, I want this committee to be activist: Let's move!'" Of course the White House busied itself in setting the agenda for social legislation. Ribicoff, Goldberg, Willard Wirtz (who succeeded Goldberg) — the minds in the cabinet were thinking quickly. And the president himself was a voracious reader. He had read Michael Harrington's impressive document about poverty, *The Other America,* and it had moved him.

Committee members and their staff people quickly realized that Powell was quick of mind (some concluded that he had a photographic memory) and that he wanted them to be quick. Ideas were taking off like jets. With Kennedy in the White House, Adam Clayton Powell was in the White House. He saw only the big picture; minutiae bored him. For eight years the Republicans had sat on social legislation; now he meant to move it. Sometimes he assigned the same task to several different members of the committee, then took the best report and ran with it.

Chairman Powell launched an all-out assault on discrimination in the unions. He hired young, energetic Herbert Hill to do research. Hill had worked with the NAACP on labor issues — had in fact immersed himself in the issue of jobs for whites and blacks, writing pungent essays, submitting revealing statistics. And middle-aged men from the FDR days were still around, men such as Wilbur Cohen, who worked on domestic legislation, and Robert Weaver, who worked on housing — men whose candles still burned. Powell made Weaver nervous. "Socially, he was like he was professionally — unpredictable," Weaver explained. But he understood that Powell knew what he was doing with the committee: "I think he was smart enough to realize that this was where he'd make his mark."

Powell told his troops — he had thirty-one congressmen on his committee — that there would be hearings from one end of the United States to the other. "We are not looking for headlines," he said beneath the headlines. There would be hearings about job discrimination, hearings about labor disputes. The upper echelons of labor unions pained him; "the cocktail, black-tie, Milquetoast diplomatic set," he called them. Whole buildings went up in Manhattan without a black hand touching a red brick. He held hearings on the minimum wage, then told the Kennedy administration that he was unhappy with its proposal (one dollar an hour with ten cents added over the next two years) because it was too meager. "This bill does not measure up to what I expected," he complained. Still, he personally selected its floor managers. He loathed a bill that would exclude southern laundry workers, men and women barely removed from the cotton fields; Adam Clayton Powell wanted the minimum wage raise, paltry as it was, to reach their hands. The bill was passed — one of many early victories the administration claimed — but there was a compromise: the southern laundry workers were excluded, dealt a cruel blow by the alliance of Dixiecrats and labor officials. Still, victory was victory. Powell's committee members were exultant. "All I want is legislation without pride of authorship," Powell humbly told Lawrence Spivak during an appearance on NBC's *Meet the Press.*

"Powell's genius was allowing his committee members their place in the sun," explained Richard Donohue, a Kennedy aide. Donohue first saw Powell at the West Wing of the White House, alighting from an automobile. "He steps out of his car — double-breasted blue blazer, beautiful slacks. I was struck by a guy representing one of America's poorest districts dressed like that. I didn't appreciate it at the time."

Donohue spent a lot of time in Powell's office, being harangued for yet another perceived slight from the administration. "I remember he was railing at me," said Donohue. "He said, 'This president has got to remember one thing: I was the first Protestant clergyman to support him.' " And whenever Donohue was sitting in Powell's office, he was impressed by the view: "In his office, you could look right over and see the Capitol dome." When reporters found out that Donohue had established a working relationship with Powell, they hunted him down for information. "The press would want me to tell them anecdotes about how irresponsible Powell was," he explained. "I'd say bullshit. He's quick as a wink." Powell's speeches also impressed him. "I can remember him making speeches about the importance of Kuwait. Part of this was his very strategic position on anti-Semitism. He just in-stinctively knew politics."

In Philadelphia, Powell told an NAACP audience that he would strangle any legislation favorable to labor unions until labor "gets in step with democracy." Many in the audience were concerned about the freedom riders in the South, who were being attacked. Powell insisted that their concerns be merged with bold dreams: "We not only want to sit at the lunch counter; we want to work behind it. We not only want to ride the buses; we want to drive them."

⟨～∞～⟩

As busy as he was in Washington, Powell introduced himself into the 1962 mayoral campaign in New York City, a campaign being waged for the very soul of the city's (and the state's) Democratic Party. There had long been a rivalry among New York Democrats: regular machine Democrat versus reform Democrat. Powell gave perfect allegiance to neither camp. After his victory over Tammany Hall in 1958, he formed the United Democratic Leadership Council, whose goal was to prevent a regular-versus-reform schism among Harlem Democrats by ensuring that they would follow only one Democrat: Adam Clayton Powell. As Louis Martin, who kept a keen eye on party maneuvering across the country while at the Democratic National Committee, put it, "Adam was a free spirit."

When Powell allowed Ray Jones into his political camp at the beginning of his 1958 campaign, he did so with the awareness that Jones, never a passionate ally and always a nervy political operative, could turn on him. In 1959 Jones ran for district leader, winning, with Powell's muted support; Powell gave a speech here, one there, repaying his debt. As a district leader, Jones began training younger Harlem politicians — Charlie Rangel, Percy Sutton — because he knew they were hungry. Sutton had even referred to the Powell-Jones alliance in 1958 as "the same cynical old Tammany crowd." Jones heard the complaints of the young men and did not dismiss them; Powell did.

In 1961 Jones made the maverick move that Powell had been wise enough to expect: he gathered his forces in support of Mayor Robert Wagner's re-election bid. Wagner and DeSapio had once been allies but now had tired of each other. In order to survive, Wagner would have to engage in a bruising battle, and there were many who thought he lacked the stomach for such a contest. Jones became a valuable asset, scouring Harlem and claiming talent. He tapped Robert Seavey, a recent law school graduate who loved hanging around Harlem picking up political pointers, to shore up the Jewish vote, and used Rangel and Sutton to tap the black voters, giving the novices their first real taste of political deal-making.

By supporting Wagner, Jones was not only working against Arthur Levitt, the New York state comptroller, who was running against Wagner; he was working against the Powell machine. Powell could not support Wagner because Jones supported Wagner, so he was forced into bed with DeSapio and had to throw his support to Levitt. Emotions swelled, and new enemies were made. "Ray Jones," recalled Seavey, "was running against Adam — and evil." If Wagner won, he was sure to continue the Esplanade housing project, which Seavey had invested money in; Levitt had no attachments to it. "This election was for all of the marbles," explained Seavey. "Control of the city — and Harlem."

One Saturday young Seavey followed Adam Clayton Powell around Manhattan as he visited half a dozen churches, stumping for his Harlem candidates and Levitt. Seavey could not understand Powell, the grip he had on his people — "He was a charlatan; he would lie" — and he could not understand how the people voted for him again and again. But on that Saturday, trailing Powell around Harlem, he began to understand Powell's aura. The congressman would alight from his car, wade into crowds, make himself immediately at home in any church, at peace as controversy swirled around him, raising his voice, using Harlem as the great metaphor for all black hopes and aspirations throughout America. "He would be able to mesmerize me!" Seavey said. "He had me clapping. He would just talk, he had a cadence; he had great illustrations. I couldn't envision Adam as a black man. He spoke Park Avenue English, Colgate English. He never spoke down to the people."

This time Powell's influence was not enough, however. Wagner won the primary against Levitt, and the general election months later, carrying Harlem in both encounters. The Powell forces in Harlem had suffered a setback. "I was crying for joy," recalled Seavey. But the Ray Jones–Robert Wagner jubilation went only so far. "I want peace with Adam," Jones told Seavey, and instructed him to deliver the message. "I had visions that Adam would be broken up," remembered Seavey. "I thought to myself I'd hold Adam, thinking of how I would assuage his feelings." Seavey walked through the doors of the Red Rooster and heard raucous laughter from a table; it was Powell and his entourage. "Adam was sitting at a round table in shirt sleeves, feet up on the table, no shoes on, and seven or eight beer bottles in front of him. He says, 'Bobby, Bobby, have a drink!' It didn't faze him. He was telling jokes. Not a word about the primary. I was so dismayed I walked out.''

Wagner's victory had come at a price: it served to expose the disintegration of New York City's Democratic forces by bringing the warring factions out into the open, where they henceforward stayed. Wagner won with the majority of the reform organizers, the Lehman-Roosevelt factions; Levitt's loss was blamed on the disintegrating powers of DeSapio and the bosses. Liberal Republicans scanned the terrain and saw the open wounds, and as La Guardia had done decades earlier, they realized it was time to begin plotting their strategies to retake City Hall by summoning the old coalition. John Lindsay would be their hope.

Powell began to wash his hands of the internecine wars of New York Democratic politics. He too could tell the fissures would be hard to mend.

⟨※⟩

In Washington Powell continued to segue from inquiry to inquiry. In October 1962 in a Manhattan office he sat across from Harlem barmaids, many of whom he knew personally, and heard them liken their working conditions to slavery. "A lot of the girls are fearful of coming down here," one of them nervously told him. Chairman Powell promised protection: anyone receiving threats for testifying should "call this committee immediately." If he could help barmaids in Harlem, he could help barmaids in St. Louis and Chicago, in Los Angeles and Newark. He liked flying into cities, showing up at scheduled hearings flanked by aides, or, more often than not, sending the aides ahead to do preliminary work, which allowed him to show up alone, just him and the driver; and as soon as he walked into a conference room, the papers would begin shuffling, aides would gather, witnesses would sit upright. Listening to witnesses, threatening recalcitrant individuals with subpoenas — it was exciting, better even than campaigning. "Next week we will hold hearings on the performing arts. . . . On Tuesday we will go into the question of discrimination in television and radio. . . . On Wednesday we are having hearings concerning discrimination in vaudeville and music. We are having Carmen Morales, Puerto Rican dancer and singer, Carla Pinza, Nat King Cole, and Martha Flowers testify . . ."

The hearings Powell's committee had with David Dubinsky, of the ILGWU — the garment industry union — grew heated. The seventy-year-old Dubinsky did not take lightly to being challenged, and struck back by having his union support Powell's 1962 GOP congressional opponent, Mae Watts. Powell crushed Watts without campaigning. In November 1962 he ran the hearings with black and Puerto Rican entertainers, who were woefully underrepresented in the industry. Sidney Poitier and Ossie Davis told of the hardships they suffered in trying to make a living. Powell summoned Otto Preminger, the director, who admitted that there were problems but let drop that he was preparing to direct a movie about politicians and was currently looking for a black actor to play an executive assistant to a southern senator. "I resent the fact that you did not let me try out for the southern senator's part," Powell quipped.

Powell's committee then attacked the large advertising agencies. "I'd like to see a major agency dare, just once," Powell said, "to use a beautiful, beautiful Negro girl and see what happens." He reminded them of the Powell amendment, that he had the president's ear, that he aimed to go the full distance in an effort to fix matters.

It was common knowledge that school systems across America still were not complying with the 1954 school desegregation decision, and Powell dispatched aides to probe and warn. "We had our own plane," recalled Russell Derrickson, the only Barden aide whom Powell kept. When Powell found out there were few blacks on the planning committees for the 1964 World's Fair, to take place in New York, he promised to hold hearings. ("And then we have the professional integrationists," snapped the imperious builder Robert Moses, "who charge us with color bias because we don't appoint Negro vice presidents.")

The Harlem congressman genuinely liked his job. The profiles in the national press were suddenly laudatory; they spoke of a new Powell, more disciplined. "The legislation passed was probably 50 percent better because of Powell's influence," Congressman James Roosevelt said about the bills that came out of the Education and Labor Committee during the first two years of the Kennedy administration — bills for the arts, vocational education, the minimum wage. "He knew his subject. He could show that half a loaf was not as good as a full loaf. He could arouse enthusiasm." Many committee members saw that Powell possessed an unyielding dedication to ending poverty.

The Harlem congressman could not help but like his job. It had its frustrations, true enough; much legislation was primed, only to be halted at the door of Howard Smith's powerful Rules Committee. But this was politics, and Powell had been training for it from the moment he had taken over his father's church, swaying the minds of old men, men who didn't agree with him. Minds would have to bend, and if they would not bend, they would have to be broken — strategically, forcefully, deceptively.

Reporters sought out the powerful chairman for interviews and were kept waiting; the chairman was busy! And he had tired of the endless questions about his social life. Arnold Sawislak and John Beckler were two wire service reporters based in Washington. Sawislak was energetic and talkative, Beckler more reserved and methodical. Being put off by Powell only made Sawislak work that much harder for an interview. Finally Powell said to him, "If you want the cooperation of the chairman, don't ask about my running around the country with women. Then you'll get my cooperation." Powell established a rapport with Sawislak and Beckler, inviting them to committee meetings, allowing them to see how legislation was put together; Sawislak found the experience exhilarating. "The Gold Dust twins," Powell began calling them.

One evening Sawislak was walking down the corridors of Congress with his attractive girlfriend. He decided to take her by to meet Powell. Sawislak sat and watched Powell's show — rising, greeting him and his girlfriend with such warmth, as if they were very important people. He asked them if they wanted anything to drink, and Sawislak's girlfriend asked for a beer. "I have Beck's, from Germany," Powell said. Sawislak had never heard of Beck's. Everyone loved the taste, and the girlfriend thought the congressman was so warm and special. "Good thing you were there," she said to Sawislak later. "I would have propositioned the man."

There was also the White House, where the social affairs boasted easy elegance and effortless sophistication. Kennedy was an arts patron; poets and musicians were regularly invited to the White House. The social calendar was busy. Powell, a frequenter of opening nights on Broadway (he told his colleagues which plays were good, which bad), easily made the Kennedys' guest lists. At one affair he arrived at the White House wearing a green Austrian evening jacket; his cuff links were prized Franz Josef coins. Marian Javits, Senator Javits's wife, could hardly take her eyes off him. She teased him, accusing him of dressing like an Austrian conductor. "He would have had to buy that jacket in Austria," she recalled. "He looked chic and, again, a little opportunistic." The Javitses, of course, knew Powell from New York City, and Marian had become a convert. "You felt everything he was saying was real, the truth," she remembered. "When he would quote from the Bible — well, what more would you want!"

ⲟⲱⲭⲟ

One might well have wondered what Vincent Sardi, of the New York theatrical restaurant, was doing before Powell's committee. Walking in and out of the restaurant for years, Powell had noticed more than celebrities; he had noticed waitresses, the kitchen help, and now Vincent Sardi was appearing before his committee because Chairman Powell was concerned about labor practices and fair treatment. The congressman had such a disarming manner. "Relax and be informal," he told Sardi. "Smoke if you want to." Then he began to grill. He said, "This is in New York City. Testimony will be brought out that waitresses receive thirty cents an hour."

"I remember having to appear before his committee down in Washington," recalled Robert Wagner. "He'd give you a hard time when you had to be a witness before his committee." But then, just before Wagner left the committee room, he was handed a note from Powell: "I hope you . . . can drop down after this and have a drink."

There was hardly a day when someone did not come by the committee office looking for work, dropping off a résumé. Many were handled with dispatch by Maxine Dargans, Powell's secretary. In Washington since the mid-fifties, she had acquired shrewdness. Years of working for a popular congressman had given her a bluntness that she made seem almost graceful. She could hardly stop Powell from hiring whom he wanted to hire, but she did come up with a disparaging term, "charity cases," for those whom the staff concluded had been hired as some form of political payoff — or because of the vibrant personal interest of the congressman himself.

Dargans knew enough to be warm toward Maurice Rosenblatt on the day he dropped by to help his friend Tamara Wall find a job. Rosenblatt was Powell's first campaign fund raiser, and he had come by to introduce his friend. He was now living in Washington and working as a congressional watchdog. He also had a crush on Wall, a young lawyer with dark Mediterranean features. Rarely did she talk of her own background: she had survived Siberian imprisonment as a young girl in Russia; her mother and brothers had not. Powell could hardly refuse Rosenblatt, and hired Wall as an assistant counsel. "Find something for her to do," he said to Dargans. Wall soon found herself telling friends and acquaintances that the Harlem congressman was far more than his critics claimed, that he was intriguing, bright, a hard worker. Rosenblatt could tell that she was enamored of Powell.

Wall's abilities were evident, and she escaped the charity-case label. Corrine Huff did not. Huff had been a fashion model and beauty contestant in Ohio. When she came into the Education and Labor Committee's office, in a green outfit and a matching pillbox hat, the men could hardly take their eyes off her. She was twenty years old and beautiful. Her eyes were narrow and her cheekbones high; Don Berens thought she was Hawaiian or Polynesian. Corrine Huff was neither; she was black. Powell instructed that she be hired as a secretary. Staff members chuckled; a charity case, sure enough. "Mr. Powell made her go to school," recalled Louise Wright. "He made her learn to type. It took her all day to write a letter."

In August 1962 — such a hot month to be in Washington — Adam Clayton Powell asked Tamara Wall and Corrine Huff if they would like to accompany him to Europe, where he would undertake a study of economic conditions for women in the workplace. It took the two women, who had become friends, little time to answer; they were delighted. Rosenblatt, who knew the tremors that gossip could cause along the Potomac, urged his friend not to go. Believing him paranoid, she dismissed his worries and eagerly packed.

They sailed on the *Queen Mary*. Huff and Wall were already aboard by the time Powell strolled along the dockside and then boarded. After five days at sea, where they saw up close how he liked the glamour of the huge ocean liner, how he ingratiated himself with the staff, they docked in London. Then the two young committee members were treated to the European Adam Clayton Powell. They went to the theater in London, avoiding the shows that he had seen on Broadway, then off to Paris, where a chauffeur whisked them along the boulevards to the wide doors of their elegant hotel. It was late summer, and many of the French had left for the countryside; they nearly had Paris to themselves. Among the hottest tickets in Paris was the risqué after-dinner show at the Lido, where the women danced practically nude. Powell led them to their seats as if he owned the nightspot. Later they went to Venice for two days, then Rome, among Powell's favorite cities, for three days. Soft winds blew along the streets of

Rome; umbrellas shielded them from the sun; the food was wonderful. Then they were off again, to Athens, then to Madrid, beautiful Madrid.

Both young women could see it: the power Powell had in Washington was somehow transformed here, in Europe, in such a sensual way; the world seemed his oyster. As a European, Tamara Wall did not have preconceptions of Powell as a black man; her vision and interpretation were formed on her own, without the influence of stereotype. She found the congressman fascinating. (The wily Maurice Rosenblatt had been right in assuming that Powell was having an affair, but he guessed the wrong woman. It was Corrine Huff who slept with Powell during the journey; Wall had been brought along not only to do legal research but as a buffer against incrimination: two women presented the veil of work.)

Back in America after this trip, Powell was confronted by older congressmen who wondered about his motives; they demanded to see the reports, evidence of research. Drew Pearson, the Washington reporter (some believed him more muckraker than reporter, but his column was widely read), had played the hell out of the journey in his columns. Powell ignored the uproar. There was so much to worry about: the legislation constantly being written, then presented to the full House; the hearings — the fun of riding shotgun on the New Frontier. Nevertheless, it was things like this — the griping, the gossip, the kinds of stories he had warned Beckler and Sawislak to avoid — that pained him and made him wonder if it was all worth it. The victories during the first two years of the administration were better than anything else he had seen on the domestic front, but it was obvious that foreign crises — foremost, the Bay of Pigs invasion — had sidetracked the administration. The legislation that had passed was not enough; he wanted more, demanded more. Howard Gamser, whose background was in labor law as a mediator, sometimes urged caution. Often he tried to bring the liberals and the conservative southerners together. Powell could grow temperamental. He wanted the southerners brought to their knees. "Whatever you say, Mr. Chairman" became Gamser's typical response when another clash loomed. After a year Gamser left Powell's staff. At times tension gripped the committee; some aides were so overworked that they began to take their lunches at their desk. It was work, and more work; Powell wanted victories.

One would have thought that with all their knowledge of Adam

Clayton Powell, members of Kennedy's administration would have become accustomed to his unpredictable habits. But they had not. They simply found it hard to fathom that on some days, when they needed the chairman of the Education and Labor Committee, he was nowhere to be found. He was in fact down in Puerto Rico — at home, with his new wife and new baby.

☙

Shortly after Hazel Scott journeyed to Juarez, Mexico, to obtain her divorce in 1960, the congressman phoned Yvette Flores in San Juan. He was flush with the election victory at the time. "December is a good time to get married," he said — and that, as she remembered, was his proposal. It was a small ceremony, with no more than sixty in attendance. (Powell's staff presented him with a silver tray as wedding gift. It had the names of his committee members on it.) The couple honeymooned on the island. Adam squired Yvette in and out of the fashionable nightclubs. At one of the clubs Harry Belafonte stopped in midperformance after spotting Powell and extended greetings from the stage; Yvette was impressed.

Before the Bay of Pigs invasion, Powell took his wife across to Cuba, and there was laughter and partying beneath bright lights in the huge hotels. She briefly went to work for him in Washington as his secretary. With his Puerto Rican constituency growing, he needed someone to translate his mail. (In addition to professing love, Adam Clayton Powell seemed to gain politically from his marriages. Isabel had attracted the entertainment crowd; Hazel, the West Indian powers of Harlem; and now Yvette, with her Puerto Rican ancestry, forged ties to Spanish Harlem.) But Yvette's tenure in Washington was brief; Washington seemed another world to her. She returned to Puerto Rico and gave birth to a boy, Adam Diego Powell (Adamcito), in 1961.

The congressman loved the ocean, loved walking in the sand. He began to dream by the water. Perhaps it was dangerous to dream by the water, but he could not help himself. Few men can avoid dreaming by the water, no matter how dangerous. In a rural area thirty-five miles outside San Juan known as Cerro Gordo, where tobacco and sugar farmers still worked in fields, where oxen still struggled under the morning sun, Powell spotted land for a home. Unsure whether he should buy it, he consulted with his friend Laurance Rockefeller, who was busy buying up stretches of land and building hotels along the Puerto Rican coastline. Rockefeller thought the purchase wise. Then

Powell summoned his son Adam III to help him draw up designs. When the house, in Dutch Indonesian style, was finished, it had Italian marble floors, a sprinkling fountain, several guestrooms; the rush of ocean was only yards from the front door. A quartet of servants tended to the family. Powell called his new home Villa Reposa — "peace and quiet."

The hundred-mile island had both a proud and a tortured history. In 1898, following the Spanish-American War, Puerto Rico came under U.S. jurisdiction. But hostilities over its direction festered through the decades. One faction, led by the Nationalists, formed in 1922, advocated independence. At times their methods of expression turned violent. There were uprisings in 1950. In 1953 the island did gain its right to self-government. Then, in 1954, in a bizarre assault inside the House of Representatives in Washington, Nationalists who opposed Truman's policies opened fire on U.S. congressmen, wounding five.

To Powell, granting Puerto Rico commonwealth status was little more than the extension of colonialism. He began to clash with local politicians opposed to his view. "Sing the 'Borinquefia,' but first sing 'The Star-Spangled Banner'!" he told a group of prominent Puerto Ricans. "Speak the native tongue of Spain, but also make mandatory the teaching and usage of the English language!" There were times when the words of the congressman from Harlem sounded all but condescending. "Whether you are conscious of it or not, there is rapidly developing in the psyche of Puerto Rico an inferiority complex," he said to a local gathering. "This would happen to any people who must continually come in the back door. I am sure it must be embarrassing to you to see other peoples, in increasing numbers, walking in the front door through statehood." Slowly, then obviously, Powell began throwing his weight around as chairman of the Education and Labor Committee, telling local politicians that they were playing a dangerous game with him because they were putting federal funds at risk. His message was stark: to oppose him was to put Puerto Rico at financial risk from Congress. (Powell used to joke with island politicians that his committee's budget was bigger than the entire budget of Puerto Rico.)

Powell saw independence as a mere ode to nostalgia. Local politicians, especially Governor Luis Muñoz Marín, whose political roots were pro-commonwealth, did not take the threats lightly. They muttered among themselves, wondering what ulterior motives the Harlem congressman had. (Marín's wife once stopped off at a school that was flying an American flag. She demanded that the flag be lowered and taken off. When it was, she laid it on the ground and began dancing on it.) When the local politicians cornered Powell and demanded to know why he was so insistent on Puerto Rican statehood, he would tell them about his son: he wanted his youngest son to grow up to be president of the United States, and now he could not, because Puerto Rico was not a state, only a territory. The questions about motives pained him. "If there is a lynching in Mississippi, I, as an American citizen and as a member of Congress, have an interest in it and express myself," he tried explaining to a reporter. "If there is a violation of civil rights among the Mexican migratory workers in southern California, I take an interest in that. I'm an American citizen. Puerto Rico is a part of the United States of America, and if anything goes on there, just like in any of the fifty states, I take an interest in it." There were those on the island who began wondering if Powell was an opportunist — and a carpetbagger.

Secretly, Adam Clayton Powell told his older son that if the territory were to achieve statehood, he would run for United States senator from the island. His wife was Puerto Rican; he had a home on the island; the dream was rational. It would, of course, be such a coup, to walk from the House over to the Senate, to take a seat with senators — southern senators, Dixiecrat senators — to fly over them and their states on the journey back to Puerto Rico, a drink in hand, comfortable and happy.

In early July 1962 a small group of men, a faction of the pro-independence movement, appeared on the Powells' lawn. Yvette's husband was away in Washington. She heard the voices rising in volume. "They came over and made a big show in front of the house," she recalled. "Told me I sold myself for money, started throwing money on the grass, started saying 'Yankee Go Home.'" She stayed behind her door, peering through windows and watching the commotion. There was no phone yet; it hadn't been installed. Soon the demonstrators left. As evening grew near, she kept her baby particularly close. Later that night rocks came hurtling through the glass windows. Startled, she jumped, reaching for the baby. The demonstrators had returned. The rocks kept coming; glass shattered; the dogs began barking wildly. Without a phone, she could not summon police. All of her life, Yvette Powell had lived on this island, and it had come to this: her love of Puerto Rico was being threatened. That night she was afraid for her life and, more important, for the life of her little son. Finally the demonstrators disappeared; the dogs stopped barking. Yvette reached a telephone the next morning and quickly called her husband in Washington. Powell was livid. He called Governor Marín and said that if anything happened to his wife and son, there would be severe reprisals for the whole island. Marín rushed police guards to the Powell compound. For an entire year he kept them there as protection.

There was little peace and quiet at Villa Reposa for the Harlem congressman. Reality began to dim his visions of statehood.

᠃

The Democrats lost seats in the House after the 1962 elections. The losses were expected — a president's usual midterm setback. Nevertheless, they weakened Kennedy's domestic agenda, already burdened by his ill-fated foreign forays. "The Democrats got the responsibility," Jim O'Hara was told, "and the Republicans got the power." Kennedy's victories on the domestic front had never been resounding; the minimum wage battle had been bruising. Powell's committee wrote an omnibus school bill; reluctantly, the chairman withdrew the Powell amendment in hopes of gaining passage, but the bill failed anyway. Powell began wondering if he hadn't been right to oppose Kennedy, as he had done in the spring of 1960; he blamed Kennedy and his staff for not being able to muscle the Dixiecrat votes, for being less than persuasive in the art of arm-twisting.

Legislative woes were hardly Powell's only problems in early 1963. Power alone could not curb the explosive manner in which race and sex cut through the nation's capital and the country itself. House members began snickering about his European jaunt in the cloakroom; there were whispers and asides about a ménage-à-trois. Omar Burleson, the Texas Democrat who controlled the House Finance Committee — the committee that funded committees — demanded an exact accounting of Powell's trip. In March he rebuffed Powell's request for a committee budget of $697,000, allowing only $200,000. Powell bitterly complained, to no avail. The attack on a chairman's power reached over onto the Senate floor — a rare event. Senator John Williams, of Delaware, rose to attack Powell, and Senator Wayne Morse, of Utah, rose as quickly to defend him.

Under attack both from fellow politicians and in the courts, where Esther James was pursuing her libel suit, Powell expected support from civil rights organizations. When it didn't come (the organizations considered their efforts to lobby on behalf of civil rights legislation far more important than Powell's problems), he went on the offensive, accusing the NAACP of being run by whites out to get him, assailing the blacks who worked for it. Stung, the NAACP quickly issued a booklet, "The NAACP and Adam Clayton Powell," listing its differences with the congressman. It called Powell "completely ignorant" of NAACP strategies. "We're not separatists," announced Roy Wilkins, whose debates with Powell went back two decades. Jewish leaders, whose support had always proved valuable, joined in the chorus of attacks on Powell. Anti-Powell editorials, many of which showed raw venom, began to appear frequently in the *New York Times*. "And, of course, the *New York Times* is very, very biased," Powell said, "and it's unfortunate that it's biased when it's owned and operated by a minority group."

In Harlem a new, magnetic figure had begun making his presence felt on the streets: Malcolm X. Curious, Powell began making appearances with the former convict, who was building an edgy following among urban dwellers who appeared attracted to his Muslim preachings. But Powell's curiosity was brief; a political loner, he soon turned away from Malcolm X, giving his attention to what he perceived as a more dangerous threat. Looking downtown, he realized that Mayor Wagner was now backing Ray Jones for a seat on the city council — a merger that could usurp his power. Powell coaxed his impressionable lawyer, Henry Williams, into the city council race, but Williams was humiliated. The defeat didn't seem to slow Powell down.

At a sit-in waged by black parents protesting an all-white school in Englewood, he advised the group to hold on, and he said that he was not going anywhere, that Congress could not get rid of him, could hardly tell him, Adam Clayton Powell, what to do. He was flying, in fact, to Paris in a few days, and he was flying as he always flew, first class. Paris was beautiful that summer. Powell enjoyed himself, and made predictions. "This is the year of truth" for America, he said. "The white man discovered in Birmingham that his naked power is no longer of any value. Now he is afraid of his conscience."

⚭

For several months veterans of the civil rights movement, led by A. Philip Randolph, had been vowing to hold a massive demonstration in Washington, a march. The Kennedy administration balked but could do nothing, in the end, to stop it. For Adam Clayton Powell the possibility of a march was glorious. He made plans to host the leaders in his committee chambers; he would show King, Randolph, Granger, his critics, what power really meant. But without his knowledge, the march organizers were planning to exclude him from all facets of the meeting. They considered him too dangerous and unpredictable; his attacks on the NAACP had not been forgotten.

Hundreds of thousands of people, many of whom had been valiant in the southern civil rights struggle, arrived in Washington on August 28. The United States had rarely witnessed such a mass of human beings. They surrounded the Mall. Speaker after speaker spoke of the gulf of race and the sad lot of black Americans. The Kennedys listened nervously by radio in the White House. No speech, however, resonated like that of Martin Luther King, Jr. The minister had a beautiful voice, musical in its cadences, and he used it to full effect in his historic "I Have a Dream" speech. At the conclusion of his address, America knew it had a genuine prophet in its midst. The young minister's status rose perceptibly. Some in the crowd asked about Powell, who was in attendance but had nothing to do. The Harlem congressman was clearly pained by the way he had been treated.

Adam Clayton Powell and Martin Luther King, while both ministers, could not have been more different. King, a southerner, had relied on an elegant education — a bachelor's degree from a seminary, a doctorate from Boston University, and the teachings of Kant and Gandhi — to guide him. He aimed to alter a nation's moral fiber from the ground up. With his arms twisted behind his back in yet another arrest, his straw hat atop his small head, he served notice to America that his imprisonment was everyone's imprisonment, that higher forces indeed guided him and his followers. Politics and politicians seemed almost to bore him; he was more interested in changing hearts. When King was in Powell's presence, one sensed his nervousness as well as his deference. One also sensed his higher moral fiber.

Powell, twenty-one years older than King, could not alter his condescending attitude toward the southern minister. He particularly did not like the civil rights movement's new emphasis on the South, to the exclusion of the North. Powell knew problems persisted in the North. He did not surround himself with a phalanx of men as King did, to help hone his strategies. The Harlem congressman was a lone operative. More important, Powell was a politician first and a minister second. He saw limitations in the ministry, opportunity in politics.

Look what he had done in the minimum wage fight — one bill, *one bill,* and it had already started boosting American paychecks. If you had been making seventy dollars a week and were living in Biloxi, Mississippi, you were now bringing home eighty dollars a week. The increase might provide an extra pair of shoes; over a month, an extra winter coat; over a year, a down payment on a truck. Adam Clayton Powell had sent millions of dollars into the homes of working people with hardscrabble jobs. And he had done it by fighting the same forces King was fighting — Dixiecrats, southern conservatives — only he was fighting them in Washington, the nation's capital, and he was fighting them to win a decision on the law books.

Shortly after Powell returned from Paris, he warned a Southern Christian Leadership Conference in Richmond that there would be no civil rights bill from the Kennedy administration. They did not have the votes, and he knew it. Then, in a move that spoke of desperation, he told the conference he was offering Martin Luther King, Jr., a copastorship of his church. It was an offer that King never seriously considered.

Back in April, Esther James had won the first phase of her libel suit against Adam Clayton Powell. Rarely at a loss for words, she made comments that now took on a unique pungency. "I was afraid of [Powell] in Harlem," she said after the verdict, "but I found out this is America." Powell told his Harlem lawyer, Henry Williams, to appeal. "Don't give the bitch a dime," he said. Williams followed his advice, setting off on a tortuous legal odyssey.

Powell was forbidden to enter New York City, except on Sundays, until he paid the libel award. Seen in Manhattan on any other day, he faced arrest. (Many began linking the popular show tune "Never on Sundays" to the Harlem congressman.)

As a fugitive minister, Powell began to peer into the future. He thought of retiring from both pulpit and Congress, the pulpit at the end of 1963, Congress a year later. Such news was too much for his congregation to take all at once, so Powell informed them only of his plans for the pulpit. "You can get another minister tomorrow," he tried to explain, "but it takes twenty years to get a chairman!" The congregation shuddered at the thought. He told his journalist friend Mike Wallace that he might try Madison Avenue advertising. "He was going to be a consultant," Wallace recalled. "He always talked about wanting to make money." At times he told his son Adam III that he wished the Kennedy administration would appoint him to an ambassador's post; he preferred London — the ambassador to the Court of St. James's — but would accept Paris.

He began to feel despondent and defensive. He admonished his black critics who felt he had done little for New York City blacks to walk across Harlem, from river to river, and peer inside the stores, "and every Negro they see in a store is there because I helped put him there." America could either identify with Harlem or assail it. Presidential candidates came to Harlem; it was no longer a community to ignore. By sheer power, Adam Clayton Powell had put the tip of Manhattan on the political map. He had made Harlem a political rallying cry, while more and more he was thinking of leaving the community. Vice President Johnson had his ranch, the LBJ Ranch, in Texas; Powell had his spread, Villa Reposa, in the foothills of Puerto Rico, by the water. Who would not enjoy such scenery, such a climate?

◦ ⋙◦

Of course the bullets in Dallas changed so much for everyone, not least the Harlem congressman. It was with a feeling of heavy remorse that Adam Clayton Powell climbed into his pulpit following John Kennedy's assassination. The choir had been instructed to sing something memorable, and they did — "We Shall Meet at the River." Tears fell and voices rose. "Weep not for Jack Kennedy," Powell told his congregation. "Weep for America. Weep for a land that does things to people because they are black. Weep for a state that can bomb seven churches in one day."

His sermons continued to embody his never-lost vigor. Heading to a fund raiser one evening with his son, he stopped to tend to a vagrant who was lying near the Waldorf-Astoria. Powell motioned to a police officer, then made a scene, vowing not to leave until the man was given assistance. The policeman didn't recognize the congressman, and asked why he was so worried about the vagrant. "Adam Clayton Powell will never step over someone who has fallen down," he replied. The next morning, in the Abyssinian pulpit, Powell began his sermon by alluding to the incident: "The good people of Park Avenue were stepping over a man — and he wasn't even black . . ."

That December, shoulder to shoulder with rent strikers in Harlem, Powell felt that some of the old rebelliousness had faded in his long absence. "Let's give Harlem the old spirit it used to have," he suggested.

Powell had been the first black national figure to support Lyndon

Johnson, as early as 1959. In Johnson he did not see what he loathed in politicians, timidity; he saw shrewdness and guile. Now Johnson was president. Adam Clayton Powell heard LBJ's men, Lawrence O'Brien and Jack Valenti, coming down the hall to tell him of Johnson's heightened domestic agenda, to tell him to get ready. "We're going to start moving around here," Valenti said. Powell had long been ready; he was past ready.

In preparing for the final triumph of his life, Adam Clayton Powell would go into battle once again against the Dixiecrats, and against any liberals who stood in his path. He sensed glory on the horizon, unaware of how heavy the price for victory would be.

VI

AND THE
POWER
1964–1966

B OTH LYNDON JOHNSON and Adam Powell had come to Washington — Johnson in 1937, Powell in 1945 — with memories of the Depression fresh in their minds. In their early years, both so eager and enthusiastic, they wanted to get things done. They raced from door to door; they pounded podiums; they picked the brains of their allies, and their allies were the New Dealers, the idealists, the men and women who welcomed them to Washington. They were both huge men, but neither Johnson nor Powell was a gangly figure. There was something controlled about their size; they were men who realized what it meant to be big. Their outstretched arms, their wide wingspread, was used alternately to bear-hug and to make a point, and yet at times it seemed as if they were summoning the whole world into their universe and their personal grasp. They filled rooms like helium in a balloon, and the cautious politicians quickly took note.

Both Johnson and Powell became astute at reading political winds. Trying to change minds, they risked attack by racing ahead of the wind. Their speed sometimes produced angst; other men wondered what drove them, wondered exactly what their ambitions were. Few in Washington at the beginning of 1964 realized how much this president from Texas and this New York City congressman were alike, how much they had in common, how far each would go to have his way, to push the kind of legislation that mattered to both.

They were born in the same year, 1908, and came into adulthood during the Hoover years. When Hoover fell from grace, they began their respective rises in the New Deal. The America that existed before the spread of FDR's legislative shadow was an uncompromising America, and they did not like it. Their reputations were made against the backdrop of grieving widows and haunted veterans and hungry children — of poverty itself. When Adam Clayton Powell was marching from street corner to street corner, from one end of Harlem to the other, the young Lyndon Johnson, down in Texas, was a congressional secretary trying to help farm women with electrification, trying to help farmers by forestalling bank closures, which swept the plains of Texas during the Great Depression. As Robert Caro has written, "Johnson reaped for his district every dollar it could provide. He urged district farmers to repay their 1933 crop reduction loans as quickly as possible, so that they could get new loans."

When those around them would not let them move fast enough, Johnson and Powell struck out on their own. And while Johnson's career in the House was shortened by a successful Senate campaign, his streak of independence showed during the 1957 civil rights debate, when he disagreed with other southerners and asserted that the civil rights bill was needed. He did not go as far as Adam Clayton Powell, who supported Eisenhower during the 1956 election, but he too had surprised fellow politicians.

Neither was a lawyer. They believed they were smarter than most lawyers; and they knew also that in the end it did not matter whether you were a lawyer or not, but whether you could get the bill passed.

At the Democratic national conventions, older party leaders realized that Johnson and Powell could be unruly. Both always seemed ready to bolt, in this or that direction; both listened intently, but if they did not hear what they wanted and needed to hear from others, they merely obeyed their own voices. By sheer virtue of their unpredictability they instilled fear in other men, especially those quiet, obsequious congressmen of whom there seemed to be no shortage in Washington.

In time they learned which buttons to push, how to claim a newspaper's headline, how to work the press, which votes to hold; they learned how to talk to Sam Rayburn and when to ignore Sam Rayburn; they certainly learned how to manipulate John McCormack, Rayburn's successor in 1961. "Johnson and Powell were great politicians, great believers in knowing which way the winds were blowing," explained Jack Valenti. Neither man had really loved a president since Roosevelt, had felt a president's power, the kind of power they liked and appreciated, coming out of Washington. Roosevelt had proved to them that power was a unique tool that, when used correctly, could work wonders. It is little wonder that Johnson and Powell did not particularly like John Kennedy, because, having been in Washington for years, they did not see battle dust on his shoes. Johnson thought him a lightweight, and the animus between the two men never really evaporated, although there were signs of grudging respect if not real warmth.

Few politicians in America had come to know the country better than Lyndon Johnson and Adam Clayton Powell. Powell realized in 1960 that big-city bosses would never back Lyndon Johnson's presidential run, but he backed Johnson anyway, and he took unbridled ridicule from fellow blacks. While he knew that the big southerner had not made his reputation as a liberal, he was a resourceful politician, and once he had claimed his ground, he looked for others to recruit. Whenever Powell was having a problem with a southern congressman, "he'd go to Johnson," recalled George Reedy, one of Johnson's aides. Once both men, Johnson and Powell, traveled to Jamaica for that country's independence festivities. Johnson was then the vice president. At the hotel one evening, Johnson got drunk and collapsed into sleep. Powell, who held his liquor extremely well, nudged up to Reedy and began asking questions — a lot of questions, Reedy said — and they were all about Johnson, his likes and dislikes, strengths and weaknesses.

For many years in Washington one couldn't help but hear Johnson and Powell coming. They made an impression; they entered rooms to win, and when they did not win, one had the feeling that they would be back, that one day the tide would turn. Others may have hated the backstabbing and the political intrigue of the Capitol, but these two men liked it, relished the day-to-day battles. At its best, Washington meant that the hungry would be fed, the sick cared for, the elderly tended, black Americans given hope. Now, in the dawn of 1964, with domestic legislation about to become as important as it had been in the days of the New Deal, two of the most important men in Washington were Lyndon Johnson and Adam Clayton Powell. The jagged edge of destiny had touched them. And both were sure of what they had to do.

～∞～

When Johnson announced his War on Poverty in March 1964, it created a unique opportunity for Powell. Johnson's Council of Economic Advisors had issued him a daunting report. One fifth of Americans were poor, going to bed hungry at night; nearly half of these were blacks and other minorities; the heads of six out of ten of these households had only a grade-school education; a third of the poor families were headed by senior citizens. Obviously, education and labor were the key factors in attacking the woes of poverty. If a person could get an education, he could get a job, and thus lift himself up from poverty.

Lyndon Johnson liked to communicate directly with Democratic chairmen, often bypassing his own cabinet members. Congress represented America, but deep in the House of Representatives sat twelve chairmen of committees, and the real power lay with them. The barons held the kind of power that got dams constructed, roads paved, hospitals built in one community and not the next community over; they were the men who could unleash legislation or bring it to an agonizing halt. There were 435 representatives and 12 chairmen, which meant that each chairman was as powerful as a bloc of 36 congressmen. Johnson assigned members of his staff to maintain direct contact with the chairmen and other powerful members of Congress — in effect, to keep them as happy as possible. Jack Valenti was assigned to Adam Clayton Powell, among others. "What that meant was that when they called in, I had carte blanche authority to put them through to the president," he explained. "I took care of them."

Now, after so many years, Powell was both hopeful and giddy. He had long been a soldier in the war on poverty and discrimination — had been a soldier, in fact, before the war had been officially declared. Now the government was joining his war. He had a president behind him, a president who knew Washington, who knew the southern senators and southern representatives, who had kept his arm around the shoulders of the liberals when he had to; a president who had already, in late 1963, sent a multimillion-dollar pilot youth grant (a precursor to the Office of Economic Opportunity) into Harlem, creating the Harlem Youth Opportunities Act, in the district of the chairman of the Education and Labor Committee.

Many on Powell's committee and staff were simply amazed at how he took over all poverty hearings. He set up the subcommittee hearings and did most of the speaking. Hearings were speeded up; critics of the poverty program were given scant time to testify, then dismissed, and Powell rebuffed conservatives, treating them rudely. Striding down the corridors with his aides in tow, he gathered more statistics, in addition to the studies he had ordered during the Kennedy years; he harangued more mayors; he threatened more city officials and lobbyists; he began warning of new federal powers that would come his way when the president's economic acts were passed.

In August, Johnson's Economic Opportunity Act of 1964 became law. Powell was given a great deal of credit for the way the bill was rammed through the House. A phone call came through his office, from Texas. Jeanne Thomson, one of his staffers, answered it. "Johnson was calling to congratulate him on getting it through," she said. Powell had controlled the hearings ruthlessly; the pounding of his gavel echoed throughout committee meeting rooms as he swiveled left, then right in his high-backed chair, reaching for a cigarette, nodding to aides. Republican debate and response was limited. He conferred with the White House only when he needed to — rarely, as it turned out. He had begun joking with critics that he had enough votes — had so many, in fact, that he could now give votes away. Once he was so arrogant as to lock Republicans out of his hearings. They tacked a note on the door: "Open the door, Adam." He did; he flashed a smile, then abruptly closed it again.

The Economic Opportunity Act, among other things, created the Office of Economic Opportunity (OEO); Powell was its authorizing committee chairman. The office included a stunning array of programs. There was Community Action, designed to give the poor and voiceless, especially in southern communities, a chance by offering jobs; Head Start, which gave young women and their babies help in childbirth and in early schooling; a novel program called Upward Bound, which reached deep into the ghettos of America, pulled out high school students with academic potential, and sent them to a college for the summer to become acclimated to college life. There were work-study programs for college students, both poor and middle-class. "There is no more senseless waste than the waste of brainpower and skill of those who are kept from college by economic circumstance," Johnson had said in his March address. There were programs for Native Americans, for farm workers, and for farmers. There was a massive Job Corps program, which sent impoverished students to work and train in communities.

Lyndon Johnson would now be able to care for not just the old women of the hill country in Texas, women whom he had seen and remembered, but old women everywhere, women who had been children during the Depression, whose mothers he knew in the way that anyone with feeling knows the poor when roaming through poor cities and towns and villages. Powell, in tandem, would be able to help not only the women of the Harlem tenements, the women who had scrubbed the floors of the rich in Manhattan townhouses, but poor women everywhere, the women who had come out to see him in the churches across America.

Johnson appointed Sargent Shriver, the Peace Corps director during the Kennedy administration, to run the OEO. Shriver was skillful and smooth. He had worked in Chicago in the Kennedy family business, had become involved in the problems of urban America, and had put in time on the tough Chicago school board. His ambitions were as big as Johnson's, as big as Powell's.

No longer on the defensive, Adam Clayton Powell was now often beaming. "He had this suite of offices," recalled Mike Wallace. "He had a kitchen, a refrigerator. He was so proud of it." Daniel Rappaport, a wire service reporter, got a thrill out of stopping by Powell's office to keep an eye on him. Rappaport didn't mind being kept waiting; there were always the secretaries to look at (like many others, he had a crush on Corrine Huff). Then Powell would appear and move quickly out the door, Rappaport on his heels. "He glided along the carpet," said Rappaport. "He always looked like he was in shape."

The plan to cut Powell's committee budget, launched in 1963, was moot with the new Congress. LBJ was not about to allow Powell to be embarrassed, and Powell hired even more staff members, more lawyers, more researchers. Résumés were coming into his office at an astounding clip. Donald Anderson's credentials — University of Michigan Law School, London School of Economics — were so impressive that the committee was surprised to see that he was not white but black. "I was afraid I would have to work for a bureaucracy, which would bore me to death," Anderson remembered. After his interview, he parked his car at the base of the Jefferson Memorial, sat behind the wheel, and tried to decide whether to return home or stay in Washington. When Powell hired him as assistant labor counsel, his work was anything but boring — poverty legislation, labor laws, the very things he wanted to do in Washington. It was becoming evident that Adam Powell was attracting the cream of black talent from all over the country.

Michael Schwartz was fresh out of law school in Florida when he was hired by Powell. "When you first met him, you almost didn't hear him," recalled Schwartz. "You were shocked by the charisma, the glitter in the eyes." Powell's talent was in making those intimidated by him feel at ease. So there he was, the tall Powell, throwing his arms around the short Schwartz, asking him what his specialty was, what he really wanted to do, education or labor. Schwartz said labor. Schwartz had rented an apartment adjacent to Powell's own Washington apartment on Guessford Court. Some nights Powell would knock on the walls, and that would be Schwartz's cue: he was being invited over. When he arrived, Powell would start talking about legislation, this War on Poverty, and their discussions would last late into the night. "He had visions of what those bills would do, could do," said Schwartz. Months after the enormous program went into effect, Powell sent him around the country to see how the War on Poverty was playing: "He wanted to know what the people felt!" So there was Schwartz, meeting with ordinary people, telling them that he had been sent by Adam Clayton Powell himself, and seeing the proud looks on their desperate faces. Sometimes the meetings would start off with anger — "Let's kill the white boy." Then Schwartz would calm them and start talking about Powell, about the bills that would soon mean jobs and money, for that is what the War on Poverty meant to Powell. "He never talked in terms of number of bills," explained Schwartz. "He talked in terms of the money he could put into the system to help people."

The War on Poverty program in effect opened entire communities up to governmental action. Southern congressmen committed to states' rights had their fears. John Flynt, of Georgia's fourth district, told the administration that the War on Poverty was simply a ruse to foster racial integration, that it was "government by decree." All across the South now, blacks and whites began working side by side in community centers, in Job Corps programs.

On July 2 Johnson signed the most sweeping civil rights legislation since Reconstruction, since the days just before the first black congressmen had arrived in Washington. The Civil Rights Act of 1964 outlawed discrimination in public places and in employment. It stipulated that federal funds could no longer be used to foster segregation — a sweeping bow to Adam Clayton Powell and his decades-old amendment. "Let us close the springs of racial poison," Johnson said to the nation about the bill. He could sense, however, the dangers inherent in the legislation, and knew that some southern whites would rise up in protest. "The purpose of this law is simple. It does not restrict the freedom of any American so long as he respects the rights of others. It does not give special treatment to any citizen. It does say the only limit to a man's hope for happiness and for the future of his children shall be his own ability."

☙❧

Before the Democrats gathered in Atlantic City for the 1964 presidential convention in late August, the Republicans convened in San Francisco. Theirs was not a smooth convention; it was nearly disastrous. Senator Barry Goldwater, of Arizona, representing the extreme right wing of the party, won the nomination over the more moderate forces of William Scranton, the Pennsylvania governor. Moderate Republicans sensed doom.

Senator Eugene McCarthy, in Atlantic City for his party's convention, told delegates (they were wild with enthusiasm) that Goldwater's vision was one in which "calendars have no years, clocks have no hands," a world "where it is impossible to distinguish between the white horse of victory and triumph and the pale horse of death and destruction." Lyndon Johnson showed up late and prosperous; it was his convention, and just as in 1936, when the Democrats were sure of their choice (FDR), there was no roll-call vote. The only drama was who Johnson's vice presidential choice would be. He leaned toward Thomas J. Dodd, a senator from Connecticut, but finally chose Senator Hubert Humphrey, from Minnesota. Powell showed up with an entourage, wearing a smile on his face and packing a pistol: since President Kennedy's assassination, letters threatening his life, which he had always received, had begun to multiply.

There were telling scenes on the Atlantic City boardwalk — gawkers, and many young people from the Deep South, come to protest. Some of the black southerners obtained passes from sympathizers so they could get into the convention. Robert Moses, the brilliant student organizer, recalled locking eyes with Powell, whose delegate's pass was dangling from his neck, and wondering if Powell was going to offer it; when Powell smiled a mischievous smile, Moses knew that he was not giving it up. The Harlem congressman needed to be inside. (But Powell had a keen eye for talent. He offered Moses a job on his staff, which Moses turned down.) In reality, the kids on the boardwalk were not Adam Clayton Powell's kids. They were undeniably closer to Martin Luther King, and because Powell had not reconciled with King, or any of the civil rights leaders, he did not wade among them. Their path was moral; Powell's was political.

Robert Kennedy appeared at the convention, relying heavily on the powerful New York delegation. Robert Wagner, Averell Harriman, the New York City bosses, all realizing the damage done to their state's Democratic coalition by infighting, had convinced Kennedy that the moment was ripe for him to launch a run for the Senate.

∽∾

A month after the convention, Adam Clayton Powell was fêted in Harlem, given a day all his own, a salute to his achievements. It was a festive occasion with a sixty-car caravan, Powell riding in a shiny black Cadillac and pumping his fist in the air and toward the crowds lining the streets. It was the kind of parade that evoked memories of the parades of the past — a hero's parade. And it gave Powell a chance not so much to heal wounds but to explain why he had had to intervene in local politics in the first place. When Governor Wagner's forces had wanted to name their own person to head the Harlem Youth Opportunities program, Powell had threatened the administration in Washington that he would hold up the entire poverty program unless he could hand-pick his man. Kenneth Clark, who originally headed the program, had an esteemed reputation; he had been one of the key witnesses as a psychologist during the 1954 testimony in the *Brown* v. *Board of Education* decision. But by challenging Powell's power he had waded into dangerous waters. "Clark was over his head with Powell and tried to undercut him," said Clifford Alexander, who briefly worked with the program. "You don't undercut a powerful member of Congress." To Powell, Clark represented the downtown crowd, "hungry ivory-tower leaders." Powell appointed Livingston Wingate to head the program instead.

Powell told Harlemites of the bills, the legislation, the money — nearly $7 billion in domestic legislation that had come across his desk, had flowed across America, had flowed here, to Harlem, down these very streets. "But I am not content," he said. He wanted more — more money to make the Great Society even greater. So passionate was he about the program that he admitted he must make a sacrifice; he would once again forgo his own House campaign to campaign instead for President Johnson, for the Great Society.

Powell hit the road, traveling from city to city — Cleveland and Chicago, Los Angeles and Philadelphia, Detroit and San Francisco, traveling with money on his fingertips, because in Washington he could talk money now, he could talk millions and millions of dollars for communities. And he urged blacks to get to the polls, because there was fear of a white backlash against Johnson and against the civil rights bill.

There was in the end no backlash. Johnson took 63 percent of the national vote, a stunning 93 percent of the black vote. In Harlem Powell took 84 percent of the vote, without campaigning. Democrats picked up seats in the House. Johnson now had what could only be interpreted as a mandate. Powell called it a "sidelash" against Goldwater and his policies. Only seven other congressmen in America had done as well as or better than Adam Clayton Powell, who received a congratulatory phone call from the president on his victory.

Powell switched vacation locales — ignoring his home in Puerto Rico for the moment — and flew to Hawaii. He was accompanied by Corrine Huff and Robbie Clark, the wife of his aide Odell Clark. Daniel Inouye, a young local politician, played host. When reporters tracked Powell to an island restaurant, where he was seated at a beautifully set table, his head partially shielded by a tall plant, Corrine Huff sitting next to him, he became angry and threatened physical retaliation. He called a press conference and announced that he was leaving the island at once, which he did, his elegantly coiffed mistress at his side.

◈

Lyndon Johnson was smart enough to realize that his mandate from the American public would in time dwindle. The public was fickle, and he had to move while momentum was behind him. Because Johnson had increased the number of House Democrats from the North and Northwest, he figured the time was ripe to go to the mat with a major education bill; he could stave off southern sentiments. He did not want the sort of piecemeal legislation that had come out of the Eisenhower and Kennedy administrations; he wanted a full-blown education bill that could be muscled past the religious zealots, the southerners, and anyone else who harbored illusions that the federal government would ruin education by becoming involved in it. A former schoolteacher, he had seen schools where books were too few, where children were hungry, where supplies were nonexistent, where teachers struggled to live on paltry salaries. In the 1940s and 1950s it was not uncommon for school years to commence with lengthy teacher strikes because of low wages. But Johnson's biggest hurdle was the zeal with which communities guarded their school systems.

In many communities, schools were located close to a church; just as citizens did not want anyone upsetting their church, where they prayed, they did not want anyone upsetting the makeup of their school systems.

Johnson summoned top officials to his office, notably Francis Keppel, the education commissioner. He told the group he could well lose a million votes a month if he went ahead with his domestic agenda, but that wasn't the point, of course — the point was to race ahead of the inevitable loss of votes. "Therefore, you fellas get over there and get your bills and hearings in fast," he said, according to Keppel. Keppel sensed problems. "We all sat there pale," he recalled. "I mean, you don't get legislation that fast." Keppel envisioned the education bill as a house of cards, and believed that various factions — religious or southern legislators, or white parents who did not want their children sitting next to black children — were capable of caving the house in. But Johnson knew who his key men would be in getting the bill passed: the gruff and unyielding Wayne Morse on the Senate side, the unpredictable Adam Powell, just back in Washington from warmer climes and quite tanned, on the House side.

Powell's first step was to look at the budget for his committee. He had asked for $440,000 and was surprised to find that the House leadership had offered far less. He needed the money to keep sending Odell Clark and Michael Schwartz out to warn local officials that if they wanted money to build, money for jobs, then they would have to get their communities in order, to institute fair play. Angry at not receiving his requested budget, Powell balked, and told his committee there would be no education bill. Johnson cursed; White House aides conferred; fellow committee members, especially Frank Thompson and Samuel Gibbons, were furious.

There was no better blackmailer on Capitol Hill than Adam Clayton Powell. The White House aides pondered staging a coup and taking the committee from him, then realized the folly of such a plot. There was no one else on Powell's committee who could do what Powell could do on the floor of the House. The House, pressured by Johnson, relented; Powell received every cent he demanded. The Harlem congressman promised to do everything he could to get the education bill passed.

It is little wonder that Powell rose so enthusiastically to the challenge. For him, an omnibus education bill represented the culmination of a decades-long battle to force the federal government to close the gulf between white and black education in America. He had personally wrecked Eisenhower's school construction bill for this very reason: the bill, however well-intentioned, would have fostered inequality. The new Elementary and Secondary Education Act would promote it.

Powell looked around the House and began to count the votes. He ruled that there would be no unannounced committee meetings on the bill, a move that reduced the opportunity for southern House members to mass against it before it reached the floor. The hearings were both grinding and swift. Grace Hewell, an educator who worked for Powell, recalled the experience: "It was the hardest job I ever had. Two or three o'clock in the morning I was on the floor of the House." The chairman himself most surprised Hewell. Her eyes would begin to get bleary; the sessions would exhaust her. And she would look around and see Powell still going, full of steam, still badgering aides to make the legislation better, quizzing the experts. He refused to have the hearings drone on. The ground had been plowed before, he said. He limited debate by critics of the bill to five minutes, then came the echo of his pounding gavel: next witness. A successful part of the White House strategy, which he fully exploited, was constantly to link the bill with antipoverty measures. It was not just black districts that would receive help, but any district, and there were plenty of poor white school districts that needed money.

Powell was able to get the bill through his committee very swiftly. Larry O'Brien, now a White House aide, thought his performance "remarkable." But then a problem arose with Edith Green, the committee member from Oregon. When she threatened to add an amendment to the bill that would open it to judicial review because of conflicts between church and state (the kind of amendment that would play right into the hands of the southerners who did not like the bill), Powell told the administration that he knew how to deal with her: he would fire her sister from the committee staff, or he would take away her chairmanship of the vocational education subcommittee. Powell giveth and Powell taketh away. He even allowed the young and brainy John Brademas to sponsor the bill on the floor.

Francis Keppel was still nervous on the day of the vote. "I was worried with Edith down there with her wrecking machine," he said. Keppel scanned the floor for Powell, the bill's orchestrator, and when he didn't see him, he panicked. But Powell eventually strolled into the

House chamber, "looking wonderfully healthy," Keppel recalled. Keppel knew that the huge bill was fraught with traps — a house of cards, as he had put it. "I wondered how much he knew about each card, how they related," he said about Powell. "I needn't have worried. Mr. Powell read the bill as if he were reading a detective story!" Keppel couldn't help but notice Powell's many references to "the commissioner of education." "It was a gorgeous performance," he recalled.

House members who backed the bill were urged to stay on the floor during the vote as a show of force. Howard Smith, an archconservative Virginia congressman and an opponent of the bill (Virginia's schools had closed rather than obey the 1954 desegregation edict), was given precious little time for rebuttal. He rose on the House floor, dumbfounded, with White House aides looking on. "You know," he said, "some of us are treating this bill like it just came down from heaven." "Rep. Adam Clayton Powell Rams Johnson Bill Through House," the headlines said.

Powell's steering of the bill to passage was described as "an awesome show of naked, raw power." If it tore at both North and South, at both Catholic and Protestant, then so be it, because in Washington, it was one thing to have power, another thing to have seniority. To have both was to be flat-out feared. "You have to give him his due," a Republican said, pointing to all the legislation Powell had helped the White House pass: "manpower retraining, antipoverty, and higher education bills."

Powell didn't want to prepare children to enter black colleges. He had, in fact, been an ardent opponent of the United Negro College Fund, which raised money for black colleges, and he believed that these institutions fostered educational segregation. He was a Colgate man, and proud that he could point out to black leaders that he did not look upon Fisk, Morehouse, Clark — their alma maters — with the same warmth and reverence they did.

For Lyndon Johnson and Adam Clayton Powell, the bill was among their grandest achievements. For more than one hundred years the debate had raged about having the federal government help public school systems. If, as Carl Elliott had said in 1958, upon passage of the National Defense Education Act, the federal government had slipped the key in the lock, now it had turned the key and opened millions of schoolhouse doors. "What Johnson and Powell were good at was knowing the political situation in every state in the United

States, then shaping the bill," recalled George Reedy. "That is the fine art of legislative tuning." And, he added, "Johnson had very high respect for Powell. He always talked about show horses and work horses. He thought of Powell as both."

Lyndon Johnson liked to send for congressmen who had helped him get important legislation passed. Once, sitting in his office with Powell, surrounded by aides, everyone cackling after yet another celebration, another legislative coup, he picked up a cigarette lighter from his desk and threw it to Powell: a souvenir to be cherished. "Now Adam," the president said, "don't go losing this in no whorehouse." The president's men laughed — hard, then harder. But not Powell. "Mr. President," the Harlem congressman said, "Adam Clayton Powell doesn't have to buy pussy." Hard laughter turned to nervous laughter. Adam Clayton Powell would be the butt of no one's witticisms, not even the president's.

⟨⟩

If you cared about domestic legislation, 1965 was a glorious time to be in Washington. That year, according to Jim O'Hara, was "the highlight of every Democrat who was there." The Republicans were being beaten back time and time again, and a great many credited Adam Clayton Powell. "He shot out the higher education bill in twenty minutes," one cried, "and the antipoverty bill in one morning." The White House was happy; Valenti was ecstatic. "We couldn't have done it without Adam," Valenti said. "He was the key, the chairman."

After the big victories, Powell would rush back to his office for a celebration. Aides would be instructed to call the Capitol Hill catering service, and trays of food would soon arrive. "He was a great one for giving committee parties," remembered his aide Jeanne Thomson. Personally, Thomson saw a graciousness in Powell that bowled her over. She wanted her seventy-year-old mother to meet the chairman during a visit to Washington. When they arrived at Powell's office, he was heading out to a press conference. Instead of making them wait, he took Thomson's mother by the arm and escorted her, and when they got to the conference room, he seated her not in the audience but right on the dais next to him. It made the elderly woman feel so important. Jeanne Thomson could only smile. And even though every year each member of Powell's staff was forced to give a hundred dollars to his re-election campaign ("It was illegal," admitted Thomson), she was able to smile about that too, because, well, it was so enjoyable being around the Harlem congressman.

It was expected within the Johnson administration that criticisms would arise once the antipoverty program had begun to take hold. As it turned out, the critics were the poor themselves, who complained that they did not have equal opportunities to get the antipoverty jobs and that when they did, they were treated in a condescending manner. Not long after Powell had gained passage of the president's antipoverty legislation, he anointed himself its ombudsman. He dispatched his investigators to places where the complaints were most frequent (Chicago, the Deep South) and threatened to withhold funds if grassroots organizers were not given opportunities to partake in the administration of the programs. He was investigating the very programs he had championed. "Powell Probing . . . Powell!" said one headline.

Powell's investigators told him what he feared: that many local and state governments had been "seduced by politicians" who were merely funneling OEO money to "political hacks" — feeding at "the trough of mediocrity," the Harlem congressman termed it. He called more hearings; any program he had initiated, he had the power to derail. He complained of bloated salaries for the antipoverty administrators. He sat in his high-backed chair at the hearings and ruled serenely and majestically, motioning witnesses to seats, waving them onto the dais itself, leaning over and snarling at them, wanting to know why the poor were not getting some of the top jobs. Then the phone would ring — he had a phone placed at his elbow during the hearings; the president might well call — but after the call, he would quickly get back to the business at hand, waving a farewell, summoning someone else to a seat, then ending the hearing and walking away, trailed by aides. Watching it all gave one onlooker the feeling that he had just watched a "nightclub host" in action.

Powell's biggest investigative targets were the Chicago administrators, the people who worked for William Dawson, for Mayor Richard Daley. One witness's meandering testimony was not tolerated. "Answer yes or no!" Powell snapped. Roman Pucinski, the Chicago Democrat on the Education and Labor Committee, grew nervous, because he did not want to be a party to embarrassing Mayor Daley. Powell was merciless toward Deton J. Brooks, the political appointee who headed the Chicago antipoverty program. There was not one poor person on the Chicago Committee on Urban Planning, the fifty-four-member agency that managed the huge program, Powell pointed out. "Who represents the poor people of Chicago?" he wanted to know. Brooks became flustered and could not shape an articulate answer.

Powell also caused some problems for the White House. At one point he summoned Sargent Shriver, who was both Peace Corps director and head of the OEO, and suggested that Shriver give up one of his two jobs, the intimation being that he lacked the mental toughness needed to do both. In New York City, Mayor Wagner sought to control the administration of antipoverty programs; in a bizarre move, Powell told the White House that he would withhold New York City's funding unless Wagner's influence was lessened. The White House put pressure on Wagner, who announced that only sixteen of the sixty-two members of the committee that actually handled the funds would be city officials; the remaining jobs would go to community organizers. Only then was New York able to receive its $18 million. And a Powell ally, Arthur Logan, was named to head the antipoverty program.

Powell had secured $1.5 billion for the 1965 antipoverty program — double the administration's goal. He had not only released more money into the communities but provided for more control by the poor. An Ohio Republican accused him of having used "steamroller tactics" to get the bill passed, and accused Shriver of unwittingly abandoning leadership of the OEO and allowing Powell to take "the driver's seat."

If Powell had painted Shriver and the administration into a corner — which he had, at one point boldly asking, "I want to know just where the administration stands on poverty" — they could not complain too openly. The previous year the antipoverty bill had passed by a slim margin — twenty-eight votes in the House — too slim for comfort. Victory was all, and Powell was notching up the victories. "Adam put a spotlight on several of the most difficult problems that we who are running the program have bumped into," remarked one of Shriver's aides.

Powell arrived in Harlem one sunny day with committee members and had a section of the street cordoned off so he could conduct hearings outside, in the open air. In shirt sleeves and sunglasses, he sat on a metal chair, high on a platform at West 114th Street and Eighth Avenue, so the people could see. He wanted to hear about abuses in the antipoverty programs. He nodded toward aides to write it down, all of it, as he waved witness after witness into a seat and listened. There were stories of mismanagement, of uncooperative downtown officials, of discrimination in the labor unions. He wanted the hearings to echo all the way downtown, because in reality he meant to be judge and jury. For Adam Clayton Powell, it was the intertwining of the glory and the power, one so wondrously feeding the other.

Later he stood before a Chicago audience and told them about legislative power: "I use myself as an example because this is the audacious power I urge every black woman and man in this audience to seek." Not long after this he threatened to withhold federal funds from Chicago because of the "de facto segregation" in its school system. His hand was on the money in Washington, and he knew it. The threat forged another split between Powell and Roman Pucinski. Powell cared little. He appointed a three-member committee to look into Chicago's school system and blithely said that Pucinski would not be one of the members because he, Powell, was looking for someone "more neutral." Pucinski thought this was an example of "bold, brazen power."

Daley's men intimidated anyone coming into Chicago. Those causing a disturbance, halting traffic, were subject to arrest. "I've been blocking traffic for a long time" was Powell's response. Chicago's citizens and politicians, and especially its editorial writers, could hear Adam Powell coming. The scathing editorials flew; demonstrations against him were threatened. He switched the hearings back to Washington — his turf. Victims of the city's segregation traveled all the way to testify before his committee. Daley's so-called populist image took a beating; Pucinski was unable to shield him. In an effort at fair play, Powell invited those opposed to and those in favor of segregated education in Chicago to testify. One witness took her seat and scoffed that the hearing was stacked. "If it were stacked," snapped Powell, "how do you think you got here?"

Robert Weaver, a housing expert, had first come to Washington during the New Deal, when he had taken a position in the lower reaches of the government. He became one of the few professional blacks to hold a position of some appreciable rank. A staid and solid man, Weaver did not attempt to keep company with Adam Clayton Powell during the 1940s, 1950s, and certainly not the exploding 1960s. "We were not bark from the same tree," he explained. Back in Washington again with the Johnson administration and destined to be the first black named to a cabinet position, Weaver nonetheless understood why Powell was pushing so hard for the success of the OEO program. During Weaver's first tour in Washington, the complaints had always been that blacks lacked the experience to work and be promoted in government. "That program got a lot of political activity, and gave blacks jobs they never had before," he recalled of OEO. "It also developed a large number of blacks at the level where they could go higher in government."

❧

When Adam Clayton Powell asked for more money for the antipoverty program in 1966, he risked defeat. The Vietnam conflict now claimed the front pages of American newspapers. "The possibilities of defeat are real," he acknowledged. "I've stood alone before." The administration threatened to cut education funding in the program, but Powell and Senator Wayne Morse threatened all-out resistance.

Although his goals were quite serious, Powell toyed constantly with the administration. He wanted more black judges. When the administration told him they were searching but coming up short, he didn't believe it, advising them, "Seek and ye shall find." And they looked harder. He wanted to know why the bright black women in the federal government were confined to low-level jobs; he laid the proof across the desks of Johnson's aides. "A Negro woman, Phi Beta Kappa, *cum laude,* A.B. in economics," he said, had been confined for twenty years to a GS-5 position — why?

The administration tried hard to stay in his good graces. Powell fretted and wondered aloud whether he was truly appreciated. He wanted credit for beating back the likes of House Republican Charles Halleck (and his protégé, Gerald Ford), who had tried over and over to derail the antipoverty program. Howard Bell, a member of the Alfred Isaacs Club, a Harlem political club that slavishly backed Powell, confided to the administration Powell's feelings of underappreciation. A letter was quickly drafted and signed by Johnson, praising Powell for his "brilliant" leadership of the Education and Labor Committee and citing the forty-nine pieces of "bedrock" legislation the Harlem congressman had by now guided into law.

The appreciation did not quiet Powell's criticism of Sargent Shriver. Shriver was a tireless worker and deeply committed to curbing poverty. But the task was huge, and he had angered mayors around the country by diluting their clout in administering the antipoverty programs. They complained to Powell, who now suggested that Shriver should be fired and that Willard Wirtz or Robert McNamara should replace him. Robert Kennedy had been elected to the Senate, from New York, and Shriver was his brother-in-law. Kennedy called Powell before his committee, and Powell happily went. Kennedy reminded him that not long before he had praised Shriver. Powell said that that had been merely campaign oratory. Kennedy asked Powell if his present criticism of Shriver was anything but campaign oratory, if he was campaigning now. The Harlem representative assured the senator that he rarely campaigned anymore, and not at all for himself; the last time he had campaigned, truly campaigned, felt the thrill and sting of it, had been for the senator's brother Jack, when he was running for president. And Adam Powell, his black hair glistening, puffed on his cigarette and blew smoke rings.

On November 3, 1965, just back from Vietnam, Johnson strode into the White House to sign eight more pieces of Great Society legislation — for schools, medical assistance, all in one flourish, $15 billion worth of legislation. After the signing, he looked around for Powell, because most of this legislation had gone through Powell's committee and because Powell had always been there, hovering over his shoulder, his arms crossed, a Cheshire Cat grin on his face, as if he could already hear the money flowing, jangling across America. Johnson didn't see Powell because he wasn't there; Chuck Stone, an aide, had come in his place. So he summoned Stone over, and he gave him a pen and told him to give it to Powell and to tell Powell he had done "a right great" job in getting the legislation passed.

By the end of 1966 this kind of legislation was profoundly altering the American landscape. It touched not only the poor but the middle class, and some of Powell's allies thought that was ironic: the middle class, who had always feared him, was now being helped by him, because middle-class children needed loans for college. The old southern congressmen in their wicker chairs, looking out across the countryside and sipping iced tea served by their black maids and butlers — maids and butlers now benefiting from the minimum wage — could not have imagined a few scant years earlier the way the winds would shift. Now even the men and women in the cotton fields, tired men and women who had been in those fields for years, were covered by the minimum wage; 8.1 million Americans had had their incomes boosted overnight to minimum wage levels, which would be raised by thirty-five cents beginning in 1968. "I never thought I'd see the day," Powell said jubilantly, "when a sharecropper would be covered by the minimum wage."

The nation had turned a corner. From day care to vocational education, from college scholarships to new college construction, a different country was coming into view. Before, college for the poor had been all but unimaginable. Now it was a real possibility. The college grant-in-aid had the same thrilling impact on the mid-sixties as the GI bill had had on returning veterans two decades earlier. For years Powell had been urging citizens to hold on, vowing to them that the dam would one day break. Now it had broken — and even now he would not let up. In the summer of 1966 Adam Clayton Powell sent an aide to Miami to investigate discriminatory labor practices. Evidence pointed to the National Labor Relations Board. Enough paper had been shuffled; Powell vowed an in-depth probe. "This will mark the beginning of a much needed and long overdue investigation of the NLRB, which I shall personally conduct," he threatened.

Another investigation that he ordered took place in New Bern, North Carolina, the home of Graham Barden, Powell's predecessor. A great deal of federal money had been poured into the area to lift up both poor blacks and poor whites. By early 1966 the community had undergone profound changes. There were VISTA volunteers and Neighborhood Youth Corps workers, a small business development center, and a public health nursing and education program. A few lines from staff member Leon Abramson's report to Powell tells of the difficulties faced in forcing the Deep South to change, however. "There also appears to be a problem in getting the poor whites to involve themselves in the program," Abramson wrote. "Negro participation has been extremely good, but the poor whites are being led to believe, by the white middle class, that the poverty program is for Negroes only. The poor whites are not organized. The only white organization is the KKK. As one interviewee put it, 'The poor whites are scared of the Klan. The Negroes are just plain scared.' "

By the end of 1966, both Johnson and Powell were facing other demons, demons that sidetracked their missionary zeal in combating poverty. Johnson's guns began to compete with Powell's butter, and Powell began to compete with himself as his personal life started to collapse. Hadn't the Harlem congressman warned of a possible Vietnam after the Bandung conference, so many years before?

That Adam Clayton Powell had accomplished so much while his

own life was unraveling, while turmoil was everywhere, while the bloodletting began, makes his accomplishments all the more remarkable. "Without Adam," said William Ayers, the Ohio Republican who was a member of Powell's committee, "there would have been no War on Poverty."

∽✸∾

Esther Collemore was born on Christmas Day 1904 in the Montego Bay section of the island of Jamaica. In 1931, impoverished, she immigrated to New York City, with the dreams of any immigrant for work and a better life; unfortunately, she landed in the lap of a nationwide depression. Her only work experience was as a maid and domestic, the kind of work that paid little in Harlem. So she drifted, and ran afoul of the law. Her first arrest came upstate, in Buffalo, in 1933, for second-degree assault. The arresting officer noted that she had "maroon" eyes and a bald spot on the back of her head, the result of a hammer blow during a scuffle. She escaped indictment. She married and became Esther James. Her husband, who had been one of A. Philip Randolph's Pullman porters, died in 1952; Esther, forced to fend for herself, was determined not to return to domestic work. From her stoop on Amsterdam Avenue she could see men and women dropping off numbers in the illicit gambling trade. There was money to be made, and Esther James began dropping off money for numbers runners in their little cat-and-mouse games with the police. At times, however, she turned against them, informing on them; thus she could make money from two sources.

Such work, of course, had its risks. On a Sunday morning in 1956, in broad daylight — the streets were filled with churchgoers — Esther James was shot three times with a handgun, a .22. She recovered, and the police, for their own reasons, charged no one. Three years later James found herself in another strange fix. On July 13, 1959, she pulled a knife from her purse and stabbed a man, the knife gashing his head above the right eye. A complaint was filed, but the case was dismissed in court.

On the streets of Harlem, Esther James had the countenance of a grandmotherly woman. She was partial to flowery dresses and huge purses, which swung from her wrist as she walked the streets, using her weight aggressively. Her eyeglasses dominated her face. Marvin Fullmer, one of the investigators whom Powell had hired to find out about James after she filed her libel suit against him, reported to Powell that "she allegedly sleeps a good part of the day but can usually be found on her doorstep after 4 P.M. She also allegedly wears a black wig. It is suggested that a surveillance be placed on Esther James to determine if she still makes contact with the twenty to twenty-five gamblers operating in her area and from whom she allegedly has extorted monies in the past."

Goaded by her attorney, Raymond Rubin, James clung to the Powell libel suit with a vengeance. Powell was elusive, and Rubin found it difficult to serve papers on him, going so far as to employ locals to stake out his Harlem haunts and report back when Powell turned up. Rubin offered a five-hundred-dollar bounty to anyone who spotted Powell in Harlem and contacted him in time for him to serve Powell with court papers. No one was quick enough to claim the reward. Rubin's persistence, however, paid off, and handsomely. A New York Supreme Court jury sided with Esther James, and a judgment — the first of many — was issued in April 1963, granting James $245,000. "The King is dead," James crowed, smiling. "This is America."

Powell, busy in Washington, ignored the ruling and refused to pay. He believed that his battle lay with the New York City Police Department, not with Esther James. Lawyers on his staff — Howard Gamser, Don Anderson, and especially Michael Schwartz, whose father offered to pay the award for Powell — encouraged him to settle. He rebuffed them, determined to root corruption from the force. "If you don't pay this, it will ruin you," Anderson warned him.

One sympathetic judge encouraged Powell to get a good negligence lawyer and suggested Harry Lipsig. Lipsig, a bantam of a man and a shrewd lawyer, may well have been the best negligence lawyer in New York City during the 1960s. Rubin was not in his league. Powell and Lipsig met in an Italian restaurant on Madison Avenue to discuss the case. Lipsig had a strategy. He wanted to go to trial and put Esther James on the stand. "She was a picture of villainy," Lipsig recalled. By exposing James to a jury, he thought he could swing sentiment away from her and toward Powell: "I'd have torn her apart with her past record." Powell chuckled, then told Lipsig what he had told others: he would not pay any judgment, since he believed that victory would come to him on appeals. Lipsig warned him that treating the case like "a mosquito bite" would lead to calamity. "The hell with the bitch," Powell replied.

After a warrant had been put out for his arrest for nonpayment, Powell had fun eluding the New York City police. Marshals surrounded a precinct entrance one election eve, having been tipped off that Powell was about to arrive. The congressman didn't show, but later sent word that he had voted by absentee ballot, lest his constituents think he had misused the right to vote. His antics hardly affected Raymond Rubin, who remained relentless, charging in and out of court, demanding payment for his client. (Powell himself went to the highest echelons of government, imploring both the FBI and Nicholas Katzenbach, the attorney general, to investigate James and Rubin. Both kept firmly distanced from the entire affair.)

Powell finally found a lawyer he liked, that is, a lawyer whose mind he could bend to look at the case as he did — as a fight to the end, without compromise. That lawyer was Henry Williams, who had an office above the Apollo Theatre on 125th Street. Both his mother and sister had been married by Powell, and Williams had strong emotional ties to both community and church. If he felt that it was wiser to settle the suit than to fight it, he ignored his feeling. Powell had him firmly under his spell; for a young attorney, the case offered wonderful publicity.

Powell feared the aftermath of a conviction — "being put in jail," said Williams. "Perhaps it is now time to feint, parry, and weave," he told Powell at one critical juncture. "Many fights have been won using these tactics." Months and years passed, and Williams stayed with the case. He was unswayed by other attorneys, who began to question his stalling methods. "There are all manner of ways to win a war," he told his client. When he won an appeal or successfully took advantage of a loophole in the law, the tone of his letters to Powell was confident. "When do we swim?" he asked at the end of a 1964 missive sent to Puerto Rico. When the news was not so good, the endings were more ominous: "Let us pray."

On Palm Sunday 1965, when an arrest warrant could not be executed, Powell made a dramatic return to the city and his church after being away from Harlem for months. The Abyssinian congregation was still his flock, and while its numbers had been dwindling for a decade, his appearance before it oftentimes let loose sounds that would have made one think a holy apparition had been spotted: "Take my hand. The pastor's back. Pastor's back in town." He strode down the aisle of the old stone church, which always looked beautiful, especially on Sundays. Abyssinian was packed. Maybe District Attorney Frank Hogan had subpoenaed church records, maybe the public glare was on this congregation, maybe Powell was a fugitive minister, but he was *their* fugitive minister. "Lo, the dreamer cometh," he preached, beautifully. "He was unworthy. Through thirty-five years of preaching in this place he has become worthy." He admonished the congregation to think big, think black, think like children of God. He had thought such thoughts, and look at his rise, the minister who had once played stickball out on Seventh Avenue. "I control the War on Poverty," he told them. "The president asked for two billion. I'm gonna push for three. Think big." And the choir, his choir, their voices good and stronger now because he was back and they wanted to impress, were swaying, shoulders touching shoulders in the balcony. The voices caught his attention, and he glanced toward the balcony and spotted a familiar face — Charlie; yes, Charlie. "Sing it, Charlie!"

❧

Cartoonists and editorial writers used their skill to skewer Powell as a scofflaw, a lawmaker breaking the law and on the run. Many in Congress, however, were not bothered by the Esther James case: it was personal. Many of them had had personal problems, had begged forgiveness from their fellow congressmen, and had received it.

But if House members were not bothered by Powell's courtroom drama, another phenomenon of his political life did bother them — in fact, it frightened them, because it was so foreign to them. In 1964, the very year the Johnson-Powell social legislation was unleashed, riots swept the nation — in Philadelphia, in Daley's Chicago, in New Jersey, and in Powell's Harlem. A year later, five days of deadly rioting engulfed the Watts section of Los Angeles. Malcolm X, the angry apostle of the black ghettos was assassinated on February 21, 1965. The congressmen had never known anything like it; the riots were quicker and fiercer than the peace marches through the South. And now, to their amazement, when they looked behind the veil of this strange new phenomenon, they saw none other than Adam Clayton Powell, the very man who had given the movement its psychic energies and who, in a major address at Howard University in 1966, coined the phrase that it hinged on: *black power*.

He first saw it displayed as a kid on the streets, when the Garveyites wore plumed hats and paraded through Harlem like heroes. Marcus Garvey, their leader, was a somber man, jet black in complexion. Little Adam Clayton Powell saw, from rooftop, doorway, street corner, their parades and their pride. It seared his consciousness, this blackness. Even now, as a powerful congressman, when he entered a room, he would scan it, then reach for the darkest-skinned person, as if he were reaching for something terribly bruised and beaten and submerged so he could bring it up and into the light — he, a man of pedigree and privilege, a near-white man, identifying with the blackest of the black. He had recently looked out over a Washington church audience and said, "Look at those glittering black bodies out there." They were glittering bodies, all right, but they did not glitter enough to appear in newspaper and magazine advertisements around the country. Edward Peeks, a Washington journalist who often listened to Powell's speeches, was amazed by the faces of the men and women Powell sometimes attacked — Washington's elite. So many were light-skinned, but they were not angry; they seemed, in fact, to delight in his attacks, as if his words inched them closer to solidarity with their darker-skinned brethren. Two decades earlier, of course, Powell had called himself "a marching black," and that was when the word *black* was not in vogue as a racial identification; *Negro* was the preferred term. But he had grabbed that word, *black,* and wouldn't let go. In the pulpit of his own church, he once turned to a light-skinned minister and said, "Yellow Negroes like you and myself, we gotta think black."

Powell had presented a paper on the "black urban crisis" and his ideas about how to solve it to the administration, but it fell on deaf ears. He admonished a group of fine black Oklahoma ladies to shake off their "mink coat mentality," warned them to "put on your work clothes and organize the black women of this country into a force so mighty that nothing can stand between you and the righteousness of your cause." He knew that the phrase "black power" struck fear in the hearts of not only whites but many blacks as well. Black power was not folksongs and it was not gospel music. "Black people are tired of waiting," Powell warned, "tired of being told they live in the castle of first-class democracy when in fact they are relegated to the dungeon of second-class citizenship." There were limits to movements. "Black power may not be the final solution. But if it is nothing else, it is a requisite interim call to moral arms for black peoples themselves to do something about the punishing inequity which dominates their lives."

Powell was curious about the Young Turks of the black power movement. There was something about them, the way they raised a clenched fist on a moment's notice. They reminded him of himself, years ago. He could use the black power movement to keep his competitor, Martin Luther King, at bay. When King planned to bring his southern crusade into Harlem in 1965, the plan angered Powell, who told King that Harlem was not susceptible to his brand of leadership. "You're dealing with more sophisticated Negroes up here," he said. When King finally did appear in Harlem, at Powell's church, the relationship was noticeably strained. In Powell's pulpit, King did little more than shower the congressman with praise.

King was hardly the only civil rights figure Powell attacked. He dismissed the National Urban League, claiming that it did not "represent the masses." "This is no time to be sipping martinis in the homes of the suburban white families," he uttered, "when black families are starving in the inner cities."

The phrase "black power" rushed into the national consciousness with the sweep of fire. The 1964 riots pained Powell, who warned that when fires were set in the ghettos, blacks were setting "our own clothes on fire." The separatists and nationalists who were plotting from Oakland to Greenwich Village, behind the facades of tenements and in coffeehouses, were talking about black power. But it was different from Powell's version of black power. They advocated physical power, the congressman power of the mind. "Burn, baby, burn" became their mantra; "Learn, baby, learn," Powell urged instead. But for many it was hard to differentiate between Powell and this "new breed of cats," as he called them. When the young who were on a march looked at the head of the line, they saw twenty-five-year-old Stokely Carmichael (even his name had an edgy resonance) and Dick Gregory, a young Chicagoan whose comedy was as shocking and real as Lenny Bruce's; and they remembered Malcolm X. Adam Powell harangued the older civil rights leaders for not joining their cause. King and Wilkins and Granger didn't understand this movement, he said; they were out of touch, they were "ailing aristocratic colonials" tottering with indecision.

Radicals began to walk down Seventh Avenue, make a right on 138th, and walk into the renowned Abyssinian Baptist Church. Thirty years earlier Adam Clayton Powell could not turn the Communists away; he did not care to turn the radicals away now. Then as now, the deacons became nervous. Powell retaliated, and ruthlessly. Wyatt Walker, an esteemed young minister who had worked for Martin Luther King, was serving an interim term in the Abyssinian pulpit. The congregation had grown affectionate toward him, and rumors floated that he might well be Powell's heir apparent. Powell fired him, giving no reason. Then he turned on the deacon board and threatened to leave the church himself and take the congregation with him. Harry Sease and the others on the board were shocked. Days later, down in Washington, the deacons sat in Powell's chambers, waiting among the trappings of power: the mounted fish on the walls, the pictures of Powell and Kennedy, Powell and Johnson. They were finally ushered in. Powell knew why they had come: they had come to apologize, to ask forgiveness, to assert their confidence in his leadership, to plead with him to remain as the Abyssinian minister.

In September 1966 Adam Clayton Powell called a black power conference in his offices on Capitol Hill. It had the passionate aims of the old Niagara Movement, which Du Bois and others had formed early in the century. He invited Wilkins, King, and James Farmer, of the Congress of Racial Equality, but they cited other commitments. The old guard had prevented him from participating in the March on Washington in 1963; this would be his revenge — a meeting in the seat of democracy, in his spacious chambers. The Harlem congressman relished the danger of it. Powell's arms spread wide, and the Young Turks were welcomed in. "They came from all over," recalled Henry Williams. Outside Powell's chambers the Capitol police stood guard, braced for anything. The congressman played genial host, and couldn't help but marvel at the youth and vigor on display. Never before had so many blacks gathered inside the Capitol in such a daring expression of both rage and hope.

As the conference got under way, there was a bit of dissension. Powell surely expected a lively debate, but he was perhaps surprised to find himself, the host, placed under immediate attack. Someone blurted that he was too light-skinned to lead such a movement as they were planning. Powell was startled, and knew he needed a quick rejoinder, which he provided. "Black is the way you think," he said rapidly, "not the way you look."

Afterward, the group released a position paper to the press, calling for more money for the cities, better voting rights protection, and a more aggressive attitude on the part of blacks who wanted to become part of the political system. Powell had legitimized their movement, allowed them to hitch themselves to him. When the reporters rushed up to him to ask questions, he blew rings of cigarette smoke and smiled, delighting in the scene he had just staged in the halls of the United States Congress.

John Brademas warned Don Anderson of the committee staff that Powell's links to the black power visionaries were dangerous. He said that these were not only his own views but worries that had been expressed by other members of Congress. Anderson told Powell, who ignored them both. (On the staff, Don Anderson was inexplicably underrated. He also had a peculiar habit that became more noticeable as dissension about Powell became more open: he quoted Shakespeare, aloud — *Macbeth,* and especially *Hamlet.* The habit made people nervous.)

Rumors began to ricochet on Capitol Hill that the Education and Labor Committee was going to strip its chairman of some of his powers. Suddenly the Esther James affair did not seem so insignificant anymore, not when it was joined to the black power conference and taken together with Powell's autocratic manner. When committee members showed up late for meetings, Powell continued his habit of slamming his gavel down. He never could get the name Brademas correct, and made fun of it by pronouncing it "Braydemas," thus infuriating the Indiana congressman. But the rumors did not seem to worry him. When a vote to limit his powers as chairman was announced, he tried to set his Harlem congregation at ease. "God works in mysterious ways," he said, adding that he was looking forward to the vote. "You have to go into the lion's den, and come out."

Samuel Gibbons, a representative from Florida and a hard-nosed former Marine, engineered the effort to curtail Powell's powers, a bold move rarely launched against a sitting chairman. Gibbons had long been angry at Powell for delaying the antipoverty bill to get more funds for the committee. Other committee members found themselves with more reasons than ever to try to upset the seniority system, from which Powell had benefited. The vote was twenty-seven to one. Committee members strained to tell Powell that it wasn't a vote against him but a vote against the old southern seniority system, but Powell took the rebuff personally and said that he was especially shocked at Gibbons, whom he had put in charge of the poverty subcommittee. "Legislative fame," he said, had been his gift to Gibbons; now this, a Gibbons-led revolt.

William Ayers was the only congressman who voted against the changes. The reasons were coldly political. As the ranking GOP member of the committee, Ayers stood to gain a chairmanship if the rules were kept in place and if the White House and the House of Representatives fell to Republicans. Following the vote, he and Powell walked down the corridor, chased by reporters. Powell fastened his tie, poked his chin out, drew a puff, turned to Ayers, and said, "When you prune the tree, it grows back stronger."

Many congressmen dismissed the vote, which would only be in effect for the duration of the current Congress, as meaningless. It would have to be taken up again by the full House the following January, and in the full House, the rules of seniority were sacred. There were some, however, who saw it as an ominous sign.

∽≫≪∽

Adam Clayton Powell frightened the men and women of Congress. He had always wanted bold men to be bolder, courageous men to show more courage, gamblers to gamble more. Those who went to the edge, right to the edge, he appreciated, but he wanted them to go further. They would hear his disappointment, the arrogance in his voice, rising from the well of the House. "He did it with the greatest of ease," recalled Carl Albert, who was then the majority leader. He held mirrors up to them and pointed out that the reflections he saw were not reflections of courage. And they didn't like it. Sam Rayburn, who struck fear in newcomers, could not terrify Powell. Rayburn had warned Powell not to throw bombs, but he threw them anyway.

The congressman from Harlem frightened the others because he was uncontrollable. He took counsel from no one. He considered himself among the smartest of the smart in the House. Discussion of everything from foreign policy to American race relations energized him. "To him it was intellectual," said Marjorie Lawson of his debates about race. To many in Congress he remained mysterious and unfamiliar. "Adam didn't pay much attention to new members," explained the Ohio representative Wayne Hays. "He kind of lived in a world of his own." When Roman Pucinski came calling one day, trailed by other committee members, to relay some of his constituents' complaints, Powell listened, then pointed to the picture of his family that sat atop his desk. "Talk to my mother," he advised them.

To one Senate staffer who later became a member of Johnson's inner circle, Powell was "a jet setter before there were jets." His reputation as a *bon vivant* was earned, but not in Washington. Few, in fact, saw Powell out on the party circuit in Washington, D.C. Now and then he would show up at Billy Simpson's restaurant-club on Georgia Avenue. Simpson had a little loft upstairs, out of the way, and those who did not want to draw attention downstairs, in the main dining area, went up there. "That's where Powell would hang out," recalled Art Carter, a journalist who sometimes trailed Powell for tips and scoops. According to Wayne Hays, "The guys in the House cloakroom would talk about him — preaching, living with different women. They were jealous."

Powell frightened people because he did exactly what he promised he would do with what Morris Udall termed "cold, raw political power." He investigated America. The hand of his committee was suddenly in their own communities — in Georgia and Alabama, in Mississippi and Louisiana, along the highways and the back roads; Adam Clayton Powell took the federal government places it had never been before. He investigated the powerful unions. He liked money, this they knew, especially when it worked for him and his committee, when he could send lawyers out into America, when he could summon the wrongdoers before his committee.

He threatened to investigate Congress itself: he wanted to know why other representatives' staff were segregated. "I thought he felt contemptuous of most members," recalled Congressman Hays. "The deep southerners hated his guts. They couldn't stand him." Sometimes he would enter the House chamber, stop, and offer a little Japanese-like bow, and his colleagues didn't know whether it was a form of respect or mockery. But there were also those southern congressmen, admirers of charm and gentility, who found it difficult, when one-on-one with Powell, to dislike him. "I'd see southern congressmen eating out of Adam's hand at cocktail parties," said Franklin D. Roosevelt, Jr.

Sometimes they had only to walk to the congressional garage and look at his Jaguar convertible, and that would be enough to allow their anger to grow. He often told his fellow representatives that the men in the Senate — he would physically point toward the south wing of the Capitol — were more courageous than they were when it came to progressive legislation. There he was in 1965, meeting with the owners of professional baseball teams, demanding statistics on the number of blacks they employed in the front offices. He knew the numbers — near zero — before he met with them, but at least a meeting had been held; his presence was felt.

Few in the House had the ability to sway the press the way he did. When Congressman Charles Diggs received several weeks' worth of uninterrupted publicity, Adam Powell said to him, "Okay, you've had enough," and went out and grabbed three weeks' worth of publicity for himself. "He could dominate the news anytime he wanted to," explained Diggs.

There were those he admired in Washington, certain representatives and senators — Wayne Morse, who was fearless; Eugene McCarthy, a visionary; Stuart Symington, because he had gone to the edge in taking on defense contractors; Lyndon Johnson, because Johnson understood America and the conundrum of race. But there were too few of them around. He drank with them, the men of Congress, invited them to his offices and poured them drinks beneath the huge fish he had landed and had stuffed, but he would not socialize with them. "He was strange that way," recalled Hays. "He didn't seem to have any real friends. He was a loner."

When they ran into him in Paris, at the risqué nightclubs, he smiled. He knew what sex meant to them, that it scared them, made them do foolish things, so when he spotted them in the nightclubs he just smiled, because he had come easily to sex, wore it lightly. Hadn't he hired Mary Ellen Terzin, a former Playboy Club bunny? He quickly and confidently announced that the attractive blonde could type ninety words a minute. He had fun with sex; his sex was out in the open. The way his colleagues' wives looked at him, sometimes the way their daughters looked at him, caused him to smile, but he saw what it did to the men: it pained them. Once Powell arrived at a Washington soirée thrown by Maurice Rosenblatt, his New York friend. The affair was populated by congressmen and ambassadors and their aides. Mendel Rivers, the South Carolina Dixiecrat, arrived late. His wife was already there. When Rivers walked in, his eyes stopped at the sight of his wife — with Adam Clayton Powell. "Adam was sort of having a jolly little tête-à-tête," Rosenblatt said. Rivers stiffened; Powell kept on smiling.

Roger Wilkins, the nephew of the NAACP leader Roy Wilkins, worked as an attorney with the Johnson administration. Whenever he found himself in Powell's presence, he felt nervous, yet proud. "He was the most powerful black man ever in Washington," Wilkins explained. "I viewed him as a king, was in awe of him. When I was brought into his presence, I was more impressed than with any cabinet officer."

On occasion Adam Clayton Powell invited congressional colleagues to Harlem, to his church, but he warned them that they'd better arrive early, because it was often overcrowded, and there would be no VIP section for them; the church was for the people, common man and common woman. "Mr. Chairman, I'm going to New York next weekend. I wonder if you'll be preaching?" James Corman, the California congressman, once asked him. Powell replied that he would be preaching, then added, "It'll be too crowded. You won't get in."

He had been asked at times about running for president, and he took the question far more seriously than those who posed it. It was, however, an inevitable line of thinking for any powerful politician. For a black politician, the question took on different hues. There was a tinge of wonder within Powell. He would blink, thinking, then confess that the United States wasn't ready for a Baptist minister to be president; he loved the ensuing laughter.

Powell had often thought of leaving the House. But his plans for statehood for Puerto Rico had collapsed, and by 1965 he had abandoned his third wife, severing important ties with the island's political figures and with them his idea of running for the Senate. His pipe dream of an ambassadorship to the Court of St. James's had dissolved when Kennedy had been killed. So he remained in the House, tasting raw power and executing legislation. "I am only one," he told his fellow congressmen, "but I am one." He wanted the liberals to hold on to their consciences. When they compromised, they became his enemies; his shoulders hunched, his hands held out, he wailed — he wanted explanations. Slowly they began to turn against him. The forceful and savvy Richard Bolling, of Missouri, turned; Emmanuel Celler turned; Frank Thompson turned. Powell had supported Albert instead of Bolling in the House fight for majority leader, had pained Celler by his 1956 support of Eisenhower, and had confused his soulmate Thompson by holding the antipoverty bill hostage.

But they had to give him his due as a legislator. Every year Adam Clayton Powell traveled to Europe, to Paris and London. Few knew, however, that in London he always participated in serious business. He was a member of the World Parliamentarians for World Government, an organization devoted to studying ways to pass legislation. Not only was he a member, he was the vice president. In the American Congress, representatives had in their midst a master parliamentarian — his more than four dozen bills attested to the fact.

Now it seemed that the Harlem congressman was taking particular glee in frightening his colleagues. *Esquire* needed a House member to write an article about ethics. Cash-strapped Americans were tired of hearing about gallivanting congressmen spending taxpayers' money on frivolous outings. Strangely enough, Powell was given the assignment. The principal point he made was that congressmen, himself included, were less worried about ethics than they were about getting re-elected. The piece garnered wide attention. An artist's sketch of a sepia-toned figure reclining under palm trees accompanied the piece.

The Democrats were having to contend not only with questions about ethics and a Republican resurgence during the 1966 midterm elections but with the Vietnam War. They had had enough. Omar Burleson, the Texas Democrat, went into motion, demanding an investigation of why Yvette Powell, estranged from her husband and living in Puerto Rico, remained on his payroll. As chairman of the House Finance Committee, Burleson had the power to do more than merely demand an investigation; he could authorize the funds to pay for it, and he did. Wayne Hays was named to head it. (Powell had once spotted Hays in Paris, at the Lido. They exchanged glances; Powell smiled.)

Before Hays had completed his report, a visitor telephoned, wishing to see him. When Maxine Dargans walked in, she showed him used airline tickets that had been stamped by the Education and Labor Committee — tickets that had sent staff members on vacations. Expecting immunity, Dargans confessed that she had taken some of these trips. Hays's investigators concluded that people on Powell's payroll had been on an inordinate number of journeys to Florida, San Juan, and Bimini. The report was not conclusive, but it did suggest that further investigation was warranted.

The Harlem congressman ignored the flak; the "War on Powell," he summed it up, vowing that it would do nothing to diminish his beloved War on Poverty. He ran his congressional staff in much the same manner he ran his church staff, alternating between laissez-faire and autocracy. When staffers in either church or congressional office had performed well, had shown unyielding loyalty, he sent them to Puerto Rico, to Bimini, to Florida, authorizing use of church or committee funds for the tickets. Sunshine was wonderful therapy for the mind.

Now Powell's critics needed someone to step up and determine what action, if any, was to be taken on the Hays report. It was a dangerous assignment. The country was engulfed in racial turmoil; Powell was its highest-ranking black politician. If a member of Congress was to accuse him, better it was a liberal, someone with unassailable credentials in the civil rights arena, lest he be besmirched with a charge of racism.

Always the Harlem congressman had looked trouble directly in the eye, and when trouble swirled, as it was now doing, he would tell his fellow congressmen to "keep the faith." It wasn't just "keep the faith," however; it was more than that, it was "keep the faith, baby," and it was the "baby" that goaded them, that reduced the insecure to something less than congressmen. A great many of the Democrats went down to defeat in 1966.

As fall gave way to winter, Powell could look around and hear the running hooves. He asked Speaker John McCormack to protect his seat, because if his seat was vulnerable, it meant that Congress itself was vulnerable, that the entire seniority system might be wrecked. But congressmen were rallying now, behind closed doors, and some in the open. Lionel Van Deerlin, a Democrat from a conservative San Diego district, in only his second term in the House, announced that he would step forward during the opening of Congress in January to deny Powell his seat. The threat caught Congress off guard. It would take just one voice to stop a fellow congressman from being seated. Lionel Van Deerlin? He was among that group, young and unknown, that Powell considered arrivistes. Powell knew nothing about him. Once, however, more than a year before the current turmoil, Van Deerlin had emerged from a building on Capitol Hill with a group of other congressmen. He remembered it as cherry blossom season, and he was walking next to Adam Clayton Powell. The cherry blossoms, of course, were precious, on the trees one week, gone the next; tourists came from miles away to enjoy their beauty. Powell turned to the young man, as both were admiring the blossoms, and said, "Isn't it a shame that that which is so beautiful is sometimes so fleeting?" Then he walked away.

As winter descended on Washington, the running hooves grew louder. Blacks across America, the young urban blacks, tensed up, wondering what would happen to Powell. But the civil rights leaders — Wilkins, King, Farmer, Randolph — were quiet; Powell would have to take his medicine alone.

Powell wanted to know what the Johnson men would do for him. He wanted to remind them of what he had done for the president — the legislation, the campaigning, the early support when the voices, especially the black voices, were going the other way, into any camp other than Johnson's camp. He was too proud to ask himself. So he sent Corrine Huff to see Jack Valenti, to inquire what the president was doing to help him. (Valenti had an appreciation for beautiful young women, and Powell knew it.) After she had left, Valenti phoned Powell and told him that he had indeed liked the messenger but could do nothing regarding her plea for help. Under the separation of powers, the will of Congress would have to be played out.

Adam Clayton Powell was being wounded, and Lyndon Johnson, a veteran of the House, realized it. Johnson was fond of telling his aides that there was nothing worse than a wounded politician, because the enemies of a wounded politician, smelling blood, felt no pity. Blood had already spilled, and Johnson told his aides that there would be more, much more.

⟡

The Harlem congressman found a new refuge in Bimini, the tiny island south of Florida that Hemingway had dramatized in his posthumously published novel, *Islands in the Stream.* On Bimini, Powell was far from the turmoil and the press. However, a *Life* photographer traced him to the island in December, then out on the waters in a chartered boat. A chase ensued. Powell knew the backwaters and, revving the engine, evaded the photographer, who nevertheless gave a good chase, clicking his camera en route, water spraying everywhere. Later, on land, the photographer finally caught up with Powell and began an approach. Powell brandished a shotgun — the one he kept to ward off sharks while deep-sea fishing — and threatened to kill the *Life* man, who was wise enough to retreat, all the while clicking away. Powell got in the back of a car, and bursts of dust rose as it sped down a scuffed dirt road, the shotgun poking from the window, the automobile showing a New York license plate. Of course *Life* got more than it bargained for, and presented the story and photographs as a high-speed chase unfolding on an idyllic island.

Not long after, Gene Miller, a *Miami Herald* reporter, arrived on the island in search of the shotgun-wielding congressman. Miller knocked on the door of Powell's tucked-away home. Getting no answer, he scrawled a message and taped it to the door. It was a request for an interview and a nod toward Powell's notoriety: "Anybody who can threaten a *Life* magazine photographer with a shotgun must be an OK person."

VII

THE FALL

1967–1968

A s AN AMERICAN COMMUNITY, Harlem, the strip of Manhattan that hovered between the poetic and the explosive, was more mercurial than most. To outsiders it could be as mysterious as another time zone. In the mid-1960s there were 1.1 million blacks living in Harlem: it was its own city, and certainly held tight its own state of mind. Many Manhattanites rarely ventured uptown, past 125th, into that sea of black faces. Some had read books by Harlem figures: James Weldon Johnson's *Black Manhattan,* Claude McKay's *Home to Harlem,* James Baldwin's trenchant *Notes of a Native Son,* Langston Hughes's *I Wonder as I Wander.* Some then strolled Harlem with curiosity in their eyes. There ran the little children, there peeked the old women from raised windows, there sat the old men in two-toned shoes on metal chairs; there sat vendors on the back of idling trucks on Seventh Avenue, selling vegetables, and there walked the hipsters with their wavy hair, hair that had been pomaded back, like Ellington's hair, like Billy Eckstine's hair, like Powell's hair. Visitors could come into Harlem on Sundays and see a proud city, dressed beautifully, could turn on 138th Street and walk into the massive Abyssinian Baptist Church and see a still-proud congregation.

On the streets of Harlem, however, there remained constants: religion, culture, hope, and crime. The roving ministers — "holyroller ministers," Baldwin called them — were still fighting for corner space, each hawking his or her religion. Langston Hughes and Arna Bontemps were finally getting due recognition from white America. Baldwin returned to visit family and friends, to engage in spirited dialogue with the Kennedys, but mostly to live in the Village and commiserate: Harlem was still a hard place to live. Musicians continued to wail.

Powell had been instrumental in getting New York musicians involved on the cultural exchange circuit with foreign countries. The Apollo was doing a nifty business in rhythm-and-blues acts, but the big-band stalwarts were long gone.

The rents were still high, slum landlords still pocketed huge amounts of money, and crime had not diminished. In late 1966 an intruder broke into the Abyssinian church, held two secretaries hostage, raped one, snatched money and jewelry, and fled. By this time, as a consequence of better job opportunities — and for this many Harlemites could thank their congressman — an exodus had begun, out to Long Island, over to New Jersey, Harlemites taking their belongings from their old apartments on Sugar Hill and leaving. Some of the big churches were losing members of their congregations. Another slow exodus led from the Abyssinian church over to Brooklyn, where people joined Gardner Taylor's huge and prestigious Concord Baptist Church. In the 1930s and 1940s Abyssinian membership had climbed as high as fifteen thousand; now it dipped as low as nine thousand.

Yet the pews remained filled. Many in the congregation were tourists, curious to see the legendary church, to get a glimpse of the fugitive minister and powerful congressman. There was no hiding the fact that the Abyssinians were aging: old deacons and old women sat in the pews, and the West Indian David Licorish, Powell's assistant, loyal to the bone, still with fire in his throat, was still in the wings, waiting desperately to be summoned to take over the pulpit, as he had been waiting now for two decades. On November 29, 1966, Adam Clayton Powell celebrated his fifty-eighth birthday, and he had still not anointed a successor. Licorish's role was appreciated, but Licorish made the mistake of confusing appreciation with admiration; the congregation demanded a forceful leader, as they had been used to. Behind his back there was snickering and ridicule.

Abyssinian remained a mighty church because the community still needed it. The Harlem that had exploded in riot in 1935 and 1943 had exploded again in 1964, in a brutal riot set loose when a white policeman shot an unarmed black youth. Businesses were burned, stores looted; there were more reasons than ever to leave. The despair could be traced to "the rats, the roaches, the futility, the despair that comes from being down, down," one resident remarked after the 1964 rioting. Harlem politicians had a mighty task, and that was to keep the voices lifted, the anger sharp, the waters roiling. "So long as the water is troubled," Baldwin wrote, in talking of the Harlem politician's lot, "it cannot become stagnant."

For all of its explosiveness and enduring pain, the community was never short of pride. As the new year dawned in 1967, its residents sensed trouble down in Washington. The pursuit of their congressman, the first and only congressman they had ever had and ever known, had reached their ears. Many remembered when there was no congressman. They would have to go to Washington, to throw their voices against the powerful men of the nation's Capitol who were trying to take the seat of their congressman — because the latest gossip, coming over the radio, in the press, was that Congress was going to attempt to deny their representative his rightful seat.

They painted placards: POWELL SPELLS CHAIRMAN; JUSTICE FOR POWELL AND HARLEM. They took their civil rights for granted; they were the "more sophisticated Negroes" Powell had told King about. They had long battled for better schools, better hospitals, integrated bus lines, integrated stores. Through the years, their congressman had led the way. During the 1966 elections their congressman had been besieged with woe, and they knew it, and they had sent him back to Congress with the eighth highest victory margin in the country — 74 percent, the widest he had ever received. That was their warning to Congress, their manner of slaying distant enemies — the march to the ballot box.

There was that special way he would come to them, following so many of his victories — renting a ballroom and holding a celebration with his staff, the entourage; then, when enough drinks had been consumed, enough backs slapped, when the liquor had entered everyone's bloodstream and made them giddy with delight, laughter, and accomplishment, he would look around and say to his staff, his whole body turning as if on an axis, "All right, let's go." And he'd be gone again, out the door, taking huge strides, back to Washington, to fight the others, with his constituents' fight in him.

In the days leading up to January 10, the day that all members of Congress would be sworn in to take their seats, Harlemites planned to go to Washington and protest on behalf of their congressman. They were used to protesting. It was time, too, for Harlem's younger political figures to show their mettle and step forward. Men like Percy Sutton, now the Manhattan borough president, and Charlie Rangel, now a legislator in Albany, would have to become involved in the community's protest, because it was their Harlem as well.

Rangel, who ate on the run because he was always so full of ideas, for himself and for Harlem, was a veteran of the Korean War, a bright young man. He and the other bright young lawyers would have settled the nuisance case brought by Esther James. Because Henry Williams was fighting it, they disparaged him. Rumors went around that Williams drank, that he had allowed his legal sense to wilt in the face of Powell's persona. The young lawyers were spending time in the Harlem clubhouses after work, into the dark hours, slapping one another on the back and looking down the road into the future. They were hungry, and they had more than their law degrees. The kittens had ambition, and something more: they had claws. They could look at Adam Clayton Powell and look right past him. But they could not overthrow the powerful congressman just yet. First they had to try to save him, to show their support, because he was still dangerous; he could tear them apart by merely feigning to; he could draw blood with a phone call. Now was the time to show support and sway with the emotions of the community.

So on January 10, Harlemites boarded chartered buses to roll en masse toward Washington. William Booth of the New York Human Rights Commission had reached into his own pockets (because the commission would not) and provided the money for the buses. When he had been a little boy, Booth's parents had taken him to Harlem and paraded him up and down the street in front of Woolworth's department store, and pointed to the tall man in the suit leading the picketers in front of Woolworth's, and explained to little Billy that Adam Clayton Powell was doing important work for Harlem, fighting for rights. Now, boarding the eight buses in the predawn darkness were men in snap-brim hats and long coats, women in wool and fur: it was cold. Other caravans were on their way, from Pennsylvania, New Jersey, even Ohio. Simultaneously, thousands in Washington were making their way toward the Capitol. (More than five thousand had gathered to show support two days earlier at Washington's Metropolitan Baptist Church.)

Powell was in Bimini. "Must Adam Leave Eden?" *Newsweek* asked in a cover story. Of course he must, and he arrived in Washington on January 8. He looked rested, tanned. He sauntered past a gauntlet of well-wishers on the Capitol walkway to the Democratic Club, his hand reaching out and gently touching the hands of women, touching their hands just for a split second and moving on, the tips of his fingers lying against the tips of their fingers, his other hand busy with a cigarette, pointing out the familiar faces from the Capitol Hill corridors who were now out on the sidewalks as well; his well-groomed head nodding to the men lined up, men who wanted to be like him, men who could not understand him, inquisitive men with their hands in their pockets in the January chill, men with coats on their backs — but not Adam Clayton Powell, coatless and smiling, the well-manicured hand opening and closing like a bird's wing and the women reaching for it.

Once inside the Democratic Club, he sidled up to the bar, spotting friends, Frank Thompson and others, committee members who were huddling, men turning to him one moment, then away the next, whispering. The closer he got, the more their voices dropped. He knocked back a martini. It was good to be back in Washington.

❧

Upon the death of Sam Rayburn, in 1961, the Speaker's gavel fell to John McCormack, the high-ranking Massachusetts congressman who had been a member of the House since 1929. McCormack came from Boston's gritty South End. He pushed himself through law school at night as a young man, then entered the hurly-burly world of Boston's Irish-dominated politics. He lost his first congressional race, but not the second. When he arrived in Washington, he checked into the most inexpensive hotel he could find. The Depression scarred John McCormack, and friends knew him as an ardent penny-pincher. There was a gaunt look about him, reminiscent of the men in the WPA photographs of the 1930s, haunted men, men who didn't know where their next dollar would come from. Those very men were the John McCormacks of America, and he knew it — only John McCormack had been one of the lucky ones: law school, and now Congress.

In Washington McCormack became a protégé in turn of John Nance Garner and Sam Rayburn, the two hard-bitten Texas congressmen whose careers in the House brought them the speakership and fame. McCormack's respect for them, for their way of thinking about the House — blindly partisan, unwaveringly loyal — shaped his own bearing. When Rayburn died, the House became McCormack's, and all the southern Democrats knew that if John McCormack was not a segregationist, like many of them, he understood how to work together and get legislation passed. Rayburn had risen to power with youth still on his side; John McCormack was seventy years old when he picked up the Speaker's gavel.

Many of the young congressmen, like Frank Thompson and John Brademas and James O'Hara, did not give their blind loyalty to John McCormack, because they wanted to upend the rules of the House, the very rules that had kept the southern Democrats in power for so many years. Blamed for much of the failure of the Kennedy domestic agenda because of his alliance with southern Democrats, and thus his inability to frighten them into line, McCormack endured the sniping. (His enmity toward the Kennedy dynasty, however, was long and unforgiving. In 1962 Edward Kennedy had beaten Edward Mc-Cormack, the Speaker's nephew, for a U.S. Senate seat.) Time and time again the young liberals stung McCormack. Because he was a friend of labor, McCormack desperately wanted a bill that would limit on-site picketing; more important, his president, Lyndon Johnson, wanted the bill. He assured the administration that the bill would emerge intact from the Education and Labor Committee. But he was stung again, this time by Powell, who held the bill hostage because labor leaders would not accede to his demands that blacks be given fair opportunity in union jobs. McCormack had plenty of reasons to want to discipline the congressman from Harlem.

But when considering how to measure a member's intraparty betrayal against the interests of the whole House, McCormack chose to give his loyalty to the institution. The member, in this case Powell, would have to be spared, at all costs. John McCormack knew that was what Rayburn would have done, what Garner would have encouraged, what constitutional precedent called for. John McCormack planned to stop the Young Turks' foolish talk of refusing Adam Clayton Powell his seat.

Nevertheless, late in 1966, when the clamor began to rise, McCormack's manner was aloof, and no one sensed it better than Richard Bolling, the powerful member of the House Rules Committee. Few knew Congress, the actual soul of Congress, as well as Bolling did. Born in New York City but raised in Huntsville, Alabama, Bolling had traveled the East Coast as a young man with the jazz impresario John Hammond, who discovered Billie Holiday. They were two jazz hounds looking for talent. (It was Hammond who introduced Bolling to Hazel Scott in a New York City nightclub; "I thought she was beautiful," Bolling said.) When he finally settled in Kansas City, Richard Bolling had added a politician's vision to a bohemian's toughness: he would champion the helpless and fight the cause of the liberal Democrats.

In Kansas City he was the first to organize a branch of Americans for Democratic Action. The move made him no friend among those who were used to political bosses. Still, Bolling found enough independent voters to elect him to Congress in 1948. His election confused those who had a hard time figuring him out, who measured him, as he recalled, as a cross between "a Communist and a gangster." In Washington, Bolling courted and was courted by the labor crowd, and he also became one of Rayburn's favorites. (Actually, Rayburn admired the young congressman more than the young congressman admired the aging Speaker.) Bolling was one of the first members of the House to speak out against Senator Joseph McCarthy, and he later brought his energy and wisdom to the Democratic Study Group, liberal House members who wished to unlock legislation that had been blocked during the Eisenhower years.

But Bolling found that his quest to pass legislation was thwarted at times by the liberal congressman from Harlem and his Powell amendment. Richard Bolling did not wish to be preached to from the floor of the House about the direction or depth of his own conscience. He wanted to defeat the Dixiecrats as much as Powell did. He saw the light in their eyes when they crowded around Powell, mischievously voting for his amendment, knowing that it would kill any legislation they did not like and at the same time make them appear to be voting for civil rights. The little trick enraged Bolling, who yearned for Powell to realize that those who were manipulating his amendment were doing so out of vindictiveness.

But Adam Clayton Powell did not need Richard Bolling. The point was painfully brought home to him in the winter of 1961, when Bolling made a spirited run against Carl Albert for House majority leader. Rayburn was gone. Since John McCormack had no genuine grip on the House, Bolling found himself soliciting support from powerful Democratic congressmen, from the chairmen, men like Adam Clayton Powell. But Powell threw his support to Albert, whom he credited with being instrumental in helping him pass the 1961 minimum wage act. He then went on to assail Bolling's alliance with labor leaders — the very labor leaders who decried his legislation and would not champion the cause of civil rights — as his primary reason for not backing Bolling. He convinced the entire New York congressional delegation to support Albert. Albert had gone into the race as an underdog and emerged as the victor. Bolling never forgave Powell; Albert never forgot.

Thus, Richard Bolling would not now go out on a limb for Adam Clayton Powell, but he would warn McCormack of the danger, of the looks on the faces of the southern men he served with on the House Rules Committee. "They asked me what to do," he said of the congressmen lining up in support of Powell. "I said 'Go to McCormack,' thinking he would do the same as Rayburn would do. I was used to a Speaker like Rayburn, who, when we had a member in trouble, would step in and be a one-man committee on ethics." There was an additional factor in Bolling's decision to play no major role in the effort to save Powell. One of the goals of the Democratic Study Group was to diminish the powers of chairmen. Powell believed wholeheartedly in the seniority system, which had ensured his rise, and the study group's way of expressing displeasure was to gather enough votes to change the House rules. Bolling was their spiritual leader.

Richard Bolling had studied the House for years, even writing incisive magazine articles about the workings of Congress. Change came slowly to that body. But now so much was coming together, at the expense of turmoil: McCormack's power was brittle; the young liberals were angry; the House rules were under attack; and the most powerful black politician in America embodied all of Richard Bolling's frustrations with the House. Adam Clayton Powell now represented the old guard, autocratic power.

John McCormack also could not control Lionel Van Deerlin. In his native California (he was born in Los Angeles but spent his adult life in San Diego), Van Deerlin had been a journalist, rising to city editor of the *San Diego Journal*. From there he began a career in television, as a commentator. It did not take him long to realize the wonders of television; his name recognition was unbelievable. When eight new congressional seats were created in California after the 1960 census, Van Deerlin, whimsically, and without any political experience, ran for one. He was as surprised by his victory as anyone. He arrived in Washington in 1963 with no set agenda; he was happily naive. His top aide had been a sports reporter at his television station. But Lionel Van Deerlin did not plan on sitting around Congress anonymously, not after years in the hot glare of television, not after having people on the streets of San Diego stop and yell his name. He was used to the spotlight and felt comfortable in its beam.

John McCormack, who still lived in an inexpensive hotel room in Washington, prided himself on being a nine-to-five congressman. His social life revolved around his wife, on whom he doted. There were times when he might amble around the Hill, having drinks with fellow House members, but more often than not he was invisible after hours. At seventy-five, he never rushed to get anywhere.

On January 7, McCormack finally made his presence felt regarding Adam Clayton Powell. Many felt that he had waited too long. But he knew what he had to do; he had to save the House from itself. He had returned to Congress with a plan. Powell was going to be saved; the Young Turks were going to be taught a lesson; tradition would prevail. McCormack had worked with the southerners long enough to know them well, and he knew that more blood would be spilled if discipline was not administered. As Speaker of the House, he had to give the appearance of impartiality.

Realizing that he could not count on Richard Bolling, McCormack recruited Morris Udall to carry out his plan. According to Udall, the Speaker called it a "two-rocket" plan: the first rocket would be to have Powell stripped of his chairmanship, thus satisfying the Republicans; the second rocket, sent up right after the first, would be to have Powell seated in the House, satisfying his national constituency and the Democrats, who had scheduled a meeting on January 8. McCormack was, of course, putting Udall in a tenuous position, asking him to lead the fight to strip one of his colleagues of power. John McCormack was wilier than he appeared, however; there were very few blacks in Udall's Arizona district. Udall did not have to worry about reprisals.

Before the Democrats convened the next day, Speaker McCormack had a word with Lionel Van Deerlin. Neither man knew much about the other. Van Deerlin's naiveté was so genuine it was almost spectacular: he had no fear of John McCormack. "Now, Van, you really don't think the House is going to deny Powell his seat, do you?" Van Deerlin was smart enough to realize that this was less a question than a warning. He could care less. "Mr. Speaker," he said, "you've been up in Boston. I've been here. You don't understand the temper of the House." John McCormack was taken aback by such arrogance.

On January 8, in tweed suit and knit tie, Adam Clayton Powell strode gallantly through the halls of Congress to meet with his fellow Democrats. Beneath his arm he carried a copy of Jack Anderson's recently published book, *Washington Exposé*, which detailed the shenanigans of many House members, Powell included. The Harlem congressman was not afraid of what might happen in a glass house. But the Democrats voting against him were not the Democrats who had been exposed in Anderson's book. They were the new Democrats, who had suffered under the archaic rules of the seniority system; those who had been made nervous by Powell's overtures to the black power proponents; those who were tired of the Esther James stories. They had grown weary of trying to contact Powell and having to go through his assistant, Chuck Stone, the mercurial figure who served as Powell's liaison with the black power groups, who thought the congressman's phones were bugged, who mixed his martinis.

Udall's motion to strip Powell of his chairmanship was adopted swiftly by the House Democrats. Powell was stunned; a glazed look appeared in his eyes. The strategy of stripping him of his cherished chairmanship, the very vehicle that had enabled him to rack up legislative victories for his party, had eluded him. Hadn't he passed the legislation? For Kennedy? For Johnson? It was such a rare move to deny a chairman his chairmanship as to be near-unprecedented. As Powell had once told his congregation, it took him sixteen years to become chairman. And he had had such plans for the 90th Congress — more antipoverty funds, a more disciplined Office of Economic Opportunity; there was going to be an attempt to unify all civil rights organizations. But now the power was gone.

Adam Clayton Powell knew he was wounded, and wounded badly. He needed his people, his Harlem. In less than twenty-four hours he would have to face the entire Congress: now his seat itself was at stake.

❧

Lionel Van Deerlin and his assistant had for weeks been poring over records of House members who had been excluded, looking for precedents, as Van Deerlin recalled years later. Neither Van Deerlin nor his top assistant had legal training; both had come to politics from television journalism. In the documents they saw what they wished to see: valid reasons to exclude. They went about their work in a relentless fashion, ignoring the icy looks of the black secretary in the office.

Van Deerlin's mission had given him an ample amount of hubris. He had ventured up to New York City to attend a conference of television executives in December 1966. After the conference, many moved to Sardi's for drinks. News spread quickly of Van Deerlin's presence on Powell's turf. When he emerged, a phalanx of reporters and cameras greeted him. Van Deerlin was surprised at the commotion, but in front of television cameras Lionel Van Deerlin, the old TV pro, a veteran of the medium, was hardly one to wilt. He came alive. Looking directly into the cameras, he announced that he indeed planned to go ahead with his threat to deny Powell his seat, citing Powell's outstanding arrest in the Esther James matter.

On New Year's Eve, 1966, Van Deerlin picked up a ringing telephone in his home. It was yet another angry telephone call, threatening him with physical harm if he went through with the Powell motion. There had been many calls, but this one unnerved the congressman so much that he cut his finger as he was trying to affix his stickpin. Lionel Van Deerlin also got a call from Alabama House member William Dickinson, who told him that he had heard rumors that Van Deerlin would pull out at the last moment and not offer a motion to block Powell's seating. Van Deerlin assured the southern Democrat that that was wrong, that he had not at all changed his mind.

⊙꧁꧂⊙

The buses began arriving in Washington on the morning of January 10. Descending from the buses on the east side of the Capitol, the throngs began hoisting their placards: JUSTICE FOR POWELL; POWELL SPELLS CHAIRMAN. "Chairman Powell" buttons were attached to their coats. Percy Sutton and Charlie Rangel, the young Harlem politicos, were conspicuously on the front line. Extra police had been summoned.

John McCormack would now see whether his two-rocket strategy was wise. As the members of the House began filing into their chamber, the mood was somber. Democrats still maintained a 248–187 majority in the House, but Republicans had picked up forty-seven seats in the last elections. Now, before the glare of national television, the Democrats were twisting about the manner in which to punish one of their own on the volatile issue of ethics.

It had been twenty-two years since Adam Clayton Powell had first arrived before this body. The men and women (they were overwhelmingly men) filing into the chamber to be sworn in wore spectacles, thin ties and white shirts and dark-colored suits. Many had followed Rayburn's dictum, "Go along to get along." Many, too, were worried about America, the unrest on the streets, the rioting, the war in Vietnam. In the Senate, the fearless Democrat Wayne Morse, Powell's staunch ally on domestic legislation, rose up and broke ranks with Lyndon Johnson over the Vietnam War. Now, outside the Capitol, the Capitol they revered, were massed thousands of protesters, waving placards. The times were not so simple anymore.

There were quiet conversations on the floor among members as they took their seats — chatter about the just-past holiday season. The tall representative with the crew cut and bow tie was Morris Udall, whom Speaker McCormack had entrusted to set this complex and explosive matter straight. This was the hour when Morris Udall had to prove to Adam Clayton Powell that his move the day before, to deny Powell his chairmanship, was calculated to save Powell's seat. Like Richard Bolling, Morris Udall had an acquaintance with black America that distinguished him from most others. During World War II he had been stationed on an army post in Louisiana, a young white officer in charge of an all-black outfit. The more time Udall spent with the men, the more he realized they were not that different from himself — everyone was lonely, no one wanted to go to war; lanterns burned at night in camp as they all wrote letters home. A camaraderie was formed, and for Morris Udall, it was profound. Though he came from a Mormon background and Mormons did not advocate integration, when he returned home to Arizona, Udall engaged family members in discussions about race, his belief in integration colliding with their belief in segregation. Morris Udall had come to Congress this day fully realizing that Powell was not the only one on trial; the House was, as well.

Powell moved along the railing in the rear, fully aware that Udall would have to carry the day. He strolled over to the Arizona congressman. "I want my seat, baby," he said. Then he showed Udall a speech he had written on a piece of paper. Udall thought it so eloquent and contrite that he assured Powell that he would have no problem retaining his seat after giving such a speech.

John McCormack had a habit of instructing members how to vote with the direction of his cigar: if the cigar motioned up, vote yes; if it motioned down, vote no. The cigar did not matter this time. McCormack was preoccupied with thoughts of insurrection. Two powerful House members, Wayne Hays and Emmanuel Celler of the Judiciary Committee, had warned their colleagues that to refuse Powell his seat would be to attack the Constitution itself. Celler especially had to swallow his pride in pushing for Powell to be seated: the Brooklyn Democrat had battled with Powell about New York anti-poverty funds only to have Powell taunt him about the Bedford-Stuyvesant area of his district, one of the most impoverished ghettos in all of America, which seemed to get worse each year. Celler loathed such criticism, because it was an attack on his honor, and everyone in Congress knew that Manny Celler was an honorable man. But Manny Celler was also a lawyer, and the law was the law; Powell must be seated because he had been duly elected, Celler insisted.

Any House member who wanted to stand and speak out on the Powell matter could do so. The alphabetical roll call began. As Carl Albert approached the lectern, many lamented that he had not been around more to partake in the behind-the-scenes debate. He might have made a difference. But Albert had suffered a heart attack in late 1966. He looked wan and a little tired, and many could see that the illness had taken its toll. Still, among Powell's allies there was some hope that he could now help. After all, in college he had been a champion debater, and on the floor of the House he had often performed masterfully. But he had returned to a House clearly divided, and the stress was evident. "The American way is first to give a man a trial and then to convict him," Albert said. His faux-pas elicited gales of laughter, and did little to aid the cause.

Many others stood after Albert, and their words had an edge to them; there was anger in the voices. Congressmen spoke of ethics and the scorn heaped on Congress because of Powell. They spoke of his arrest warrant in New York City, of the angry mail they had received from constituents, mail that battered them about both Johnson's war and the Harlem congressman. And they were passionate in claiming that their upcoming vote would have nothing to do with race, that they were merely reflecting the sentiments of the American public. Congressman after congressman addressed the crowded House, and it became quite clear that momentum was against the Harlem congressman.

Powell, Udall, and Van Deerlin spoke after most others, because their names fell late in the alphabetical roll call. When Powell's name was called, just as he turned to head toward the lectern, he crumpled the piece of paper containing his eloquent speech and tossed it to the ground. Udall's worry grew grave. "There is no one here who does not have a skeleton in his closet," Powell began. This was not the contrite, apologetic Powell whom Udall had hoped would address the gathering; it was the familiar ferocious Powell. "I know, and I know them by name," he said. Then he told his fellow representatives that he hoped however they voted, they would be able to have a good night's sleep.

There was nothing Udall could do about Powell's defiant tone. He still had to try to convince the members to seat Powell, and he moved that Powell be seated and that an inquiry into his activities be undertaken. The Harlem congressman had made his now desperate mission no easier. But the moment was vitally important for Morris Udall. Standing there, his long arms rising and lowering, his hand jabbing the air, Udall realized how much was at stake; after all, he had led the forces to strip Powell of his chairmanship, and if he failed here, in the second phase of McCormack's approach, the Democrats would have thrown Powell, one of their own and already wounded, to the Republicans. Enough punishment had been meted out, Udall told his colleagues, pleading in a merciful tone for the seating of "the gentleman from New York."

It was now left to Lionel Van Deerlin; if he offered the motion to deny Powell his seat, it would have to be voted on. When John McCormack called on him, Van Deerlin looked around the chamber for Powell. Their eyes locked, because Powell was looking directly at him. Powell hoped that his stature in the House would prevail, that the young congressman, a fellow Democrat, would not do as he had threatened. But Van Deerlin did, and his utterance, his opposition to the seating of "the gentleman from New York," had to be voted on.

The vote on Udall's motion to seat Powell while an inquiry took its course failed. The vote on Van Deerlin's motion to deny Powell his seat until after the inquiry was swift and brutal: 364 in favor and 64 opposed. Van Deerlin had achieved his aim. McCormack's strategy had been beaten, and beaten badly.

So much seemed to have gone wrong that a bit of the very foundation of Congress itself seemed to have cracked. The Speaker had been badly bruised; seniority had been dismissed. Andrew Jacobs, a young Democratic congressman from Indiana, didn't know what to make of it. He had felt all along that Powell would be seated; the people, not the House, decided who would serve in Congress; the concept was older than James Madison, who had written the words. Jacobs knew that something had gone wrong and "wanted to cry" as he watched Powell leave the chamber, the necks craning. "A person with all that talent and mission for oppressed people," Jacobs thought to himself, was now leaving, and who knew when, if ever, he would return.

Udall walked over and picked up the piece of paper Powell had crumpled and thrown to the floor — his undelivered speech. Powell walked past McCormack in silence. "Those sons of bitches," he said in the hallway. "They really did it."

For the moment at least, the Harlem congressman could no longer frighten them.

Congress had not denied a duly elected member a seat since 1807. There were only seven members in the House who had amassed more votes than Adam Clayton Powell in the 1966 elections.

Outside the Capitol, word quickly raced to the milling protesters, and their voices rose in anger. To avoid the protesters, Van Deerlin slipped out the side door. Then Powell appeared, standing before the masses — his people. He waded into the crowd, heading for his waiting sedan. But they wanted something from him — a balled fist, defiance, words; they needed to know what to do next. He made the usual threats about forming a third party. Because they now had no representative in Congress, he told them to consider withholding their taxes. Some youths opened wallets and burned their draft cards; vulgar comments were heard against LBJ. Lady Bird, the first lady, looked out on the crowd from a nearby window, alarmed to see such a large demonstration.

Meanwhile, at the other end of the Capitol there was a celebration, forced into muteness because of the Powell commotion. Republican Edward Brooke, from Massachusetts, the first black since Reconstruction to be elected to the Senate, had just been sworn in. Brooke's ascendancy was measured with mixed emotions by many blacks. It was a glorious step forward for Brooke, but a painful step backward for Powell and his followers.

Powell compared being denied a seat in Congress with French history, telling the gathering that he was a "black Dreyfus." (Alfred Dreyfus was a French army captain accused in 1894 of high treason. The evidence was nonexistent, and the accusation could be traced to anti-Semitism. Dreyfus was convicted and imprisoned on Devil's Island. In 1906, two years before the birth of Adam Clayton Powell, Jr., he was pardoned.) Powell ducked into the waiting black sedan. People rushed close to the windows; inside, hanging from the rearview mirror, they could see a swinging miniature Jesus Christ figurine.

The embattled congressman's office staff had already been tipped off by a reporter. Powell arrived, called a quick gathering, and told the gloomy staff members that he would try to protect their jobs — something he was not able to do. (Maxine Dargans, who had voluntarily given information to Wayne Hays, was given a job on the staff of Carl Perkins, the Kentucky Democrat named to replace Powell as chairman of the committee.) In the background, Odell Clark began riffling through drawers and file cabinets, packing documents and papers and files, grumbling to himself. His action gave the entire scene, with its distraught staff members, uncertain futures, anger, the emotional urgency of a harried getaway.

Lawyers appeared quickly. Powell had told them to be available. Herbert Reid, the distinguished Howard law faculty member, had arrived. So had William Kunstler from New York City, and Frank Reeves, and Jean Camper Cahn of the Antioch law school. Every one of them had antiestablishment credentials, and most had been involved in the successful court battle of the young Georgia legislator Julian Bond to be returned to the Georgia statehouse after being refused his seat. "Adam was leaving for Bimini right away," recalled Kunstler. "He came in, said he'd like us to set up a team. He pressed a $2,500 check into my hand." Kunstler knew what that retainer meant. "We had a course of war."

Powell made a stop at his Guessford Court home, to pack personal belongings. Louis Martin, who was now working for the Democratic National Committee, came by. Martin felt the despair that had engulfed Powell, who was trying vainly to console Corrine Huff. "It was a sad, sad occasion," said Martin. "Corrine was unhappy. I remember seeing her fur coat on the bed. He was really down."

In New York, both senators — Robert Kennedy and Jacob Javits — voiced their outrage that Powell had been denied his seat. The anger spread quickly. The city councilman Edward Koch introduced a resolution to open the Esther James investigation again, "to clear the air as to where the truth lies." Nowhere was the anger more raw than on the streets of Harlem. In the decades of hurt and pain, this was among the most deeply felt blows. Harlemites told inquiring reporters virtually the same thing over and over: that their congressman meant a lot to them, had lifted a community's spirit and hopes, had marched. "Why," one woman said, "I remember a store here and it didn't hire colored people and so Adam said in 1939, 'Come on, children, let's walk,' and so we picketed and now there's as many colored working there as white."

It was January in Harlem — and very cold again.

ᑎᗯᑌ

John McCormack needed someone he could trust. There were men in this Congress who were saying to themselves that he was genuinely out of step with his own House. Many had seen it coming — the volatile showdown between Powell and his enemies. And they had wanted McCormack to stop it all; but McCormack was old, and the criticisms heaped on him during the Kennedy years — that he allowed the southern Democrats to outmaneuver him — were blowing in the wind once again.

McCormack had little time to ponder the criticisms. He had to find someone to head the select committee to investigate Powell's fitness to return to Congress. It was essential that whoever he selected have bipartisan respect and support. Also, he needed a veteran of the House, someone who revered the House's traditions, someone who was imbued with a sense of respect for Congress, for what it stood for despite the pens of the pundits. As important, McCormack could not select a southerner, nor a northern conservative. Above all else, the chairman of the select committee had to be above potential charges of racism.

McCormack found his man in Emmanuel Celler. Few were as highly esteemed on the Hill. Although Celler's voice had been drowned out when he requested that Powell be seated, with punishment, perhaps he could repair some of the damage. Celler, who quickly accepted the assignment despite his confrontations with Powell in the past, knew that Powell's seat had to be saved, for the sake of the Constitution.

The Brooklyn congressman chose a nine-member select committee, five Democrats and four Republicans. There was only one southerner on the committee, Claude Pepper, of Florida, and one black, John Conyers, of Detroit. As the hearings got under way, it quickly became clear that it was Manny Celler's show. His aides sat at either end of the table at the meetings, which took place in the spacious House Judiciary Committee conference room. Lack of levity was an essential Celler trademark. As Andrew Jacobs, a committee member, recalled, "Celler gave me the impression of Winston Churchill. His discourse was always formal." His strategy was plain enough: witnesses would be summoned, the allegations would be repeated, other witnesses would have a chance to rebut them, and afterward, the committee would come to a conclusion based on the testimony and offer its recommendations to the full House, with the full expectation that whatever conclusions and suggestions it reached would be accepted.

As Celler's committee prepared to begin hearings and call witnesses, many grew nervous. "I ain't going to jail for Adam," Robbie Clark told her husband, Odell. Powell had no apartment in Harlem, where he needed a voting residence, so he listed his residence as the Clarks' address. As it happened, the Clarks did not have to appear before the select committee, but many Powell staff members did.

The spotlight glared. Chuck Stone admitted to using committee funds to buy plane tickets and asserted energetically that Powell had signed the tickets. (Powell's supporters labeled him a turncoat.) Don Anderson expressed shock that his name had been forged on tickets. Russell Derrickson couldn't help thinking that his career had come to an ignominious juncture as he faced the lights and answered the questions. The committee produced travel logs from Chalk Airlines, which flew to Bimini, and names of the staff members showed up frequently. Celler's committee could not be persuaded that Education and Labor Committee staffers had to go to Bimini on business on behalf of the American taxpayer.

Powell and Corrine Huff refused to make the committee's assignment easy. Exiled on Bimini, Huff grew more nervous and exhausted by the day. She had left home for Washington with so much promise, and now relatives were seeing her name linked to a governmental inquiry. The subpoena addressed to her by the select committee sent her into even deeper depression. She tossed it away and imagined herself a fugitive.

Nearly a month to the day after he had been denied his seat, Powell appeared in Washington to face the inquiry. Flanked by lawyers, he took a seat and proceeded to answer no questions save his name, citizenship, and birthdate, the sole information an elected congressman had to offer before being seated. Emmanuel Celler was confused. He wanted testimony, and a dash of repentance would not hurt either; he wanted Powell to see that he was on his side. His had been one of the strongest voices urging that Powell be seated. But to Adam Clayton Powell, Emmanuel Celler was yet another soft liberal, another liberal imprisoned by his own well-meaning conscience. Powell looked on Celler as an enemy, not a friend, and Celler, getting only silence from

Powell, glared back. The two veteran New York congressmen, one seventy-eight, the other fifty-eight, two steadfast liberals, refused to give an inch.

Powell had arrived at the hearing with the intention of naming others who had relatives on their payrolls, others who had taken trips with no purpose other than leisure. He had said he knew where the skeletons were. But the judicial Celler would not allow such commentary. So Powell's testimony was nontestimony, and afterward, in the hallway, he asked anyone who was within earshot, "Where is the great American sense of fair play?" He quickly left Washington.

Celler's committee was particularly interested in talking to Powell's estranged wife, Yvette, who was eager to appear. Her reasons were twofold: to redeem her reputation, and to save her husband, whom she still loved. The night before she was questioned by the committee (she had stepped off the airplane from San Juan wearing sunglasses and looking radiant), she sat in her hotel preparing for her appearance with her attorney, Joseph Rauh. Though the hearings were getting wide press attention, the fevered atmosphere did not intimidate Rauh, who was familiar with such climates. He had been Arthur Miller's lawyer when Miller had appeared before the HUAC; he had also defended the playwright Lillian Hellman before a House committee. As he and Yvette discussed her appearance, the phone rang. It was Adam Clayton Powell. Yvette started talking quickly, telling her husband about their son, wanting to know when he was planning to return to San Juan, to Villa Reposa, to the family. As she spoke, her eyes darted back and forth to Rauh. But Powell did not want to talk about his young son or Villa Reposa; he told Yvette to say nothing to the committee. Rauh could see her tighten.

"When I walked into the hearing room," Rauh said about the next morning, "it was absolutely full. I never saw that many flashes go off in my life." Rauh's strategy with his client was simple: she was to be absolutely honest with the committee. "Probably she committed a crime as well as Adam," said Rauh. "She took money from the committee for no services. I knew enough to know this was touchy ground we were on." Celler and the committee wanted to know about the checks that Yvette kept receiving from her husband even after she left the committee staff and returned to San Juan. She had brought the check stubs with her. Rauh handed them over. "You should have seen the flashes go off," he recalled. There was no punishment for Yvette; the committee merely wanted to gather all the evidence it could. She made impassioned pleas for Congress to return her husband to his seat, and before leaving the hearing room, Joseph Rauh told the committee that many relatives of House members were on the House payrolls, doing little or no work. The Committee did not seem very interested in the claim.

It was becoming quite clear that no smoking gun would be found. Powell had no secret bank account, as rumored. Questionable airplane tickets had been handed out, and there would have to be punishment for the waste of taxpayers' money, but that practice, as Celler and others on the committee knew, was not uncommon. As for the James libel case, Henry Williams was making efforts to pay the settlement. Through dogged appeals, he had had the judgment whittled down from $245,000 to $46,000.

Celler's position continued to mirror his earlier stance — that it would be violating the Constitution to deny Powell his seat. He received a strong nod from Republican Arch Moore, who warned of the dangers of tampering with the provisions of the Constitution regarding the seating of House members. Celler then proposed a stiff fine for Powell: $40,000 for the fifteen months his wife had remained on his payroll and for the misused airline tickets. In addition, Powell would be denied his seniority, and thus permanently punished. Celler did not have to worry about the Republicans on his committee; they all were in agreement with him. There were two Democrats who were not.

Claude Pepper was the lone southerner on the committee, and from the beginning of the discussions it was obvious that he favored outright dismissal of Powell from Congress. In the early 1940s, Pepper had received a degree of national acclaim as a liberal southern senator and a strong supporter of Franklin D. Roosevelt. But there was one issue on which he broke ranks with FDR, and that was the FEPC, the antidiscrimination bill. As a southerner, Pepper knew that supporting the legislation would surely lead to his defeat. When he made an appearance in New York City, he was attacked for this stance by none other than Adam Clayton Powell. (Pepper was eventually defeated for the Senate and later elected to the House, where he served until he died in 1989.) The verbal clash was written about in the press; Pepper resented it, and never forgot.

The other Democrat who gave Celler problems was young John Conyers, the only black on the committee. Conyers simply believed that the fine and the denial of seniority were too stiff; he could accept one or the other, but not both. Thus it came down to the differences between a black and a southerner — the Powell way. Time was running out, and Manny Celler had to file his report. He convinced everyone to sign the final recommendations, but he allowed Conyers and Pepper to attach their dissents to the document.

☙❦❧

In late February, following the preparation of the report — which would be voted on by the full House in early March — Celler shared the document with House Republican leader Gerald Ford. Democrats Lyndon Johnson and Adam Clayton Powell had gone to Congress to upset the status quo; Republicans Gerald Ford and Thomas Curtis had gone to uphold it. Ford and Curtis were trained lawyers, conservatives from the Midwest — Ford from Michigan and Curtis from St. Louis. They leaned toward the Taft wing of the party and joined the rock-ribbed Republicans led by Charles Halleck. Halleck had noticed Ford and given him prominence in Republican affairs, and Ford had recently noticed Curtis and appointed him to a House-Senate body exploring ways to organize an ethics committee. The work suited Tom Curtis just fine.

Back in St. Louis, Curtis had worked on the board of law examiners, prosecuting dishonest attorneys. (Before that he had waged battles against public housing, promoted by the likes of Harry Truman.) He stayed up late at night poring over documents regarding lawyers who he knew were cheating — but what good would it do to know it if he couldn't prove it? Curtis found many wrongdoers, and delighted in bringing them down. To Tom Curtis, rules were rules. When he went to Congress, he studied the arcane rules of the House with the kind of dedication that approached religion. Others preferred the challenge of passing legislation; not Tom Curtis. It was as if he saw no people, no humans, behind the purpose of Congress, merely rules and more rules. He had no chief of staff, only four women with whom he ran his office. He knew the rules so well that he was adept at applying them to blocking liberal legislation. President Kennedy loathed the Missouri congressman; "a real bastard," he once called him.

Tom Curtis was out in St. Louis when word of Ford's intention to accept the bipartisan committee's recommendations reached him. Powell would be fined, stripped of seniority, and seated. When a reporter told Curtis, he turned red. Curtis wanted Adam Clayton Powell expelled from Congress. He raced back to Washington, looking for Ford. "Gerry," he said, "you can't do this." And Tom Curtis began haranguing Gerald Ford in that Tom Curtis way — a nonstop discourse about the law, about wrongdoers. He told Ford that he was mistaken and that he, Curtis, planned to do something about it. He didn't quite know what he would do yet, but he was sure he would do something. He was so angry that he told his wife one evening he would have to consider leaving Congress if he couldn't change Ford's mind, because Tom Curtis was not going to stay in a Congress that allowed a wrongdoer to reclaim his seat.

Curtis would not let up, and his discussions with Ford grew more heated by the day. He drew up his own resolution, an expulsion resolution, and waved it in front of Ford and told him that it was the answer. Then Gerald Ford began to look at the whole affair the way Tom Curtis was looking at it: Powell would have to be expelled; not only did they both now believe it, but 54 percent of the American people, according to a Louis Harris poll, also believed it.

On March 1, Congress convened to vote on the Celler committee's report. Celler felt confident, as did McCormack; Powell remained in Bimini. Tom Curtis aroused some attention when he arrived bearing a copy of the Ten Commandments. To McCormack's surprise, the recommendations of the Celler committee were defeated, 222 to 202. The anger against Powell was so deep that neither Celler nor McCormack had recognized its depths. This marked the first time that the House had ever ignored the recommendations of a bipartisan committee.

The liberals who had wanted merely to punish Powell now faced the possibility of ending his career altogether. Curtis's resolution for outright expulsion was voted on. It passed, 248 to 176. Emmanuel Celler grimaced. The old liberal thought he knew this place, this sanctuary, where he had served since 1924. But this action was vindictive and needless. Claude Pepper had fooled him and abandoned the bipartisan report to vote for Powell's expulsion, the only member of the committee to do so. Prejudice seemed to be at work; the last time that Congress had denied a duly elected member his seat was in 1921, when Victor Berger, from Milwaukee, was accused of being a socialist.

Not only had the most powerful black politician in America been stripped of his chairmanship, he had been denied the right to take the seat to which he had been overwhelmingly elected. Tom Curtis was exultant; his work behind the scenes had paid off. Ford grew defensive and gruff. Powell's lawyers prepared a legal challenge, vowing to take it all the way to the Supreme Court if necessary.

The next day there were ominous hints in the press that the House of Representatives had overstepped its bounds. "If the House can refuse to seat Powell for peccadilloes of middling gravity," asked the *Detroit News*, "what limit is there on its power to exclude anybody, on any grounds a simple majority may decide to use, even membership in the wrong party? The Powell precedent is grave." From the *Washington Post*: "Despite the enormity of Mr. Powell's offenses, we think this outcome was emotional, vindictive, and foolish." The *Chicago Daily News* wondered if Congress had provided the means to drive a wedge "deeper between Negroes and whites" in America. And in an editorial headlined "Haunted House," the *New York World-Journal-Tribune* said, in part, that though Powell "may be politically finished, his case is not. It is a major piece of unfinished business that will haunt the House."

❧

The voices of King, Wilkins, Farmer, and Ralph Bunche, of the United Nations, were slow to rise in reaction to Powell's expulsion, and when they did, they rose with caution. Adam Clayton Powell had disdained them for so long. Wilkins, always a methodical man, had admitted at the beginning of the inquiry that he had spent no "sleepless nights" wondering about Powell's fate at the hands of his congressional colleagues.

There was, however, one voice among the old guard of the civil rights movement that did rise, and it rose higher than all the other voices. It was the voice of a man who remembered the old days in New York City, a man who had watched young Adam Powell march downtown to City Hall and protest on behalf of Harlemites, a man who knew how high the wall had been against blacks who tried to integrate the unions and who had seen Adam Clayton Powell lower that wall considerably with threat and intimidation, with political power. A. Philip Randolph still had an office in New York City, and he picked up the phone and sent out the rallying cry. He was now seventy-eight, and he moved more slowly than he had, but his clipped voice was still sure and confident. He summoned not only the civil rights leaders but the entertainment community — Lena Horne, Sammy Davis, Harry Belafonte, Louis Armstrong. Gallantly, A. Philip

Randolph announced plans for a "Negro summit." It would evoke the *esprit de corps* of the March on Washington; the destruction of Adam Clayton Powell's power would not be tolerated.

But a strange thing happened. There was no rush to Randolph's side. The esteemed leader of the Pullman porters heard excuses, heard men and women telling him about their busy schedules. He had to watch his call for a Negro summit on Powell's behalf being reduced to fitful church meetings and union hall gatherings here and there across the country.

One such meeting at the Abyssinian Baptist Church drew 4,500 members. In the glory days there might well have been twice as many for an emotional protest rally. But even the 4,500 gathered in the church made David Licorish nervous. With his eye on the Abyssinian pulpit, aware that the congregation now looked for leadership from within, Licorish was eager to disprove the nay-sayers regarding his own abilities. But there was little he could do when so many non-Abyssinians were flocking to the church, angry young men calling themselves black nationalists, dressed in berets and denim, young men whose talk leaned toward revolution more than piety.

Unpitied by both Congress and the mainstream civil rights leaders, Adam Clayton Powell had one last recourse: to rely on the young radicals. They visited him by the dozen on Bimini, to offer support, but more than that, to seek balm and guidance, for Powell's overthrow had imbued him with the rough glitter of a living martyr. They had to go to him from Miami, across the ocean, to a little backwater island that was British territory, which gave their journey the true feeling of a mission. There, at journey's end, stood Adam Clayton Powell, surrounded by islanders, spreading his arms wide, welcoming them. So many went: Julian Bond, from Georgia, articulate, handsome, witty; Dick Gregory, from Chicago via Mississippi, now less the comic and more the political activist; Floyd McKissick, of the Student Non-Violent Coordinating Committee, who had shown such courage in the Florida civil rights battles; Mervyn Dymally, a Californian who had no links to the southern movement but came to forge such links. The ousted congressman regaled them with stories about Congress, the war in Vietnam, his planned comeback. But they quickly found that he was not one for idle banter. There would be little intimacy; he would not complain if they left when the press left.

New York governor Nelson Rockefeller was required by law to call a special election to fill Powell's vacant seat. The election was called for April 1967. There was speculation in Manhattan about whether Powell would even enter the race. Still wanted for contempt of court in the Esther James case (even though he had settled the financial judgment), he might find it risky to go to New York to sign his election petition. Possible arrest was not the only worry. Aides had warned him that there might be riots in reaction to his ouster. The New York press was missing out on the story, unaware of Powell's plans and motivations.

Thomas Johnson had joined the *New York Times* from *Newsday.* Earlier in his career, he had written from New York for the *Pittsburgh Courier.* He had gotten to know Powell. Johnson looked around the *Times* newsroom and quickly realized that there was no one to whom Powell might talk more easily than to him. He approached Abe Rosenthal, the managing editor, and said, "I can talk to Adam Powell." Rosenthal dismissed him: "No one can talk to Adam Powell." But Johnson was experienced enough to know that most editors could be convinced to let a reporter chase a story if they felt the reporter had a passion and energy for it. "Rosenthal liked the macho stance," recalled Johnson, who repeatedly badgered Rosenthal to let him go down to Bimini. A short while later he heard Rosenthal's voice on the end of a telephone: "How soon can you get there?"

Johnson left right away. For several days he trailed Powell, getting the occasional quote, capturing the scene, and filing dispatches. Johnson wanted to gain Powell's confidence — not a simple endeavor, inasmuch as his newspaper had been a forceful critic of Powell. But Johnson stayed as close as he could, close enough that Powell started acknowledging him at news conferences, introducing him as "Uncle Tom . . . Johnson of the *New York Times.*" Johnson knew enough to take the barb as one might take a harmless joke.

Evenings, he found himself being invited over to Powell's home on South Bimini for off-the-record visits. Thomas Johnson found a different Adam Clayton Powell at home, very different from the Adam Clayton Powell of the news conferences. In his home at night, swirling his rum, when the cameras were no longer turned on him, Powell talked longingly of Congress ("He said he was a member of an exclusive club," recalled Johnson); of his father, Adam Senior; of Marcus Garvey, whose own career had come to such a painful end; and of America, which he believed to be on the verge of social revolution.

"He had a conversational range from outrageous to very insightful," said Johnson. A great deal went through Johnson's mind as he sat there watching Powell, knowing as well as Powell knew that things would never be the same again. Johnson had covered some aspects of the Esther James case while at *Newsday*. He had talked to policemen who told him that Powell was correct, that James was a bagwoman; but the police officers were hardly going to come to the rescue of Adam Clayton Powell.

Powell turned to Johnson one evening and told him to be ready to fly the next morning. He did not mention the destination. It was the moment Johnson had been waiting for, and his heart began to race. The next morning he boarded a plane with Powell and Floyd McKissick at the edge of the island. Johnson knew they were not going far, because the plane flew low, just above the blue-green waters. Powell played the mystery out for all it was worth. When they landed in Miami, he led Johnson into the airport terminal, moving swiftly, and Johnson moved swiftly to keep up. Since Powell was wanted on an outstanding warrant, he could be arrested by U.S. marshals. Baggage men — his people — waved to him, and he waved back, smiling. Then he ducked into a room where Jean Camper Cahn, one of his Washington-based attorneys, was waiting. She handed him the petition that he had to sign in the presence of a notary public to enter the special election in New York. Johnson snapped a photograph and handed the film to McKissick to deliver to New York, where he was headed.

After Powell scrawled his signature, he turned and walked back through the terminal, a red handkerchief hanging from his hip pocket. Back on the plane with Johnson, he said, "Uncle Tom, did that satisfy you?" He told the reporter that he would get his story on page one. "I'm going to make your career, nigger. Going to make your career!" The plane took off to the roar of Powell's laughter. Johnson was impressed. He wrote his story up, and no one else, least of all the Florida reporters, had it. Johnson knew Abe Rosenthal would like this kind of scoop.

With a Republican governor, Rockefeller, in Albany and a Republican mayor, John Lindsay, in City Hall, New York Republicans intended to claim Powell's seat, held by his party since 1945. To them, Harlem looked winnable for the first time in years. Jackie Robinson, who was now a community affairs adviser to Rockefeller, warned early that a move to take advantage of Powell's downfall might well backfire, but Rockefeller was willing to take the chance, telling Robinson that it was Democrats against Republicans and that the battle had to be launched.

The Republicans imagined that the bandleader Lionel Hampton, an acquaintance of Rockefeller's, would be a formidable candidate. Hampton, however, was honest about his shortcomings; he was a musician, not a politician, and declined. Then, in what they concluded was a brilliant stroke, the Republicans decided to extend full backing to a young Columbia Law School student who was also an army veteran: James Meredith. Meredith represented both tragedy and hope in America. He had been forced to walk a gauntlet shielded by federal marshals at the University of Mississippi, which he integrated in 1962. Then, on June 6, 1966, while embarking on a voting rights march in the South, he was shot. Moving north, to New York City, Meredith entered Columbia Law School. He was a shy young man, and painfully aloof; the latter attribute gave acquaintances the feeling that he was either a stark visionary or had suffered unbearable mental stress which had permanently marked his personality.

"The Republican Party made me an offer: full support for the seat, in every way, everything," recalled Meredith. Meeting in the comfort of swank hotel rooms with men sent by Rockefeller himself, Meredith found the overtures inviting; victory was made to look, and sound, quite possible. Access to the state's top Republicans gave him a heady feeling: "I didn't deal with details, and I didn't deal with people who didn't matter." He announced his candidacy.

Harlemites knew little of James Meredith; his presence had not been felt in the community. His currency as tragic hero meant nothing to local people, who saw him as a dupe of the Republicans. Their anger raged in his ears. Floyd McKissick knocked on the door of his New York City apartment one day and assailed his candidacy. Meredith found himself in the middle of yet another furor, and these were not white southerners railing at him, they were black New Yorkers. He thought the harsh glare of the press was as bad as what he had gone through in Mississippi. Pummeled with criticism from both Harlemites and national organizations such as SNCC and CORE that were sympathetic to Powell, Meredith was forced to retreat within a week's time to rethink his position. Even in absentia, Adam Clayton Powell loomed large.

As unpredictably as he had entered the race, James Meredith shocked state Republicans and withdrew. "The Lord moves in mysterious ways," Adam Clayton Powell wisecracked when he heard the news. The Republicans searched frantically for another candidate to place on the ballot for the special election. They found her in Lucille Williams, a Harlem grandmother and a member of the Abyssinian Baptist Church. There was precious little time for Williams to mount a serious campaign, and she knew it. She breezed around Harlem with a devil-may-care attitude, sometimes talking about her grandchildren, sometimes speaking glowingly of her opponent.

Adam Clayton Powell won re-election in the April 11 contest by a seven-to-one margin. The news was delivered to him in Bimini. Harlemites had sent yet another message to Washington: they would accept no one other than their man, Adam Clayton Powell.

Manny Celler vowed to fight for his right to be seated, but he did not realize that there would be no congressman to fight for. Powell was willing to take back his seat only on his own terms. Convinced that he had been robbed of his seat unconstitutionally, he vowed to continue his fight in the courts. The House had not only denied him his seat, it had overridden the wishes of black Harlem, his Harlem, his people. Thus, he would have to do as he had done when he first arrived in Congress in 1945; he would have to do exactly what Rayburn had cautioned him not to do: he would have to throw a bomb. Adam Clayton Powell was intent on holding Congress hostage; once again he would pin the conscience of House liberals to the wall. He would refuse to show up in January 1968, choosing self-imposed exile and depriving the liberals of their chance to put the House back in order.

⟨⟩

Soon the young blacks, "the new breed of cats," stopped going to Bimini. (Oftentimes Powell had paid for their hotel rooms, and with no income, no link to any civil rights organization's treasure chest, his finances were becoming strapped.) They all had other battles anyway. Dodging the draft, Stokely Carmichael was on the run from the FBI. Mervyn Dymally was involved in political organizing in California. Dick Gregory was amassing an interesting following — radicals and fervent protesters and those who found deep truth in his grim and sometimes comic asides about the American political structure. Gregory returned to Chicago to run for mayor against Richard

Daley, having received Powell's endorsement beneath a banyan tree on the island of Bimini.

In July 1967 Powell was booked to appear at a black power conference in Newark. He sent word at the last minute that he would not appear. He was wanted on a warrant; authorities had warned him of possible riots. Adam Clayton Powell III appeared instead. A shy man, not blessed with his father's quick tongue, he was booed.

Powell himself continued to float threats that he might emerge to form a third political party — threats that vanished without a trace. His lawyers urged patience. They were fighting his case with a missionary zeal, but the judicial system worked ever so slowly. Days and weeks and months passed on Bimini.

The island of Bimini, a strip of land seven miles long and a mile wide, sits sixty miles off the coast of Miami. For generations it had served as a fishing playground for well-heeled Europeans on holiday, who ran their huge boats across the seas to compete in its leisurely run fishing tournament. Adam Clayton Powell gave it the aura of a hideaway. Cars zoomed down the scuffed dirt road; tourists sampled the rum (one of the bars had the perfect name, End of the World) and the renowned conch chowder; visitors frolicked on the white sand. As the island had only one main switchboard, communication was often a task — just the way many residents preferred it.

Powell's home was on South Bimini, around the curve formed by an inlet of water, gently screened by palm trees. He had no telephone at all, and some visitors thought the living arrangements were a bit challenging for him. While his lawyers fought his expulsion from Congress, Adam Clayton Powell fished. He took the sport more seriously than had his father, who had also been an able fisherman. On Bimini Adam Junior entered fishing tournaments, taking pride in battling huge game fish to the end. "He never liked to lose a fish," explained Wesley Saunders, Powell's boat captain. Powell kept notes of his nautical activities and each outing's take. On the water, he preferred white dress: white shoes, white shirt, white shorts — "a beautiful dresser," according to Saunders.

The islanders took to the exiled congressman, wondering if the increased tourism was directly attributable to the wide attention he was bringing to their home. In the Biminians, Adam Clayton Powell saw a distressed people given little aid and attention by the British government. When Hurricane Betsy pounded the tiny island in 1965, he contacted his powerful friends in Washington, who quickly got in touch with the coast guard. Aid was immediately sent. Islanders appreciated his concern.

At one point Powell pulled together twelve of his followers — his disciples, as they were known — and recorded an album of sermons. Recording equipment had to be flown from the mainland to the island. The disciples served as background voices; Captain Saunders enthusiastically supplied a falsetto. The album, recorded live, was called *Keep the Faith, Baby!* and consisted of six sermons, among the more intriguingly titled of which were "My Dear Colleagues" and "Handwriting on the Wall."

Shortly after Powell's album appeared, Esther James released her own album. She was no longer living full-time in Harlem; it had become too risky. Once a gambler standing near James had been shot dead; knowing the wrath that many Harlemites felt toward her, she wondered if the bullets had been meant for her. She began shuttling back and forth between various New York State residences and her childhood home in Jamaica, which, of course, put her within reach of Powell's Bimini residence. James had once even showed up at a Nassau court in a flowered dress, a huge purse swinging from her arm, to inquire whether Powell had transferred property titles to the Jamaican courts. She was sent away.

James's album was called *No Man Is Above the Law — I Have Kept the Faith.* In tribute to her Caribbean upbringing, she recruited a calypso band for background vocals; the backup singers called themselves Lord Faith and the James Men. Among the titles that appeared on the album were "Hold the Dough," "Harlem Farewell," and "Bimini Boat Song." Both albums were released in a carnival-like atmosphere.

Sunday mornings — the haze lifting off the water, the fishermen long gone out to sea, the sun shining bright — often found Powell standing on the Bimini tennis courts, or dockside, giving sermons. "He'd call a prayer line, and he'd get pretty fired up," remembered Stanley Pinder, a young island minister. Biminians might well have been confused by some of Powell's sermons, particularly the ones he read directly from his House rules manual. Often, after the sermon, he would lead his gospel troupe in a rendition of "Amazing Grace." Rev. Adam Clayton Powell was far away from his own church. "It would bring tears to his eyes," recalled Thomas Johnson.

As the weeks and months passed, the sense of being a fugitive, on the lam, gnawed deeper. The emotional strain took its toll on Corrine

Above: Esther James at the trial of her $1 million libel suit against Powell in 1963. He did not testify in court.

Left: Powell about to be sentenced to thirty days for contempt of court, November 1966

Democratic leaders convening for the 90th Congress, January 1967. *From left to right in front:* Dan Rostenkowski, Carl Albert, Hale Boggs (behind Albert), and John McCormack

Below: Powell's legal team. *From left to right:* Jean Camper Cahn, William Kunstler, and Arthur Kinoy

Facing page: The Celler committee. *Standing from left to right:* Vernon Thomson, Charles Teague, Clark Mac-Gregor, Claude Pepper, John Conyers, and Andrew Jacobs; *sitting:* Arch Moore, Emmanuel Celler, and John Corman

THIS PAGE: *Left:* On the way to preach after being stripped of his powers as committee chairman, 1966

Middle left: On Bimini, reading the rules of the House of Representatives to a crowd of reporters, 1967

Below: Protesters surround Powell on the Capitol steps upon his exclusion from Congress, January 10, 1967

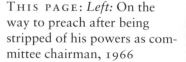

FACING PAGE: *Top:* Speaking in Watts, January 9, 1968, months before the riots

Below left: On *The Dick Cavett Show,* 1969, with his Haile Selassie medal and the inevitable cigarette

Below right: After reinstatement in the House, 1969

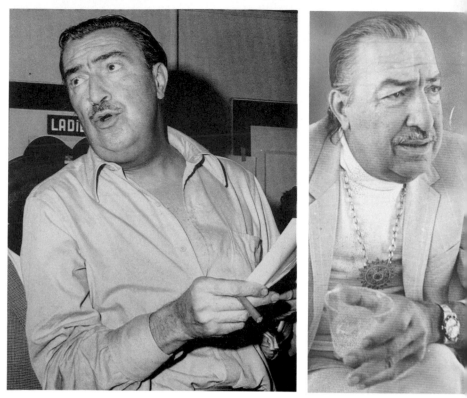

Above left: Reading the returns at his Harlem headquarters on primary night, June 23, 1970. Charles Rangel won by 150 votes.
Above right: Aboard *Adam's Fancy* in 1971 — never far from a drink or an interviewer
Facing page: Raising a fist in the black power salute at the Long Island House of Detention, October 3, 1970.
Below: With Darlene Expose, Adam III, and Beryl Powell, 1971

Hazel Scott, with Adam Clayton Powell III looming behind her, leaving the Abyssinian Baptist Church after Powell's funeral, April 9, 1972. Rev. David Licorish is at the right.

Huff, who was, in her own words, "a small-town girl from New Castle, Pennsylvania." After moving with her family to Ohio, she had entered local beauty pageants. She came in second as Miss Ohio but replaced the winner when a problem over the winner's age arose. Her mere appearance as a black woman in the beauty contest drew curiosity. Hollywood called. She did readings, and was saddened when producers told her that she was too light-skinned to portray blacks in movies.

In 1961, Huff became a fashion model for the Ebony Fashion Fair, a fashion troupe that originated in Chicago, the brain child of magazine publisher John Johnson. Every year a group of black models were selected to tour America. Huff was aghast at the segregation she found on the road in the Deep South; she had not suffered such indignities in Pennsylvania and Ohio.

After modeling, she ventured to Washington and onto the staff of Adam Clayton Powell. Their affair sometimes left her speechless. For her twenty-first birthday he took her to New York City — to "21." However, that had not been the original intention. Originally he had purchased tickets to a Broadway play. En route, spotted by a group of people milling about and encouraged to chat with them, he couldn't refuse and hopped on top a soapbox. As he wailed away, time passed; Huff grew angry, realizing that they would miss the play. In the end, he whisked her off to "21" instead. She was dazzled. She was outright amazed when he presented her with a fur coat. Then, of course, there had been the 1963 journey to Europe. When she turned twenty-six, he gave her twenty-six bottles of perfume. In Washington she grew giddy over entering nightclubs with him, because he always arrived just after the show began, so as not to cause a disturbance; the maître d' would lead them to the reserved table amid whispers and nods of acknowledgment. They drove together, fast, to New York Jets football games, "no matter the weather," she recalled. He had left his wife, Yvette, for her, and the web he pulled her into — Washington, New York, Paris, Rome, Athens — was so magnetic, it was impossible to pull away.

But now, on Bimini, Corrine Huff was understandably nervous. Not only had she ignored the House committee's subpoena (Chuck Stone had told the committee that she had traveled on numerous occasions under the names of other committee members), but it was widely known that Gerald Ford was pushing for a Department of Justice investigation of Powell, and her name had also been mentioned in that probe. Pictures of her as a beauty contestant were appearing in newspapers across the United States — specifically, a picture of her in a swimsuit. That particular photograph seemed to say something unsavory about her lifestyle, and she knew it; it fed the gossip in Washington and everywhere else. Tourists began to make her edgy. She imagined that government spies had stalked her to the island. Sometimes on the anchored boat, *Adam's Fancy,* the sound of footsteps was more than enough to send her scurrying belowdecks.

One day she received a letter from Hazel Scott, encouraging her to hold herself together. The hand of sisterhood made Corrine Huff feel better and a little stronger.

⟨∾⟩

Some Harlemites were bothered by Adam Clayton Powell's refusal to return to Washington after his victory in the special election. Most, however, allied themselves with his cause: to prove the House wrong by court action. The spirits of Powell's lawyers were considerably boosted when the Supreme Court agreed to hear his case. But legal maneuvers did not carry weight with everyone. In October, six months after the special election, the leader of the National Urban League, Whitney Young, appeared in Wyatt Walker's Manhattan pulpit and urged Harlemites to let go of their "sentimentality" about Powell and look to the future. The black power proponents, leaning heavily on anger and sentimentality, dismissed the likes of Young and vowed continued support for Powell.

In Washington, the liberals found themselves sorely missing Powell's stewardship of the Education and Labor Committee. Domestic legislation was taking a pounding because of the financial resources needed to fund the Vietnam War. As Congressman Richard Bolling put it in the summer of 1967, when the conflict was steadily escalating, "Good causes have been rebuffed." But the Johnson administration refused to concede criticism of its domestic agenda easily. A presidential aide feared that Carl Perkins, Powell's replacement as chairman — more and more often accused of capitulating to House Republicans — was being compared to Powell and coming up short. The aide urged Johnson to write a letter, to boost Perkins's spirits and the committee's as well.

On Bimini, Adam Clayton Powell began to long to go home. A presidential campaign loomed; wide-eyed idealists were mentioning him as a 1968 favorite-son candidate. There were rumblings across the country of the social revolution he had predicted — increased sit-ins, antiwar demonstrations, a burgeoning radical student movement. Some of the old guard didn't understand the movement, thought it too radical and lacking in proper strategies. Powell understood, and wanted to return to ride its crest. Moreover, Adam Clayton Powell, idling on Bimini, was running out of money. He had counted on his album to bring in royalties, but distribution problems crippled sales. It provided enough to pay off the Esther James judgment at last, but his contempt-of-court citation stood; Powell was still a wanted man, dodging a ninety-day jail sentence.

Needing money and predicting a revolution, Powell booked a series of speeches across America. The students were so vigorous in their rage, so rebellious against the status quo; "the old man of the black revolution," as he called himself, was encouraged. Actually, the travel plan was quite grandiose: after an extended American tour, he would tour Europe, beginning with an appearance at Oxford University, which quickly booked him. He knew he could gather crowds in Europe; the strategy was to take remuneration wherever he could get it.

Operating as his manager, Corrine Huff made calls to the mainland. There was considerable interest in the exiled Harlem congressman, and an itinerary came together quickly. They would begin on the West Coast, then move on to the Midwest; from there they would swoop south. Powell wanted badly to "awaken white young people" to the movement, to pass on to them whatever vestiges were left of his own rebellious vigor. "The old generation is finished," he said.

Adam Clayton Powell left Bimini in early January 1968, after nearly a year in exile, to return to the United States in the role of angry eminence. Corrine Huff was by his side, imagining the tour as salvation and hardly underestimating her own contributions. "I had to get him there," she recalled of the appearances, "and on time."

The reporters mobbed Powell at the Los Angeles International Airport. He looked dandy — tanned, wearing a sport coat, an ascot, a light-colored shirt. He had come out of exile, he announced, to take part in "the second civil war." California, despite having a conservative governor in Ronald Reagan, had mustered a teeming undercurrent of student radicalism, driven by the children of those who had elected Reagan. In Oakland, the Black Panthers were engaged in community activism and general revolt. California was angry and mystic, fertile ground for the exiled politician.

His first stop was Watts. Gliding through the battered streets, peering at the bobbing heads, Adam Clayton Powell was surrounded, then mobbed, by a crowd of mostly young men, young men in headbands and sunglasses, puffing on cigarettes in the coolish Los Angeles air. It took little time, still, for him to remove his coat, to loosen his tie, to begin jabbing the air with his fist, to summon the old fire. "We have not the democracy today that we used to have," he bellowed, the crowds trailing him. He paused and lectured on the street one minute, on the back of a flatbed truck (a quick, reflexive jump had put him up on it) the next. "It's a democracy for the upper class, white and black." Cheers greeted him at every turn. "We're not going to have the kind of America we should have," he said, "until they recognize that people like you are the backbone of what once was America." When he reached the core of Watts, where the worst of the 1965 riots had taken place — and this was Rev. Adam Clayton Powell at his best — he raised his arm, asking for quiet, then silence, "in memory of our soul brothers and sisters who died here." Then the procession went on. It had been a long time since he had heard hale and hearty voices on his behalf, since he had been grabbed, mobbed, idolized. "Those cats got my fifteen-dollar John Fredericks necktie and tore up my Brooks Brothers oxford button-down pin-striped shirt," he grumbled later.

Principally, Powell had gone to Los Angeles to kick off his speaking tour on the UCLA campus. When he arrived at Pauley Pavilion, escorted by Lew Alcindor (who later changed his name to Kareem Abdul-Jabbar), the school's Harlem-born premier basketball player, he was greeted by a round of applause from more than seven thousand students. This was the student vigor he had heard and read so much about. UCLA BLACK STUDENTS UNION WELCOMES BROTHER POWELL, read one placard. The students, sitting in stands, on bleachers, even standing, were hungry for something. He fully knew what they were hungry for — for guidance and understanding. "You must not scorn the black revolution," he urged them. "You must not scorn black power." He made references to Marcus Garvey, a plea to the "white bright youth" who mostly populated the audience. He ticked off the names of the black radicals fanning out across America — H. Rap Brown, Stokely Carmichael, Floyd McKissick — urging the students to listen to them. "We are a new breed of cats," he told them, at times staring off into the distance, at times making sentimental references to his own age (fifty-nine) and telling them how pleased he was to know he could still draw a crowd.

A day later he was wildly applauded on the San Diego campus of the University of California, where he pointed to white students and urged them to join the black revolution. His next stop was Berkeley, a hotbed of ferment, on the edge of its own revolution against the campus administration. Corrine Huff, however, noticed something: the congressman was tiring already. She wondered how long the hectic pace could continue.

In Berkeley, appearing outside Sproul Hall on the renowned "Free Speech" plaza, Powell faced six thousand students sitting on rooftops, on the ground, at his feet, listening to his antiwar tirades: "How dare we try to impose on the lovely people in Southeast Asia a way for democracy we are not practicing here?" He presented himself as an example of someone who had taken on the establishment, only to be reviled and ousted from Congress. "You young people are frustrated with your preachers, your politicians, and your parents, who have created this decadent society in which we live," he told them.

Stanford was next on the itinerary. But Powell was exhausted; the three-mile walk through Watts, the speeches, the tugging — it had all drained him. The change in temperature from Bimini to northern California had saddled him with flulike symptoms. The crowds had been good, and they seemed to respond energetically to his message, but now his body was giving out on him. In Washington he had always gone to the House gymnasium to stay in shape. On Bimini he had merely fished and drunk; now his stamina was gone. The Stanford speech was canceled, and so was the midwestern portion of the journey. He had been booked at schools in Florida and North Carolina. Those engagements too were canceled, but only temporarily. Ailing, Adam Clayton Powell left California only days after he had arrived, vowing to continue the tour at a later date. Corrine Huff was worried — she noticed the pallor of his skin, his extreme tiredness — and insisted that during their layover in Miami, he see one of his doctors.

In his law office above the Apollo Theatre, Henry Williams continued to work through the spring of 1968 to arrange for Powell to return to Harlem without arrest. For several years Williams had been ridiculed by other lawyers who questioned his tactics in the James case. It was often said around Harlem that he was a heavy drinker; that he was so mesmerized by Powell that he was unable to exercise sensible legal judgment. "Shut up," Powell had once snapped in his Bimini home when Williams had begun to question his motivations for delaying the payment to James. The exiled congressman coarsely told his lawyer just to keep him out of jail. But Henry Williams had to point out that through dogged appeals he had reduced the original judgment to less than $50,000 before finally paying it off.

Henry Williams was a proud lawyer, and he was fighting against Raymond Rubin, a downtown lawyer, a lawyer in a law firm. Henry Williams was still above the Apollo, with his lone secretary. Why did he take verbal abuse from Powell? Because he knew that there were many who had told Powell, more than once, to replace him with better-known lawyers — white lawyers — and Powell had refused. Powell's belief in him was encouragement enough.

In March, Williams made an impassioned plea to New York justice Arthur Markewich. The two talked about Powell's fate. Williams was persuasive, mentioning the possibility of extensive riots if Powell was jailed. A deal was made: Powell would go directly to Judge Markewich's Riverside Drive home, be greeted and arrested by a waiting marshal, and then immediately released upon the promise that he would appear on future court dates. Williams rushed to Bimini to deliver the news and bring Adam Clayton Powell home to Harlem.

They arrived in New York City on Friday, March 22, 1968. The weather was rainy and the air crisp; the press was unaware of his arrival. After the visit to the Markewich home, where Powell was arrested and immediately released, they rode uptown to Harlem and waltzed through the door of the Renaissance Ballroom. Patrons, shocked to see Powell, rushed to his side; drinks were ordered. Word swept Harlem: he was back; after fifteen months away, Adam was back in Harlem. The news raced along the streets, from 125th to 145th, from the Hotel Theresa to the Red Rooster, from Small's Paradise to the Apollo, from the Apollo to the Harlem YMCA, from stoop to stoop, from restaurant to restaurant: he was back.

They did not let him remain in the Renaissance for long. They wanted him out on the street, which is really where he wanted to be, and by the time he appeared on the street, the crowd, thousands, had amassed. He began the stroll up 125th and Seventh, his street — Adam Powell back among his people, free of worry from arrest. Horns honked; apartment doors swung open. There were so many who wanted to touch him, but the crowd kept swelling, and he kept walking, grinning the hard grin of the wounded hero. The scene had the fervor of the old campaign rallies, back in the 1940s — cameras clicking, crowds growing, his voice booming, the women grabbing. More than three dozen police officers had gathered to protect him, and their presence added an uneasy tension, because Powell was ringed by black power advocates led by Charles Kenyatta, a self-proclaimed revolutionary. Kenyatta played the role to the hilt: he wore a helmet and revolutionary garb; he also carried a Bible. Someone set up a ladder and Powell took to it effortlessly, his long body lithe, his jump upon it catlike. He waved a copy of the report of the President's Commission on Riots. It was a devastating indictment of society, citing urban disorder and the gulf of inequality that stained America. "We are in the midst of the second civil war!" he cried out, the rain falling. "The period of nonviolence has come to an end." He excoriated black political leaders in Harlem, then across the country, specifically citing King. Then he walked over to his church, trailed by the kind of angry young men who made the deacons so uneasy, and called for renewed strikes, an alliance with radical blacks; and he dared anyone to challenge him in the upcoming election. Finally he retired across the street to the Red Rooster, for drinks and the bonhomie of old friends whom he had so long missed.

The proud Abyssinian men and women — especially the women who really ran the church, women like Hattie Dodson — prepared the church for Powell's Sunday morning sermon. Since he had been away, the Sunday services had been reduced from two to one. The pews had begun to show wide spaces; the playing of musical chairs in the pulpit had taken a toll on devoted worshippers. But now the congregation was energized, and the women rushed to decorate the pulpit, to clean the fountain, to welcome him back. It had been a long fifteen months.

On his first Sunday, Powell was greeted by an overflow gathering. A huge banner stretched across the entire length of his father's pulpit:

WELCOME HOME ADAM C. POWELL • OUR PASTOR AND CON-
GRESSMAN THE MEMBERS AND THE OFFICIALS GREET YOU.

The choir regaled him with beautiful singing. Overcome with emotion, he dabbed at his eyes with a handkerchief. The congregation did not know quite what to think of the armed men who had encircled the pulpit, guarding him — Kenyatta's foot soldiers. The young men had their arms folded; some wore leather jackets and sunglasses; all were unsmiling. It bothered the older members of the church.

In the pulpit Powell seemed a different minister. Gone was the old idealism, the reach for distant dreams. He spoke of hobbled black leaders and of "Judases" within the Abyssinian Baptist Church. The congregation listened uneasily. They were told that the young militants would be the future leaders of America. The deacons also sat and listened, but they would not stand for this type of preaching for long. It was too shrill and too dangerous. They would not allow revolution to be launched from their pulpit. They would begin taking their orders from the memory of Adam Clayton Powell, Sr., who had said it was a community church, a church for the masses, not a church for particular political interests. Hadn't the younger Powell said to them the day before, out on the street, that "the stones in this community cry out in shame that you don't have the guts of your fathers"?

Following his sermon, the embattled minister took to the streets, waving to form a parade. He felt like marching. Nothing was more revealing of Adam Clayton Powell's loosening grip on Harlem and his church than the lackluster reaction to his summons for a march this day. Many in the church were old now, and walked with canes. Those who didn't use canes walked slowly. They could not take to the streets as in the old days, when they had followed the wave of his huge hand, chanting behind him as he strolled down Seventh Avenue, stopping traffic with a gesture. And so they stood and watched on the Harlem streets as he swept by them, surrounded by young militants elbowing for space, policemen braced for riot. The deacons made note.

Before he left Harlem, Adam Clayton Powell let it be known that he was running for re-election. The younger politicians would have to put their ambitions on hold.

⟆⟆⟆

The warm weather of Bimini had been a perfect tonic, and in April Powell lifted himself again to reignite his barnstorming tour. This time, however, the venture was more modest, confined to southern schools. In Tallahassee, a crowd of feverish students awaited him on the campus of Florida A and M University. "I'm calling this evening for total revolution of young people, black and white, against the sick society of America," he cried. In Florida he also called for the immediate withdrawal of American troops from Vietnam. Adam and Corrine Huff were whisked to and from airports and campuses, the students praising him, the young reporters sticking microphones in his face, the campus security men sending reports to the Justice Department, where it was believed that Powell was visiting campuses merely to incite riots. It was all worth it, because he had a message; furthermore, the bank account was nearly depleted.

On April 4 he traveled north from Florida to Durham, North Carolina, where he was scheduled to speak on the Duke University campus. After checking into a hotel room, he unpacked, then grew tired and sickly from chest pains. Students had been gathered in an auditorium for thirty minutes when word came that he had suffered a mild seizure and been rushed to a hospital. He remained conscious, however, and found out at the hospital that Martin Luther King had been assassinated on the balcony of a hotel in Memphis, Tennessee, where he had gone to help organize sanitation workers. Powell had long been a critic (and an angry one of late) of King, but he realized that King possessed extraordinary gifts. Imagining — and fearful of — a conspiracy to assassinate black leaders, he left Durham in a hurry and returned to Bimini.

Three weeks later, Powell underwent surgery for prostate cancer in Miami's Jackson Memorial Hospital. Released after less than a week with encouragement for a full recovery, he sought another brief rest in Bimini.

⟨✴⟩

When Adam Clayton Powell surfaced weeks later in New York City to launch his re-election campaign, he was constantly surrounded by guards. He had long been distrustful of all but a few of his male aides, believing that the others were potential enemies. The assessment proved correct in the case of John Young. Young had performed public relations duties in the past for Powell; now he emerged as, of all things, his Democratic primary opponent. Young was quick to launch salvos at Powell — about his ouster, his time away from Harlem, his health. Powell won the primary, virtually ensuring his election, but the turnout was low (11,052), and the margin of victory — 6,665 to 4,387 — was slim by the majestic standards of the past.

When Columbia University began moving into Harlem, taking over buildings and dislocating the poor, in the spring of 1968, it ignited angry student demonstrations. Administration buildings were stormed; students were handcuffed and paraded off to jail. It was the kind of demonstration made for Powell's politics. He called meetings in his church basement and delivered a paper attacking the administration: "The Massacre of Harlem by Columbia University." Students stopped by the church looking for him, seeking advice. The young were rallying every day, it seemed, picking up causes everywhere. They were also gassed and beaten that summer, nowhere more brutally than in Chicago at the Democratic convention. Chased by helmet-wearing police, they were run down and beaten with nightsticks. Powell's prediction for the year 1968 proved true: it all got worse. Antiwar demonstrations took on an intensity all their own. Riots swept Philadelphia, Kansas City, and Washington, D.C. (though Harlem was quiet). On June 4, Robert Kennedy won the California presidential primary. Two days later he too was dead from an assassin's bullets.

Powell sought to join the Poor People's Campaign, but that had been King's idea, and he finally thought better of it. Fired by the students' energy and his own passions, he kept moving, from Harlem to St. Louis, where he urged boycotts of stores that would not hire blacks. "Nobody can control us anymore," he told a St. Louis gathering. "We're in the saddle and we're going to stay there." The young certainly had other heroes — Benjamin Spock and Eugene McCarthy and Julian Bond among them — but now was no time for Powell to stand still. Back in Manhattan, in the August heat, he patrolled Times Square with Muhammad Ali, who had been stripped of his boxing championship for refusing to go to Vietnam. "We're here to shake hands with people and show them what the land of the free and the home of the brave has done to two champions," Powell said. "I'm not in Congress and he's not in the ring."

Henry Hall, a political novice, was Powell's opponent in the November election. Powell campaigned — casually, as usual. He conferred with his campaign aides in their homes, where he sometimes fell asleep. Charlie Rangel remembered that after one political meeting, Powell stood up and asked for a ride home. Rangel was surprised, and even more surprised when someone asked Powell where, exactly, he was living. He had a little apartment, one bedroom, above Jack Duncan's funeral home, around the corner from the Abyssinian church. Rangel gave him a lift. The two talked little — Powell's distrust of the young politician was obvious — but Powell did mention that he was worried about his congressional pension and wondered how much of it he would get.

There were still those in Harlem who remembered, those who had nothing to forgive Adam Clayton Powell for, because they had never accused him, and they walked into the voting booths that November and sent him back to Washington, D.C., to Congress. He beat his opponent 36,973 votes to 7,290 votes. On the surface it was a land-slide, but there were danger signs. In 1964, 94,200 people had voted for Powell. Two years later, in 1966, 45,300 had given him their support. It was obvious that the voter rolls in Harlem were shrinking as people moved away. (In 1962, when Albany, with Rockefeller's support, had tried to enlarge Powell's district, pushing him further downtown and away from Harlem, he had stopped the effort by going to court and filing a gerrymandering suit. For Powell, the smaller his district, the better: it was more controllable. The strategy was sensible, but there was a down side: any potential opponent in the future, waging battle in Powell's district, a district growing smaller in pop-ulation, would have only so many voters to impress. Also, the district could not shrink indefinitely.)

Of course, in 1969 there would be a new president in the White House, an old Powell enemy dating back to the Education and Labor Committee of the 1950s. During his lecture tour, Powell had predicted that Richard Nixon would be elected. For Nixon it was a galvanizing victory. He had finally achieved his ultimate political dream, having surmounted (but, as the country would find out in due time, still containing) the demons of his political past.

Adam Clayton Powell looked forward to his return to Washington. He wanted, more than anything, redemption. He wanted to show the young politicos of Harlem that he could come back; that, stripped of power, he could still make a difference; that there was still fight left in him. And, of course, there were scores to settle. His return to Washington was not unlike Nixon's return to Washington: a ghost of things past.

VIII

REDEMPTION BY THE
CONSTITUTION

1969–1972

WHEN CONGRESS GATHERED in January 1969, there was no crowd from Harlem in the galleries. Lolling in the back of the House chamber before the swearing-in ceremony, Powell smiled and greeted old allies and old enemies. There were the congressmen and the press, and relatives of congressmen looking on; there were the new members, seeing for the first time, in person, the legends of the House — Carl Albert, John McCormack, Charlie Halleck, Gerald Ford — the men and women who wrote the bills. The old southerners were breathing easy now. The pendulum had swung; Nixon's energetic campaigning through Dixie had paid off in rich dividends. They viewed his conservatism as a godsend.

The young liberals — Brademas, O'Hara, the wily Richard Bolling — had been working hard behind the scenes, within the Democratic Study Group, to block McCormack's renomination as Speaker. This was the very reason they abhorred the seniority system: it nudged the gavel once again into the trembling hands of John McCormack, eighty years old now. McCormack knew how to cash in chips. He rallied southern conservatives and loyal northern Democrats and crushed the planned revolt. And Manny Celler, himself eighty years old, the light in the chamber glinting off his thick bifocals, was vowing to have the gentleman from New York, Adam Clayton Powell, Jr. — leaning on the back railing of the chamber, alone, always alone — sworn in and seated. Celler, however, was not without opposition.

Gerald Ford still opposed any effort to seat Powell, and he was vociferously joined by H. R. Gross of Iowa, who rose out of his seat to carry on about the possibility of Powell's being allowed to take the oath. Gross considered himself as well schooled in the rules of the

House as Tom Curtis of Missouri: rules were not to be broken; rule breakers like Powell must be punished. But there was also Morris Udall, rising again and pleading with the House to give Harlem its representative. For two years it had been the only district in America without representation, its voters forced to take their pleas for help to neighboring congressmen. Repeatedly, through one special election and one regular election, they had told the House who their choice would be: the same person they had been sending to Congress since 1944, the gentleman in the two-piece gray suit at the back of the House, listening once again to a debate about his fitness to sit in this legislative body.

Manny Celler could not lose again. He would not tolerate the continued opposition to seating Powell. For two years, ever since his recommendations had been defeated and Powell had been refused his seat, Celler had been under pressure in his Brooklyn district. A good many Brooklyn voters had begun to wonder whether Celler was too old now, whether he had lost a step; and Celler certainly heard the rumors that had begun two years before about the powerful Brooklyn minister Gardner Taylor, about a movement for Taylor to take him on — rumors that Taylor himself did nothing to still.

Celler looked around at his House colleagues. "He who is without sin in this chamber, let him cast the first stone," the Brooklyn congressman said. Then he listened as the stones were cast on a first motion, to deny Powell his seat without punishment. The motion carried. Then another motion was quickly offered, to seat Powell with punishment. This time 160 representatives still voted against seating Powell, but 261 were in favor. After two long years, the ordeal was finally over. Adam Clayton Powell was back in Congress, although with stipulations: a stiff fine of $25,000, which would be docked from his salary, was imposed, but more significant, he was stripped of his seniority. He was Adam Clayton Powell, freshman member of the House.

The proud congressman from Harlem strode toward the front of the chamber to be sworn in, the walk of an ocelot still there. He broke stride momentarily to bow and kiss the hand of Brooklyn's Shirley Chisholm, the first black congresswoman. Now and then he shook a hand or patted a back, but the House he had so often awed in the past was mostly quiet as he went up to the Speaker to be sworn in. It was his longest walk since entering Congress. But he was back.

He took a smaller office. Gone were the lawyers who had served under him as chairman, the huge committee staff, the perks. Now he was a freshman with two secretaries and Odell Clark, his long-time trusted aide. He had no agenda, no legislation to draft or pass, although his lawsuit against the House of Representatives was headed for a hearing at the Supreme Court. He was still taken with the idea, which he pushed, of investigating antipoverty programs across America, but he lacked the clout to lay claim to such an undertaking. His beloved OEO program and the overall War on Poverty were not decimated under Nixon at first, but they did not grow. The pendulum was certainly swinging, and Powell and others could feel it. (Eventually Nixon eviscerated both the OEO and the War on Poverty, but Powell's bills remain law, a legacy written on the American landscape.) Stained by his two years away and his loss of power, Powell found little comfort in the nation's capital. Still, he planned to find some way to be heard. "For Zion's sake I will not hold my peace; for Jerusalem's sake, I will not rest," he told his Abyssinian congregation in January.

Back in Manhattan, Powell could not resist the political jockeying taking place. A mayoral race was shaping up. A number of individuals were competing with John Lindsay, the genteel progressive Republican who had upset the Democratic establishment four years earlier by drawing votes across party lines; among the districts he had won was Adam Clayton Powell's district in Harlem. ("People would listen when Lindsay spoke," said Robert Seavey, "but they would march when Adam spoke.") Congressman James Scheuer was planning to tilt after Lindsay; so were Mario Procaccino, the city comptroller, and William F. Buckley, Jr. The most interesting competition, however, was the novelist Norman Mailer. Before entering the race, Mailer had been partying with legal and literary friends in his Brooklyn Heights apartment. There was drinking, and ideas were offered. Someone suggested that the group back Adam Clayton Powell for mayor and put Mailer on the ticket. Mailer nixed the proposal, lashing out at Powell for being too old and undependable. But he did enter the race, and his selection for running mate was as wild as Mailer's own entry: the journalist Jimmy Breslin, who had been at the party. Thus two ego-driven writers threw themselves into the mix of New York City politics.

Powell scanned the list of mayoral candidates and wasn't impressed, not with Mario Procaccino, not with James Scheuer, and certainly not with Mailer and Breslin, whose candidacy he thought beneath the dignity of comment. To him, the Mailer-Breslin team did not represent serious politics. They might keep the likes of William Buckley at bay, but Adam Clayton Powell had played the game in Washington for keeps, and played it with men far, far bigger than William Buckley. Scanning the list, then, he found no one he could endorse. However, when he inched his way toward endorsing the incumbent, a Lindsay emissary quickly visited William Epps, one of Powell's aides, and begged Powell *not* to offer an endorsement.

So Adam Clayton Powell sent out word that he was contemplating a mayoral run of his own. "I think Adam wanted to be mayor of New York City," recalled his friend Mike Wallace. By mid-March Powell was claiming that he had gathered fifteen thousand signatures, and had begun leaning toward radio microphones to intimate that he was days away from an announcement and that all he needed was a call from the electorate and $1 million for the campaign kitty. Neither ever came. Many realized that running the largest city in America was a young politician's job; Adam Clayton Powell was now sixty years old. His mayoral dreams died ignominiously.

In April, back in Washington, Powell walked over to the Supreme Court and watched as his antiestablishment attorneys argued against the government's attorneys in his suit against the United States House of Representatives, *Powell v. McCormack* (as Speaker of the House, John McCormack's name was on the suit). The legal camps could not have been more different.

The leadership of the House had been stunned by Powell's suit, and even more stunned when the Court declared that it had merit and should be heard. (Gerald Ford's animus toward the Warren Court was huge; he was gathering documentation for a personal investigation of liberal justice William O. Douglas.) Claude Pepper told his fellow House members that they should hire the best attorneys in the country. In Pepper's estimation, those attorneys worked in New York City, at Cravath, Swain & Moore.

The firm agreed to take the case and assigned its house legend, Bruce Bromley, to it. For decades Bromley had been a highly respected attorney, not only in New York but across the nation. He routinely performed legal chores for IBM and Westinghouse, working brutal hours. He was now seventy-six, and he still worked the brutal hours, rising in predawn darkness in his home outside New York City, dressing quietly (always in black, according to his son, Peter), and heading off for the law firm. In court, where he was always flanked by younger lawyers from the firm, he had a habit of looking at his colleagues before delivering his final arguments and saying, "No way we'll win this case." And the younger attorneys would quickly grow paranoid. "It will take a miracle," he would add. Then of course he would make his arguments and would win, and the younger lawyers had their miracle, compliments of Bruce Bromley himself.

Around the law firm, talk about *Powell v. McCormack* was energetic. Such a case challenged the very foundations of governmental powers. "All the young lawyers wanted to work on it," recalled Jack Hupper, one of the lucky ones. In the weeks leading up to the opening of the trial, John McCormack often summoned Bromley and his team to his Washington office. Bromley would frequently be met by various House members, most notably Carl Albert and Gerald Ford. Adam Clayton Powell had forced Democrats and Republicans to forge an alliance to defend the House. Lloyd Cutler, another lawyer who assisted Bromley on the case, remembered, "While we were sitting around, McCormack would pass around fifteen-cent, terrible-tasting cigars." A few congressmen emerged as leaders in propping up the government's position; "Ford was pretty active," recalled Cutler.

The lawyers went back and forth, debating the case, convincing themselves whenever the issue arose that the case had nothing to do with race. Cutler even reminded himself that he had supported a petition signed by various attorneys assailing the segregationist positions of Alabama's governor, George Wallace. But Adam Clayton Powell was not only putting Congress on trial; once again, he was forcing its members to recheck their consciences, as Cutler had done, on the pivotal question of race.

The Cravath legal team did not frighten Powell's attorneys, who had trained and lived for this very kind of challenge. Although their collective veneer may well have been antiestablishment — they were labor, NAACP, quintessential activist lawyers — and "the legal betting was that we didn't have a chance," as Herbert Reid explained, they knew the law, and they knew it well. There was Jean Camper Cahn, who had served as co-dean of the avant-garde Washington, D.C., Antioch Law School. A black woman confident enough to have married a white man, she dismissed any criticisms of her interracial union and remained deeply, soulfully immersed in the spirit and actions of the civil rights movement. Herbert Reid, while a student at Harvard Law School in the 1940s, had once rushed to an auditorium on campus to hear Adam Clayton Powell, Jr., whose speech made a deep impression on him. Reid was now on the faculty of the esteemed Howard University Law School. The tall, gangly William Kunstler, fearless defender of draft dodgers, Vietnam protesters, Black Panthers, a canny lawyer with a radical's heart, was also on the team. Clients rarely got out of Kunstler's office without being given a huge emotional bear hug. Frank Reeves was an NAACP lawyer, working for Powell without that organization's blessings or encouragement. The NAACP had a long memory.

And there was Arthur Kinoy. After weeks and months of plotting the case, the team received a painful setback when the Court of Appeals for the District of Columbia, led by Warren Burger, ruled against Powell. Powell urged his attorneys to appeal further, to the Supreme Court. During those tense months, Arthur Kinoy began to emerge as the spiritual leader of the case, its very soul. He was a constitutional lawyer, and while he suspected that racial prejudice had had more than a little to do with Powell's ouster, he had quickly judged the action as nothing less than an affront to the U.S. Constitution.

Short, frumpy, and Jewish, Kinoy had been born in Brooklyn, the son of two schoolteachers, and had attended Harvard during the Depression, when he had sometimes walked along the banks of the Charles River feeling unhappy. The rich students on campus intimidated him, with their gilded last names, with that predestined look in their eyes. Kinoy had had to scratch his way into Harvard. His political beliefs quickly became apparent. He became president of the John Reed Society and distributed antiwar leaflets in Harvard Yard. Academically, he was precocious, becoming after graduation a Junior Fellow of Harvard, a prestigious honor. After that he entered Columbia Law School (grittier than Harvard Law) and set out on his life's work at the bar: defending union activists, those accused of being Communists, the doomed Rosenbergs. When the 1950s rolled over into the 1960s, he found himself in Mississippi, Georgia, and Alabama, defending bus boycotters and student protesters. In 1968 he defended the Chicago Seven, always reminding himself that "a Jewish boy from Brooklyn could do as well as New England aristocrats."

Arthur Kinoy came to Adam Clayton Powell's case with a sense of mission. "We saw the case as part of the movement," he explained. "It was a fight that had to be made." On April 21 he made his way over to the Supreme Court to argue against Bruce Bromley.

Members of Congress may well have convinced themselves that Powell's expulsion had nothing to do with race, but it was an argument some of the justices found incredible. Justice Hugo Black was the first to broach the subject, asking Bromley whether, in fact, Powell had been excluded because of his race. Bromley said that he had not and that Congress had a right to determine whether those elected were fit to be seated. The answer confused Chief Justice Earl Warren, who wanted to know from Bromley just who had the ultimate right to draw the line. The House, said Bromley, except in cases of "perversion." "What could be more perverse," Warren wanted to know, than excluding someone because of the color of his skin?

Jack Hupper, the young Cravath attorney, detected a shift, something he did not like. He thought the questioning from the justices was harsh and pointed, and it focused far more than expected on the issue of race.

Arthur Kinoy, considerably more animated than Bromley, told the justices that the case struck "at the very heart" of representative government. The people govern, Kinoy reminded the court, going on to point out that to ignore that edict would be "to turn history on its head." He kept on, wheeling between the deep strands of history and his reverence for the Constitution. He wanted the justices to ponder nothing less than an attack on the Constitution itself, the document written to thwart unchecked arrogance and power within the government. He alluded to the classic case of John Wilkes, excluded from the British Parliament in 1768 — a case so resounding that James Madison had cited it at the Philadelphia convention as a pure example of wrongful legislative intrusion. To allow the Wilkes example to become a common part of American life would be to allow the republic to turn itself into an "autocracy or oligarchy," Kinoy said.

The young Cravath attorneys found themselves listening to every word of Kinoy's argument. "He was very good," Hupper admitted. Many in the courtroom that day felt that Kinoy had more than held his own; there was even a tingling feeling that Arthur Kinoy might well have been the best lawyer in the courtroom that day. "Beautiful," Powell gushed to him outside the courtroom, throwing his long arms around the exhausted attorney. Now the case rested in the hands of the justices. There was nothing to do except wait for them to hand a decision down.

෧᎒ᲜᲘᲔ

Adam Clayton Powell looked forward to the wedding of his son Adam III, which would take place in Washington on May 30, 1969.

After Powell and Hazel Scott divorced, Adam III spent much of his time with his mother. As he grew, he showed no interest in politics, music, or religion, though he did like to read *Variety*, the entertainment magazine. Judging him against his parents, who both had an instant rapport with strangers — a rapport he didn't possess — many labeled him aloof. His connections to Harlem were limited. He was raised in White Plains, sent to private schools, and felt comfortable in the capitals of Europe. The rhythms of Harlem eluded him — no drinks and talk of politics at the Red Rooster, no wrapping of arms around strangers.

Adam's father wanted him to attend one of the military academies — West Point or the Naval Academy. The boy chose MIT. One day he was sitting in his dorm room listening to the campus radio station. He thought it was awful and marched over to tell the management. They asked if he thought he could do a better job. He said yes, and he did, drawing raves for his management of the station. He chose communications as his major.

During Adam's college days, his father was the subject of an enormous amount of press coverage, much of it negative — first from the Hays committee, then from the Celler committee. Often the young man would return to his dormitory and find government investigators waiting to question him: his name appeared on some of the airline tickets to Bimini. He was shrewd, and refused to answer any questions unless a friend sat in on the sessions as a witness. He also placed a tape recorder in front of the government investigators, taping the sessions.

After graduating from MIT, Adam Powell III returned to New York City, where he took a job working for Mike Wallace at CBS. Attending a party, he eyed a young woman, moved closer, and began a conversation, which led to dating. He took her to hear his father preach; it was so far removed from her world that she was fascinated. Beryl Slocum had been a Radcliffe girl. She had family roots that stretched back to the founding of Rhode Island and on through tobacco and banking interests. The Slocums were in the Social Register. The young couple's romance was talked of less for its interracial composition than for the mingling of two notable bloodlines. When the couple announced their engagement, Congressman Powell blessed them more quickly than the Slocums did. In the end, there was little for the families to do except come together and wish them well.

So on May 30 sleek cars began arriving at National Cathedral in Washington for the wedding. The congregation was a mixture of power and high society, with journalists in formal wear. "On either side of the aisle were some of the mighty of Washington," recalled Mike Wallace. Hazel Scott, beaming, arrived with her Harlem friend Wesley Carter. She was dressed in a green chiffon dress and a lime-green hat, but her outfit was no match for her former husband's: Adam Clayton Powell arrived in a flowing ministerial robe, turning heads, wading through the assemblage, smiling. He had attended no rehearsal, but he would offer to say something, a little prayer; this was his son, his namesake. The robe billowed, drawing attention. (The *Washington Post* editor Ben Bradlee looked particularly hard at Powell. He was quite curious about the rumor that Powell was naked beneath the robe. He wasn't.) Corrine Huff, who arrived with Powell, could not help noticing the staring, which made her feel both uncomfortable and proud. But she also looked at him with pride. He wished on this day to appear not as politician but as minister.

Just before the service began, Rev. Adam Clayton Powell introduced himself to the minister who was to perform the ceremony, saying that he wished to say a few words, to bless the event in the form of a prayer. The fellow minister shook his head, explaining that the litany would be followed to the letter and there would be no time for impromptu prayers. Powell appeared stunned. Beryl Slocum was quickly told of the imbroglio. She had thought there might be a scene, and she did not want a scene on this day; she wished to be married without incident. Powell would not speak. Corrine Huff felt embarrassed for him: "He looked like a fool up there in his robe."

If Powell felt shamed and hurt, he was good at concealing it. He waltzed into the Georgetown reception in an exuberant mood. Mike Wallace thought his entrance grand: "There was more attention paid to him than to the bride and groom." Hazel Scott gave an impromptu performance, sitting at the piano and playing such hits as "People Who Need People" and "Windmills of My Mind."

As a wedding gift, Powell gave his son and daughter-in-law an all-expenses-paid trip to Bimini. Years later, when Beryl Powell thought about her wedding day, she regretted slighting him in the church. "Now I think it was appalling," she said. "If I had been more independent, I would have said that Adam should say a prayer. I was cowardly."

⚬⚭⚬

On June 16, in a sweeping rebuke to the House of Representatives, the Supreme Court issued a seven-to-one decision in favor of Adam Clayton Powell. The sixty-two-page opinion, authored by Chief Justice Warren, was written in strong, precise language. "It is the responsibility of this Court to act as the ultimate interpreter of the Constitution," Warren wrote. By excluding Powell and by believing that it had the ultimate authority to do so, the House had exhibited a "dangerous" misuse of its powers.

The decision, which the New York Times called "historic," drew quick and angry reaction from Republicans in Congress. Gerald Ford vehemently denounced it. Meeting with fellow members, Ford vowed that the House would not abide by the decision. Inasmuch as Powell had already taken his seat, however, Ford's logic sounded a bit flawed. (Ford next began promoting a Justice Department investigation of Powell.)

Not only had the Court decision (which made no mention of Powell's loss of seniority or pay but did allow for further legal challenge) rebuked the lawyers in the House, it had laid the issue of racial discrimination squarely at the door of Congress. The ruling was the last decision handed down by Warren himself. His years on the Court had seen numerous sweeping decisions on behalf of civil liberties and personal freedoms. For years there had been protest against many of these decisions, prompting IMPEACH WARREN signs to appear by the sides of country roads. The Brown desegregation decision of 1954 had been among Warren's first landmark decisions; the Powell decision was his last. The California jurist stayed true to form to the end.

The House could hardly have been pleased either with the preliminary bill sent by Cravath, Swain & Moore: it was for $213,000. The final accounting was still being prepared.

For Arthur Kinoy and Herbert Reid and Powell's other attorneys, the decision was a cause for jubilation. Having packed bottles of champagne, they boarded a plane and flew to Bimini to share the news. When they arrived, they were surprised to find a subdued Adam Clayton Powell, in sunglasses, addressing a bank of microphones beneath palm trees. "I have kept the faith," he said. He claimed that the reward of the decision was not his but America's. There was no gloating, inasmuch as the decision did not restore his seniority or award him back pay. But the Court had reaffirmed that the people govern, and the people lived in the Harlems of America. So he celebrated with his lawyers, and at times he could be seen staring out at the waters.

When Kinoy and the others left Bimini, many talked about the fact that Powell did not look well. He looked tired and sickly; he seemed melancholy. Kinoy had spotted an oxygen tank on his boat. Powell had yet to tell his friends, but he had been diagnosed with cancer of the lymph glands. He had never been one to complain and wasn't about to do so now, even when confronted by an illness that often proved fatal. No, he would not complain. He would pack. He would return to Washington, to Congress, because he belonged there; he had earned the right, yet again, to be there; he needed for Congress to know that he had lasted, that he had fought yet another battle, and won.

He found that his colleagues shrugged off the decision. To many of them it was painful; many others took comfort in the possibility that the Department of Justice investigation of him might yield indictments. Adam Clayton Powell's return to Washington was not triumphant. Looking around, he realized that there was little for him to do on Capitol Hill. He avoided committee meetings. Ghosts seemed to be everywhere. There was no one in the Nixon White House in whom he could confide.

In the past his office had always been crowded, with constituents sitting in the chairs seeking help, reporters outside the door, staff members waiting and milling about. Now hardly anyone came by. He donned glasses and pored over his mail. His staff was down to four. Sometimes in his office he took to humming gospel tunes; "Oh Happy Day" was a favorite. But he would not wilt. As long as he could walk he would make a stand. In June he made his way to the Capitol steps, carrying a Bible. He took a seat on the steps and led a group of Quakers in an anti–Vietnam War protest and prayer, his hands clasped against his forehead.

The young found in him an antiestablishment hero. Whatever his frailties, they knew he had opposed the status quo. On the college campuses a year earlier, the size of the crowds (overwhelmingly white except when it was a black college) had genuinely impressed him. The young had rushed to listen to him as he mixed political discourse with personal opinions. They saw in him a battler, a tilter at windmills, someone who had taken on several presidential administrations, had challenged both Democrats and Republicans. Adam Clayton Powell had no illusions about why the young were on the march. "They want a new world," he said. "They're tired of these wars and dying, not just in Vietnam, but all over the world. And they are tired of the fake morality of their parents. They've seen what goes on in the country clubs and exurbia." To a sixty-year-old congressman from Harlem, their goals and aims represented nothing less than "a beautiful dream," a dream he felt he had kinship to. "I've lived through [this] before, in the 1930s, and somehow I've been able to bridge the gap for the students today. They're in revolt against everything their parents, their preachers, and their teachers have told them."

Already looking ahead to 1972 and Nixon's Democratic challengers, Powell announced — a full three years before the next presidential campaign season — his backing of an Edward Kennedy–Julian Bond ticket. He called for a huge anti-Nixon convention — "A National Conference to Save the Republic," he called it — and whenever he mentioned it to students, they clapped wildly. Nixon's Justice Department was threatening to cut off financial aid for students who were arrested during campus demonstrations, and Powell vowed that he would personally challenge such a move, in the courts if necessary.

Four thousand students turned out to hear him on the University of Alabama campus in Tuscaloosa. "If the Democratic Party is not ready for a Kennedy-Bond ticket in 1972, then I say it's time for a third party," he declaimed. Deep in Dixie, he cautioned against the anger building against black power: "It doesn't mean antiwhite unless you are antiblack." His addresses oftentimes drifted from fiery speech to quiet sermonizing.

Many might well have wondered about the significance of the large piece of gold jewelry hanging from his neck. It was a piece of jewelry that Adam Clayton Powell was quite proud of. The national civil rights honors — the Whitney Young Medal and the Spingarn Medal, bestowed by the NAACP — had gone to King and Wilkins. Powell had long been a critic of that organization, and it was not about to present him with its most prestigious honor. The National Urban League, which Whitney Young headed, had also been the victim of some of Powell's most caustic attacks. But more than a decade earlier, Powell had received the Golden Cross of Ethiopia, bestowed on him in the pulpit of the Abyssinian Baptist Church by Haile Selassie — emperor, freedom fighter, international figure, rebel. Selassie awarded the cross to Powell for his work on behalf of the poor. To have the honor bestowed by the emperor himself bore deep meanings: Selassie was a true Abyssinian, like the founders of the church. Selassie spoke in French from the church stage as he presented Powell with the medal; Hazel Scott interpreted for the congregation. Now, roaming the country from college campus to college campus, Powell was never without his medal. It was a reminder to himself of what he had done, of how he had been recognized by an emperor.

On the campus of Washington, D.C.'s Howard University, he attacked. The faculty, he charged, was "coming up with the same tattered notes they've been using for ten years." He ridiculed the administration; "it has no leadership." At the University of Missouri, in Columbia, he urged students to boycott classes and make plans to seize the 1972 Democratic National Convention. Back in New York he delighted in addressing the graduating class of Benjamin Franklin High School. "Don't think it's hopeless," he told the graduates. "Nineteen seventy-two is our year, when Ted Kennedy will run for president and Julian Bond will run for vice president. You go out and march together, fight together, picket together, and by God, we'll win together."

In late October he arrived on the Wayne State University campus in Detroit, an hour late. By now Corrine Huff, tiring of these travels, had returned to Bimini. But he soldiered on, arriving to see the impatient students he had kept waiting, then bringing them to their feet. "Whites have to deal with a new breed of cats," he said on the Wayne State campus, "who are no longer second-class citizens." He cautioned against the criticisms of Senator Kennedy's personal life: "I've been judged on rumors the last nine years."

Leaving Detroit, he flew east, to the Bronx, to address a group of Fordham University students. For several years student activists had been protesting the Vietnam War on the campus, and they were proud of their unity in this cause. The Fordham students wanted to know why Powell had endorsed Johnson in 1968. That was not all they wanted to know, either; they asked about Powell's own position on Capitol Hill, wanting to know what bills he had offered, what new legislation was his. "I'm unable to operate on the floor of the House because of the unholy alliance that is now in charge," Powell claimed, but his explanation was not accepted. The questions kept coming, hard and fast. "There's no way of my putting through any legislation of importance," he went on to say. Angry hisses began floating from the mostly white crowd.

At times black students, especially on mostly white campuses, found themselves wrestling mentally with how to react to Powell when around white students. If they accepted him wholly, they risked being viewed as coddling a one-time fugitive congressman. They had gone to college to show white students that they could learn, to be up-standing citizens. Some of their parents had talked shamefacedly of Adam Clayton Powell — of the women, the cars, the government investigations. Black Fordham students were forced to decide on Powell's contributions for themselves. When several white students in the audience stood and walked out on him, several black students joined them. In all, two dozen students walked out on the man who had been instrumental in, who had insisted on, increasing student loan expenditures.

"Powell was crushed," recalled William Epps, who was traveling with him. "Bill," Powell said, shaken, walking to the waiting car, "they just don't know." The car rolled from the Bronx into Harlem, past the tenements, the sights of despair on the streets, the ongoing decay. "Your generation must do something about this," he said, pointing to the streets of his Harlem.

⟨∾⟩

Powell returned to Bimini, only to find that Corrine Huff had left him — had, in fact, taken up with Patrick Brown, an islander who had done some boating off and on for the congressman. The notoriety of living with Adam Clayton Powell had finally driven the young woman away. First Powell laughed at her decision to see Brown, believing it to be a passing fancy. "The beauty and the beast," he dubbed the couple. When Huff married Brown, he realized that she was not coming back. Adam Powell left women; women did not leave him. His pride was deeply wounded.

Lolling on the island, Powell would wait until Patrick Brown went off to work, then visit Huff and try to woo her back. He would sit down and ask for something to eat. She would fix him a meal but tell him that he couldn't stay long because she was trying to start a marriage. "I told him he could not come around and use this place as a watering hole," she said.

Living on the island, alone again, he fished, drifting for hours.

Weeds grew high around his little home. Sunny days turned to moonlit evenings. He caroused with fishing buddies, empty gin bottles pointing to the day's waste. The sight of Patrick Brown and Corrine Huff together caused him pain. Adam Clayton Powell packed yet again; he missed Manhattan.

Once there, he looked up old friends, summoning long-ago revelries. There was Toots Shor's place, and the bars and restaurants along Seventh Avenue ("He liked to dine, rather than to eat," recalled Henry Williams.) Jazz still held his interest, and he whiled away time in jazz clubs. But he was thrilled by the success of the 1969 New York Knicks and was a frequent visitor to Madison Square Garden. Of course, he had played basketball in his youth. ("He never passed the ball," remembered William Rowe, a childhood friend.)

The Knicks were a uniquely synchronized team, a team of players like Bill Bradley and Walt Frazier, Willis Reed and Dick Barnett. They were a group of individualists who had managed to put the concept of team first. And Adam Clayton Powell admired their savoir-faire. The attraction was mutual: the Knicks adopted Powell as their unofficial chaplain. They played their home games at the Garden. It was the new Garden, as opposed to the old Garden, scene of so many of Powell's own triumphs — of the big war bond rallies, the freedom rallies, the rallies where his voice thundered, rallies that sent New Yorkers into the streets talking up his name. So there he would be after Knicks games, in the locker room, cigarette in hand, looking up at the huge bodies as if they were sequoia trees, patting individual players on the back. "They treated him like a king," said William Epps.

He appeared on many talk shows, often dressed in black, the huge piece of jewelry, more and more a conversation piece, dangling from his neck. He told Dick Cavett that he had undisclosed information about the John F. Kennedy and Martin Luther King assassinations, hinting at a government conspiracy in both deaths. But he decreed that the time was not right to provide such evidence. Cavett looked perplexed.

There was another reason for being in New York: Powell was spending time at New York Hospital's Cornell Medical Center for treatment of his cancer. "He took the news very well," Aaron Wells, Powell's physician, remembered. "We gave him chemotherapy and radiation." The treatments, however, sapped his strength. In a friend's Harlem apartment one evening, with talk of politics in the air — Charlie Rangel and Percy Sutton were in attendance — Powell stood up, raised his shirt, and showed the scars left from radiation treatment, showed where hair had been lifted from his scalp. It would have seemed too cruel, right at that moment, to ask if he was running for re-election, so no one did, according to Rangel. Rangel offered him a ride home — two politicians, one surely rising, the other wavering in nostalgic winds. Adam Clayton Powell could not look at Charles Rangel as an adversary during that ride. Who was Rangel but another lawyer trying to wage battles in Harlem, years after the hardest battles had been fought? They passed the time talking about Congress again, about pension benefits — an increasing worry for Powell — until they reached Powell's one-bedroom apartment above the funeral home.

For weeks on end during the winter of 1969, Adam Clayton Powell vanished from Harlem. Many imagined that he was in Washington, tending to his congressional duties, but they finally realized that he was back in Bimini, by the water. A bone-chilling winter in Harlem offered little comfort to someone suffering from cancer. On Bimini he could revive himself, and from Bimini he could make strategic forays into Washington and Harlem, looking tanned and healthy.

It seemed an unnecessary bit of vindictiveness, but as Congress reached the close of business in 1969, Kenneth Heckler, a West Virginia Democrat, offered yet another resolution to have Powell expelled from the House. The resolution withered away, but it seemed to represent just how little respect some members of the House held for the Supreme Court decision.

While Adam Clayton Powell was away, the young men of Harlem, the kittens who had been studying politics for years, began to think of the upcoming June primary, of Powell's re-election chances. It was inevitable they would think such thoughts; they were young, and thinking of Harlem's future.

༺✶༻

In exile Powell could do nothing. He had no phone in his Bimini home; his phone messages were left at a hotel, and he rarely responded to them anyway. He was still the subject of a criminal investigation. Paranoia set in. Gradually Harlemites began to grow angry; their congressman had taken up self-imposed exile. In late 1969, still months before the 1970 primary, Governor Nelson Rockefeller appealed to Charlie Rangel to travel to Bimini and encourage Powell to return, to focus his attentions on the needs of his constituents. Floyd

McKissick, the former student leader who had allied himself with Powell immediately after his 1967 ouster, was holding breakfast meetings and touting himself as a successor to Powell's seat.

Rockefeller admired Rangel and had been instrumental in placing him on the Republican as well as the Democratic ticket during Rangel's 1968 state assembly re-election campaign. Rangel accepted the mission. He simply had to discuss Powell's future and tell him of the political movements taking place in Harlem. Perhaps the ailing congressman would remove himself from the upcoming race; there would surely be a huge testimonial dinner in New York, something grand at the church as well.

Rangel set off for Bimini with a sense of purpose, fully realizing that it would not be an easy journey. "He was my idol," he said of Powell. "I was always the guy in the crowd listening to Powell." But Rangel realized how legitimate the worries about Powell were. "There was a time when we thought Adam was paranoid, not wanting to return to the district," he recalled. "It just didn't make sense." Sometimes all the Harlem voters needed was someone to make a phone call on their behalf; decades earlier, voters in upper Harlem had felt similar frustration with Fiorello La Guardia. "We started feeling the pain," said Rangel, "of not having a congressman."

Like many who arrived on Bimini, Rangel had to wait until Powell returned from his day's fishing. Charlie Rangel was not a fisherman, and he wondered how Adam Clayton Powell could float out there on his boat for hours on end. It seemed such a lonely activity. He did not particularly mind waiting; his wife had accompanied him to the island, and they could stroll around together.

When Rangel finally caught up with Powell, it was at the End of the World — wooden chairs and tables, sand on the floor, the smell of rum and sea. Powell was surrounded by his followers, his disciples. Cheerily, he ordered drinks for everyone — himself, his disciples, Rangel, and Rangel's wife. Rangel thought the atmosphere was a bit too sunny; he had come with serious business on his mind. When he finally got Powell's attention, he told him of the political maneuverings taking place in Harlem. He warned Powell of two potential primary foes: Jesse Gray, who had acquired a following by leading rent strikes, and Floyd McKissick, now openly courting Harlem ministers to support his planned campaign. Powell played coy about his own plans and dismissed Gray and McKissick as unworthy adversaries.

Rangel did not like Powell's cavalier attitude. So he shared a little bit more news with Powell — that he himself, Charlie Rangel, might well consider running for the congressional seat. Looking across the table, Powell smiled at him. He opened the palm of his hand, lifted it toward Rangel's face, and began patting him on the cheek, rather condescendingly. "Do what you have to do, baby." And right then and there, Charlie Rangel realized that Adam Clayton Powell was telling him that he was not a formidable foe either. Rangel did not like the way Powell patted his cheek, the way someone strokes a kitten, and he did not like Powell's doing it right in front of his wife. It was belittling.

Rising, Powell gathered his clan, offered farewells, passed a few words with the bartender, and left. When Rangel looked around, the bartender was looking at him, the tab in his hand. Powell had left Rangel the bill "for thirty people," Rangel recalled, halfway between mirth and bitterness.

Charlie Rangel returned to Harlem and started setting up meetings with his allies. J. Raymond Jones, the Fox, had taught him well. Rangel had been helping Harlemites over the past several years with rent and utility bills and had been providing legal counsel to parents whose children had been arrested during civil rights and antiwar demonstrations. It was sometimes drudgery, but he never shrank from it. Many in New York knew that he had political potential beyond the state assembly. Charlie Rangel knew he did not deserve to be treated as he had been treated by Adam Clayton Powell. Charlie Rangel would do what he had to do.

༒

It was more than the 1970 primary season that encouraged Powell to leave Bimini again and return to Harlem. There was turmoil at the Abyssinian Baptist Church, a veiled move afoot to take the pastorship from Powell and anoint a successor. The plan struck Powell as heresy. It was his pulpit. Before him, it had been his father's pulpit. His mother had cried in this pulpit over the loss of her only daughter. Time and time again he had announced plans to retire, to hand the reins to someone else, but he could not bring himself to do it.

Back in 1965, he had hired Wyatt Walker to keep the church together while he battled with Esther James. But he had felt betrayed by Walker. Increasingly, Walker's sermons had been about marriage, the sanctity of marriage, and divorce, and the sin of fornication. And the parishioners had sat there and listened and become nervous in their seats. Walker had done, in fact, what other ministers stepping into the pulpit always knew not to do, and that was thrust the Bible in Adam Clayton Powell's direction. "Those touchy kinds of subjects where you knew Adam was guilty, you didn't deal with them," said William Epps, who knew the reason for Walker's dismissal: "Wyatt dealt with them." And there was something else about Wyatt Walker. He was a man in a hurry. He wanted his own church; the Abyssinian was a pulpit to be treasured. But he misjudged the congregation. While they sat and listened, and while his sermonizing made sense, it grated on them to hear him talk, even indirectly, about the sins of their minister, their Adam. "Nine out of ten of those folks loved Adam," said Epps. In just three months Walker had made his presence felt; he had also been fired. To Powell he was a traitor.

David Licorish was always a possible successor to the throne, but it worried members that he was not married (he was a divorcé), as they believed that a minister needed a wife, the comfort of home and family. Some in the congregation found it hard to understand Licorish's West Indian accent. William Epps, who served as Powell's chief aide, had attended the Andover Newton Theological School in Massachusetts and made a name for himself in radical Boston student circles. When he had arrived at the church to interview with Licorish, Licorish had offered a warning: "Don't you do to me what Wyatt Walker did to me. Wyatt Walker tried to take this from me." Epps assured Licorish that he merely wanted a chance to serve as an apprentice at the church. (Powell liked young Epps. He was articulate and fiery, but his emotions were under control; he reminded Adam Clayton Powell of the young Adam Clayton Powell.)

The long-time deacon board members opposed to Powell began to agitate. At a meeting of the diaconate, one said that they must put an end to paying Powell his salary because his absences from the pulpit were becoming longer and longer. "We don't want to pay him to come in on weekends and just preach," the deacon said. And then another deacon rose in anger and said that he would not have it, that it was wrong, "after all Adam has done for us." He began talking about the church, the jobs in Harlem: "He got me a job in the post office." And the other deacons lowered their voices and let their protests fade.

News of the discontent reached Powell, who had his spies in the church and on the board, principally Odell Clark and his wife, Robbie. So Adam Clayton Powell, Jr., back from Bimini, with news of church dissension all about him, squared his shoulders in his pulpit and laid a piece of paper on the lectern. It was a resignation letter. He said that anyone who wanted to resign from the church or who wished the minister to resign should come up and sign the letter. Not a soul moved.

He shared the news of his cancer with the congregation: "It may be just a matter of time until the Old Man will knock on my door." But he was satisfied at how crowded the church was; he still saw looks of appreciation on the faces of the old women. They told their minister that they would pray for him, that they still believed, that he was still their Adam. That is what he needed to hear: the echo of their voices; he needed to hear them say his name, Adam, because for so many years, whenever they said it, they said it in such a breathless, hopeful tone, and now they were saying it again, because he was sick, he looked uncertain, he had been shaken by reports that his church would be taken from him. Confidence came to him again. They would not take his church, and, looking around Harlem, he decided that they would not take his congressional seat either.

Adam was back in Harlem — home to do battle.

He announced that his cancer was in remission. All the talk from the primary foes — there were five in the race now — about his absence from Congress and Harlem irritated him. No one was talking about the bills, the legislation, the billions of dollars that were still pouring out of the federal government to help the poor and needy, black and white and Hispanic. Charlie Rangel and Percy Sutton, a Rangel supporter, drew his ire — "yellow Uncle Toms," he called them (both Rangel and Sutton were light-skinned). Powell envisioned a new wave of boycotts, marches, fiery protests: he had done it all thirty-five years earlier; it was time to light the match again. William Epps was instructed to recruit new church members, who in turn would work in the campaign. Odell Clark, who had worked in the early campaigns, the campaigns of the 1940s, was still around, and Odell knew what to do.

Powell was preparing to go into battle against opponents half his age. They would be reminded that in the 1930s, 1940s, and 1950s, long before the emergence of this new breed of cats, there had been a king of the cats: Adam Clayton Powell, Jr., leading marches and protests, wailing from one end of America to the other, striking fear into representatives, senators, and presidents; going abroad, stretching his reputation, returning to America with all eyes on him, stalking through Harlem in blazing suits, the women dashing down stairwells to see him, to hear his voice rising to them through the bullhorn he held in his hand right there on Seventh Avenue beneath the star-filled sky.

He set up campaign headquarters in the basement of the Abyssinian Baptist Church. He began making appearances in an elegant suit and tie — never mind the recent look of turtleneck and sport jacket — and there was a flurry of activity. He made the rounds of the bars and restaurants — Small's Paradise, the Red Rooster, the Apollo — rallying those willing to be rallied. He climbed the steps of the *Amsterdam News* and chatted with the reporters, the ones who he had always made sure were among the first to receive news from his office, so they would feel as important as the white reporters. But Jesse Walker, the *Amsterdam News*'s political reporter, looked at Powell sitting on a desk and saw a sick man. He wondered if Powell could go through the rigors of a campaign. Still, Powell left with the newspaper's endorsement. "We endorsed him out of respect for the past," recalled Walker.

Powell began to notice how much the landscape had changed. Many of his political allies were gone. The labor leaders had latched on to other candidates and other causes. The black radicals, too, had vanished, having cast their eyes on Powell once again and pronounced him a lapsed radical. Some musicians talked of a Powell fund raiser, but many of the old Harlem musicians he had once depended on were gone, some off playing the European jazz festival circuit, some dead. He began to find that he could not depend on church members as he had in the past. Many resented his return to the church, as church member Olivia Stokes explained, because he seemed to expect everyone to drop everything they were doing to take up his campaign cause.

And there were evenings when Powell disappeared into yet another bar to campaign, and hours passed by. Epps began telling him that he was drinking too much, and Powell explained that the alcohol dulled some of the pain caused by the radiation treatments.

He campaigned on, facing primary foes he could not bring himself to respect. With the full support of the New Frontier Democratic Club, which drew much of its money from old Kennedy supporters and Upper West Side Jewish organizations, Charlie Rangel began to emerge as a formidable opponent, having picked up the endorsements of both Shirley Chisholm, the Brooklyn congresswoman, and Mayor John Lindsay. But Powell questioned the commitment of every one of his foes — their fight, their Harlem roots. At one campaign stop, he took to the podium at the Americana Hotel, and one could hear the old fire in his voice: "The first man to put black men into jobs in the bus company was yours truly, Adam Clayton Powell. The first man to put blacks into jobs at the telephone company was yours truly, Adam Clayton Powell." So many had forgotten, so he went on, the voice thundering. "First to author the Federal Voter Registration Act . . . to establish the amendment barring federal aid to segregated schools . . . the law to establish a teaching hospital at Howard University." And when his memory slipped — because there had indeed been a lot of legislation; how was he to remember every single piece of legislation? — he simply said "And there's more! More!"

Epps could see the campaign taking its toll. Powell simply could not match the feverish pace of his opponents. Some mornings he had to go to Cornell Medical Center for treatment. He missed television appearances, missed radio interviews. But he kept reminding listeners of his past legislation. Toward the campaign's end, he donned his medallion again and strolled down the streets of Harlem, the huge piece of jewelry bouncing on his chest. Years and cancer had slowed the gait, added pounds to his face, which was now jowly. His primary opponents demanded debates, but Adam Clayton Powell did not debate opponents. Now, finally, he was giving Harlemites a genuine campaign, taking it down to the wire, the kind of campaign he had denied them for so many years. He was campaigning not only for his seat but for his pride as well.

As the election returns began flowing into his campaign headquarters, Powell was optimistic. The returns from central Harlem looked strong; so did the returns from Spanish Harlem. His gathered staff looked optimistic. But then, as the evening wore on, it became more and more evident that there would be no landslide for Adam Clayton Powell in this election, and he had come to expect landslides. He donned his glasses and began squinting at the returns. Young Rangel was also piling up numbers of votes. There were blocks on the western edge of Harlem where gentrification had begun and where Powell was not doing so well. Shirt loose and opened, eyes peering harder and harder at the numbers on the returns, because he knew, finally, that Harlem might be slipping away from him, Adam Clayton Powell predicted victory all evening long.

The final returns that night showed that he had lost to Charles Rangel by 203 votes. Aides moved in close, trying to console, but he would not have sympathy. "Fuck it," he said to his son. "I'll go fishing." A day later the fighter in him surfaced. It had been too close to concede. He demanded a recount. Ballot boxes were gathered and sealed; yes, the old congressman would give nothing up. Showing up at a press conference dressed in white, his medal swinging from his neck, his eyes heavy-lidded, he pointed his finger, scolding, charging that the election had been stolen.

A recount showed he had been defeated by Rangel by only 150 votes. Adam Clayton Powell vowed court action, then said he would form a third party, a People's Party, to get on the November ballot. Signatures were gathered, but then the cancer pain slowed him again. He lashed at his critics, "the new Negro bourgeoisie." Rangel's primary victory was equivalent to a November win, but Powell could not bring himself to endorse Rangel. A maverick to the end, Adam Clayton Powell endorsed Charles Taylor, the Liberal Party candidate.

It was a lonely autumn. William Epps often went by Powell's apartment to visit and found Powell staring at a blinking television screen, all alone. Jawn Sandifer, a good friend who had done some legal work for Powell and whom Powell had helped to get a judgeship, went by one day, and before he reached the apartment he saw a car parked at the curbside and a man sitting inside by himself. The engine wasn't running. It was Adam Clayton Powell, just sitting behind the wheel of the car. Sandifer could not bring himself to go over to say hello. "It was one of the saddest moments for me," he recalled. And there were days when Adam III dropped by and found his father rereading sermons his own father, Adam Senior, had written forty years earlier.

Some mornings Powell found the strength to rise and look for missions. In October, following a riot at the Long Island House of Detention, he ventured out there to play mediator and quiet the anger. After talking to the convicts, he went out to the courtyard. He stood alone, the arm raised, the fist balled, the echoing voices of convicts raining down upon him as he stood there surrounded by concrete and barbed wire. This is what he could still do: be a symbol, give hope. The congressman who had lost all his actual power stood there alone, because he still had presence, and it showed from the middle of the prison yard as he raised his right arm and balled his fist, giving the black power movement's salute.

That November Charles Rangel was elected as the second congressman from New York's eighteenth district. The long reign of Adam Clayton Powell was now officially over.

There were a few things to pack in Washington. He bade farewell to some old friends, Frank Thompson among them. Recently Powell had been seen with Darlene Expose, a young secretary who had worked for Congressman Thompson. He thanked Thompson for introducing him to her. Expose had told Thompson that she needed Fridays off, that there was a man living in New York, a doctor. "Turned out to be Dr. Powell," said Thompson.

⌒∾⌒

By springtime he was back in New York City. During his last days in Manhattan he was often escorted by a plainclothes police officer; the times were violent, and the landscape had been stained by assassinations. He had a drink in midtown with Henry Williams, the lawyer in the Esther James case. When he went to get his coat, Powell found that someone, probably mistakenly, had taken it. There was a nip in the air and he could not go out without a coat, so he lifted a coat off the rack — stole it — and walked outside. He turned the collar up, and Henry Williams never saw him again.

Powell's relations with his church remained strained. A successor was to be named, but he offered little help in making the choice. The deacons went about the task on their own. There was much squabbling and backbiting. David Licorish, who had served the church for twenty-eight years, still imagined himself the front-runner, although he realized that there were those who did not support him. He engaged Powell's help. "Adam told me that I'd get the church and a twenty-five-thousand-dollar salary," he recalled. But Licorish would have been surprised at what Powell actually told the deacon board. He told them that David Licorish was a good man but that he did not see the big picture, a good man but not a leader. Powell liked his assistant, William Epps, but Epps was too young and inexperienced. Also, the congregation wished for a quiet voice in the pulpit; Epps struck many as being cut from Powell's cloth. "I think toward the last days something began to wear thin in that church," explained Rev. Gardner Taylor, the respected Brooklyn minister. "Many Sunday mornings Licorish did not know he was to preach until eleven."

The deacons offered the pastor's job to Samuel Proctor, a highly respected educator who sometimes filled in for Powell at the church, but he turned it down — twice. Proctor also had considerable administrative experience, having worked in the OEO in Washington. He thought it odd that Powell had never sought to establish a friendship, had never invited him over for dinner. Licorish fumed, believing that the deacons had discriminated against him because of his background. "Maybe they didn't want a West Indian," he speculated.

On Easter Sunday of 1971, Powell made his last appearance in the Abyssinian pulpit. Emotions stirred throughout his low-key sermon. Afterward Rev. Adam Clayton Powell, Jr. — using the title with which he had begun his adult life — walked outside, along Seventh Avenue. Children had once followed him up and down the Avenue, pocketing the coins he tossed to them. As he was walking along Seventh Avenue that final Sunday, a passerby said, "My man Adam," and the remark had a sentimental longing to it, that special call and recognition, so familiar in the old days. Powell looked up and down the street and turned to Epps. "Seventh Avenue," he said. "Yeah, this is my street." The two walked along together, then went into an apartment and had a drink.

They had taken his congressional seat, and they were now giving his church to another minister. Both Washington and Harlem now belonged to others. Strolling in Manhattan during those very last days, Powell held the hand of his lady friend, Darlene Expose, tightly. She was his last romantic coup, a woman from deep Mississippi, a woman who had been one of twelve children of sharecroppers, who had "paid her dues," as he put it — a daughter of sharecroppers, the very people to whom he had fought to give the minimum wage. How proud he was of this coal-black woman, this ordinary woman. He had given her a string of pearls, black and white pearls, telling her that they represented the thought of integration. Others stared as they walked the streets hand in hand, because they looked so much like an interracial couple.

❧

Many mornings on Bimini, Powell lacked the strength to raise the anchor on his boat, *Adam's Fancy*, and sail off into the distance. The boat remained dockside; Powell remained in bed at home. Soon enough, however, he began to realize that he was running out of money. He rewrote his will several times, at times torching versions of it, growing paranoid as he pondered the depth of his friends' loyalty. He wrote feverish letters to Henry Williams, wondering if the time might not be ripe to make a movie deal with a Hollywood studio for his life story. He wrote to his literary agent, offering up several book ideas at once. Then, realizing that even if all such proposals were accepted he would still receive most of the money later, and he needed money now because the IRS was hounding him about back tax payments, he scrapped the ideas and arranged speaking engagements. He could still command $1,700 per speech. Besides, he enjoyed the students, the cacophony. The students had been able to shake up his anger, and he saw how enthused they became when watching him summon the old fire. And there was still plenty to talk about: Nixon (the presidential campaign was a year away), the new conservatism, the dismantling of the antipoverty programs, the anger across America.

He reached for the medallion, put it around his neck, took Darlene Expose by the arm, and left the island to seek out the students. He was a slow barnstormer now, dressing in black, slipping unobtrusively through airports, for the most part unrecognized, his hair longer than it had ever been, hanging down his neck. The crowds were overwhelmingly white; black students had begun ignoring him. So he regaled the students who came to hear him with stories about Congress, his victorious legislation, his Supreme Court victory ("The history books may try to make me out a scoundrel, but they'll have to put this in too," he said about that), shaking his fist in their faces, encouraging them on, his eyes looking sleepy at times, a thin cigarette always in his hand.

Following an appearance at the Ruby Diamond Auditorium on the Florida State University campus, in Tallahassee, he saw that the students were overcome with emotion, rushing backstage to touch him. He could still move a crowd. His tired eyes scanned the faces and he spotted a friend, Michael Schwartz, his one-time lawyer from the Education and Labor Committee. "Meet me at the Rooftop Lounge, Holiday Inn, half an hour," he whispered. He had given Schwartz his first job out of law school, and now Schwartz was a Tallahassee lawyer. There was much talk, and drinking, at the Rooftop Lounge that night — talk about Congress, the legislation that had passed through the committee, the work that had been done. Powell had once sent Schwartz to Florida to investigate discrimination in unions, and Schwartz, so young, so idealistic, had thought it was the best job in the world. That night Michael Schwartz kept waiting to hear Powell talk about his hardships, but he never did. "We closed the place down," recalled Schwartz. "One thing about Adam, you never knew when he was suffering."

But again the barnstorming was brief. He suddenly wanted to get back to Europe; he had loved Europe so much. Maybe there were too many sad memories in Paris — memories of the years with Hazel — because for his last trip abroad he chose Rome. Walking along the Via Veneto with Expose, he ran into Gore Vidal, who later remembered that he was with a woman, "very young, very black." But the writer couldn't help but see a different Adam Clayton Powell. "He seemed very low," said Vidal. "I felt sad. He did not have the fire anymore."

When Powell had seen enough of Europe, he left, returning to Bimini. Word about his failing health began to reach friends in the States. Some visitors arrived, taking the Chalk Airlines flight from Miami. One day Samuel Proctor showed up, along with Odell Clark. "He looked lonely and depressed," Proctor said, "like people had deserted him. He talked about the church. The church then was in a troubled state."

Edward Bennett Williams arrived, then wished he hadn't. "He was just sort of vegetating there," recalled Williams. Franklin D. Roosevelt, Jr., wanted to go but couldn't bring himself to do it. "I was afraid I'd be a little bit disappointed," he explained. "He was always a hero to me."

But Powell brightened at the sight of his son Adam III and his daughter-in-law, Beryl. There was a new addition to the Powell family, a grandson, Adam IV. Powell sat in his boat rocking the baby in his arms as the water rocked both. He strolled along the dirt roads of the island proudly, baby in his arms, son and daughter-in-law beside him. As he ducked into the End of the World to show off his grandson, Beryl Powell winced, but she didn't dare ask him not to take the baby inside the bar.

Gone were the inquisitive newspaper reporters. In a way he missed them, missed the attention. One sunny day he was in his boat and heard footsteps along the dock. He had dubbed his hideaway Buccaneer Point. The sun forced him to squint, and he reached for his sunglasses. He saw a man with a camera coming his way. "CBS? NBC?" he called out. It was a wire service reporter by the name of Strat Douthat, come to write up a little feature story about a once-powerful congressman in exile.

On days when Powell had the strength, he sought out a place with shade and struck up a game of dominoes with friends. Adam Clayton Powell, Sr., had preferred chess, a methodical game won by carefully planned movements; the son preferred dominoes, a game where the wrong move caused everything to crash to the playing board. Everything had crashed down upon him in his own life. He complained to Adam III that he had spent much of his life building up, then, because he had had three wives, he had had to give most of it away.

By dusk, as the sun slipped below the horizon, he was often on his back at home, wracked by pain. The rushing noise of the tour boats sent waves lapping against his dock, just beyond the front yard. One time Maurice Rosenblatt left Miami, where he was doing some planning for the 1972 Democratic convention, and went to Bimini in search of Powell. There was no phone, so he could not phone ahead. Someone pointed out the roof of Powell's little home, which he could see through the palms from the balcony of the Yacht Club. He made his way over. He found Powell looking exhausted. Darlene Expose sat in a corner, "crouched like an animal, a panther," said Rosenblatt, who felt that his visit had startled her. "Powell was sitting in a wicker chair, not quite the John Barrymore I had known. He was bloated and in pain. The light would go on and off in his eyes." There was small talk, nostalgia. Rosenblatt kept looking at Expose ("You could tell she didn't want anyone around him"), and she kept her eyes on him. One minute, recalled Rosenblatt, Powell seemed happy, the next sad; when he began looking at his watch, Rosenblatt felt he was trying to tell him he should leave. But Powell rose, turning his body, still huge, toward the water, and said that he wanted to go fishing. Rosenblatt accompanied him down the dock: "He got on board, chug-chugged off into the blue." That was the last Maurice Rosenblatt saw of his old Harlem friend.

During the first week of March, Expose noticed that Powell's health had worsened; his pain was becoming unbearable. She made her way to a telephone on March 7 and dialed the coast guard. He was airlifted to Jackson Memorial Hospital in Miami, where he and Expose were given a secluded room at the end of a hallway. For a time Adam Clayton Powell assured himself that he would rally. When Congressman Carl Albert phoned, Powell said that he would pull through. "He was an optimist, you know," recalled Albert. He wanted no publicity, and the hospital staff was instructed not to release his room number.

Bea Hines, a reporter at the *Miami Herald* who had contacts at Jackson Hospital, was nonetheless able to wangle Powell's room number from a nurse. She was feeling sentimental. When she was seventeen years old, she had been taken to the swank Sir John Hotel to see a pianist, Hazel Scott. For the first time, Bea Hines saw black royalty, in the form of Scott and her husband, Adam Clayton Powell, who had accompanied her on that trip. Scott knew there were many blacks in Miami who could not afford to attend her Sir John performance, so a day later, on a Sunday, she held a free jam session, and Bea Hines went and appreciated every second of the performance. Every time Hazel Scott went to Miami, she remained for a day and gave a free performance, and Hines attended as often as she could.

Now Bea Hines found Adam Clayton Powell's hospital room. "It was an un-air-conditioned room, in an old section of the building, a little cubbyhole of a room where he had asked to be," she remembered. "His lady friend was there with him. He was sitting on the side of the bed. She was combing his hair. He was in such pain, rocking back and forth. He wouldn't cry out. I asked him for an interview and he said, 'Sweetheart, I don't feel up to it now. Come back later.' "

Hines knew the chances of getting the kind of interview she wanted were slim, yet she did not leave that hospital room particularly sad. What impressed Bea Hines, a very dark-skinned woman, was that Powell's lady friend, Darlene Expose, was as dark as she was. "I felt so many men of his complexion looked down on darker-skinned women," she explained.

Powell's condition continued to grow worse. He had new prostate gland troubles as well as the spreading cancer. In late March doctors scheduled surgery. Under heavy sedation following the operation, he awoke in pain and a violent rage. He was sedated again. But his vital signs showed no real improvement; he was steadily weakening. Finally he slipped into a coma and was placed on a life-support system. The hospital could no longer keep his presence secret, and it quickly became known that the former congressman was in grave condition.

Jesse Jackson, the young activist then working in Chicago, came to visit; but Powell would never recognize another visitor. Corrine Huff came to Miami; when she was told that he was dying, she suffered a nervous breakdown and had to be hospitalized herself. Powell's youngest son, Adamcito, born to Yvette Flores, was summoned from military school in San Juan. When mother and son arrived in Miami, they were denied visitation rights by Expose, who claimed that Powell had married her in the Bahamas. Yvette produced a marriage license and appealed to the hospital administration; she and Powell had never been legally divorced, and she wanted her son to see his father. Adamcito was nine years old. Today he recalls a man hooked up to tubes, a man whose hair had gone all white. Frightened, the little boy backed away.

There was more than a little irony in the fact that Powell lay dying in a hospital bed in the Deep South — in Florida, where he had sent his labor investigators to probe allegations of job discrimination; in the district of the very congressman, Claude Pepper, who had been his fiercest critic on the Celler committee. He was in enemy territory, yet his bitterness had been curbed by the large and jubilant crowds of students who had greeted him here in Florida, causing him to smile, to joke again, to encourage.

On April 4, 1972, Adam Clayton Powell, Jr., suffering from massive internal bleeding, drew his last breath and died. He was sixty-three years old and not quite alone. He was miles from Harlem.

Following his death, there was a flurry of court activity, with different wives claiming custody of the body. A Miami judge ruled that the body was in the charge of Darlene Expose. Abyssinian church officials appealed to her to bring it to Harlem so it could be viewed. Howard Bell, a member of Powell's political organization in the early 1960s, and a group of Abyssinian officials were allowed to go out onto the tarmac when the plane arrived from Miami. Jack Duncan, the undertaker, wheeled his hearse up to the back of the plane as the door opened, revealing the casket. Adam III and a few others helped lift the casket into the hearse. One of the old church ladies walked up to it, leaned over, and said, "Adam, you're finally home."

☙⚭❧

They came from Harlem tenements and Manhattan townhouses, from Brooklyn brownstones and the double-deckers in Queens to view the body; they came from the chandeliered offices of downtown politicians; they came from the stores he had forced to integrate decades before. They came from California and Michigan and Florida, from many states and many cities. They came because all his life he had been true to his word as a politician, and they had to concede him that. He had come from that trail-blazing line of Harlem politicians who carved national reputations: first La Guardia, then Marcantonio. But he proved more politically adept than either.

More than a hundred thousand people came to view the body on Saturday, April 8, a day before the funeral. The old and the young advanced through the wide doors of the Abyssinian Baptist Church, coming up 138th Street in the bitter winds of a cold Harlem spring, taking their place in the long line, resting their arms on the police barricades. All day long they came, walking past store windows that displayed a picture of him with the galvanizing smile that somehow seemed both to comfort allies and to challenge enemies. They came because they remembered how Harlem had been, how he had taken Harlem in a new direction. A great many were old enough to remember him during the Depression, when he had once been grabbed at by a vagrant while walking down the street. The man needed food. Powell led him into the first restaurant he spotted. "This man is hungry," he told the owner. "You give him anything he wants and just give me the bill."

Inside the church, the foot of the coffin was draped in an African flag, and the casket was covered with white and red carnations. So many bent over and kissed Adam Clayton Powell on the cheeks that one of the church nurses covered his face with a net, lest it be smudged beyond recognition.

After all the people had departed, after the sun's glint had gone from the wide windows of the old stone church, Isabel Powell, his first wife, was allowed a moment alone with the body. She had grown to love him even more — it was the manner in which he led his life, the battles that led to victories, the way he always held his head so high. Recently she had begun telling friends that if their marriage had lasted, his life would not have ended as it had. His first wife, the former actress, lowered herself onto her knees. "Adam," she whispered, "now I finally know where you are."

The next day thousands crowded inside the church for the service, and thousands had to be turned away when there were simply no more seats. There was Jackie Robinson, white-haired, stoical; and there was John Lindsay, and Shirley Chisholm, running for the presidency, the first black woman to do so. Hazel Scott, who earlier had led a paradelike walk through the streets of Harlem, sat next to her son, Adam III. There were old Pullman porters, union allies, and visiting ministers. There were businessmen whose stores Powell had picketed three decades before. Nigel Bowe, his Bahamian attorney, was struck by one thing in particular, and that was the old women. There were so many; they seemed to be everywhere, and the soft cries that filled the streets and sidewalks was a sound he heard all day long. They were the old women who had voted for Powell, the ones who had waited so long for a minimum wage and finally got one, the ones who now saw their grandchildren getting enough aid to go on to college. They were the old women who had known Adam Senior, who remembered when the old man had stepped aside so the boy could rise up.

Corrine Huff saw snippets of the funeral on television. She was shocked that the casket was open. Powell had confided to her that seeing his mother and father buried in open caskets had alarmed him, and he had left instructions, now being ignored, that his own casket should be closed.

Gardner Taylor came over from Brooklyn to deliver one of the eulogies, and his seemed to capture the spirit of the day best. There were those across the country, in Baptist circles, who considered Taylor the finest preacher alive. His cadence was deep, pure southern (he was from Louisiana), and sweet. Taylor's beautiful voice swept the church, saying of Powell, "You bore your burdens in the heat of the day." He linked Powell with Mother Nature, who, he said, had "put fire in his mouth and trumpets in his throat." At the end of his eulogy, Taylor turned to Powell in the casket and said, "Sleep on, sweet prince. Sleep on."

A white-gloved navy guard, snapped to attention, stood in the church beside the body. Powell had sponsored the first black for admittance to the U.S. Naval Academy, in 1945. Then he had spread the word in Washington that the young man was being harassed because he was black. The complaints went to the top of the Defense Department, and an investigation was launched. Told that his complaints had no foundation, Powell admitted that they were not quite true, that he had made them up in order to make sure the young man would *not* be harassed.

Powell had always smiled at David Licorish when the Abyssinian choir sang "Jesus Savior, Pilot Me," and Licorish instructed the choir to sing it this day. The final musical selection was "Blessed Are They [That] Die in the Lord," from Brahms's German Requiem. The pallbearers, who included Odell Clark, his long-time aide; Aaron Wells, one of his doctors; and Chester Bagley, who had been one of the original members of the Young Thinkers, that iconoclastic group Powell had formed in the basement of his father's church so many years ago, lifted the casket and carried it past a line of saluting police officers and weary Harlemites. While sitting inside the church, the Powells' friend Wesley Carter had heard a rumor that black militants planned to kidnap the body on the way to the airport — why, he could not imagine. He quickly scribbled a note to Adam III. Police were warned of the rumor and were put on special alert as they escorted the body to the airport for its return to Miami.

❦

More than a few ministers sat around after Adam Powell's death trying to figure out what his truest motivations in life had been. They were intrigued by how passionately he had sought to prove his own identity, revealing it on so many occasions almost as a prize, something that had been won through contest. "Some of us used to joke sometimes," recalled Gardner Taylor, "that one of Adam's drives was his determination to be *black*."

Adam Clayton Powell's stock in certain sectors of America at the time of his death was quite low. He died four years to the day after Martin Luther King, Jr., which prompted many editorial writers to compare him to King. Measured against King's life, Powell's life was narrowed to his moral shortcomings. Roger Wilkins, on the editorial board of the *Washington Post,* became aware that his paper was preparing a rather negative editorial about Powell, and he figured he would cut its author off at the pass. He phoned the Education and Labor Committee and asked for a compendium of the bills Powell had passed. He knew he could not put them all in an editorial, so he "put in the biggest bills." Philip Geyelin, Wilkins's editor, did not like his editorial, which he judged to be too favorable. So Wilkins and Geyelin went back and forth, until the editorial struck the tone Wilkins wanted it to, praising the significant legislation that had come out of Powell's committee and noting how his had been a singular voice for so many years.

When Roger Wilkins himself had doubted Powell's contributions to American society, his uncle, Roy Wilkins, the esteemed head of the NAACP — the organization that Powell had wittily referred to as the National Association for the Advancement of Adam Clayton Powell — had pulled him aside and told him that Powell had refused every offer to buy him off, every offer to line his pockets with money, when he had been fighting merchants in Harlem in the 1930s. Roger Wilkins remembered that conversation as "a powerful endorsement" for Adam Clayton Powell.

When a *New York Times* editorial appeared — it was short and negative, and invidious comparisons with King were made throughout — a group of protesters demanded a meeting with John Oakes, the editorial page editor. Oakes listened. He reread the editorial and concluded that it might indeed have been a bit harsh, but by then he knew what the protesters knew: the ink on the editorial had long dried.

Those who thought Adam Clayton Powell radical for the wrong reasons should have been on the University of Michigan campus in 1969. By then he had lost the power; by then he believed in the youth. "This is a nation I am proud of," he told the students seated before him, holding a cigarette — damn the cancer — limply in his hand. "Don't take some of the things I have said tonight to mean I don't love America. I do."

⌒⟰⌒

Adam Clayton Powell's body was cremated at the Lithgow Funeral Home in Miami. Gardner Taylor thought it odd that Powell would wish to be cremated: it was an unusual act for Baptists, and there was an empty plot in the Queens cemetery next to his family members; now he would not join them. But then Taylor figured that the desire to be cremated was in Powell's maverick nature; it was "the final act of who Adam Powell was."

Powell had wanted his ashes sprinkled over Bimini, so Adam III chartered a plane, a twin-engine Widgeon, from Chalk Airlines. It was a sunny, beautiful day when the plane took off from Nassau, where Powell's lawyer, Nigel Bowe, had kept possession of the ashes. They flew at about one thousand feet. Adam III pointed out a spot where his father had liked to fish, and the pilot swooped low and nearer. Adam III then opened the window and began to upend the urn. But he was surprised by the wind, and ashes blew back onto him. Startled, he yelled at the pilot before he could realize that it was hardly the pilot's fault. He dusted himself off, trying to regain his composure. The remaining ashes floated away.

His friends had wondered how Adam Clayton Powell could take to the water on his boat and drift for hours and hours in silence. Having led a life of chaos and challenge, in the end Powell sought only quiet. "My life has been devoted to carrying the heavy end of the log," he once said, "and to catching the big fish." The comment represented more than metaphorical sentiment; it told of a life fully lived.

⌒⟰⌒

Here in Bimini, weeks before he had been airlifted to Miami, Adam Clayton Powell had been engaged in an epic battle with a game fish. Wearing a white glove on his left hand — always a bit of style — he leaned over the side of his vessel as the fish pulled him from his chair. He held tight to his fishing gear, the strength of the fish ripping through his insides, tender from the cancer. Grimacing, he finally let go. Afterward, he rarely emerged from bed, the pain becoming more severe by the day, until finally the coast guard helicopter was summoned. His friends convinced themselves that his battle with the fish had hastened his death.

Introduced to the water as a young boy, Adam Clayton Powell held a Melvillean affection for it his entire life. Martha's Vineyard and Long Island Sound; the great lakes of Germany and the waves of Cerro Gordo in Puerto Rico; then Bimini. The rushing and receding fascinated him, the way the water swept out from dry land into the distance — so wide open out there, so free.

EPILOGUE

ᐉᐍᐍᗉ AFTER HIS FATHER'S DEATH, Adam Clayton Powell III went to Bimini to retrieve Powell's personal belongings. He found windows ajar and the door unlocked. The home had been burglarized. His father's personal papers and many personal items, among them the valued medallion from Haile Selassie, were gone. A Bahamian police investigation yielded nothing.

Hazel Scott stayed in America after her return from Europe in the early 1970s. For a brief period she settled in Los Angeles, where she found intermittent work in television dramas. She was also able to renew her friendship with the jazz critic Leonard Feather, which had begun decades earlier in Greenwich Village. Feather invited her to his home for dinner one evening. He could tell she had been smoking marijuana. After the meal, a guest spotted a piano in the living room. Turning to Scott, he asked if she wouldn't mind playing a song or two. She exploded, cursing violently. She had come to eat, not play; Hazel Scott was still demanding respect more than applause.

Invited to the Abyssinian church a short time after Powell's death, she stood in the pulpit, her eyes scanning the church. She began to speak; then her words trailed off into whispers, and she stopped, unable to go on. Powell's estate was hounded by the IRS, and she allowed her son, Adam III, to sell her Steinway piano and some of her diamonds to pay the debt. Having flirted with several religions in her life, Buddhism among them, Scott now considered herself a student of world religion and wore trinkets with religious symbolism. Black radicals grew bored with her, believing that her marriage to a white European, Ezio Bedin, had undercut her progressivism.

As the rock craze spread, there were not as many jazz clubs, or jazz patrons, as there had been in her heyday. But she still managed to work in Manhattan, backed by her own trio. She added vocals to her compositions, and though her circle of admirers grew smaller, they remained reverent enough to form what could only be called a cult following. She appeared at the King Cole Room at the St. Regis and filled in for Bobby Short at the Café Carlyle. The *Times* review of her stint at the Carlyle mentioned that her rendition of "Send in the Clowns" was "not only different from most interpretations — a combination of rhythmic phrasing over an insistent beat with easy, unforced projection — but also conveys an appreciation of what the song is about."

She had long dreamed of a room, a jazz room, to call her very own in Manhattan, a place where she could go and play without worrying about subsequent engagements. She found it at Kippy's, where she played in quiet, elegant surroundings with her back to the wall. No longer asked to bastardize the classics, she played what she wished to play, striking sentimental chords late into the evening. Adam III by now had two sons, Sherman and Adam IV, and she doted on them, waltzing them in and out of Manhattan toy stores, insisting that they get the biggest toys. At times she showed up at their schools to give recitals. Desperately wanting the children to recognize what she played, she began playing "The Star-Spangled Banner."

While performing at Kippy's one evening, Scott felt a sharp pain in her stomach. Doctors thought it was a tumor; it turned out to be pancreatic cancer. She was confined to Mount Sinai Hospital. Her mind began to wander, and in the evenings she would tap her fingers on the bedsheet, trying to remember her most cherished numbers. When her condition worsened, Dizzy Gillespie, a friend during the Paris years, came to visit. He pulled out his trumpet and began playing "Amazing Grace"; feigning to want quiet, nurses rushed in, but merely stood by and listened.

Hazel Scott died on October 2, 1981. Many of her friends — mostly actors and musicians, including Gillespie and the crooner Johnny Hartman — attended her funeral. There was talk of her courage and her musical genius, first spotted when she was a mere child. A poem that Langston Hughes had written for her years earlier — "To Be Somebody" — was read aloud. "Poor child," muttered the actor Robert Earl Jones. "It should have been me." Bobby Short thought this comment odd, and attributed it to Jones's sentimentality.

Isabel Powell, who never remarried ("Who could follow Adam?" she once cried out), continued to summer at the Oak Bluffs retreat she had shared with Powell in the 1930s, and kept his fishing gear on the walls through the years. During the school year she taught children in the Harlem Head Start program. Among the first things she did as a teacher was to ask the youngsters if they knew who Adam Clayton Powell was. Of course they did not; they were too young. It gave her the opening she needed to lecture them about Powell, demanding that they remember the name — Adam Clayton Powell — and pointing to their meals and explaining that he had had a hand in putting them there.

Yvette Powell remained in San Juan, allowing her ambitions for Puerto Rican statehood — ambitions driven by her husband's political desires — to dim with time. Corrine Huff, who eventually divorced Patrick Brown, moved from Bimini to St. Thomas in the Virgin Islands; she was skittish about returning to the mainland, as she still feared the possibility of facing criminal charges.

Before Powell's death, Arthur Kinoy had begun legal proceedings to force Congress to pay Powell the more than $55,000 in back salary that he had been denied when he was unconstitutionally removed from the House. Kinoy was confident of victory, but he dropped the challenge after Powell died.

In 1970 Congress wrote itself an in-depth ethics act, citing the case of Adam Clayton Powell as impetus: the Harlem congressman continued to haunt the House of Representatives. Liberal members of Congress were finally able to adopt a new set of rules that diluted the power that chairmen could wield over Congress. After Powell's reign, chairmen's powers were never the same again.

Also in 1970, Whitman Knapp was appointed the chairman of a full-scale investigation of corruption within the New York City Police Department. The investigation, which Powell had called for back in the 1950s, lasted two years. Among its findings was a link between police and numbers running — the same charges that Powell had aired not only in the Esther James case but years earlier. The commission prided itself on beginning to root out the notorious "code of silence" that had allowed corruption to flourish within the department for many decades. Esther James left Harlem for good in 1968; Harlemites never saw her again.

After being offered the Abyssinian pastorship three times, Samuel Proctor finally accepted, becoming the first minister other than a Powell to lead the congregation on a full-time basis since 1908. "Maybe the Lord wants me to do it," he told himself.

Two months after Powell's death in Miami, the Democratic national convention was held in nearby Miami Beach, where George Mc-Govern became the party's nominee. Republicans also held their convention in Miami Beach, and renominated Richard Nixon. Both presidential candidates had at one time served with Powell on the Education and Labor Committee.

In 1989, while going through some news clippings in the *Miami Herald* newsroom, I came across a small story that mentioned a recent auction of the personal belongings of former congressman Adam Clayton Powell, Jr. The article identified the sole buyer as Marilyn Perry. Days later I tracked Marilyn Perry to her home in Tampa. Her phone number was unlisted, but the address was not, and I showed up unannounced. The home sat back off an unpaved road. A woman answered the door, demanded some identification, and said that she was indeed the Marilyn Perry who had been mentioned in the article. She invited me in. She had met Powell while fishing on Bimini, she said. She also felt compelled to tell me that Powell had told her one day that he knew Liz Taylor. When I asked about the personal belongings, she began displaying some of the items she had purchased at the auction: Powell's dominoes, some of his speeches, his Bible. Halfway through my brief visit she brought out a tape recorder, turned it on, and placed it in front of me. I eagerly awaited sight of the gold medallion that Powell had received from Haile Selassie. When it didn't appear, I asked about it. Marilyn Perry said she knew nothing at all about the medallion that had hung on the chest of Adam Clayton Powell in those last proud and desperate years.

NOTES

BIBLIOGRAPHY

INDEX

NOTES

Unless otherwise noted, all quoted material is drawn from interviews the author conducted with those cited in the text.

MANUSCRIPT SOURCES

American Baptist Historical Society Papers, American Baptist–Samuel Colgate Historical Library, Rochester, New York
Graham Barden Papers, Duke University, Durham, North Carolina
Chester Bowles Papers, Yale University, New Haven, Connecticut
Dwight D. Eisenhower Papers, Eisenhower Presidential Library, Abilene, Kansas
Gerald R. Ford Papers, Ford Presidential Library, University of Michigan, Ann Arbor, Michigan
Herbert Hoover Papers, Hoover Presidential Library, West Branch, Iowa
Stanley M. Isaacs Papers, Municipal Archives, New York, New York
Lyndon Johnson Papers, Johnson Presidential Library, Austin, Texas
John F. Kennedy Papers, Kennedy Presidential Library, Dorchester, Massachusetts
Fiorello H. La Guardia Papers, Municipal Archives, New York, New York
Newbold Morris Papers, Municipal Archives, New York, New York
Papers of the National Association for the Advancement of Colored People, Library of Congress, Washington, D.C.
Adam Clayton Powell, Jr., Collection, Schomburg Library, New York, New York
Franklin D. Roosevelt Papers, Roosevelt Presidential Library, Hyde Park, New York
Bayard Rustin Interview, The Bayard Rustin Fund, New York, New York
Harry S. Truman papers, Truman Presidential Library, Independence, Missouri

U.S. Department of State Records, National Archives, Washington, D.C.
Mike Wallace Papers, George Arents Research Library, Syracuse University, Syracuse, New York

PROLOGUE: THE YOUNG THINKERS

PAGE
1 "codfish cakes": Powell, Jr., *Adam by Adam*, p. 17.
2 "Fats": Kisseloff, *You Must Remember This*, p. 275.
4 "a bit strange": Powell, Sr., *Against the Tide*, p. 145.

I. COLGATE, 1926–1930

12 "Some of the boys": Thomas Patterson, personal interview.
13 "the angel factory": Howard Armstrong, personal interview.
16 "You've got to have": James Nelson, personal interview.
17 "ordained": Hull, *Give Us Each Day*, p. 429.
    "there never was": Samuel Proctor, personal interview.
18 "Do not fool": Colgate University archives, Hamilton, New York; unidentified newspaper clipping, June 6, 1930.
    "Never let that": Jawn Sandifer, personal interview.

II. YOUNG ADAM POWELL, 1930–1945

25 "No man can": *Amsterdam News*, February 12, 1930.
    28,500 free meals: Powell, Sr., *Upon This Rock*, p. 44.
26 "all the God-given energy": *Amsterdam News*, October 19, 1932.
    "hypocritical prayers": Powell, Sr., *Against the Tide*, p. 229.
    "The preachers, churches": Ibid., p. 228.
    "In his magnificently furnished": Ibid., p. 232.
    "Let not": Ibid., p. 246.
28 "Take your money": Isabel Powell, personal interview.
30 "enshrined in our hearts": Page Smith, *America Enters the World*, p. 167.
32 "Drive carefully": Mitgang, *The Man Who Rode the Tiger*, p. 254.
34 "the butcher shop"; "the morgue": Ottley, *New World A-Coming*, p. 85.
    "When I take": *Amsterdam News*, March 8, 1933.
35 "Go on back": Ibid.
    "If nothing is": Ibid.
36 "incompetency, inefficiency, and prejudice": *Amsterdam News*, April 26, 1933.
    "members of my church": *Amsterdam News*, June 7, 1933.
39 "Don't vote for me": Howard Bell, personal interview.
40 "Are you trying": Kessner, *Fiorello La Guardia and the Making of Modern New York*, p. 250.

PAGE

41 "He is young": *Amsterdam News,* November 8, 1933.

43 "stands four-square": Anderson, *A. Philip Randolph,* preface.
"My newspapering days": Wilkins and Mathews, *Standing Fast,* p. 111.

45 "walk out with": Anderson, *A. Philip Randolph,* p. 260.
"truly a lost": Weisbrot, *Father Divine,* p. 176.

47 Not long after: Fiorello H. La Guardia Papers, Box 3529, letter dated April 20, 1934.

48 "This very conventional": Kessner, *La Guardia,* p. 371.
"Fusion has done": *New York Post,* August, 15, 1935.
"What is worse": *New York Evening Post,* March 27, 1935.

49 "It was like": Hycie Curtis, personal interview.

50 "Missed you in": Preston Powell, personal interview.

51 "They had bourbon": Olivia Stokes, personal interview.

55 "The Florida pines": *Amsterdam News,* April 18, 1936.
"mordant": Wilkins and Mathews, *Standing Fast,* p. 120.
"provocateurs": Ibid., p. 125.
"publicity and power": *Pittsburgh Courier,* February 2, 1934.

56 "I wonder what": Edward Peeks, personal interview.

57 "like Tennyson's brook": Powell, Sr., *Upon This Rock,* p. 47.

58 "I acquiesce": Abyssinian Baptist Church, "The Retirement Reception" (brochure), November 1937.
"high ideals": *New York Times,* August 9, 1936.

INTERLUDE: ADAM CLAYTON POWELL, SR.

58 The land in: For background information on Llewellyn Powell and his twenty-one slaves, see U.S. Census, 1850; *Rocky Mount News,* November 16, 1967; Roy Talbert, Jr., Gary Lee Cardwell, and Andrew Baskin, *Studies in the Local History of Slavery,* essays prepared for the Booker T. Washington National Monument, Ferrum College, 1978, p. 5; and Emmie Ferguson Farrar and Emilee Hines, *Old Virginia Houses: The Piedmont* (Charlotte, N.C.: Delmar, 1975), pp. 178–79.

60 "handsome and brilliant": Powell, Sr., *Against the Tide,* p. 7.
"lynched or murdered": Ibid., p. 14.

61 "bayonets gleaming": A. A. Graham, comp., *History of Fairfield and Perry Counties* (Chicago: W. H. Beers, 1883), p. 41.
"lawless and ungodly": Powell, Sr., *Against the Tide,* p. 14.
"wicked heart": Ibid., p. 15.
"hoist sails": Ibid., p. 17.

63 "Away to the": Powell, Sr., "A Souvenir of the Immanuel Baptist Church, Its Pastors and Members" (New Haven, Conn.: Clarence H. Ryder, 1895), p. 51.

PAGE
63 "a freer air": *New Haven Negroes*, p. 286.
"spiritually dead": Powell, Sr., "A Souvenir," p. 73.
65 "too full of": Powell, Sr., *Against the Tide*, p. 45.
"the only man": Powell, Sr., *Upon This Rock*, p. 9.
"real sermons": Powell, Sr., *Against the Tide*, p. 47.
"life and fire": Ibid.
66 "a cloud has": New York Baptist Association Minutes, 1835 Convention, Vol. 1831–1850, p. 25.
67 "a year of": Ibid., 1864 Convention, p. 15.
"a terrible town": Edel, *Henry James*, pp. 611, 613.
68 "ravening wolves": Jervis Anderson, *This Was Harlem*, p. 19.
"a valley of": Ibid.
"gospel bombardment": Powell, Sr., *Upon This Rock*, p. 8.
"like a football": Kisseloff, *You Must Remember This*, p. 296.
69 "trying to kill": Powell, Sr., *Upon This Rock*, p. 15.
"the symbol of": Ibid., p. 16.
70 "extortionate charges": Ibid., p. 18.
71 "the pastor and": Ibid., p. 24.
"You could find": Powell, Sr., *Against the Tide*, p. 89.
72 "Preach with all": Powell, Sr., *Upon This Rock*, p. 51.
74 $147,000: Maurice Rosenblatt, personal interview.
76 "suave, handsome young": Powell, Jr., *Marching Blacks*, p. 94.
78 "The hour for": Shaw Commencement address, 1938; Vol. VII, Shaw University archives, Raleigh, North Carolina.
"The time has": Colgate *Maroon*, March 18, 1938.
80 "brilliant": Paul Klein, personal interview.
82 "brilliant": Newbold Morris Papers, letter dated October 29, 1941, titled "Why New York Needs a New City Council."
83 the shouting: Ottley, *New World A-Coming*, p. 232.
84 "Powell Leads City": Powell, Jr., *Adam by Adam*, p. 69.
"extraordinary": *New York Herald Tribune*, November 7, 1941.
"two surprises": *New York Times*, November 13, 1941.
"amazed Manhattan politicians": *Time*, January 12, 1942.
85 "It may seem": Stanley M. Isaacs Papers, letter dated December 12, 1941.
86 "varies in loyalty": Kessner, *La Guardia*, p. 549.
"dividing up the": Caro, *The Power Broker*, p. 20.
"You cannot isolate": *Boston Globe*, February 9, 1942.
87 "taken out of": *Current Biography*, 1942.
91 In Harlem: See Franklin D. Roosevelt Papers, Official Files, Box 21, "Survey of Racial Conditions in the United States."

PAGE

92 "all but one": Nichols, *Arna Bontemps–Langston Hughes Letters,* p. 100.

93 "It was because": *The People's Voice,* June 19, 1942.
"My cry today": Ibid.

94 "had run off": Nichols, *Bontemps–Hughes Letters,* p. 100.
"dirtiest, muck-racking": Anderson, *A. Philip Randolph,* p. 268.
"much concerned": NAACP Papers, Box 241 (People's Committee), letter dated April 14, 1943.

95 "return to a Democracy": Department of Army Intelligence files, Washington, D.C., #100-51230-4, dated May 11, 1943.
"the new Negro": *The People's Voice,* April 10, 1943.

96 "Is there any": NAACP Papers, Box 241 (People's Committee), letter dated April 23, 1943.
"mutual": Ibid., letter dated June 5, 1943.
"The question that": *The People's Voice,* June 26, 1943.
"If a riot": *The People's Voice,* July 3, 1943.
"These are dark": Ibid.

97 "It seemed to": Baldwin, *Notes of a Native Son,* p. 85.
"It is harder": *PM,* August 3, 1943.
"Had it been": Ibid.
"blind smoldering resentment": *The People's Voice,* August 14, 1943.
"lunatic fringe": *New York Journal-American,* August 6, 1943.

98 "I helped you": *The People's Voice,* August 7, 1943.
"looking like Hollywood": *The People's Voice,* October 30, 1943.

99 "men on horseback": *The People's Voice,* November 11, 1943.
"a very decent": Roosevelt Papers, PPF files, Box 8633, letter dated January 18, 1944.
"compromises": *New York Times,* April 19, 1944.
"for the four": FBI files, HQ100-51230.

100 "bloodshed": *New York Times,* April 13, 1944.
"I had lunch": *The People's Voice,* March 25, 1944.
"You get nowhere": *New York Times,* May 13, 1944.
"we'll give her": *New York Times,* May 23, 1944.

101 "political machine backing": *New York Herald Tribune,* May 15, 1944.
"spellbinder": *Time,* May 22, 1944.
"This is a year": *The People's Voice,* June 17, 1944.
"an unceasing war": *The People's Voice,* May 14, 1944.
"Let's go friend": *The People's Voice,* May 6, 1944.
"The cloistered hall": Adam Clayton Powell, Jr., Collection, Reel #F-1, 1944–1946, dated May 7, 1944.

102 "love song": Ibid., June 30, 1944.
"pal of the poll-tax": *The People's Voice*, July 1, 1944.
"principles, issues, and men": Adam Clayton Powell, Jr., Collection, Reel #F-1, 1944–1946, dated July 10, 1944.
103 "so-called Big Negroes": *The People's Voice*, August 26, 1944.
"Luce talk": *Boston Globe*, October 23, 1944.
"The people have": *The People's Voice*, August 12, 1944.
"When Powell goes to Congress": *The People's Voice*, August 5, 1944.
104 "I thought you": Lloyd Dickens, personal interview.
"During the past": *The People's Voice*, October 14, 1944.
"His claim to": Adam Clayton Powell, Jr., Collection, Reel #F-1, 1944–1946, dated October 10, 1944.
"cheered by crowds": *New York Times*, November 2, 1944.

III. THE RISE OF A PHOENIX, 1945–1952

110 "Phoenix-like": Aptheker, *A Documentary History of the Negro People in the United States*, Vol. 3, p. 627.
111 "I have no": Ibid., p. 628.
112 "the Negro chosen": *Pittsburgh Courier*, January 13, 1945.
"the virgin Hattie": Paul Klein, personal interview.
113 "Just wait": Franklin D. Roosevelt, Jr., personal interview.
115 "lost souls": MacNeil, *Forge of Democracy*, p. 129.
"Don't try to": Ibid.
"Adam, everybody thinks": Powell, Jr., *Adam by Adam*, p. 72.
"They convinced me": *Pittsburgh Courier*, January 20, 1945.
117 "the most southern": Green, *Washington*, p. 485.
118 "a little kike": Brinkley, *Washington Goes to War*, p. 222.
"Last week democracy": *Pittsburgh Courier*, February 24, 1945.
"dirty liar": *Pittsburgh Courier*, March 3, 1945.
"The time has": Ibid.
119 "Those opposed to": *New York Times*, March 1, 1945.
"suitable for framing": *The People's Voice*, February 17, 1945.
"An ideal preacher's wife": *Amsterdam News*, April 28, 1945.
120 "Born of landed gentry": *Amsterdam News*, April 21, 1945.
"soon as possible": Harry S. Truman Papers, General File, telegram dated April 16, 1945.
"I never felt": *Amsterdam News*, July 28, 1945.
122 "Everyone wants to": Mike Wallace Papers, interview with Hazel Scott, Box 9, p. 2.
123 "My stuff is": Hazel Scott, *Current Biography*, 1943, p. 679.
124 "knows and can play": *Chicago Daily News*, December 13, 1943.

PAGE

125 "Park Avenue's women": *Amsterdam News*, August 11, 1945.

126 "Hazel was pretty": Olivia Stokes, personal interview.

127 "warm, golden brown": *Ebony*, January 1949.

128 "flew like birds": *Amsterdam News*, October 6, 1945.
"Request immediate action": Truman Papers, Official File, Box 438, dated October 1, 1945.

129 "Tea for Fifty Ladies": *Newsweek*, October 22, 1945.
"the last lady": Acy Lennon, personal interview.
"That damn nigger": Donovan, *Eisenhower*, p. 148.
"In light of": Truman Papers, Official File, Box 438, dated October 13, 1945.
"perpetuation of racial": *New York Times*, October 20, 1945.
"Mrs. Luce's Action": *New York Times*, November 2, 1945.

130 "Minnesotans Criticize DAR"; "A Problem Haunts"; "It can't stand": Truman Papers, Box 438, "DAR."

131 "the drawing": *New York Times*, October 17, 1945.
"the political ropes": *Amsterdam News*, October 20, 1945.
"On the other hand": Truman Papers, Box 438, "DAR," dated October 19, 1945.
"no hand-picked Negro": *Amsterdam News*, October 27, 1945.

132 "from within": *Amsterdam News*, November 3, 1945.
"this good man": *Amsterdam News*, November 17, 1945.
"About June": *Amsterdam News*, December 1, 1945.
"How they can": Ibid.
"enigmatic, unpredictable": *Amsterdam News*, December 29, 1945.
"I never posed": *The People's Voice*, March 30, 1946.
"The South evidently": Powell, Jr., *Marching Blacks*, p. 178.

133 "Many good causes": *New York Times*, February 3, 1946.
"However, and I say": *The People's Voice*, February 2, 1946.
"white liberals": *The People's Voice*, March 30, 1946.
"Walk out": Powell, Jr., *Marching Blacks*, p. 180.

134 "a lot of": *Congressional Record*, May 1946.

141 "first real test": *Amsterdam News*, March 9, 1946.
"deplorable conglomeration of": *New York Post*, March 12, 1946.
"antagonistic attitude": *Amsterdam News*, March 9, 1946.
"Keep punching": *New York Herald Tribune*, August 22, 1946.

142 "Powell Setback": Ibid.
"awakening": Ibid.
"I'm already resting": *Amsterdam News*, August 24, 1946.

143 "betrayal": *New York Times*, August 26, 1946.

144 "Bitter": *New York Times*, November 4, 1946.

PAGE

144 "move in on terrorists": Ibid.
  "I've been in bed": *Amsterdam News,* November 9, 1946.
  "He's somewhere": Marjorie Lawson, personal interview.
145 "The thousands of dollars": *Amsterdam News,* November 9, 1946.
146 "or resign": *Amsterdam News,* November 16, 1946.
  "I believe": *Congressional Record,* January 1947.
147 "the grand jury": Ibid.
  "I make no": Ibid.
148 "The issue": Rubinstein, *I Vote My Conscience,* pp. 236–37.
  "If you must know": *New York Post,* February 8, 1947.
  "severe and sudden": *Amsterdam News,* May 24, 1947.
149 "The best price": *New York Times,* October 9, 1947.
  "back in shape": *The People's Voice,* January 10, 1948.
150 "follow his conscience": *New York Times,* January 5, 1948.
  "my civil rights": *New York Times,* February 4, 1948.
  "pioneer work": *New York Times,* March 20, 1947.
152 "knock the whole town": *Amsterdam News,* October 16, 1948.
  "from top to bottom": Ibid.
  "His hands still drip": *Amsterdam News,* October 30, 1948.
153 "is not in the good graces": *New York Post,* October 26, 1948.
154 "It's been grand fun": Richard Norton Smith, *Thomas E. Dewey and His Times,* p. 49.
  "First Negro to Preside": *New York Herald Tribune,* May 11, 1949.
155 "young, pink-faced": Powell, Jr., *Adam by Adam,* p. 83.
  "unconstitutional": McCoy and Ruetten, *Quest and Response,* p. 179.
156 "anti-Catholic": *New York Times,* September 2, 1949.
  "Let me speak": *Congressional Record,* August 1949.
  "Here is our": *Congressional Record,* March 1949.
157 "First, I have fallen": U.S. Department of State Records, #033.1119, dated December 19, 1949.
  "We are living": Ibid.
158 "There can be": Ibid., December 21, 1949.
  "I know this": U.S. Department of State Records, #442.112, dated November 9, 1950.
159 "I welcome you": *Amsterdam News,* July 13, 1946.
160 "a small part": Manchester, *The Glory and the Dream,* p. 520.
  "to give dignity": *New York Times,* February 23, 1950.
  "the Negro down": *Daily Worker,* June 2, 1950.
161 "like a cobra": Manchester, *The Glory and the Dream,* p. 532.
  "I have said": Duberman, *Paul Robeson,* p. 388.

PAGE

161 "In the hour": *New York World-Telegram*, April 25, 1949.
162 "you are the wife": U.S. House of Representatives, Subcommittee of the Committee on Un-American Activities, p. 3611.
"headline-seeking superpatriots": Ibid., p. 3613.
"Now that you": Ibid., p 3614–15.
164 "I want to": *New York Times*, November 8, 1950.
"a dupe of": *New York Times*, October 12, 1950.
"We have launched": *New York Times*, October 2, 1950.
166 "ancient warriors": *Amsterdam News*, January 5, 1952.
"Negroes must fight": *Amsterdam News*, January 12, 1952.
"We will list": *Amsterdam News*, February 2, 1952.
167 "have again crucified": *Amsterdam News*, March 29, 1952.
"We are going": *Amsterdam News*, June 21, 1952.
168 "Can we elect": Isaacson and Thomas, *The Wise Men*, p. 562.
"I am the Democrat": Ibid., p. 561.
169 "a Republican type": *New York Times*, July 21, 1952.
"Re-examine your hearts": Manchester, *The Glory and the Dream*, p. 617.
170 "the stark reality": Ibid., p. 623.
"the great tragedies": *New York Times*, July 27, 1952.
"on ice": *New York Times*, July 27, 1952.
"I am not": *Amsterdam News*, August 2, 1952.
"confused in his thinking": Ibid.
171 "walls and ceiling": *Amsterdam News*, August 30, 1952.
"down the river": *New York Times*, August 4, 1952.
172 "We are 100 percent": *New York Times*, August 30, 1952.
173 "on an unbroken record": *Amsterdam News*, October 11, 1952.
"There are too many": Ibid.
"the white supremacy candidate": *Amsterdam News*, October 18, 1952.
"double-dealing": *Amsterdam News*, November 1, 1952.
"Stevenson Wildly Cheered": *New York Times*, October 28, 1952.
174 "Here, my friends": Manchester, *The Glory and the Dream*, p. 621.
175 "From the beginning": *Amsterdam News*, November 8, 1952.
"80-Year-Old": *Amsterdam News*, February 9, 1946.

IV. SHIFTING GROUND, 1953–1957

180 "no recollection": *New York Times*, March 1, 1953.
181 "Negroes do not want": Dwight D. Eisenhower Papers, Official File, Box 731; *Reader's Digest*, July 16, 1954, p. 7.
"He built": Olivia Stokes, personal interview.

PAGE

182 "New Deal lawyers": Ambrose, *Eisenhower, The President,* p. 20.

185 "How can we": Eisenhower Papers, General File, Box 910, telegram dated February 5, 1953.

"They are serving": Ibid., May 4, 1953.

186 "legally, or logically": Watson, *Lion in the Lobby,* p. 244.

187 "The hour has arrived": Eisenhower Papers, Official File, Box 731, telegram dated June 3, 1953.

188 "Max, I've been": Maxwell Rabb, personal interview.

"a single step": Eisenhower Papers, Official File, Box 731, dated June 10, 1953.

189 "a Magna Carta": Ibid.

"troubled hours": Ibid.

190 "knew or knew of": Ibid., June 23, 1953.

"bear witness": *New York Herald Tribune,* October 12, 1953.

191 "You might be interested": Eisenhower Papers, Alpha File, Box 2485, dated November 2, 1953.

192 "a rough, tough": Elliott and D'Orso, *The Cost of Courage: The Journey of an American Congressman,* p. 133.

193 "to the status": Eisenhower Papers, Official File, Box 731, dated March 29, 1954.

"This is the first": Kluger, *Simple Justice,* p. 656.

194 "In these days": Ibid., p. 710.

"democracy's shining hour": *New York Times,* May 19, 1954.

"There is no place": Eisenhower Papers, Alpha File, Box 2485, wire service article dated October 6, 1954.

"As a Democrat": Ibid., dated July 16, 1954.

196 "Republican-sponsored drive": *New York Times,* September 28, 1954.

198 "an intricate tax scheme": *New York Times,* December 17, 1954.

199 "There are no Communists": *National Party Conventions, 1831–1984* (Washington, D.C.: Congressional Quarterly, 1987), p. 100.

200 "I'm known throughout": U.S. State Department Records, #611.70/4-1653, letter dated April 16, 1953.

"Ike doesn't want": Adam Clayton Powell III, personal interview.

202 "two generations removed": *New York Herald Tribune,* April 19, 1955.

"Before Powell had": Homer Bigart letter to author, May 9, 1987; also personal interview.

"vigorous": *New York Times,* April 23, 1955.

"It is perfectly obvious": *New York Herald Tribune,* April 21, 1955.

"In our opinion": *New York Daily Mirror,* April 20, 1955.

PAGE

202 "an anti-white": *New York Times*, April 23, 1955.

203 "One of the really": *Dayton Daily News*, McGill column, April 22, 1955.
"who appears": *New York Times*, April 23, 1955.
"first worldwide": *New York Times*, April 27, 1955.
"did more than": *New Republic*, May 2, 1955.
"showered American racial policies": *Pittsburgh Courier*, June 4, 1955.
"annihilate the propaganda drive": *New York Daily News*, May 12, 1955.

204 "Who is this": Wesley Carter, personal interview.

205 "Negroes constitute": *Washington Post*, November 22, 1987.

206 "a big, open-hearted fella": Carl Elliott, personal interview.
"I was out": Ibid.

207 "This is no place": *New York Times*, June 18, 1955.
"Bias Issue Blocks": *New York Times*, June 6, 1955.
"persuasion": *New York Times*, June 25, 1955.
"No one believes": *New York Herald Tribune*, June 13, 1955.
"being lost": *Washington Post*, June 10, 1955.

208 "with the echo": *Washington Afro-American*, July 9, 1955.
"walk by the monument": Ibid.
"Even if unintentionally": *New York Times*, July 3, 1955.
"social reforms": *New York Times*, March 30, 1955.

209 "Liar": *New York Times*, July 21, 1955.
"encourages segregation": Eisenhower Papers, Official File, Box 731, dated August 8, 1955.
"We have been": Ibid.

210 "The verdict": *New York Herald Tribune*, September 28, 1955.
"I don't think": *Greensboro Daily News*, February 3, 1956.
"Mr. Powell": Ibid.
"a vote against": Ambrose, *Eisenhower, The President*, p. 303.
"the lifeline": *New York Times*, February 13, 1956.

211 "It is this tight clique": flyer dated May 10, 1956, *New York Times* clipping file.

212 "a victory": Eisenhower Papers, Official File, Box 733, dated February 22, 1956.
"opportunist": Eisenhower Papers, Official File, Box 731, dated February 27, 1956.
"physically fit": Eisenhower Papers, Alpha File, Box 2486, dated March 2, 1956.
"passing the buck": *New York Times*, March 3, 1956.
"We'll decide": AP dispatch, March 24, 1956.

PAGE

213 "Bigoted, stupid people": Bayard Rustin Interview, p. 11.
"North and South": *New York Times,* May 25, 1956.
214 "Dear Adam": Bayard Rustin Interview, p. 11.
"I have a note": Ibid.
215 "allergy": *New York Times,* February 12, 1956.
"Evidently what they want": Martin, *Adlai Stevenson and the World,* p. 256.
"I ask this question": *New York Times,* February 17, 1956.
"a palace guard": *New York Times,* March 31, 1956.
"gazing into the fairways": Sherman Adams, personal interview.
216 "We are going": *New York Times,* March 5, 1956.
217 "wide-open": *New York Post,* October 3, 1956.
"As a Democrat": *Newsweek,* October 1, 1956.
218 "disillusioned liberal Democrats": *New York Times,* October 12, 1956.
219 "if he is": *New York Times,* October 12, 1956.
"thrown away": *New York Times,* October 31, 1956.
"even if it means": *Newark News,* October 20, 1956.
"My quarrel": *Los Angeles Times,* October 24, 1956.
220 "Anyone who is": Ibid.
221 "In 1956": *New York Times,* October 29, 1956.
"The Party of Eastland": Lyndon Baines Johnson Papers, James Rowe, Box 100.
"Let's put it": *Time,* November 26, 1956.
222 "The isolated move": *New York Post,* November 19, 1956.
224 "anyone who goes": Eisenhower Papers, General File, Box 811, dated February 8, 1957.
225 "dangerous game": *New York Post,* March 22, 1957.
"Not behind": Eisenhower Papers, Official File, Box 731, dated March 28, 1957.
226 "this day of destiny": *New York Times,* April 15, 1957.
"We are getting": Eisenhower Papers, Official File, Box 731, memo dated April 17, 1957.
"inexcusable": *New York Times,* April 22, 1957.
227 "We are sick": FBI files, HQ 100-51230, Vol. 16.
"the rank and file": Eisenhower Papers, Official File, Box 731, dated June 4, 1957.
228 "We disagree": Eisenhower Papers, Official File, Box 731, undated stack of telegrams.
"lip service": Eisenhower Papers, Official File, Box 9, dated July 12, 1957.
"After eighty years": Ibid., dated August 30, 1957.

PAGE

228 "I have just returned": Eisenhower Papers, Official File, Box 733, telegram dated September 17, 1957.

229 "I must say": Eisenhower Papers, Official File, Box 731, dated September 27, 1957.
"This is giving": Ibid., dated October 27, 1957.

232 "Honey": Paul Klein, personal interview.
"You tell": Ibid.
"Get out of here": Wesley Carter, personal interview.

234 "Once you've played": *New York Herald Tribune*, July 6, 1960.

V. THE GLORY, 1957–1963

237 "playing basketball": Manchester, *The Glory and the Dream*, p. 788.
"disturbingly small-minded": Ibid.

238 "another Little Rock": *Chicago Sun-Times*, January 30, 1958.

239 "Seven months": Dwight D. Eisenhower Papers, Alpha File, Box 2486, dated January 28, 1958.
"broken promises": Ibid., dated February 7, 1958.

240 "When those old ladies": *New York Post*, March 13, 1958.
"the beginning": *New York Times*, February 25, 1958.

241 "for the same thing": *New York Times*, May 21, 1958.
"When Crump first": Charles Rangel, personal interview.
"If Jack refuses": *New York Times*, May 21, 1958.

242 "at the lowest ebb": *New York Post*, March 13, 1958.
"independent Negro leadership": *New York Post*, April 24, 1958.
"Let the poor man": *New York Times*, May 12, 1958.
"We call": Ibid.

243 "As we near": Ibid.
"God bless you": *New York Post*, May 16, 1958.
"We will dump": Ibid.
"We won't do": *New York Times*, May 19, 1958.
"black leaders": *New York Times*, May 18, 1958.

244 "I don't know": *New York Post*, May 23, 1958.
"Nothing could be deadlier": *New York Post*, May 26, 1958.
"Negroes would reflect": *New York Post*, May 28, 1958.

245 "We must act": *New York Daily News*, May 8, 1958.
"stood up": *New York Times*, June 7, 1958.
"It is a high price": *New York Times*, May 31, 1958.
"to the very end": *New York Times*, June 31, 1958.
"Love those": *New York Times*, June 23, 1958.
"assailed with desperate weapons": *New York Post*, June 18, 1958.

PAGE

246 "Rabble-Rouser": *Newsweek*, June 2, 1958.
247 "Harlem in the thirties": *New York Post*, August 7, 1958.
  "rising quietly": *New York Post*, August 8, 1958.
248 "influence events": *New York Post*, August 14, 1958.
  "In a close": *New York Times*, August 17, 1958.
249 "I will name": *New York Times*, October 21, 1958.
  "where slave labor": *New York Times*, October 23, 1958.
  "Averell's a Democrat": Isaacson and Evans, *The Wise Men*, p. 585.
250 "chaos at the top": *New York Post*, December 1, 1958.
  "The Negro": *New York Times*, June 30, 1959.
251 "Ain't Got Time": *New York Times*, October 19, 1959.
253 "a phony roundup": *New York Times*, January 6, 1960.
  "I am against": *New York Times*, January 4, 1960.
254 "I don't need": *New York Times*, January 11, 1960.
  "pauperizing": *New York Times*, January 13, 1960.
  "continued and shocking disregard": *New York Times*, January 14, 1960.
  "protecting white gamblers": *New York Times*, February 4, 1960.
257 "true to form": *Charlotte News and Observer*, September 1, 1960.
  "This opens up": Chester Bowles Papers, Box 214, letter dated January 29, 1960.
  "Public Enemy No. 1": *New York Times*, January 26, 1960.
258 "terrible": *New York Times*, February 9, 1960.
  "sheer stupidity": *New York Times*, February 19, 1960.
259 "They were all men": *New York Post*, March 10, 1960.
260 "far greater magnitude": *New York Times*, March 10, 1960.
261 "You know Cherio's": *New York Post*, March 30, 1960.
  "It must have been": *New York Post*, April 18, 1960.
  "These mistakes": *New York Post*, April 19, 1960.
262 "boss-free": Lyndon Baines Johnson Papers, Senate File, Box 52.
263 "wallowing in the": Chester Bowles Papers, Box 214, dated May 2, 1960.
264 "For a man": *New York Times*, June 26, 1960.
265 "Peccadilloes, my boy": Gore Vidal, telephone interview.
266 "revolution of passive": Edward Sylvester, telephone interview.
  "You watch": Ibid.
  "let's burn the place": Gore Vidal, telephone interview.
  "Do not leave": Martin, *Adlai Stevenson and the World*, p. 527.
  "The woods are lovely": Ibid., p. 525.
269 "of our troubled": McKeever, *Adlai Stevenson*, p. 463.
  "uncharted areas of": Sorenson, *Kennedy*, p. 167.
  "a turning point": Ibid.

PAGE

270 "smoldering resentment": *New York Times*, July 20, 1960.
"We need": Harris Wofford, personal interview.

271 "shocked and amazed": *New York Times*, September 26, 1960.
"The persecuted cannot join": *New York Post*, September 19, 1960.

273 "They don't quote": Wofford, *Of Kennedys & Kings*, p. 64; also Louis Martin and Harris Wofford, personal interviews.
"Gentlemen, I bring": Raymond Jones, personal interview.

274 "We stand today": *New York Times*, November 4, 1960.

275 "There's a saying": *New York Times*, January 30, 1961.

276 "I worked": Sam Rayburn Papers, dated November 10, 1960.

277 "The place is crawling": *New York Herald Tribune*, March 13, 1961.

278 "We are not looking": *New York Times*, April 11, 1961.

279 "the cocktail, black-tie": *New York Times*, February 28, 1961.
"This bill": *New York Times*, February 18, 1961.
"All I want": John F. Kennedy Papers, interview in folder of clippings marked "P," dated February 12, 1961.

280 "gets in step": *New York Times*, July 15, 1961.
"the same cynical": *New York Times*, June 6, 1960.

282 "A lot of the girls": *New York Times*, October 26, 1962.
"Next week": 87th Congressional Hearings, Fair Labor Standards Act, October 22, 1962, p. 139.

283 "I resent the fact": 87th Congressional Hearings, Fair Employment Hearings, October 23, 1962, p. 31.
"I'd like to see": *New York Times*, November 3, 1962.
"And then we have": *New York Times*, March 12, 1962.

285 "Relax": Fair Employment Hearings, October 23, 1962, p. 31.
"This is in New York": Ibid., p. 32.

286 "Find something": Barringer, *Flight from Sorrow*, p. 126; also Maurice Rosenblatt, personal interview.

287 "Whatever you say": Doris Gamser, personal interview.

289 "Sing the Borinquefia": *San Juan Star*, clipping of speech dated February 21, 1960.

290 "If there is a lynching": *San Juan Star*, clipping of interview dated December 19, 1961.

292 "completely ignorant": *New York Times*, April 20, 1963.
"And, of course": *New York Times*, April 4, 1963.
"This is the year": *New York Times*, May 30, 1963.

294 "I was afraid": *New York Times*, April 5, 1963.
"You can get": *Look*, May 7, 1963.

295 "and every Negro": *Ebony*, June 1963.

PAGE

295 "Weep not": *New York Times,* November 25, 1963.
"Adam Clayton Powell": Adam Clayton Powell III, personal interview.

VI. AND THE POWER, 1964–1966

300 "Johnson reaped": Caro, *The Years of Lyndon Johnson,* Vol. I, p. 259.
303 "Open the door": *New York Herald Tribune,* May 8, 1964.
"There is no more": *New York Times,* March 17, 1964.
305 "government by decree": Lyndon Baines Johnson Papers, Official Files, Moyers papers, 2 of 2.
"Let us close": *New York Times,* July 3, 1964.
306 "calendars have no years": *Life,* September 4, 1964.
307 "But I am": *New York Times,* September 20, 1964.
308 "sidelash": *Tuesday* magazine, *Philadelphia Bulletin,* February 1966.
310 "remarkable": Johnson Papers, Official File, Box 38; also Lawrence O'Brien, personal interview.
311 "You know": *Philadelphia Bulletin,* March 29, 1965.
"Rep. Adam Clayton Powell": Ibid.
"an awesome show": *Philadelphia Inquirer,* March 1, 1965.
"You have to": Ibid.
312 "Now Adam": Clifford Alexander, personal interview.
"He shot out": *New York Herald Tribune,* December 17, 1965.
313 "Powell Probing": *New York Journal American,* September 5, 1965.
"seduced by politicians": *Washington Post,* April 12, 1965.
"nightclub host": *Washington Star,* April 13, 1965.
"Answer yes or no": *Chicago Sun-Times,* April 16, 1965.
314 "steamroller": *New York Herald Tribune,* May 14, 1965.
"I want to know": *Washington Daily News,* December 16, 1965.
"Adam put": *Chicago Daily News,* May 14, 1965.
315 "I use myself": *Chicago Tribune,* May 29, 1965.
"more neutral": *Chicago Sun-Times,* June 25, 1965.
"bold, brazen power": Ibid.
"I've been blocking": Ibid.
"If it were stacked": *New York Times,* July 29, 1965.
316 "The possibilities": *Washington Post,* March 31, 1966.
"Seek and ye": Johnson Papers, Executive Files, letter dated August 5, 1965.
"A Negro woman": *Washington Star,* November 18, 1965.
"brilliant": *New York World-Telegram,* March 24, 1966.
317 "a right great": *New York Times,* November 4, 1966.

318 "I never thought": *New York Herald Tribune,* Jimmy Breslin column, September 23, 1966.

"This will mark": Michael Schwartz personal papers, letter dated June 1, 1966.

"There also appears": Ibid., report dated March 1, 1966.

319 "maroon": Henry Williams personal papers, letter dated August 4, 1933.

320 "she allegedly sleeps": Ibid., letter dated August 24, 1961.

"The King is dead": *New York Times,* April, 1963.

321 "Perhaps it is": Williams papers, letter dated March 2, 1965.

"There are all manner": Ibid.

"When do we swim?": Williams papers, letter dated June 11, 1964.

"Let us pray": Ibid.

"Take my hand": *Life,* April 23, 1965.

323 "Look at those": *Washington Post,* March 29, 1965.

"Yellow Negroes": *Life,* April 23, 1965.

"mink coat mentality": *New York Times,* July 30, 1966.

"Black people are": *New York Post,* August 31, 1966.

"Black power may not be": *New York Post,* August 31, 1966.

324 "You're dealing": *New York Post,* July 28, 1965.

"represent the masses": *Washington Post,* May 9, 1966.

"This is no time": *Washington Daily News,* March 25, 1966.

"our own clothes": *New York Times,* October 10, 1966.

"Learn, baby, learn": Ibid.

"new breed of cats": *New York Times,* July 19, 1966.

"ailing aristocratic colonials": Ibid.

325 "Black is the way": Henry Williams, personal interview.

326 "God works": *New York Times,* September 19, 1966.

"Legislative fame": *New York Times,* September 16, 1966.

327 "a jet setter": George Reedy, personal interview.

328 "cold, raw political power": Morris Udall, personal interview.

330 "I am only one": *New Republic,* March 6, 1965.

VII. THE FALL, 1967–1968

337 "holyroller ministers": Baldwin, *Notes of a Native Son,* p. 65.

338 "the rats": *Life,* July 31, 1964.

"So long as the water": Baldwin, *Notes of a Native Son,* p. 59.

340 "Must Adam Leave Eden?": *Newsweek,* January 16, 1967.

345 "Now, Van": Lionel Van Deerlin, personal interview.

348 "I want my seat": Morris Udall, personal interview.

349 "The American way": *New York Times,* January 11, 1967.

"There is no one": *Congressional Record,* January 10, 1967.

PAGE

351 "Those sons of bitches": *Life,* January 20, 1967.
"black Dreyfus": *New York Times,* January 11, 1967.
352 "to clear the air": *New York Times,* January 21, 1967.
"Why, I remember": *New York Times,* January 12, 1967.
354 "I ain't going": Robbie Clark, personal interview.
355 "Where is the great": *Washington Post,* February 9, 1967.
357 "a real bastard": Bradlee, *Conversations with Kennedy,* p. 217.
"Gerry, you can't": Tom Curtis, personal interview.
359 "If the House": *Detroit News,* March 3, 1967.
"Despite the enormity": *Washington Post,* March 2, 1967.
"deeper between Negroes": *Chicago Daily News,* March 3, 1967.
"may be politically finished": *New York World-Journal-Tribune,* March 3, 1967.
"sleepless nights": *New York Times,* January 15, 1967.
364 "The Lord moves": *New York Times,* March 14, 1967.
368 "Good causes": *New York Times,* July 2, 1967.
369 "the old man": *Life,* April 23, 1965.
"awaken white young people": *New York Times,* January 12, 1968.
"the second civil war": *New York Times,* January 9, 1968.
370 "We have not": AP dispatch, January 10, 1968.
"Those cats got": *New York Times,* January 12, 1968.
"You must not scorn": *New York Times,* January 11, 1968.
"We are a new breed": *Los Angeles Times,* January 11, 1968.
371 "How dare we": *New York Times,* January 13, 1968.
"You young people": *Washington Post,* January 13, 1968.
"Shut up": Thomas Johnson, personal interview.
373 "We are in the midst": *New York Daily News,* March 23, 1968.
374 "Judases": *New York Times,* March 25, 1968.
"the stones": *New York Times,* March 24, 1968.
"I'm calling": *Washington Post,* April 1, 1968.
376 "Nobody can control": UPI, August 19, 1968.
"We're here": AP, August 24, 1968.

VIII. REDEMPTION BY THE CONSTITUTION,
1969–1972

382 "He who is": *New York Times,* January 4, 1969.
383 "For Zion's sake": *New York Times,* January 6, 1969.
385 "No way": Jack Hupper, personal interview.
386 "a Jewish boy": Arthur Kinoy, *Rights on Trial,* p. 43.
387 "perversion": *New York Times,* April 22, 1969.
"at the very heart": Arthur Kinoy, personal interview.
"to turn history": Arthur Kinoy, personal interview.

387 "autocracy or oligarchy": Kinoy, *Rights on Trial,* p. 312.
"Beautiful": *New York Times,* April 22, 1969.
390 "It is the responsibility": *New York Times,* June 17, 1969.
"I have kept": *New York Times,* June 18, 1969.
392 "They want": UPI, March 14, 1969.
"If the Democratic Party": *Washington Evening Star,* April 11, 1969.
393 "coming up with": *Washington Post,* April 26, 1969.
"Don't think": *New York Daily News,* June 25, 1969.
"Whites have to deal": *Detroit Free Press,* October 23, 1969.
"I'm unable to operate": *New York Daily News,* October 25, 1969.
399 "We don't want": William Epps, personal interview.
400 "It may be": *New York Times,* December 1, 1969.
402 "The first man": *Ebony,* June 1972.
403 "the new Negro bourgeoisie": *Jet,* July 16, 1970.
405 "paid her dues": Ibid.
406 "The history books": *Miami Herald,* June 27, 1969.
410 "Adam, you're finally home": Howard Bell, personal interview.
411 "This man": Bayard Rustin Interview, p. 12.
412 "You bore your burdens": *Los Angeles Times,* April 10, 1972; also William Epps, personal interview.
414 "This is a nation": Gerald R. Ford Papers, Box 136, undated clipping of 1969 student newspaper.
"My life": *Ebony,* June 1963.

EPILOGUE

418 "not only different": *New York Times,* September 5, 1977.
"Poor child": Bobby Short, personal interview.

BIBLIOGRAPHY

Adams, Sherman. *First-Hand Report: The Story of the Eisenhower Administration.* New York: Harper & Brothers, 1961.

Ambrose, Stephen. *Eisenhower, The President.* Vol. II. New York: Simon & Schuster, 1984.

Anderson, Jervis. *A. Philip Randolph: A Biographical Portrait.* New York: Harcourt Brace Jovanovich, 1973.

———. *This Was Harlem: A Cultural Portrait, 1900–1950.* New York: Farrar, Straus & Giroux, 1983.

Aptheker, Herbert. *A Documentary History of the Negro People in the United States.* Vols. III and IV. New York: Carol, 1973.

Baldwin, James. *Notes of a Native Son.* Boston: Beacon Press, 1955.

Barringer, Felicity. *Flight from Sorrow: The Life and Death of Tamara Wall.* New York: Atheneum, 1984.

Bernstein, Barton J., and Allen J. Matusow, eds. *The Truman Administration: A Documentary History.* New York: Harper & Row, 1966.

Brademas, John. *The Politics of Education.* Norman: University of Oklahoma Press, 1987.

Branch, Taylor. *Parting the Waters: America in the King Years, 1954–1963.* New York: Simon & Schuster, 1988.

Brinkley, David. *Washington Goes to War.* New York: Knopf, 1988.

Buckley, William F., Jr. *The Unmaking of a Mayor.* New York: Viking, 1966.

Caro, Robert A. *The Power Broker: Robert Moses and the Fall of New York.* New York: Knopf, 1974.

———. *The Years of Lyndon Johnson.* Vol. I: *The Path to Power.* New York: Knopf, 1982.

Carr, Raymond. *Puerto Rico: A Colonial Experiment.* New York: Random House, 1984.

Cashman, Sean Dennis. *America in the Gilded Age: From the Death of*

Lincoln to the Rise of Theodore Roosevelt. New York: New York University Press, 1984.

———. *America in the Twenties and Thirties: The Olympian Age of Franklin Delano Roosevelt.* New York: New York University Press, 1989.

Clifford, Clark, with Richard Holbrooke. *Counsel to the President: A Memoir.* New York: Random House, 1991.

Connable, Alfred, and Edward Silberfarb. *Tigers of Tammany: Nine Men Who Ran New York.* New York: Holt, Rinehart and Winston, 1967.

Cooper, John Milton, Jr. *Pivotal Decades: The United States, 1900–1920.* New York: W. W. Norton, 1990.

Dahl, Linda. *Stormy Weather: The Music and Lives of a Century of Jazz Women.* New York: Pantheon, 1984.

Diggins, John Patrick. *The Proud Decades: America in War and Peace, 1941–1960.* New York: W. W. Norton, 1988.

Donovan, Robert J. *Conflict and Crisis: The Presidency of Harry S Truman, 1945–1948.* New York: W. W. Norton, 1977.

———. *Eisenhower: The Inside Story.* New York: Harper & Brothers, 1956.

Duberman, Martin Bauml. *Paul Robeson.* New York: Knopf, 1988.

Edel, Leon. *Henry James: A Life.* New York: Harper & Row, 1953.

Elliott, Carl, Sr., and Michael D'Orso. *The Cost of Courage: The Journey of an American Congressman.* New York: Doubleday, 1992.

Feather, Leonard. *The Jazz Years: Earwitness to an Era.* New York: Da Capo, 1987.

Flaherty, Joe. *Managing Mailer.* New York: Coward-McCann, 1969.

Foner, Eric. *Reconstruction: America's Unfinished Revolution, 1863–1877.* New York: Harper & Row, 1988.

Friedrich, Otto. *City of Nets: A Portrait of Hollywood in the 1940s.* New York: Harper & Row, 1986.

Green, Constance McLaughlin. *Washington: Capital City, 1879–1950.* Princeton, N.J.: Princeton University Press, 1963.

Halberstam, David. *The Best and the Brightest.* New York: Random House, 1972.

Hardeman, D. B., and Donald C. Bacon. *Rayburn: A Biography.* Austin: Texas Monthly Press, 1987.

Harding, Vincent. *There Is a River: The Black Struggle for Freedom in America.* New York: Harcourt Brace Jovanovich, 1981.

Heckscher, August, with Phyllis Robinson. *When La Guardia Was Mayor: New York's Legendary Years.* New York: W. W. Norton, 1978.

Hull, Gloria T., ed. *Give Us Each Day: The Diary of Alice Dunbar-Nelson.* New York: W. W. Norton, 1984.

Isaacson, Walter, and Evan Thomas. *The Wise Men: Six Friends and the World They Made.* New York: Simon & Schuster, 1986.

Jacobs, Andy. *The Powell Affair: Freedom Minus One.* New York: Bobbs-Merrill, 1973.

Judis, John B. *William F. Buckley: Patron Saint of the Conservatives.* New York: Simon & Schuster, 1988.

Kessner, Thomas. *Fiorello H. La Guardia and the Making of Modern New York.* New York: McGraw-Hill, 1989.

Kinoy, Arthur. *Rights on Trial: The Odyssey of a People's Lawyer.* Cambridge, Mass.: Harvard University Press, 1983.

Kisseloff, Jess. *You Must Remember This: An Oral History of Manhattan from the 1890s to World War II.* New York: Harcourt Brace Jovanovich, 1989.

Klehr, Harvey. *The Heyday of American Communism: The Depression Decade.* New York: Basic Books, 1984.

Kluger, Richard. *Simple Justice: The History of* Brown *v.* Board of Education *and Black America's Struggle for Equality.* New York: Knopf, 1975.

Lasky, Victor. *J.F.K.: The Man and the Myth.* New York: Macmillan, 1963.

Lemann, Nicholas. *The Promised Land: The Great Black Migration and How It Changed America.* New York: Knopf, 1991.

Lewis, David Levering. *When Harlem Was in Vogue.* New York: Knopf, 1981.

MacNeil, Neil. *Forge of Democracy: The House of Representatives.* New York: David McKay, 1963.

Manchester, William. *The Glory and the Dream: A Narrative History of America, 1932–1972.* New York: Bantam, 1973.

Mann, Arthur. *La Guardia Comes to Power, 1933.* Philadelphia: J. B. Lippincott, 1965.

Martin, John Bartlow. *Adlai Stevenson and the World.* New York: Doubleday, 1977.

McCoy, Donald R., and Richard T. Ruetten. *Quest and Response: Minority Rights and the Truman Administration.* Lawrence: University Press of Kansas, 1973.

McCullough, David. *Truman.* New York: Simon & Schuster, 1992.

McElvaine, Robert S. *The Great Depression: America, 1929–1941.* New York: Times Books, 1984.

McFeely, William S. *Frederick Douglass.* New York: W. W. Norton, 1991.

McKeever, Porter. *Adlai Stevenson: His Life and Legacy.* New York: Morrow, 1989.

Mitgang, Herbert. *The Man Who Rode the Tiger.* New York: Viking, 1963.

Morris, Roger. *Richard Milhous Nixon: The Rise of an American Politician.* New York: Henry Holt, 1990.

Moscow, Warren. *The Last of the Big-Time Bosses: The Life and Times of Carmine DeSapio and the Decline and Fall of Tammany Hall.* New York: Stein and Day, 1971.

Moses, Robert. *La Guardia: A Salute and a Memoir.* New York: Simon & Schuster, 1957.

Naison, Mark. *Communists in Harlem during the Depression.* New York: Grove Press, 1983.

Nevins, Allan. *Herbert Lehman and His Era.* New York: Scribner's, 1963.

Nichols, Charles H., ed. *Arna Bontemps–Langston Hughes Letters, 1925–1967.* New York: Dodd, Mead, 1980.

O'Connor, Richard. *Heywood Broun: A Biography.* New York: Putnam's, 1975.

Osofsky, Gilbert. *Harlem: The Making of a Ghetto.* New York: Harper & Row, 1968.

Ottley, Roi. *New World A-Coming.* Boston: Houghton Mifflin, 1943.

Pearson, Drew, and Jack Anderson. *The Case Against Congress.* New York: Simon & Schuster, 1968.

Pfeffer, Paula F. *A. Philip Randolph: Pioneer of the Civil Rights Movement.* Baton Rouge: Louisiana State University Press, 1990.

Powell, Adam Clayton, Jr. *Adam by Adam: The Autobiography of Adam Clayton Powell, Jr.* New York: Dial, 1971.

Powell, Adam Clayton, Sr. *Against the Tide: An Autobiography.* New York: Richard R. Smith, 1938.

————. *Upon This Rock.* New York: Abyssinian Baptist Church, 1949.

Puryear, Elmer L. *Graham A. Barden: Conservative Carolina Congressman.* North Carolina: Campbell University Press, 1979.

Rappaport, Daniel. *Inside the House.* Chicago: Follett, 1975.

Ravitch, Diane. *The Troubled Crusade: American Education, 1945–1980.* New York: Basic Books, 1983.

Reedy, George. *From the Ward to the White House: The Irish in American Politics.* New York: Scribner's, 1991.

Rubinstein, Annette T., ed. *I Vote My Conscience: Debates, Speeches, and Writings of Vito Marcantonio.* New York: Vito Marcantonio Memorial, 1956.

Schuyler, George S. *Black and Conservative.* New Rochelle, N.Y.: Arlington House, 1966.

Sevareid, Eric. *Candidates 1960.* New York: Basic Books, 1959.

Shapiro, Herbert. *White Violence and Black Response, From Reconstruction to Montgomery.* Amherst: University of Massachusetts Press, 1988.

Shumway, Floyd, and Richard Hegel, eds. *New Haven: An Illustrated History*. Woodland Hills, Calif.: Windsor, 1981.

Sitkoff, Harvard. *A New Deal for Blacks: The Emergence of Civil Rights as a National Issue*. Vol. I: *The Depression Decade*. New York: Oxford University Press, 1978.

Smith, Page. *America Enters the World: A People's History of the Progressive Era and World War I*. Vol. 7. New York: McGraw-Hill, 1985.

Smith, Richard Norton. *Thomas E. Dewey and His Times*. New York: Simon & Schuster, 1982.

Sobel, Mechal. *Trabelin' On: The Slave Journey to an Afro-Baptist Faith*. Princeton, N.J.: Princeton University Press, 1979.

Socha, Evamarie, ed. *National Party Conventions, 1831–1984*. Washington, D.C.: Congressional Quarterly, 1987.

Sorenson, Theodore. *Kennedy*. New York: Harper & Row, 1965.

Washburn, Patrick S. *A Question of Sedition: The Federal Government's Investigation of the Black Press During World War II*. New York: Oxford University Press, 1986.

Watson, Denton L. *Lion in the Lobby*. New York: Morrow, 1990.

Weisbrot, Robert. *Father Divine*. Boston: Beacon Press, 1983.

White, Theodore H. *The Making of the President 1960*. New York: Atheneum, 1961.

Wicker, Tom. *JFK and LBJ*. New York: Morrow, 1968.

Wilkins, Roger. *A Man's Life: An Autobiography*. New York: Simon & Schuster, 1982.

Wilkins, Roy, with Tom Mathews. *Standing Fast: The Autobiography of Roy Wilkins*. New York: Viking, 1982.

Williams, Howard D. *A History of Colgate University, 1819–1969*. New York: Van Nostrand Reinhold, 1969.

Wofford, Harris. *Of Kennedys & Kings: Making Sense of the Sixties*. New York: Farrar, Straus & Giroux, 1980.

INDEX

Abdul-Jabbar, Kareem (Lew Alcindor), 370
Abramson, Leon, 318
Abyssinian Baptist Church: at West 40th Street, 1, 11, 57, 67–69; moves to Harlem, 2, 57, 69–72; ACP delivers first sermon at, 17; ACP understudies father, 23; ACP administers work relief bureau at, 25; and the Depression, 25, 46; and ACP's relations with Communists, 44–45; size of congregation, 56, 321, 337; ACP Sr. retires, 56–57; ACP succeeds father, 56–58; founding and early years, 65–67; mortgage paid, 72; and ACP's first congressional campaign, 99, 101; as ACP's Harlem headquarters, 116, 149, 158; response to Hazel Scott, 126; and ACP's congressional career, 160, 167, 181, 196–97, 219, 240, 242–43, 339; and church segregation, 167; Joe Ford and, 196–97; tax preparation scandal, 196–97, 222; and Montgomery boycotts, 212; ACP thinks of retiring, 294–95; and

ACP's libel case, 321–22; ACP threatens to abandon, 324–25; and black radicals, 324–25, 373–74; ACP invites fellow congressmen to, 329–30; in mid-1960s, 337, 338–39; and succession to ACP, 338; response to ACP's expulsion from House, 360; and ACP's return from exile, 373–74; Haile Selassie awards ACP medal at, 393; conflict over successor to ACP, 398–401, 404–5; ACP's final appearance at, 405; and ACP's funeral, 410–13; Proctor becomes pastor, 419
Adams, Julius, 207
Adams, Sherman, 209, 212, 224, 227, 237, 249; and ACP, 187–88, 189, 191, 220, 225, 226
African Meeting House, Boston, 66
Agar, Herbert, 80
Age, 54
Alabama: civil rights movement in, 204, 205, 206, 212–13
Alabama, University of: ACP speaks at, 392
Alabama Education Association, 206

Albert, Carl, 327, 343, 349, 381, 385, 408
Alden, Robert, 201, 202
Alexander, Clifford, 307
Alfred Isaacs Club, Harlem, 316
Ali, Muhammad, 376
Alpha Phi Kappa, 12, 17
Amalgamated Meatcutters, 246
American Cliosophic Society, 263
American Labor Party, 30, 101, 161; endorses ACP for reelection, 142
Americans for Democratic Action, 192, 343
Amsterdam News, 54–55, 88, 89, 401
Anderson, Daniel, 304
Anderson, Don, 320, 326, 354
Anderson, Jack, 345
Anderson, Marian, 128, 221
Anderson, Merton, 9–10, 11, 18
Andrews, T. Coleman, 222–23, 261
Andrews, William T., 100
Anti-Defamation League, 79
antilynching bills, 80–81, 95; ACP presses for, 119, 131, 148
antipoverty programs, 301–6, 313–16; LBJ and ACP join forces on, 301–6, 313–16; Vietnam War effect on, 316
anti-Semitism, 40, 79–81, 263, 279, 351
antiwar movement, 369, 374, 391, 392; 1968 demonstrations, 376
Apollo Theater, Harlem, 338
Arkansas: civil rights movement in, 228–29
Armstrong, Howard, 12–13, 15, 16, 17
Armstrong, Lil, 121
Armstrong, Louis, 359

Associated Negro Press, 186
atomic weapons, 199, 201
Ayers, William, 192, 319, 326

Badillo, Herman, 248
Bagley, Chester, 412
Bailey, Cleveland, 208–9, 274–75
Baldwin, James, 97, 233, 337, 339
Baltimore, Richard, 173, 175
Baltimore Afro-American, 89
Bandung, Indonesia, conference (1954), 200–203, 225
Bankhead, John, 213
Bankhead, Tallulah, 213
Bankhead, William, 213
Baptists: and southern civil rights movement, 204–5. See also Abyssinian Baptist Church
Bard, Albert, 31, 56
Barden, Graham, 156, 208; ACP and, 191, 193, 256, 276, 318; chairs Education and Labor Committee, 191–93, 223–24, 238, 255–57; background, 192, 193; retires, 256–57; and minimum wage bill, 257
Barnett, Dick, 395
Bartenders Union, 246
Bates, Ruby, 34
Bay of Pigs invasion, 287, 288
Beaux Arts Club, 3
Beckler, John, 284, 287
Bedford-Stuyvesant district, New York, 347–48
Bedin, Ezio, 417
Belafonte, Harry, 288, 359
Bell, Howard, 46, 95, 101, 316, 410
Berens, Donald, 277
Berger, Victor, 358
Bergman, Ingrid, 87
Berkeley: ACP speaks at, 371

Bethune, Mary McLeod, 57, 72, 105
Between the Lines (TV), 254–55
Bigart, Homer, 201, 202
Bimini, 365–66; ACP in, 333, 340, 361–62, 364–67, 368–69, 372, 374, 390–91, 394–95, 396–97, 405–6, 407, 414–15
Black, Justice Hugo, 387
black colleges, 311
black judges, 316
Black Manhattan (Johnson), 337
black nationalists, 324
Black Panthers, 369
black power movement, 322–26
  ACP and, 323–25, 360, 364, 373, 392, 412
  WASHINGTON conference, 325
  AND ACP's speaking tour, 369–70; at Fordham, 394
blacks
  LIGHT-SKINNED vs. dark-skinned, 10–11, 400
  AND political parties, 30–31
  SHIFTING allegiance to Democratic Party, 30–31, 46–47
  AND Communists, 44–45
  MIGRATION north, 68, 111, 133
  RELATIONS with Jews, 73–75, 78–81
  AND WWII war effort, 81, 86–87
  AND Reconstruction, 109–10
  AND Korean War, 161
  AND Eisenhower administration, 182–83, 190, 228–29
  AND Third World conference, 200–201
  AND 1956 presidential campaign, 214–15, 217, 218, 219–21
  AND ACP tax evasion charge, 223
  VOTER registration drive, 228
  AND labor unions, 246, 258
  AND John Kennedy, 262, 264, 267, 269–72
  AND 1960 presidential campaign, 264, 265–66, 269; Democratic, 265, 267, 269, 272–74; Republican, 269, 273
  EDUCATIONAL concerns, 274
  AND ACP's chairmanship, 275–76, 277–78
  ACP attracts to congressional work, 277–78, 304–5
  ACP launches labor discrimination investigation, 278–79, 282–83
  AND poverty in America, 302
  AND Johnson education bill, 310–12
  AND ethic inquiries on ACP, 332
  RESPONSE to ACP's expulsion, 359–60
  SEE also civil rights movement; desegregation; Harlem; segregation
black separatists, 324
Blumstein's department store, 74
Bogart, Humphrey, 124–25
Boland, Thomas, 259
Bolling, Richard, 192, 330, 348, 368, 381; ACP and, 49, 343–44, 348; career of, 342–43; and House Rules Committee, 342–44
Bolshevik Revolution, 44
Bolton, Charles, 70
Bond, Julian, 352, 360, 376, 392, 393
Bontemps, Arna, 337
Booker, Jimmy, 219
Boone, J. T., 185

Booth, William, 340
Bourne, Gwen, 37
Bourne, St. Claire, 29, 88, 89, 148
Bowe, Nigel, 411, 414
Bowles, Chester, 257
Brademas, John, 250, 256, 310, 326, 342, 381
Bradley, Bill, 395
Brandy, Robert, 96
Breslin, Jimmy, 383
Brice, Fannie, 143
Bricker, John, 211
Britt, Mai, 275
Bromley, Bruce: and ACP's case before the Court, 384–85, 386
Brooke, Edward, 351
Brooks, Delton J., 313–14
Brooks, Dorothy, 112
Brotherhood of Sleeping Car Porters, 246
Broun, Heywood, 34, 54
Brown, Earl, 132, 161, 193; and 1958 congressional election, 241, 244, 247, 248
Brown, H. Rap, 370
Brown, John, 64
Brown, Patrick, 394, 395, 419
Brownell, Herbert, 183, 200, 210, 216, 220, 222–23, 238, 259
Brown v. Board of Education, 193–94, 202, 208, 226, 243, 307, 390. See also school desegregation
Bruce, Herbert, 42, 43–44, 46, 53, 54, 77, 82, 83, 87, 91, 94, 100, 104, 130, 135; early career, 44
Bruce, Lenny, 324
Bryan, Judge Frederick vanPelt, 258–62
Buchanan, Bessie, 241

Buchanan, Charlie, 88
Buckley, Charles, 268
Buckley, William F., Jr., 223, 259, 383, 384
Bull Moose Republicans, 30
Bunche, Ralph, 359
Burger, Judge Warren, 386
Burleson, Omar, 291, 330
Burroughs, Nannie, 57
Burton, Harold, 152–53, 195–96, 245
Byrd, Harry, 222

Caccione, Peter, 84
Café Society, New York, 122–24, 159, 162
Café Society Uptown, New York, 124
Cahn, Jean Camper, 352, 362, 385
California: ACP's speaking tour in, 369–71
Campbell, Al, 14
Cannon, Joe, 115
Carmichael, Stokely, 324, 364, 370
Caro, Robert, 300
Carroll, Diahann, 234
Carter, Art, 328
Carter, Elmer, 164
Carter, Wesley, 231, 389, 412
Carver Democratic Club, 167
Cavett, Dick, 395
Celler, Emmanuel, 115, 150, 181, 219, 268, 330; and case against ACP, 348–49, 388, 410; and hearings to expel ACP, 353–57, 358; effort to reseat ACP, 362, 381, 382
Chicago: 1944 presidential conventions in, 101–2, 138; 1952 presidential conventions in,

168–71; South Side blacks, 169, 244; 1956 presidential convention at, 216–17; 1960 Republican presidential convention, 269; ACP investigates antipoverty programs, 313–14, 315; 1960s riots, 322; 1968 Democratic convention protests, 322

Chicago Daily News, 359
Chicago Defender, 89
Chicago Tribune, 153
China, Communist, 199, 201
Chisholm, Shirley, 382, 400, 411
Chou En-lai, 201, 202
Civil Rights Act: *1957*, 250, 264; *1964*, 305–6
Civil Rights Commission, 184
civil rights legislation: Reconstruction and, 109–10; Truman introduces, 150; under Eisenhower, 193–94, 202, 207–8, 227–28; Johnson and, 250, 264, 305–6
civil rights movement, 92–94
AND 1948 presidential campaign, 150–51, 152
AND 1952 presidential campaign, 169–70
ACP and, 204–6, 221–22, 225–26, 292–95; and ethics inquiries, 332; response to his expulsion, 359–60
SOUTHERN, 204–6, 225–29, 262, 280
AND 1956 presidential campaign, 214–15, 217
1957 prayer pilgrimage to Washington, 226–27
VOTER registration drive, 228
EISENHOWER meets with leadership, 246

STUDENT boycotts, 262
1963 march on Washington, 292–93
SEE also *individual leaders*
Clark, Kenneth, 307
Clark, Odell, 94, 132, 308, 309, 352, 354, 383, 399, 400, 407, 412
Clark, Robbie, 308, 354, 399
Clayton, Buck, 233
Clinton, Miss., massacre, 110
Coca, Imogene, 123
Coffee, John, 130
Cohen, Wilbur, 278
Cohn, Roy, 222
Cole, Nat King, 152, 232, 282
Colgate, James, 18
Colgate-Rochester Seminary, 13
Colgate University: ACP at, 5, 9–19
college education: Great Society and, 318
Columbia University: 1968 student protests, 375–76
Committee Against Jim Crow in Military Service, 138
Communists: ACP and, 44–45, 98, 101, 147–48; and Harlem politics, 44–46, 47, 55, 56, 76, 98; HUAC and, 146; and 1948 election campaign, 151; Hiss case, 156, 160; Truman era persecutions, 160–63, 184; and 1950 election, 163; Eisenhower era persecutions, 184; and Third World conference at Bandung, 199, 203
Community Action, 303
Concord Baptist Church, Brooklyn, 338
Con Edison, 77

Congress
79th, 113, 115, 117–19
80th, 146–48
81st, 154–57
SENIORITY system, 192, 256–57; move against, 326–27
85th, 223
SEE also House of Representatives
Congress of Racial Equality, 325
congressional elections: 1944, 94–105; 1946, 131, 135, 139–46; 1948, 152–53; 1950, 163–65; 1952, 172–75; 1954, 194–96; 1956, 221; 1958, 238, 239–50; 1962, 283, 291; 1964, 307–8; 1966, 331, 332, 339, 347; 1968, 375, 377; 1970, 398, 400–403
Constitution Hall, Washington, D.C.: ACP and segregation at, 128–31
Conyers, John, 353, 356–57
Cooke, Marvel, 54, 88, 89, 147
Coolidge, Calvin, 31
Cooper, Ralph, 102
Corman, James, 330
Costello, Frank, 258
Cotton Club, 27, 51, 122
Court of Appeals for the District of Columbia, 386
Courts, Gus, 213
Cravath, Swain & Moore, 384–85, 386, 387, 390
Crisis, The, 42, 138
Crosby, Daniel, 10, 11–12, 13, 14–15, 17, 18, 25
Crump, Elijah, 241
Curran, Thomas, 245
Curtis, Hycie, 51, 53
Curtis, Tom, 200, 357, 381; and case against ACP, 357–58
Cutler, Lloyd, 385
Cutten, George, 13, 16

Daily Worker, 259
Daley, Richard, 313, 315, 364–65
Dargans, Maxine, 105, 132, 155, 188, 285, 286, 352
Daughters of the American Revolution (DAR): and segregation, 128–31
Davis, Benjamin, 42, 43, 46, 54, 88, 94, 98, 101, 144, 147, 162, 259
Davis, Benjamin, Sr., 43
Davis, Christine, 111, 116, 117
Davis, Ossie, 283
Davis, Sammy, Jr., 232, 265, 275, 359
Dawson, William, 111, 116, 118, 169, 170, 171, 257, 313
Debs, Eugene V., 43, 264
Delaney, Hubert, 39, 42, 138
Democratic Club, Washington, 340–41
Democratic Party
ELECTIONS: see congressional elections; presidential elections
BLACKS shifting allegiance to, 30–31, 46–47, 111–12, 143
1933 NYC mayoral election, 38–41
1944 election, 99–105
IN South, 109–10, 117–18, 151, 220, 256.See also Dixiecrats
ACPS conflict with southerners, 118, 132, 134–35, 215, 218–19, 287, 296, 328
1948 election, 150–54
1952 presidential campaign, 167–72
1956 presidential campaign, 214–20
ATTACKS ACP for 1956 election disloyalty, 221–22

REFORM vs. regular, 239; in
New York City, 280
1960 presidential campaign,
249, 262–74
1958 congressional elections,
249–50
1962 NYC mayoral election,
280–82
EFFECT of 1962 congressional
losses, 291
1964 presidential convention,
306–7
AND campaign to unseat ACP,
349–50
1968 presidential convention
protests in Chicago, 376
1972 presidential convention,
420
Democratic Study Group, 343,
344, 381
Depression, 23–25, 45–46
DePriest, Oscar, 46, 47, 99, 111
Derrickson, Russell, 193, 283,
354
DeSapio, Carmine, 172
AND Tammany Hall, 163, 165,
196, 239–46, 282
AND 1956 presidential campaign, 216, 218, 220–21
AND ACP, 216, 217, 220–21,
239–41, 242, 243, 244, 245;
in 1958 campaign, 239–41,
242, 243, 244, 245, 248
AND 1960 presidential campaign, 265, 268
AND 1962 mayoral election,
280–82
desegregation: and Harlem hiring
practices, 75–78; ACP pursues
for D.C., 134; at Truman's inauguration, 154; military, 186,
189–90 (see also military desegregation); school, 193–94,

215 (see also school desegregation); southern civil rights
movement, 204–6 (see also
civil rights movement). See also
segregation
Detroit: antiwar riots, 96; sends
black to Congress, 195; black
Democrats in, 219
Detroit News, 359
Dewey, Thomas E., 80, 131, 183;
and ACP, 49, 135, 139, 146,
182; as governor, 97, 135, 145,
164, 173; 1944 presidential
campaign, 99, 102, 103, 104,
138, 139; and 1946 Harlem
congressional election, 135,
138, 139–40; and 1948 campaign, 139, 145, 150, 151,
153–54, 193; and Grant Reynolds, 139–40
Dial Press, 132
Dickens, Lloyd, 49, 77, 241
Dickinson, William, 347
Diggs, Charles, 195, 224, 238,
328
Dirksen, Everett, 169
District of Columbia. See Washington, D.C.
Divine, Father, 45
Dixiecrats, 156, 221, 228, 248,
274, 291, 296 (see also Democratic Party; States' Rights
Party); and 1952 election, 169;
and 1956 election, 214–15,
219–20, 221, 223
Dodson, Hattie, 2, 55, 72, 105,
197, 373; as ACP's Washington
secretary, 112–13, 116–17; devotion to ACP, 112–13; experiences Washington segregation,
116–17; and church tax preparation scandal, 197–98, 199,
222–23, 248, 260

Dodson, Howard, 198
Dollinger, Isidore, 180
Donohue, Richard, 279
Donovan, James, 163, 164
Dood, Thomas J., 304
Dorsey, Tommy, 87
Douglas, Helen Gahagan, 163, 164–65, 181
Douglas, William O., 384
Douglass, Frederick, 64
Douthat, Strat, 407
Dreyfus case, 351
Drug Store Clerks and Pharmacists Union, 246
Dubinsky, David, 173, 283
Du Bois, W. E. B., 42–43, 46, 64, 86, 161, 164, 325
Dudley, Ed, 140
Duke, Angier Biddle, 275
Duke University: ACP speaks at, 375
Dulles, John Foster, 199–200, 202, 203
Duncan, Jack, 410
Dunnigan, Alice, 186
Dunning, Millie, 59
Dunning, Sally. See Powell, Sally Dunning
Dymally, Mervyn, 360, 364

Eastland, James, 220
Ebenezer Baptist Church, Philadelphia, 62
Eckstein, Billy, 337
Economic Opportunity Act (1964), 303
education: and Soviet-American competition, 237–38; ACP and LBJ join on bill, 308–12. See also school desegregation
Education Committee. See House Education and Labor Committee

Eisenhower, Dwight, 150; 1952 election campaign, 167, 168, 169, 170, 173, 174; campaigns in Harlem, 173; and Republican hegemony, 182–84; cabinet, 182–84; and ACP, 184, 185, 186, 188–89, 190, 203–4, 228–29, 239; approach to government, 184; background, 184; and military desegregation, 184–86, 187, 189–90; and civil rights legislation, 193–94, 202, 207–8, 227–28; and school desegregation, 193–94, 210, 215; and Third World conference, 200; and military reserve bill, 207–8; and school construction plan, 208–9, 210–12, 310; 1956 reelection campaign, 214, 217, 218–19, 221; suffers heart attack, 214; ACP supports in 1956, 218–21; and civil unrest in South, 225–27; and Little Rock confrontation, 228–29; meets with civil rights leaders, 246
elderly: antipoverty programs for, 303
elections. See congressional elections; New York City, mayoral elections; presidential elections
Elementary and Secondary Education Act, 308–12
Ellington, Duke, 87, 98, 122, 202, 337
Ellington, Maria, 152
Elliott, Carl, 192, 193, 205, 206, 209, 211, 223, 238, 257, 274, 311
Emergency Work Bureau, New York: ACP and, 25–26
Emperor Jones, The (O'Neill), 27
Enoch, John, 10, 12, 14

entertainment industry: 282, 166–67; segregation in, 166–67

Epps, William, 384, 394, 395, 399, 400, 402, 403, 404

Esquire: ACP writes on ethics for, 330–31

evangelists: in Harlem, 45–46

Evans, Bernice, 79

Expose, Darlene: relations with ACP, 404, 405, 406, 407, 408, 409–10

Fair Employment Practices Commission (FEPC), 81, 82–83, 131, 138, 154, 160, 164, 188, 356; ACP chairs subcommittee on, 154–56, 160, 173

Farmer, James, 325, 332

Faubus, Orval, 228

FBI, 99, 162; NYPD and, 180

Feather, Leonard, 123–24, 417

Federal Housing Administration, 195

Ferguson, Homer, 201

Ferguson brothers, 152

Field, Adrian, 277

Field, Marshall, 89

Fifteenth Amendment, 109

Fitzgerald, F. Scott, 14

Flores, Yvette. *See* Powell, Yvette Flores

Florida A and M University: ACP speaks at, 374

Florida State University: ACP speaks at, 406

Flowers, Martha, 282

Flynn, Edward, 37, 38, 39, 42, 49, 99, 165

Flynt, John, 305

Folsom, James, 205–6; ACP and, 206

Ford, Gerald, 203, 316, 381, 385; and case against ACP, 357–58, 367, 381, 384, 390

Ford, Joe: relations with ACP, 53–54, 77, 85, 91, 94, 100, 132, 196; and church tax preparation scandal, 196–97, 199

Fordham University: ACP speaks at, 393–94

Forrestal, James, 264

Frankfurter, Justice Felix, 193

Frazier, Walter, 395

freedom rally: Madison Square Garden (1942), 92–94

Frost, Robert, 266

Fugitive Slave Act, 66

Fulbright, J. William, 115, 165, 237

Fullmer, Marvin, 319

Fusion Party, New York, 38–41, 42, 47, 48

Gail, Mo, 88

Gamser, Doris, 230

Gamser, Howard, 230, 287, 320

Gandhi, Mahatma, 204

Garner, John Nance, 115, 341, 342

Garrison, William Lloyd, 64

Garvey, Marcus, 11, 45, 69, 322–23, 361, 370

Gavagan, Joseph, 39, 71

Gaynor, William, 179

Geyelin, Philip, 413

Ghana: ACP visits, 224–25

Giamo, Robert, 250

Gibbons, Samuel, 309, 326

GI Bill, 184

Gillespie, Dizzy, 233, 248, 418

Goldberg, Arthur, 275, 278

Golden Cross of Ethiopia, 392–93, 417, 420

Gold Street Baptist Church, New York, 65, 66

Goldwater, Barry, 145, 269; 1964 presidential campaign, 306, 308
Gore, Albert, 215–16
Granger, Lester, 225, 246, 293, 324
Grant, Ulysses S., 59, 110
Gray, Jesse, 397
Great Society: ACP campaigns for, 307–8, 317; legislation for, 317–18
Greeff, J. G. William, 36
Green, Edith, 274, 310
Gregory, Dick, 324, 360, 364–65
Gross, H. R., 381–82

Haile Selassie, Emperor, 393, 417, 420
Hall, Henry, 376
Hall, Leonard, 191
Halleck, Charles, 316, 357, 381
Hamid, Sufi, 45, 79
Hammond, John, 342
Hampton, Lionel, 363
Hampton, William, 195, 197
Handy, Mildred, 14
Hannegan, Robert, 114
Harlem
  SOCIAL conditions in: during the Depression, 23–25, 44–46; evangelists in, 45–46; blacks moving to, 67, 68, 69; 1940s southern migration to, 133; crime and decay in, 158–60, 337; barmaid working conditions, 282; loss of population, 377
  POLITICS in: relations with Tammany Hall, 34–37, 43–44, 53–54; and 1933 mayoral election, 38–42; political activism in, 42–46; Communists and, 44–46, 47, 55, 56; new gener-
ation of politicians surfaces, 248
  RACIAL riots: 1935, 47, 179, 338; 1943, 96–97, 179, 338; 1964, 322, 338–39
  AND news media, 54–55
  PICKETING against antiblack hiring practices in, 73, 75–77
  JEWISH control of business, 73–75
  AND anti-Semitism, 78–81
  22nd district congressional seat: created, 92–94; ACP campaigns for, 93, 94–105
  CONGRESSIONAL campaigns: 1944, 94–105; 1946, 131, 135, 139–46; 1948, 151, 152, 153–154; 1950, 164; 1952, 172–175; 1966, 339; election for ACP's vacated seat, 362–64; 1968, 375, 376–77; 1970, 398, 400–403
  TRUMAN campaigns in, 152
  ACP moves from, 158, 159
  ACP visits after travels, 158
  POLICE and organized crime, 179–80
  NUMBERS playing in, 252–55, 419
  JOHN Kennedy in, 272–73
  REACTION to ACP: ACP feted in 1964, 307; support for ACP under attack, 339–41, 347; response to ACP's unseating, 352–53; support for ACP after special election, 368
  ACP investigates antipoverty programs, 314–15
  IN mid-1960s, 337–39
  ACP returns from exile to, 372–74
Harlem Hospital, 24; controversy over services at, 33–36

Harlem Renaissance, 69, 130, 265

Harlem Youth Opportunities Act, 302, 307

Harper, Solomon, 90–91

Harriman, Averell, 39–40, 41, 44, 307; and 1952 election campaign, 167, 168; elected governor, 196; and 1956 election campaign, 215, 216, 217; and 1958 gubernatorial election, 239, 240, 244, 248–50; and 1960 election campaign, 239, 268

Harrington, Michael, 278

Harrington, Ollie, 88–89, 90, 91, 98

Harris, George, 100

Harrison, James, 257

Hartman, Johnny, 418

Hawkins, Coleman, 98, 122

Hays, Wayne, 327, 328, 331, 352; and congressional investigation of ACP, 331, 348, 388

Hazel Scott — Relaxed Piano Moods, 233

Head Start, 303, 419

Health, Education, and Welfare, Department of, 184, 186–87, 208; and integration, 186–87

Heckler, Kenneth, 396

Hedgeman, Ann, 213

Hellman, Lillian, 354

Hemingway, Ernest, 333

Herndon, Angelo, 43

HEW. *See* Health, Education, and Welfare, Department of

High, Stanley, 193, 194

Hill, Herbert, 278

Hill, Lister, 205

Hillman, Sidney, 83

Hines, Bea, 408–9

Hines, Earl, 123

Hiss, Alger, 156, 160, 163, 199

Hitler, Adolf, 78, 79, 81, 83, 94

Hobby, Oveta Culp, 183–84, 185, 186–87, 208

Hobby, William, 183

Hobe, John, 18

Hoffa, James, 256

Hogan, Frank, 321

Holiday, Billie, 122, 124

"Hollywood Ten" case, 148

Home to Harlem (McKay), 337

Hook, Frank, 118

Hoover, Herbert, 26, 33, 117, 299

Hoover, J. Edgar, 161, 275

Horne, Frank, 96

Horne, Lena, 87, 359

House Education and Labor Committee

  ACP on, 191–93, 223–24, 237–39, 245, 246, 255–57, 413, 420; and seniority, 256–57, 344

  DURING Eisenhower era, 191–94, 223–24, 237–39, 250

  SUBCOMMITTEES, 223–24

  FRESH Democrats join in 1958, 250, 255–56

  ACP chairs, 274–80; expands research, 276–77; hires staff, 277–78, 304–5; and War on Poverty programs, 302–3; and education bill, 309–12; revolt against, 326–27; loss of chair, 346

  MCCORMACK and, 342

  AFTER ACP's expulsion, 368

House Finance Committee: inquiries on ACP's expenses, 291–92

House Interior and Insular Affairs Committee: ACP on, 251

House Labor Committee: ACP on, 115, 146, 154

House of Representatives RECONSTRUCTION blacks and, 109–10

79th Congress, 113, 115, 117–19

ACP sworn in, 113

80th Congress, 146–48

AND 1948 presidential election, 151

CHAIRMANSHIP power, 192, 302; diluted, 419

SENIORITY system, 192, 256–57, 344, 350; rebellion against, 326–27, 342, 344, 381

COMMITTEES, 256; southern control of, 256, 342

EFFECT of Democratic 1962 congressional losses, 291

AND urban riots of 1960s, 322

ACP in: reputation, 327–33; investigation and effort to unseat, 331–33, 342–51, 353–58; self-defense, 349–50; hearings, 353–58; expulsion, 358–59; reseated, 381–82; *Powell* v. *McCormack*, 384–87, 390–91

POWER struggle under McCormack, 341–50

WRITES ethics act, 419

SEE also congressional elections

House Rules Committee, 156, 284; and ACP, 342–44

House Un-American Activities Committee, 146, 162; Hazel Scott testifies before, 162–63

Houston, Rev. D. B., 61

Hoving, Walter, 142

Howard University, 61–62; ACP speaks at, 393

Huff, Corrine, 286, 308, 332, 352, 354, 409, 412, 419; affair with ACP, 366–68; manages ACP's speaking tours, 369, 371, 374, 393; breaks with ACP, 394, 395

Hughes, Langston, 90, 94, 125, 231, 337, 418

Humphrey, Hubert H., 153, 170, 264, 306

Hupper, Jack, 385, 387

Hurston, Zora Neale, 141

Ickes, Harold, 128

Imes, Rev. William Lloyd, 76, 80

Immanuel Baptist Church, New Haven, 63; ACP Sr. at, 63–65

Impelliteri, Vincent, 168

Indian Affairs Committee: ACP on, 115

Indochina, 199. *See also* Vietnam

Indonesia, 199

Inouye, Daniel, 308

integration. *See* desegregation; segregation

international affairs: ACP and, 200–204, 224–25

International Ladies' Garment Workers' Union, 283

Irgun (Zionist underground), 81

IRS: and Abyssinian Baptist Church tax preparation scandal, 196–97; and ACP tax evasion charge, 222–23, 260

Isaacs, Stanley, 31–32, 41, 44, 56, 82, 85, 86, 97, 182, 244

Isherwood, Christopher, 265

Italians: and Harlem, 39, 69

I Wonder as I Wander (McKay), 337

Jack, Hulan, 241, 243–44

Jackson, Rev. George, 63

Jackson, Harrison, 104, 243

Jackson, Jesse, 409

Jacobs, Andrew, 350, 353
Jamaica: ACP and LBJ in, 301
James, Esther: and ACP libel case, 255, 291–92, 294, 319–22, 326, 340, 346, 356, 361, 362, 369, 371–72, 398, 404, 419; background of, 319; releases album, 366
James, Henry, 67
Javits, Jacob, 145, 180, 181, 220, 221, 240, 263, 352
Javits, Marian, 233, 284–85
Jefferson, Thomas, 273
Jews
  AND Harlem, 39, 45, 69; control of business, 73–75
  AND NYC politics, 40
  ANTISEMITISM, 40, 79–81, 263, 279, 351
  CRITICISM of ACP, 292
Job Corps, 303, 305
John, Eardlee, 100
Johnson, Arnold, 76
Johnson, Jack, 223
Johnson, James, 260
Johnson, James Weldon, 337
Johnson, Lyndon B., 153, 183, 215, 342
  AND civil rights: legislation in Eisenhower era, 228; blacks and, 264
  ACP and, 250, 257, 262, 263, 295–96, 299–301, 329, 393; and 1964 campaign, 307–8; and education bill, 309–12; and ethics inquiries on ACP, 332–33; and War on Poverty, 302–6, 316
  IN Congress: as majority leader, 228, 257; and 1960 presidential campaign, 250, 262, 263, 264, 267, 268; pre-presidency career, 299–301

ASSUMES presidency (1963), 295–96
  AND War on Poverty, 301–6, 313–16
  AND chairmen of congressional committees, 302
  1964 presidential campaign, 307–8
  AND Great Society, 307–8, 317
  AND education bill, 308–12
  LEGISLATIVE successes of 1965, 312–16
  AND Vietnam War, 316, 317, 347
Johnson, Thomas, 361–62, 366
Jones, J. Raymond, 267; background, 241–42; as ACP's campaign manager, 242, 246–47; and future Harlem politicians, 248, 273, 280–81, 398; usurping ACP's power, 292
Jones, Robert Earl, 418
Josephson, Arthur, 122, 123, 124
Josephson, Barney, 120, 122–23, 124, 158, 162
Justice Department: and ACP tax evasion case, 222–23, 258–62

Kansas City: 1968 antiwar demonstrations, 376
Katzenbach, Nicholas, 321
Keating, Kenneth, 181
Keep the Faith, Baby! (ACP album), 366
Kefauver, Estes, 168, 214–15
Kempton, Murray: and ACP's tax evasion trial, 258–59
Kennedy, Edward, 342, 392, 393
Kennedy, John F., 357; ACP and, 49, 250, 262, 264, 269–72, 274, 278, 279, 291, 301; elected to Congress, 146; elected to Senate, 250; 1960

Kennedy, John F. (*cont.*)
presidential campaign, 250,
262, 264, 267–69; and blacks,
262, 264, 267, 269–72, 273;
Catholicism issue, 264, 269,
270, 271, 279; in Harlem,
272–73; presidency, 274, 278,
284, 287, 291, 292; assassinated, 295, 330
Kennedy, Robert: ACP and, 270,
317, 352; ties with blacks,
273; as senator, 307, 317, 352;
assassinated, 376, 395
Kennedy, Stephen, 254
Kent, David, 195–96
Kenyatta, Charles, 373
Keppel, Francis, 309, 310–11
King, Martin Luther, Jr., 204,
206, 212, 213, 214, 218, 223,
224, 225, 226, 227, 228, 238,
245, 246, 376; and 1960 Democratic presidential campaign,
265–66, 273; Kennedys help
release from jail, 273; ACP
and, 293–94, 323–24, 325,
332, 359, 373, 413; and 1963
civil rights march on Washington, 293–94; assassinated, 375,
395; awards to, 392
Kinoy, Arthur, 419; and ACP's
case before the Court, 386–87,
390–91
Klein, Paul, 154–55, 174, 231, 232
Knapp, Whitman, 419
Koch, Edward, 352
Korean War, 157, 161, 169, 174,
199
Ku Klux Klan, 184, 318
Kunstler, William, 352, 386

Labor Committee. *See* House
Labor Committee
labor discrimination: ACP

launches investigations, 278–
79, 282–83, 318
labor unions: support ACP in
1958, 246; and ACP's chairmanship of Labor Committee,
257–58, 275, 328; ACP
launches discrimination investigation, 278–79, 280, 282–83
La Follette, Robert, 31, 79, 80,
264
La Guardia, Fiorello, 31, 44, 84,
85, 90, 140, 179, 398, 410;
and Harlemites, 38–39, 42, 46,
47–49, 76; 1933 mayoral election, 38–41; and ACP, 48–49,
85–86, 96, 182; and 1943 racial riots, 96–97; death, 165
Langer, William L., 96, 181, 208
Lawford, Peter, 265
Lawson, Belford, 75–76; and
ACP, 113, 115, 116; back-
ground, 114
Lawson, Marjorie, 76, 270; and
ACP, 113, 115–16, 119, 143,
144, 176, 327; background,
114
Lee, Robert E., 59
Lehman, Herbert, 239, 268, 272,
282; governor of New York,
33, 37, 40, 87, 91–92, 93,
268; as senator, 165, 168, 170
Leibowitz, Samuel, 39, 75
Leigh, Janet, 265
Lennon, Acy, 84, 93, 132, 158,
195, 196, 198–99
Lesinksi, John, 154, 155–56
Levitt, Arthur, 281
Lewis, John L., 256
liberals: ACP's relations in 1930s
with, 49
Licorish, David, 41, 98, 243,
338, 360, 399, 404, 405, 412
Life, 126, 333

Lincoln, Abraham, 30
Lindsay, John, 245, 282, 362, 383, 384, 400, 411
Lippmann, Walter, 210
Little Rock, Arkansas: integration confrontation, 228–29
Lodge, Henry Cabot, 183, 269, 272, 273
Loftus, Joseph, 256
Logan, Arthur, 314
Lollobrigida, Gina, 265
Los Angeles: 1960 Democratic presidential convention, 265, 266–69; Baptist convention in, 273; on ACP's speaking tour, 370
Loughlin, Edward, 100
Louis, Joe, 74, 141, 223
Lovett, Robert, 249
Luce, Clare Boothe, 103, 128, 129, 142, 143
Lucy, Autherine, 213, 214
Lynch, John, 110
lynching, 55; antilynching bills, 80–81, 95

Macaluso, Leonard, 12
MacArthur, Douglas, 161, 166, 169, 249
Madden, Owney, 179
Madden, Ray, 203
Madison, James, 387
Madison Square Garden, New York: 1942 freedom rally, 92–94; 1956 civil rights rally, 212–14
Mailer, Norman, 265, 383
Malcolm X, 292; assassinated, 322
Marcantonio, Vito, 39, 95, 98, 125, 145, 148, 152, 161, 163, 181, 410; relations with ACP in Congress, 115; 1950 elec-

tion, 163–65; postcongressional career, 164
Marching Blacks (Powell), 132–34, 141
Markevitch, Arthur, 372
Marín, Luis Muñoz, 251, 289–90, 291
Marshall, Thurgood, 138, 241
Martin, Joseph, 208, 210
Martin, Louis, 105, 145, 237, 238, 270, 271, 272, 273, 280, 352
McCafferty, John, 202–3
McCarran Act, 161
McCarthy, Eugene, 262, 266, 306, 329, 376
McCarthy, Joseph, 184, 203, 222, 258, 259, 262, 264, 343
McCormack, Edward, 342
McCormack, John, 131, 208, 300, 332, 381
CAREER of, 341
AS Speaker, 341–42; and effort to reform House rules, 344–345; effort to block renomination, 381
AND ACP, 342, 344–45, 347, 348, 350, 353, 358, 384, 385
McGill, Ralph, 203
McGovern, George, 223; presidential campaign, 420
McKay, Claude, 337
McKee, Joseph, 33, 37–38, 39–40, 41, 42, 44, 82, 99
McKinney, Ernest, 142
McKissick, Floyd, 360, 362, 363, 370, 397
McLaurin, Dunbar S., 242
McNamara, Robert, 317
Mead, James, 130, 168
Means, Inez, 175
Meany, George, 257–58, 275, 276

Mencken, H. L., 54
Meredith, James, 363–64
Metcalf, Lee, 223
Metropolitan Life Insurance, 77
military desegregation, 186, 189–90; Powell amendment and, 184, 185–86; 1960 reserve bill, 184, 185–86, 207–8
military segregation, 135–36, 138, 181, 184–86, 194; school, 184, 185–86
Miller, Arthur, 354
Miller, Gene, 333
Mingus, Charlie, 233
minimum wage bill, 257; ACP supports, 279, 291, 294; for sharecroppers, 317–18
Minnelli, Vincente, 125
minorities: NYC votes for proportional representation, 56; and poverty in America, 302. See also blacks; Puerto Ricans
miscegenation: ACP and, 5, 10–11, 18; slavery and, 59
Mississippi: in Reconstruction, 110
Missouri, University of: ACP speaks at, 393
Mitchell, Arthur, 46–47, 111
Mitchell, Clarence, 186, 205, 208, 226
Monaghan, George P., 180
Montgomery, Alabama: civil rights movement, 205, 206, 212–13
Moore, Arch, 356
Moore, Frederick, 54
Morales, Carmen, 282
Morris, Rev. Charles S., 65, 67
Morris, Edward, 60
Morris, Newbold, 41, 44, 56, 82
Morrow, E. Frederick, 182–83,

212, 219, 220, 224, 227, 228, 239
Morse, Wayne, 291, 309, 316, 329, 347
Morton, Frederick, 34, 36, 44
Moses, Robert, 32, 38, 41, 48–49, 86, 97, 283
Moses, Robert (student organizer), 306
Mostel, Zero, 123
Murrow, Edward R., 182
Myrdal, Gunnar, 90

NAACP, 27, 43, 76, 83, 138, 164, 213, 278; and Harlem Hospital controversy, 34; The Crisis, 42, 46; Spingarn Medal, 92, 392; and 1944 Harlem congressional campaign, 94; and 1946 Harlem congressional campaign, 144; ACP's relations with, 154–55, 186, 263, 265–66, 280, 292, 386; and FEPC, 154–55; and "Powell amendment" on school construction, 211; and 1958 Harlem election campaign, 243–44; and 1960 Democratic presidential campaign, 265–66. See also Wilkins, Roy
Nasser, Abdel, 201
National Conference of Constitutional Freedom, 272
National Council for a Permanent FEPC, 155
National Council of Churches, 167
National Defense Education Act (1958), 238, 311
National Education Association, 210
National Labor Relations Board,

275; ACP seeks inquiries on, 318

National Review, 259

National Urban League, 324, 368

Native Americans, 119; antipoverty programs for, 303

Native Son (Wright), 134

navy bases: desegregation of, 189–90

Neal, Clarence, 53, 91, 100, 105, 165

Negro Actors' Guild, 103, 166

Negro Labor Council, 258

Negro Labor Victory Committee, 99

Negro-March-on-Washington, 81

Nehru, Jawaharlal, 201

Neighborhood Youth Corps, 318

New Deal, 46–47, 111, 153, 154, 299, 301

New Frontier, 274

New Frontier Democratic Club, 401

New Haven: blacks in, 63

Newman, Paul, 233

New Negro Alliance, 75–76

New Negro Alliance v. *Grocery Co.*, 76

New Republic: on ACP, 132, 203

news media: in Harlem, 54–55; ACP's *The People's Voice*, 88–91, 94, 100, 119, 133, 147–48; laud ACP as committee chairman, 283, 284; ACP sways, 328–29; and ACP's expulsion from House, 359. *See also specific newspapers*

New York City

HARLEM: *see* Harlem

TENDERLOIN district, 1, 68–69

DURING the Depression, 25

MAYORAL elections: *1930*, 31–

32; *1932* (special), 33; *1933*, 37–42; *1962*, 280–82; *1970*, 383–84

POLITICS to 1932, 31–33

ACP enters politics of, 40–42

VOTES for proportional representation, 56, 82

TURN OF THE century, 67–69

BLACKS picket for equal hiring (1937), 75–78

SEGREGATION in, 76

1942 freedom rally at Madison Square Garden, 92–94

NEW 22nd congressional district for Harlem, 92–94 (*see also* Harlem)

ANTIWAR riots, 96–97

ANTIDISCRIMINATION housing bill, 244

MOBSTERS and numbers racket in Harlem, 253–55, 419

AND ACP's libel case, 294, 320–21, 361, 369

ANTIPOVERTY programs, 314–15

ELECTION for ACP's vacated seat, 361, 362–64

New York City Coordinating Committee for Democratic Action, 80, 83

New York City Council, 31, 82, 85–88, 244; created, 31; ACP on, 82–88

New York Daily Mirror, 202

New York Herald Tribune, 84, 100, 201, 202

New York Police Department (NYPD), 179–80; and numbers racket in Harlem, 253, 254–55; investigation of corruption in, 419

New York Post, 247

New York State
ELECTIONS: *1932*, 33; *1958*,
239–40, 248–50
DELEGATION to 1960 presidential convention, 267–68
New York Times, 84, 133, 201,
202, 203, 292; interviews ACP
after expulsion, 361–62; on
Court ruling for ACP, 390;
obituary on ACP, 413–14
New York World-Journal-Tribune,
359
New York World-Telegram, 84
Niagara Movement, 42–43, 325
Nightbeat (TV), 230–31
Nixon, Richard, 243, 406; elected
to Congress, 146; on Labor
Committee with ACP, 146,
155, 173, 420; Hiss case and
redbaiting, 156, 160, 161;
1950 congressional election,
163, 164–65; 1952 vice presidential candidacy, 169, 173,
174; Checkers speech, 174; in
Harlem, 207; 1956 vice presidential candidacy, 214, 218; relations with King, 224, 238;
and 1958 elections, 249; 1960
presidential campaign, 262,
269, 272, 273; 1968 election,
377, 381; eviscerates Democratic reforms, 383; and student protests, 392; 1972
reelection, 420
Norris–La Guardia labor act, 76
Notes of a Native Son (Baldwin),
337

Oak Bluffs, Martha's Vineyard,
51, 418–19
Oakes, John, 413
O'Brien, George, 195

O'Brien, John, 33, 35, 36, 37, 38,
39, 40, 41
O'Brien, Lawrence, 296, 310
O'Dwyer, William, 125
Office of Economic Opportunity
(OEO), 302, 303–4, 314, 316,
383
O'Hara, James, 250, 255, 266,
278, 291, 312, 342
Olivet Baptist Church, Chicago,
171
Oxford University: ACP speaks
at, 369

Packard, Jack, 254
Paine, Tom, 101
Panama: ACP visits, 157–58
Panama Canal, 157–58
Paris Blues (movie), 233
Parker, Charlie, 124
Parks, Gordon, 95
Parks, Rosa, 206
Parrish, Waldo, 116
Patterson, Howard, 10–11
Patterson, John, 264
Paul, Rev. Thomas, 66
Peale, Norman Vincent, 269
Pearson, Drew, 287
Peeks, Edward, 323
People's Committee, 76, 85, 86,
101, 164
People's Party, 403
People's Voice, The, 88–91, 94,
100, 119, 133, 147–48
Pepper, Claude, 353, 410; and
case against ACP, 353, 356,
357, 358, 384, 410; career of,
356
Perkins, Carl, 352, 368
Perry, Leslie, 138
Perry, Marilyn, 420
Petry, Ann, 89, 148
Philadelphia: 1964 riots, 322;

1968 antiwar demonstrations, 376

picketing campaigns: New York, 75–78

Pierce, Samuel, 197

Pinder, Stanley, 366

Pinza, Carla, 282

Pittsburgh Courier, 203

Poitier, Sidney, 96, 233, 234, 283

political parties: blacks and, 30–31, 109–12. *See also specific parties*

poll tax, 110, 131, 132

Pool, Rabbi David De Sola, 80

Poor People's Campaign, 376

poverty: in America, 301–2; LBJ and ACP combat, 301–6, 313–16

Powell, Adam Clayton, Jr.

  POLITICAL career. *See separate main entry following*

  CHILDHOOD and youth, 1–5; and Young Thinkers, 2–3; at Townsend Harris Hall, 3–4; at City College, 4, 5; family ancestry, 59–60; birth, 64

  SEXUAL interests and notoriety, 2, 3, 13–14, 230–32, 270, 273, 312, 329

  AT Colgate, 5, 9–19, 311; relations with other blacks, 9–13; and black fraternity, 12; and sports, 12; majors in biblical literature, 13, 15, 16; academic performance, 15, 16; early interest in politics, 15; appearance, 17

  COLORING and racial ambiguity, 10–11, 18, 87, 104, 113, 116–17, 252, 265, 325

  AND Abyssinian Baptist Church: understudies father, 23; and Communists, 44–45; succeeds father, 56–58, 72–73; first congressional campaign, 99, 101; as congressional headquarters, 116, 149, 158; effect on congressional career, 160, 167, 181, 196–97, 219, 240, 242–43, 339; tax preparation scandal, 196–97; thinks of retiring, 294–95; and ACP's libel case, 321–22; and black radicals, 324–25, 373–74; threatens to abandon, 324–25; response to ACP's expulsion from House, 360; and return from exile, 373–74; conflict over successor, 398–401, 404–5

  MARRIAGES: to Isabel Washington, 27, 49–51, 29–30, 52–53, 78, 120; premarital relations with Hazel Scott, 98, 103–4, 113–14, 116, 124, 125; divorces Isabel, 103–4, 120; to Hazel Scott, 120–21, 125–26, 146, 148; family life with Hazel, 229–30; problems and break with Hazel, 231–34; to Yvette Flores, 288–89. *See also individual wives*

  EARLY political activities: and Harlem Hospital controversy, 34–36; conflict with Tammany Hall, 34–37; and 1933 NYC mayoral election, 40–42; and Communists, 44–45, 98, 101, 147–48; and political precursors in Harlem, 44–46; rising popularity of, 46, 48; and La Guardia, 48–49; and liberals in 1930s, 49. *See also* political career

  CHILDREN of: relations with adopted son Preston, 50–51,

Powell, Adam Clayton, Jr. (*cont.*)
52, 166; birth of ACP III, 132,
141; birth of son Adamcito,
288; wedding of ACP III, 388–
90
RECREATIONS of: sailing, 51;
travels, 51–53 (*see also* political career); and New York
Knicks, 395
AS journalist, 54–55, 88–91.
See also The People's Voice
AND picketing campaign for
black hiring in Harlem, 73,
75–78
AWARDED doctorate, 78
RELATIONS with Jews, 80–81
HEALTH problems of: heart attack, 148; chest tumor, 250–
51; prostate cancer, 375;
lymph gland cancer, 391, 395–
96, 400, 402
MOVES from Harlem, 158, 159
DEATH of father, 175–76
HAILE Selassie medal, 392–93,
417, 420
FINANCIAL anxieties, 405–6
FINAL illness and death, 408–
10; funeral, 410–13; reputation at death, 413–14; crema-
tion and dispersal of ashes,
414–15; IRS hounds estate,
417; auction of belongings, 420
Powell, Adam Clayton, Jr.: *political career*
PRECURSORS in Harlem, 44–
46
RELATIONS with Truman, 48,
128–29, 131, 146
AND WWII war effort, 81, 86–
87; at 1942 freedom rally, 93–
94
NEW York City Council: campaigns for seat, 82–85;

ON city council, 85–88
AND *The People's Voice*, 88–91,
94, 100, 119, 133, 147–48
AND 1943 Harlem racial riots,
93–94
CONGRESSIONAL campaigns:
1944, 94–105; *1946*, 131, 135,
139–46; *1948*, 151, 152;
1950, 164; *1952*, 172–75;
1954, 194–96; *1956*, 220–21;
1958, 238, 239–50; *1962*,
283; *1964*, 307–8; *1966*, 339;
1968, 375, 376–77; *1970*, 398,
400–403; defeated by Rangel,
402–3
AND Tammany Hall: first
congressional campaign, 100,
105; 1946 election, 142, 143;
1952 election, 172; 1956 election, 216, 217, 218, 220–21;
1958 election, 239–46, 248,
250; crushes machine, 248,
264
AND Washington segregation,
113, 118, 128–30; desegregation effort, 134, 156
EARLY years in Congress: sworn
in, 113; settles into Washington, 113–15; first committee
appointments, 115; conflict
with southern politicians, 118,
132, 134–35, 215, 218–19,
287, 296; maiden speech, 118;
takes on DAR, 128–30; first
legislation, 134
MARCHING Blacks published,
132–34
GROWING power: use of "Powell amendment," 134, 154, 156
(*see also* Powell amendment);
chairs FEPC subcommittee,
154–56, 160; views civil rights
as issue of future, 166–67, 171

AND Communist persecution, 147–48, 161–62
CONGRESSIONAL leave after heart attack, 149
MINISTERS honor for pioneer work, 150
NAACP and, 154–55, 186, 263, 265–66, 280, 292
RELATIONS with liberals, 156
TRAVELS, 157–58, 165–66, 194, 209–10, 216, 222, 227; Bandung conference, 200–203; visits Ghana, 224–25; to Puerto Rico, 251–52; and tax evasion charges, 260; with female aides, 286–87, 291, 308; home in Puerto Rico, 288–89; accounting demands on, 291–92, 331; to Bimini, 333, 340, 361, 364–65 (see also Bimini); congressional hearings on, 354; final trip to Europe, 407
1952 elections: and Harriman's presidential bid, 168, 169; at Democratic convention, 168–71; fails to support Democratic ticket, 170–72
NYPD corruption investigations, 180
ASSESSMENT at fourth congressional term, 181–82
SELFIMAGE as independent, 182, 217–18, 329
EISENHOWERS first term: dawning of era, 182–91; relations with Morrow, 183, 191; campaign for military desegregation, 184–86, 189–91; and HEW, 186–87; influence on White House, 188–91, 203–4; writes Reader's Digest article on Eisenhower, 193, 194–95
EDUCATION and Labor Committee, 191, 223–24, 237–39, 245, 246, 255–57; and seniority, 256–57, 326–27, 344, 346, 356; as chairman, 274–80, 282–86, 326–27; expands research, 275, 276–77; holds hearings, 282–83; fame, 283; staff hirings, 285–86, 304–5; travels with aides, 286–87; defeats in 1963, 291; and education bill, 309–12; rebellion against, 326–27; stripped of chairmanship, 346
AND Diggs' congressional campaign, 195
ATTACKED on loans and ethics, 195–96
AND international affairs, 200–204
AND 1950s civil rights activities: Montgomery boycotts, 204–6, 212–13; and southern movement, 204–6, 212–13, 225–29, 246, 292; and military reserve bill, 207–8; and school construction plan, 208–9, 210–12; and 1956 Madison Square Garden rally, 212–14; and civil unrest in South, 225–29; and Little Rock confrontation, 228–29
1956 elections: and presidential campaign, 214–21; and DeSapio, 216, 217, 220–21, 239–41, 242, 243, 244, 245; support for Eisenhower, 218–21
TAX evasion of: charges, 222–23, 242, 256; trial for, 258–62
AND unions: support ACP in 1958, 246; and ACP's chairmanship of Labor Committee, 257–58, 275; discrimination investigation, 278–79, 280

Powell, Adam Clayton, Jr. (cont.)
REVIEWS his accomplishments,
247
AND 1960 presidential campaign, 250, 262–74
AND John Kennedy, 250, 262,
264, 269–72, 274, 278, 279,
284, 291, 301
AND Johnson, 250, 257, 262,
263, 295–96; career compared
with LBJ's, 299–301; and War
on Poverty, 302–6, 318–19,
322; and Great Society programs, 307–8, 317; and education bill, 308–12; and
legislative successes of 1965,
312–16; antipoverty programs,
313–16; and ethics inquiries
on ACP, 332–33
AND Harlem's numbers racket,
253–55
LIBEL case against, 255, 291–
92, 294, 319–22; warrant,
294, 320–21, 361, 369; returns
to Harlem after deal, 372–74
REVIEWS 1950s, 263
AND Robert Kennedy, 270
HOTEL Commodore send-off
party, 275–76
AND 1962 NYC mayoral cam-
paign, 280–82
AND Puerto Rico's status, 289–
91
CONGRESSIONAL ethical at-
tacks on, 291–92; investigation
of, 331–33, 342–51, 353–57;
Harlemites support, 339–41;
and McCormack, 342, 344–45,
348, 350; self-defense before
House, 349–51; departure
from Congress, 351–53;
congressional hearings on,
353–57; appears to face inquiry, 354–55; expelled from
House, 358–59; Supreme
Court hears case, 368, 383,
384–87, 390–91; seating of,
381–82; penalized and stripped
of seniority, 382–83; returns to
House after Court ruling, 391–
92
AND 1960s civil rights movement, 292–95; 1963 march on
Washington, 293; and King,
293–94, 323–24, 325, 329,
332, 373, 413
THINKS of retiring, 294–95
ASSASSINATION threats to,
306
OPPOSES black colleges, 311
AND Shriver, 314, 316–17
AND 1960s urban riots, 322–23
AND black power movement,
322–26, 360, 364, 373, 392
REPUTATION in House, 327–33
MANIPULATES media, 328–29
ADMIRERS and opponents in
Congress, 329, 330–33
PRESIDENTIAL prospects, 330,
368–69
SELFEXILE in Bimini, 361–62,
365–67; wins seat in special
election, 364; releases album of
sermons, 366, 369
SPEAKING tours: on West
Coast, 369–71; at southern
universities, 374–75; in 1971,
406; as antiestablishment hero
to students, 391–92, 393–94
AND Rangel, 376
AND 1970 NYC mayoral race,
383–84
Powell, Adam Clayton, Sr., 1, 3,
34, 46, 52, 112, 407; relations
with son, 1, 2, 16, 28–29, 40,
44, 87, 113, 160, 361; interest

in women, 16; relief work during the Depression, 25, 26–27; and NAACP, 55, 94; retires from pulpit, 56–57, 72–73; background and career, 58–72; family background, 59–60; youth, 60–61; joins ministry, 61; education, 61–62; at New Haven church, 63–65; awarded doctorate, 64; and birth of ACP, 65; assumes Abyssinian Baptist ministry, 67–68; oversees church's move to Harlem, 68–72; second marriage, 175; death, 175–76

Powell, Adam Clayton, III, 157, 194, 202, 203, 209, 229–30, 289, 290, 294, 365, 403, 407, 408, 417; birth, 132, 141; education, 388; wedding, 388–90; and ACP's death, 410, 411, 413, 417, 418

Powell, Adam Clayton, IV, 407, 418

Powell, Adam Diego (Adamcito), 288, 409–10

Powell, Anthony, 60

Powell, Beryl Slocum, 388, 389–90, 407

Powell, Blanche, 1, 4–5, 11, 64

Powell, Charles, 59, 60

Powell, Hazel. See Scott, Hazel

Powell, Isabel Washington: ACP's early relations with, 14, 23; ACP marries, 27, 29–30; background and career, 27–28; baptized, 29; marital relations with ACP, 49–51, 52–53, 78, 85, 98, 103–4; ACP divorces, 103–4, 113, 120; post-divorce feelings, 143, 204; at ACP's funeral, 411; after ACP's death, 418–19

Powell, Llewellyn, 59

Powell, Mattie Fletcher Schaeffer, 1, 3, 25, 58, 62, 63, 113, 176; marriage, 62; death, 119

Powell, Preston, 28, 29; relations with ACP, 50–51, 52, 119, 166

Powell, Sally Dunning, 59, 60

Powell, Sherman, 418

Powell, Yvette Flores: early relations with ACP, 251–52; ACP marries, 288–89; estrangement, 330, 331, 367; and ACP's expulsion hearings, 355–56; and ACP's final hospitalization, 409–10; after ACP's death, 419

Powell amendment, 134, 224, 343; FEPC and, 154; military segregation and, 207–8; and school construction plan, 208–9, 210–12; joins lexicon, 211–12; Stevenson's 1956 election campaign and, 214–15, 216; and ACP's labor discrimination investigations, 283

Powell v. McCormack, 384–87

Pravda, 201, 202

prayer pilgrimage: to Washington (1957), 226–27

presidential elections: 1932, 26, 32–33; 1940, 80; 1944, 99; 1948, 150–51, 153–54; 1952, 166, 167–75; 1956, 214–21; 1960, 249, 250, 262–74; 1964, 306–8; 1968, 377, 381; 1972, 392, 420

President's Commission on Riots, 373

prison segregation, 146

Procaccino, Mario, 383

Proctor, Samuel, 52–53, 404, 407; becomes pastor at Abyssinian Baptist Church, 419

Progressive Party, 30, 78, 79, 151, 153; blacks and, 30–31
Prohibition, 14, 15, 53
Prosser, Seward, 25
Pucinski, Roman, 250, 256, 313, 315, 327
Puerto Ricans: and Harlem congressional campaigns, 242, 243; ACP and, 251, 283; ACP's marriage and, 288
Puerto Rico: ACP in, 251–52; ACP's married life in, 288–89; ACP's Villa Reposa home, 289, 290–91, 295; ACP and politics of, 289–91, 330; commonwealth status, 289–91; demonstration against ACP, 290–91
Pullman porters, 92–93, 94

Rabb, Maxwell, 183, 193, 208, 218, 224; ACP and, 187–88, 190–91, 200, 220, 226
racial relations, 3, 4; ACP at Colgate, 9–13, 18; skin tone and, 11, 52; and ACP's travels, 52; miscegenation, 59; ACP's personal experience of racism, 113; in Europe, 216; and campaign to unseat ACP, 348–49; and ACP's case before the Court, 387, 390. *See also* desegregation; segregation
racial riots
 HARLEM: *1935*, 47, 74; *1943*, 96–97
 NEW York (1863), 67
 OF 1960s, 322–23, 370
 PRESIDENTS Commission on, 373
radio: segregation in, 166; discrimination in, 282
Rainey, Joseph H., 109

Randolph, A. Philip, 42, 43, 80, 83, 99, 138, 244–45, 246, 248, 266, 275, 332; early career, 43; and FEPC, 81, 82, 92–94, 138, 155; and civil rights movement, 92–94, 213, 225, 226, 227, 292–93; honored at 1942 freedom rally, 92–94; and ACP's chairmanship of Labor Committee, 258; supports ACP on expulsion, 359–60
Randolph, Mrs. A. Philip, 141
Rangel, Charles, 248, 280, 281, 339, 347, 376, 400; as rising star, 339–40; ACP and, 376, 396–98; pursuit of ACP's seat, 397–98, 400, 401, 402–3; defeats ACP, 402–3
Rankin, John, 118, 130, 131, 147; ACP confronts, 118
Ransier, Alonzo, 110, 156
Ransom, Reverdy C., 58, 68
Rappaport, Daniel, 304
Rauh, Joseph, 134, 211, 217, 355–56
Rayburn, Sam, 115, 130, 156, 185, 221, 224, 250, 257, 267, 276, 300, 327, 341, 343, 364; relations with ACP, 115; death, 341
Reader's Digest: ACP writes for, 193, 194–95
Reagan, Ronald, 369
Reconstruction, 60, 109–10, 117, 156, 351
Recovery Party, New York, 39–40
Reed, Willis, 395
Reedy, George, 164, 301
Reeves, Frank, 266, 352, 386
Reid, Herbert, 352, 385–86, 390
Republican Party: blacks and,

30–31, 109–11, 182–83, 190, 218, 219, 221; 1944 election, 99, 100–101; and Reconstruction, 109–10; 1946 Harlem congressional campaign, 135, 139–46, 154; gains in 1946 congressional election, 145; 1952 presidential campaign, 167, 169, 171; 1952 Harlem congressional campaign, 173–75; ACP's relations with, 182, 217–21, 238–39; and beginning of Eisenhower era, 182–84; 1956 presidential campaign, 214, 218–19, 221; 1958 congressional elections, 249–50; 1964 convention, 306; and campaign to unseat ACP, 350; and election for ACP's vacated seat, 362–64

Reuther, Walter, 219

Revels, Hiram, 110

Reynolds, Grant: challenge to ACP in 1946, 135, 139–46, 154; background and career, 135–39

Ribicoff, Abraham, 263, 275, 278

Richardson, Benjamin, 95, 133

Rivers, Francis, 47

Rivers, Mendel, 329

Roach, Max, 233

Robeson, Paul, 27, 42, 86, 90, 95, 124, 161

Robinson, Bill "Bojangles," 125, 140, 223

Robinson, Fannie, 140–41

Robinson, Jackie, 227–28, 249, 362–63, 411

Robinson, Sugar Ray, 262

Robson, Morton: and ACP's tax evasion trial, 258–61

Rockefeller, Laurence, 288

Rockefeller, Nelson A., 200, 240, 254, 377, 396; 1958 gubernatorial election, 248–50; and 1960 presidential election, 262, 269; and election for ACP's vacated seat, 361, 362–63

Romulo, General Carlos, 201

Roosevelt, Eleanor, 86, 91, 95, 123, 217, 220, 225, 226, 239, 266, 268, 275; support of black causes, 123, 128, 143, 212–13, 214, 225, 272

Roosevelt, Franklin Delano, 95, 273, 282, 300; as governor of New York, 26, 32–33; 1932 election, 33; and blacks, 46–47, 117; 1940 election, 80; and antilynching bills, 81; and FEPC, 81, 356; and black politicians, 91, 117; 1944 election, 99, 102, 138, 139; fourth term, 113; relations with Congress, 117; death, 120

Roosevelt, Franklin Delano, Jr., 123, 127, 165, 168, 170, 241; relations with ACP, 127, 159, 170, 328, 407

Roosevelt, James, 275, 283

Roosevelt, Theodore, 30, 64, 182

Rosenblatt, Maurice, 285–86, 287, 329, 408; relations with ACP, 79–80, 83–85, 86

Rosenbloom, Rabbi Jerome, 80

Rosenman, Judge Samuel I., 45, 75

Rosenthal, Abraham, 361, 362

Rowan, Carl, 201

Rubin, Raymond: and libel case against ACP, 255, 320, 321, 372

Russell, Richard, 229

Russian education, 237–39

Rustin, Bayard, 205, 213, 214, 265

St. Louis: ACP speaks in, 376
Saltonstall, Leverett, 207
Sample, Elizabeth, 59
San Diego: ACP speaks in, 371
San Francisco: 1964 Republican convention, 306
Sardi, Vincent, 285
Saunders, Wesley, 365
Sawislak, Arnold, 284, 287
Scheuer, James, 383
school construction plan, 208–9, 210–12, 310
school desegregation: military, 184, 185–86; Warren Court and, 193–94, 208, 211, 215; and 1956 election campaign, 214–15; at Little Rock, 228–29; and Soviet-American education competition, 237–38; noncompliance, 283; and 1964 education bill, 308–12
school lunch program: ACP's amendment, 134
Schultz, Dutch, 179, 253
Schuyler, George, 54, 55–56; ACP and, 55–56
Schwartz, Michael, 304–5, 309, 320, 406
Scott, Alma, 121
Scott, Hazel, 87, 89, 98, 113, 202, 342, 368, 393, 408, 411; early relations with ACP, 98, 124, 125; premarital affair with ACP, 103–4, 113–14; marriage to ACP, 120–21, 125–26; background, 121–22; early career, 122–27; career after marriage, 127–29, 130, 157, 158, 184–85; as congres-

sional wife, 128, 146, 148, 175, 288; and Washington segregation, 128–30; birth of son, 132, 141; and West Indian vote for ACP, 145; travels, 157–58, 172, 260; testimony at HUAC, 162–63, 232; performs for veterans, 184–85; family life, 229–30; problems and break with ACP, 231–34, 288; career problems in 1950s, 232–33; moves to Paris, 233; and the movies, 233–34; and marriage of ACP III, 389; after ACP's death, 417–18; death, 418
Scott, R. Thomas, 121
Scottsboro boys case, 34, 75
Scranton, William, 304
Seabury, Judge Samuel, 31, 32, 38, 56
Sease, Edith, 76
Sease, Harry, 2, 73, 76–77, 325
Seavey, Robert, 239, 280–81, 383
segregation: and Harlem hiring practices, 75–78; in Washington, 87, 116–17, 128–31, 134, 154; in WWII, 87, 135–36; DAR and, 128–31; military, 135–36, 138, 181, 184–86, 194; in prison, 146; in entertainment industry, 166–67. See also civil rights movement; school desegregation
Senate: committees of, 256
seniority rules. See Congress; House of Representatives
Shaw, Artie, 233
Shaw, George Bernard, 57
Shaw University: awards ACP doctorate, 78
Sheppard, Harry, 221
Short, Bobby, 418

Shriver, Sargent, 270; and OEO, 304, 314; ACP and, 314, 316–17

Siegel, Bugsy, 233

Simpson, Billy, 327–28

Simpson, Helen, 84–85

Simpson, Kenneth, 85

Sinatra, Frank, 265

Sing Out the News, 121

slavery, 59, 109

Smalls, Robert, 109, 156

Smaltz, Audrey, 261

Smith, Ferdinand, 88, 98

Smith, Howard, 284, 311

Smith Act, 147

Socialists, 30

Sokolsky, George, 223

Souls of Black Folk (Du Bois), 42–43

South: segregation (*see* segregation); Democratic Party in, 109–10, 117–18, 151, 257 (*see also* Dixiecrats); Reconstruction, 109–10; civil rights movement in, 204–6, 225–29, 262, 279 (*see also* civil rights movement); black voter registration drive, 228; Great Society changes in, 317–18; ACP's speaking tour at universities, 374–75

Southern Christian Leadership Conference, 294

Southern Manifesto, 215

Sparkman, John, 170, 171–72, 173, 174, 175

Speaks, Sara Pelham, 100, 101, 102

Spellman, William, 67

Spingarn Medal, 92, 392

Spivak, Lawrence, 279

Spock, Benjamin, 376

Sputnik, 237, 238

Stassen, Harold, 167, 168

States' Rights Party, 151, 153, 222. *See also* Dixiecrats

Stern (Zionist underground), 81

Stettenheim, Frederic R., 80, 83

Stevens, Thaddeus, 110

Stevenson, Adlai, 153; ACP and, 49, 171, 172, 216, 217–18; 1952 election campaign, 167, 168, 170, 171, 172, 173, 174, 175; campaigns in Harlem, 173; oratorical style, 174; and Powell amendment, 214–15, 216; and race issue, 214–15; 1956 election campaign, 214–18, 219, 221; and 1960 presidential campaign, 264, 266, 267, 268

Stokes, Olivia, 73, 76, 112, 119, 120, 196, 198, 400

Stone, Chuck, 317, 346, 354, 367

Stork Club, New York, 159

Street, The (Petry), 89, 148

student movement, 369; ACP's speaking tour in California, 369–71; ACP's speaking tour in South, 374–75; ACP as antiestablishment hero, 391–92, 393–94

Sukarno, 199, 201

Sullivan, Ed, 132

Sulzberger, C. L., 203

Sumner, Charles, 110

Supreme Court: and school desegregation, 193–94, 202, 210–11; hears ACP's expulsion case, 368, 383, 384–87, 390–91

Sutton, Percy, 248, 280, 281, 339, 347, 396, 400

Swanson, Gloria, 139

Sylvester, Edward, 266, 269, 270
Symington, Stuart, 237, 329; and 1960 presidential campaign, 250, 262, 264, 267, 268

Taft, Robert, 153, 167, 169
Taft, William Howard, 30
Tallmadge, James, 134
Tammany Hall
AND corruption in NYC politics, 31–33, 38, 48, 139, 179–80
RELATIONS with Harlem, 34–37, 43–44, 53–54, 82, 91, 165, 242, 247–48; Harlem Hospital conflict, 34–37
AND 1933 mayoral election, 37–42
AND ACP: first congressional campaign, 100, 105; 1946 election, 142, 143; 1952 election, 172; 1958 election, 239–46, 248, 250
DESAPIO and, 163, 165, 196, 239–46, 248, 250
AND 1956 presidential campaign, 218, 220–21
ACP defeats, 248
Tatum, Art, 123
Taylor, Charles, 403
Taylor, Gardner, 205, 338, 382, 412, 413, 414
Taylor, Glen, 151
Tenderloin district, New York, 1, 68–69
Terzin, Mary Ellen, 329
Third World conference (1954), Bandung, 199–203, 225
Thomas, Charles, 189–90
Thompson, Frank, 192–93, 223, 268, 275, 309, 330, 341, 342, 404
Thomson, Jeanne, 303

Thurmond, Strom, 151
Till, Emmett, 209–10
Time, 84, 174
Townsend Harris Hall: ACP at, 3–4
Truman, Bess, 128, 129, 146, 184
Truman, Harry, 216, 221; ACP and, 49, 128–29, 131, 146, 182; and 1944 election, 102; succeeds to presidency, 120; ends war, 126; civil rights program, 150, 184; and 1948 election, 150–51, 152, 153–54; campaigns in Harlem, 152, 173; integrated inauguration, 154; and Communist threats, 156–57, 160–61, 167; loss of popularity, 165; decides not to run, 167
Truman, Margaret, 129
Turner, Benjamin, 110
Turner, Joe, 123
TV: segregation in, 166; discrimination in, 282
Twenty-fifth Regiment, 30

UCLA: ACP speaks at, 370
Udall, Morris, 328; and House attack on ACP, 345–46, 348–51; career of, 348; and effort to reseat ACP, 382
unions. See labor unions
Union Theological Seminary, New York, 23, 25
United Democratic Club, New York, 34
United Democratic Leadership Council, 280
United Nations Ball, 167
United Negro College Fund, 311
Upward Bound, 303
U.S. Naval Academy, 412

Valenti, Jack, 296, 300, 302, 312, 332–33
Valentine, Lewis, 96
Van Deerlin, Lionel, 332; and attack on ACP, 344, 345, 346–47, 349–50, 351; career of, 344
Van Vechten, Carl, 125
Vaughan, Ray, 10, 11–12, 14
veterans' facilities: segregation at, 184–85, 186
Vidal, Gore, 265, 407
Vietnam War, 316, 317, 318, 331, 347, 368, 369, 374; antiwar movement, 369, 374, 391, 392; 1968 protests against, 376
Vincent, Conrad, 33, 34, 35
Vinson, Carl, 208, 247
Vinson, Chief Justice Frederick, 193
Virginia Union University: ACP Sr. at, 34, 52, 62; awards ACP Sr. doctorate, 64
VISTA, 318
Voorhis, Jerry, 146
voter registration drive, 228
voting rights: Reconstruction and, 109–10; literacy and poll tax barriers, 110

Wagner, Robert: as judge, 71; as senator, 80, 130, 155, 268
Wagner, Robert, Jr.: NYC mayor, 241, 254, 268, 285, 292, 307, 314; 1962 mayoral campaign, 280–82
Walker, A'Leia, 74
Walker, Jesse, 401
Walker, Jimmy, 31–33, 38, 47, 165
Walker, Wyatt, 324–25, 368, 398; and succession to ACP, 398–99

Wall, Tamara, 285–87
Wallace, George, 385
Wallace, Henry, 100, 102, 104, 119; and 1948 presidential election, 150–51, 152
Wallace, Mike, 230–31, 294, 304, 384, 388, 389
Waller, Thomas "Fats," 2
Wall Street crash, 17
War on Poverty, 301–6, 313–16, 319, 383
Warren, Chief Justice Earl: and 1948 presidential election, 151, 193; appointed to Supreme Court, 151; and ACP's case, 387, 390; impeachment movement against, 390
Washington, Booker T., 30, 42, 58, 64
Washington, Fredi, 27, 88, 147, 288
Washington, Isabel. See Powell, Isabel Washington
Washington Evening Star, 187
Washington Exposé (Anderson), 345
Washington Post, 359, 413
Washington, D.C.: 1937 black picketing campaign in, 75–76; segregation in, 113, 116–17, 128–30, 134, 154, 156; black population, 117–18; ACP introduces desegregation bill, 134, 156; 1957 prayer pilgrimage, 226–27; 1963 civil rights march, 292–93; Harlemites support ACP in, 340; protests on ACP's unseating, 351; 1968 antiwar demonstrations, 376
Watson, James, 241
Watts, Mae, 283
Watts: 1965 riot in, 322, 370; ACP speaks in, 369–70

Wayland Theological Seminary, 62

Wayne State University: ACP speaks at, 393

Weaver, Robert, 278, 315–16

Webster, Preston, 27

Webster, Preston, Jr.. *See* Powell, Preston

Welles, Orson, 95, 134

Wells, Dr. Aaron, 227, 395, 412

West, Mae, 125

West Indians: and Harlem congressional campaigns, 242

West Point academy: ACP at, 181; race issues at, 181, 186

White, George, 110, 111–12

White, Josh, 231

White, Walter, 97, 138, 150, 164

Whitener, Basil, 221

Whitney, John Hay, 142

Whitney Young Medal, 392

Wilkerson, Doxey, 90, 147

Wilkes, John, 387

Wilkins, Roger, 329, 413

Wilkins, Roy, 42, 43, 46, 54, 55, 77, 83, 94, 97, 138, 212, 213, 221–22, 226, 229, 246, 266, 292, 324, 325, 329, 332, 359, 413; early career, 43; awards to, 392

Williams, Edward Bennett, 243, 407; and ACP's tax evasion trial, 258–62; named Harlem Man of the Year, 262–63

Williams, G. Mennen "Soapy," 219

Williams, Henry, 395, 404, 405; and ACP's libel suit, 292, 294, 321, 325, 340, 356, 371–72

Williams, John, 291

Williams, John Bell, 223, 254

Williams, Lucille, 364

Williams, Mary Lou, 98, 233

Willkie, Wendell, 80

Wilson, Dooley, 125

Wilson, J. Finley, 102, 103

Wilson, Teddy, 123

Winchell, Walter, 118

Wingate, Livingston, 307

Wingee (ACP's chauffeur), 52

Winston, Harry, 124

Wirtz, Willard, 278, 317

Wofford, Harris, 270, 271

Wolfe, Deborah, 277–78

Wolff, Lester, 254–55

Wood, John, 162

Woodward, Joanne, 233

work-study programs, 303

World Parliamentarians for World Government, 330

World's Fair, New York (1964), 283

World War I, 86

World War II, 80, 81, 86; blacks and war effort, 81, 86–87; segregation and, 87; antiwar riots, 96–97; war rallies, 98, 104

Wright, Louis, 34

Wright, Louise, 276

Wright, Richard, 90, 134, 201

Yale University, 63, 64

Yergan, Max, 147

Young, John, 375

Young, Whitney, 368

Young Thinkers, 412; ACP and, 2–3

Zelenko, Herbert, 204, 275

Zionist movement, 81

8